AN AGRICULTURAL STRATEGY FOR POLAND

REPORT OF THE
POLISH • EUROPEAN COMMUNITY • WORLD BANK
TASK FORCE

Library of Congress Cataloging-in-Publication Data

Polish-European Community-World Bank Task Force.
An agricultural strategy for Poland: report of the Polish-
European Community-World Bank Task Force.
p. cm.
ISBN 0-8213-1708-3
1. Agriculture and state—Poland. 2. Rural development—
—Government policy—Poland. 3. Capitalism—Poland.
I. International Bank for Reconstruction and Development.
II. Title.
HD1995.7.Z8P64 1990
338.'8438—dc20
90-21181
CIP

Foreword

In April 1990, the Polish government decided that it urgently needed to formulate a strategy for the agricultural sector. During discussions with the World Bank, it was agreed to appoint a joint task force to help prepare a proposal, which was to be submitted to the government by the end of July 1990. The Commission of the European Communities supported the effort by financing consultants.

This document is the result of the work of the Task Force. It was submitted to the Ministry for Agriculture and Food Economy, which, after review, presented it to the Council of Ministers for its consideration. The document is divided into a main report and 21 annexes. The main report combines the Task Force findings and recommendations; it assumes the reader is conversant with Poland's economic background and the main characteristics of its agricultural sector.

Because of the short time available to the Task Force (May 28 to July 27, 1990), the proposed strategy is only a broad framework. It covers essential actions and decisions to be taken immediately or in the near future, but does not pretend to cover completely the detailed actions that must accompany and complement these major decisions. Wherever possible, the main report identifies those areas where further studies and review are required.

While many of the strategic recommendations imply that decisions should be taken in the near future, the strategy proposes the creation of structures and methods that will take at least a few months to establish.

The Task Force was chaired by Mieczyslaw Stelmach, Undersecretary of State, Ministry of Agriculture and Food Economy, and led by Claude Blanchi. The other members of the Task Force were:

Gottfried Ablasser, Zdzislaw Adamczyk, Karol Adamik, Ronald Anderson, Pascale Binon, Franciszek Blok, Tadeusz Borek, Karol Borzuta, Barbara Dabrowska, Cornelis de Haan, Jean-Jacques Dethier, Andrzej Dygnarowicz, Piotr Eberhardt, Malgorzata Ellert, Izoslaw Frenkel, Maria Halamska, John Hayward, Manuel Hinds, Oskar Honisch, Stanislaw Jablonski, Zdzislaw Jablonski, Ulrich Koester, Andrzej Kolodziej, Wladyslaw Korcz, Tadeusz Kowalak, Tadeusz Kowalski, Odin Knudsen, Andrzej Kwiecinski, Marian Krol, Gary Luhman, Wladyslaw Lukasik, Wales Mack, Stefan Malecki, Jan Malkowski, Kamil Matuszewski, John McCarrick, Krystyna Milewska, Adrian Moens, Knud Munk, Maria Nowak, Peter Oram, Jan Pawlak, Zdzislaw Piasek, Andrzej Pilichowski, Elzbieta Piotrowska, Jerzy Plewa, Lorenz Pohlmeier, Wlodimierz Rembisz, Ryszard Rozwadowski, Orlando Sacay, August Schumacher, Anna Tuz, Roman Urban, Jerzy Wilkin, Nick Young, Montague Yudelman, and Ryszard Zrobek.

Warsaw, July 1990

LIST OF TASK FORCE MEMBERS

Task Force Chairman:

Mieczyslaw STELMACH — Undersecretary of State, Ministry of Agriculture and Food Economy, Warsaw

Task Force Leader:

Claude BLANCHI — Senior Operations Adviser, Europe, Middle East and North Africa Regional Office, The World Bank, Washington, D.C.

Task Force Members:

Gottfried ABLASSER — European Department, The World Bank, Washington, D.C.

Zdzislaw ADAMCZYK — Ministry of Agriculture and Food Economy, Warsaw

Karol ADAMIK — Dairy Institute, Warsaw

Ronald ANDERSON — Université Catholique de Louvain, Louvain-la-Neuve, Belgium

Pascale BINON — Technical Department, The World Bank, Washington, D.C.

Franciszek BLOK — Ministry of Agriculture and Food Economy, Warsaw

Tadeusz BOREK — Independent Farmers' Solidarity Trade Union, Warsaw

Karol BORZUTA — Institute of Meat and Fat Industry, Warsaw

Barbara DABROWSKA — Consultant, The World Bank, Washington, D.C.

Cornelis de HAAN — Agriculture and Rural Development Department, The World Bank, Washington, D.C.

Jean-Jacques DETHIER — European Department, The World Bank, Washington, D.C.

Andrzej DYGNAROWICZ — Ministry of Agriculture and Food Economy, Warsaw

Piotr EBERHART — Institute of Geography and Spatial Organization, Polish Academy of Sciences, Warsaw

Malgorzata ELLERT — Ministry of Agriculture and Food Economy, Warsaw

Izoslaw FRENKEL — Institute of Village and Agricultural Development, Polish Academy of Sciences, Warsaw

Maria HALAMSKA — Institute of Village and Agricultural Development, Polish Academy of Sciences, Warsaw

John HAYWARD — Technical Department, The World Bank, Washington, D.C.

Manuel HINDS — Technical Department, The World Bank, Washington, D.C.

Oskar HONISCH — Technical Department, The World Bank, Washington, D.C.

Stanislaw JABLONSKI	Ministry of Agriculture and Food Economy, Warsaw
Zdzislaw JABLONSKI	Institute of Meat and Fat Industry, Warsaw
Odin KNUDSEN	Agriculture and Rural Development Department, The World Bank, Washington, D.C.
Ulrich KOESTER	University of Kiel, Kiel, Germany
Andrzej KOLODZIEJ	Institute of Planning and Organization of Rural Areas, Agricultural Academy, Wroclaw
Wladyslaw KORCZ	Ministry of Agriculture and Food Economy, Warsaw
Tadeusz KOWALAK	COPA-COGECA-EFA Committee for Agriculture and Rural Development in Poland, Warsaw
Tadeusz KOWALSKI	Ministry of Agriculture and Food Economy, Warsaw
Marian KROL	Institute of Crops, Fertilizers and Soil Science, Pulawy
Andrzej KWIECINSKI	Warsaw University, Warsaw
Gary LUHMAN	European Department, The World Bank, Washington, D.C.
Wladyslaw LUKASIK	Council of Ministers, Warsaw
Wales MACK	University of California, Berkeley, USA
Stefan MALECKI	Ministry of Rural Welfare, Warsaw
Jan MALKOWSKI	Institute of Agriculture and Food Economics, Warsaw
Kamil MATUSZEWSKI	Independent Farmers' Solidarity Trade Union, Warsaw
John McCARRICK	Dairy Consultant, Dublin, Ireland
Krystyna MILEWSKA	World Bank Resident Mission in Warsaw, Poland
Adrian MOENS	University of Waageningen, Waageningen, The Netherlands
Knud MUNK	Commission of the European Communities, Brussels
Maria NOWAK	Caisse centrale de coopération économique, Paris, France
Peter ORAM	International Food Policy Research Institute, Washington, D.C.
Jan PAWLAK	Institute of Building, Mechanization and Electrification of Agriculture, Warsaw
Zdzislaw PIASEK	Zootechnical Institute, Krakow
Andrzej PILICHOWSKI	Institute of Sociology, Lodz University, Lodz
Elzbieta PIOTROWSKA	Institute of Sociology, Lodz University, Lodz
Jerzy PLEWA	Institute of Human Nutrition, Agricultural Academy, Warsaw
Lorenz POHLMEIER	Technical Department, The World Bank, Washington, D.C.

Wlodimierz REMBISZ — Central School for Planning and Statistics, Warsaw

Ryszard ROZWADOWSKI — Ministry of Agriculture and Food Economy, Warsaw

Orlando SACAY — Technical Department, The World Bank, Washington, D.C.

August SCHUMACHER — European Department, The World Bank, Washington, D.C.

Anna TUZ — Supreme Cooperative Council, Warsaw

Roman URBAN — Institute of Agriculture and Food Economics, Warsaw

Jerzy WILKIN — Department of Economics, University of Warsaw

Nick YOUNG — Centre for European Agricultural Studies, Wye College, University of London, Wye, United Kingdom

Montague YUDELMAN — World Wildlife Fund, Washington, D.C.

Ryszard ZROBEK — Institute of Planning and Organization of Rural Areas, Agricultural Academy, Olsztyn

Table of contents

An agricultural strategy for Poland

List of annexes

An agricultural strategy for Poland

Poland embarked on the road toward a market economy with its economic reform program of January 1990, aimed at stabilizing the macroeconomy. The productive sectors, including agriculture and related industries, will be able to build on the solid foundations of this program. But the productive sectors are difficult and time consuming to reform, and it is not always easy to identify the actions that will bring about the desired changes and differentiate them from those that slow down the reform process. Both categories often look dangerously alike. A strategic plan is needed to help orient decision-makers in the maze of complex relations and detailed actions that are constantly required. The agricultural sector, because of its social and economic importance, has the potential to be either a brake or an engine for the reform program. The present farm crisis is only a reminder of this fact.

This report is an attempt to define such a strategy for agriculture. It is articulated around a few basic ideas:

• The immediate problems of agriculture reside mostly in the agribusiness sector and not on the farms themselves.
• The key to solving agribusiness problems lies in the privatization and demonopolization process pursued by the government, which will force an increase in efficiency through increased competition.
• Rural development is indispensable to help the rural sector keep its population, develop employment, and relieve pressures on the urban sector until the latter adjusts to the new economy.
• Technical improvements at farm levels are possible but will occur only if the proper environment is created.
• While the government must not interfere with production and marketing, it has an essential role to play in creating favorable conditions for agricultural and rural development.

One of the major and most unfortunate legacies from the previous social system is the scarcity of Polish personnel, both in the public and private sectors, trained in modern economic and financial concepts. Another is the habit of dependence on the state for everything — combined with a fundamental distrust of the state's actions. Training and education in the new concepts must be an essential activity. Developing public and private staff capable of creating the conditions for change will depend on the success of these programs.

The macroeconomic context of Polish agriculture

When the Mazowiecki government took power in September 1989, it inherited a difficult economic situation. Inflation was reaching triple digit rates, the budget deficit was about 8% of GDP, and debt service was five times export

1

earnings. Subsidization of the economy, and particularly of state enterprises, which composed 70% of the industrial sector and controlled virtually all exports, was so high and disproportionate to budget revenues that the budget deficit reached 29% of expenditures in the first half of 1989. Per capita income had declined by about 20% over the previous 10 years, although farmers and part-time farmers were in a better position than the rest of the population, as their real incomes had declined by only 3% and 1% respectively. The economy was essentially bankrupt.

The first actions taken by the new government were to regain control over the budget and introduce bankruptcy procedures to let the worst state enterprises fail. This was accompanied by a package of fiscal and monetary restraints and a massive devaluation and complete liberalization of trade. Market mechanisms were then expected to select the most efficient enterprises. It was recognized that this process would create unemployment, but that it was expected to generate a drive toward efficiency through competition. Agriculture was expected to become more efficient and competitive, to deliver products to local markets at prices closer to world levels without the previously existing shortages, and to take advantage of the devaluation by increasing agricultural exports, despite the decrease or elimination of subsidies. The sector was also expected to help absorb the unemployed in the short term by transforming some of the part-time farmers (40% of the farming population) into full-time farmers.

Despite employing 28% of the work force, agriculture in Poland creates only 12% of GDP. This relatively low figure hides the fact that Poland depends on agriculture for 87% of its food consumption. Similarly, 20% of industrial output derives from agro-industries, which in turn depend on agriculture for 90% of raw materials. The sector is thus much more important to the economy than its size would indicate. Present projections assign an important role to the sector; it is supposed to grow at 3-4% per annum over the next five years, and is also expected to increase its exports substantially, to 30% of its contribution to GDP. The ambitious targets, which few if any countries have achieved, will require major changes in the agricultural production and processing sectors. Sustained agricultural growth on that scale cannot be expected to occur through normal gains in productivity. The expectation in Poland is that the changed economic system, and particularly the increased efficiency that can be expected from a market economy, will unleash hitherto repressed productive forces and that this can happen quickly.

Until very recently, the agricultural sector in Poland was closed and inward-looking. Agricultural policy was based on notions of income parity with the urban sector and on food self-sufficiency. To achieve those objectives, prices were manipulated, subsidies were given, production targets were established, and imports and exports were controlled with little consideration given to economic costs. Since prices were not allowed to reflect scarcity, central allocation had to be used, resulting in large distortions and waste. Although about 75% of total agricultural land in Poland is farmed by private farmers, they were entirely dependent on state agencies and state-controlled cooperative sectors for input purchases and sale of their products. In the state and cooperative sectors, capital was immobilized, since investment was always a government decision and bankruptcy of public firms was not allowed. Similarly, labor was immobilized because housing and other social benefits were linked to employment, itself considered a basic right. The result was a highly distorted sector that was unable to realize its economic advantage.

The social context of Polish agriculture

Unlike many countries of Western Europe, the Polish rural sector is of major importance to the social and economic equilibrium of the country. Its main characteristics, which should be kept in mind while designing an agricultural strategy, are described in the following paragraphs.

The rural population has remained approximately at the same level (15 million) since 1950 and is now 40% of the population. This population stability, largely the result of easier access to housing and food, is a major advantage for the economy during the present crisis. Theoretically, it may enable the rural sector to act as a buffer and absorb some of the unemployed. However, beyond a certain level, this can only be done at the expense of agricultural efficiency.

The average farm size is 6 ha. The approximate breakdown of holdings is as follows:

	Size of farms	% of farms
Very small	0.5 to 2 ha	24%
Small	2 to 5 ha	27%
Medium	5 to 10 ha	28%
Large	over 10 ha	1%

There are 21 persons per 100 ha in Poland, about three or four times the number in EC countries. However, it must be noted that wide regional differences exist, resulting from the history of partition of the country into three regions as well as from unequal regional industrialization and development.

Although the rural population is generally stable, its composition has changed with time. The share of the rural population working outside agriculture increased from 15.7% in 1950 to 40.7% in 1988. Only 20% of the actively farming population derive their income exclusively from farming; 40% supplement their income with outside activities, and the rest are part-time farmers. This high level of nonfarming activities directly related to the small size of farms is a major structural characteristic of the rural population. It represents flexibility, an asset for the future that can help develop rural economic activities upstream and downstream from agriculture.

The Polish rural sector represents a unique combination of the private economy, dominant at the farm level (75% of area, employing 85% of the active agricultural population), and cooperatives and state enterprises, dominant in activities other than agriculture (92% of the active nonagricultural population). Historically, this combination of decentralized and centralized economies is a result of the failure of agricultural collectivization and of the subsequent policy of indirect collectivization. It should be noted however that, in addition to the official private sector outside agriculture, there is an important unrecorded informal sector.

The rural population lives in 2,121 *gmina* (counties), comprising 42,000 villages, 82% of which have fewer than 500 inhabitants. Except for a recently developed road network, infrastructure and public services are much less developed than in the cities. The weakest aspects are water supply (only 29% of villages have a piped water system), sewerage, and telephone (only 8% of villages). The quality of schools and health services is also weaker than in the cities. The poor quality of rural infra-

structure and the low quality of life are important determinants of migration of women and young people.

The behavior of the rural population is a direct consequence of a perverse system in which private farming had to survive in a centralized environment. This semicapitalist, semisocialist system, as well as the policy of repressive tolerance, has created behavioral patterns that are often contradictory and can be described as follows:

• farm management that is based principally on a logic of survival rather than on a logic of development. This is expressed in a propensity to minimize risk rather than maximize profit, to ensure self-financing mostly through multiple employment, and to take advantage of all labor resources of the family;

• an attitude of resistance to, but also dependence on, the state. This behavioral dualism expresses itself in rejection and distrust of anything that derives from the state, yet, at the same time, in complete dependency vis-à-vis the administration. It also creates a habit of unlimited demands by farmers on the state as well as an acquired helplessness toward market regulation by the state;

• differences in behavior between the private and state sectors. Private farmers are tied to the land and this enables them to remain independent. In contrast, farm workers in state farms are wage earners benefitting from specific advantages, particularly housing. The same differences exist between private farmers and workers in cooperatives upstream or downstream from agriculture.

Structural changes in agriculture are likely to be slow, given that farms are small and the agricultural population is aging. Small farms, contrary to what is commonly thought, will not be eliminated by the crisis. They will simply withdraw from the market and only disappear when their owners retire without successors. Commercial farms (which are more dependent on the market) will be in a difficult situation, with a risk of economic regression. They will have to use labor-intensive methods, yet at the same time reduce their costs and improve quality to survive and develop in the medium term.

However, the population's habit of off-farm work and the semiprivate character of the rural economy offer the possibility of more rapid development of private initiatives and investments, both in the upstream sectors that sell to or service agriculture and in downstream sectors that buy from it. This potential needs to be actively tapped, as it represents an essential ingredient for the progress of agriculture itself. It also represents the possibility of generating rural employment (not agricultural employment, which is likely to decrease when on-farm efficiency increases), thus helping reduce overall unemployment while creating a market economy. The rural sector could thus play a social role, in addition to its traditional productive one, and make a significant contribution to the economic reform process.

Implementing a new agricultural strategy presupposes a gradual reduction in the dual perspective of farmers and, particularly, the adoption by farmers of market-related behavior. It also presupposes a reduction in the antagonism between farmers and the state, an antagonism which, under present circumstances, could be exacerbated by the sudden fall in agricultural income and by the uncertainties linked to the absence of market signals. The only solutions to reduce the antagonism are:

- immediate definition of clear economic rules to enable farmers to define their own holistic strategy in a stabilized environment;
- establishment of transition mechanisms to buffer the collapse of prices; wherever possible, use of welfare policies that increase demand for food;
- development of rural employment, based on the creation of gainful activities centered around, and servicing, agriculture.

Poland's agriculture possesses many positive characteristics which should help it through the transition from a command economy to a market economy:

- Compared with other countries in transition, the private farm sector is large and has deep-rooted traditions.
- Polish farmers have consistently demonstrated their resilience and survival abilities; although the economic transition is difficult and sudden, they have the imagination, strength, and willingness to make it on their own — essential ingredients for future entrepreneurs.
- There is an abundant, albeit not always adequate or well-distributed, farm infrastructure, a well-developed rural road network, and electricity available in nearly all villages. Heavy farm subsidies during the past 10 years have at least equipped the sector with machinery, without creating much indebtedness at the farm level. This should alleviate the need for costly investments in the immediate future.
- Poland is geographically well situated for export markets in both the West and the East, possesses an appropriate exchange rate and a convertible currency, and has a largely free trade regime.
- Most important, Poland has a good technical knowledge base, and a substantial number of farmers, particularly younger ones, are well educated. Crop husbandry is sound, but can be substantially improved: although yield increases have been high over the past 10 years, they remain largely below their potential. Animal husbandry is basically sound and veterinary standards are high.

The obstacles to transformation

Despite some signs of adjustment in the sector, particularly evidence that exports have increased despite an end to export subsidies, the agricultural sector is presently beset by major obstacles to transformation that are outside the farming sector itself. Symptoms of these obstacles are that price transmission mechanisms have not functioned: there are large gaps between Polish and world market prices for agricultural products; stocks have accumulated (dairy products, grains); little competition is present on agricultural markets; and credit remains so expensive that many agro-industries are facing acute difficulty and farmers are unwilling to borrow.

The rural sector, although mostly private, was, and still is, totally dependent on the state and cooperative sectors for the procurement of all inputs and services and for the sale of all production. The previous economic system had successfully discouraged private wholesale and retail trade, and producers were tied to cooperatives that enjoyed territorial monopolies. All marketing systems, whether for grain, milk, or animals, were and still are largely vertically integrated. The producers had no access to markets above the level of their cooperatives, which in general they did not control. In practice, therefore, a largely private rural sector was in fact completely dependent on an omnipresent state and cooperative sector that enjoyed monopolistic and monopsonostic privileges.

This situation has not changed significantly since the economic reform program was started. The upstream and downstream agribusiness structure remains the same as before, and no actual competition has emerged to challenge the powers of existing enterprises, which are operating fully independently. The state and cooperative agribusiness sectors still respond to the same pre-reform incentives and not to market incentives. Their primary objective, since they are managed by labor, is to maintain the labor force at pre-reform levels, and to retain all social benefits. In this, they have largely succeeded, as can be seen by the very low number of jobs lost in the state and cooperative sectors. They still have no incentive to maximize return on capital invested, since there is no advocate for efficient capital utilization in their management. Because they still enjoy monopolistic privileges, their preferred solution, when confronted with a decrease in demand, is to keep their margins constant by manipulating prices, rather than by increasing efficiency through a reduction in costs and an increase in sales at lower prices. It even seems possible that some state industries (not only in the food sector), by extending credit to each other through excessively delayed payments, are contributing to the perpetuation of inflation.

This situation, worrisome in itself, is made worse by the fact that the food-processing sector (the downstream sector for most of the farmers), is particularly inefficient in Poland. It ranked second to last in a review of the 17 major Polish industrial groups, declining in productivity by 5.1% from 1978 to 1982. During the overall resurgence in output growth between 1982 and 1985, food industry sector productivity grew by 1.2% but still ranked second to last in growth. Nationally, the food industry showed negative value added at world prices in 1986, and 90% of the loss-making public enterprises were in the food-processing sector. This gross inefficiency means that there is no incentive for farmers to improve their quality or productivity since those gains are likely to be confiscated by subsequent processing. This inefficiency also further reinforces self-sufficiency attitudes in farmers, with negative consequences for productivity.

The consequences of inefficiencies in the agribusiness sector go much beyond the agricultural sector. In fact, they threaten the stabilization program. Farmers find it difficult, if not impossible, to sell their products; consumers see no decrease in food prices; dairies are unable to purchase milk; and buying prices are not being announced by purchasing agencies. Farmers therefore ask with increasing insistence for government-guaranteed crop prices. Because of very low prices, sometimes much below production costs, and, as in the case of milk, well below world prices, farmers feel justified in demanding minimum prices or even minimum income guarantees. Because the cost of credit has remained at prohibitively high levels, farmers are also asking for preferential credit at fixed and lower interest rates. The government recognizes that the crops must be bought at reasonable prices, and in the very near future. Because time is so short before harvest, the government has few practical options to modify the faulty structures, to create new ones, or to let the private sector find its own ways. It is, therefore, under considerable pressure to return, at least partially, to the old system of direct government interventions. This would, however, be a severe setback to the establishment of a market economy. The very large and sudden cash outlays demanded from the Treasury would fuel inflation. The entire economic program would be in jeopardy.

It is, thus, clear that the agribusiness sector is critical to the development of agriculture, and indeed of the economy, and that the roots of the present agricultural crisis are to be found there, rather than on the farms themselves. The present crisis is clearly not one of lack of production at the farm level: the government has to deal with a glut rather than a shortage. Certainly, on-farm efficiency needs to improve and can do so. However, farmers are not going to make the needed efforts if the benefits are lost to an inefficient trade and processing industry. It would not be efficient to invest at the farm production level if downstream industry and trade are not capable of handling the products more efficiently. Government priority actions should therefore be directed toward increasing agribusiness efficiency.

Market prospects for agricultural products

DOMESTIC DEMAND FOR FOOD

Households have experienced a 30-40% reduction in real income in the first quarter of 1990 as a result of the removal of food subsidies and the liberalization of food prices. Their overall consumption of food has declined by 10-15%. Households spent on average 55% (65% for pensioners) of their incomes on food in January-April 1990, compared with 39% last year. Fifty-four percent of food expenditures was spent on meat and dairy products, compared with 45% last year.

The fall in household demand for most food items is lower than commonly thought. This is due to hoarding by households of nonperishable food before the price increases of October 1989, and to households having reduced or deferred their nonfood expenditures. Households have restructured their expenditures according to relative price changes but have attempted to maintain approximately their past food consumption levels.

Average nutritional intakes compare favorably with those of Western European countries. However, average figures mask the increasing number of people who are below the poverty line and nutritionally at risk as a result of the fall in their real incomes and limited income opportunities due to rising unemployment. The percentage of households below the poverty line is estimated to be 37% among pensioners and 30% among workers' households.

There is thus a need to reinforce and expand the existing social welfare system by transferring income to low-income groups and by expanding existing targeted nutritional programs for vulnerable groups to cover those nutritionally at risk.

During the period of economic adjustment, real incomes can be expected to fall until they attain a macroeconomically sustainable level. Projections have been carried out for two scenarios: the more optimistic predicts a 14% decline in real terms in 1990 followed by growth at a real rate of 5% thereafter; the more pessimistic predicts that real GDP will decline by 20% in 1990 and by 5% in 1991, will not grow in 1992, and will then grow at an annual real rate of 3% thereafter. Estimated income elasticities show that the relationship between income and consumption in Poland is typical of middle- to high-income countries, that is, that consumption increases quickly at low levels of income, stabilizes, then remains constant at higher levels of income. The projections indicate that, in per capita terms, food demand grows at an average rate never exceeding 1.2%. Because of population increase, however, total food demand shows a more pronounced upward trend.

The projections indicate that, in the long term, total food demand in Poland will be mainly driven by population growth. On a per capita basis, and in both income growth scenarios, food demand will not increase at high rates. Moreover, increased prices and better food availability will reduce food wastage.

The transition to a market-based economy is likely to induce a worsening distribution of income for three to four years. Demand for basic food items will be higher than the projections indicate in view of this worsening income distribution. As real incomes increase after 1993 and more people move to higher income groups, the food budget share and the income elasticity will decline sharply, and the latter may come close to zero, as in the high-income OECD countries. When the economy recovers, growth in food demand will slow down, implying that projected figures are biased upward for the years 1993-2000. As income increases and the share of the poor in total income decreases, demand for more processed and more expensive food items will increase and demand for primary, unprocessed food will decline.

Supply-side factors, such as the opening of the economy and the restructuring of the food sector, will have a profound effect on consumption patterns. There will be a reduction in seasonal consumption fluctuations linked to the seasonality of processing industry production and to the virtual absence of food imports. In the short term, food demand is expected to adjust to relative consumer price changes until food markets are in equilibrium. There will also be substitution over time within major food groups. The availability of imports, together with the greater choice and quality of consumer products, will lead to a differentiation of consumer tastes and a consequent differentiation of food markets.

FOREIGN TRADE PROSPECTS

Poland's agrifood exports account for about 20% of total exports, but the share of exports compared with total agricultural production is relatively small: 9.5% in 1989 and 1990. The Polish trade balance became positive over the first five months of 1990, partly due to an increase in exports of agricultural products, but mostly because of a decrease in imports (mainly feedstuffs), which is a dangerous development for future meat and dairy production. Agrifood exports were supported in the past by disproportionately large export subsidies and enjoyed a greater effective rate of protection than other sectors. There are indications that exports of processed food are less competitive than exports of agricultural commodities. Profitable exports of processed products will therefore depend on the ability of agro-industry to increase efficiency. Inefficient food-processing sectors will have to be reorganized and restructured. Export markets are important for Poland's agriculture, and the shift to a market economy should help the industry consolidate and improve its position on the world markets. However, there are serious limitations arising from the characteristics of those markets that should be kept in mind.

Although it would be good for Poland to obtain increased access to European Community (EC) markets, increased tariff quotas are unlikely under the generalized system of preferences (GSP) or other schemes, since it is unlikely that the Common Agricultural Policy of the EC will be modified to accommodate Poland. Of course, Poland could negotiate special agreements allowing privileged access for Polish products that have a comparative advantage (such as fruits and berries); in return, privileged access to the Polish market might be granted for other EC products, including agricultural products not produced in Poland. However, the possibilities of significantly expanding agricultural exports toward the EC are not great.

The prospects for exports to the Soviet Union and other Eastern European countries are better. Experience proves that exports are greatly facilitated if the exporter enjoys a strong and stable domestic market. Given that income levels in those countries and in Poland are similar, the quality requirements for export of agrifood products will probably be similar to those of Poland's domestic market. This would permit the expansion of exports. However, these markets are unlikely for some time to offer prices higher than, or even equal to, world markets.

Most Polish agricultural products are not competitive in export markets, largely because of upstream and downstream inefficiencies. A strategy of export expansion would require large export subsidies or other forms of subsidies and is not affordable in the present context. But the export potential for specialized agricultural products for which Poland currently has an advantage in terms of low labor costs should be identified and exploited. Improvements in quality standards could assist in promoting such specialized exports. A socially acceptable way to reduce excess capacity in agriculture would be to aim to produce somewhat below self-sufficiency. In such a case, the sector would not require major government intervention or financial outlays. Such an option would imply that consumer prices in Poland would fluctuate around import parity levels, and still be well below prices paid by consumers in the European Community. It would also mean that Polish taxpayers would avoid the costs of export subsidies or other government support programs for agriculture.

The future of rural Poland

With the above background in mind, it is possible to set goals for the development of agriculture and the rural sector, and for government actions.

Agriculture in Poland should become open, nationally and internationally, to ensure flexibility and responsiveness to market signals, to exploit its comparative advantage, and to produce competitively for both domestic and export markets. This means that the drive for domestic autarky, which is the traditional strategy of Polish farmers, must progressively give way to a production pattern that is mostly outwardly oriented.

Agriculture and its upstream and downstream sectors should strive for efficiency and allow mobility of labor and capital. Labor and capital markets should be developed and should function as freely as possible.

Agriculture should be driven by market forces and be private; agricultural production should be on land that is essentially private. Similarly, marketing, transport, processing, and storage activities should be private; as for prices, they should be determined by market forces.

Agriculture should be free to use all trade possibilities, both domestically and internationally, since this is the only way it can fully exploit its comparative advantage at any given time.

The rural sector should be a dynamic and integral part of society; it should provide diverse sources of income by creating employment outside the farming sector and should consistently improve the quality of life in rural areas; holistic rural development should thus be a priority goal to help create employment in the rural areas outside of, but connected to, agriculture. This would compensate for the loss of rural employment and possibly also help absorb some of the urban unemployed.

The foreseeable long-term structural changes in the sector (increase in average farm size, decrease in overall farming population, increased specialization of production) will be progressive. These changes should be promoted by government action but not forced upon the rural population. For some time to come, an increasingly modern and high-performance agriculture, not only on the large farms but also on small, modern, and highly intensive ones, will coexist with the more traditional small-farm sector. The interests of both must be safeguarded.

Since parts of the rural population will suffer from the consequences of those changes and may not be able to be self-employed, non-market-distorting social safety nets should be designed, principally through subsidies uncoupled from production and prices.

Agriculture should be protective and supportive of the environment; appropriate regulations and incentives should be designed and enforced.

As will be described later, major changes in the structure of agricultural production cannot be foreseen. Grains and livestock (including, of course, dairy) will remain prominent for social and technical reasons. There are no miracle crops waiting to take over the Polish fields once markets are free, but changes can be expected with new demand for more elaborate food (fruits and vegetables); a lower consumption of animal fats will probably induce more demand for vegetable oils (rapeseed); and changes in modern agro-industries may create changing demands for new crops (including industrial ones such as flax). Government research, at the cutting edge of development, should be on the lookout for opportunities, and agriculture (including its supporting services) must be positioned to respond to changing market needs. The best way to achieve this is to ensure that the agricultural sector is given the freedom to decide how and where to invest, as well as access to all the tools and information that allow farmers and processors to make informed investment decisions and to reap the benefits (as well as bear the costs) of their decisions.

Strategy for the agribusiness sector

MODIFYING OWNERSHIP AND PRIVATIZING STATE ENTERPRISES

Improving the efficiency of the agribusiness sector should be the first priority of an agricultural strategy. The causes of the present inefficiencies are well known and understood in Poland. They are to be found in their structure rather than in the quality of management or equipment. While both need great improvements, these cannot be achieved until the structures are profoundly modified. At present, the state enterprises dealing in agro-industries and input supplies do not respond to market incentives because they were built to be large monopolies insulated from market pressures by an almost total lack of competition. Furthermore, because they are generally vertically integrated and large, they prevent the introduction of new entrants into the market.

State enterprises do not respond to profitability incentives because they are controlled by workers' councils. However ambiguous the ownership of the enterprises remains, the owner (the state in the case of state enterprises, and an undefined owner in the case of enterprises previously belonging to the cooperative unions) in the final analysis is responsible for enterprises' losses. Until now, this system has allowed workers and managers to extract a maximum from enterprises under the form of various compensations, and the state has always covered losses.

In such circumstances, it is clear that those who control the enterprises have no reason to take, or accept, decisions that could harm their immediate interests, and a drive for demonopolization and increased efficiency would clearly harm a part of the work force, even if, in the long term, it might benefit those who stay. Their strategy is therefore to reinforce their control of the enterprises through acquisition of the shares at the occasion of the privatization drive; and to obtain capital either from the state, banks, or foreign partners (through joint ventures) to renew and augment the enterprises' fixed assets, which are seen as the only reason the enterprises face difficulties. Their rationale is to maintain the monopoly situation they inherited.

Remedies to these structural problems lie in the privatization objectives of the government and in the law that has been recently voted by Parliament. The entire agribusiness sector, and particularly those parts of it which are most important for farmers, such as product marketing and processing, transport, services and input supply, should be demonopolized and privatized as a matter of urgency. Moreover, this process should affect the entire sector in the same fashion: it would be harmful to leave some monopolies-monopsonies intact for some time, for this could induce distortions and undesirable shifts in production patterns. Such distortions would cause imbalances that would be costly to correct. The privatization drive should affect the agribusiness sector homogeneously. Several basic decisions should be taken following the enactment of the Privatization Law.

First, public ownership must be reestablished. Following the reestablishment of public ownership, temporary new government agencies should be created to control the management of enterprises until these can be transferred to new owners. The temporary agencies should be geared to maximize economic return and minimize the time needed for the next step, privatization. They should be sufficiently small to avoid creating very large holding agencies that could accumulate too much economic and thus political power and be able then to develop their own agendas.

Conglomerates, *agrokombinats,* and all other monopolies and monopsonies should be broken down into smaller concerns to promote competition. The present integration allows compensation of losses between different units at the cost of overall efficiency. The conglomerates should be divided into profit centers capable of operating independently.

While this recommendation is largely outside the scope of an agricultural strategy, it should be mentioned that the promulgation of a modern accounting and auditing system capable of clearly measuring the profitability of enterprises is an urgent priority. Public enterprises not yet privatized and those not immediately subject to privatization should apply this new system as soon as possible. Private enterprises will not need to be forced to do it since the sanction for nonprofitability is bankruptcy.

Enterprises should also be relieved of the social functions and goals they now carry as a result of the previous social organization in Poland. Such functions are not compatible with a market orientation. Social security, such as medical coverage, insurance, pensions etc., should be assumed at the community or national level, and not as an adjunct to an employment contract, except for the normal employer's contribution. Similarly, housing should not be a consequence of an employment contract. The stock of housing belonging to enterprises should, therefore, be separated from other assets, and distributed in full ownership to their occupants either free or on very favorable terms. This would ensure that the loss of jobs that will come with the efficiency drive is not rendered more painful for the worker by loss of housing. Such a decision would remove one of the major worries that workers have regarding privatization of enterprises. A housing distribution program would also help create a housing market and develop labor mobility in Poland.

Rapid and massive privatization should be initiated in the agribusiness sector, particularly in the food-processing, transportation and farm input sectors.

Criteria for appraising investment proposals should be developed to ensure that public sector enterprises targeted for privatization do not continue to claim public resources unless they demonstrate their ability to use them efficiently. Access to financial resources either public or private, other than self-financing, should be submitted to strict a priori controls by the controlling institutions.

There are many ways to approach the complex issue of privatization and very little relevant experience on which to draw lessons. The Polish situation is difficult to compare with that of other countries that have privatized part of their public sectors, if only because of considerations of scale. The principles which should govern any privatization can be stated as follows:

• The privatization drive's main goal is to improve enterprise management and result in an optimal dispersion of ownership. This dispersion should be sufficient to create an active capital market, improve income distribution, and avoid too much economic concentration, which would lead to inefficiencies. It should not be so large as to dilute ownership excessively and prevent owners from exercising their control over management.

• The process should be as rapid as possible. The present inefficiencies of the agribusiness sector are crippling for the economy and hamper stabilization and economic growth. They also threaten consumers with food shortages and high prices, while imposing low prices and glut conditions at the farm level. Moreover, the public enterprises remain the responsibility of the government, which bears the blame for their inefficiencies and, eventually, will have to cover their losses. Speed in the process is also necessary to limit the process of spontaneous privatization that is now taking place and is an undue appropriation.

• The privatization process should be equitable. Poland is on the verge of distributing assets accumulated over 40 years (and more) and paid for by the population through low standards of living. This distribution, whatever form it takes, should be equitable, if it is not to create future social tensions. If shares are transferred without payment (in part or in totality), they should be given equally to all citizens. If they are sold, buyers should pay the right price for them.

Enterprises should not be technically improved before being transferred. Privatization is the prerequisite for management and efficiency improvement, and before this happens, there is no certainty that the amount spent on refurbishing the assets of the enterprise will be recouped through its sale.

MODIFYING OWNERSHIP AND PRIVATIZING STATE FARMS

Although state farms are not principally part of the agribusiness sector, their role in agroprocessing is large, and their situation is similar to that of state enterprises. There are 1,300 state farms, consisting of 5,000 agricultural units and enterprises, on about 4 million ha, providing employment to more than 470,000. They account for about 24% of agricultural output, and 35% of marketed output, and are responsible for about 25% of agricultural exports. It is clear that such an important subsector must be included in any reform of agriculture. State farms benefit from government subsidies, estimated at about $100 million a year. But state farms are not particularly efficient; although they tend to have better yields than private farms, their overall efficiency of use of production factors is below that of the private sector. A number of them are integrated horizontally and vertically (*agrokombinats*), which allows for compensation of losses between units, at the cost of overall efficiency.

State farms, particularly the largest ones, cannot easily be broken down into medium-size units without a major temporary loss of efficiency. Their lands cannot be distributed without creating a major population migration that would be socially and financially costly in the short term. Moreover, suddenly placing large tracts of land on a narrow land market would seriously depress land values. It is therefore advisable to take a gradual approach to state-owned land distribution, synchronized with the development of a land market and related institutions. Apart from those state farms that are structurally unprofitable and could be sold to adjacent private farmers, the others should be allowed to operate as large enterprises, but with some fundamental changes to free the state or its agencies from the task of running agricultural production units and covering their losses, and to ensure that the new units are as efficient as possible. To achieve the above, the following strategy is proposed:

• As with other public enterprises, housing should be delinked from state farms and distributed to the workers, after which the state farms should be legally repossessed by the state and the managerial power of workers' councils rescinded (this would probably be covered as part of the legislation on public enterprises). A new management control system should be established, through holding companies, as in the case of other public enterprises.

• Ownership of land and buildings should be legally separated from the right of usage of these assets. The land and buildings should be transferred to a state land agency, whose only mandate would be to own state land and buildings, to make sure that they are maintained in good agricultural condition, and to lease or sell them to private farmers or industries. A state land-leasing policy should be developed to ensure that the leases are fixed at levels representing their true economic value. Such a policy would also influence the prices of private lease agreements.

• The conglomerates (*agrokombinats*) should be broken down into smaller, independently managed units that would operate as autonomous, financially independent, cost and profit centers.

• Privatization of management should be initiated for each of the independent units. The industrial parts of state farms should be treated as industrial public enterprises. The agricultural parts should be offered on lease to private enterprises, including workers' cooperatives. Leaseholders would take the entire commercial responsibility for management of production units. A bidding system should be developed to ensure equity of opportunity to purchase.

• As with other privatized public enterprises, state farms not yet under private management should not have unrestricted access to new financing and should not be given preferential treatment over private farms.

• To facilitate and guide this effort, a state farm agribusiness restructuring group should be constituted from the current state farm task force, with members from MAFE, Treasury, BFE and state farms.

Part of the land belonging to state farms could be used to start a land market. Land at the periphery of state farms could be offered for sale to neighboring farmers to enable them to increase the size of their enterprises to viable levels. Smaller state farms might be sold in their entirety. In some cases, lessees may not wish to take over all land previously belonging to the state farm. In this case, residual land should remain with the State Land Agency, which will lease it or sell it to private farmers. Land found unattractive to leaseholders might be turned over to public forestry or conservation activities.

Restructuring cooperative enterprises of liquidated unions

Many agro-industries, and especially the dairies and fruit-processing ones, were created and owned by the cooperative unions, which were dissolved at the beginning of 1990 and are undergoing liquidation. It appears that the primary cooperatives are the legitimate owners of those enterprises. The reasons for this are as follows:

• The primary cooperatives organized and registered these unions with the courts as pro-vided by the Cooperative Law of 1982. It follows that since the primary cooperatives own the cooperative unions, all assets of the cooperative unions, including the industrial assets accumulated over the years in the industrial enterprises are owned by the primary cooperatives.

• It cannot be claimed that the assets of these enterprises were financed by state subsidies. Subsidies were passed on to consumers and cooperatives were heavily taxed. In 1988, 27% of the income of cooperatives went to pay taxes. Cooperatives were also indirectly taxed, as 21% of their income was spent for social purposes.

• The cooperative system was largely self-financed. A total of 32% of the income of cooperatives was allocated to different funds (resource fund, 14%; investment fund, 9%; and development fund, 9%). The development fund, which averaged 9% but was as high as 25% of income for individual cooperatives, went to the central unions and in turn was used to finance the establishment and operation of enterprises.

• These enterprises (agroprocessing, wholesaling, transport, etc.) are part of a marketing chain. To suddenly break these linkages would create further disruption in the system and aggravate the already difficult situation in the food industry.

• Appropriation of these enterprises by the state would be a step backward for the privatization process. Primary cooperatives are private enterprises and retaining the assets of cooperative enterprises by primary cooperatives would have the effect of privatization or reprivatization. Privatization in this sense means releasing these enterprises from state control.

The state had control of these enterprises through the cooperative unions, but this does not establish its proprietary rights. Neither is there justification for favoring the takeover of these enterprises by their workers, as the liquidation law permits. These assets should be kept within the cooperative system, but the enterprises should be transformed into joint-stock companies with the primary cooperatives as shareholders and operating exactly like private firms, without special privileges. Those that operate unsuccessfully will go bankrupt. Those not claimed by primary cooperatives should be treated as public enterprises and liquidated if they are redundant.

The liquidation process under the Cooperative

Law of January 1990 has had negative consequences for the entire cooperative system because marketing linkages, previously managed by the unions, have been severed. Thousands of economic enterprises owned by cooperative unions have been orphaned and operate without effective ownership representation. Their access to financing is in doubt and their ability to enter into joint-venture arrangements has been crippled.

Those appointed to liquidate the unions have been given full authority to decide on future ownership of the unions' enterprises and to manage them until new owners take over. It is clear that these liquidators are not prepared to assume these decisive roles and have no clear guidelines or supervision to perform their duties. Some 400 unprepared liquidators operate largely individually in restructuring most of the country's agroprocessing and trade enterprises.

To prevent further deterioration of the situation, it is proposed that any decision to award ownership of cooperative unions' assets be delayed until a cooperative restructuring organization including regional restructuring teams is formed. It is proposed that the cooperative restructuring organization be managed by a national committee of representatives of the Ministry of Finance and the Supreme Cooperative Council (composed of 98 elected representatives of primary cooperatives). At the regional level, the committee should have a similar organization. These bodies would have the responsibility of immediately ensuring professional management of cooperative enterprises with the participation of the legitimate owners. This would allow more time for restructuring enterprises along efficient lines, proper evaluation of assets, and identification of prospective buyers and joint-venture arrangements.

Strategy for strengthening the rural infrastrucutre

DEVELOPING AND DIVERSIFYING THE RURAL ECONOMY

The rural sector in Poland contributes much more to the economy than food and fiber. It houses a large proportion of the population, and has the potential to create employment through the reestablishment of a network of productive and trade activities normally associated with agriculture. Any development strategy must, therefore, go beyond production aspects to encompass the full spectrum of rural activities. What is needed is a rural development strategy. The objectives of such a strategy can be described as follows:

• in the short term, maintenance of the productive potential of agriculture and of its role in providing employment; the rural sector should act as an employment buffer for the economy as a whole;

• in the medium term, creation of a rural market economy through privatization and development of nonagricultural activities; this rural economy would be an engine of growth for the economy as a whole. This will be achieved through the development of local markets, of itinerant trade, of handicrafts, of cottage industries, and of rural services. In addition to small and medium-size enterprises, there will be self-employment and many microenterprises, corresponding to the investment and management capabilities of individuals;

• in the long term, regional planning and multisectoral development of rural areas will raise rural living standards and decentralize the national economy; this will improve utilization of productive factors and promote a more harmonious regional distribution of rural assets.

In the short term, over the next few months, the following actions should be undertaken:

• incorporate the specific requirements of the agricultural cycle in fiscal, credit and privatization policies as they apply to the rural sector;

• reduce the present instability of the rural economy through measures leading to stabilization of producer prices and interest rates, by developing access to storage of products and by disseminating information about prices and markets to increase market transparency. Such measures should not involve direct interventions in price fixing or direct buying by the state or its agencies.

In the medium term, incentives for private initiative to develop must be put in place. Normal mechanisms to create a network of small production units, entrepreneurship and capital accumulation in rural areas have been blocked for 45 years. Outside of agriculture, where multiple jobs and the liberal credit policy of the Gierek period have permitted savings to develop, the only means of accumulating capital were informal. They included: illegal appropriation of means of production (private use of public resources, including workers' time, assets and inputs); informal trade made possible by distortions in the economy; and unrecorded remittances from labor abroad. The creation of a rule of law and of a market economy presupposes the elimination of distortions and privileges, but also deprives economic agents of these previous sources of cheap capital.

The reform policy, and particularly the drive for increased efficiency, will create massive unemployment, estimated at 2 million by the end of 1990. Clearly, the policy cannot be limited to simple welfare, which wastes human potential and perpetuates and increases dependence on the state. State involvement in welfare is at present limited to a small part of the population. The economic reform program calls for a more active policy, supporting the disadvantaged and giving everyone an opportunity to generate employment. This supposes that access to capital is facilitated. Obviously, resource limitation means that such a policy must be precisely targeted. It is also a powerful tool for reawakening private initiative and for developing local markets in which the income of one creates the market for another. It is also a means of providing opportunities for entrepreneurs.

This kind of self-employment policy is unusual in industrialized countries, where wage labor has killed the concept of independent labor and where society accepts the need to offer permanent support to a high percentage of unemployed. It nevertheless reflects the modern industrial revolution, in which a multiplicity of technologies and markets fosters a new production model based on closely linked small production units. This development is facilitated by progress in telecommunications and information technology. This model, in the medium term, could be the objective of rural job creation.

The three major instruments of such a self-employment strategy are:

• a training policy with two basic components: a reawakening of private initiative through management seminars based on developing individual strategies, management and marketing (the use of active and participatory training methods, until now unknown in Poland, would be very efficient); and group action-training for small rural activities, delivered at the work place;

• a financing policy facilitating access to credit by new economic agents. Since interest rates should not be subsidized, it is necessary to create mechanisms to compensate for the new entrepreneurs' lack of equity contribution or assets by granting temporary exemption from taxes and social security contribution (without reduction in benefits), by giving them start-up grants to help in project preparation, and by supervising the start-up of their activities. These two mechanisms necessitate two forms of subsidies, one at the level of the entrepreneur and the other at the level of the bank or local development agency. Both would require financing from the state budget;

• a favorable environment. For this it is necessary to eliminate useless regulations and modify the administration's arbitrary and slow behavior; to develop a clear, coherent legal and fiscal framework (this is currently being elaborated); to implement an information policy regarding markets, technologies and new behavioral patterns; to facilitate access to appropriate machinery by reorientation of national production toward small-scale equipment, permitting the import of small-scale machinery, including secondhand equipment (given the high relative cost of such equipment in Poland, it would be helpful to create the legal framework for the development of leasing contracts); and to facilitate access to land and building to establish workplaces.

To prepare for the long term, it will be necessary:

• to put in place a capacity for regional planning and undertake the development of rural infrastructure; priority should be given to the supply of piped water, energy and telephones, and also to cultural, educational and health infrastructure;

• to enact regional development policies and land set-aside policies for reforestation, hunting, fishing, and tourism;

• to promote decentralization of the industrial structure, following the privatization of monopolies, for storage, transport and processing.

To implement such a strategy, the state must provide a legal and administrative framework and necessary budget allocations. Local agencies and governments should take responsibility for economic and social development at the local level. Both state and local governments should avoid getting directly involved in economic activity. Local rural organizations and nongovernmental organizations (agricultural chambers, the Church, foundations) can play an important role, particularly in information transfer and training.

Changing the role of government

MARKET REGULATION

Government will always be called upon to intervene in market regulation. The case can be made that, until the transition period is over, domestic markets being imperfect and monopoly forces still existing in the country, government intervention is necessary to provide some degree of stability and predictability to prices both for commodities and credit. Interventions should be designed to promote responsible actions by the private sector, avoid the creation of unjustified rents, and limit open-ended and unsustainable budgetary commitments. The interventions and protection granted by OECD countries to their agricultural sectors are often given as examples for Poland. It should be remembered, however, that Poland's industrial and service sectors are not yet generating value-added surplus that can be transferred to agriculture. Similarly, the capacity of urban dwellers to pay high food prices is severely limited. In such circumstances, lasting protection over average world prices cannot be sustained financially. Such interventions also distort production patterns. The basic rules to follow should be as follows:

• avoid direct state intervention in buying, storing and selling commodities in favor of negotiable financial instruments and deferred purchasing contracts. Avoid price fixing, which creates state purchase obligations if the private sector does not buy above the level fixed;

• make sure that budget transfers for price stabilization mechanisms are explicit and decided ex ante;

• ensure that the level of price stabilization is not above the average c.i.f. world price available to Poland, so that exports can cover the cost of stabilization when purchased products cannot be sold on domestic markets.

In the medium term, Poland will need to establish a system to limit major fluctuations in domestic prices principally for grains, pigs, poultry and dairy products. Since Poland will be close to self-sufficiency and will switch from imports to exports, domestic price fluctuations will be induced by world market price fluctuations and, more important, by the f.o.b.-c.i.f. differential. In addition, small farmers undergoing modernization and specialization will need relatively stable prices. Social reasons also justify price stabilization. Border measures will play an important role in such a policy. The temptation to remonopolize part of the trade to avoid inter-Polish competition, which may sometimes occur in such a situation, is dangerous and not justified by the relatively small size of the export sector compared to the domestic market. However, minimum export prices can be imposed at the borders to prevent Polish exports at unnecessarily low prices.

Modern trading techniques used in national and international trade are not developed in Poland. Financial matters must be separated from physical possession of assets. For instance, traders should hold certificates of ownership or supply contracts, not grain or oil. Introducing those modern techniques and setting up a system for buying and selling such certificates are essential steps for developing trade in Poland; it is the indispensable complement of the privatization drive and of the modernization of Poland's banking sector and accounting and auditing profession. A speedy modernization of the Commercial Code, making it compatible with the laws, regulations and practices in force in Poland's trading partners, is urgently needed.

SOCIAL INTERVENTION

One of the most important roles of government is to provide a social safety net for those adversely affected by economic adjustment and those who cannot benefit from new opportunities for job creation or self-employment. Such a safety net is being developed by the government, and there is little to add here, except concerning the following:

• As stated previously, it is advisable to separate the provision of housing from employment contract, and to distribute, under favorable terms, the present stock of state farms' and state enterprises' housing;

• Social benefits over and above the public norms are often distributed by firms on an ad hoc basis. It would be desirable to have those regrouped progressively into national or regional schemes, again to avoid the dispersion of activities inside enterprises. In any case, when enterprises have to adjust to the new economic conditions, they are likely to reduce social expenses to be competitive. It will be a serious economic and social loss if the infrastructure created is not managed to the benefit of the community at large.

• Assistance is justified for those who are less able to adjust to the new economic circumstances. The government has introduced unemployment compensation and special centers to deliver food to the poor and unemployed. Food distribution to, or income supplementation of, the poorer segment of the population can increase overall demand for agricultural products, since the poor have a high marginal propensity to purchase food. This form of assistance is technically preferable to general food subsidies, which tend to distribute benefits both to those who need it and to those who do not. Its budgetary costs can be defined in advance and kept under control. The target population needs to be clearly identified, and the distribution well focused on intended beneficiaries only. Several ways exist, including: food stamps, which were envisaged by the government in the fall of 1989 and have been successful in other countries, school and pensioners feeding programs, and direct distribution to the neediest. The assistance of philanthropic organizations in identifying target groups and in distributing food would greatly help the government, reduce its costs and increase the distributional efficiency. To avoid creating open-ended entitlement, benefits should not be given for fixed periods of time and renewable. They should be financed by ex ante budget allocations.

Welfare mechanisms to implement a social policy already exist in Poland. They are: unemployment benefits included in the Labor Fund (of unlimited duration); the social security status of farmers, which is presently undergoing revision to ensure pension and health care while favoring, through noncoercive means, the transfer of farms; and welfare centers, which are being created in the countryside and cities to channel financial aid, in-kind help and food aid; all these channels are appropriate and need only to be developed.

Agricultural research

Research has a major role to play in helping farmers increase productivity, find new opportunities, and catch up with other countries. The agricultural research sector is large (six central laboratories, 16 institutes, 90 substations, and 80 testing stations). It employs more than 8,300 people and appears to be overadministered and underfunded. Polish scientists are of a high scientific and technical level, and have achieved important scientific results. The major constraints seem to be the following:

• lack of a comprehensive agricultural research policy;

• lack of coordination and duplication in research because there is no central management, such as an agricultural research council;

• inconsistencies in financing (all research is program-based) have produced distortions in long-term research;

• the Ministry of Agriculture and Food Economy (MAFE) system is too dispersed and lacks integration and focus;

• research has been until now largely production-oriented, geared to large state farms and cooperatives. This has created an increasing gap between actual and potential yields. The system is not attuned to economic analysis;

• major gaps exist in research coverage;

• linkages between research and extension need reappraisal and reinforcement;

• scientific salaries and operating budgets are very low by world standards, thus promoting a dangerous brain drain, and most of the equipment is obsolete. Core funding of key scientific salaries is essential to promote continuity of effort.

Poland does not merely need an adaptation of existing agricultural production techniques, but a fundamental realignment of agricultural policy with emphasis on private farms and on economic efficiency rather than maximizing yields. Research will be essential to find solutions to those problems at the conceptual level and to develop more cost-efficient methods of production. Additional investment in basic science is unnecessary at this time as Polish science should first adapt international findings to its own needs. Significant economies and increases in efficiency are possible if a significant reordering of research resources is carried out. The main recommendations for immediate actions are the following:

• shift the emphasis of research policy toward economic efficiency at farm level. Examples are: efficient use of inputs, minimizing pollution hazards; more responsive crop varieties; more efficient feed conversion factors for livestock; integrated pest management; all production research should involve an assessment of economic response levels. Research on the social acceptability of technical findings is essential;

• reinforce MAFE procedures for policy formulation and resource allocation to agricultural research by creating a policy-making and management unit to coordinate the national system through the establishment of a national agricultural research council under a deputy minister;

• establish sound procedures for evaluating research proposals before their submission to the National Scientific Research Council for funding;

• develop a blueprint for a more rational structure of agricultural research;

• initiate new research programs as a component of an agricultural research policy, with the aim of closing gaps in crop research, economic evaluation, animal feeding, and environmental management.

For the medium term, actions to be taken are as follows:

• establish a new regional research organization based on well-equipped centers in each of the country's seven main agro-ecological zones to replace the uncoordinated mass of more than 200 substations;

• strengthen technology transfer by improving linkages between research and extension. Extension should not undertake research on its own;

• update scientific and management competence, to meet the new knowledge and changing technological and socioeconomic dynamics. Improve exchanges and networking arrangements between Polish scientists and foreign research institutions;

• structure training efforts for institute staff, especially to bridge major disciplinary and subject matter gaps;

• institute an award system for demonstrated research achievements, particularly for evidence of adoption and impact rather than for academic publications.

Given the present inefficiencies in the system, the above strategy can be substantially achieved by reallocating existing resources and redeploying staff. It is expected that the national cost of agricultural research would decrease, but its contribution to farming would increase.

AGRICULTURAL EXTENSION

The existing extension service (WOPR) is inefficient, fragmented, and uncoordinated. Like the research system, it is geared toward maximization of output and production targets, and not efficiency. Extension mostly disperses its activities into larger production units, analogous to state farms. Overall, it is mistrusted, particularly by small private farmers. However, the rural sector is now subject to dramatic shifts in farm input/output price relationships which generate great uncertainties regarding farm management decisions; these shifts will bring different pressures to bear on different groups of farmers. In these circumstances, there is a great need for an effective extension service, capable not only of passing information to farmers, but also of informing the research establishment about problems at farm level.

The government is considering a proposal to transfer ownership of extension to farmers through the Chamber of Agriculture (COA) at voivodship level. The proposal seems fraught with problems, principally regarding:

• the mixing of public and private funds, and the private system for disbursing them;

• the dominant role that large farmers will play in these COAs, which may perpetuate a lack of attention to smaller farmers' problems;

• possible conflict of interest situations;

• the risk that the COAs will become self-serving, profit-making organizations with little relevance to the needs of the majority of farmers.

Although the concepts of coordinating public and private sector activities and increasing farmers' influence over advisory agencies are sound, the present plan to entrust extension responsibilities to the COAs needs to be critically reviewed and modified. The following is recommended for the immediate future:

• Extension should immediately be redirected toward efficiency and away from achievement of high production targets. No production target goals should be issued.
• Extension staff should be retrained toward business orientation and efficiency of farm management, using technical assistance.
• Performance criteria should be designed and published on the basis of an identification of the service needs of representative farms. Technical assistance will be needed.
• WOPR advisory functions should be separated from its production units, which should then be treated as state farms. The advisory service should be renamed to reflect its new role and break with the past (suggested name: Agricultural Service Agency, Agencja Uslug Rolniczych(AUR));
• Staff levels at the AUR level should be reviewed. A ratio of one advisor to 250-400 farmers, depending on the region, seems appropriate. The AUR should be supported by appropriate budget commitment, and operating budgets must be kept at a proper level vis-à-vis salaries (65:35 seems appropriate).

For the medium term, the recommendations cover the diversification of extension activities to respond to the needs of almost all rural communities, not only farmers. Also essential is the revision of agricultural school and university curricula to emphasize farm economics and rural development. It will be necessary to review AUR operations and develop a full cost assessment to permit phasing over the longer term of full-cost payment for agricultural advice and service. The AUR should be coordinated at voivodship level by advisory boards of farmer representatives, government agencies and private agribusiness. The AUR may need reequipping to allow it to perform efficient analysis and diagnostics. Finally, it will be necessary to study the operation of the Chambers of Agriculture in appropriate Western countries (Spain, Austria), and test the validity of the approach in Poland.

The consequences of the above strategy would be that:

• The government and the voivodships would be faced with the responsibility of retrenching the number of staff. The remaining staff would have to be fully funded by government.
• Technical assistance would be needed for a variety of tasks.
• Commercial farmers could expect better farm management advice and more efficient diagnostic facilities, but at full cost that they could possibly offset against taxes. Smaller farmers would have greater interaction with AUR staff, whose performance evaluation criteria would be geared toward more farm efficiency. All farmers would gradually increase their influence over extension through the Agricultural Advisory Board and the Chamber of Agriculture.

Financial and technical assistance from bilateral and multilateral sources is likely to be available, often on a grant basis, to support reforms of the research and extension system.

Developing rural institutions: cooperatives and rural financial systems

Two sets of rural institutions are particularly critical for the future of the rural sector: the cooperatives and the rural financial system. It is essential to envisage their transformation to make them responsive to the evolving needs of agriculture.

Agricultural cooperatives

Initiated in the middle of the 19th century, primary cooperatives are an important part of the economy, contributing about 11% of GNP and employing almost 2 million people. Cooperatives figure prominently in agriculture: they channel consumer goods and production inputs in rural areas; they serve as purchasers as well as processors of 60% of agricultural products; and they controlled until recently the entire dairy and most of the horticulture industries. Cooperatives collectively hold the largest assets in rural areas. In the absence of an active private sector, and also to make sure that they are not entirely dependent on a few traders, Polish farmers, like most farmers in Western Europe, generally recognize the need to keep their cooperative organizations, principally for procurement of inputs and sale of products.

Primary cooperatives were mostly controlled by the state over the last 45 years. They were not member-owned business organizations and until 1987 they were regrouped into regional cooperative unions, tightly controlled and operated by the state. While they often enjoyed monopolies, cooperatives were heavily taxed and had to make involuntary contributions to cooperative unions. Large portions of their incomes were allocated for social purposes. But they managed to accumulate significant assets, to the point where members' initial equity contribution became insignificant. The result was that the cooperatives owned themselves and their assets took the form of socialized property.

In the new economic environment, cooperatives must succeed as business enterprises. They must be restructured to increase their efficiency and enable them to respond to market signals and members' needs, protect members' rights and encourage efficient management. Many cooperatives have already embarked on this path, and increasing competition is developing between agricultural cooperatives. Cooperatives, compared with other market players, including state and parastatal enterprises, are relatively advanced in reacting to the new economic conditions.

Because of the liquidation of regional and central unions, the cooperative system has been decapitated. Training, management advice and auditing has stopped. The Supreme Cooperative Council could play a major role in the establishment of regional cooperative service centers to serve primary cooperatives. Aside from direct contributions of primary cooperatives for services rendered, this apex institution could identify sources of funds to continue these vital services. One possibility would be the sales proceeds of some of the assets of cooperative unions. External financial and technical assistance should also be explored. In the medium term, the functions of the cooperative service centers would be taken over by new cooperative unions freely established by primary cooperatives.

New cooperative legislation is urgently needed to ensure the revival of an efficient and truly private cooperative system. This legislation should ensure independence of cooperatives from government intervention; cooperative principles should be reaffirmed, recognizing that cooperatives are business enterprises requiring capital and needing to generate profits for members. The duties and responsibilities of members, management and workers should be well defined. Wide consultation with the successful cooperative systems of other countries is recommended. Assistance of international agencies in formulating legislative proposals should be sought.

In the interim period, there is need for a cooperative policy declaration to address the most urgent issues facing primary cooperatives, to establish the cooperative restructuring organization and its regional teams, and to provide the basis for establishing cooperative service centers. Redesigning the unions' liquidation and restructuring process and establishing cooperative service centers are very urgent tasks that require professional input from local and expatriate consultants. The offers of many international and bilateral donor agencies and nongovernmental organizations to provide cooperative business consultancies on a grant basis should be immediately explored.

RURAL FINANCIAL SYSTEM

The financial system will play a crucial role in the transformation toward a market-driven economy. Since the creation of a two-tiered banking system, the development of the banking sector has progressed steadily. The National Bank of Poland (NBP) has assumed full central banking functions while its credit activities have been transferred to nine regionalized commercial banks. All banks are now allowed to operate in all sectors. So far, 26 licence applications for new commercial banks have been approved by NBP.

Major distortions in the previous economic system prevented efficient financial intermediation. Deposit rates were higher than lending rates; the difference was subsidized by the government. Credit was allocated, which meant that the use of deposits was restricted. Interest rates have now been liberalized and real interest rates are no longer negative. The policy adopted is to eliminate preferential interest rates although there still remain pockets of subsidized programs in agriculture. Subsidizing agricultural credit would be a major constraint to developing the financial system and would have many negative consequences.

The demand for credit has declined precipitously because of high nominal interest rates since the beginning of the year. It appears that the supply of funds is adequate to meet this reduced demand. This, however, is a temporary situation and it is expected that credit demand will grow to meet the requirements of restructuring and modernization of enterprises and of an expanding private sector. It is thus necessary that the capacity of financial institutions to perform financial intermediation be strengthened. A major effort will be needed to generate resources through deposit mobilization if agricultural production and investment are not to be unduly constrained by a shortage of credit.

It is indispensable to integrate the rural financial system with the financial sector. But, despite rapid progress in the financial sector, the Bank for Food Economy (BFE) and Cooperative Banks (CBs) will remain for some time as the dominant financial institutions in rural areas. These institutions provide 23% of total credit. The BFE has experience in lending to large state and cooperative enterprises through a network of 95 branches. However, the BFE has certain limitations: little experience in risk analysis and no experience in lending to the private sector. It is overly dependent on NBP resources, which constitute 60% of loanable funds.

The CBs have a widespread membership of about 2.5 million people; about 75% of the members are farmers and the rest are artisans, employees of the social sector, and other residents of rural communities. There are 1,660 CBs, which are the only financial institution providing both deposit and credit services to the private sector in rural areas. Some have traditions dating back more than a century. It is estimated that about two-thirds of deposits of private individuals were generated by CBs.

After a long history of state control, CBs also have major weaknesses. The BFE was imposed as their apex organization. As a result, they were able to lend only 40% of the deposits they generated and the rest were siphoned off by BFE and lent to the social sector. Over the years of government control, CBs were not permitted to accumulate capital, resulting in a situation where their equity base became insignificant, thereby placing their financial stability in a very precarious position. The financial resources of CBs are large if taken in their totality. But individually, they cannot meet the equity requirements for medium-size and large loans.

Furthermore, they have little experience in enterprise analysis.

In view of their separate histories and their different sets of clientele, it seems likely that BFE and the CBs will evolve into separate structures. With its base of clients and branches, BFE should focus initially on its traditional clients in the social sector and seek to meet the full range of their financial needs. It should analyze its loan portfolio, recapitalize, and develop a business plan. It should also undertake a major institutional development program.

There are various options for developing the Cooperative Banks system, but the best would be the development of regional apex banks as full-service banks independent of the government. These banks would expand the lending capacities of CBs, increase deposit mobilization, and promote regional development. They would also have access to NBP refinancing facilities. They would assist in upgrading and computerizing accounting systems, provide training for management and staff, coordinate retention of external auditors and perform other support services for CBs. There are now various initiatives to form such banks. The Supreme Cooperative Council should take the lead in helping the CBs federate into such regional cooperative banks.

The capitalization of CBs is presently very low, at less than 1% of total resources. Additional capital is needed to allow individual banks to operate satisfactorily in the new environment and meet the capital requirements of regional banks. In the short term, CBs need to obtain additional capital from their members. Many have initiated this process by raising the value of shares from the low levels resulting from past inflation. The payment of dividends providing a positive real return to shares would aid this effort. In the medium term, CBs might consider requiring borrowers to contribute a small percentage of their loans to equity.

These measures would strengthen the rural financial system and enable it to mobilize domestic resources to meet the credit demand for investment. This would strengthen the credit delivery system of banks in the short term, move toward a financially viable position in the medium term and eventually achieve financial independence.

Farm structure is likely to change — slowly over the next five years, then at an accelerated pace. A decline in the number of small farms is to be anticipated, mainly through the retirement of their owners and part-time farmers finding full-time work in the nonfarm rural economy. However, it is neither likely nor desirable that this decline in farm numbers take place in the early part of the decade as the overall restructuring of the nonfarm industrial and service sector is likely to create extensive unemployment and related social dislocations. This will put pressure on the rural sector to act as an employment sponge, and delay the needed structural changes. Thus, a strategy for adjustment and land ownership restructuring is proposed, especially for the partial breakup of the small or bankrupt state farm or cooperative farm sector. This strategy is phased to take the labor absorption need into account.

Several changes are required in the short term to legalize and improve on the functioning of the private land market and to foster legal transfers of public land to the private sector:

• eliminate the 100-ha administrative restriction on private sector holding ceilings. A substantial increase in the limit should be permitted if it is felt that complete removal of ceilings would lead to short-term inequities;

• permit farmland to be purchased or leased by anyone, rescinding the requirement of farmer qualification. Such a restriction is not justified in a market economy where the acid test of financial success will soon return farmland not productively used to the market. This should enable individual workers and firms to acquire freehold or long-term leases on farmland and enable persons, especially younger farmers, to gain entry into farming;

• establish modern regulations for leasing farmland to protect equally the interest of owners and renters, to encourage renters to invest in their farms, and to provide for divestiture by the state through leasehold transfer of land now managed by state farms and production cooperatives;

• consideration should be given to introducing a land tax aimed at promoting productive use of land.

Other restructuring measures should be undertaken in the short term.

• A state land holding agency should be organized, perhaps through the reorganization of the State Land Fund. The agency should receive all land (as well as other immovable assets) previously belonging to state farms, and be empowered to divide, lease, and sell, by public auction or negotiation. It should be entirely self-financing. Incentives should be given to managers to encourage the sale of land. The land now belonging to the National Land Fund that is not of adequate agricultural quality or does not find a buyer or lessee should be consolidated into regional land and conservation management agencies for conservation purposes, in both grass or, in appropriate cases, forestry. Grazing and forest cutting should be limited to environmentally sound practices.

• Farmland belonging to the National Land Fund (or to the land holding agency, if one is created), should be first offered for sale or lease to farmers in the vicinity, through an auction or bidding system.

• To assist land consolidation, which is indispensable to allow productivity increases, modestly expanding the present program of land consolidation to 100,000 ha per annum is recommended, with improvement in administrative efficiency and addition of a Global Positioning System (GPS) computer mapping facility. Poland should study the experience accumulated by the French SAFER (Société pour l'Aménagement Foncier et le Remembrement), which has successfully conducted large-scale land consolidation in France. Assistance from SAFER could help define the best approach for Poland. For conservation and reforestation programs, linkages to the Bureau of Land Management and to the Forest Service in USDA or equivalent offices in Canada would be profitable.

• A review of forestry and land conservation issues should be undertaken without delay to define a strategy for those subsectors.

Sector-specific strategies

AGRICULTURAL PRODUCTION

The present situation

Significant progress has been made in the last 10 years in crop production. Cereal yields have increased 37%, rapeseed 69%, sugar beet 17%, and potatoes 105%. However, considerable scope remains for further improvements in productivity, for raising product quality and for increasing cost-effectiveness by greater attention to economic efficiency. It may be misleading to draw inferences as to Poland's future yield potential simply by comparing current Polish levels with those in other European countries, especially Western Europe, because Poland has more difficult soils and climate and a very different agrarian structure. Nevertheless, differences in productivity within Poland between the favored state farms and relatively neglected private farms confirm that overall yields could be much higher.

With good crop husbandry, yields of all the major cereals could be increased within a few years by at least 15-20%. The major constraints are low levels of fertilizer use and lack of adherence to the optimal agricultural calendar, particularly to recommended sowing dates. There is good potential for root crop improvement: yield increases over the next three to five years of at least 20% in potatoes and 10% in sugar beets do not seem unrealistic, provided essential inputs can be secured. An augmentation in rapeseed yield of at least 10% should be feasible through improved plant nutrition, timely field operations and crop protection. There is good potential for further improvement in vegetable yields, which is likely to come from expansion of greenhouse and plastic cover technology, and better crop protection, in combination with improved agronomy.

Apart from triticale, attempts to introduce new crops (sunflower, soya bean, hybrid maize) have had little success. While this does not mean that attempts to diversify the agricultural economy should be abandoned, it suggests that for the immediate future Poland should continue to capitalize on its comparative advantages by reinforcing research and extension on wheat, triticale, rapeseed, potatoes, grain legumes, fodder crops (including maize), and horticultural crops while striving to improve its considerable area of poorly managed permanent pastures.

The typical small Polish farm has evolved into a balanced combination of crops, livestock, and family labor, well suited to low-input risk aversion technology, but not well equipped to cope with the demands of market-driven modern agriculture. Medium- and large-size farms (5-40 ha) are generally highly mechanized, have the best genetic quality livestock, and possess the best animal husbandry skills; such farms are essential elements in the future development of livestock and especially dairy development in Poland.

The livestock sector plays a key role in Poland's agriculture. It provides nearly half the value of agricultural production and half of agricultural exports, uses 70% of all domestically produced grains, and is the main source of cash income for well over a million small farmers. In addition, Poland's 10.5 million cattle, 20 million pigs, 67 million poultry, 5 million sheep, and 1.4 million horses provide critically important organic fertilizer and the essential power for many small-farm operations. With livestock, as with crops, the genetic base for improvement is good, but there is scope for improvement in nutrition and for better feed conversion that should facilitate economies in concentrate feed utilization. Better management of pastures and fodder conservation should both raise the quality of feed and reduce costs of livestock production.

Farm profitability. A preliminary analysis of farm profitability, using mid-1990 prices and costs, suggests that a small private farmer can make a living equal to that of an industrial worker. Below about 10 ha, farm size is less critical than either the choice of agricultural activities, the soil type, or the quality of management. Pigs are by far the most profitable enterprise at present and dairy cattle the least rewarding: increasing the number of cattle on a farm has no beneficial effect on profit. An analysis of 18 typical farm models clearly shows that the most successful farms are those that combine satisfactory levels of productivity with cost containment. This confirms the need for research and extension to pay more attention to efficiency and cost-saving rather than yield maximization. Farm modeling is an indispensable tool for modern farmers. However, models are only as good as the data available and must be up-dated to match the movements of the market. Extension services should be equipped with the necessary facilities to help farmers make decisions in a climate of economic uncertainty.

Major areas of untapped potential

Coping with natural constraints. Crop yields, and the productivity of grazing livestock, are depressed by inadequate drainage and soil acidity over much of Poland. Investment in their alleviation both benefits yields directly and has an indirect multiplier effect through improving responses to plant nutrients, widening the crop range, and facilitating access to land for mechanization. However, more rapid progress implies improving machinery for drainage and lime spreading, and closer attention to the economics of these practices. More attention may also be needed in the longer term to mitigating climatic constraints by means of irrigation and the wider use of plastics, especially for horticultural crops. The introduction of more quickly maturing crop varieties, changes in cropping systems, mechanization to facilitate more timely field and harvesting operations, and improvements in drying and storage, especially on small private farms, can also contribute to this objective. An approach along these lines is consistent with the goal of increasing efficiency through reducing losses.

Raising the efficiency of input use. Fertilizer application in Poland is not well balanced in terms of the elements applied, mainly due to weaknesses in formulation by manufacturers. There are also large regional differences in levels of application. Evidence as to the optimum economic levels of use is lacking, reflecting serious weaknesses in economic research throughout Polish agriculture and the production-oriented mentality in the socialist sector. Much remains to be learned before the real potential contribution of fertilizer and lime to agricultural growth can be determined, but it appears considerable. This knowledge has to be related to specific agro-ecological zones of Poland and farming conditions, rather than to broad national averages or administrative units.

Inflation and the removal of subsidies have increased input prices sharply and farmers have cut back on their use. Cutbacks have extended to seeds, most significantly to seed potatoes, which represent about 25% of potato production costs. Spraying against potato blight has also been reduced, and the repercussions on future yields could be serious. Sales of certified cereal seeds have also fallen, which may have serious implications for future yields and quality.

In Poland little information is available to show how costs could be reduced without reducing yields. Privately sponsored research suggests that considerable economies are feasible in tillage and seeding practices, that

wider use of herbicides and seed treatments could have a high payoff at relatively low cost (weed populations are high and only about 50% of cereal area received seed treatment), and that possibilities of combining herbicide and fertilizer application and introducing integrated pest management practices should be explored.

Mechanization. There is also considerable scope for reducing costs without reducing yields through more effective mechanization. On nonmechanized farms, labor costs are higher and timeliness of practically all farm operations is more difficult to achieve. Thus yield losses are higher than on mechanized farms during the growing season and at harvest. Poland's inefficiently designed and poorly serviced machinery also leads to higher farm costs and reduced yields. Large state farms and private farms are already well mechanized; small private farms, however, have been neglected until recently, both by the farm machinery industry and by research and extension services. As a result, there is a shortage of appropriate modern tractors and equipment and a serious lack of spares to maintain machinery, much of which is old and in poor condition. Priority must be given in the immediate future to designing or importing machinery that meets the requirements of such farms, and particularly to promoting contract operations on smaller units of land. In addition, agricultural land tax policy should be used to stimulate amalgamation of holdings and consolidation of plots, which would help achieve economies of scale in farming.

Animal feed. For the livestock industry it is clear that rationalizing the feed industry and improving supply management and markets are essential to intensifying smallholder animal production and enhancing economic standards of production on medium-size farms. For crop production, the upgrading of processing standards is no less essential. For example, the expansion of rapeseed production of domestically processed high-value concentrate feed is limited by lack of processing capacity; similarly, inefficient industrial extraction of sugar from beets negates the benefits expected from breeding for higher sugar content.

Areas for action

Because of Poland's lack of strong comparative

advantage in export crop production, the present strategic orientation toward the supply of basic food for the population and provision of feedstuffs for animal production should continue. About 70% of crop production (including cereals and potatoes) directly or indirectly supports livestock production, and the rest is essentially used in human consumption. Whether these proportions should remain or whether there should be changes should be determined entirely by market decisions. Crop area and production targets should not be prescribed by the state.

In technical terms, the following actions are recommended:

• concentrating cereal development mainly on intensification of wheat and triticale;

• expanding the production of double-zero rapeseed, accompanied by a corresponding expansion of crushing capacity;

• concentrating potato production on the most suitable agro-ecological areas; improving genetic resistance to potato blight;

• raising the efficiency of sugar extraction from beets by introducing differential payments to producers based on sugar content and improving factory processing standards. Concomitantly increase breeding efforts for higher yields and sucrose contents;

• double (at the least) the grain legume area, notably in private sector farms, in order to provide more high-value vegetable proteins for human and animal consumption and to improve soil structure and fertility;

• improving grassland management through better research, crop nutrition, and introduction of appropriate harvesting and conservation techniques;

• exploring the justification for increased production of some of the more important minor crops having either export or export substitution potentials, such as malt barley, hops, tobacco, flax, and hemp;

• increasing small-farm production of vegetables, flowers, fruits, and berries, to supply increased domestic and export demand.

Livestock will remain an integral part of farming; diversification and intensification of livestock production should be encouraged, especially on small farms, and greater production efficiency encouraged on medium-size farms. The major constraint to livestock efficiency is the provision of quality feed throughout the year. Stricter quality standards need to be introduced for feed production units. Improvement in product quality and marketing will be essential to make Polish livestock products more competitive on world markets and livestock production must be backed up by more efficient input supply, marketing and support services. In particular, research on livestock husbandry and pasture management requires greater emphasis: current allocations do not reflect the importance of the livestock sector either socially or economically.

To avoid the well-known periodic fluctuations in pig population and prices, it is suggested that an industry-financed and -managed price stabilization program be introduced, by imposing a levy on all animals slaughtered. The reference price should be tied to the world market price. Such price stabilization methods work well in other European countries.

Environmental issues. Polish agriculture is not a major contributor to rural environmental degradation. Farm chemical use in Poland is about 20% of levels applied per ha in EC countries. Industry is by far the greatest source of rural pollutants. There is no effective legislation on the use of restricted products or enforcement of laws related to the use of such products. Also, there appears to be no enforcement of laws regarding the disposal of older, unused or deregistered pesticides and pesticide containers. As farm chemical use expands in the coming decade, it is critical that Poland establish a code of conduct to ensure that pesticide regulations are brought to international standards, and that imported and locally produced farm chemicals meet international standards for registration, both on crops grown for domestic consumption and for export. Training should be undertaken in careful pesticide use by farmers. Initial efforts in integrated pest management and biological control need to be expanded.

Agricultural marketing

The crucial importance of the agricultural marketing and processing system for the Polish economy and for the agricultural production sector has already been mentioned. This sector is mostly owned by the state and cooperatives (principally the former unions). Its present inefficiencies (poor resource allocation, long dependence on large and increasing subsidies that rewarded loss-making enterprises, monopolistic-monopsonistic organization, low-quality production, absence of responsiveness to market signals) have also been reviewed. The structural causes have been identified and recommendations made to start reforming the structure through rapid change of ownership structure, modification of management systems, and rapid privatization. Those measures are to be complemented by more specific actions and policy decisions applying particularly to the sector.

In addition to forcing the enterprises to make the structural changes mentioned above, the following actions are necessary to increase competition:

- Antitrust regulation should be designed and implemented. Competitive conditions should be monitored; this should extend at the regional level and throughout the food chain. An antitrust law has been introduced by the government, an agency is in place, and the agricultural sector is at the top of its priorities. It needs reinforcement and technical support to work efficiently and rapidly.
- Barriers to entry should be lowered to enhance competition. This can be achieved by encouraging joint ventures, establishing a new cooperative law, and making special provisions for new entrants. The latter is justified by the importance of the food sector, the nature and magnitude of the existing barriers, and the fact that privatization of the existing enterprises may not, without additional measures, increase competition, but rather help create private monopolies. Small- and medium-scale enterprises could be given temporary tax concessions and help to get access to finance through the establishment of a business development fund providing partial guarantees once banks have accepted the feasibility of an operation. The fund could also provide technical assistance to the new entrepreneurs and to the banks.
- No special concessions or treatment should be given to established enterprises, particularly to state and cooperative ones.
- Competition from imports should be allowed in some product areas, while taking appropriate measures to protect against dumping, in agreement with GATT regulations.

Measures should be taken to improve marketing infrastructure and institutions. The main aim is to facilitate development of a comprehensive market information service and rational spot, forward and futures market exchanges throughout the food chain. Information should be collected and disseminated to all players. A specific and detailed study is essential and urgent. Local retail market facilities should be encouraged and inspected for public hygiene. Finally, market exchange facilities at the producer/primary wholesaler and processor level must be established and encouraged. These activities require public investment (at state and local government levels), but the operation of the market should become self-financing.

Marketing services should be developed. Neither the state nor local governments should involve themselves in the direct operation of the market system — their intervention should be limited to the regulatory level. Direct operations are the responsibility of the professionals and of their associations. The establishment of interprofessional organizations (IOs) by major commodities, as exist in the Western countries, should be encouraged, and for this, appropriate enabling legislation may be necessary (models can be found in Holland, France, Germany, or Belgium). Those IOs should help establish quality standards and provide market analysis and information services to their members. They can organize storage and transport. They can also play an important role in the organization and promotion of exports, replacing the present Foreign Trade Organizations, which restrict competition, discriminate against other players and suffer from conflicts of interest when they are also importers or exporters. Those organizations should be fully privatized and prevented from monopolizing their activities. It is important to separate marketing promotion activities, to be undertaken by the IOs, from trading, which is the responsibility of the traders. Public support for the export-marketing drive is useful to help establish the reputation of Polish products abroad. Finally, IOs can play an important role in market regulation, not only through their information and advisory services, but also through interventions financed by the profession itself (and thus budget neutral).

Development of human resources is a particularly critical need, since one of the worst economic legacies of the previous regime is an absence of people trained in commercial operations or having the right attitude toward the exigencies of a market economy. A coordinated program for the development of the food industry should be prepared, and technical assistance from foreign countries will be essential. These programs should be targeted at young middle managers. Development of business school education has high priority.

Rational investment should be encouraged in the agrifood sector. Many opportunities for efficiency-improving investments will be created once the structural changes are implemented. There might soon be a lack of funds to finance those investments. It might be advisable to consider retaining tax concessions to facilitate and encourage self-financing. Enterprises not yet privatized should not have automatic access to those concessions until they demonstrate their ability to manage their business profitably.

Further research. The following areas deserve further examination:

* detailed description of the structure and channels of distribution and ownership;
* detailed examination of comparative advantage, and particularly up-to-date assessments of strategic marketing opportunities; this is work requiring specialized expertise not available in Poland;
* review of the market information requirements of the sector and the establishment of a formal market reporting and service agency;
* exploration of the feasibility of establishing more commodity exchanges in the Polish food chain.

The special case of the dairy sector

The importance of the dairy sector is well known. With a production of over 15 billion liters (19% of agricultural GDP), the sector is the main source of cash for more than 1.1 million small farmers. The dairy industry employs 110,000 people in 712 plants spread over the rural areas. The sector suffers from extreme fragmentation of production (average delivery per farmer is 12 liters at more than 10,000 assembly points). Dairy equipment is largely obsolete, and it produces a very narrow product mix. The price structure gives very low importance to quality, no importance to protein content, and limited premium to winter milk. Finally, quality enforcement is inadequate, with only 30% of milk collected actually qualifying as class I. Polish dairy products are of low quality and suffer a heavy discount when exported.

The economic stabilization program has exacerbated those problems by dramatically reducing the subsidy on milk products, which dropped from US$1 billion in 1988 to about US$70 million in 1990. The remaining subsidies were applied to low-fat milk and stimulated the production of butter. The liquidation of cooperative unions, hitherto responsible for stock management and financing, has obliged primary cooperatives to find the financing for their stocks themselves. The interest rate policy adopted at the beginning of 1990 confronts butter-producing primary cooperatives with high interest charges at the same time that their low-quality product can only be sold at prices that, in terms of milk equivalent, are only one-third the price paid by dairies producing cheese, skim milk products, and other exportable products. These low prices threaten the solvency of the dairies and specialized dairy farmers, who may be forced to sell their cows. Those farmers have the best genetic stock and hold the future of the Polish dairy sector. If measures are not taken rapidly, the present distress sales of butter on world markets at severely discounted prices will continue, resulting in butter shortages during the winter season.

The Polish dairy industry's strengths are in the husbandry skills of its farmers and the excellent health condition and genetic potential of its herd, which are at par with other world producers; in addition, the sector benefits from low labor and energy costs. But food demand projections and comparisons with other European countries suggest that domestic demand for dairy products will not regain the levels of the 1980s before the end of the century, although product mix will change. Predicting export market possibilities is difficult given the protection afforded to their producers by the OECD countries; but with the present quality and processing technology of the Polish industry, only modest prospects exist.

The strategy proposed is, after a necessary stabilization period of a few months, to steer the industry toward the production of a full range of quality products, to enable the industry to hold the domestic market and export as opportunities arise while providing a viable income to a maximum number of farmers.

For the short term, industry confidence should be restored and distress sales prevented. An inventory of available stocks and their quality should be taken, and the government should guarantee a price level to exportable quality butter that would increase from the present level to 80% of the world level by next spring. On the basis of present world prices, this means a guarantee of US$1,000 per ton equivalent by March 1991. The guarantee would cover the difference between the domestic price in March and the guaranteed price. The price guarantee would increase the collateral value of stocks and facilitate their financing. The state guarantee would be dependent on:

• dairy industry's assurance that a new pricing structure increasing the premium for quality and decreasing the premium for fat is implemented;
• the scheme being valid only until 1991;
• implementation by the industry of a quality improvement scheme.

Dairy industry restructuring should start immediately and strive to achieve economies of scale, product flexibility, and better sales and export organization. For this a regional rationalization is recommended to create a dozen or so milk pools by amalgamating dairy cooperatives. Temporary (2-year) collection exclusivity could be granted to accelerate the process. Legislation may be necessary. Technical assistance will be needed to help organize the milk pools, plan for regional organization, and convince farmers and financiers that the plan is workable.

The industry should move as fast as possible toward higher quality standards. Change in price structure, a well-targeted investment program, and an extension effort will be necessary. Strict enforcement of international standards should be introduced. Those dairies not complying with quality standards (particularly regarding milk contaminated with antibiotics) should be excluded from government support. Strict suspension rules should be applied to producers. An investment program to improve chilling facilities on farm and other on-farm improvements and improvements to the dairies and stock management facilities should be designed with the banks. A dairy export promotion board should be created, and export coordination mechanisms reviewed. Particularly, the role of the present export agencies should be reassessed.

It is expected that the above set of measures will bring the price of milk in a range nearer to Zl 900/liter (generally assumed to be the present production cost of milk), improve quality, and reduce the price discount for Polish dairy products in the world market. The emphasis on quality would tend to exclude smaller producers who could not afford the cooling equipment. Similarly, the milk pools will tend to exclude producers in low-density areas; a number of dairy plants will become redundant.

In the medium term, rationalization of the industry should continue around the milk pools. At the end of the 2-year collection exclusivity given to regional dairies, new entrants should be let in the market to develop niche products and markets and maintain the competitiveness of the industry. A study should be undertaken to prepare an industry-wide stock management and export system. The milk subsidy should be abolished; it could be replaced by measures such as distribution of milk to schools and vulnerable population groups.

Postscript: Addressing the present surplus production crisis

The 1990 grain harvest is only a few weeks away. The flush season for milk is in full swing. The food industry, still monopolistic and managed as before the reform, is not yet obliged to compress its margins to face competition. The farmers, who went out of debt in February 1990 when interest rates increased and became variable, have not borrowed since then and have by now exhausted their stocks of inputs; they need to replenish them for the next planting season. Yet they do not know at what prices the coming crops will be bought, and much less what the prices for next year's crop will be. Milk producers are unable to obtain remunerative prices for their product. At the same time, dairies are choking on a glut of unsalable butter they cannot finance. Dairy farmers have started selling cows that are uneconomic to maintain, and the present glut may, by winter, become a shortage of milk and butter. Pig production seems to be the only large-scale activity still doing reasonably well.

The government is asked by farmers to intervene directly to correct those problems and substitute itself for the apparently failing market system. It is pressed to reintroduce price-, marketing-, and even income-guarantee mechanisms. Grain stocks are still large because of inventory carried over due to last year's bumper crop, and commodities from imports and food aid. The shortage of capacity to dry and store the incoming grain harvest could create a problem of crisis proportions. The government is urged to guarantee the purchase of grain and commit itself to open-ended financial support. The impending agricultural crisis threatens the very objectives of the economic reform program, since a relaxation of fiscal discipline may restart inflation.

In the course of its work, the Polish-EC-World Bank Task Force was confronted with current problems, and its advice was sought on measures to alleviate the present crisis. The most pressing problems are being faced in:

- grain purchases;
- milk and dairy restructuring;
- credit policy;
- cooperative union liquidation.

While the Task Force did not fully examine all the subtleties and ramifications of these problems and is not privy to the negotiations between the government and the farmers, it has looked into these issues and can offer the following recommendations:

- An amendment to the present credit policy, particularly regarding the predictability of interest rates, is essential for farmers. No farmer will borrow if interest rates remain as variable as they have been since the beginning of this year. If interest rates remain too high, they will strongly discourage borrowing. It is during this period that farmers make their planting decisions and replenish their stocks of inputs. It appears that the government has already decided to freeze interest rates for this year.
- It is urgent to negotiate with Poland's food aid donors to obtain a relaxation of the interdiction on reexporting grain in order to provide space to dry and store the 1990 grain harvest with the existing facilities;
- Purchasing grain at guaranteed minimum fixed prices should be avoided at almost any cost. Rather than trying to manipulate supply and demand through an import-export policy, Polish farmers and traders should be provided incentives to store the grain in Poland. For this, it is proposed to create deferred purchase contracts, with a guaranteed price at six or nine months calculated to be remunerative for the

farmer but still below world markets. The newly established Agricultural Marketing Agency could offer such contracts. This system could lead to the establishment of a futures market for grain in Poland. A solution along those lines is being considered by the government.

- For butter, a similar course is recommended, including resistance to calls for fixing prices at cost-plus levels. Dairies should be offered deferred purchase guarantees at prices slowly increasing to about 80% of world market level by March 1991; they should use these contracts as collateral to borrow from banks to finance their stocks.
- The process of liquidating the enterprises formerly owned by the cooperative unions should be suspended and amended. A cooperative restructuring organization should be created to manage and restructure these cooperative enterprises.

Agriculture is a crucial sector in most countries, and probably more so in Poland. Today, it is not an exaggeration to say that agriculture holds one of the keys to the success of Poland's economic transformation. The path to a reformed, efficient and market-driven agriculture will be difficult. Old habits, mentalities, and structures must change if Polish agriculture is to catch up with the rest of Europe. The sector needs far-reaching reforms and structural changes that will be beneficial to most, but onerous to some. Polish farmers can certainly cope with this situation and even take advantage of these changes if the country pursues the right policies. To define these policies, a strategy is as essential to decision-makers as a map is to the traveller in unknown territory. But, unlike a map, a strategy needs to be adjusted from time to time, and modified according to experience gained from success as well as from failure. The Task Force hopes that this document will contribute to the process of mapping out the future of agriculture in Poland.

Endnote

This report was written by Claude Blanchi on the basis of the documentation, data and analysis prepared by the Task Force.

Annex 1

The macroeconomy and agricultural adjustment

Normally, when middle-income countries embark on major policy reforms of the macroeconomy — real devaluations, liberalization of prices, reductions in inflation, and trade liberalization — agriculture prospers. The real devaluation of the exchange rate raises the price of all tradeable commodities in comparison with nontradeables. Since agriculture produces largely tradeable commodities, this devaluation raises relative agricultural prices while lowering the costs of labor; agricultural producer incentives are thus boosted. Liberalization of prices eliminates the implicit taxation of farmers coming from price controls that normally foster urban consumption. It also allows a relative price adjustment between various commodities, permitting farmers to use resources more efficiently, and thus raising their incomes. Reductions in the inflation rate reduces uncertainty in prices and should lower real interest rates, permitting stockholding and on-farm investments to be less costly and risky. Finally, trade liberalization allows domestic farm prices to be linked more closely to world prices, expands markets for agricultural commodities, and lowers input costs.

In many countries, these macroeconomic reforms have resulted in agricultural growth that has exceeded growth in other sectors. While construction may suffer or import-substituting industries endure the adjustment costs of the transition to more export orientation, agriculture responds quickly and normally booms. Governments initiating these reforms can point to their

agricultural sector as illustrating the initial successes of their programs and argue that these successes will soon spread to the rest of their economy.

But this has not been the case in Poland. Although the reform program is still new — prices liberalized in August 1989 and macrostabilization in January 1990 — there exist few indications that success will be achieved in the next several years, unless there are substantial additional reforms. Agricultural incentives have declined significantly despite relatively high international commodity prices, a massive devaluation, and price and trade liberalization. Despite inflation having fallen dramatically, resulting in a more stable real interest rate, farmers and merchants have failed to borrow. Stockholding has become entirely involuntary, a result of being unable to sell previously acquired stocks. Many agro-industries are suffering from high debt, exacerbated by large stocks of unsold commodities and low throughput. As a consequence, Polish agriculture is in crisis.

The purpose of this annex is to analyze why Polish agriculture is not responding positively to the economic reforms, to suggest a short-term strategy for alleviating the farm crisis, and to present a medium-term strategy reliant on a private agro-industrial sector. To do this, the annex is divided into five parts. After this introduction, the second section describes the macroeconomic crisis and its effects on agriculture. The third section presents three options for dealing with the short-term farm crisis. The fourth section addresses the medium-term strategy, in particular the role of privatization and trade. The fifth and concluding section summarizes the elements of the economic strategy and draws some broad conclusions.

The macroeconomic crisis and stabilization

The government that took power in September 1989 faced an extremely difficult economic situation. Inflation was accelerating at triple digit rates, fueled in part by a massive budget deficit equal to 8% of GDP. External debt amounted to 80% of GDP; debt servicing was five times export earnings. Growth had stagnated, with per capita income now lying below 1978 levels, while government expenditures had grown by over 30% in real terms in the last decade (see Table 1.1).

Complicating the macroeconomic situation was the structure of the economy. Over 70% of the industrial sector was owned by the state. Exports were canalized by a few large enterprises that had survived on massive export subsidies. But even more critical was the nature of decision-making in these enterprises. In 1981, the Polish Parliament gave wide powers to the workers' councils, among them the power to hire and fire management. Management and labor had merged into an explicit collusion, with the government, the nominal owner of capital, having lost control of costs and production while it retained the ultimate obligation to fund the losses of these enterprises. Because of large subsidies to state enterprises and a substantial fall in revenues, the fiscal deficit reached 29% of budget expenditures in the first half of 1989.

The government had then inherited in the fall of 1989 an essentially bankrupt economy — unable to service its debt, in macroeconomic free-fall, and with a state sector outside of its control. It had few options. Over 40 years of communist rule had culminated in a rigid economic structure in macroeconomic ruin.

The new government decided to launch a critical two-pronged attack on the unstable economy. In the first part of this strategy, the government attempted to gain control over the budget and prepare for the next phase by making some institutional and legal changes, mainly introducing unemployment compensation and bankruptcy procedures. On January 1, 1990, the second phase of the program was launched. The crux of this phase of the government's program was a standard IMF-type stabilization package — fiscal and monetary restraints, a wage freeze, and a massive devaluation followed by a fixed nominal exchange rate to serve as a nominal anchor. The stabilization package was designed to bring down inflation rapidly and put pressure on inefficient state enterprises. With budgetary constraints in place, the government expected that the market would select inefficient state enterprises for bankruptcy and initiate the rationalization of the state sector. Unemployment was expected to rise, but this could be viewed as a sign of the success of the process — enterprises would be trimming labor costs by reducing employment levels and controlling wages. With improvement in efficiency and reduced costs, the cost-push part of inflation would be brought under control. Following macroeconomic stability, the real adjustments in the economy were expected to follow through a gradual process of enterprise restructuring.

Table 1.1 Evolution of the economy, 1978 - 1988

Change / Macro variables	Change / Per capita (%)	Household survey data	Per capita (%)
Gross domestic product	-1.4	Real income of farmers	-3.1
Domestic absorption	-8.6	Real income of farmer/workers	-1.1
Consumption	0.7	Real income of workers	-24.7
Government expenditures	31.7	Real income of pensioners	-16.9
Gross fixed investment	-29.3	All households	-19.9

	Year	%
Farmers' income as a percentage of workers' income:	1978	90.8
	1988	116.9

Agriculture's role in this stabilization program was envisaged to be three-fold. First, it was expected to respond rapidly to the new incentives. It was anticipated that agriculture, being largely a private sector (about 75% to 80% of arable land is held by private farms), would follow the incentives of higher relative prices and deliver food to urban areas at prices closer to world prices. Although higher food prices would mean drops in real wages, these would be moderated by the increased availability of both greater quantities and varieties of food. Furthermore, the hidden costs of food — waiting in long queues — would be eliminated. Second, agriculture was expected to boost exports, easing pressure on the balance of payments. Although export subsidies were eliminated, it was expected that about 80% of remaining exports would be competitive at world prices. Furthermore, the devaluation of the real exchange rate would compensate for the loss of export subsidies. And finally agriculture would hold back rural-to-urban migration and perhaps absorb some of the unemployed from the industrial sector. With about 50% of the small-farm population being part-time farmers employed in local state enterprises, a more prosperous agricultural sector was expected to absorb part of these displaced workers.

THE ACTUAL OUTCOME OF THE STABILIZATION

By most macroeconomic indicators, the stabilization program was a great success. Inflation crumbled under the stringent monetary and fiscal restraints from a monthly rate of 79% in January to 24% in February to about 5% in May. Budgetary controls and increased revenues (from several reforms on enterprise taxation) produced a budgetary surplus, projected to be between 1 and 3% of GDP. Monthly interest rates followed the decline in inflation, undershooting inflation in January but becoming real and positive in February by 14 to 16% and falling to 1 to 4% in May. The massive devaluation in January of about 100% (compared with the December rate) held: zlotys became readily convertible in Poland and foreign exchange reserves expanded. Driving the foreign exchange accumulation was a contraction in imports and a rapid expansion of exports (imports contracted dramatically by 27% and exports expanded by 14.5% from convertible currency areas in the first five months of 1990).

But there were also signs of trouble (see Table 1.2). Real wages fell dramatically by 40% in the first quarter of 1990. Output declined by 30% in the socialized sector (29% below its level in May 1989)[1]. Food expenditures rose from about 39% to 55% of total expenditures (compared with the first four months of 1989), reflecting the immediate pressure of food price rises on household real income. Unemployment, however, did not increase as expected. By the end of April, unemployment stood at only 2.6% of the labor force. Only a few enterprises had declared bankruptcy. Nevertheless, real debt was increasing rapidly by 12% in March, 18% in April, and 3% in May (see Table 1.3). Also, there were various reports of lengthening delayed payments and of indebtedness between enterprises. It appears that the restructuring program had not

Table 1.2 Industrial production[a] and unemployment, 1990

	Jan	Feb	March	April	May	Jan/June
Changes in percent with respect to the same month in 1989	-28.7	-31.5	-31.9	-31.9	-28.6	-30.1
Changes in percent over previous month	-10.1	-14.2	10.5	-8.6	3.5[b]	
Total registered number of unemployed ('000)	55.8	152.2	266.7	351.1	443.0	
Percentage of work force unemployed[c]			2.0	2.6	3.3	

a. Output sold by socialized sector.
b. Correcting for different working days, the increase in May is zero.
c. National work force calculations; do not include employment in agricultural sector.
Source: GUS data.

Table 1.3 Bank credit to public enterprises, 1990
(billions of zlotys)

	Dec	Jan	Feb	March	April	May
Total nominal	30.6	31.79	39.45	46.09	58.78	63.5
percentage increase in month		3.89	24.10	16.83	27.53	8.03
Total real	30.60	17.80	17.83	19.89	23.47	24.14
percentage increase in month		-41.83	0.15	11.59	17.96	2.89
Percentage change in real credit						
since 1/90			0.15	11.74	29.70	32.59

Source: Calculated on figures supplied by National Bank of Poland.

yet hit the state enterprises — labor was largely being retained and enterprises were holding on despite the magnitude of the macroeconomic adjustment.

The signs of problems with the macroeconomic program were most evident in the agricultural sector, where the greatest successes had been hoped for. The very strengths of the agricultural sector that were to lead to its success — its largely private nature and its ability to respond quickly to incentives — rapidly brought forth the difficulties facing the macroeconomic adjustment program: the inability to achieve stability and a supply response through macroeconomic policies when the real structure of the economy remains distorted and economically concentrated.

THE EFFECT OF THE ECONOMIC PROGRAM ON AGRICULTURE

Agriculture in Poland is a small sector, contributing only about 12% of GDP, so it would appear at first consideration that agriculture would most likely be affected by the economic program but would not in turn influence the program's success. But this is turning out not to be the case. The effect of the economic program is straightforward. With the domestic market consuming about 87% of agricultural production, it is not difficult to foresee that the macroeconomic program and the resulting sharp recession could significantly affect the market for farm products and hence the sector's economic well-being. But agriculture also has strong feedbacks to the general economy through employment (28% of the work force) and through affecting the real wage rate (food expenditures range from 35 to over 50% of all expenditures depending on income class). Furthermore, about 20% of

industrial output comes from agro-industries, which in turn are dependent for 90% of their raw materials on domestic agriculture. The agricultural sector is thus more important to the economy than its economic size would indicate.

When the economic program began, the agricultural sector was highly protected and subsidized. From 1986 to 1989, food subsidies ranged from 3.4 to 4.8% of GDP (see Table 1.4). Although part of this subsidy was nominally for consumption, it was in part brought about by high producer prices. For example, producer prices for wheat during the late 1980s ranged from 10 to over 30% above equivalent border prices. For the state sector, which produced most of the marketed wheat, the price support

Table 1.4 Agricultural subsidies in terms of GDP, 1986 - 1990
(percent of GDP)

	1986	1987	1988	1989	1990(est)
Food	3.5	8.4	4.8	3.8	0.2
Meat products	0.8	0.8	1.4	1.2	
Chicken	0.1	0.0	0.1	0.1	
Fish products	0.1	0.1	0.0	0.0	
Milk and					
milk products	1.6	1.4	2.1	1.6	
Flour	0.7	0.9	0.9	0.4	
Sugar	0.0	0.0	0.1	0.1	
Vegetable oil	0.2	0.2	0.2	0.2	
Baby food	0.0	0.0	0.0	0.0	
Milk bars	0.0	0.0	0.0	0.0	
Agro-inputs	1.1	1.0	0.9	1.3	0.3
Fodder		0.4	0.4	0.3	0.0
Fertilizer		0.4	0.4	0.8	0.3
Tractors		0.0	0.0	0.0	0.0
Pesticides		0.1	0.0	0.2	0.0
Credit to					
agriculture	0.2	0.1	0.1	0.1	0.1
Total	4.8	9.5	5.8	5.2	0.6

was even higher — averaging about 50 to 60% above world prices. In the case of milk, the producer support was nearly equally generous, from 24 to 50% above world prices depending on the year. As with wheat, the support was concentrated in the state sector. This support through output prices was supplemented by input subsidies for fertilizers, pesticides, and animal feed at the rate of about 1% of GDP. Credit subsidies also were provided to the agricultural sector. Furthermore, export subsidies were given for certain commodities at a rate often half the value of the goods exported.

Aggregating these subsidies for the different crops results in what is referred to as the producer subsidy equivalent (PSE), or the total income supplement offered farmers and the state farm sector. In the state sector for wheat, this PSE constituted nearly 70% of the value of the wheat produced; for rye, about 50 to 70%; for sugar, about 50%; for rapeseed, about 40 to 50%; for pork, about 40%; and for milk, about 40 to 80% (see Table 1.5).[2] In other words, support for agriculture and processing on a per unit value basis was about at the level of many industrial economies. Agriculture, especially the state sector, was sheltered and heavily subsidized. In 1988, average farmers' income exceeded that of urban workers by 17% (compare this to Hun-

gary and Yugoslavia, where farmers' income is below that of urban workers by 4 and 20%, respectively).[3]

This subsidization ended abruptly with the macro-stabilization program and the reduction of state expenditures. Food subsidies fell from about 4% of GDP in 1989 to less than a budgeted 0.2% for 1990. Agricultural input subsidies are to decline from 1.3% of GDP in 1989 to 0.3% in 1990. Furthermore, credit subsidies and export subsidies were nearly eliminated. In less than a year, a once highly supported agricultural sector (with support near Western European standards) had been released to survive in a deeply recessionary economy, still struggling to establish a market economy.[4]

Partly compensating for this near elimination of direct subsidies should have been the devaluation of the exchange rate. The real exchange rate (the nominal exchange rate corrected for inflation) was devalued nearly 50% compared with its 1989 level. If this devaluation were to be transmitted to farm-gate prices, then the net effect would have been a much more neutral adjustment in producer support.

But the price transmission did not occur — in part because of deliberate government policies and in part because of economic concentration in agro-industry. With inflation running ram-

Table 1.5 **Producer subsidy equivalents (PSEs)**
(percentage)

	Wheat	Rye[a]	Barley[a]	Beets[b]	Seed[c]	Pork	Beef[d]	Milk
1988 Poland								
Private	34.2	28.1	32.0					
State	—	—	—					
EC	30.0	34.0	34.0	71.0	59.0	6.0	56.0	60.0
1987 Poland								
Private	47.1	48.1	58.7	31.0	43.5	.	39.1	22.7
State	67.4	69.3	75.2	49.7	69.0	.	3.9	41.1
EC	66.0	63.0	63.0	80.0	67.0	5.0	46.0	68.0
1986 Poland								
Private	46.2	37.8	64.9	32.8	50.1	28.1	15.7	57.1
State	68.2	62.3	87.3	56.7	75.5	36.6	4.0	77.9
EC	63.0	66	66	76.0	57.0	5.0	50.0	73.0

a. Coarse grains used for ECs PSE data.
b. Refined Equivalent of Sugar used for ECs PSE data.
c. Soybeans used for ECs PSE data.
d. Beef and veal used for ECs PSE data.
Source: Polish data calculated by the Foreign Trade Research Institute in Warsaw. EC data published in *Agricultural Policies, Markets and Trade*, OECD (1990).

pant, the cooperative structure in disarray (the cooperative unions were dissolved), and a collapse in real producer prices, farmers withheld grains from the market in early- and mid-1989 (for the first nine months of 1989, agricultural supplies to cities were reportedly down by 30%). The specter of a food shortage in urban areas was of deep concern to the government. Exports of essential foodstuffs were prohibited and food aid urgently procured. With the blockage of exports, the arrival of food aid, and the sales of farmers to the milling industry increasing (because of the cooling down of inflation and rising interest rates), scarcity quickly turned to abundance. Exacerbating the situation was the decline in domestic food consumption brought about by rising retail food prices and declines in real income. Stocks of grains and milk products accumulated and farm gate prices plunged. Because of low demand for agricultural inputs, animal feed, and fertilizer sales also sharply declined.

Further aggravating the fall was the behavior of agro-industry. Although on an economywide basis it appears that the grain industry (the grain monopoly was broken up into 41 separate companies) and the milk industry are quite fragmented and competitive, at the local level they are highly concentrated. Years of accumulated collusive behavior (encouraged by past governments in order to meet the objectives of a state-coordinated sector) continued after prices were liberalized and most subsidies removed. The breakup of national monopolies created local monopolies and a system of cost-plus pricing continued. Instead of lowering prices to encourage sales, agro-industry restricted throughput, raised selling prices and forced back on producers (through lower purchase prices) most of the industry's higher per unit operating costs. In May/June 1990, wheat prices were at 60% of the border price; oilseeds at 80%; pork at 70% of its export price; and cattle for slaughter at 59% of the f.o.b. export price. The ratio of flour to wheat prices rose from about 3 to 1 on January 1, 1990, to 6 to 1 by the end of June 1990.

Heavy government support to agriculture had turned to indirect taxation through export controls, food aid, and oligopsony behavior. The government, recognizing the rapidly deepening farm crisis, lifted the ban on most agricultural exports except grains (where it remained bound by its food aid agreements to prevent reexport). For butter given as food aid, it cancelled its request and sought the substitution of feed corn. But the crisis was now deeply imbedded in the sector. Meanwhile the flush season for milk began and the grain harvest began to loom on the late summer and fall horizon. High nominal and real interest rates made stockholding extremely expensive, adding to the indebtedness of agro-industry. Dairy cooperatives, the potato industry, feedmills, sugar processors, and part of the horticultural industry were particularly hard hit. Farmers and some state farms, fleeing high interest rates and debt, quickly sold off durable goods and farm implements. Most dairy farmers received only extremely low and delayed (sometimes for months) payments for their milk. Agriculture, the only largely private sector in Poland, had been brought to its knees. But to rescue agriculture through subsidies meant opening the floodgate of subsidization elsewhere in the economy, since the austerity program now was beginning to take hold in other state sectors. In a collective consciousness, state managers began to contemplate the day of restitution of their state enterprises by the government. Macroeconomic stability was being threatened by the problems of a relatively minor sector (in terms of GDP): agriculture.

The short term (one year) — diminishing options

As the agricultural season proceeds, the government's options are becoming limited. The major harvest comes once a year; the cows reach their peak milk production during the summer months when feed is usually abundant. When the fall comes, the carrying cost of the herd increases and slaughter becomes a more prominent option.

To deal with the farm crisis and the threat of its intensification, the government basically has two options. One is to let market forces take their toll — some farmers go broke, many agro-industrial enterprises sink deeper into debt, and eventually, as domestic supplies diminish, imports begin once again. Since c.i.f. import prices are higher than f.o.b. export prices, prices to consumers, and possibly to farmers, will eventually rise. For consumers, the shift from f.o.b. to c.i.f. prices could add as much as 20% to the cost of food. For farmers, the results in terms of farm-gate prices would be uncertain, depending on whether agro-industry fully passes on the higher costs of competing imported food to producers. But the adjustment is likely to be swift — a major realignment of the sector followed in several years by a leaner agricultural sector with a sharply dual structure consisting of subsistence farmers producing for their own needs and large farms producing for the market. But this outcome may not result in an economically efficient sector. Market signals would be distorted by the economic concentration of agro-industry, causing an overreduction in the size of the sector and a distortion in the relative shares of crops under production.

The second option is to intervene through injecting lower cost liquidity in agriculture, stimulating demand for some foods, circumventing the oligopsony strength of agro-industry, and possibly in an indirect way providing some subsidization for agriculture. In this way, the sector is brought through the summer and fall and allowed to adjust at a slower pace.

The first option is relatively straightforward — hold the course and let the market bring about a different agriculture. But the risks are great — when the sector hits bottom, strong political forces will demand once again subsidies for agriculture and direct intervention to raise agricultural prices.

The second option is more complex, requiring delicate management by the state. Its primary danger is that the interventions that are intended to be short term — to get agriculture through the immediate adjustment — stick and become permanent and are viewed as an entitlement by farmers and agro-industry. The key to the second option is to intervene in a manner that does not create permanence to the intervention and ideally promotes the development of the market. The short-term intervention options suggested have three elements: first, the promotion of market and price transparency and inducements for private storage; second, the reduction of the uncertainty in real interest rates; and third, the promotion of demand through targeted food programs.

THE FIRST INTERVENTION OPTION — DEALING WITH PRICE UNCERTAINTY AND STORAGE

The first of these interventions is for the grain market. It is really an attempt to promote the development of a more transparent market that circumvents the local monopoly power of the state grain enterprises. Already the government has established legislation (in May 1990) authorizing an agency to intervene in the grain market. This agency (Agencja Rynku Rolnego, Agricultural Marketing Agency) has been assigned the following objectives:

- increase storing and drying capacity
- increase competition in grain merchandizing
- stabilize grain prices.

As originally conceived, the proposed agency would buy grain from qualified organizations; clean, weigh, test, and dry grains; pay to have the agency grain stored by qualified organizations; and sell grain to processors, merchandisers, and exporters. To fulfill these functions, the agency would establish purchase prices, qualify storage facilities, finance investment in storage, inspect grains at purchase and during storage, and monitor market conditions. The agency would have a governing council of 21 seats, 12 of which would be held by producers, processors and traders. Budget proposals call for 1 million tons of storage (transferred from the former state grain trust, PZZ) and an allocation of Zl 876 billion (or about US$87 million).

The prospects for the financial survival of the agency are not strong. If the coming harvest is large, a rough calculation indicates that the agency is likely to generate large losses (unless the government bails it out) because of storage costs and the inability to support prices when the crop is large. Also, it is likely that storage losses will be high since those storing the grain do not have an incentive to preserve it (it is owned by the state). Furthermore, by overstabilizing prices (announcing a fixed procurement price), private storage will be discouraged (one incentive to store grains is price fluctuations) and budgetary costs could quickly expand because the government has made a commitment through the agency to buy all grains at a fixed spot price.

However, the agency could fulfill its objectives without overly disrupting the market by altering the way it operates.[5] Instead of physically procuring and storing the grain (or paying others to store it), the agency could reduce price uncertainty, encourage private storage, and add competition in the grain market by creating a forward market in bonded storage certificates.[6] Although the proposed alternative operations of the agency appear to be complex, in essence they are relatively simple.[7]

The key to the alternative operation of the agency would be the bonding of storage certificates. Farmers or merchants would either sell their grain directly at the going price or put it into storage for later sale (when possibly prices will be higher). If they place their grain in a bonded warehouse, they will receive a certificate that guarantees that the grain will be properly dried and of a specified quantity and quality. The farmer or the merchant would be able to sell this certificate or use it as collateral for a loan for a percentage of the current value of the grain in storage (for example, 60 or 70%). The trading of this certificate would allow farmers to seek the highest prices for their grain among different merchants or millers.

To create a market for these certificates and to make their value more certain, the agency could be set up to trade in these certificates. The agency could offer both a present price or spot price and a future price for delivery of the grain at some specific dates in the future. Instead of selling their grain, farmers or merchants could make a sales contract with the agency for delivery of the grain at some specified future date at a stated price (the agency would maintain a list of prices for future delivery). This sales contract for future delivery would put a lien on the grain (if the grain is not delivered, the agency would have a legal right to confiscate the grain) but the ownership and, hence, responsibility for the storage of the grain would rest with the farmer or merchant. The agency could resell the contract to a merchant (domestic or foreign) or could sell back the contract to the owner of the grain at a price (the offset price) attractive to the owner. In this way, the agency would never have to take actual delivery of the grain. By acting in this way, the agency would be establishing a futures market in grains by acting as a market-maker in futures contracts.

Through these actions, the agency would be facilitating the trade in bonded storage certificates and establishing a futures price that would reduce price risk to storers of grain. Since the sales contract has a specified price, the sales contract has known value and could also be used as collateral for loans. By daily setting the futures price (the price by which the agency will buy futures contracts) and the offset price (the price at which it will sell these contracts), it is able both to control its losses (losses would depend on its pricing policy and how the spot market develops) and to avert the actual delivery of grains.

To make the market more transparent and less arbitrary, the agency could state its futures prices in terms of US dollars, convertible to zlotys at the official exchange rate. The futures prices could be directly related to the futures prices trading in the Chicago Board of Trade, corrected by quality and marketing costs and other discounts. By setting the discount, the government could establish the subsidy for grains in the country. The agency could sell the futures contracts to an exporter if it is necessary to remove excess stocks from the domestic market. The agency and sophisticated traders could hedge their price uncertainty in the Chicago Futures Market.[8]

Although the system appears complicated, for the farmer or merchant it would be rather simple — store grain in a bonded warehouse and then decide whether to sell the bonded certificate of storage today or hold it for later sale or contract for delivery to the agency at a stated futures price. The agency would be basically a trading agency in contracts for delivery — it could be a small office staffed by traders (such as those who buy and sell foreign exchange for the central bank). Spot and futures price lists would be publicized throughout the country to make the market more transparent. If the government decided to subsidize the price it would do so through setting the discounts or premium from the Chicago Futures price (this subsidy would appear through the losses of the agency).

There are several advantages to dealing in storage certificates and futures contracts over buying and storing grain directly. These are:

• Ownership of the grains would be retained by farmers or merchants who have a stake in maintaining quality;
• Prices, both present (spot) and future, would be known and publicized and related to world present and future prices;
• Collateral would have been created that would reduce the banking risks of loans and hence lower interest rates on borrowing; and
• Farmers would be able to hedge their price risks.

Both alternative operations of the agency could provide temporary price support through subsidies. Subsidization through futures contracts would be more controllable, however, as the agency would have greater ability to offset its position in the market by selling delivery contracts. An additional advantage is that after about three years or so, the agency could be transformed into an actual futures market with private traders, rather than the agency, arbitrating the market. It should be noted that for both proposed operations of the agencies, it would be necessary to certify storage facilities and inspect storage. A trained field staff would be required for both operations. Furthermore, storage would need to be separated from milling, with storage facilities and silos sold (preferably) or rented to private merchants or cooperatives.

THE SECOND INTERVENTION OPTION — REDUCING REAL INTEREST RATE RISK

Preferential interest rates have been largely eliminated beginning in 1990, and banks have been allowed to set their own loan rates (see Table 1.6). But two preferential rates continue

to exist for agriculture. Farmers can receive credit at fixed rates of 24% for six months (3.7% per month) and 36% for nine months (3.5% per month). The government has allocated Zl 750 billion (about US$80 million) to finance the difference between these interest rates and the market rates. In addition, counterpart funds from the EC are available at 75% of the prevailing rate for small-scale production, trading, and processing. The remaining credit available from the Bank of Food Economy is at prevailing rates of interest, which are set monthly based on anticipated inflation. Real rates on these funds were negative in January and February and positive the months thereafter.

With high and variable real interest rates, only the stout of heart or the foolish carry stocks financed through banking credit. If the prices of the goods stored do not increase near the nominal rate of interest, high losses will occur. Given that the monthly interest rates are currently at about 5%, miscalculation can be disastrous. Because the rates are variable based on anticipated monthly inflation, the risks are even greater. Voluntary stockholding by traders under these circumstances will be very limited.

Table 1.6 Monthly nominal and real interest rates, Jan-March 1990

	Jan	Feb	March	April	May
			Nominal		
Central Bank discount rate	36.0%	20.0%	10.0%	8.0%	5.5%
Demand deposits	7.0%	5.5%	3.0%	3.0%	2.0%
6-month time deposits	17.0%	13.0%	6.5%	5.0%	3.4%
1-year credit					
minimum	36.0%	20.0%	9.0%	7.5%	5.0%
maximum	62.0%	23.0%	12.0%	9.5%	8.0%
Bank for Food Economy					
1-year credit	39.0%	20.0%	10.0%	8.0%	5.5%
6-month credit	39.0%	23.0%	10.0%	8.0%	5.5%
			Real[a]		
Central Bank discount rate	33.9%	14.0%	3.7%	1.4%	1.4%
Demand deposits	-48.0%	0.2%	-2.9%	-3.3%	-1.9%
6-month time deposit	-43.1%	7.3%	0.4%	-1.4%	-0.6%
1-year credit					
minimum	-33.9%	14.0%	2.7%	0.9%	1.0%
maximum	-21.3%	16.8%	5.6%	2.8%	3.8%
Bank for Food Economy[b]					
1-year credit	-22.0%	-3.1%	5.1%	2.9%	0.5%
6-month credit	-22.0%	-0.7%	5.1%	2.9%	0.5%

a. Real rates according to point-to-point index.
b. Real rates according to average index.
Source: Gazeta Bankowa, No. 27 1990.

But stocks must be held or exported. The harvest comes in over a short period while the processing of the grain takes place over the entire year. If export controls are fully released on grain, it can be expected that stocks will be quickly exported and grain imported later as needed. In other words, stockholding will be effectively carried abroad, by those paying lower and more certain real interest rates.

The problem for the economy is that exporting and importing both carry costs, represented by the difference between f.o.b. and c.i.f. prices (costs of transport, distribution, and insurance, etc., cause price differences). Furthermore, distress exporting (as is currently seen for butter stocks) brought on by the high and risky costs of storing could find only low prices, below what could be expected as normal f.o.b. prices.[9]

The government must then continue to maintain some constraints on exports of grains and provide some additional incentive to hold stocks until real interest rates stabilize at lower levels.[10] The proposed agency, by offering a futures price, will provide an incentive to hold stocks. But unless the futures price is above the costs of carrying the grain, including interest charges, stocks will not be voluntarily carried. If PZZ companies are forced to hold stocks (they remain state enterprises), losses will accumulate and at some future date subsidies may become necessary.

Since the harvest comes once a year and at a time when great uncertainty still remains over real interest rates, it seems reasonable for the government to continue to offer a fixed nominal interest rate for a period of six or nine months to agriculture and agro-industry. The rate of interest should be set at a projected positive rate but at one below what the market rate is currently demanding (the monthly rate varies but has been as high as 30% real). To further induce stockholding, this interest rate could be offered to loans collateralized by the futures sales contract to the agency. Since banks receive secured collateral for the loan, some inducement to making the loan at lower real rates should be present.

The government should make it clear that this preferential rate is a short-term offer, one that is made to alleviate the current crisis, and one that will be withdrawn once real interest rates stabilize at lower levels. It should not be viewed as an entitlement for agriculture or agro-industry.

THE THIRD INTERVENTION OPTION — SELECTIVELY STIMULATING FOOD DEMAND

It is generally accepted that the economic adjustment will be difficult, with unemployment increasing and real incomes falling. Already food expenditures, especially among pensioners, have fallen in the first quarter of 1990. It can be expected that the austerity program will take a heavier toll among the less skilled and the old. Furthermore, in large families with several children, the food budget could be severely hit with the result that older children are kept from school in order to find menial jobs. No one set of programs can fully alleviate the suffering that could accompany a reform of the magnitude that Poland is attempting. Some assistance to those less able economically to defend themselves in this adjustment is called for. Already (since January 1990) the government is beginning to prepare assistance through unemployment compensation and special centers to provide food to the poor and unemployed.

In this assistance, agriculture can also be aided by increasing the demand for food. Families at lower income levels have a higher propensity to consume food; that is, for every zloty spent a higher proportion goes to food than at higher income levels. Thus, supplementing the incomes of low-income families increases food demand. One way of supplementing their income is through food stamps, or coupons which can be spent only on food. The advantage of stamps over direct income supplements is that there can be a higher propensity to consume food out of the implicit income transfer of food stamps. [11]

One option then is to initiate a food stamp program targeted to the poor and other vulnerable groups. Stamps could be redeemable for selected essential commodities in stores or through farmers markets. Stores and farmers receiving food stamps for the foods they sell could redeem the stamps through banks but only through direct deposit in accounts (for later monitoring of abuses). In rural areas, these banks could be the cooperative banks. Stamps should also be made available to the vulnerable in rural areas, possibly through the Church, charity groups or other social bodies (compensation and food stamps given only in urban areas creates an incentive to migrate to the cities). To prevent the program from being an entitlement, family eligibility for food stamps should be for a fixed period (six months, renewable depending on circumstances). Stamps should be redeemable for a certain value of food (if based on quantity, then inflation could raise budgetary costs).[12]

Another possibility is to initiate school feeding programs and expand pensioner feeding programs. Food could be procured from excess stocks for direct distribution, again supplementing the demand for food.

These types of programs help to buffer the call for general food subsidies which tend to distribute benefits to rich and poor alike. By setting up the basis for target intervention, farmers and the poor could be assisted. The key to success in the targeting will be achievement of the maximum gain both in food demand and social welfare.

Since part of the purpose of these interventions is to stimulate demand for domestically produced food, food aid should be limited. Ideally, food aid should be used to substitute directly for commercially imported food; that is, it should be part of commercial foreign assistance, and not an instrument to impoverish farmers. To ensure this, food aid should only be accepted for those commodities that can be freely exported or imported without quantitative restrictions.[13] The government should distribute the food aid at commercial or market prices. The best way to ensure this outcome is to open the acquisition of food aid stocks to competitive bidding, instead of the current system of distributing it to state controlled agro-industry for sale.[14]

All three options described above have relevance for both the short and the longer terms. The (futures) agency, by dealing in futures contracts and encouraging private storage, promotes the development of a viable rural market economy supported by both spot and futures markets. The preferential credit line based on longer term (six- and nine-month) credits will become more the norm when inflation and interest rates stabilize; that is, the term structure of interest rates will naturally evolve to offering longer term, fixed interest rate loans. And the food stamps and other target food programs are the safety nets offered by most industrial and some developing countries for their most vulnerable groups. The interventions, while directed at the short-term farm crisis, do not unduly compromise the future by setting precedents of unlimited government support for agriculture. In this way, these interventions would support the medium-term vision and options presented in the next section.

The medium term — two to five years

To describe the options for the medium term, it is necessary first to present a vision for the agricultural sector and to define in broad terms the role of the government in fulfilling this vision. To contrast this new vision (one largely held by the current government), the past approach to agriculture needs to be presented first.

In the 1980s, the vision of agriculture held by the government was one based upon income parity and self-sufficiency. Farmers should be receiving prices that guarantee an income more or less commensurate with urban wages. Furthermore, imports and exports should be restricted so that Poland would become food self-sufficient. This policy produced a highly distorted sector that was unable to follow its natural economic progression — that is, one that would produce a diminishing share of GDP with a lower portion of the work force (agricultural employment remains extraordinarily high at about 30% of the labor force for an agricultural sector producing only about 12% of GDP).

Poland in the mid-1980s, then, had an agricultural sector that was relatively large and employed more labor than countries of comparable real income per capita (especially if income comparisons are made on a purchasing power basis). This large sector did not come about by chance or through absolute advantage — Poland's soils are only of moderate fertility and its growing season is short. It came about by conscious government policy to promote income parity at nearly any cost through subsidies and guaranteed prices. In fact, on a per unit of value basis, subsidies, especially to the state sector, were equal to or higher than in the EC and the United States. This highly supported agricultural sector now faces a new reality — that of market forces and world prices. The sector must adjust; the only question is how quickly it can do so.

If other sectors of the Polish economy were not in recession and such a desperate need to export did not exist, then the adjustment in agriculture could be leisurely, with the sector allowed a soft landing. According to World Bank estimates, the economy, after a decline in GDP of 14% in 1990, must grow at a rate of 5 to 6%. Exports must expand to 26% of GDP by 1993. For agriculture's share of GDP to decline at a reasonable rate, agriculture would need to grow at a rate of 3 to 4% per year. To meet the targets on exports, agricultural exports would need to expand from about 12% to 25 to 30% of agricultural GDP.[15] Most observers of Polish agriculture believe that such growth rates and export orientation are optimistic.

Besides the technical obstacles to raising productivity growth to these rates, two other major impediments prevent the achievement of such performance in agriculture. The first is the state sector and its control of food processing and inputs. The second is the external barriers facing agricultural trade.

THE STATE-CONTROLLED AGRO-INDUSTRIES AS BARRIERS TO GROWTH

In Poland, the efficiency and productivity of agro-industry is as critical to agricultural performance as good farm technology and management. An estimated 75% of food is processed and almost all agricultural inputs come from domestic industry. Between these upstream and downstream industries lies agriculture. Its farmers are dependent for their share of wholesale food prices on the efficient and competitive operation of food processing and distribution. Farmers also require high quality and low cost inputs such as seeds, fertilizer, and other chemicals from their input suppliers. Without the efficient operations of these industrial sectors, agriculture is helpless and investments in improving farm productivity are nearly useless.[16]

Unfortunately, agro-industry in Poland is grossly inefficient and, worse, generally unresponsive to market forces. In terms of factor productivity growth, food processing ranked second to last in a sample of 17 industrial groups, with a decline in annual growth of 5.1% in productivity from 1978 to 1982 (see Table 1.7). With the overall resurgence in output growth between 1982 and 1985, food industry productivity growth became positive at 1.2% but still ranked second to last in growth. In terms of international comparisons of competitiveness (as measured through domestic resource coefficients), the food industry displayed the least international competitiveness of all of Poland's industries (see Table 1.8).[17] In fact, the DRC measure for food processing was negative, indicating that the value of inputs exceeded the value of outputs when measured in world prices.[18] Field visits to agro-industrial enterprises tended to confirm these numbers on lack of efficiency. Processing plants were generally a decade and a half behind in technology.

This lack of efficiency shows up in other measures. In a 1988 sample of 500 of the largest state-owned industrial enterprises, about 10% were found to be loss-making in the absence of subsidies and taxes (see Table 1.9). Of this 10%, about 90% were in the food processing industry. Of other industries that made losses, about 70% supplied agricultural inputs, animal feeds and fertilizer. While part of this loss-making is attributable to price controls, major responsibility must also be assigned to the agro-industries' inefficiencies and antiquated technologies.

Beginning in August 1989, the government began the liberalization of prices with the objective of allowing the market to determine which

Table 1.7 Total factor productivity growth, 1978 - 1985

1978-1982		1982-1985	
Best Performances			
(1) Precision instruments	2.7%	(1) Precision instruments	6.3%
(2) Pottery and china	2.4%	(2) Pottery and china	4.8%
(3) Engineering	1.9%	(3) Electrical engineering	4.4%
(4) Metal products	0.7%	(4) Engineering	3.6%
(5) Wood	0.4%	(5) Textiles	3.5%
Worst Performances			
(17) Building materials	-5.3%	(17) Paper	-0.5%
(16) Food processing	-5.1%	(16) Food processing	1.2%
(15) Wearing apparel	-2.1%	(15) Nonferrous metals	1.2%
(14) Nonferrous metals	-1.6%	(14) Ferrous metals	1.2%
(13) Basic metals	-1.0%	(13) Building materials	1.4%

Source: Konovalov, 1989.

Table 1.8 DRCs and value added, 1986

(millions of zlotys)

Industry	Value added domestic prices	Value added world prices	Short run DRCs	Long run DRCs
Metallurgical	15,411	5,785	1.15	4.00
Electro-engineering	89,208	70,802	0.55	1.32
Chemical	23,581	18,786	0.41	1.25
Mineral	8,981	9,177	0.49	1.05
Wood and paper	9,226	8,399	0.54	1.04
Light	40,601	30,373	0.61	1.01
Food	6,048	-3,803	-1.47	-3.40
Grand Total	193,226	139,518	0.62	1.45

Source: Konovalov, 1989.

Table 1.9 Loss-making enterprises in 1988

Sample of 500 largest state-owned industrial enterprises[a]

Total number of loss-makers of which:	56
Food Processing, of which:	43
meat products	23
food-oil products	6
poultry products	5
grain products	5
sugar products	3
Other Industries, of which:	13
fodder production	6
fertilizer production	3

a. Coal mining excluded.
Source: Konovalov, 1989.

enterprises are efficient and which are not. Unfortunately, the drive for efficiency through price liberalization confronted another barrier — the oligopolistic structure of agro-industry (see Table 1.10). Agro-industry is highly concentrated, at both the aggregate and regional levels. For example, in a 1987 sample, it was found that two enterprises had 47% of the market in food concentrates, 41% in oils and fats, 51% in potato products, 30% in vegetable and fruit products, and 30% in sugar products. In other industries, such as dairying, milling, and meat processing, the two-firm concentration ratios were lower (in the range of 2 to 20% of the market), but these low percentages concealed the regional oligopsony nature of the enterprises. With transport difficult to obtain and costs high, single buyers dominated many regional markets. Also, there is a strong possibility of collusive behavior among these state enterprises. One of the legacies of central planning is that a large number of enterprise directors and managers are accustomed to formal and informal economic coordination.

To complete this bleak picture, it is necessary to describe the response of enterprises to the economic reform program. Despite a dramatic fall in throughput and increasing indebtedness of enterprises, only one agro-industrial enterprise has gone bankrupt and few have significantly reduced their labor force. With workers' councils having the right to select and fire managers and with the state still the nominal owner and thus eventually obligated to bail out failing enterprises, no manager has the incentive to reduce his labor force or for that matter close the enterprise. In many ways, price liberalization has contributed to the worst case scenario — inefficient oligopoly and oligopsony enterprises pricing largely as they wish to compensate for lower output and not reducing costs. It is impossible to conceive of a vibrant agricultural sector while it is hostage to such an uncompetitive and inefficient agro-industry.

Table 1.10 Economic concentration ratios of state firms, 1987

(fraction of market sales)

	One-firm	Two-firm	Four-firm
Outputs			
Food concentrates	0.31	0.47	n.a.
Oils and fats	0.28	0.41	0.66
Potato products	0.27	n.a.	n.a.
Fruit and vegetable products	0.23	0.31	0.40
Flour milling products and pasta	0.09	0.14	0.24
Eggs and poultry	0.08	0.15	0.28
Milk and milk products	0.02	n.a.	n.a.
Sugar and sugar products	0.19	0.30	0.51
Inputs			
Tractors	0.90	0.96	n.a.
Fertilizer	0.22	0.43	0.73
Farm machinery	0.15	0.23	0.35
Animal feed	0.14	0.26	0.51

Source: Rocznik Statystyczny Przemyslu, 1988.

DEALING WITH UNCOMPETITIVE AND INEFFICIENT STATE INDUSTRIES

The government in confronting this situation has basically two broad options: keep agro-industry in the state sector or privatize it.[19] Economic theory says little about the benefits arising from one ownership structure over the other but, auspiciously, experience throughout the world with state ownership of agro-industry has demonstrated that government ownership simply does not work. Agro-industry, when dealing with such an economically sensitive product as food, is unable to withstand political influence. Inevitably, prices are controlled by the state either directly through laws or directives or indirectly through more informal requests. Controlled prices lead to subsidization and to the disincentives that come from knowing that the state is the controller of prices and stands by as the ultimate source of financing for losses. These observations on state behavior and the need for privatization are shared widely in Poland both by the government and the public.[20] The reliance on state enterprises is a legacy of the past; the only outstanding issue is how to privatize and with what speed.

In privatizing agro-industry and, for that matter, other state enterprises, the government has three broad options: first, a slow piecemeal privatization such as Britain has been attempting; second, a more rapid enterprise-by-enterprise privatization; or third, a broad-based privatization based on holding companies or mutual funds.[21]

In the piecemeal approach to privatization, enterprises are sold off to investors, to groups such as workers, or to other enterprises. The essential determinant for privatization of enterprises is the market. As the market reveals through bankruptcy which enterprises are not being managed properly, they are sold off to the private sector. The state remains the owner of enterprises that are competitive under a market economy while ridding itself of inefficient and badly managed enterprises. The process is then orderly and Darwinian. Unfortunately, the process is also long and costly and subject to a major risk — the soft-budget option. Enterprises that find themselves unable to compete will attempt to rally political support in defense of their survival. The political temptation will be to continue to subsidize inefficient enterprises or invest in their rehabilitation. Without a clear owner financially liable for losses and benefitting from gains, it is doubtful that investment will be economic.

A variation of the piecemeal approach is to privatize quickly all enterprises but on a company-by-company basis. Each enterprise is made into a joint shareholding company with the state initially the only owner of shares. The state would then sell off the shares to various parties: workers, the public banks, etc. The problem with this scheme is that the state would retain only the enterprises that no one wants to own while having divested itself of the profitable ones. Also, if employees or banks have controlling interest, the enterprise may be managed either to the workers' or banks' benefit, neither of whom may have the preservation of the assets of the enterprise at heart.

The last suggested option is to create holding companies initially to take control of the shares of a variety of enterprises; at the next stage, the shares of the holding company are given or sold to the public at large with the state retaining a minority and noncontrolling allotment of the shares. The public having now received shares is free to sell them to other parties as it wishes. Equity selling and buying would lead to controlling interests by various private parties. Once the shares have achieved value and management is under the control of private owners, the state can divest itself of its remaining shares. This method of privatization allows the state initially to reclaim control from the employees over the management of the enterprise, maintain continuity in management until private ownership exerts itself, and then receive a return on its initially retained shares. The public also gets a share of the state enterprise pie in an equitable distribution. The holding companies, then, control a wide variety of enterprises, some profitable and some loss-making. Based upon

Table 1.11 The share of agrifood exports in total exports
(percentage shares)

Zone	1989		Jan-May 1990	
	Food	Agrifood products	Food	Agrifood products
Nonconvertible	1.6	2.0	1.5	1.3
Convertible	13.8	5.8	12.5	7.1

Source: Annex 4.

its criteria of return to its private owners, the holding company can sell or close enterprises. Eventually, the holding companies would be dissolved with shareholders receiving directly shares in companies under holding company ownership.

A MAJOR BARRIER TO AGRICULTURAL RECOVERY — EXTERNAL TRADE CONSTRAINTS

Poland's farmers have two markets: the internal market and the world market.[22] The demand for food products in the internal market will largely be set by income growth; if Poland's income per capita recovers quickly from the severe recession and future growth is rapid, the domestic market will expand at a rate much less than overall income growth. Because of the severe fall in incomes in 1990 and slow growth forecast for 1991 and some of the later years, projections indicate that domestic consumption of food will not reach 1989 levels until the year 2000.[23] That is, farmers can expect that the domestic market's ability to absorb domestic farm produce will be limited; nevertheless, domestic consumers will have to remain the primary market for most food output.

The export market for certain products — meat and fruits and vegetables — will remain strong but will be limited by external trade restrictions. Poland's agricultural exporters face variable import levies, quotas, minimum prices, and voluntary export restraints for most of its agricultural exports to hard currency areas. These restraints to trade are particularly pronounced in the EC, which currently constitutes about 50% of Poland's agricultural export market (see Table 1.12). Agricultural exports to non-convertible currency areas remain small, about 1 or 2% of total exports to these areas. Some expansion in these markets can be expected as the Soviet Union adjusts its agricultural policies but, to say the least, the prospects are highly uncertain (it is expected that in

Table 1.12 Agricultural and food exports mainly to hard currency countries, increasing share of EC countries
(percentage shares)

	1975	1984	1989
Convertible zone of which:	67.4	77.2	81.9
EC countries	31.1	34.6	50.1
USA	12.1	12.8	10.5

Source: Annex 4.

January 1991, this trade will become convertible).

Polish exporters also face the constraint of a highly concentrated export trade — five state enterprises dominate agricultural exports. These enterprises are resistant to new competition yet continue to maintain old channels for trade and methods of doing business. Without additional private sector competition in exporting, agricultural exports will remain confined and diversification in terms of both products and markets will be hindered.

On the positive side, the real exchange rate has depreciated significantly, giving a strong incentive to export. However, inflation persists, and each day it appreciates the real exchange rate (as long as the nominal exchange rate remains fixed), reducing export competitiveness. The race is then between devaluations and an inflation rate that erodes export competitiveness, but eventually each feeds on the other. At a 5% rate of monthly inflation, incentives offered by a 50% undervalued exchange rate will evaporate in less than nine months without further nominal devaluations.

A STRATEGY FOR AGRICULTURAL EXPORTS

Agricultural exports are important to the prosperity of Polish agriculture — without growth in exports, farmers face a stagnant or only slow-

Table 1.13 Oligopolistic position of foreign trade organizations (centralas) in agrifood import and export
(percentage shares)

Centralas	Animex	Rolimpex	Rybex	Agros	Polcop	Total
Export	31.6	21.1	10.0	9.5	4.9	77.1
Import	9.1	39.9	5.0	20.8	3.0	77.8

Source: Annex 4.

growing domestic market. Three steps are needed to expand and diversify exports.[24] The first step is privatization of agro-industry and export enterprises and the removal of all formal barriers to entry by new private enterprises. Without this step, exports will be bound by traditional ways of trading and new products and markets will be difficult to develop. The second step is political negotiation with major trading partners for market access. The European Community gave Poland GSP status, but this concession, while cutting tariffs by 50% for some products, still imposes quantitative restrictions (quotas are shared by other GSP countries so the concession is minimal) and variable levies. Bilateral donors cannot just give financial and technical assistance to Poland; they must provide market access. Otherwise, it is equivalent to putting one foot on the accelerator while the other presses down hard on the brake. Poland cannot survive such contradictory signals. It is hoped that the Uruguay Round of trade negotiations will make some progress in reducing trade barriers but this will be a long process. In the meantime, donors must take a more favorable stance to market access for Polish agricultural exports.

The third step is maintaining the real exchange rate at a somewhat undervalued level (see Table 1.14). If the exchange rate becomes overvalued, then Polish farmers will not only face the barriers to trade outlined above, but will be confronted by an implicit export tax. It is unlikely that Poland can compete in the world agricultural markets with this additional handicap.

Conclusions

Poland's agriculture has gone from a highly protected and subsidized sector to a somewhat indirectly taxed sector almost overnight. Besides this abrupt transition, agriculture faces a difficult macroeconomic situation resulting in falling domestic food demand and high interest rates. Overshadowing even these difficult problems is the legacy of inefficient agro-industries and lethargic export enterprises. Finally, many export markets remain constricted by protectionist policies of trading partners. Under such circumstances, it is difficult to be optimistic about the prospects of Poland's agricultural sector.

An additional danger that exists is a potential overreaction by the government that could exacerbate the economic situation — by imposing price controls and guarantees, by creating state enterprises to intervene in the market, by providing large subsidies and by enacting excessive import and export controls. These interventions taken at the height of a farm crisis could become the barriers to achieving a more efficient economy in the future.

This danger does not mean that the government should be inactive in addressing the current farm crisis. Some actions have already been suggested: creating an agency to trade in futures contracts based on certificates of storage, providing incentives to store butter (see Annex 21), providing longer term loans at fixed nominal interest rates (but at real interest rates), and stimulating food demand through food stamps and direct feeding programs for school children, pensioners and other vulnerable groups initially harmed by the economic reforms. On the trade side, the government should continue to maintain an attractive exchange rate for exports and attempt to negotiate market access for its products. On the technical side, many suggestions are offered in the other annexes.

Finally and most importantly, it must privatize. With output markets, external trade and input supplies dominated by state enterprises responding to noncommercial incentives, it is difficult to imagine a vibrant agricultural sector. Because the problems of agriculture are intensifying — the farm crisis is already upon the sector — privatizing agro-industry must occur soon and rapidly.

Table 1.14 Effective real exchange rate, 1981-1990[a]

	1981	1982	1983	1984	1985	1986	1987	1988	1989	1990
Real exchange rate	110.65	137.95	167.55	163.85	140.95	110.30	79.55	72.73	76.95	43.29(est)

a. A decrease indicates depreciation.
Sources: IMF, World Bank.

Endnotes

This annex was prepared by Odin Knudsen, assisted by Wales Mack.

1. These numbers may overstate the severity of the fall as production in the private sector is not recorded.

2. Some caution should be exercised in interpreting PSE numbers for Poland as the exchange rate is a confounding factor. However, if estimates of the real exchange rate from the World Bank and IMF are used to correct the PSE numbers then the level of subsidization actually increases for 1987 and 1988 because these estimates point to an undervalued exchange rate (compared with 1980) for those years (see Table 10.14). From 1982 to 1985, the exchange rate was overvalued (compared with 1980); subsidies helped compensate for this overvaluation in those years.

3. In the first quarter of 1990, farmers' income was 86% of workers' income. Caution should be exercised in interpreting these ratios as other intangibles such as housing and seasonality may not be uniformly or consistently applied to the data.

4. This is most evident in the dairy sector where subsidies reached nearly US$1 billion in 1988, fell to US$70 million in 1989 and nearly disappeared in 1990. This sector contributes 19% of agricultural GDP and provides an important source of cash to over 1 million small farmers.

5. A legal opinion would be needed to establish conclusively whether the proposed alternative operations of the agency are consistent with the legislation establishing the agency.

6. This intervention is described more fully in Annex 9.

7. A similar concept of price stabilization is proposed for butter but using a more guaranteed price intervention by the government (see Annex 21).

8. See Annex 9 for qualifications and greater details on these operations.

9. This problem is described more fully in Annex 4.

10. Some temporary licencing of exports would need to be maintained. The licenses could be auctioned or taxed to prevent excessive profits for exporters.

11. Although the income supplement from food stamps is partially fungible, this higher propensity is thought to originate because the stamps are used primarily to supplement the expenditures of the primary food purchasers who tend to have a higher propensity to buy food than others in the family. Income supplements are spread wider in the family and therefore follow more conventional intrafamily distribution patterns.

12. See Annex 2.

13. Imposing tariffs on imports and exports would be all right since domestic prices would then be equal to the world price plus the tariff with corrections for transport, etc., regardless of the amount of food aid. Since domestic prices would be unaffected, domestic supply would not be discouraged. Of course, one of the assumptions implicit in this discussion is that competition exists, an assumption that currently does not hold in Poland. In later sections of this annex, this lack of competition will be discussed in more detail.

14. Under the current system, state agro-industries sell the food aid on behalf of the government. Proceeds from the sale go into a counterpart fund after distribution and handling costs are retained by the enterprise. Under the current system, these enterprises have little incentive to reduce costs or follow market pricing in the distribution of food. Competitive bidding would offer some competition for the food aid, although collusive bidding would need to be prevented.

15. Source: World Bank President's Report No. P-52-94.

16. The reverse is also true — agro-industry depends on the efficiency of agriculture. This also has broader economywide implications since the food industry share of all industrial output is about 20%, of (convertible) exports 13%, and of employment roughly 10%.

17. These results are based on results from V. Konovalov, *Poland: Competitiveness of Industrial Activities: 1961 - 1986*, August 1989, The World Bank.

18. There was considerable variability of results, with the dairy and meat industry is being the least competitive and soft drinks and milling products being more competitive.

19. The issue of privatization of the state farms and cooperative industries is dealt with in Annexes 6 and 7.

20. Polls taken in March and April 1989 by the Center for the Study of Public Opinion show that between 80 and 90% of workers and managers support privatization of most small- and medium-size industries. For large industries, the number declines to about 57%.

21. This section is based on discussions with Manuel Hinds and Polish counterparts. For more details, see the annex on privatization of agro-industrial enterprises.

22. See Annex 4 for a more elaborate analysis of Poland's agricultural trade and its prospects.

23. See Annex 3 for details on the projections.

24. Other steps are of course necessary. Annex 8 gives suggestions in this regard.

Rural development strategy

Initially, the Task Force had planned to limit the scope of the strategy to agricultural policy issues. But it soon realized that it was necessary to broaden the strategy and include issues related to rural development because of the importance of the rural sector in the Polish economy and of the possibility of sustained development in rural areas.

The main objectives pursued by a rural development strategy are:

• increasing employment and labor mobility, and
• quickly privatizing and creating small production units.

Because of the limited time available, the Task Force was not able to examine in detail the wide range of economic, sociological and cultural issues related to rural development. Some of these are discussed in other annexes, while others still require a more systematic analysis before policy conclusions can be drawn. This annex focuses mainly on characteristics of the rural population and on proposals for the short term regarding:

• the awakening of economic initiative and the creation of an alternative labor market;
• the implementation of a social safety net for the rural population.

The level of analysis which is applied to the various issues discussed in this annex does not reflect their relative importance, but rather the access to data necessary for the analysis during the work of the Task Force. Therefore, this annex should be viewed as a general outline of rural policy development based on a selective approach to different issues.

This annex is mainly based on information provided by the members of the Task Force. It has also benefitted from discussions with — and reports provided by — representatives of the Ministry of Agriculture, Ministry of Rural Welfare, Ministry of Labor and Social Policy, and Ministry of Finance.

Demographic and sociological determinants of rural change

In contrast to the situation in many Western European countries, the rural sector in Poland continues to be an essential component of the national economy and of social equilibrium. Its main characteristics are discussed in this section.

STABILITY OF THE RURAL POPULATION

The rural population has been very stable. It has remained approximately at the same level — 15 million — since 1950. Today, despite the strong demographic increase, the rural population still represents 40% of the total population and 36% of the productive-age population (see Figure 2.1). The structure of the rural population differs considerably from that of the urban population (see Figure 2.2) and is much

Figure 2.1 Total and rural population, 1950 - 2000

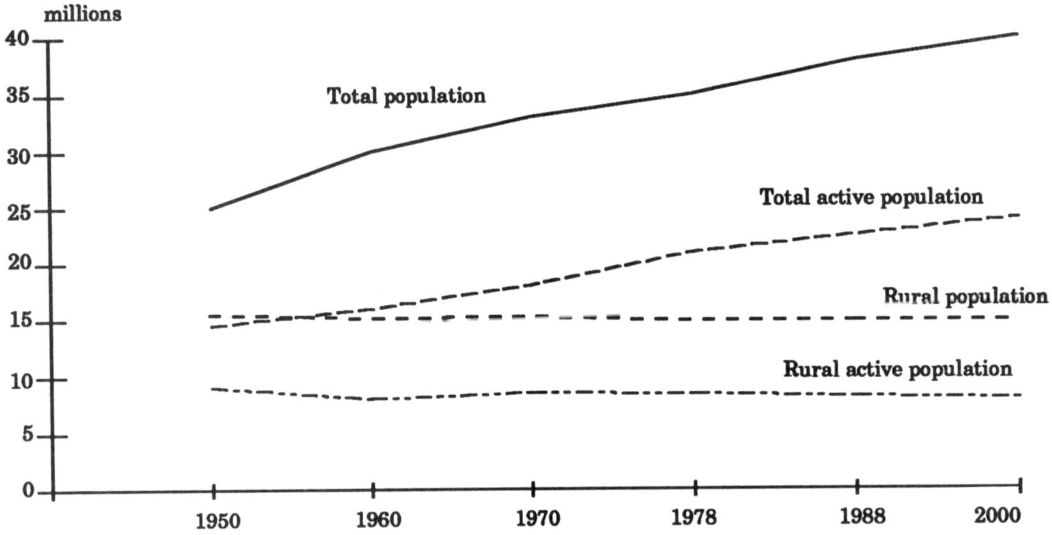

older as a result of migration. The farm population in rural areas is older than that working outside the farms. More than 20% of farmers are of post-productive age, and this is an important constraint on agricultural productivity increases. The percentage of old people is particularly high in northern, central and central-eastern voivodships (see Map 2.1). The shortage of women of marrying age (see Figure 2.2) will slow down the process of farm takeover and farm management. This farmer's wife problem is strongest in the northeast, where the number of women of marrying age is 65 per 100 men. It is a major reason for depopulation in rural areas (see Map 2.2).

There are also wide regional differences. As an example, the high rural population density in the central and southern parts of Poland contrasts with the low density in the horseshoe-shaped area comprising the eastern, northern and western border territories. In parts of the horseshoe and in several regions of central Poland (accounting in total for one-third of the Polish territory), the depopulation process is ongoing. It gives rise, as in several other European countries, to difficult economic and political problems.

DIFFERENCES IN FARM SIZE

The average farm size is 6 ha. Farms can be broken down into four groups of approximately equal size, as follows:

Size of Farm	Percent of Total
Very small (from 0.5 to 2 ha)	24%
Small (from 2 to 5 ha)	27%
Medium (from 5 to 10 ha)	28%
Large (more than 10 ha)	21%

There are important regional differences in farm structure. The average farm size varies from 2.4 ha in the Katowice district to 11.8 ha in the Suwalki district. These differences can be explained by the country's partition into three regions during the 19th century and by the unequal pace of regional industrialization and development.

ACTIVITIES OF THE RURAL POPULATION

Although the rural population has remained stable, its structure has changed over time. The share of farm population has decreased while the off-farm population living in rural areas and working either there or in cities has increased. From 1950 to 1988, the percentage of rural population working outside agriculture has increased from 15.7% to 40.7% (see Figure 2.2). Almost 2.3 million rural inhabitants work outside the *gmina* (county) where they live, and more than half of the rural population works in cities. Table 2.1 shows the distribution of the active population by place of employment and by economic sector. Rural areas not only absorb surplus labor from farms but also provide shel-

Figure 2.2 Population structure

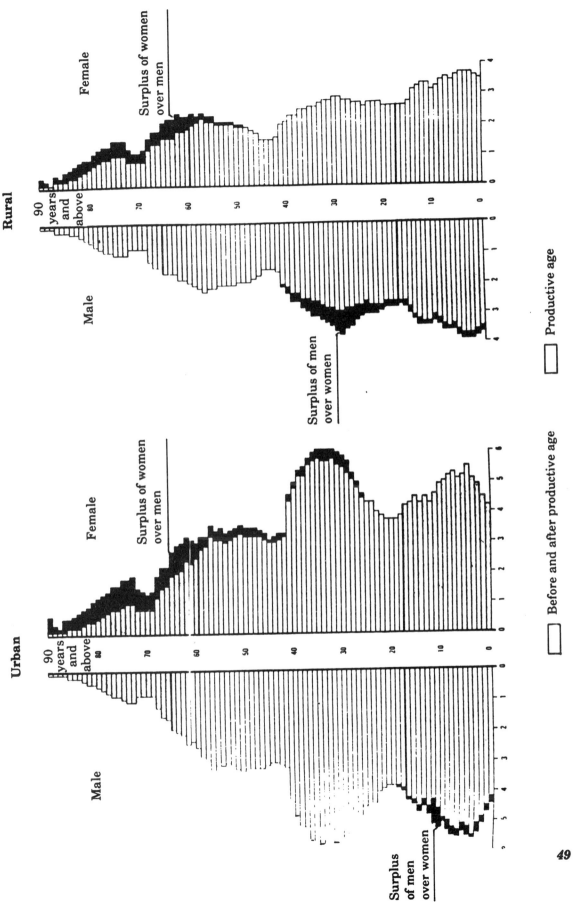

Rural

Female

Surplus of women over men

90 years and above

80

70

60

50

40

30

20

10

0

Male

Surplus of men over women

Urban

Female

Surplus of women over men

90 years and above

80

70

60

50

40

30

20

10

0

Male

Surplus of men over women

Productive age

Before and after productive age

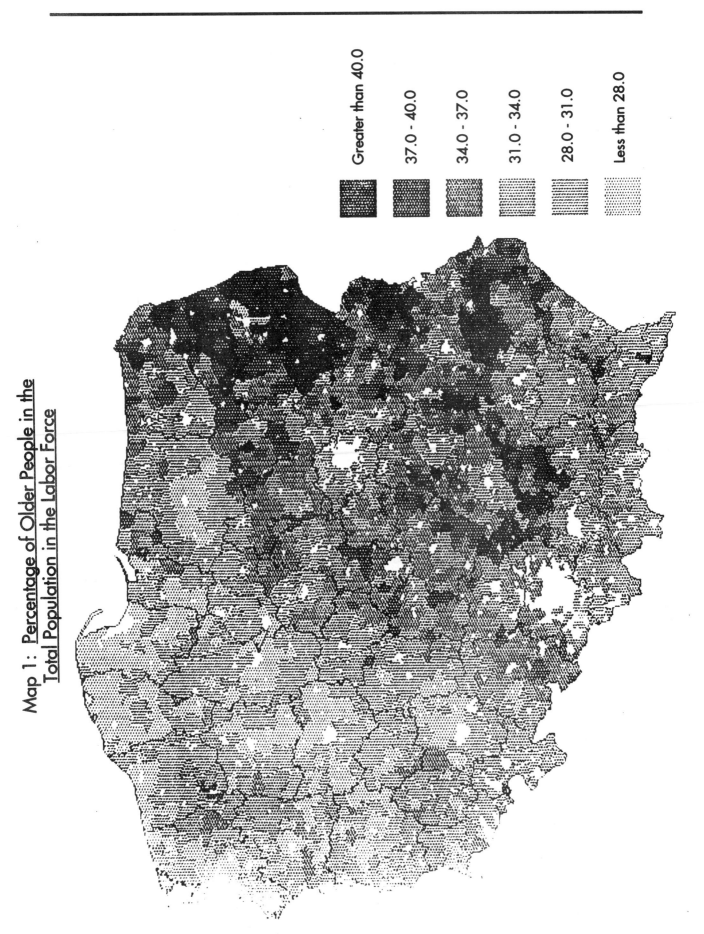

Map 1: Percentage of Older People in the Total Population in the Labor Force

Greater than 40.0

37.0 - 40.0

34.0 - 37.0

31.0 - 34.0

28.0 - 31.0

Less than 28.0

Map 2: Number of Women per 100 Men

Greater than 95.0

87.5 - 95.0

80.0 - 87.5

72.5 - 80.0

65.0 - 72.5

Less than 65.0

Map 3: <u>Density of Population</u>

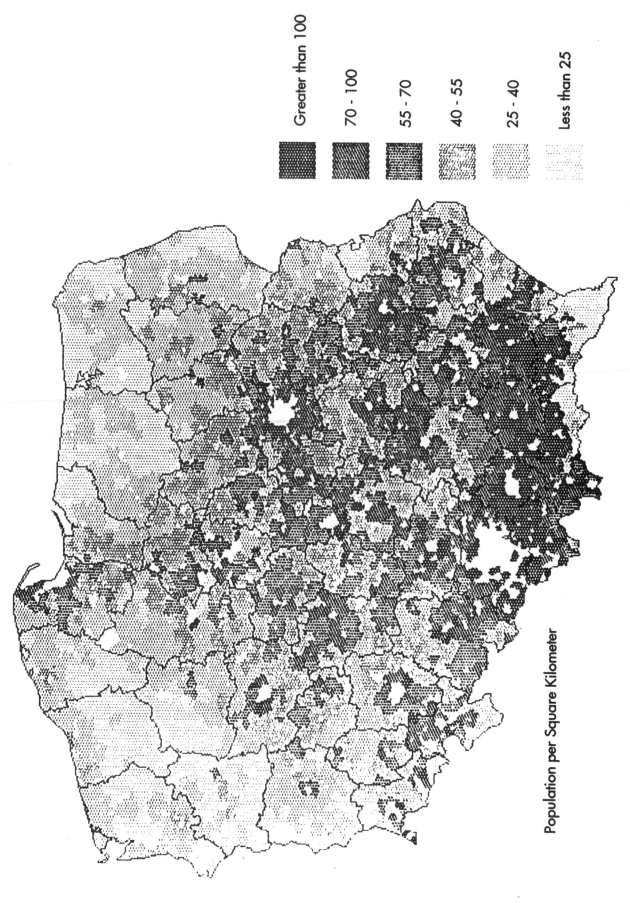

Greater than 100

70 - 100

55 - 70

40 - 55

25 - 40

Less than 25

Population per Square Kilometer

Map 4: <u>Farms with Main Source of Income</u>
<u>in Agriculture</u>

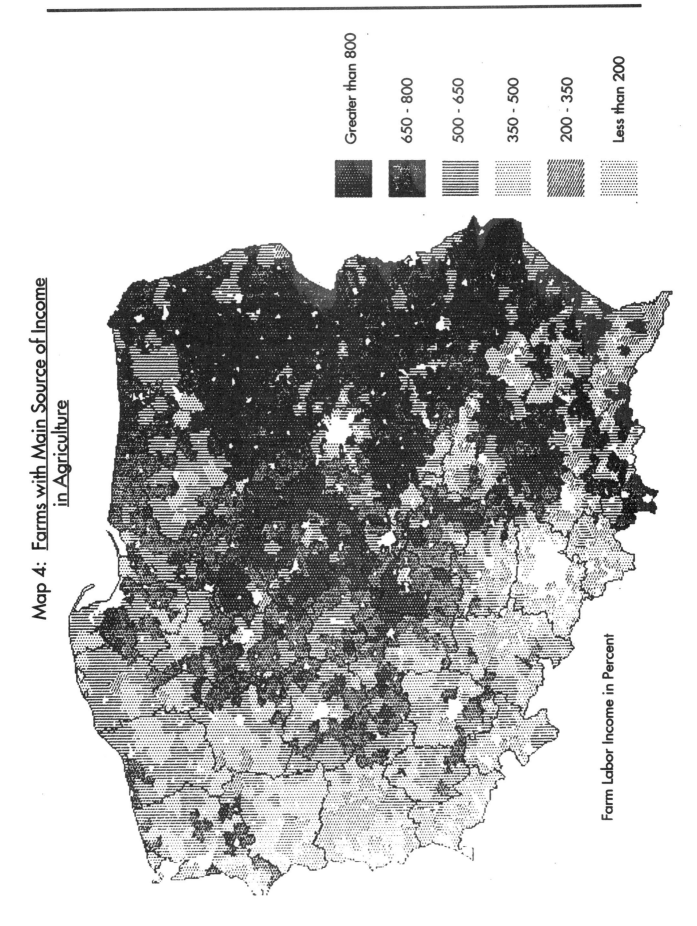

Greater than 800

650 - 800

500 - 650

350 - 500

200 - 350

Less than 200

Farm Labor Income in Percent

Table 2.1 Percentage of nonagricultural population by place of employment and by economic sector, 1978

(in percentage)

Economic sector	Total	Working in the gmina where they live	Commuting outside their gmina		
			Total	to cities	to other gminas
By workplace					
Total	100.0	36.8	63.2	56.8	6.4
Industry	100.0	30.2	69.8	63.1	6.6
Housing	100.0	26.2	73.8	65.5	8.3
Forestry	100.0	60.0	40.0	23.8	16.1
Transport and communication	100.0	23.4	76.6	68.9	7.7
Trade	100.0	50.7	49.3	44.7	4.6
Municipal and housing management	100.0	18.8	81.2	78.8	2.4
Science, education and culture	100.0	73.1	26.9	23.2	3.6
Health and social care	100.0	42.0	58.0	54.1	3.7
Tourism and recreation	100.0	49.0	51.0	46.1	4.9
Other sectors	100.0	59.4	40.6	36.2	4.4
By economic sector					
Total	100.0	100.0	100.0	100.0	100.0
Industry	43.2	35.5	47.6	47.9	44.6
Housing	12.3	8.7	14.3	14.1	16.0
Forestry	2.5	4.1	1.6	1.1	6.4
Transport and communication	11.2	7.1	13.6	13.6	13.6
Trade	11.3	15.6	8.8	8.9	8.1
Municipal and housing management	2.9	1.5	3.8	4.1	1.1
Science, education and culture	6.9	13.8	2.9	2.8	3.9
Health and social care	3.5	4.0	3.2	3.4	2.1
Tourism and recreation	0.7	1.0	0.6	0.6	0.6
Other sectors	5.3	8.6	3.4	3.4	3.7

ter for an important fraction of the population that is employed in urban areas and commutes daily as much as one hundred kilometers (because of housing problems in cities and the relative ease of constructing houses in the countryside). This situation implies high industrial production costs and transportation costs of the labor force.

Along with an increase in the rural labor force working outside agriculture, there has been an increase in the level of multi-activity of the farm population (see Figure 2.3). The number of households that derive their main income from outside agriculture (peasants working in the state-owned or cooperative sector, peasant-workers, and retired peasants) has increased greatly. In 1988, only 20% of farm families derived their income exclusively from farming and 40% mainly from farming.

COEXISTENCE OF THE PRIVATE, COOPERATIVE AND STATE-OWNED SECTORS

The main characteristic of the countryside — a result of the long-term struggle of the peasantry against collectivization — is the coexistence of private farming with a public sector that is dominant in extra-agricultural activities. As Table 2.2 shows, the private sector accounts for 85% of the active population employed in agriculture. The remaining 15% are state farm employees (47%), agricultural services employees (30%) and production cooperatives employees (23%). Outside agriculture, the situation is different: 92% of the active population work in the state sector, and only 8% in the private sector. Although the latter figure is low, it must be pointed out that it has tripled over the past 10 years and that it does not include the informal

Table 2.2 Rural population working in agriculture and in other sectors, 1978 and 1988

		Total	Rural population working in agriculture	Rural population working outside agriculture	Proportion of those working in agriculture
Total in '000	1978	8040	4771	3269	59.3
	1988	7749	4348	3401	56.1
	1978 = 100	96.4	91.1	104.1	x
State sector	1978	3899	747	3152	19.2
	1988	3788	647	3141	17.1
	1978 = 100	97.2	86.6	99.7	x
Private sector	1978	4141	4024	117	97.2
	1988	3961	3701	260	93.4
	1978 = 100	95.7	92.0	222.6	x
Private sector, as percentage of total	1978	51.5	84.3	3.6	x
	1988	51.1	85.1	7.6	x

sector, which is sizeable, especially in handicrafts, housing and transportation.

Table 2.3 shows the frequency of occurrence of registered industrial and service units in rural areas as well as their form of ownership. It can be seen that most agricultural marketing enterprises and most agro-industrial enterprises are part of the state sector: this is an effect of the so-called indirect collectivization carried out by the state after the failure of direct collectivization efforts in the early 1950s. On the other hand, it should be pointed out that despite a policy aimed at destroying handicrafts, services and private trade enterprises, many skills remain available in the countryside and allow the rural population to perform necessary tasks in construction, mechanics, carpentry, etc. This work is most often carried out on the basis of assistance from neighbors or as informal (unregistered) work.

WEAKNESSES OF THE RURAL INFRASTRUCTURE

The settlement network includes 42,000 villages divided into 57,000 rural localities. Villages are small: about 82% have fewer than 500 inhabitants. Administratively, villages are grouped into 2,121 *gmina*, one-third of which have between 5,000 and 7,000 inhabitants.

Village-level infrastructure is insufficient. The greatest problem is water supply (only 29% of villages have a water supply system) and access to a sewerage system (5.3% of villages). About 8% of villages do not have telephones. There are two telephone owners per hundred inhabitants,

as compared with 40 in Western Europe.

The level of education and health care is much lower than that in urban areas. The education network includes about 13,000 schools, but the education level is poor because of lack of skilled personnel and poor organizational conditions. The situation is similar in the 3,311 health centers, which lack doctors and medical equipment. The weaknesses in the socioeconomic infrastructure in the countryside result in difficult living conditions and are the main cause of women's and young people's migration to town and of the negative selection of the remaining population.

AMBIGUOUS BEHAVIOR AND ATTITUDES OF THE RURAL POPULATION

The attitudes and behavior of the rural population are the consequence of a perverse system in which private enterprises worked in a centrally planned economic environment and the state discriminated against private farming rather than trying to create conditions for its growth. This mixed economic system and the policy of repressive tolerance toward peasant farming has created behavioral patterns that are often contradictory.

Peasant way of management. The management behavior of peasants is based on a logic of survival and not on a logic of development. It expresses itself in a propensity to minimize risk rather than to maximize profit, to ensure self-financing mostly through multiple employment and to take advantage of all labor resources of

Figure 2.3 Breakdown of rural population, 1960 - 1988

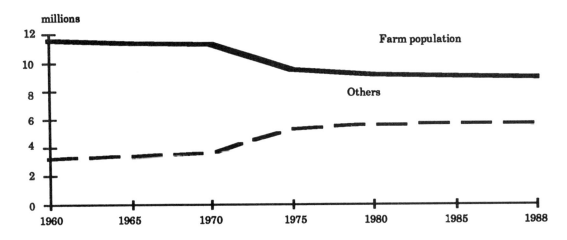

Figure 2.3 Breakdown of rural population, 1960 - 1988

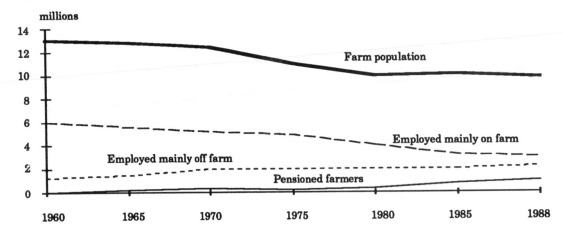

the family. It nevertheless allows some flexibility in behavior.

Resistance to and dependence on the state. On the one hand, farmers have developed a strategy of resistance toward changes coming from above and their behavioral patterns enable them to maintain the independence of their activities and private initiative. On the other hand, they are completely dependent on the administration. Farmers are accustomed to unrestricted food demand sustained by the centralized marketing organization and food subsidy system. They show an acquired helplessness and seem unwilling to undertake actions independent of the public sector.

Differences in behavior between private and state-owned sectors. Private farmers are emotionally tied to the land, which allows them to remain independent and in charge of their own farms. By contrast, state farm workers are wage earners carrying out passively and in a repetitive fashion the tasks set out for them. They are mainly concerned with their public employee status, their salary and their perquisites (housing, bonuses, paid vacations, child care, etc.) The same asymmetry of behavior exists between private farms and those enterprises in the cooperative sector (samopomoc chlopska, agricultural circles, and others) responsible for agricultural marketing and services. In a small number of such cooperative organizations, the self-government elections held in March 1990 led to a change in the balance of power in favor of cooperative members and to the subordination of the goals and activities of the cooperatives to the interest of these members. In most cooperative organizations, however, such changes did not take place.

Table 2.3 Frequency of industrial plants and services in *gmina* and ownership status in 1987

	Percentage of localities with	of which: percentage of private plants
Industrial plants		
Construction materials	1.8	41.7
Construction ceramics	2.1	71.5
Concrete	5.0	82.6
Sawmills	2.7	61.3
Slaughterhouses and Meat processing plants	2.1	29.3
Dairy processing plants	0.6	4.6
Mills	3.3	48.2
Bakeries	5.0	50.0
Potato processing plants	0.4	4.4
Fruit, vegetable and Mushroom processing	0.9	64.6
Soft drink plants	1.4	51.9
Feed plants	1.7	7.1
Other plants	12.6	79.0
Centers purchasing Agricultural products:		
Animals	6.1	x
Cereals	5.9	x
Potatoes	5.5	x
Beet	1.9	x
Fruit and vegetables	8.3	x
Milk	21.5	x
Other products	5.7	x
Commercial outlets (consumer goods)	68.5	4.7
Restaurants	7.3	22.02
Gas stations	4.3	x
Agricultural machinery and implements	0.2	x
Construction materials	5.2	x
Services		
Mechanical and electro-technical	1.3	60.5
Fitting and smithing	13.7	92.5
Cars	9.2	89.2
Repair of agricultural machinery	3.4	54.6
Radio and television	3.2	46.3
Glazier	1.7	53.2
Carpentry, furniture and upholstery	15.5	95.2
Tailoring	6.7	92.8
Shoemaking	1.6	94.3
Plumbing	8.1	64.7
Construction repairs	33.1	96.0
Electrical installation	9.5	96.1
Drycleaning and dyeing	2.2	55.5
Hairdressers and Beauty parlors	2.8	56.8
Photographers	1.3	91.4
Other services	19.3	97.2
Railway station	7.3	x
Intercity bus station	71.6	x
Post office	12.1	x
Cooperative bank	5.8	x
Primary school	21.4	x
Health care centers	7.3	x
Pharmacists	3.2	x
Hotel, shelters, tourist house	5.0	x

POTENTIAL AND CONSTRAINTS OF THE RURAL SECTOR

Some conclusions regarding the potential for change and constraints in the rural sector can be drawn from the observations made above. Both the negative and the positive aspects of the present situation must be considered.

Structural changes will be slow at the farm level because of the fragmented farm structure and the old age of farmers. Small farms may not be eliminated by the present crisis and may simply wither away. Commercial farms — that are more dependent on the market — face a difficult situation involving the risk of regression. They will have to use more labor-intensive techniques, reduce costs and improve the quality of their products. Some rationalization of the agrarian structure can be achieved through a shift of part of the state sector land to the private sector, land consolidation in private farms and a better combination of factors (see Annex 14). But the attitude of state farm employees preclude the use of an agrarian reform-type solution.

The multiple activities of the population and the semiprivate character of the rural economy can contribute to relatively fast rural development. The privatization of supply and marketing functions is necessary for the adjustment and development of agriculture in the new market economy. This will have to take place in a context of growing unemployment related to the restructuring of the industrial and cooperative sectors, coinciding with the increase of the population of productive age.[1] The rural sector should play the role of buffer sector for the unemployed and make a significant contribution to the economic reform process because of its stability and its capacity to absorb labor.

The implementation of a new, efficiency-oriented policy presupposes the gradual reduction of the ambiguous behavior of the farmers and a more dynamic attitude toward the market economy. It also presupposes a reduction of the antagonism between farmers and the state, presently exacerbated by the sudden fall in agricultural incomes and by the uncertainty regarding prices. An improvement in relations between the farmers and the state depends on three factors:

• the definition of (and information about) clear economic rules, enabling the farmers to carry out their personal strategies and giving them a large amount of freedom in a more stable environment;

• the creation of transition mechanisms to buffer the collapse of agricultural prices; and

• a policy of rural development and social welfare. The outline of such a policy is discussed in the remainder of this annex.

Outline of a rural development strategy

The strategy for rural development should be developed taking three periods into account: the very short term, which will be a period of uncertainty and regulatory vacuum; the short-term, during which the legal and institutional framework of the new economic system needs to be built; and the long-term, during which the new economic mechanisms put in place will produce their effects, leading to structural and functional changes.

STRATEGIC GOALS

The basic goals of the strategy for the very short term should be:

• maintenance of the productive capacity of agriculture; and

• protection of the main source of income for a large part of the population.

For the short term, the goals should be:

• reduction of the structural asymmetry between agriculture and its environment; and

• creation of a rural model of market economy.

For the long term, the goals should be:

• regional economic planning and balanced population distribution;

• multisectoral development of rural areas;

• revival of an active social life in the country-side;

• rationalization of structures in agriculture itself and in activities that are upstream and downstream from agriculture, based on a better combination and spatial allocation of factors.

ELEMENTS OF THE STRATEGY

The implementation of the above goals requires various means and actions. In the very short term, fiscal and social policies should accommo-

date the specific requirements of the agricultural production cycle. The rural strategy should be coordinated with the establishment of the new market economy. Because of the strong dependence of the agricultural sector on state and cooperative supply and marketing institutions, a quick privatization and demonopolization of these institutions is recommended (see Annexes 5 and 6). There should also be a reduction of the level of price uncertainty in the rural economy through measures aimed at the stabilization of agricultural markets (in particular, through the Agency for Agricultural Marketing (see Annex 9)).

In the short term, and at the heart of the rural development strategy, are measures leading to the reawakening of economic initiative and the creation of a network of small and medium-size economic units in and around agriculture. Specifically, this means the creation of genuine cooperatives (see Annex 6); the development of a competitive agricultural processing industry (see Annex 8); and the development of cottage industries and services, which now exist mainly informally, and of local and itinerant trade and craftsmen. (This point is discussed below.) This includes a set of measures aimed at creating incentives for the development of private initiative and the promotion of various forms of economic activity.

In the long term, the objectives of rural development are, first, to make rural areas more attractive as a place of work, housing and recreation, and improve living standards; second, to shift the public investment structure in favor of radical improvement of the socioeconomic infrastructure in rural areas; third, to change the programs and methods of agricultural education; fourth, to improve the starting conditions for the employment of the rural youth; and, finally, to develop regional planning and set-aside areas.

Short-term strategy — components and instruments

REAWAKENING ECONOMIC INITIATIVE IN RURAL AREAS

For more than 40 years, the normal mechanisms of economic activity based on entrepreneurship and capital accumulation have been blocked. Outside of agriculture, the possibilities of capital accumulation by the rural population were mainly informal and often illegal. They included:

• illegal appropriation for private use of productive factors belonging to state enterprises (including equipment, raw materials and workers' time);
• informal trade, taking advantage of the distortions and irregularities present in the economy, and in particular exchange rate distortions;
• periodic, and usually illegal, work abroad.

The restoration of the rule of law and the establishment of a market economy imply that these distortions be removed, that privileges related to a political or administrative rank be abolished, and that respect for public property be restored. However, at the same time, the change of economic and political system deprives economic units of easy access to capital. The economic reform program will lead to increased unemployment. Assuming that the 2 million unemployed forecast by the end of 1990 include an equal proportion of rural nonfarm and urban workers, unemployment in rural areas could be as high as 300,000 to 400,000 persons. The situation of these jobless workers could be particularly difficult, considering the fact that labor supply in the countryside is very limited and that labor mobility is low because of the lack of housing.

The state faces a choice between welfare policies based on unemployment benefits that perpetuate the dependence on the state and policies giving a large place to self-employment. Self-employment promotion policies are not common in industrialized countries where wage-labor has gradually destroyed the concept of independent labor and where societies became used to supporting a large number of unemployed. However, it is increasingly recognized that self-employment can fill in labor market gaps resulting from economic rigidities. It also follows the modern evolution of industry. The availability of many technologies and the differentiation of markets have contributed to the collapse of the Fordist mass production industrial model and to the development of a new model based on a network of small, flexible production units, easily adapting to market demands thanks to telecommunications and information technology. This model can be one of the objectives of rural development.[2]

The three main components of the self-employment strategy are a training policy, a financial policy, and a set of measures to create a favorable regulatory environment.

TRAINING POLICY

The two areas deserving consideration in the training program are changing economic behavior and training for new jobs. During the communist period, a lot of damage was done to the work mentality of the population. Nobody can estimate this fully, but it will remain a fact to be taken into account for some time to come. It would be an error to think that simply changing the economic system will change attitudes and behavioral patterns created by 40 years of lies, fear, resistance and cheating. Apart from the transformation of property rights, the essential problem of the transition period is to adapt mentalities and attitudes to the new reality. In rural communities, this requires organizing short courses aimed at freeing people from the constraints imposed by the previous system, opening up a real dialogue and awakening their initiatives, showing potential micro-entrepreneurs how the market economy functions and assisting them at the same time to define their own economic strategy. This would require high-quality trainers, able to use modern, participatory training methods not widely used previously in Poland.

Vocational training is currently carried out by the extension service (WOPR) for farmers and by the Vocational Training Units (ZDZ) for workers, apart from the education system. Training for new activities related to the market economy will require that new solutions be found, within or outside of the framework of these institutions. In the new situation created by the economic and political changes, it must be noted that the goal of training is changing. The purpose is not to update one's knowledge, but rather to change skills or to train for a new kind of job. Rapid action is required given the number of workers who risk losing their jobs, but the directions of new training are difficult to determine beforehand. Training funds, until now included in the overhead of enterprises — at least as far as ZDZ are concerned — are becoming increasingly limited. Training costs could be partly covered by the Labor Fund, but have to be met mainly by the trainees themselves. The available training personnel are not prepared to train new — that is, independent and reliable — economic operators.

Given this situation, the principles of vocational training should be as follows:

• Training should correspond strictly to the existing or envisaged jobs, including, in the rural areas, small-scale trade, crafts, cottage industry, etc.

• Training should be concentrated on essential know-how and essential tasks, and be limited in time.

• Training teams should be mobile and flexible. To the extent possible, training should be practical on-the-job training and trainers should be able to provide technical advice on the choice of technology and equipment.

Changing economic behavior. Courses helping the rural population to understand the new economic environment, and to initiate new forms of activity, require a relatively small number of trainers with the ability to adjust to educational needs. Above all, the work of this group should be directed at local self-governments and at the various forms of rural organizations. The creation of a small team, perhaps called a team for instigating changes in rural areas, would have two main goals: training of instructors in charge of short courses for the emulation of economic activity in the countryside, and accumulating experiences allowing a better understanding of the social psychology and setting up progressively a strategy for change.

The creation of such a team in itself would raise one of the main issues of post-communist societies — which is a preliminary condition for its solution — and would also facilitate dialogue between the state and the farmers.

At the same time, such a team could more easily identify cheaters who will be interested no doubt in this new market. Obviously there is a risk of falling into dull — and inefficient — propaganda. Therefore it would be desirable that the team be outside the state administrative structure (for example, within the framework of the Agency for Local Initiatives, discussed below) and facilitate contacts with the extension service and the mutual exchange of experiences. Given the usefulness of multidisciplinary approaches, this team should consist of experts from different fields. It is clear that it would not have any kind of monopoly and should cooperate in various initiatives with lo-

cal and foreign institutions. Several existing initiatives are good initial steps in this direction, for instance, the Plunkett Foundation course on economic activity, French minibuses traveling in the Polish countryside with audio-visual data on French agriculture, etc. The participation of foreign experts in the team for instigating changes in rural areas would probably contribute to a better understanding of the market economy model, on the one hand, and of rural realities and attitudes, on the other.

Retraining for a new job. The best basis for training as far as adaptation to new standards and economic (agricultural or not) activities in the countryside goes is without doubt the WOPR extension service. Its basic goals and the suggested reforms to its organization are specified in Annex 12. The WOPR is currently providing different kinds of training for carpenters, fitters, drivers, mechanics, tailors, etc. In changing its structures and modes of operation, it should consider the future increase in the demand for new crafts in the countryside and the need for extension regarding purchases of new technical equipment.

FINANCIAL POLICY

Problems related to small loans to small producers. In most countries, banks avoid providing credit for small investments for three reasons: the relatively high cost of distribution and administration of these small credits, the lack of down-payment and collateral from the borrower, and the low level of economic know-how on the part of customers who do not know how to present the project or how to fill in the necessary forms. Some programs set up to finance small enterprises show that these problems can be overcome by using appropriate methods and that, in contrast to the general opinion, loans for microenterprises created by poor people entail low financial risk.

Principles of small investment credit. These principles, based on the experience of many countries, can be summarized as follows:

• Small credit is based, above all, on the customer and on the local market. Project evaluation requires common sense rather than complex financial analysis. Nevertheless, the precondition for a credit to be granted is that the profitability of the enterprise allows repayment of capital and interest. It is clear that rates of interest currently prevailing in Poland do not allow investment credit to expand in the rural population.

- The methods and procedures of granting credits must be based on knowledge of the local community and on the needs and constraints of customers. This applies to collateral and to forms and schedules of repayment. Apart from mortgaging farm land, which applies only to farmers, the main collateral used in rural areas is warranty. It is a serious guarantee in small local communities where people know each other well and are able to evaluate not only the efficiency and honesty of the potential entrepreneur but the project itself. Apart from warranty, a good way of collateralizing a credit would be to introduce equipment leasing, which currently does not exist in Poland (although it is envisaged by the newly founded Bank for Socioeconomic Initiatives — BISE).

- The interest rate to be used should be the market rate and should be positive in real terms. A lower rate would bring about a rapid decapitalization of banks. The main disadvantage of preferential interest rates is that they are available only to a limited number of borrowers and that they attract customers to whom they were not initially targeted. Thus, they do not ensure that all economic operators, including poor people, have permanent access to credit. Therefore, it is preferable not to interfere with banking mechanisms. Instead of giving preferential interest rates, the state could give separate subsidies to assist small entrepreneurs in building up the necessary equity, as well as subsidies allowing banks to cover complementary costs connected with small credits.

- Credits should not be forgiven. The condition for granting production credit to all groups of the population is the strict observance of repayment rules. Credit forgiveness makes people think that credits do not have to be repaid.

- Progressiveness is an important principle of small credit. This principle applies both to the amount of individual loans (the first loan should be relatively low so as to check the efficiency of the entrepreneur and his behavior with respect to the bank) and to the number of loans in a given area. The good performance and repayment on the part of the first clients then becomes a model for the followers. At the same time, first

loans permit methods and procedures to be adapted to customers' needs and constraints.

There is a necessity to provide advisory services. In general, and in particular in a country in transition toward a free market, the financing of small enterprises requires:

- assistance in preparing the project and presenting it to the bank;
- services for economic activity such as accountancy and tax advice;
- supervision of economic activity allowing faster diagnosis of difficulties and assistance in solving them.

Offering advice of this type goes beyond the tasks of a bank and should be offered by separate institutions. Several organizational schemes for the credit system are possible. The necessity of using existing means and institutions leads us to make the following proposals:

Credit institutions. Labor Offices currently provide small amounts of credit for setting up one's workshop. This can be only a transitory solution. Presently, Labor Offices attempt to develop contracts with banks so that the latter can evaluate professionally the reliability of the borrower and the profitability of the project.

Banks are the usual institutions offering credit. In the rural community, cooperative banks exist in almost all *gmina* (there are 1,663 banks for 2,121 *gmina*). These banks, which are relatively sound from a financial viewpoint, operate mainly with the deposits of the rural population, who find them more reliable than other cooperatives. Using this network of small cooperative banks would make it considerably easier not only for the customer but also for the state budget. Credit could be refinanced by the National Bank — the BISE — created by initiative of the Ministry of Labor or the Bank of Food Economy.

Financial mechanisms. Cooperative banks operating with member deposits must be able to meet additional costs related to distribution of small credit and to risk. A guarantee fund should be set up to cover part of the risk. The share covered would be relatively high at the beginning (about 50% depending on the requirements of cooperative banks), and would fall as the banking techniques for this type of credit improve, thus permitting a better repayment rate. The guarantee fund could gradually be replaced by local mutual guarantee funds. Each borrower would pay 10% of his loan into this fund and bear, to this proportion, the risk of all credits taken by members of the group of borrowers. It must be noted, however, that the creation of funds of this type, based on mutual guarantee, requires time, since they are possible only on a small, local scale, where people know each other.

According to normal cooperative principles, loans are granted to members having some personal contribution. This contribution could be covered by a single bonus for creating one's own new workplace. The guarantee fund and bonuses allowing the creation of the equity could be provided by the Labor Fund. However, it is necessary for the people who have not been laid off (for example, young entrants in the labor market or small farmers without sufficient means of subsistence) to be able to gain from this system.

Economic advisory system. At present, there is almost no advisory system. Organizing one would require ample funds. In this instance also, emerging initiatives should be followed up on. One of them is the Agency of Local Initiatives, created to assist the BISE. This agency is part of the Fund for Development of Local Democracy and aims at creating initially 17 regional agencies. Considering the fact that there are 2,121 *gmina*, the range of each agency would be too wide for it effectively to carry out advisory functions at the local level. To solve this problem in a budgetarily cost-effective manner, there are various options that could be tested experimentally (and may differ depending on the voivodship). The two main options would be:

• to increase the personnel through cooperation with other local institutions (chambers of commerce or industry, agricultural organizations, etc.) through encouragement of social work by retired people, and through the use of the graduates that are employed in the intervention work financed by the Labor Fund. All those potential advisers would have to be trained appropriately and demonstrate not only occupational skills, but also the ability to perform social and enterprise-oriented work.
• to group borrowers. The creation of rural business "circles" would reduce advisory costs and enable the consolidation of advisory services,

such as accounting, and the creation of a basis for mutual guarantee funds. These groups could follow the tradition of the old "agricultural circles," based on solidarity and mutual cooperation. This would allow the development and progress of rural areas.

CREATION OF A FAVORABLE ENVIRONMENT

Training and financing policies for rural areas will only yield results if the environment is favorable to change. The following measures can contribute to the creation of a favorable environment in rural areas.

Revision and / or abrogation of all unnecessary laws and regulations preventing the development of economic activity. In this respect, the systemic changes induced by the privatization law and the revision of the civil code recently passed by Parliament are essential. But there are also many regulations preventing the development of economic activity by private entrepreneurs that should be abolished. A list has been prepared by the Office of Property Restructuring. In itself, the existence of a set of consistent regulations offering maximum freedom to economic subjects, protective of the public good, and translated into a language understandable to the average citizen, is necessary for the good performance of the economy. But legal changes alone will not imply the end of the dictatorial attitude or of the inertia of the administration. In this field, the dependence observed until now must give way to citizen action against all kinds of abuse.

Simplification of the tax system and tax exemptions for new enterprises. The present tax system for small-scale economic activity has three main shortcomings: it is complicated, it is an excessive burden for new enterprises, and it changes too often. Apart from the turnover tax, there is currently an income tax (or wage tax, paid by the employer), a surtax, a tax on special fields in agriculture, a real estate tax, a land tax, etc. As of January 1991, an income tax will replace the salary tax and the surtax. A year later, it is envisaged that the turnover tax will be replaced by a value-added tax. These changes are important not only because they rationalize the taxation system, but also because they mean the progressive elimination of a system in which scores of poorly understood regulations enabled the Nomenklatura to decide that private businessmen had not fulfilled all of their tax obligations and to destroy their businesses through unexpected fines.

The stabilization plan was not a fortunate transition from this point of view. Higher taxes, rents and prices of raw materials and energy, combined with lower demand and payment delays, have eliminated many small enterprises. In the first quarter of 1990, the number of handicrafts in Poland dropped by 7.8% and that of businesses run by physical persons by 5.6%. Many of the businesses have shifted to speculative trade. A decree dated May 18, 1990, of the Minister of Finance decided to suspend for one to five years taxes on new private businesses registering before the end of the year. This decree, however, does not apply to all enterprises and partly only solves partly the problem of tax exemptions for new businesses. Encouraging setting up small enterprises and legalizing many activities in the so-called hidden economy would be facilitated by the temporary suspension of taxes and Social Security dues (which amount to 43% of wages, plus 2% for the Labor Fund).

Making it easier for an enterprise to find a location. The fact that state supervision of rents to be paid by private firms was terminated has had a very negative effect on many small enterprises, in particular in cities. In the countryside, this problem can be solved more easily. Farmers often have buildings that can be used for workshops, and local self-government bodies own many buildings used by the state and cooperative sector. The Office for Property Restructuring sent a circular to communes on June 1, 1990, suggesting that they should repossess their properties and sell or lease to the private sector. At the same time, communes were advised to pay more attention to the need to develop market places and street commerce and to facilitate the obtainment of lots for new buildings. These directives (which are not mandatory since power is in the hands of self-governments) will be implemented in a more or less quick fashion depending on the situation of the local government but represent a step in the right direction.

Facilitating access to appropriate equipment and machinery. Small rural enterprises need small, cheap and easily accessible equipment. For a long time, Polish industry mainly produced

equipment for large plants and access to equipment depended on arbitrary decisions. It is therefore no wonder that there is a mismatch between supply of equipment and the needs and financial capacity of small businesses. However, this market is slowly organizing itself. The department of agroprocessing of the Ministry of Agriculture provides, for instance, useful information on prices and supply outlets to interested parties. Domestic industry is slowly adjusting to the needs of small businesses: for example, small trucks have been equipped with cold storage equipment to be used for street commerce. Imports of small equipment (for example, small dairy facilities) are growing.

It would be recommended that the extension service (WOPR) and trade unions contact cooperatives and chambers of commerce of West European countries in order to organize imports of secondhand equipment that could be useful for Polish microenterprises. Such contacts exist for agricultural machinery from Germany.

It should be stressed, however, that the essential problem is the high cost of the equipment compared with average income levels. The BISE estimates that an investment of Zl25 to ZL35 million zlotys is necessary for the creation of a workplace. This represents three to four times the average annual salary. The introduction of leasing, mentioned above, could be one option to make it easier to purchase equipment.

Developing an information policy. This policy is a necessary complement to the training policy and is particularly important in the transition period. With respect to the uncertainty prevailing in the countryside, it is preferable to know clearly what the future holds, even if it is difficult, than to be afraid of unknown dangers with respect to which the difficult but certain present feels safer. Having appropriate information allows people to have reference points to carry out their activity in the new market economy.

Rural areas obtain information mainly through radio and television. Since the beginning of the crisis, fewer copies of agricultural newspapers are being sold. Therefore, emphasis should be put on those media. Radio and television broadcasts devoted to agriculture (for example, *Notowania* — Rates, in English) should be expanded and should cover other branches of economic activity which can be developed in the countryside, providing information on markets, technologies and sources of supply of machinery and raw materials.

The important thing, for people living for over 40 years in a system restricting their personal initiative and setting the standards of activity from above, is to break the imagination barrier. Therefore, another essential initiative should be to give concrete information on the principles and performance of a market economy from the point of view of economic units (for example, how Mr. X went about setting up a private bakery in the countryside). The purpose of this information would be to alter the negative prevailing attitudes with respect to private operators and to show what specific possibilities exist and what rules apply for small-scale businesses. This information, supplied by the mass media, should be supported by manuals guiding potential entrepreneurs through the necessary steps.

Developing public works. The development of agriculture and rural areas requires urgent investment in land irrigation, water supply, telephone and telecommunication systems, market places and transport. Given the tradition of collective action existing in rural areas, many roads, schools and health centers have been built with unpaid work from the rural population — amounting to one-third of construction costs (the remainder being covered by the state budget and other financial sources). The Labor Fund could finance the salaries, for six months, of unemployed persons within the framework of the existing intervention work. The combination of these elements could form the basis for a rural works policy which could be carried out by local self-governments with the assistance of local organizations and existing foundations (such as the Foundation for Supplying Water to the Countryside, and the Agricultural Committee of the Church). Such works would not only provide employment for those taking part in them, but would also create the infrastructure necessary for the development of the countryside. They would also have a positive income effect and offer opportunities to local small entrepreneurs. These initiatives could be an important complement to the self-employment policy.

SOCIAL WELFARE POLICY

Though maximum attention should be paid to employment policy, the state must also fulfill its obligations in matters of social welfare and protection of vulnerable groups. Social policy in the countryside entails specific problems related to (1) the large number of old people living in rural areas, and therefore, the problem of pensions and organization of health care services required by these people; (2) the large proportion of part-time farmers, who will be in all likelihood the first to be dismissed from their workplaces, although they often work in the occupations requiring the least skills; and (3) the low level of education and health care services, and therefore the poor initial conditions for the rural youth.

The policy of rural development aims at gradually improving living conditions in the countryside and shares this aim with welfare policy. A policy of social protection would include three main components.

Unemployment fund. Labor Fund unemployment benefits are available only to farmers having less than 5 ha. Part-time farmers do not receive unemployment benefits, but the Labor Fund pays their insurance fee. (Since 1989, part-time farmers have been exempt from pension payments paid to the Peasant Insurance Fund, since insurance was automatically paid by their workplace. Pensions for farmers are currently about Zl480,000 per person and Zl75,000 per hectare.) Part-time farmers are also authorized to obtain a retraining allowance when changing jobs in rural areas, and part-time farmers having less than 3 ha may obtain a loan amounting to six times the average monthly salary for setting up an extra-agricultural workplace in the countryside.

In reducing funds available to part-time farmers, account was not taken of the fact that they represent a specific category for whom work outside the farm is an economic necessity. The fact that many of them will be laid off before others seems unavoidable but it would seem less justified, from the point of view of social justice, to restrict funds available to them. The shortage of funds for creating new workplaces outside agriculture and the unnecessary flow of labor toward the farm sector is liable to have negative effects on rural development. At any rate, the system of financing and advising small enterprises should be open to all potential candidates.

Reform of farmers' insurance. In 1978, social insurance for farmers was introduced. This was an important step from the point of view of welfare policy. However, there were several shortcomings. There was no correspondence between the fee paid and the value of the funds. The real burden on farms increased continually because of the decreasing number of farmers paying fees. There was no relationship between the social objective and the economic objective to stimulate production (the pension amount being dependent on the value of the agricultural product sold). And social insurance had rigid effects on structural and generational changes in agriculture (the right to pension being in force only when the farmer stops farming).

The reform now being proposed by the Ministry of Rural Welfare consists mainly of three elements. First, an independent Peasant Social Insurance scheme would be created, specializing in services for the agricultural system, with farmer interests represented by farmers' councils, operating under the supervision of the Ministries of Agriculture and Finance. This institution would be able not only to collect funds but also to perform previously nonexistent financial functions (investing surpluses, carrying out economic activities, applying for loans, managing deposit funds paid to farmers, etc). Second, old age and disability pensions would be separated. Third, the contributory pension fund (where the choice of insurance premium and pension amount depend on the farmer's decision) would be separated from the state pension. The contributory pension would be available at retirement age (though premia can still be paid in order to obtain a higher pension). The state pension, paid by the state budget and amounting to 35% of average wage, would come after 60 years when the farmer stops farming and transfers the farm to someone else.

If passed by Parliament, this reform would represent a great improvement over the current situation because it represents a better balance between farmers' contributions and contributory pension, as well as between state pension and giving up farming. However, several objections could be raised concerning the economic activities of the bank, which does not seem to be the most effective or safest way of dealing with funds.

Social welfare, including food assistance. The state of rural social welfare is worse than in cities. Benefits for private farmers are lower than those for employed persons. For example, since May 1, 1990, the family allowance for farmers' children has been set at the same level as workers' children, but only a handful of farmers' children are entitled to such an allowance.

Because of the dispersed settlement network, transport difficulties and late introduction of a free health care system for farmers (in 1972), the countryside lags behind considerably in terms of welfare services, of particular importance for the elderly. The recent transfer of social welfare functions to the Minister of Labor and Social Policy, who will share responsibility with local self-governments, and the preparation of a new law to replace the social assistance bill of 1923 should improve the situation, although this takes place at a time of widespread increase of poverty in the countryside.

Social welfare centers now handle 1.5 million cases, out of which about 40%, or 600,000 persons, live in the countryside. There is no doubt that this number will increase, since the number of poor people has been estimated at 8 million. Since funds are limited, it is important to determine, first, who should be priority beneficiaries and, second, what means of assistance are the most efficient. At the initial stage, on both counts, much initiative was left to the centers themselves. But this state of affairs cannot be sustained in the long run because it places too much responsibility on social workers and can lead to abuse.

From the point of view of an agricultural policy, emphasis should be placed on food distribution to the neediest people, and distribution should be organized in such a way that it does not interfere with the market mechanism. Food distribution for welfare purposes should enlarge demand without inducing an artificial decrease of prices. At present, social centers carry out such functions, for example, through school canteens. They also distribute food parcels and free meals, issuing so-called milk bar coupons. The rural housewives' circles have taken part in such actions in the countryside.

In the autumn of 1989, the Ministry of Labor

proposed the introduction of food stamps throughout Poland but the project was dropped because of opposition from banks and the lack of interest on the part of retailers. At present, the main constraints to the distribution of food stamps are the fact that retailers are used to cash transactions and the perceived stigmatization of the poor, who would feel more than ever marginalized. The system of food stamps to the poorest should be tested on a small scale, in *gmina* where prices of agricultural produce are particularly low and local governments would agree to simultaneous creation of marketplace development and introduction of food stamps redeemable for all agricultural products.

RESPONSIBILITIES OF THE RURAL ACTORS

A dynamic rural development strategy requires the cooperation of all the actors involved in the countryside. This section outlines the main responsibilities of the key actors in rural areas.

The state is responsible for:

• creating a legal framework to provide social protection without perpetuating unemployment and to allow independent private businesses to develop
• ensuring budgetary support for training, extension, a guarantee fund, infrastructure and social welfare
• creating a favorable environment for the socioeconomic development of the countryside.

After many years of investment in large-scale industry and city development, state policy should make an about-face toward the agricultural sector, small- and medium-sized industry located in rural areas, and a decentralized network for commerce, transport, storage, handicrafts and services. In economic terms, these policies would have the highest returns on investments and would contribute to a reduction of unemployment, complete the process of privatization and reactivate the economy.

Local authorities are responsible for:

• defining a development strategy at the local level
• helping in the development of new economic activities and participating in social welfare policy
• implementing a policy of sociocultural development.

Local finances will not be defined before the end of the year. At present, this fact greatly constrains any action at the local level. What may turn out to be a long-term problem is the desire of many local self-governments to perform economic activities, which would allow them to earn necessary funds but reduce private initiative. Such a policy would represent, at the local level, a repetition of the errors of the centrally planned system. Increases in the budget of local governments should be sought through the development of private economic activity in rural areas rather than through public economic activity.

All rural organizations are currently undergoing an identity crisis. Despite the fact that the Farmers Union, agricultural circles (such as those of rural housewives), and rural organizations officially have 1,200,000 members, have large assets, and count on an experienced apparat, they lack authenticity and activism. Rural organizations tend to be regressive rather than constructive. This attitude, related to the enormous difficulties of agriculture during the transition period, is characteristic of the National Union of Farmers, agricultural circles and organizations, and a large faction of rural Solidarity (almost 400,000 members in 2,000 communes).

A renewal of authentic rural organizations, the goals of which would be not only to maintain a dialogue with the state and popularize information on rural areas and agriculture for public opinion, but also to take part in the promotion of progress, education and enterprise, is necessary for the success of a policy of rural development.

The Church still plays an important role, not only through its charitable action, but also through various foundations — notably the Water Foundation —in the development of infrastructure in the countryside. The Church's agricultural committee envisages many training and financing projects. In an initial stage, training policy could use the network and experiences of the Church committee for farmers, which has had an important educational role during the martial law period.

Finally, the rural community itself will play a decisive role through social pressure, through private initiative and through the transformation of the hidden-economy activities into more formal activities. Social committees exist in many villages and collective work also remains an important instrument for a program of rural development.

RESEARCH PROGRAM

The national rural development program could be facilitated and accelerated through research carried out in three different areas: Wielkopolska District (advanced agriculture); Kielce District (small farms and part-time farmers); and Eastern Border (depopulated and poor regions).

In each of the chosen areas inhabited by about 50,000 people, the program would include studying the constraints and opportunities for development; training, with contribution from existing institutions; experimental developmental work based on local resources and initiatives, financed by existing banks and funds; and conclusions and generalizations.

This program could be carried out with the assistance of local self-governments. The main goal would be to create appropriate conditions for activities by private farmers and small entrepreneurs, without trying to replace them. The history of rural development projects and programs all over the world shows how easily they can be prey to bureaucracy and vanish along with the funds which helped their emergence. What is at stake here are not projects of this type but rather studies and actions from which general conclusions can be drawn. The team responsible for this program should consist of representatives of universities and research institutes and local representatives.

Concluding comments

This annex is a first attempt at defining a rural development strategy for Poland. We have emphasized the necessity to base the strategy on the current reality and on human factors, taking into account the demographic and psychological features that are observed in rural areas. We would like to stress that changes in the behavior and mentality of the rural population will be as critical to the success of the reform process as changes in property rights and ownership. Finally, we would like to point out that reforms must create favorable conditions and opportunities for all economic agents, including the self-employed, and small and medium-size enterprises, and should avoid concentrating economic initiative in the hands of the state, local governments or other established institutions.

Endnotes

This annex was prepared by Maria Nowak (Caisse centrale de coopération économique/consultant, EC), assisted by Piotr Eberhardt (Institute of Geography and Land Policy), Izoslaw Frenkel and Maria Halamska (Institute of Rural and Agricultural Development), Wladyslaw Lukasik (Council of Ministers), Stefan Malecki (Ministry of Rural Welfare), Andrzej Pilichowski and Elzbieta Piotrowska (Institute of Rural Sociology, Lodz University), and Jerzy Wilkin (Warsaw University).

1. The trend for the population in productive age was decreasing — reaching a low level of 300,000 persons during 1986-1990 — but will increase and reach 700,000 persons in 1991-1995, and up to a million in the next period.

2. The most often cited example illustrating this model is the area of Bologna in northern Italy where an extensive mechanical and textile industry based on small flexible units has developed over the past 30 years. Many small enterprises have been constituted by creating narrowly specialized workshops with managers who were trained in large plants. There are examples of this approach to creating small production units in Poland. In the area of Konskie where the metallurgic industry has a 300-year long tradition, and where there are three large metallurgic plants (foundries and mechanical working plants) employing some 5,000 workers, about 100 small fitting, mechanical, and pressing production units have been created in recent years.

Changes in food demand, January 1989 — April 1990, and food demand projections

This annex presents an analysis of the changes in food consumption that have taken place in Poland largely as a result of the liberalization of agricultural markets and removal of food subsidies in 1989. The analysis is based on monthly Household Budget Survey estimates for January 1989 - April 1990 from the Central Statistical Office (see appendix on data sources).

The annex also presents food demand projections for 1990 - 2000. These long term projections are done, at constant prices, on the basis of exogenously given income and population growth rates, using income elasticities by income group estimated for this annex. Two different scenarios (high and low income growth) are presented. The final section of this annex summarizes the findings and discusses the projections.

Policy reforms affecting food consumption

Important policy reforms implemented in 1989 have affected prices and quantities of agricultural products consumed by Polish households. The reforms, carried out in several stages, are briefly summarized in this section.

• At the end of 1988, the state monopoly of procurement of grains and livestock products was abolished. The food subsidy system, however, was still in place so that this reform hardly affected quantities and prices of food consumed by households. Subsidies on food (accounting for 3.45% of GDP and making up 31% of total consumer subsidies in 1987) were in effect for
- milk and dairy products (40% of food subsidies in 1987);
- meat, meat products and fish (27.5%);
- cereals (25.6%);
- sugar;
- fats and oils.

The overall subsidy rate for food (value of subsidy divided by value of retail sales) was 32.5 % in 1987. Potatoes, vegetables and fruits were not subject to state procurement and were not subsidized.

• During the period January-July 1989, prices of most food products were not controlled but the system of subsidies (and meat rationing) was still in operation.

• On August 1, 1989, official fixed procurement prices for farm products and retail prices for food products were replaced by a system of market-based prices. Subsidies on food products and on industrial feed for animals were not yet removed but were frozen (until their elimination the following October). Between August and October, the increase in the retail prices of food was much higher than the increase in the producer prices of meat, dairy and crops delivered to the food-processing industries.

• On October 1, 1989, all consumer subsidies on food (with the exception of subsidies on low-fat cottage cheese, 2% fat milk and baby food) and the subsidy on concentrated feed were removed.[1]

• On January 1, 1990, the stabilization plan was implemented: it included many measures that have further affected agricultural markets.

• First, a major devaluation of the exchange rate (Zl 9,500 per US$ versus an average 1989 rate of Zl 1,400 per US$);

• Second, the elimination of the system of centrally allocated foreign exchange and the liberalization of all current account transactions; the reduction of most barriers to export and import. Many trade restrictions have been removed although, in December 1989, a new customs law (consistent with GATT) allowing the imposition of quotas, licenses, surcharges and higher tariffs was adopted;

• Third, sharp increases in nominal interest rates (monthly rates of 36% in January, 20% in February, 10% in March, 8% in April, 5.5% in May versus a yearly rate of approximately 100% for 1989);

• Fourth, an anti-inflationary income policy,

with reductions in real wages enforced through high marginal tax rates on wage increases;

• Fifth, reductions in subsidies of agricultural inputs (to one quarter of the level of 1989) and an abolishment of the Price Equalization Fund for foreign trade and thus the elimination of the corresponding subsidies. Other subsidies affecting agriculture, such as those for energy, are still in place.

As described in the following sections, these reforms have considerably affected levels and patterns of income, expenditure and consumption by households.

Changes in food prices

As a result of the measures summarized in the previous section and of other (policy- and non-

Table 3.1 Monthly consumer price indices, January 1988 - April 1990.

		Jan	Feb	March	April	May	June	July	August
Consumer price index									
	1988	128.40	138.20	143.20	146.00	147.90	149.40	150.90	152.20
Previous Year = 100	1989	183.20	176.20	175.50	176.10	178.20	180.70	184.40	198.10
	1990	1,189.70	1,281.40	1,296.80	1,298.20				
	1988	103.70	117.20	105.70	107.10	102.40	102.90	103.20	100.60
Previous Month = 100	1989	111.00	107.90	108.10	109.80	107.20	106.10	109.50	139.50
	1990	178.80	123.90	104.70	108.10				
Consumer food price index									
	1988	123.40	136.00	142.30	144.30	145.70	146.10	146.50	146.90
Previous Year = 100	1989	164.20	154.10	152.20	155.10	159.20	162.20	166.60	191.20
	1990	1,654.90	1,735.00	1,713.00	1,691.10				
	1988	101.70	123.00	106.40	103.80	101.90	102.30	100.80	97.70
Previous Month = 100	1989	105.70	108.00	108.10	114.40	109.80	104.30	107.10	180.40
	1990	179.00	118.10	100.00	112.40				

		Sept.	Oct.	Nov.	Dec.	Jan./Dec.
Consumer price index						
	1988	153.60	155.40	157.60	160.20	160.20
Previous Year = 100	1989	219.60	258.10	300.30	344.10	344.10
	1988	102.80	102.60	103.80	104.90	
Previous Month = 100	1989	134.40	154.80	122.40	117.70	
Consumer food price index						
	1988	147.50	148.00	148.80	150.10	150.10
Previous Year = 100	1989	227.90	290.50	353.20	412.60	412.60
	1988	101.20	101.70	104.40	104.30	
Previous Month = 100	1989	144.50	165.10	117.40	111.60	

Notes: "Previous year" means corresponding period of previous year on accrual basis.
Consumer price index is based on all goods and services.
Consumer food price index is based on retail prices of food items.
Source: Central Statistical Office, *Informacja Statystyczna*, May 1990.

policy-related) factors, the official price index for food increased sharply after August 1989 and at the beginning of 1990. Table 3.1 shows the official indices for retail prices of (1) all goods and services (CPI) and (2) food items for the period January 1988-April 1990.

The increase in retail prices of goods and services translates into higher costs of living for Polish households: in the first quarter of 1990 (I-1990), the cost of living was 13-14 times higher than in the same quarter in 1989 and approximately two and a half times higher than in IV-1989. Price increases have affected households differentially. This is shown in Table 3.2 for four different types of households: workers, farmer-workers, farmers, and pensioners. For farmer and farmer-worker households, the index does not take into account the value of the food that is produced on-farm and consumed by the household.

Table 3.2 Cost of living increase in I-1990, by type of household

Worker Households	I-1989 =100	IV-1989 =100
Total	1,319	236
Food	1,757	212
Alcoholic beverages	1,144	184
Nonfood products	1,022	259
Services	1,304	384
Farmer / Worker Households (*)		
Total	1,351	248
Food	2,090	237
Alcoholic beverages	1,139	188
Nonfood products	1,076	271
Services	1,244	329
Farmer Households(*)		
Total	1,341	254
Food	2,119	248
Alcoholic beverages	1,138	189
Nonfood products	1,096	276
Services	1,254	317
Retiree / Pensioner Households		
Total	1,434	246
Food	1,850	218
Alcoholic beverages	1,138	184
Nonfood products	1,049	284
Services	1,251	360

Note: * = excluding food from own farm.
Source: (GUS).

Table 3.3 Nominal (average monthly per capita) income in I-1990 and comparison with I-89 and IV-89

Household Type	ZL Thousand	I-89 = 100	IV-89 = 100
Worker	396.60	821	172
Farmer/worker	387.30	837	140
Farmer	340.06	860	110
Retiree/pensioner	341.70	985	199

Changes in incomes

Nominal income estimates calculated by household category on the basis of family budget surveys and national accounts data indicate great differences in average per capita monthly income and in changes in average monthly income depending on the household category (see Table 3.3).

Compared with the same quarter one year ago (I-1989), average nominal income has grown most in pensioner households and least in worker households. This has reduced disparities in per capita income levels between the different types of households. The relatively low growth of income in I-1990 as compared with IV-1989 in farm households, shown in Table 3.3, is due to the production cycle: the lowest levels of farm income in any year are always recorded during the first quarter.

Retail consumer prices increased much more than nominal incomes in I-1990 compared with IV-1989. Price increases amounted to 248% causing an average decrease of about 29% in purchasing power during the period.

Real incomes have declined by 30-37% between March 1989 and March 1990, depending on the type of household. In other words, the capacity of households to satisfy their needs at a level similar to I-1989 has been limited to 63-70% (see Table 3.4).

SOURCES OF HOUSEHOLD INCOMES

Changes in the structure of nominal income have also been significant. There has been a reduction in the share of wages from 45.2% in I-1989 to 39.1% in I-1990 and an increase in social security benefits from 13.3% to 19.4%, respectively (see Table 3.5).

Compared with I-1989, there has been a decrease in the share of wages in total income in all types of households: in worker households from 87.7 to 83.6%, in farmer/worker households from

Table 3.4 Real (average monthly per capita) income in I-1990 compared with I-89 and IV-89

Household Type	I-1989 =100	IV-1989 =100
Worker	63	73
Farmer/worker	64	57
Farmer	66	44
Retiree/pensioner	70	82

Table 3.5 Structure of nominal income, I-1989 and I-1990

(in percent of total)

	I-1989	I-1990
Total Income	100%	100%
of which:		
Wages	45.3%	39.1%
Social benefits	13.3%	19.4%
Revenue of private economy, except farming	12.4%	12.2%
Other incomes	29.0%	29.3%

Table 3.6 Frequency distribution of household per capita income in worker and pensioner households, December 1989 and March 1990

(in percent)

Income Group (per capita monthly income)	Household Type	
	Worker	Retiree/ Pensioner
December 1989		
100,000 Zl - and less	0.8	3.9
100,001 - 150,000	7.3	15.5
150,001 - 200,000	17.0	24.6
200,001 - 250,000	19.5	24.3
250,001 - 300,000	17.3	16.2
300,001 - 350,000	13.6	7.1
350,001 - 400,000	9.0	4.1
400,001 - 450,000	5.2	1.8
450,001 - 500,000	3.5	0.9
500,001 and over	6.8	1.6
March 1990		
150,000 Zl - and less	0.4	1.3
150,001 - 200,000	2.2	4.3
200,001 - 250,000	5.9	8.0
250,001 - 350,000	21.4	25.7
350,001 - 450,000	23.0	27.0
450,001 - 550,000	18.5	18.1
550,001 - 650,000	12.3	7.8
650,001 - 750,000	6.5	4.0
750,001 - 850,000	4.6	1.7
850,001 - and over	5.2	2.1

Note: Preliminary estimates.

56% to 52.8%, and in pensioner households from 14.7% to 9.4%. By contrast, in all household types, the importance of social benefits has increased — mainly as a result of the reevaluation of retirement benefits and an increase in social benefits for farmers. In I-1990 social benefits amounted to 86.3% of pensioner households' income, 14.9% of farmers', 14.5% of farmerworkers' and 13.9% of workers'. This represents an increase of 5.9, 3.8, 2.9 and 3.6 points, respectively, compared with I-1989.

In the case of farm households, the share of income from the farm in total income has fallen from 87% in I-1989 to approximately 81% in I-1990. In farmer/worker households, the ratio had remained almost unchanged (about 31%). It is difficult to ascertain whether this is due to changes in the terms of trade facing farmers or to difficulties in valuing farm output during the first quarter of the year (some GUS statisticians consider that incomes from the farm in I-1990 are underestimated by 20 to 30%).

SIZE DISTRIBUTION OF INCOME

Preliminary information on the size distribution of incomes in December 1989 and March 1990 is available for workers and for pensioners (see Table 3.6). It must be noted, however, that December is not a typical month either with respect to incomes (because of wage premia payments, increases in retirement payments and pensions, profit shares, awards and allowances) or with respect to spending (because of the holiday season).

The Polish Institute of Labor and Social Affairs calculates quarterly a poverty line called the social minimum. It is based on a basket of goods considered necessary for subsistence, with an additional 10 percent for discretionary household spending, and is adjusted quarterly to take inflation into account. The data published by the Institute indicate an average per capita minimum income of Zl 150,000 for 1989.[2] Among workers, 8% of households were below this poverty line and among pensioners 19% of households. Considering that the increase in consumer prices over the December-March period was 132%, the level of the minimum income for March 1990 may be taken at Zl 300,000 per capita. Using Zl 300,000 as a poverty line, one may consider that 30% of worker households were below this level and 39% among pensioner households in March 1990.

Changes in expenditure patterns

FOOD AND NONFOOD EXPENDITURES

It is estimated that, in real terms, total household expenditures in I-1990 have decreased by 33% with respect to the previous year and, in comparison with IV-1989, by 30-40% (see Table 3.7).

Important changes in the structure of household expenditures have been forced primarily by the higher increase in food prices compared with nonfood prices (especially housing which is subsidized). Inflation-driven purchases of goods and hoarding, which was observed during the hyperinflation of 1989, has stopped and the high prices of goods and services caused some households to forego purchases or defer them to the future.

The change in the structure of household expenditures and average monthly expenditures during I-1990 are presented, by type of household, in Table 3.8 below. Nominal average per capita expenditures by households in I-1990 increased almost 8-fold compared to the previous year, with food expenditures increasing

Table 3.7 Real per capita expenditures in I-1990

Household Type	I-1989 = 100	IV-1989 = 100
Worker	65	69
Farmer/worker	67	61
Farmer	68	54
Retiree/pensioner	67	78

Table 3.8 Household expenditures for major products, per capita, in I-1990

Expenditures	Worker	Farmer / Worker	Farmer	Retiree / Pensioners
I-1990, average monthly expenditures in Zl '000				
Total	339.6	311.5	344.1	312.0
Yearly increase (I-1989 = 100)				
Total	853	873	883	936
of which:				
Food	1,166	1,177	1,253	1,200
Clothing and shoes	489	510	500	529
Housing	802	789	706	769
Fuel/electric power and heating	959	733	630	940
Personal hygiene and health protection	716	771	824	771
Culture, education, upbringing, sport, tourism and others	650	749	507	559
Transport and telecommunications	850	1,014	1,141	986
I-1990 structure of expenditures (percent of total)				
Food	51.9	50.6	52.4	60.3
Clothing and shoes	10.9	11.1	9.0	8.4
Housing	9.6	12.0	10.5	8.7
Fuel/electric power and heating	2.8	2.9	3.2	6.0
Personal hygiene and health protection	2.9	2.2	2.0	3.5
Culture, education, upbringing, sport, tourism and others	6.7	4.3	3.4	3.7
Transport and telecommunications	5.3	6.4	8.0	4.2
I-1989 structure of expenditures (percent of total)				
Food	38.0	37.5	36.9	47.0
Clothing and shoes	19.0	19.0	15.9	14.8
Housing	10.2	13.3	13.2	10.6
Fuel/electric power and heating	2.5	3.5	4.4	6.0
Personal hygiene and health protection	3.5	2.4	2.1	4.2
Culture, education, upbringing, sport, tourism and others	8.7	5.0	5.9	6.2
Transport and telecommunications	5.4	5.5	6.2	4.0

Figure 3.1 Food share in total expenditures, November 1989 - April 1990
(percent of total)

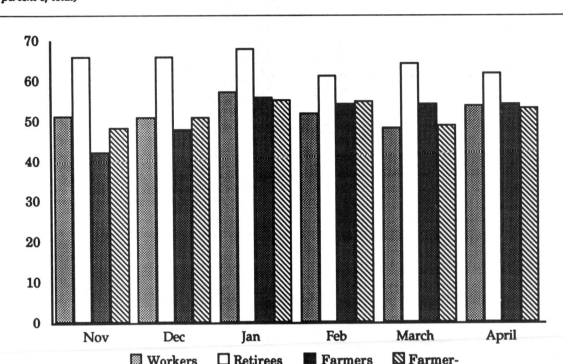

much more than other products and services. Changes in the share of food in total expenditures by household type for the 6-month period November 1989 - April 1990 are shown in Figure 3.1.

As a result, the structure of expenditures compared with I-1989 has changed greatly with the food share in the budget increasing by 13-16%. Expenditures on nonfood products and services (clothing, culture, education, upbringing, sport, tourism and others) have been reduced correspondingly (see Table 3.8).

CHANGES IN FOOD BUDGET SHARES

Table 3.9 shows monthly changes in the budget share (expenditures by food item in percent of total food expenditures) of an average household for 17 food groups for the period January 1989 to April 1990. Meat and dairy products alone account for nearly half of household food expenditures. Figures 3.2 and 3.3 show monthly changes in the budget share for dairy products

(milk, butter, cheese) and meat (pork and beef) over the past 16-month period.

Changes in household food consumption

DIFFERENCES ACROSS HOUSEHOLD TYPES IN FIRST QUARTER OF 1990

Average monthly per capita consumption of basic food items (in kg) in I-1990 is given in Table 3.10. Changes in average monthly consumption with respect to I-1989 are given in Table 3.11. These amounts exclude consumption in restaurants, bars and canteens and refer, properly speaking, to monthly acquisitions of food and not to consumption of food. Households participating in the survey fill out a questionnaire indicating on a monthly basis quantities purchased, gifts, or consumption from own production. For valuation, food products acquired without payments (own production or gifts) are valued at the average price recorded for the same item in the voivodship. The differ-

Table 3.9 Food expenditure shares, January 1989 - April 1990.
(percent of total food expenditures)

| | 1989 | | | | | | | | | | | | |
	I	II	III	IV	V	VI	VII	VIII	IX	X	XI	XII	Average
Cereals	6.22	6.12	4.97	5.99	5.74	5.16	4.55	8.24	5.62	6.64	8.08	7.47	6.23
Potatoes	2.85	3.08	2.50	3.25	2.96	4.28	4.70	6.29	6.36	5.87	1.99	1.23	3.78
Pulses	0.48	0.46	0.33	0.31	0.23	0.12	0.32	0.42	0.22	0.20	0.24	0.25	0.30
Vegetables	6.56	6.97	7.83	11.38	16.00	15.89	17.52	23.38	8.89	6.20	4.57	4.29	10.79
Fruit and products	10.40	8.52	7.64	5.67	4.28	12.19	14.20	15.71	6.18	3.84	4.90	6.71	8.35
Meat and products	29.17	29.65	33.21	29.35	28.50	24.72	22.49	50.69	39.32	39.61	39.62	38.24	33.71
- Pork	7.52	7.45	8.75	7.60	7.46	6.17	5.94	10.45	10.41	10.09	9.89	10.32	8.51
- Beef	2.35	2.58	2.03	2.46	2.33	1.91	1.87	3.51	3.57	3.42	3.48	2.70	2.68
- Poultry	3.49	3.79	3.86	4.16	4.20	4.13	3.99	4.87	4.21	4.17	3.76	3.05	3.97
Fish and products	2.55	3.21	2.77	2.34	2.03	1.71	1.45	2.11	1.43	1.52	1.79	3.71	2.22
Butter	4.80	4.50	3.99	4.53	4.14	3.53	3.27	7.55	6.74	8.73	7.02	4.76	5.30
Animal fat	0.98	0.95	0.81	0.81	0.76	0.69	0.72	1.67	1.53	1.95	2.09	1.56	1.21
Vegetable oils	1.29	1.33	1.32	1.38	1.15	0.95	0.88	1.33	1.26	1.64	2.10	2.09	1.39
Eggs	5.78	5.60	5.33	4.77	4.34	3.97	4.58	6.95	3.69	3.29	3.62	4.06	4.66
Milk	15.23	15.36	13.67	16.96	17.77	16.33	13.15	22.01	13.25	14.92	14.69	11.95	15.44
Cheese	3.05	2.92	2.30	2.53	2.41	2.04	1.85	4.22	3.36	3.62	3.47	2.41	2.85
Sugar	8.02	8.36	8.96	9.00	8.36	8.33	7.84	9.91	4.55	6.17	8.42	10.25	8.18
All Food Items *(share of total expenditures)*	39.11	39.91	39.97	38.20	39.33	40.95	44.41	52.33	52.27	55.92	51.66	52.92	45.58

| | 1990 | | | | Average 1990 (I-IV) | Average 1989 (I-IV) |
	I	II	III	IV		
Cereals	12.64	13.76	12.96	10.06	12.35	5.82
Potatoes	1.54	1.55	1.42	1.10	1.40	2.92
Pulses	0.25	0.27	0.24	0.18	0.24	0.39
Vegetables	3.02	3.35	3.58	4.35	3.57	8.19
Fruit and products	4.40	4.59	5.14	4.24	4.59	8.06
Meat and products	38.97	39.37	40.95	47.82	41.78	30.34
- Pork	10.16	9.86	9.86	11.85	10.43	7.83
- Beef	3.72	4.04	4.52	3.28	3.89	2.35
- Poultry	3.47	3.39	3.46	4.31	3.66	3.82
Fish and products	1.68	2.31	2.20	1.71	1.98	2.72
Butter	4.75	3.59	3.25	2.80	3.60	4.46
Animal fat	2.12	2.16	1.90	1.60	1.95	0.89
Vegetable oils	2.39	2.00	1.76	1.52	1.92	1.33
Eggs	4.34	3.45	2.73	2.96	3.37	5.37
Milk	14.74	5.30	16.09	16.17	13.07	15.31
Cheese	3.14	3.26	3.21	2.23	2.96	2.70
Sugar	8.50	7.48	7.30	3.73	6.75	8.59
All Food Items *(share of total expenditures)*	58.83	53.57	50.14	55.34	54.47	39.30

Figure 3.2 Share of dairy in food expenditures (January 1989 - April 1990)

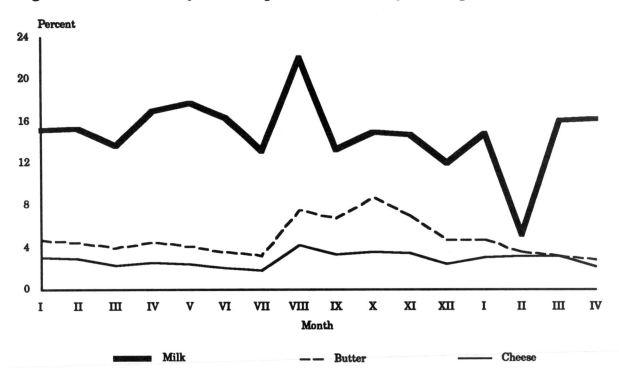

Figure 3.3 Share of meat in food expenditures (January 1989 - April 1990)

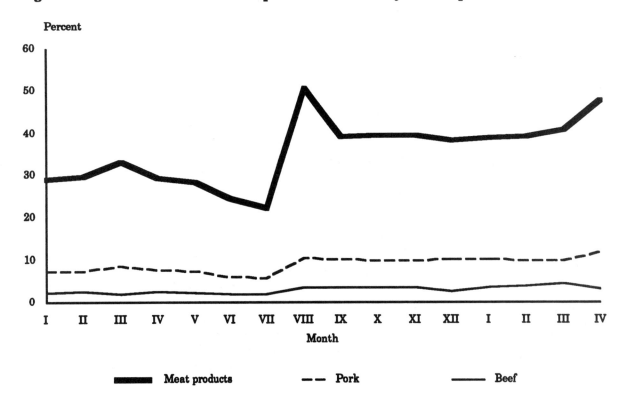

Table 3.10 Average monthly per capita consumption of basic food products in I-1990

Product (in kg)	Worker	Farmer	Farmer/ Worker	Retiree/ Pensioner
Flour	1.10	2.20	2.46	1.82
Bread	6.97	7.90	8.38	8.26
Noodles	0.14	0.07	0.08	0.20
Rice and cereal flakes	0.29	0.47	0.49	0.66
Potatoes	4.46	9.58	10.90	6.59
Pulses, vegetables, mushrooms and processed products	3.25	4.42	5.03	4.72
Fruit and processed fruit	2.60	1.75	1.85	2.93
Meat and processed meat	4.79	4.96	6.18	5.64
Meat	2.62	3.11	4.16	3.28
Processed meat	2.17	1.85	2.02	2.36
Fish and processed fish	0.39	0.23	0.49	
Fats	1.47	1.53	1.80	2.02
of which:				
Butter	0.67	0.59	0.60	0.78
Animal fat	0.37	0.55	0.79	0.59
Milk	7.11	10.10	12.78	11.44
Cream and sour cream	0.43	0.72	0.89	0.58
Cheese	0.80	0.86	0.91	1.09
Eggs	15.04	19.23	22.92	20.02
Sugar	1.47	1.78	2.00	2.06

Household type

Table 3.11 Changes in average monthly per capita consumption, I-1990 compared with I-1989 (I-1989=100)

Product	Worker	Farmer	Farmer/ Worker	Retiree/ Pensioner
Flour	92	105	102	89
Bread	102	97	97	101
Noodles	93	70	73	87
Rice and cereal flakes	73	71	70	73
Potatoes	110	97	101	113
Pulses, vegetables, mushrooms and processed products	93	77	102	94
Fruit and processed fruit	94	84	88	87
Meat and processed meat	94	91	97	100
Meat	93	93	101	99
Processed meat	94	88	71	73
Fish and processed fish	78	70	71	73
Fats	94	92	96	94
of which:				
Butter	93	97	100	94
Animal fat	106	95	101	105
Milk	95	103	108	102
Cream and sour cream	77	92	100	72
Cheese	81	90	95	78
Eggs	86	92	97	88
Sugar	77	73	72	77

Household type

ence between acquisition and consumption is only significant in the case of nonperishable, storable items such as potatoes and we have therefore used the term 'consumption' throughout this annex.

Generally, in all types of households — but especially in worker households (with or without additional farm income) — a decrease in consumption for most food products can be observed. The most significant decrease in consumption is in sugar, fish, and rice and cereal flakes. Worker and retiree households have also greatly reduced their consumption of dairy products (cream and cheese). Farmer households have greatly reduced their consumption of pasta. Compared with I-1989, worker and pensioner households have the most increased con-

sumption of potatoes and animal fats, and farmer households of flour and milk. Farm households have a higher per capita consumption of flour, potatoes, meat, poultry and cream (low fat and normal). Worker and pensioner households consume more pasta, fruit and processed fruit, processed meat and fish (including processed fish).

In order to compare per capita food quantities consumed among different household types, one has to consider demographic differences between groups. Worker households generally have more children than farmer or farmer-worker households. Pensioner households consist mostly of two elderly adults. To take these demographic differences into account, Table 3.12 shows average monthly consumption recalcu-

Table 3.12 Average monthly consumption of basic food products corrected for differences in consumption units, in I-1990

Product (in kg)	Worker	Farmer	Farmer/Worker	Retiree/Pensioner
Flour	1.10	2.20	2.46	1.82
Flour	1.38	2.66	2.98	2.06
Bread	8.71	9.56	10.14	9.33
Noodles	0.18	0.08	0.10	0.23
Rice and cereal flakes	0.36	0.57	0.59	0.75
Potatoes	5.58	11.59	13.19	7.45
Pulses, vegetables, mushrooms and processed products	4.06	5.35	6.09	5.33
Fruit and processed fruit	3.25	2.12	2.24	3.31
Meat and processed meat	5.99	6.00	7.48	6.37
Meat	3.28	3.76	5.03	3.71
Processed meat	2.71	2.24	2.45	2.66
Fish and processed fish	0.49	0.28	0.36	0.55
Fats	1.84	1.86	2.18	2.28
of which:				
Butter	0.48	0.71	0.72	0.88
Animal fat	0.46	0.67	0.96	0.67
Milk	8.89	12.22	15.46	12.93
Cream and sour cream	0.54	0.87	1.08	0.66
Cheese	1.00	1.04	1.10	1.23
Eggs	18.80	23.27	27.70	17.72
Sugar	1.84	2.15	2.42	2.33

Table 3.13 Nutritional requirements
(monthly per capita, adult equivalent, in kg)

	Minimum	Recommended
Cereals	12.47	9.73
of which:		
Bread (mixed)	13.38	10.65
Flour/pasta	1.37	1.22
Other cereals	1.06	0.76
Milk and dairy	18.25	31.94
of which:		
Milk	9.13	15.21
Cottage cheese	0.76	1.06
Cheese	0.46	0.91
Eggs (number)	7.5	23
Meat and fish	3.65	5.32
of which:		
Meat	2.13	2.89
Sausages	0.61	0.91
Fish	0.76	1.22
Butter	0.61	0.91
Vegetable oils		
Soybean/sunflower oil	0.15	0.15
Potatoes	13.69	9.13
Fruits and vegetables		
Vitamin C-rich	5.78	7.60
Carotine-rich	3.65	4.56
Dry Pulses	0.37	0.09
Sugar	1.52	1.98

Note: The figures apply to a male adult, 21-64 years, for moderately heavy work conditions.
Source: Instytut Zywnosci i Zywienia, 1987.

lated at the level of so-called consumption units — that is, using different demographic weights to account for the population structure.

Nutritional norms. The data in Table 3.12 above can be compared with normative information on minimum food requirements published in Poland. The Instytut Zywnosci i Zywienia (Prof. Szcygiel) published in 1987 a list of dietary requirements. The data in Table 3.13 below presents both the minimum requirements (minimum levels required for an adult's normal work) and the target requirements (recommended dietary allowances) published by IZiZ. The kg figures are obtained by translating required levels of energy (2,630 cal/day) and nutrients (minerals and vitamins) into food intake at prices prevailing in 1987. Given the changes in relative prices of 1989-90, it is likely that the same dietary requirements would translate today into other combinations of food intakes.

MONTHLY CHANGES IN FOOD CONSUMPTION, JANUARY 1989 - APRIL 1990

Table 3.14 shows monthly changes in average per capita consumption. This series represents an average for the population (all household types) and reflects two influences: the price changes that have taken place in 1989-90 and the pattern of seasonality of consumption usually observed in Poland.

Seasonality is linked to several factors: absence of significant amounts of imports, climate (for vegetables and fruits, for instance), and seasonality of production (due to the poor infrastructure — cooling, storing facilities — in the food-processing industry). The level of income also affects the seasonality of purchases: poor households purchase nonperishable food (for example, potatoes in the last quarter of the year) when it is cheap and store it at home for the rest of the year. Richer households are less likely to exhibit such behavior. Figures 3.4-3.7 show the pattern of seasonality of purchases of milk, cheese, cereals, and potatoes.

Table 3.15 shows the share of total per capita consumption that originates from the farm's own production, over an 8-month period, comparing the period August 1988 to March 1989 (before the food price increases) with the period August 1989 to March 90. The share of own consumption, which was already high in 1988/89, has increased for almost all categories of goods. It is also surprising to note that, according to the survey, worker households have a high self-sufficiency ratio.

Food demand projections for 1990-2000

Food demand for a particular item depends mainly on four factors: (1) the price of that item; (2) the prices of competing items; (3) the level of per capita income; and (4) population. In a market economy, obtaining projections for food demand would require that one start from an equilibrium position in the market for a particular food product and compute the growth in demand by multiplying the respective elasticities (own-price, cross-prices, and income) by exogenous projections of prices, income, and population.

At present, Poland's food markets are not in an equilibrium position. The Polish economy is currently in a major phase of adjustment of both income levels and relative prices. It is not possible to determine from the data whether purchases by households in mid-1990 reflect normal budgeting behavior (that is, in economic terms, whether quantities demanded at prevailing prices reflect the marginal utilities that households attach to those quantities); but, in all likelihood, they do not. Prior to the removal of food subsidies, rationing was the norm — with food rations available at a below-market price and shortages since consumers could not purchase the amounts that they demanded.[3] Observed prices did not reflect demand (they did not represent a signal to producers and retailers to market more or less of the product). It is therefore not possible to use past survey data to estimate price elasticities.

The long-term forecasts that are presented in this section assume that the main factor that will influence consumption in the future is the level of income and that other factors (such as changes in prices, in the distribution of income or in family size) do not affect food consumption in a systematic (nonrandom) way. They are therefore tentative and must be interpreted with caution. In this section, we describe the models used for the projections and the results obtained. The implications of this exercise from the point of view of an agricultural strategy are presented in the following section.

Long term changes in demand for food were calculated, at constant prices, using exogenous growth rates of income and population. Two scenarios are presented. The high income growth scenario assumes that real income will decline by 14% in 1990 and then grow at an annual rate of 5% during the 1991-2000 period, with population growing at a rate of 0.6% in 1990-92 and 0.8% in 1993-2000 (with a 1989 population of 38 million).[4] The low income growth scenario assumes that real income will decline by 20% in 1990, 5% in 1991, stagnate in 1992 (0%), and then grow at a rate of 3% in real terms during the 1993-2000 period.[5] Population growth assumptions are the same as those of the high income scenario. Base levels of per capita consumption are those of 1989 presented in Table 3.14.

Income elasticities were estimated from cross-sectional data for the last quarter of 1989 (that is, when markets for food were liberalized).[6] The elasticities used for the projections are shown in Table 3.16. We use these estimates in the projections assuming that income elasticities for food decline over time, in a gradual fashion, as income per capita increases. The consumption function has a hyperbolic-logarithmic shape (that is, it approximates the shape that is usual for Engel curves in middle-income countries). Since we only had access to cross-sectional data for two types of households (worker and pensioner), in order to obtain the values in Table 3.16, we made the assumption that income elasticities for an average household are equal to the mean of income elasticities estimated independently for worker and pensioner households. (This assumption does not bias the results of the projections greatly given the relationship existing between income levels and the population shares by type of household.)

The long-term projections are presented in

Tables 3.17-18 (high-income scenario) and Tables 3.19-20 (low-income scenario). Tables 3.18 and 3.20 present the projections on a per capita basis. Tables 3.20 and 3.22 present projections of food demand for the whole population. (Note that these figures refer only to demand for human consumption and do not include demand for feed.) Finally, Tables 3.21-22 show annual growth of food demand, for each scenario.

Summary of findings

SHORT-TERM CHANGES IN HOUSEHOLD EXPENDITURE AND CONSUMPTION PATTERNS

Households have experienced a sharp reduction in real income as a result of the removal of food subsidies and the liberalization of food prices, but their overall consumption of food, in quan-

Table 3.14 Food consumption, January 1989 - April 1990
(in kilograms per capita)

	I	II	III	IV	V	1989 VI	VII	VIII	IX	X	XI	XII	1989 Total	1989 Average
Cereals	7.99	7.56	8.23	8.04	7.98	8.31	8.27	7.55	7.80	7.89	7.47	8.08	95.2	7.93
Potatoes	5.66	5.48	5.75	6.49	6.21	6.24	7.54	8.35	19.83	24.88	7.97	5.64	110.0	9.17
Pulses	0.11	0.09	0.09	0.07	0.06	0.04	0.13	0.13	0.13	0.12	0.11	0.11	1.2	0.10
Vegetables	3.85	3.73	4.11	3.19	3.51	4.91	6.83	9.32	8.10	8.31	4.94	4.51	65.3	5.44
Fruits and fruit products	2.88	2.57	2.69	1.66	1.12	3.92	5.07	4.25	4.55	3.02	2.53	2.93	37.2	3.10
Meat and meat products of which:	4.97	4.94	6.01	5.11	5.17	5.03	4.97	4.79	5.30	5.18	5.26	6.37	63.1	5.26
Pork	1.25	1.23	1.69	1.34	1.38	1.31	1.32	1.21	1.27	1.22	1.24	2.00	16.5	1.37
Beef	0.50	0.52	0.51	0.51	0.51	0.47	0.50	0.47	0.49	0.47	0.53	0.57	6.1	0.50
Poultry	0.70	0.71	0.03	0.78	0.76	0.79	0.81	0.83	0.93	0.85	0.73	0.82	8.7	0.73
Fish and fish products	0.42	0.50	0.58	0.41	0.37	0.35	0.33	0.29	0.32	0.38	0.39	1.03	5.4	0.45
Butter	0.71	0.66	0.75	0.74	0.76	0.81	0.87	0.73	0.79	0.65	0.65	0.70	8.8	0.74
Animal fat	0.47	0.46	0.45	0.41	0.40	0.44	0.50	0.45	0.48	0.50	0.49	0.49	5.5	0.46
Vegetable oil	0.51	0.50	0.60	0.51	0.49	0.49	0.52	0.41	0.49	0.55	0.54	0.63	6.2	0.52
Eggs (number)	17.30	17.71	23.45	19.39	19.39	18.27	16.51	16.12	16.73	16.11	5.27	18.25	204.5	17.04
Milk (liters)	13.80	13.27	14.67	14.64	15.71	16.19	15.18	14.27	14.34	13.63	13.16	12.78	171.6	14.30
Cheese	1.18	1.15	1.29	1.20	1.24	1.26	1.21	1.06	1.09	1.03	1.00	0.97	13.6	1.14
Sugar	2.68	2.39	3.05	3.34	2.90	3.68	3.40	2.41	2.27	2.27	2.26	3.41	34.0	2.84

	1990 I	II	III	IV	Average I-IV 1990	Average I-IV 1989	Difference
Cereals	7.92	7.05	7.86	7.50	7.58	7.95	-4.7%
Potatoes	5.91	5.72	6.33	6.84	6.20	5.85	6.1%
Pulses	0.11	0.10	0.10	0.09	0.10	0.09	11.1%
Vegetables	3.63	3.59	3.72	3.73	3.67	3.72	-1.4%
Fruits and fruit products	2.48	2.43	2.56	1.82	2.32	2.45	-5.2%
Meat and meat products of which:	4.78	4.87	5.48	5.87	5.25	5.26	-0.1%
Pork	1.18	1.17	1.27	1.54	1.29	1.38	-6.4%
Beef	0.53	0.61	0.72	0.54	0.60	0.51	17.6%
Poultry	0.67	0.62	0.72	0.87	0.72	0.56	29.7%
Fish and fish products	0.34	0.40	0.41	0.34	0.37	0.48	-22.0%
Butter	0.66	0.63	0.73	0.76	0.70	0.72	-2.8%
Animal fat	0.47	0.44	0.46	0.41	0.45	0.45	-0.6%
Vegetable oil	0.51	0.41	0.47	0.50	0.47	0.53	-10.8%
Eggs (number)	15.80	16.60	18.80	21.70	18.23	19.46	-6.4%
Milk (liters)	12.67	11.97	13.33	12.09	12.52	14.10	-11.2%
Cheese	0.97	0.93	1.05	0.87	0.95	1.20	-20.6%
Sugar	2.28	1.68	2.03	1.87	1.96	2.86	-31.4%

Table 3.15 Self-sufficiency ratios, August 88 - March 89 and August 89 - March 90
(own production as a percentage of per capita consumption)

Households	Farmer households		Worker households	
	1988/89	*1989/90*	*1988/89*	*1989/90*
Cereals	13.7	32.3	1.3	1.9
Potatoes	99.2	97.9	28.1	29.0
Pulses	92.0	90.7	41.3	41.8
Vegetables (fresh and processed)	81.5	83.1	35.5	37.9
Fruits (fresh and processed)	77.0	72.8	24.0	22.3
Meat and meat products	72.9	73.8	9.6	11.0
Fish and fish products	0.9	1.0	1.2	0.5
Butter	9.9	18.6	0.3	1.1
Animal fat	57.5	62.7	7.8	8.4
Vegetable oils	1.2	0.0	0.0	0.0
Eggs	97.8	98.4	28.3	30.2
Milk and dairy (except butter and cheese)	93.1	94.3	11.0	11.2
Cheese	35.2	51.4	0.9	1.2
Sugar and sweets	0.0	0.0	0.3	0.6

tity terms, has not declined as drastically as previously reported. While real incomes have declined by 30-40% — depending on household type — in the first quarter of 1990 (I-1990) compared with I-1989, consumption has declined on average by 10-15%. The most significant decline in consumption has been observed in sugar (31%) which accounts for 8.6% of average household expenditures at 1990 prices. In terms of expenditures, however, profound changes took place over the past year. On average, households spent 55% of their income on food in January-April 1990, compared with 39% last year. Pensioners spent as much as 65% of their income on food. More than half (54%) of food expenditures go to meat and dairy, on average, compared with 45% last year.

• Consumption of *dairy products* has been seriously affected: milk (15.3% of expenditures, compared with 13.1% a year ago) has fallen by 11.2%; cheese (2.7% of expenditures, compared with 3.0% a year ago) by 20.6%; but butter consumption (4.5% of expenditures, compared with 3.6%) has fallen by only 2.8%.

• Consumption of *meat and meat products* (representing 30.3% of total household expenditures), overall, has not been affected by price changes (fall of 0.1% in consumption). But relative price changes have led households to substitute cheaper products: consumption of fresh pork has fallen by 6.4% and represents now 7.8% of expenditures (10.3% a year ago), while fresh beef consumption has increased by

17.6%, now representing only 2.3% of expenditures (compared with 3.9% a year ago). Poultry consumption has increased by 30% and represents 3.8% of expenditures.

• Consumption of *cereals* in various forms (bread, flour, and the like) has declined by 4.7% and represents 5.8% of expenditures compared with 12.3% a year ago.

• Consumption of *potatoes*, which in Poland is not an inferior product,[7] has increased by 6% and represents 2.9% of expenditures (compared with 1.4% a year ago).

• Consumption of *fruits and vegetables*, both fresh and processed, has fallen by 5.2% and 1.4%, respectively. They represent now 8.0% and 8.2% of expenditures, compared with 4.6% and 3.6% respectively a year ago.[8]

The fall in household demand for most food items is lower than commonly thought (and reported in newspapers). This is due to two factors. First, to the fact that households had hoarded and bought nonperishable food before the price increases of October 1989. Second, households have reduced their nonfood expenditures (such as clothing, education, and durables) and deferred those expenses to the future. Households have restructured their expenditures according to relative price changes but have attempted to maintain approximately the same food consumption level as in the past. In macroeconomic terms, households have behaved over the past year as if they adjusted their consumption pattern to a lesser permanent in-

Figure 3.4 Monthly changes in milk consumption
(liters per capita per month, January 89-April 1990)

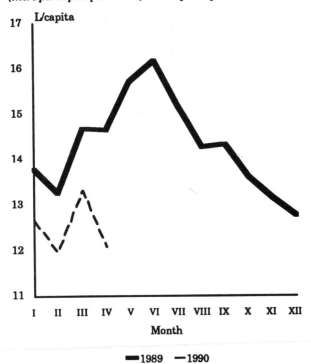

L/capita

Month

■1989 —1990

Figure 3.5 Monthly changes in butter consumption
(kg per capita per month, January 89-April 1990)

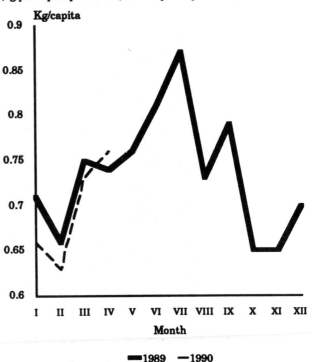

Kg/capita

Month

■1989 —1990

Figure 3.6 Monthly changes in cereals consumption
(kg per capita per month, January 89 - April 1990)

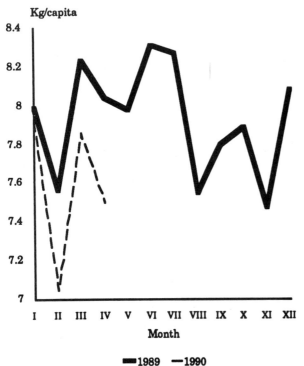

Kg/capita

Month

■1989 —1990

Figure 3.7 Monthly changes in potatoes consumption
(kg per capita per month, January 89- April 1990)

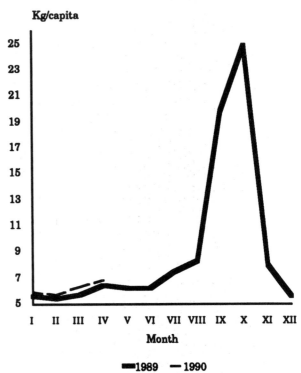

Kg/capita

Month

■1989 —1990

Table 3.16 Income elasticities used for long-term projections

A. High-income scenario	1990	1991	1992	1993	1994	1995	1996	1997	1998	1999	2000
Income level 1989=100	86.0	90.3	94.8	99.6	104.5	109.8	115.3	121.0	127.1	133.4	140.1
Flour	0.13	0.12	0.11	0.11	0.10	0.10	0.09	0.09	0.08	0.08	0.08
Bread	0.10	0.10	0.09	0.09	0.08	0.08	0.08	0.07	0.07	0.07	0.06
Other cereals	0.18	0.18	0.17	0.16	0.15	0.14	0.13	0.13	0.12	0.12	0.11
Potatoes	0.28	0.27	0.26	0.25	0.23	0.22	0.21	0.20	0.19	0.19	0.18
Pulses and vegetables	0.25	0.24	0.23	0.22	0.20	0.20	0.19	0.18	0.17	0.16	0.16
Fruits and fruit products	0.28	0.26	0.25	0.24	0.22	0.21	0.20	0.19	0.19	0.18	0.17
Meat and meat products	0.23	0.22	0.20	0.19	0.18	0.17	0.17	0.16	0.15	0.15	0.14
Pork	0.35	0.34	0.32	0.30	0.29	0.27	0.26	0.25	0.24	0.23	0.22
Beef	0.11	0.11	0.10	0.10	0.09	0.09	0.08	0.08	0.08	0.07	0.07
Poultry	0.26	0.24	0.23	0.22	0.21	0.20	0.19	0.18	0.17	0.17	0.16
Fish and fish products	0.33	0.31	0.30	0.28	0.26	0.25	0.24	0.23	0.22	0.21	0.20
Total fats	0.22	0.21	0.20	0.19	0.18	0.17	0.16	0.15	0.15	0.14	0.13
Animal fat	0.17	0.16	0.15	0.15	0.14	0.13	0.13	0.12	0.11	0.11	0.11
Vegetable oil	0.31	0.30	0.28	0.27	0.25	0.24	0.23	0.22	0.21	0.20	0.19
Butter	0.18	0.17	0.16	0.15	0.14	0.14	0.13	0.12	0.12	0.11	0.11
Milk	0.09	0.09	0.08	0.08	0.07	0.07	0.07	0.06	0.06	0.06	0.06
Cheese	0.19	0.18	0.17	0.16	0.15	0.14	0.14	0.13	0.12	0.12	0.11
Eggs	0.20	0.19	0.18	0.17	0.16	0.15	0.15	0.14	0.13	0.13	0.12
Sugar	0.16	0.15	0.14	0.14	0.13	0.12	0.12	0.11	0.11	0.10	0.10

B. Low-income scenario	1990	1991	1992	1993	1994	1995	1996	1997	1998	1999	2000
Income level 1989=100	80.0	76.0	76.0	78.3	80.6	83.0	85.5	88.1	90.7	93.5	96.3
Flour	0.14	0.14	0.14	0.14	0.14	0.13	0.13	0.12	0.12	0.11	0.11
Bread	0.11	0.12	0.12	0.12	0.11	0.11	0.11	0.10	0.10	0.09	0.09
Other cereals	0.20	0.21	0.21	0.20	0.20	0.19	0.19	0.18	0.17	0.16	0.16
Potatoes	0.31	0.32	0.32	0.32	0.31	0.30	0.29	0.28	0.27	0.25	0.25
Pulses and vegetables	0.28	0.29	0.29	0.28	0.27	0.26	0.26	0.25	0.24	0.22	0.22
Fruits and fruit products	0.30	0.32	0.32	0.31	0.30	0.29	0.28	0.27	0.26	0.24	0.24
Meat and meat products	0.24	0.26	0.26	0.25	0.24	0.24	0.23	0.22	0.21	0.20	0.19
Pork	0.38	0.40	0.40	0.39	0.38	0.37	0.36	0.34	0.34	0.31	0.31
Beef	0.12	0.13	0.13	0.13	0.12	0.12	0.12	0.11	0.11	0.10	0.10
Poultry	0.28	0.29	0.29	0.28	0.28	0.27	0.26	0.25	0.24	0.23	0.22
Fish and fish products	0.35	0.37	0.37	0.36	0.35	0.34	0.33	0.32	0.31	0.29	0.28
Total fats	0.24	0.25	0.25	0.24	0.23	0.23	0.22	0.21	0.21	0.19	0.19
Animal fat	0.19	0.19	0.19	0.19	0.18	0.18	0.17	0.17	0.16	0.15	0.15
Vegetable oil	0.34	0.36	0.36	0.35	0.34	0.33	0.32	0.31	0.30	0.28	0.27
Butter	0.19	0.20	0.20	0.20	0.19	0.18	0.18	0.17	0.17	0.16	0.15
Milk	0.10	0.10	0.10	0.10	0.10	0.09	0.09	0.09	0.09	0.08	0.08
Cheese	0.20	0.21	0.21	0.21	0.20	0.19	0.19	0.18	0.18	0.16	0.16
Eggs	0.22	0.23	0.23	0.22	0.21	0.21	0.20	0.19	0.19	0.17	0.17
Sugar	0.17	0.18	0.18	0.18	0.17	0.17	0.16	0.16	0.15	0.14	0.14

Source: Computed from fourth quarter 1989 Household Budget Survey data.

Table 3.17 Long-term projections: Per capita food consumption (high-growth scenario)

(in kg)

	1989	1990	1991	1992	1993	1994	1995	1996	1997	1998	1999	2000
Assumptions												
Per capita income growth		-14%	5%	5%	5%	5%	5%	5%	5%	5%	5%	5%
Projected consumption												
Flour (kg)	15.60	15.81	15.91	16.01	16.12	16.23	16.30	16.37	16.45	16.50	16.56	16.61
Bread (kg)	83.10	83.48	83.91	84.34	84.79	85.25	85.56	85.88	86.22	86.45	86.68	86.92
Other cereals (kg)	4.68	4.75	4.79	4.84	4.88	4.93	4.96	4.99	5.03	5.05	5.08	5.10
Potatoes (kg)	110.04	107.52	108.93	110.32	111.81	113.33	114.48	115.69	116.98	117.82	118.69	119.62
Pulses and vegetables (kg)	65.28	65.44	66.24	67.04	67.89	68.77	69.38	70.03	70.71	71.16	71.63	72.12
Fruits and fruit products (kg)	37.20	37.19	37.68	38.18	38.71	39.25	39.63	40.04	40.47	40.75	41.04	41.35
Meat and meat products (kg)	63.12	62.74	63.41	64.08	64.79	65.52	66.04	66.59	67.17	67.55	67.95	68.36
Pork (kg)	16.44	16.16	16.42	16.69	16.98	17.27	17.49	17.72	17.96	18.12	18.29	18.46
Beef (kg)	6.00	5.97	6.01	6.04	6.07	6.10	6.13	6.16	6.18	6.20	6.22	6.24
Poultry (kg)	8.76	8.69	8.79	8.90	9.01	9.13	9.21	9.30	9.39	9.45	9.51	9.58
Fish and fish products (kg)	5.40	5.33	5.41	5.49	5.58	5.67	5.73	5.80	5.87	5.92	5.97	6.02
Total fats (kg)	20.64	20.53	20.74	20.95	21.17	21.40	21.57	21.74	21.92	22.04	22.16	22.30
Animal fat	8.88	8.87	8.94	9.01	9.09	9.16	9.22	9.28	9.34	9.38	9.42	9.46
Vegetable oil	5.52	5.47	5.56	5.64	5.72	5.81	5.88	5.95	6.02	6.06	6.11	6.17
Butter (kg)	6.24	6.19	6.25	6.30	6.35	6.41	6.45	6.49	6.53	6.56	6.59	6.62
Milk (liter)	171.60	171.84	172.59	173.34	174.13	174.94	175.49	176.07	176.69	177.09	177.50	177.93
Cheese (kg)	13.68	13.68	13.80	13.93	14.05	14.19	14.28	14.38	14.48	14.55	14.61	14.69
Eggs (number)	171.60	172.00	173.65	175.30	177.06	178.85	180.09	181.41	182.80	183.71	184.65	185.64
Sugar (kg)	33.72	34.02	34.28	34.55	34.83	35.12	35.32	35.52	35.74	35.88	36.02	36.18

Table 3.18 Long-term projections: Demand for food (high-growth scenario)

(in thousand tons)

	1989	1990	1991	1992	1993	1994	1995	1996	1997	1998	1999	2000
Assumptions												
Per capita income growth		-14%	5%	5%	5%	5%	5%	5%	5%	5%	5%	5%
Population growth		0.6%	0.6%	0.6%	0.8%	0.8%	0.8%	0.8%	0.8%	0.8%	0.8%	0.8%
Projected demand												
Cereals	3,950.3	4,000.6	4,046.8	4,093.6	4,150.4	4,208.1	4,258.3	4,309.9	4,363.0	4,410.2	4,458.3	4,507.5
Potatoes	4,181.5	4,110.3	4,189.3	4,268.3	4,360.1	4,455.0	4,536.0	4,620.7	4,709.6	4,781.5	4,855.4	4,932.3
Pulses and vegetables	2,480.6	2,501.6	2,547.3	2,593.7	2,647.7	2,703.3	2,749.1	2,797.0	2,847.0	2,888.0	2,930.2	2,973.9
Fruits and fruit products	1,413.6	1,421.5	1,449.1	1,4771.0	1,509.6	1,543.0	1,570.5	1,599.1	1,629.2	1,653.6	1,678.8	1,704.9
Meat and meat products	2,398.6	2,398.3	2,438.6	2,479.1	2,526.7	2,575.5	2,616.7	2,659.6	2,704.3	2,741.4	2,779.5	2,818.9
Pork	624.7	617.6	631.6	645.7	662.0	678.9	692.9	707.6	723.1	735.4	748.0	761.3
Beef	228.0	228.4	231.0	233.6	236.7	240.0	242.9	245.8	248.9	251.6	254.4	257.2
Poultry	332.9	332.1	338.2	344.3	351.4	358.8	364.9	371.3	378.0	383.5	389.2	395.0
Fish and fish products	205.2	203.6	208.0	212.4	217.4	222.7	227.1	231.7	236.5	240.3	244.3	248.4
Total fats	784.3	784.8	797.6	810.6	825.7	841.3	854.5	868.3	882.6	894.5	906.7	919.3
Animal fat	337.4	338.9	343.7	348.6	354.4	360.3	365.3	370.6	376.0	380.6	385.4	390.2
Vegetable oil	209.8	209.2	213.6	218.1	223.2	228.5	232.9	237.5	242.3	246.1	250.1	254.3
Butter	237.1	236.8	240.2	243.6	247.7	251.8	255.4	259.2	263.0	266.3	269.7	273.1
Milk ('000 liters)	6,520.8	6,569.1	6,637.4	6,706.2	6,790.7	6,876.6	6,953.6	7,032.5	7,113.4	7,186.6	7,261.0	7,337.0
Cheese	519.8	523.0	530.9	538.7	548.1	557.6	565.8	574.2	582.9	590.3	597.9	605.7
Eggs (millions)	6,520.8	6,575.2	6,678.2	6,782.2	6,904.8	7,030.5	7,136.0	7,245.6	7,359.5	7,455.4	7,553.5	7,654.9
Sugar	1,281.4	1,300.4	1,318.4	1,336.7	1,358.4	1,380.6	1,399.4	1,418.7	1,438.8	1,456.0	1,473.7	1,491.8

Table 3.19 Long-term projections: Per capita food consumption (low-growth scenario)
(in kg)

	1989	1990	1991	1992	1993	1994	1995	1996	1997	1998	1999	2000
Assumptions												
Per capita income growth		-20%	-5%	0%	3%	3%	3%	3%	3%	3%	3%	3%
Projected consumption												
Flour (kg)	15.60	15.65	15.54	15.54	15.60	15.66	15.73	15.80	15.86	15.92	16.08	16.12
Bread (kg)	83.10	82.77	82.29	82.29	82.56	82.84	83.13	83.43	83.70	83.95	84.60	84.76
Other cereals (kg)	4.68	4.68	4.63	4.63	4.66	4.68	4.71	4.74	4.77	4.80	4.86	4.88
Potatoes (kg)	110.04	104.97	103.30	103.30	104.25	105.23	106.26	107.32	108.26	109.07	110.95	111.55
Pulses and vegetables (kg)	65.28	64.07	63.18	63.18	63.68	64.21	64.76	65.33	65.85	66.32	67.49	67.81
Fruits and fruit products (kg)	37.20	36.34	35.78	35.78	36.10	36.43	36.77	37.12	37.44	37.73	38.46	38.66
Meat and meat products (kg)	63.12	61.56	60.80	60.80	61.23	61.69	62.16	62.65	63.09	63.48	64.43	64.71
Pork (kg)	16.44	15.68	15.38	15.38	15.55	15.73	15.92	16.12	16.30	16.45	16.82	16.93
Beef (kg)	6.00	5.92	5.88	5.88	5.90	5.92	5.95	5.97	5.99	6.01	6.05	6.07
Poultry (kg)	8.76	8.50	8.38	8.38	8.45	8.52	8.60	8.67	8.74	8.80	8.95	9.00
Fish and fish products (kg)	5.40	5.18	5.09	5.09	5.14	5.20	5.25	5.31	5.37	5.42	5.53	5.56
Total fats (kg)	20.64	20.16	19.92	19.92	20.06	20.20	20.35	20.50	20.64	20.76	21.06	21.15
Animal fat	8.88	8.74	8.66	8.66	8.70	8.75	8.80	8.86	8.90	8.95	9.05	9.08
Vegetable oil	5.52	5.33	5.24	5.24	5.29	5.35	5.40	5.46	5.52	5.56	5.68	5.71
Butter (kg)	6.24	6.10	6.04	6.04	6.08	6.11	6.15	6.19	6.22	6.25	6.32	6.34
Milk (liters)	171.6	170.55	169.70	169.70	170.18	170.68	171.20	171.74	172.23	72.67	173.77	174.06
Cheese (kg)	13.68	13.47	13.33	13.33	13.41	13.49	13.58	13.67	13.75	13.82	13.99	14.04
Eggs (number)	171.60	169.18	167.33	167.33	168.38	169.47	170.61	171.78	172.85	173.81	176.25	176.90
Sugar (kg)	33.72	33.57	33.28	33.28	33.45	33.62	33.80	33.98	34.15	34.31	34.72	34.82

Table 3.20 Long-term projections: Demand for food (low-growth scenario)
(in thousand tons)

	1989	1990	1991	1992	1993	1994	1995	1996	1997	1998	1999	2000
Assumptions												
Per capita income growth		-20%	-5%	0%	3%	3%	3%	3%	3%	3%	3%	3%
Population growth		0.6%	0.6%	0.6%	0.8%	0.8%	0.8%	0.8%	0.8%	0.8%	0.8%	0.8%
Projected demand												
Cereals	3,955.2	3,968.6	3,968.0	3,991.8	4,037.8	4,084.9	4,132.9	4,182.0	4,230.4	4,278.0	4,348.7	4,392.6
Potatoes	4,181.5	4,012.7	3,972.6	3,996.4	4,065.4	4,136.6	4,210.3	4,286.6	4,358.7	4,426.4	4,538.6	4,599.6
Pulses and vegetables	2,480.6	2,449.3	2,429.6	2,444.2	2,483.6	2,524.2	2,566.1	2,609.4	2,651.2	2,691.3	2,761.0	2,796.3
Fruits and fruit products	1,413.6	1,389.2	1,376.2	1,384.4	1,407.8	1,431.9	1,456.8	1,482.6	1,507.4	1,531.2	1,573.2	1,594.1
Meat and meat products	2,398.6	2,353.5	2,338.0	2,352.1	2,387.9	2,424.9	2,462.9	2,502.1	2,539.9	2,576.0	2,635.8	2,668.2
Pork	624.7	599.5	591.3	594.9	606.4	618.4	630.9	643.8	656.1	667.6	688.1	698.3
Beef	228.0	226.2	226.1	227.4	230.1	232.8	235.6	238.4	241.2	243.9	247.6	250.1
Poultry	332.9	325.1	322.4	324.3	329.6	335.0	340.7	346.5	352.0	357.3	366.3	371.0
Fish and fish products	205.2	198.1	195.7	196.9	200.5	204.3	208.2	212.3	216.1	219.8	226.2	229.4
Total fats	784.3	770.7	766.0	770.6	782.1	794.0	806.2	818.8	830.9	842.5	861.6	872.0
Animal fat	337.4	334.1	332.9	334.9	339.5	344.1	348.8	353.7	358.5	363.0	370.2	374.3
Vegetable oil	209.8	203.8	201.5	202.7	206.4	210.2	214.1	218.2	222.1	225.8	232.3	235.6
Butter	237.1	233.3	232.4	233.8	237.0	240.3	243.7	247.1	250.5	253.7	258.6	261.6
Milk ('000 liters)	6,520.8	6,519.8	6,526.1	6,565.2	6,636.7	6,709.6	6,783.8	6,859.5	6,934.0	7,007.2	7,108.5	7,177.5
Cheese	519.8	515.0	512.8	515.9	523.1	530.5	538.0	545.8	553.4	560.7	572.4	579.0
Eggs (millions)	6,520.8	6,467.5	6,435.0	6,473.6	6,566.5	6,662.0	6,760.1	6,861.1	6,959.1	7,053.8	7,209.8	7,294.5
Sugar	1,281.4	1,283.4	1,279.9	1,287.6	1,304.3	1,321.5	1,339.2	1,357.3	1,375.0	1,392.3	1,420.1	1,435.7

Table 3.21 Long-term projections: Demand for food (high-income growth scenario)

	1990	1991	1992	1993	1994	1995	1996	1997	1998	1999	2000
Assumptions											
Per capita income growth	-14.0	5.0	5.0	5.0	5.0	5.0	5.0	5.0	5.0	5.0	5.0
Population growth	0.6	0.6	0.6	0.8	0.8	0.8	0.8	0.8	0.8	0.8	0.8
Projected growth of food demand											
Cereals	1.3	1.2	1.2	1.4	1.4	1.2	1.2	1.2	1.1	1.1	1.1
Potatoes	-1.7	1.9	1.9	2.2	2.2	1.8	1.9	1.9	1.5	1.5	1.6
Vegetables and pulses	0.8	1.8	1.8	2.1	2.1	1.7	1.7	1.8	1.4	1.5	1.5
Fruits and fruit products	0.6	1.9	1.9	2.2	2.2	1.8	1.8	1.9	1.5	1.5	1.6
Meat and meat products	0.0	1.7	1.7	1.9	1.9	1.6	1.6	1.7	1.4	1.4	1.4
Pork	-1.1	2.3	2.2	2.5	2.5	2.1	2.1	2.2	1.7	1.7	1.8
Beef	0.2	1.1	1.1	1.4	1.4	1.2	1.2	1.2	1.1	1.1	1.1
Poultry	-0.2	1.8	1.8	2.1	2.1	1.7	1.8	1.8	1.5	1.5	1.5
Fish and fish products	-0.8	2.1	2.1	2.4	2.4	2.0	2.0	2.1	1.6	1.7	1.7
Total fats	0.1	1.6	1.6	1.9	1.9	1.6	1.6	1.6	1.4	1.4	1.4
Animal fat	0.4	1.4	1.4	1.7	1.7	1.4	1.4	1.5	1.2	1.2	1.3
Vegetable oil	-0.2	2.1	2.1	2.4	2.4	1.9	2.0	2.0	1.6	1.6	1.7
Butter	-0.1	1.4	1.4	1.7	1.7	1.4	1.5	1.5	1.2	1.3	1.3
Milk	0.7	1.0	1.0	1.3	1.3	1.1	1.1	1.2	1.0	1.0	1.0
Cheese	0.6	1.5	1.5	1.7	1.7	1.5	1.5	1.5	1.3	1.3	1.3
Eggs	0.8	1.6	1.6	1.8	1.8	1.5	1.5	1.6	1.3	1.3	1.3
Sugar	1.5	1.4	1.4	1.6	1.6	1.4	1.4	1.4	1.2	1.2	1.2

Table 3.22 Long-term projections: Demand for food (low-income growth scenario)

	1990	1991	1992	1993	1994	1995	1996	1997	1998	1999	2000
Assumptions											
Per capita income growth	-20%	-5%	0%	3%	3%	3%	3%	3%	3%	3%	3%
Population growth	0.6%	0.6%	0.6%	0.8%	0.8%	0.8%	0.8%	0.8%	0.8%	0.8%	0.8%
Projected growth of food demand											
Cereals	0.3	0.0	0.6	1.2	1.2	1.2	1.2	1.2	1.1	1.7	1.0
Potatoes	-4.0	-1.0	0.6	1.7	1.8	1.8	1.8	1.7	1.6	2.5	1.3
Pulses and vegetables	-1.3	-0.8	0.6	1.6	1.6	1.7	1.7	1.6	1.5	2.6	1.3
Fruit and fruit products	-1.7	-0.9	0.6	1.7	1.7	1.7	1.8	1.7	1.6	2.7	1.3
Meat and meat products	-1.9	-0.7	0.6	1.5	1.5	1.6	1.6	1.5	1.4	2.3	1.2
Pork	4.0	-1.4	0.6	1.9	2.0	2.0	2.1	1.9	1.8	3.1	1.5
Beef	-0.8	0.0	0.6	1.2	1.2	1.2	1.2	1.2	1.1	1.5	1.0
Poultry	-2.3	-0.8	0.6	1.6	1.7	1.7	1.7	1.6	1.5	2.5	1.3
Fish and fish products	-3.5	-1.2	0.6	1.9	1.9	1.9	2.0	1.8	1.7	2.9	1.4
Total fats	-1.7	-0.6	0.6	1.5	1.5	1.5	1.6	1.5	1.4	2.3	1.2
Animal fat	-1.0	-0.4	0.6	1.3	1.4	1.4	1.4	1.3	1.3	2.0	1.1
Vegetable oil	-2.8	-1.1	0.6	1.8	1.8	1.9	1.9	1.8	1.7	2.9	1.4
Butter	-1.6	-0.4	0.6	1.4	1.4	1.4	1.4	1.4	1.3	2.0	1.1
Milk	0.0	0.1	0.6	1.1	1.1	1.1	1.1	1.1	1.1	1.4	1.0
Cheese	-0.9	-0.4	0.6	1.4	1.4	1.4	1.4	1.4	1.3	2.1	1.2
Eggs	-0.8	-0.5	0.6	1.4	1.5	1.5	1.5	1.4	1.4	2.2	1.2
Sugar	0.2	-0.3	0.6	1.3	1.3	1.3	1.4	1.3	1.3	2.0	1.1

come, attempting to preserve their past level of food consumption but reducing their purchases of durable goods.

NUTRITIONAL STATUS

In the early 1980s, average consumption per capita of cereals, meat, milk and fats fell sharply leading to a worsening of nutritional indicators (for instance, energy intake fell from 3,570 kcal in 1980 to 3,300 in 1982). But at the end of the decade, average energy and nutrient intakes were back at their 1980 levels.[9]

Average nutritional intake compares favorably with that of Western European countries. Per capita daily calorie supply in 1986 was 3,336 cal in Poland, compared with 3,326 cal in the Netherlands, 3,336 cal in France, 3,645 cal in the United States, 3,528 cal in the Federal Republic of Germany, and 3,064 cal in Sweden.[10] Even if changes in nutritional indicators were as drastic as those observed at the beginning of the eighties, this would still represent a good nutritional status for the population, on average.

However, average figures mask the fact that an increasing number of persons are below the poverty line and nutritionally at risk, presently and in the future, as a result of the fall in their real income and/or limited income opportunities due to rising unemployment. The percentage of households that are below the poverty line (evaluated by the Institute of Social Affairs at Zl 300,000 per month) is estimated to be 37% among pensioner households and 30% among worker households.

There is a demonstrated need to reinforce and expand the existing social welfare system in two directions: first, to reinforce existing programs that transfer income to low-income groups (Social Aid Centers, Labor Fund, and other institutions); and, second, to develop existing targeted nutritional programs for vulnerable groups (such as the milk bars) to cover all old persons, children, and pregnant and lactating mothers that are nutritionally at risk.

MEDIUM- AND LONG-TERM PROSPECTS

During the shock period of the transition from a centrally planned to a market-based economy, the pattern of expenditures and consumption described in the previous section is not representative of what can be expected in the medium term. What consumption profile can we then expect for major food groups over the next decade?

Projections for 1990-2000: the influence of income. During the period of adjustment of the economy, one can expect real incomes to fall until they attain a macroeconomically sustainable level. Projections have been carried out for two income-growth scenarios: the optimistic scenario considers that GDP will decline by 14% in real terms in 1990 and grow at the real rate of 5% thereafter; the pessimistic scenario considers that real GDP will decline by 20% in 1990 and by 5% in 1991, that it will not grow (0%) in 1992, then grow at an annual real rate of 3% thereafter.

Our food demand projections, under both scenarios, are based on estimated income elasticities. Our estimation shows that, empirically, the relationship between income and consumption in Poland (for example, the Engel curve) is typical of middle- to high-income countries — it increases fast at low levels of income, stabilizes, then remains constant at higher levels of income. The projections indicate the following trends.[11]

Per capita consumption. In per capita terms, the food demand curve over time is flat. After the initial shock of the decline in income, demand for food products grows at an average rate never exceeding 1.2%. Demand for cereals grows at an average rate of 0.5% in the optimistic scenario (0.3% in the pessimistic scenario); for meat at a rate of 1% (pessimistic scenario: 0.7%); and for milk at 0.4% (pessimistic scenario: 0.3%)

Total demand. When population growth is taken into account,[12] total food demand shows a more pronounced upward trend. Average growth rates of poultry, pork and fish exceed 2% per annum, but cereals grow at an average rate of 1.1% in the optimistic scenario (0.8% in the pessimistic scenario); meat at a rate of 1% (pessimistic scenario: 1.2%); and milk at a rate of 1% (pessimistic scenario: 0.8%) The average growth rate for the 1990-2000 period in the pessimistic scenario is affected by the fall in the demand for all food products in 1990-91 and the low rate of growth (approximately 0.6%) in 1992.

The projections indicate that, in the long term, total food demand in Poland will be mainly driven by population growth. On a per capita basis — whatever income growth scenario one uses — food demand will not increase at high rates. We can say that food consumption will not continue to be sustained at levels similar to those existing when the generalized food subsidy program was in effect.[13]

Other factors that will affect food demand. The long-term forecasts discussed above assume that the main factor that will influence food demand in the future is the level of income and that other factors (such as changes in prices, distribution of income, or family size) will not affect food demand in a systematic (nonrandom) way.

But food demand is influenced not only by the level of income but also by the distribution of income. During a period of 3-4 years (say, until 1993), we can expect that the change from a centrally planned to a market-based economy will — in all likelihood — effect a worsening in the distribution of income. Demand for basic food items will therefore be higher than the projections indicate. Then, after 1993, as real incomes increase and more people move to higher income groups, the food budget share and the income elasticity will decline sharply.[14] Therefore, after 1993, if the economy recovers, the overall growth in food demand will slow down, implying that our projected figures are biased upward for the years 1993-2000. At the same time, another tendency will come into play: as income increases and the share of the poor in total income decreases, demand for more processed and more expensive food items will increase and demand for primary, unprocessed food will decline.

Several other factors — not accounted for in the projections — will affect food consumption. In particular, supply-side factors such as the opening up of the economy and the restructuring of the food sector will have a profound effect on consumption patterns.

Seasonal fluctuations. First, the profile of consumption will be flatter. There will be a reduction in the amplitude of seasonal fluctuations that are observed in consumption in Poland. This seasonality in consumption is linked to the seasonality of production in the processing industry, to the absence of much food imports, and to the scarcity of storage and cooling facilities, long-shelf-life products, and so forth.

Second, the consumption trend for major food groups will be affected by important factors:

• A middle-income country like Poland (per capita income level of US$1,860 in 1988) cannot sustain over a long period an average household food budget share of 55%. This share will decline over time until it reaches a level similar to that of middle-income European countries (for instance, Portugal 34%, Greece 30%, Spain 24%, Ireland 22%);

• During the short term, we can expect food demand to adjust to relative consumer price changes until food markets are in an equilibrium position. There will be substitution within major food groups (for example, pork versus beef; butter versus margarine; animal fat versus vegetable oil; bread versus processed cereals) as a result of relative price effects;

• The availability of imports, and the greater choice and quality of consumer products, will lead to a differentiation of consumer tastes. If the supply side responds, food markets will be differentiated according to income and price elasticities of various types of consumers;

• In the long term, improvements in nutritional standards of the population, through nutrition education, will reduce high-cholesterol, high-calorie food intake and modify consumption habits.

Appendix:
Data sources

The main source used in this annex are unpublished data from the Budzety Gospodarstw Domowych (Household Budget Surveys) on incomes and expenditures, including consumption estimates (in zlotys and kg) for some 65 food items that were aggregated into main food groups. The surveys are carried out on a monthly basis by the Central Statistical Office (GUS) since 1980. The data for January 1989 - April 1990 were kindly provided to the Task Force by GUS.

The Household Budget Survey suffers from several shortcomings but is statistically reliable.[15] Stratified random sampling techniques are used with a large sample size.[16] The survey covers some 90% of the population. Excluded from the survey are persons employed in the private sector outside of agriculture, military and police. The information included in the survey is presented for four types of households made up of: workers and employees; farmers; farmers/workers (for example, rural farming households with an important share of income originating outside the farm);[17] and retirees and pensioners. Annually, the size distribution of income and expenditures (by income class: from poorest to richest) is published by GUS. Preliminary information for size distribution for workers and pensioners in 1989 and March 1990 is available (see Table 3.6).

Three important caveats must be mentioned:

• Regarding food consumption, households must fill out a questionnaire indicating quantities and value of purchases, gifts, or own production. Food products acquired without payments (own production or gifts) are valued at the average price recorded for the same item in the voivodship. Quantities therefore refer to monthly acquisitions and not to consumption of food. The difference between acquisition and consumption, however, is only significant in the case of nonperishable, storable items such as potatoes.

• Income and expenditure data for rural households (farmers and farmer-workers) mentioned in this annex must be interpreted with caution: rural income according to GUS experts is underestimated by 20-30%. This is due to the method of data collection: household net incomes and expenditures are obtained by subtracting purchases and sales related to the management of the farm from gross incomes and expenditures. Corrections to the rural data are done by GUS at the end of the year since many activities are, by nature, seasonal activities.

• Finally, it must be mentioned that GUS has not yet adapted its method of collecting data to the changes that have occurred in the economy. The private nonagricultural sector was excluded from the sample design. In the future, the coverage of the survey must be extended to include incomes coming from this source. In addition, underreporting of income generated in the hidden economy is known to exist but statistically unobservable. In conclusion, one should not expect the 1990 income data used in this annex (even when corrected for seasonal and demographic influences) to be entirely reliable since it underreports incomes.

The other sources used in this annex are *Informacja Statystyczna*, published monthly by GUS (used for price indices) and a mimeographed report from GUS dated May 1990 titled *Informacja o warunkach bytu ludnosci w I quartale 1990r.*

Endnotes

This annex was prepared by Jean-Jacques Dethier (The World Bank) and Jerzy Plewa (Warsaw Agricultural University).

The authors would like to thank Prof. Jan Kordos, Mr. Kubiczek and Mmes Gradek and Gizicka (GUS) for kindly providing them with Household Budget Survey data, and Prof. Stanislaw Berger (Warsaw Agricultural University) for advice on nutrition policy in Poland.

1. Subsidies on bread were eliminated. However, in the case of rye bread, the Ministry of Finance exercises some degree of control over the price because of the obligation for bakeries to submit a justification of cost increases if they wish to increase consumer prices.

2. The per capita survival minimum for December 1989 was:

worker households	for	1 person	=	Zl 179,000
		4 persons	=	Zl 147,900
retiree/pensioner households	for	1 person	=	Zl 156,000
		2 persons	=	Zl 138,400

3. In such a situation, subsidies do not alter demand at the margin. Conceptually they are simply transfers from the budget to the consumer.

4. See World Bank, *Structural Adjustment Loan*, Report No. P-5294-POL, June 1, 1990. The average per capita income in 1989 was Zl 2.8 million. Population projections are from the 1988 *World Bank Atlas*.

5. Production for the first quarter of 1990 has declined by 30.1% compared with the same period in 1989 (GUS estimates).

6. They represent the percentage change in food consumption induced by a percentage change in income, at various levels of per capita income.

7. According to our estimates, the income elasticity for potatoes is small but positive — unlike what is observed in Western Europe.

8. All the figures presented in this section are percent changes between January-April 1990 (average) and January-April 1989 (average).

Tables 3.9 (expenditure shares) and 3.14 (consumption) give the monthly data for 1989-90.

9. See B. Kowrygo, S. Berger and B. Sawicka, "Nutritional Implications of Changes in Agricultural Policy. Poland in the Eighties," mimeographed, Institute of Human Nutrition, Warsaw Agriculture University, n.d.

10. World Bank, *World Development Report 1990, Oxford University Press, 1990.*

11. Note that the figures for cereals and potatoes refer only to demand for human consumption and do not include demand for feed.

12. We have used the 1988 *World Bank Atlas* population projections indicating 0.6% growth until 1992 and 0.8% from 1993-2000.

13. In addition, higher food prices will lead to reduced waste. This means that total demand (= consumption + waste + stocks) will also grow more slowly as less food is wasted and/or fed to animals.

14. In market economies with high per capita income levels (OECD countries), the income elasticity for most food products — even highly processed food — is almost zero.

15. For details, see World Bank, Poland: Subsidies and Income Distribution, report No. 7776-POL, November 1989, and Branco Milanovic, "Poverty in Poland in the years of crisis 1978-87," The World Bank, mimeographed, November 1989, which uses the data to examine safety net and poverty issues.

16. In 1989, the sample included 20,555 worker families (for a population of 18.8 million) and 5,216 pensioner families (for a population of 4.9 million).

17. In the first quarter of 1990, these farmer/worker households received on average 52% of their income from wages, 31% from their farm and the rest from social security and other benefits.

Annex 4

Agricultural trade policy strategy

The Polish government's declared intention is to move Poland from a centrally planned economy to a Western market economy. This implies a desire to move to a situation where domestic prices in general will be closely related to world market prices and where trade will take place according to market forces.

However, economic liberalization should not be considered as an objective in itself, but rather as a means to achieve more basic social welfare objectives. Liberalization of markets without the appropriate government regulation may well generate effects in both the short term and the long term that are undesirable due to negative effects on production growth and the distribution of income. Accepting that liberalizing the economy in general, and foreign trade in particular, will bring major benefit in the long run does not imply that the overall process of liberalization should start with a complete liberalization of external trade, in particular not for agricultural products.

Liberalization will only produce the desired results if market-oriented institutions, which respond to market signals, exist. To create such institutions requires a change of management culture and a redefinition of property rights. The process of doing this will take a long time. During this process the use of trade policy instruments may ease the adjustment process. The use of trade policy instruments is particularly important in Poland's present situation where the government lacks other instruments to adjust the income distribution. Trade mea-

sures are normally less costly to administer than internal measures. Agricultural trade measures could therefore play an essential role in assisting the adjustment process both on the supply and the demand side.

The agricultural sector is not directly linked to the international market. Agricultural products are always traded in some processed form. Hence, the import and export parity farm prices are derived from c.i.f. and f.o.b. world market prices taking into account the costs of transforming agricultural products in form, space and time. The present inefficiency of upstream and downstream sectors in Poland taxes the agricultural sector indirectly. In connection with a high (perceived) real interest rate this is a major source of agricultural price instability (as will be argued subsequently). This can increase the adjustment costs for the agricultural sector (which in terms of employment and income generation is of major importance to the Polish economy) and will cause problems in relation to the urban sector where the price of food is of crucial importance for social stability.

The trade policy needed may appear to contradict the government's general policy to decrease government involvement in the economy, but the basic hypothesis underlining this annex is that a specific agricultural trade policy for the short and medium term could assist the adjustment process of transforming the Polish economy into a modern market economy. The formulation and communication to the economic agents of such a policy would stabilize expectations, which in itself could contribute to the realization of the government's stabilization policy.

This annex presents briefly the past and present trade regimes and describes the trade flows in recent years on the basis of available empirical evidence. External trade was very distorted in the past. Thus, the evaluation of past trade is important to evaluate whether the same pattern of trade flow should prevail in the future as in the past.

The role of the agricultural sector in foreign trade depends on the competitiveness of the sector. Hence, the main determinants of its competitiveness are investigated in the section on the effect of trade policy on the competitiveness of the agricultural sector. Of main interest is the question of whether the agricultural sector was taxed or subsidized in the past, also taking into account the effect of the inefficiency of upstream and downstream sectors. If the agricultural sector was taxed in the past one would expect the agricultural sector, and hence agricultural exports, to expand in the medium term without government support (assuming that the restructuring of the Polish economy in general will make the upstream and downstream sectors function efficiently). If, on the other hand, the agricultural sector was subsidized one would expect Polish agricultural exports to contract. It has not been possible to present definitive answers to all questions raised in this section. Nevertheless, it is hoped that the presentation will help to get a better idea of the future agricultural trade prospects and to specify the needs for further research.

The reader more interested in the policy recommendations might, however, want to move directly to the summary section, in which the strategic considerations are presented and recommendations for the medium term and short term are formulated. Trade performance would improve if measures were instituted to improve the functioning of the internal markets. However, these measures are not explored in this annex. Rather, we have focused on the question of how the agricultural sector could be influenced by trade measures in a beneficial way. Specific emphasis is laid on the grain and dairy markets. Since these product markets are the most important for Polish agriculture, assisting the adjustment in these markets through the use of trade policy instruments deserves special attention.

The trade regime

THE PREVIOUS SYSTEM

In the centrally planned economic system which prevailed before the reforms introduced by the present government, foreign trade in agricultural and food products was regulated by the following principles:

• State monopoly of foreign trade. Producers did not have direct access to foreign markets and had to operate through a few specialized state and cooperative foreign trade organizations (*centralas*). Even in 1989, after the first decentralization attempts of foreign trade, the share of the five main *centralas* in the total value of imports and exports of agricultural and food products amounted to about 80-85%.

• Trading according to plan. The volume and the price to be paid to domestic suppliers, as well as the exchange rate, was fixed by the central plan. *Centralas* were responsible for carrying out the plan. They imported goods and services on the basis of currency availability as fixed by the central plan, and in turn had to sell to the state almost the entire amount of foreign currency earned through exports. In the 1980s, however, the exporting firm was allowed to keep a certain percentage of the hard currency obtained.

• Overvalued exchange rate. During 1987-89 there was a practice of fixing the exchange rate at a level which would make 80% of total exports profitable.

• No transmission between the international and domestic prices.

• Agricultural and food exports were more heavily subsidized than exports of other products. Exports were subsidized more to the ruble area than to the hard currency area. In 1989, 88% of the exports of agricultural and food commodities to the ruble area were subsidized, as were 67% of the agricultural and food exports to the hard currency area. The average subsidy paid for agricultural and food products amounted to 40% to the ruble area and 24% to the hard currency area compared with 8% and 3%, respectively, for nonagricultural products.

THE CURRENT AND FUTURE SYSTEM

Some changes in the foreign trade regime were initiated in 1987. The changes were accelerated in 1989, but the radical liberalization of foreign trade did not take place until January 1, 1990. Since this date the external trade regime has been based on the following three main principles: internal exchangeability of the domestic currency; no central distribution of hard currencies; and free access to foreign trade.

Duties on imports of agricultural and food products are relatively low. The unweighted average of duties paid on the imports of agricultural products during the first five months of 1990 amounted to 8.3% and the weighted average (the weights being the 1989 import shares) only 2.5%; for processed food products, the corresponding figures are 13.7% and 6.8%, respectively.

There are no quantitative restrictions on imports into Poland.

Exports of agricultural and food products to the hard currency area are not subsidized.

During January 1990 quantitative restrictions were imposed on the export of some strategic products, including agricultural and food products, either by export quotas (for meat, live animals, vegetable fats, sugar, butter and full milk powder) or by discretionary export licenses (for cereals, flour, rapeseed and cheese). These quantitative restrictions were motivated by the desire to prevent excessive domestic price increases immediately after the strong devaluation of the zloty in December 1989.

At present Poland's export of agricultural and food products is only restricted in order to satisfy Poland's international obligations: the remaining bilateral clearing agreements with the COMECON countries; minimal prices for dairy products (butter, skim and full milk powder) agreed in the GATT; the ban by donor countries on the reexport of wheat and wheat flour; and restrictions on exports to the EC in return for trade concessions (for example, quotas under the GSP (General System of Preferences), reference prices for fruit and vegetables, minimal prices for eggs, poultry, live animals, and pork, and voluntary export restraints on sheep, mutton, goats and goat meat).

During the last six months of 1989 Poland obtained improved market access to the EC: the quotas imposed because of Poland's status as a CMEA country were lifted and Poland was given a number of tariff quotas (export at reduced tariffs) under the GSP arrangement. At the beginning of 1990 Poland was also given GSP status in its trade with the United States.

In the latest annual trade agreement with COMECON countries the value of trade in agricultural and food products under the trade agreement was decreased significantly compared to previous years. Agricultural and food products have been excluded from the trade protocols with the German Democratic Republic, Hungary and Romania. Exports of agricultural and food products require subsidies of up to 50%. In order to minimize these subsidies the Ministry of Foreign Economic Relations has organized auctions where the commitment to export a certain contingent is given to the enterprise that accepts the lowest subsidy. Trade in agricultural and food products in excess of the commitments under the clearing agreements is not subsidized.

From 1991 on, all trade with the COMECON countries including the Soviet Union will be conducted in hard currency. Clearing arrangements, as in the trade between the Soviet Union and Finland, are currently under negotiation.

Trade flows and trade performance[1]

TRADE FLOWS

During the first five months of 1990 Poland had a surplus on its balance of trade with both the convertible zone (US$1,605 million) and the nonconvertible zone (1,198 million rubles) countries (see Table 4.1). This represented a significant improvement compared with the same period the year before (US$1,223 million and 786 million rubles). Nearly half of this improvement is explained by improvement of the agrifood balance (see Table 4.1). The improvement of the agrifood balance is partly due to an increase in the export of agricultural products, but is mainly due to a dramatic fall in agrifood imports. The fall in food imports may, however, be overestimated due to significant private food imports. But unregistered private exports that did not clear customs are not assumed to be significant.

Trade reversal has taken place over the last 12 months for a number of products. Poland, which used to import butter, has during the first five months of this year exported it in a sizeable amount. If there had not been a ban on cereal exports, Poland would have exported wheat.

The increase in exports is not a consequence of increased production, but rather a consequence of a decrease in domestic stocks of agricultural

Table 4.1 Balance of Trade
(I: nonconvertible zone, II: convertible zone)

Total	1989 (i-v)	1990 (i-v)	% Change
Exports (I) M ruble	4313	4508	104,5
Exports (II) M US$	3361	3758	111,8
Imports (I) M ruble	3901	2528	64.8
Imports (II) M US$	2979	2154	72.3
Balance (I) M ruble	412	1198	+786
Balance (II) M US$	382	1605	+1223

Agrifood	1989 (i-v)	1990 (i-v)	% Change
Exports (I) M ruble	160	130	81
Exports (II) M US$	658	737	112
Imports (I) M ruble	103	55	53
Imports (II) M US$	787	208	26
Balance (I) M ruble	57	75	18
Balance (II) M US$	-129	529	658

Food	1989 (i-v)	1990 (i-v)	% Change
Exports (I) M ruble	73	70	95.7
Exports (II) M US$	464	471	101.7
Imports (I) M ruble	89	36	40.6
Imports (II) M US$	393	167	42.5
Balance (I) M ruble	-16	34	50
Balance (II) M US$	71	304	233

Agriculture	1989 (i-v)	1990 (i-v)	% Change
Exports (I) M ruble	87	60	69.0
Exports (II) M US$	194	266	137.1
Imports (I) M ruble	15	19	128.3
Imports (II) M US$	394	41	10.4
Balance (I) M ruble	72	41	-31
Balance (II) M US$	-200	225	425

Note: Figures only cover trade by state trading companies and private trade which has gone through customs.
Source: GUS.

products in a period when the real interest rate has changed from being negative to being positive, and when food consumption has decreased due to the sharp fall in real income of Polish households (see Annex 3).

The decrease in imports of agricultural products is mainly due to a decrease in the imports of feed stuff, which will subsequently lead to lower animal production. This will have a negative effect on the future agrifood balance.

The share of exports in total agrifood production is relatively low (see Table 4.2). Relatively small changes in production and consumption may therefore lead to quite signifi-

cant changes in the trade balance. A relatively small increase in food consumption or decrease in agricultural production may therefore easily turn the surplus into a deficit.

For these two reasons the significant increase in the agrifood surplus during the first five months of 1990 should not be taken as an indication that the Polish agrifood surplus will continue to increase. Further depreciation of the real exchange rate due to expected inflation of around 20% until January 1 will mean that the picture may change for the second half of the year.

The share of exports in domestic production of certain products such as slaughter lambs and frozen fruits and vegetables has in the past been very high (see Table A.1 in the Appendix). Whether this will continue under free market conditions remains to be seen.

The evolution of exports and imports for selected commodities from 1987 to 1990 is illustrated in Tables A.2 and A.3 in the Appendix.

Agrifood exports constitute an important share of total exports to convertible zone countries whereas the share of exports to nonconvertible zone countries is very small.

The share of agricultural products in total agrifood exports has in the past been twice that of food products. The increase in the share of agricultural products in 1990 exports may be taken as an indication that agricultural products are more competitive under free market conditions than processed products. This is consistent with the analysis below.

The shares of animal and crop products in total agrifood exports have in the past been of the same order of magnitude, but it seems that crop products are gaining in importance.

Table A.4 in the Appendix indicates that Poland's agrifood exports are very diversified.

Table 4.2 Share of exports in production

Export of	1988	1989	1990 (est)
Agrifood products % of total production	5.8	6.1	7.0
Agricultural products % of total production	3.0	3.4	4.3
Food % of total production	9.4	9.5	9.5

Source: GUS and Institute of Agriculture and Food Economics.

Table 4.3 Share of agrifood in total exports and imports

	1989 (i-v) %	1990 (i-v) %
Exports (I) ruble	3.6	2.8
Exports (II) US$	19.6	19.6
Imports (I) ruble	2.9	3.1
Imports (II) US$	26.4	9.7

Source: GUS.

Table 4.4 Share of agricultural and food products and of crop and animal products in total agrifood exports

	1984 %	1988 %	1990(i-v) %
Agricultural products	31	28	36
Food products	69	72	64
Animal products	54	47	36
Crop products	46	53	63

Source: GUS.

Table 4.5 Share of agrifood exports going to various destinations
(at official exchange rate)

	1975	1984	1989
Nonconvertible zone	33	23	18
of which:			
SU	13		
other	5		
Convertible zone	67	77	82
of which:			
EC	31	35	50
US	12	13	11
other	24	29	21

Source: GUS and Institute of Agriculture and Food Economics.

Table 4.6 Share of foreign trade by state trade organizations (*centralas*) in convertible imports and exports, 1989

	Exports	Imports
Pewex		6
Animex (animal products)	32	9
Rolimpex (grain)	21	40
Rybex (fish)	10	5
Agros	10	21
Polcrop	5	3
All	77	84

Source: Ministry of Foreign Economic Relations.

This diversification has been seen as an advantage, as it makes Poland's export earnings less sensitive to fluctuation in the price of specific products. However, this is again something that may change under free market conditions.

Agrifood exports to the convertible zone, in particular the EC countries, have been increasing over recent years, whereas exports to the nonconvertible zone countries have decreased.

This trend may very well be reversed in the future when all trade, including trade with the Soviet Union, will be in foreign currency. Polish food products, which are of relatively low quality, seem to have a better chance of competing in the Soviet market than in the EC market, where both quality requirements and trade barriers will make further expansion difficult.

In the Appendix, Table A.5 provides more detail on the country destination of Polish exports, and Tables A.7 and A.8 give information on the distribution of exports and imports for convertible and nonconvertible zone countries for selected commodities.

Foreign trade organizations (*centralas*) have in the past had a dominant position in agrifood exports and imports and still maintain it, even with expanding private trade.

EVALUATION

Up to 1989, the export of agrifood products was strongly subsidized. Subsidies amounted to Zl 748 billion, of which Zl 151 billion were subsidies for exports to nonconvertible zone countries (area I) and Zl 594 billion to convertible zone countries (area II). In 1988 the corresponding figures were respectively Zl 249 billion, Zl 62 billion and Zl 187 billion.

Agrifood exports were more subsidized than exports in general. Whereas the share of agrifood exports in total exports was 14%, (3.6% in area I, 19.6% in area II) the share of agrifood export subsidies in total export subsidies was significantly higher, 44.2% (17.3% in area I, and 74.1% in area II).

In 1989, 88% of agrifood exports to area I and 67% to area II required subsidies. In 1988, the corresponding numbers were 87% and 67%. The budget figures showing the revenue and expenses associated with the import and export of agrifood products in 1988 and 1989 are shown in Table A.9 in the Appendix. The main reason for the large budget deficit in 1989 was the huge subsidies to the import of grain and meat products (Zl 91 billion). The largest subsidies in exports to area I were associated with fruit and vegetable products and crop products. For exports to area II, big subsidies were given both to fruit and vegetable products (Zl 134 billion) and to meat and animal products (Zl 109 billion).

It is difficult to make a general assessment about export profitability in 1989. Official procurement prices which were in use up to August 1, 1989, have been increased several times but the exchange rate has not been adjusted to the same extent during this period. This caused an increase in export subsidies. Therefore most *centralas* made losses. In the last quarter of 1989, the exchange rate was adjusted, which allowed the *centralas* to cover previous losses to some extent.

An indication of the export subsidies on various products may be obtained from data on the average cost of obtaining foreign currency. In 1989, subsidies to agrifood exports were as follows:

• for exports to the nonconvertible zone countries (area I), Zl 958 had to be spent (in payment to middlemen) to obtain one ruble. Comparing this with the official exchange rate of Zl 536 ruble, this corresponds to a technical coefficient of 1.78 (= 958/536) or an export subsidy of 44%;[2]
• for exports to the convertible zone countries (area II), Zl 1,928 had to be spent to obtain one dollar. Comparing this with the official exchange rate of Zl 1,479/US$, this corresponds to a technical coefficient of 1.30 or an export subsidy of 23%.

The corresponding technical coefficients for nonagrifood exports were 1.12 (export subsidy of 11%) for area I and 1.03 (export subsidy of only 3%) for area II. These coefficients were similar in previous years.

Table A.10 in the Appendix contains technical coefficients for a number of products. These data seem to suggest that processed products, in general, required greater subsidies than agricultural products.

The effect of trade policy on the competitiveness of the agricultural sector

THE BASIC QUESTION

Poland's net exports are by definition the difference between Poland's domestic demand and domestic supply. In order to understand the evolution in trade and prospects for future trade, domestic supply and demand conditions need therefore to be considered, in particular the functioning of the upstream and downstream sectors (see below).

The prospects for future Polish agricultural trade depend on whether or not the Polish agricultural sector in the future will be competitive at world market parity prices. The basic question to be answered before discussing Poland's agricultural trade strategy (in fact, before the discussion of any aspect of Poland's agricultural strategy) is to what extent the Polish agricultural sector will be profitable without government support after the implementation of the government's restructuring program. To answer this question it is important to know to what extent Poland's agricultural sector was subsidized or taxed in the past. If the Polish agricultural sector was heavily subsidized one would expect Polish agricultural exports to contract and if it was taxed one would expect them to expand (assuming no changes in domestic household demand).

CONCEPTUAL FRAMEWORK

In a market economy, production decisions of the agricultural sector are a function of its endowment with primary factors (land, labor and capital), the prices it has to pay for its intermediate inputs (such as fertilizer, feed and machinery) and the prices it receives for its outputs (crop products, animals and animal products). The relationship between agricultural sector output prices and intermediate input prices is popularly called the price scissors. If output prices increase or input prices decrease, the price scissors open and the agricultural sector will tend to expand, and vice versa. The agricultural sector prices depend on the world market price, the exchange rate, government intervention and the functioning of upstream and downstream sectors.

The upstream sectors are the industries delivering inputs to the agricultural sector and organizations dealing with trade in these commodities. The upstream sectors include industries producing fertilizers, pesticides, feed stuffs, machinery, transport and services.

The downstream sectors are the sectors processing agricultural outputs and trading in these commodities. The downstream sectors include industries which deal with dairy, meat processing, fruit and vegetable processing, other crop processing, transport and services.

The linkages between the agricultural sector, the rest of the economy and the world market may be illustrated by the supply-utilization matrix in Figure 4.1, which shows the physical flows affecting the agricultural sector.

In a market economy these physical flows are governed by a set of prices specific to each sector. For each production sector there exists a specific set of output and input prices which are determined on the one hand by production costs, and on the other hand by government intervention in terms of taxes, subsidies and government intervention. The agricultural sector input and output prices (the price scissors) are influenced by a wide range of government policy instruments related to the various sectors:

- import: tariffs, import restrictions
- upstream sectors: for example, subsidies to

energy inputs in the fertilizer industry
- downstream sectors: for example, investment subsidies and input subsidies to the food-processing sector; consumption (food subsidies, rationing)
- export: for example, export subsidies or taxes, export bans.

The agricultural sector prices will naturally also be affected by the government's macroeconomic policies (income policy, exchange rate policy, credit and monetary policy, and public finance and taxation policy). These policies affect the agricultural sector directly, as well as indirectly through their effect on other sectors, in particular through their effect on export and household demand for agricultural products.

This framework should draw attention to two issues:

- It is extremely difficult to assess the eventual effect on the agricultural sector of the dramatic change of government policy which Poland has experienced in recent months, involving fundamental changes both of macroeconomic policy and of government intervention in relation to all sectors.
- The competitiveness of the agricultural sector depends crucially on the cost efficiency and competitive behavior of upstream and downstream sectors.

TO WHAT EXTENT IS THE POLISH AGRICULTURAL SECTOR TAXED BY THE INEFFICIENCY OF THE UPSTREAM AND DOWNSTREAM SECTORS?

To evaluate the prospects for the agricultural sector and hence for agricultural trade we need to assess the extent of the implicit taxation of

Figure 4.1 Supply-utilization account

	Import	Upstream	Agricultural Sector	Downstream	Human Consumption	Export
Food products	+x			+x	-x	-x
Agricultural products	+x		+x	-x	-x	-x
Inputs specific to the agricultural sector	+x	+x	-x	-x		
Other products	+x	-x	-x	-x	-x	-x

+ : supply
- : utilization

the Polish agricultural sector by the monopolistic and inefficient upstream and downstream sectors. This analysis is also important for understanding the role agricultural trade measures can play in the stabilization of agricultural prices. Figure 4.2 illustrates the points to be made using the situation on June 1, 1990, for rye as an example.

Economists often speak about the world market price. One of the supposed benefits of the government's policy of starting the reform process by liberalizing trade was that this would allow the domestic agents to replace the old distorted price system by world market prices for domestic transactions. The idea that there is one world market price which may serve as a guide to the domestic transaction price is a simplification which may be especially misleading for agricultural products, where Poland is close to self-sufficiency. For a given commodity there exists one relevant world market price at the closest international trading center where there is an export surplus and another one at the closest international trading center where there is an import deficit. The difference between these two prices is determined by the costs of moving the commodity from the one center to the other. At the Polish border, the export price (the f.o.b. price) will for any commodity be lower

than the corresponding import price (the c.i.f. price). The f.o.b. price is determined by the transport costs from the Polish border to the closest international trading center where there is an import deficit and the c.i.f. price by the transport costs from the closest international trading center where there is an export surplus. The domestic price will be the f.o.b. parity price (f.o.b.- for short) or the c.i.f. parity price (c.i.f.+ for short) depending on whether Poland has an export surplus or an import deficit. The f.o.b.- is the f.o.b. price minus the costs of moving the commodity to the border and the c.i.f.+ is the c.i.f. price plus the costs of moving the commodity from the border.[3] This naturally applies both to commodities that are used by the agricultural sector as an input (in this case the price transmission is through an upstream sector) and commodities produced by the agricultural sector (in which case the price transmission is through the downstream sector). Since rye is both produced by the agricultural sector and consumed as a feed input the example used in Figure 4.2 may serve to illustrate both cases. The difference between f.o.b.- and c.i.f.+ prices is greater the higher the transport costs and the more inefficient the trade and processing channels. As is illustrated by the example, the difference for Poland is for the moment quite significant. This is confirmed by the information contained in Table 4.7.

Table 4.7 shows the ratio between f.o.b. and f.o.b.- and between c.i.f. and c.i.f.+ for a number of agricultural and food products. Since Poland for the moment is in an export position for most products, f.o.b. and f.o.b.- prices are in general the border prices and the domestic (wholesale) prices, respectively. The data indicate a very inefficient price transmission between f.o.b. and f.o.b.- prices. Column (7) in Table 4.7 indicates the dramatic increases in wholesale prices which may be expected if Poland moves from an export to an import position. As our subsequent analysis indicates, this is not a purely theoretical possibility.

Two important conclusions may be drawn from this analysis:

• The level of domestic consumer and producer prices for agricultural products will, particularly in the short run where the downstream or upstream sectors are very inefficient, be significantly different depending on whether Poland is exporting or importing.

Figure 4.2 The price transmission from the world market depending on the direction of trade

	Point of consumption: Agricultural sector or household sector
processing transport costs services monopolistic profit	Farm-gate price (c.i.f.) 120 $/t
Import price (c.i.f.) 110 $/t	
	Range of domestic price variation at constant world market price
Export price (f.o.b.) 85 $/t processing transport costs services monopolistic profit	
	Farm-gate price (f.o.b.) 55 $/t
	Point of production: Agricultural sector

Table 4.7 The price transmission in June 1, 1990

	f.o.b. price (1) $	f.o.b.- price (2) $	Ratio (1/2) (3)	c.i.f. price (4) $	c.i.f.+ price (5) $	Ratio (4/5) (6)	Ratio (6/3) (7)
Pigs, live	x	961	x	910	1,226	.74	1.28
Beef	741	550	1.35	741	886	.84	1.61
Meat							
pork	1,440	1,397	1.03	1,370	1,501	.91	1.07
beef	1,470	954	1.54	1,420	1,556	.91	1.63
Ham	4,020	#4,726	.85	3,216	4,363	.74	(.92)
Calves	2250	*1,789	1.26	2,250	2,352	.96	1.31
Sheep (EC)	2,242	**	x	2,242	2,343	.96	x
Ducks	1,820	**	x	x	x	x	x
Wheat	121	88	1.38	146	161	.90	1.84
Rye	85	69	1.23	110	122	.90	1.76
Oats	95	63	1.50	120	133	.90	2.10
Lupin	150	105	1.43	195	216	.90	2.05
Beans	160	105	1.52	195	216	.90	2.05
Rapeseed	390	#684	.57	x	x	x	x
Sugar	400	#519	.77	430	498	.86	(.96)
Potato flour	320	316	1.01	340	410	.83	1.30
Casein	1,800	1,368	1.32	3,500	4,221	.83	3.08
Butter	1,200	#895	1.34	1,350	1,522	.89	(1.70)
Skim milk powder	800	453	1.77	1,500	1,960	.77	4.33
Full milk powder	1,250	579	2.16	1,600	2,010	.80	3.47
Cheese							
Cheddar	1,400	947	1.48	1,600	2,091	.77	2.21
Gouda	1,650	1,105	1.49	2,100	2,638	.80	2.39

Legend:
#: Retail prices.
*: Average price paid to exporters.
**: Revenues from exports are calculated on the basis of the export price.

Source: Ministry of Finance and author calculations.

• If stocking is neither technically nor economically feasible (due to excessive real interest rates or credit rationing), the domestic prices may change dramatically from year to year due to trade reversal and even within the marketing season due to the seasonal pattern of consumption and production.

In the two following subsections the framework presented above will be used to assess the level of protection of the Polish agricultural sector in the past and the recent developments of Polish agricultural trade.

To WHAT EXTENT WAS THE AGRICULTURAL SECTOR TAXED OR SUBSIDIZED IN THE PAST?

In the section on trade flows and performance data were presented on the border protection of

Polish agriculture in the past. The discussion above should have made it clear that the level of protection of the Polish agricultural sector in the past cannot be assessed solely on this basis. First, subsidies to agricultural sector outputs and inputs also need to be taken into account. In the past the prices were fixed administratively. The subsidies to the agricultural sector were therefore related to the losses made by food-processing companies and companies producing inputs to the agricultural sector.[4] Out of the 500 biggest state enterprises, 56 were loss making in 1988. Of these, 43 belonged to the food-processing industry and nine to the feed-processing and fertilizer industry. The profitability of these industries (the return to invested fixed capital) in 1988 was -8.5%. The strongly subsidized dairy industry is not included in these figures. The losses of the food-processing firms are a function of the ratio between farm-gate prices and the consumer prices that in the past were fixed administratively. It is difficult to determine to what extent these losses are due to too high producer prices or too low consumer prices. In other words, it is difficult to establish to what extent the losses represent subsidies to consumers, to the agro-industrial companies or to the farmers.

A rough idea of the price transmission in the past can be obtained from the data contained in Table A.11. In the past, domestic prices for the food-processing industry were in all cases higher than border prices. For grain products and live animals the farm-gate prices were also higher than border prices, whereas farm-gate prices for pork and fruit seemed to have been lower.

The price transmission does not reflect taxes and subsidies given to agricultural inputs. In assessing the level of protection of the agricultural sector in the past these should also be taken into account.

According to preliminary calculations, direct production subsidies in 1989 (including the state budget subsidy to the social security and retirement system for private farmers) for production of grains, rapeseed and sugar beets (mostly the subsidy to mineral fertilizers) amounted to one-tenth of the farm-gate prices, while subsidies to livestock production (mainly to coal and concentrate feedstuffs) constituted a third of the procurement price for slaughter swine and a tenth of the procurement price of cattle and milk.[5] Input subsidies for previous years were at a similar level.

Producer subsidy equivalent (PSE) has been calculated for Poland.[6,7] The unit PSE indicates the transfer to the agricultural sector due to border measures and subsidies to agricultural sector outputs and inputs in relation to the value of agricultural production at producer prices. These data (see Table 4.8) suggest — as one would expect since they take into account the input subsidies mentioned above — that the agricultural sector was subsidized in the past to an even larger extent than the export subsidies and price transmission data seem to indicate.

The PSE for animal products do not take into account the excess feed costs due to higher than world market prices for feed grain. The protection for animals and animal products, in particular for pork, is therefore lower than the PSE data indicate. The PSE does not take into account the effect of low energy prices on the

Table 4.8　Gross unit producer subsidy equivalents, 1987 (private sector)

	1986	1987	1988
Wheat	46	47	34
Rye	37	48	28
Barley	65	59	32
Sugar	33	31	
Rapeseed	50	43	
Pork	28		
Beef	16	39	46
Milk	57	23	

domestic prices for fertilizer. The level of protection of crop products is therefore higher than the PSE data indicate.

A more fundamental problem in interpreting these data is the role played by the exchange rate. In the PSE calculations, the world market prices have been translated into domestic prices at the official exchange rate. If the exchange rate was overvalued in relation to the equilibrium exchange rate, the level of subsidization would be overestimated. The fact that the black market exchange rate was significantly higher than the official exchange rate could support such an interpretation. Purchasing parity comparisons may lead to the opposite conclusions.

Another issue is the level of world market prices used in the calculations. For 1986 and 1987, world market prices for agricultural products were particularly low. If calculated at 1989 world market prices, the PSE would be significantly lower.

It is unclear to what extent the PSE calculations reflect the considerable efficiency gains which would arise from restructuring the upstream and downstream sectors and to what extent subsidies in the past have been eaten up by the administrative cost of the rationing scheme in force at that time.

The misallocation of resources within the agricultural sector due to rationing inputs in the past (having the effect of input taxes) should also be taken into account in assessing the level of protection.

However, on balance the evidence seems to suggest that the agricultural sector was subsidized in the past. In other words, it suggests that the removal of government intervention is likely to lead to lower agricultural production and therefore, if the fall in production is not accompanied by an even greater fall in food consumption, to lower net exports. One important implication of this is that domestic prices in Poland, if left to market forces, will move from the present level, well below the f.o.b. prices, to a level of prices above the c.i.f. prices.

However, considering the complexity of the link between the world market prices and the agricultural sector prices, it would be premature to assess the prospects for Poland's agricultural trade only on the basis of past performance as reflected by the PSE calculations.

RECENT EVOLUTION OF TRADE AND PRICES

The decrease in income and the relative price increase for certain food products have made food consumption in 1990 decrease by around 10% compared with 1989 (see Annex 3). It is unlikely that adaptation has been completed. Substitute products like quality margarine, for example, are not yet available. The consumption of butter may therefore decrease significantly if in the future it is priced at cost. Food consumption in general, however, is likely to increase to a similar level as in the past when the level of income recovers (see Annex 3 on food demand).

After having accumulated stocks during the hyperinflation in 1989, private agents (farmers and consumers) seem to have reduced stock to a bare minimum in 1990 due to the shift from a negative to a highly positive real interest rate. Farmers have decreased the use of inputs partly because of high prices and partly because of crippling high interest rates. Data gathered by the Ministry of Finance provide clear evidence of a planned reduction in herd size (although these plans have yet to be implemented) due to the low feed costs during the summer season.

This has caused an accumulation of stocks in state enterprises and trade reversal for several products, which in turn results in very low domestic prices relative to world market prices (f.o.b. parity prices). The present situation is not indicative of the future situation if the government's restructuring program succeeds in improving the efficiency of upstream and downstream sectors and if trade reversal moves prices up from the f.o.b.- to the c.i.f.+ level. Uncertainty about the government's agriculture policy and the high and uncertain real interest rate may lead 1) to destocking and running down of agricultural capital (in particular, livestock capital), which will represent a serious misallocation compared with what would be

optimal for the medium term, and 2) to price instability over the season due to price swings from f.o.b.- to c.i.f.+.

Table A.11 in the Appendix shows that the situation has changed dramatically during the first three months of 1990 compared with the previous period. The prices paid to farmers as well as to middlemen during this period were significantly lower than border prices. The increase in the exchange rate from Zl 2,990/US$ to Zl 9,500/US$ on January 1, 1990, eased the effect of the suppression of export subsidies. But as the real exchange rate depreciated (due to high inflation) the relation between output prices and input prices deteriorated.

Data gathered by the Ministry of Finance also show that the ratio of input prices to output prices has developed unfavorably during the first five months of 1990, particularly for milk, but also for grain; the evolution of input to output prices for pork, on the other hand, has been more favorable.

More detailed calculations describing the relation between farm-gate prices and border prices are presented in Appendix Table A.11 for pork, live cattle and live lamb. Appendix Table 12.1 shows that exports of pork were subsidized until 1989. The border price was lower than the price paid to the meat processing firms. During the first months of 1990 the devaluation allowed profit in the trade of pork carcasses. The domestic price has increased 389.3% while the border price has grown 510.5%. The first figure reflects the inflation rate, while the second can be attributed to the devaluation of the Polish zloty. The picture is similar for live cattle and live lamb.

RECOMMENDATION REGARDING FUTURE RESEARCH

It has not been possible within the timeframe of this study to provide reliable projections for Poland's trade prospects for the future. Trade must be seen as the interaction between external conditions and domestic supply and demand conditions. It may be possible to predict future domestic demand for agricultural products; but without knowing how the agricultural sector will react in the medium term without government intervention (which in turn depends on how much the agricultural sector has been supported in the past), it is very difficult to predict trade. We have reviewed the evidence concerning the extent of past agricultural subsidization.

Figure 4.3   The price transmission for wheat

processing
transport costs
services
monopolistic profit

Import price (c.i.f.)   146 $/t

Export price (f.o.b.)   120 $/t
processing
transport costs
services
monopolistic profit

Point of consumption:
Household sector
Farm-gate price (c.i.f.)   160 $/t

Range of domestic price
variation at constant
world market price

Farm-gate price (<f.o.b.-)   65 $/t

Point of production:
Agricultural sector

• nearly 2 metric tons of food aid 1989-90

• shift from negative to strongly positive real interest rate

• farmers, households and other private agents have shifted from building up stocks to reducing stocks and input use (feed, seed)

• reduction in household demand (less waste, less consumption) due to lower income

• domestic prices, which without food aid would have been c.i.f.+ prices, are now even below normal f.o.b

• prices due to export ban

• 2 metric tons of grain in public storage which is unusual at this time of the year. Usually only 6 metric tons out of a harvest of 25 metric tons is traded, but due to high interest rate and plans to reduce animal production, farmers may want to sell more than usual

• if exports are allowed, prices will increase but only to f.o.b.- level

• Poland will, in all cases, want to import about 1 metric ton of hard wheat for bread-making

• if export exceeds 3 metric tons, Poland is likely to move to an import
position later in the marketing year

Figure 4.4 The price transmission for butter

processing
transport costs
services
monopolistic profit

Import price (c.i.f.)   1,350 $/t

Export price (f.o.b.)   800 $/t
processing
transport costs
services
monopolistic profit

Point of consumption:
Household sector
Farm-gate price (c.i.f.)   1,500 $/t

Range of domestic price
variation at constant
world market price

Farm-gate price (<f.o.b.-)   600 $/t

Point of production:
Agricultural sector

• import at c.i.f. price of 2,000US$/t at beginning of 1989, food aid of 4,500 tons from US

• rapid decrease in consumption due to decrease in income and relative price increase and due to subsidy to low-fat milk

• Poland renounces 10,000 tons food aid in autumn 1989

• export of 40,000 tons of butter in 1990 at very low prices due to Polish-Polish export competition and collusion of EC importers

• turnover tax provides incentive for cutting out middleman dairy industry going bankrupt: cannot sell processed product at sufficient price to cover even very low milk price to farmers

• no one wants to stock butter (further problem that butter is of low quality and has very low shelf life after storage)

• prospect of dramatic increase in prices in late autumn and spring "knock-on" effect on herd size

• most efficient farmers will leave milk production

The evidence is not conclusive. It depends on how much the official exchange rate was overvalued, and on the degree to which the agricultural sector was taxed by the productive inefficiency and bureaucratic costs of the upstream and downstream sectors. On the basis of the available evidence regarding external conditions and internal supply and demand conditions, we will in the following section try to provide some recommendations for Poland's trade policy for the short and medium terms. These recommendations do, however, rest on a very weak foundation. We therefore recommended that further research should take place to assess the competitiveness of Polish agriculture, incorporating theoretical analysis of empirical evidence relating to levels of subsidization of the Polish agricultural sector in the past. The comparison between processing and trading margins in Poland and comparable countries should form an important part of such a study.

Summary propects for trade and recommendations

AGRICULTURAL TRADE

Poland's agrifood exports account for 20% of total exports. But food exports were maintained with significantly greater export subsidies than nonfood exports. Rough calculations suggest that the overall level of protection of Polish agriculture in the past was even higher than the level of protection due to border measures. There is some indication that exports of processed food products are less competitive than exports of agricultural products. Therefore, it is uncertain whether even the past level of exports will be sustainable in the medium term without government assistance, and it is likely that the structure of trade of the past, enforced by administrative decisions, will change.

Poland's agrifood trade balance has improved by more than 500 million ECU over the first five months of 1990 compared with the same period in 1989. The agricultural trade surplus is equivalent to 30% of Poland's trade surplus for this period. The surplus, however, is mainly due to a collapse of Poland's agrifood imports. Agricultural exports, which account for approximately one-third of Poland's agrifood exports, have increased significantly, but food exports that represent a greater value added have stagnated. The increase in agricultural exports may have been influenced by decisions to run down stocks below their normal level (for example, in the case of butter), including livestock capital. Furthermore, Poland's agrifood exports constituted only a relatively small share of production (around 3.5% of agricultural production and around 10% of food production). Relatively small changes in domestic supply and demand conditions will therefore eliminate this surplus. There are fears that a further depletion of livestock capital in the autumn will lead to a reduction in agricultural exports and increased food imports in the longer term.

PROSPECTS FOR TRADE

In general. It is unclear whether Poland in the medium term will be able to generate an export surplus at f.o.b. prices corresponding to current world market prices. Even in the short term the export of butter may well turn into an import deficit. The extent to which an improvement in the efficiency of the upstream and downstream sectors can improve the agricultural sector's competitiveness, however, must still be fully assessed. The negotiations in the current round of GATT concerning mutual reduction of protection in the industrialized countries are not likely to result in a dramatic improvement of agricultural world market prices.

The EC has, within the existing legal framework, provided Poland with the maximum possible privileged access to the EC market in terms of increased tariff quotas under the GSP and other schemes. The Common Agricultural Policy (CAP) is going to stay, as the conclusions from the latest meeting of the G7 countries in Houston demonstrate. For the EC to assist Poland by providing it with privileged access to commodities that the EC subsidizes at high cost is, from a purely economic point of view, very inefficient (compare this with the scheme for sugar for the Africa, Caribbean and Pacific (ACP) countries). Polish agrifood exports to the EC will either directly or indirectly lead to increased EC agrifood exports. The opportunity cost of allowing Poland access to the EC market for surplus products or for agricultural products competing with surplus products (this means almost all agrifood products which Poland is likely to produce) is the EC export restitution for these products plus the transport and other transaction costs of bringing the products from Poland to the EC and from the EC to the world market.

The ratio between the costs to the EC and the increase in the Polish national income from such arrangements is extremely unfavorable, especially if Poland's agrifood production is subsidized.

Assuming that Poland has a comparative advantage in labor-intensive fruit and vegetable production (which still has to be established), privileged access to the EC market for these products in return for privileged access to the Polish market for EC agricultural products could, from an economic point of view, be worthwhile to consider. The political feasibility of such an arrangement is, however, uncertain.

The prospect for expansion of trade with the Soviet Union and other Eastern European countries at prices that are more favorable than world market prices seems excluded in the short term, but might prove a possibility in the medium term. Creation of export markets is in general easier for products with a strong position in home markets. The level of income in the Soviet Union and in other Eastern European countries is similar to the level of income in Poland; expansion of exports to these countries might for this reason be easier than expansion of exports to Western countries, where the quality requirements (due to higher levels of income) will be higher than in Poland. Existing capacity in the food-processing industry will also be more easily exploited in expanding exports in this direction.

In the short term for key products. Butter: The high level of butter exports will continue until the downturn in butter production in the autumn if the economic conditions for storage are not improved dramatically. The currently depressed butter price (far below the f.o.b. parity price that would prevail with a well-functioning trade sector) is likely to increase significantly as the production of butter falls for seasonal reasons — even to the extent that butter exports become profitable. Poland is therefore likely to lose the difference between the parity c.i.f. price and the parity f.o.b. price; this amounts then to a loss of at least 500 ECU per ton of butter due to lack of seasonal storage (as a consequence of the high real interest rate and the uncertainty about future economic conditions).

Cereals: Without government intervention something similar might happen in the case of cereals. Left to free market forces, a significant share of the traded part of the cereals harvest (around 6 metric tons), plus the 2 metric tons surplus which is in storage due to food aid will be exported during the coming months; these cereals will eventually have to be reimported later during the marketing year, resulting in a loss to Poland corresponding to the difference between the parity c.i.f. price and the parity f.o.b. price, amounting to at least 40 ECU per ton.

Meat: Finally, without better prospects for milk, meat production will increase in the autumn as market-oriented farmers (rather than the small inefficient dairy producers who produce mainly for household consumption) will reduce their dairy herds. This will, in the short term, put further pressure on exports and reduce domestic prices well below the f.o.b. prices that would prevail under normal conditions. This will eventually lead to an increased need for meat imports and to increases in domestic prices to the c.i.f. level and will compromise the improvement in milk quality that is necessary to make the dairy industry viable.

RECOMMENDATIONS RELATED TO TRADE

Even at the high level of EC prices (compared with world market prices) many farms in Western Europe — which by Polish standards are large — are under heavy pressure. In Denmark, for example, the number of farms that have to close down because they are too small to provide an adequate return to primary factors is more than 3% per year. The value added for a large part of EC farms would be negative if production had to be sold at export parity prices. This does not mean that the EC agricultural policy is not a rational policy, but that its rationale is dependent on 1) the political desire, for reasons other than economic efficiency, to maintain the rural population at a higher level than it would be if determined by market forces; 2) the fact that, given the size of the agricultural population (around 5% of the total) and the level of income in society, the costs of such a policy are affordable.[8]

It seems that Poland does not have better natural conditions for agricultural production than the rest of Europe, but worse. It is therefore not surprising that our empirical analysis indicates that Polish agriculture will only be competitive at world market export prices with a much smaller farming sector than exists at present. The difference between the EC and Poland, however, is that support to the agricultural sector at a similar level as the EC is a luxury which — given the relative size of its agricultural sector and its general level of income — appears unaffordable for Poland in the foreseeable future.

The odds are that Poland will not, in the medium term, be able to generate an important export surplus of agrifood products even with sizeable investment in upstream and downstream sectors. The investment funds are likely to obtain a greater return in other sectors. The basic idea of this annex is hence that the Polish government should use border measures, which are in general administratively and financially less costly than domestic measures, to achieve its socioeconomic objective in relation to both the urban and rural sectors of the economy. Furthermore, this should be done without any preconceived commitment concerning the future role of agriculture in Poland's trade strategy in general. This leads us to quite different trade policy recommendations for the short and the medium terms due to the assumed difference in general economic conditions during those timeframes.

The social and political costs of providing Polish agriculture with an export-oriented role should be carefully considered. The political costs in terms of strained relations with the EC and in terms of creating a political barrier to Poland's eventual political integration with the rest of Western Europe should be one concern for the Polish government. Of greater importance are the internal political and social costs in the short and medium term. An effective export strategy would have to set domestic agrifood prices at the f.o.b. parity prices, which, even with well-functioning downstream sectors, may be more than 30% below the c.i.f. parity prices. It is beyond any doubt that a sizeable part of Polish agriculture will not be viable at f.o.b. parity prices and would therefore need government assistance. To provide such support either in terms of export subsidies or through domestic subsidies is hardly in line with the government's overall strategy for reforming the Polish economy.

We therefore suggest that the Polish government should aim deliberately for an agricultural production somewhat below self-sufficiency, if necessary by providing financial assistance to reduce excess agricultural capacity in a socially acceptable way. This would, without further government intervention or financial outlays, generate prices at the c.i.f. parity level. In isolation, this policy would naturally be seen to be against the interests of consumers. However, even c.i.f. parity prices will represent consumer prices well below those paid by consumers in other Western European countries and consumers will, in their role as taxpayers, avoid the costs in terms of high subsidies to the agricultural sector which would be the consequence of an export-oriented agricultural strategy.

The export potential for the specialized agricultural products for which Poland can exploit its advantage in terms of low labor costs should, however, be identified and exploited. Such production could include fresh fruit and vegetables, and live animals (pigs and cattle) for fattening. Export promotion, assistance to improve quality standards and marketing for such products (see the Annex on the agrifood industry) should be subsidized.

The temptation to monopolize export activities in order to avoid Polish-Polish export competition (as has been the case in New Zealand, Denmark and other countries with a big agricultural export sector) should be resisted. The costs which would result from this, in terms of monopolistic tendencies at the domestic market, are not justified for a country like Poland where the share of the export market in total production is small. Minimum export prices, however, may be considered as a short-term measure to prevent Polish export at unnecessarily low prices.

For sectors which are not economically viable, assistance for rapid restructuring and creation of alternative employment possibilities outside as well as inside the agricultural sector should be considered. Without such assistance the adaptation process will be long and socially painful and efficient producers will not have sufficient incentive to improve the quality of their production. The dairy sector seems to be such a sector. For the dairy sector to develop to the point where it can supply the domestic market with quality dairy products, it is important that sales of low-quality milk to the dairies be eliminated (see Annex 21). It is necessary to induce these producers to engage in other labor-intensive activities that are socially more profitable, such as breeding cattle and pigs. For such a transition to be socially acceptable, it seems important that small dairy producers switch to other activities voluntarily without too big a loss of income. In this context a buying up scheme of what these producers consider well-established rights to deliver low-quality milk to dairies should be considered, in parallel with the introduction of stricter quality requirements for delivery of milk to dairies. Such a scheme could involve the annual payment of a premium to these producers in return for a commitment not to deliver milk below a certain quality to the dairies. The production of milk for farmhouse consumption should not be affected. The trade aspect of such a strategy could involve an agreement with the EC to deliver dairy products, in particular skim milk powder to be mixed with high-quality Polish-produced milk, at agreed prices for as long as it will take for Poland to develop a modern dairy industry to supply its domestic market.

RECOMMENDATIONS CONCERNING PRICE STABILIZATION

For the medium term. Poland will, in the medium term, need a system to protect its agricultural sector against big fluctuations in the domestic prices for cereals, cereal-based meat production (pigs and poultry) and dairy products. The reasons are the following:

• Without such a system, year-to-year price fluctuations of 50% to 100% are likely, partly due to price fluctuation at the world market (the prices for cereals doubled between 1986 and 1988 due to changes in U.S. policies and supply conditions) and partly due to a shift from c.i.f. to f.o.b. prices resulting from Poland's switching from an export to an import position. Since Poland is likely to be close to self-sufficiency for cereals and cereal-based meat production, this is likely to happen for these products.

• Poland will, for the foreseeable future, have a lot of small farms that are not very well integrated into the financial system. Such farmers need stable prices to have sufficient incentive to specialize. Based on the EC experience, this is a prerequisite for high productivity growth in modern agriculture. Moreover, for social reasons, dramatic price fluctuations are unlikely to be politically acceptable.

Border trade measures should play an important role in such a stabilization system because such measures are easy to put in place and relatively cheap to administer. The domestic prices for the products mentioned above should be stabilized, within a price band around the trend for the corresponding world market price, by a system of variable export taxes/subsidies (to be used when Poland is in an export position) and a corresponding system of import taxes/subsidies (to be used when Poland is in an import position). Such a system would, in the long run, be close to self-financing depending on where between the f.o.b. and c.i.f. prices the reference world market price will be fixed. The financial implications would, even within a single year, be very modest since Poland would be self-sufficient for most of these products. The government should avoid being involved in intervention buying except as a matter of last resort, but should if necessary provide financial support for private storage to smooth out the seasonal price fluctuations. The institutional framework for such a system should contain strong guarantees for pegging the reference price to the world market price to prevent the stabilization system from degenerating into a price support system. Producer organizations should therefore not be involved in running the system. The system would be particularly cheap to administer in the case of a price band of +/- 15% around the world market reference price. Only if the world market price were to move out of this range would the application of border measures be needed and then only in relation to rather small trade flows (due to Poland's position of near self-sufficiency in most of these products).

For the short term. Poland faces a serious agricultural crisis for reasons which are specific to the short term and which can be related to the fact that no sector-specific strategic thinking went into the preparation of the present government's stabilization program and that the government did not create organizations responsive to market signals prior to freeing agricultural trade. The two short-term-specific factors fueling the crisis are the food aid and the (perceived) extremely high interest rate associated with extreme uncertainty with respect to the government's future agricultural policy.

Cereal prices, particularly the wheat price, are of crucial importance, not just for reasons of resource allocation within the agricultural sector (the cereals price is an anchor for nearly all agricultural prices due to its role as substitute crop and major input in animal production), but also for the balance between rural and urban interests that is of crucial importance for the political survival of the government. Because of the absence of a well-functioning tax and social security system, the wheat price is one of the few instruments through which the government can control this balance in the short term.

The government presently lacks the many instruments for income redistribution that are at the disposal of governments in developed market economies, but it is able to control the border. The government should therefore allow itself all types of border measures, including quantitative restrictions, to achieve its objectives in terms of setting the price of cereals (in particular the price of wheat) where, for political reasons, it would like it to be. Qualitative restrictions are not to be recommended as long term measures, but they have the advantage in the short term of being administratively more flexible than border taxes. (Auctions of export and import quotas should be considered if the difference between the border price and the domestic price becomes too large.) The government should also clearly announce to the economic agents where it wants the cereals prices to be over the next 12 months to prevent further uncertainty in this respect. However, for the government to be able to use border measures effectively, the incentive for private agents to hold stocks has to be created. With the extreme uncertainty about future agricultural prices and with a perceived real interest for borrowed capital between 20% and 50% p.a. nobody wants to keep stocks of agricultural products. This is particularly important because the economic agents on the Polish scene are likely to be very risk averse. Few Poles or Polish institutions have the capital to justify the risk of a substantial loss even if the expected rate of return is excellent. A possible package for ameliorating the situation could be the following. The government should:

• offer private agents credit at 4% real interest p.a. corresponding to, say, 90% of the assessed value of cereals kept in storage. The interest on the loan, however, should not be indexed according to the general consumer price index, but according to the evolution in the f.o.b. border price for the type of cereals being stored (as estimated by some independent agency);
• announce that it guarantees farmers the possibility of delivering grain to government-appointed delivery points by the end of the market season at, say, 10% below the f.o.b. price prevailing at that time;
• promote the export of 2 metric tons of grains

when the new harvest arrives in order to increase the cereals price to the f.o.b. parity price level;
• if the measures indicated above are not sufficient, restrict grain exports in order to leave sufficient grain in storage to satisfy Poland's needs for the coming year.

A similar scheme could be envisaged for butter (as suggested in Annex 21). Further export of butter should be banned this year. If this were to lead to a further reduction in the price of butter, government intervention buying should take place as a matter of last resort.

It is likely, however, that so much butter has already been exported that the butter price will increase dramatically in a few months. In this case, the government should consider intervening directly by importing quality margarine and putting this on the domestic market at subsidized prices until butter production increases again in the spring. This would assist the substitution of butter for margarine in domestic consumption, which should take place when the domestic capacity for producing quality margarine is in place.

Endnotes

This annex was prepared by K. J. Munk (EC), main author, and by U. Koester (University of Kiel), A. Kwiecinski (Warsaw University), and W. Rembisz (Central School of Planning and Statistics), assisted by M. Malawski (Economic Council), and B. Nosecha, J. Burakiewicz, G. Dybowski and M. Kisiel (Institute for Agriculture and Food Economics). The information provided by officials in the Ministry of Foreign Economic Relations and the Ministry of Finance has been essential for the preparation of the report. Help provided by W. Mack is gratefully acknowledged.

1. Much of the information in this section has been based on H. Bochniarz, M. Kudelska, A. Solyga and M. Pajor, "Polski Handel Zagraniczny Artylami Rolno-spozywczymi w Roku 1989 na tle Sytuacji Swiatowej", Foreign Trade Research Institute, March 1990.

2.. The technical coefficient is defined as the ratio between the payments to domestic suppliers in order to obtain one unit of foreign currency, and the official exchange rate.

3. Under free market conditions there will in fact not be one domestic price but many regional prices, which in turn are determined by regional supply and demand conditions and internal transport costs.

4. See E. Schaffer "State-owned Enterprises in Poland: Taxation, Subsidization, and Competition Policies," in *European Economy*, No. 43, March 1990, Commission of the European Communities, Directorate-General for Economic and Financial Affairs.

5. These calculations have been made by J. Rowinski, Institute of Agricultural and Food Economy.

6. For an explanation of the PSE methodology, see C. Cahill and W. Legg, "Estimation of Agricultural Assistance using Producer and Consumer Subsidy Equivalence: Theory and Practice," *OECD Economic Studies*, No. 13/ Winter 1989-1990.

7. See "Submission of PSE Data and Estimates. Poland". Negotiating group on Agriculture: Technical Group on Aggregate Measurement of Support and Related Matters, MTN.GNG/NG5/TG/PSE/POL/1, 22.3. 1990. See also N. J. Cochrane, "The Longer Term Effects of Major Policy Reform on Poland's Agricultural Production and Trade," in Report on Agriculture in the East and West: The Polish Case, Copenhagen, Danish Ministry of Agriculture, May 1990.

8. See K.J. Munk (1989), "Price Support to the EC Agricultural Sector: An Optimal Policy?" *Oxford Review of Economic Policy*, Vol. 5, No. 2.

Appendix Supplementary Tables

Table A.1 Share of exports in production for selected agrifood products

Table A.2.1 Volume of exports of major agrifood products in 1987-1990
Table A.2.2 Volume of exports of major agrifood products in 1988-1990 (index)

Table A.3.1 Volume of imports of major agrifood products in 1987-1990
Table A.3.2 Volume of imports of major agrifood products in 1988-1990

Table A.4 Commodity pattern of Polish agrifood exports

Table A.5 Country desination of agrifood exports

Table A.6 Exports of major agrifood products to area I and area II in 1989 and 1990

Table A.7 Imports of major agrifood products from area II in 1989 and 1990

Table A.8 Revenue and expenses of budget related to import/export activities in the domain of agricultural and food products

Table A.9 Financial coefficient in agrifood trade (domestic to border price)

Table A.10 Prices received by farmers, food processing enterprises and middlemen as percent of trade price paid and received on western countries markets

Table A.11 Export subsidies for selected commodities:
Table A.11.1:Pork carcass
Table A.11.2:Live cattle
Table A.11.3:Live lambs

Table A.1 Share of exports in production for selected agrifood products

Specification	1975	1984	1988
Slaughter cattle	8.6	9.3	13.1
Slaughter lambs	16.0	26.1	38.9
Slaughter horses	39.9	62.4	63.3
Horse meat	73.7	61.1	70.0
Poultry	14.3	8.3	6.8
Bacon	79.0	51.6	31.8
Hams and shoulders, canned	74.3	81.4	84.8
Meat, canned	19.8	18.4	16.9
Sugar	3.9	16.4	15.3
Frozen fruits	71.1	73.5	72.4
Frozen vegetables	37.4	60.2	71.6
Fish, fresh and frozen	8.7	17.2	18.0

Source: GUS.

Table A.2.1 Volume of exports of major agrifood products in 1987 - 1990

('000 tons)

	1987	1988	1989	1989 1990 (Jan - May)	
Sugar	252	79.3	190.4	47.8	5.5
Molasses	316	284.5	324.2	106.5	204.9
Rapeseed	421	382.5	93.7	120.5	326.9
Rapeseed oil	49.2	21.1	17.3	11.6	35.6
Rye	0.8	17.6	11.8	7.7	0.1
Potatoes	425.8	602.4	750.9	262.8	52.4
Fruit and vegetable products	257.3	264.6	268.8	117.1	85
Fruits and vegetables, fresh	131.8	189.1	137	79.3	86.1
Fruits and vegetables, frozen	360.5	315.6	135.9	n.a.	n.a.
Spirits [a]	560	577	659	228.3	239
Casein	21.5	20.6	15.9	4.7	6.1
Cheeses	0	1.4	3	n.a.	n.a.
Milk powder	44	46	59.5	17.0	13.8
Fish and fish products	144.2	146.1	138.3	52.3	50.6
Meat	47.6	51.3	78.9	26	30.4
Meat, horse	10.5	8.7	7.5	3.2	2.0
Meat, rabbit	4	3.1	2.8	0.9	0.5
Bacon	1.5	1.3	1.4	0.4	0.4
Ham and shoulders, canned	36.7	36.5	42.8	17.2	8.6
Meats and sausages, canned	15	15.3	1.4	7.4	7.0
Cattle for slaughter and breeding	62	86.6	81.5	0.0	0.0
Sheep for slaughter and breeding	10.3	12.7	12.1	6.7	6.5
Horses for slaughter and breeding	26.8	15.7	12.7	0.0	0.0

a. in '000. hectolitres

Source: GUS and Foreign Trade Research Institute.

Table A.2.2 Volume of exports of major agrifood products in 1988 - 1990 (index)

('000 tons)

	1988	1989	1990 (Jan - May)
Sugar	31.5	240.1	11.5
Molasses	90.0	114.0	192.4
Rapeseed	90.9	24.5	271.2
Rapeseed oil	42.9	82.0	307.5
Rye	2,220.0	67.0	1.3
Potatoes	141.5	124.7	19.9
Fruit and vegetable products	102.8	101.6	72.6
Fruits and vegetables, frozen	143.5	72.4	108.6
Fruits and vegetables, fresh	87.5	43.1	x
Spirits [a]	103.0	114.2	104.7
Casein	95.8	77.2	131.3
Cheeses	x	214.3	x
Milk powder	104.5	129.3	81.2
Fish and fish products	101.3	94.7	96.8
Meat	107.8	153.8	116.0
Meat, horse	82.9	86.2	61.6
Meat, rabbit	77.5	90.3	60.9
Bacon	86.7	107.7	96.4
Ham and shoulders, canned	99.5	117.3	50.0
Meats and sausages, canned	102.0	371.9	94.3
Cattle for slaughter and breeding	139.7	94.1	137.5
Sheep for slaughter and breeding	123.3	95.3	96.3
Horses for slaughter and breeding	58.6	80.9	156.3

a. in '000 hectolitres

Source: GUS and Foreign Trade Research Institute.

Table A.3.1 Volume of imports of major agrifood products in 1987 - 1990

('000 tons)

	1987	1988	1989	1989 (Jan - May)	1990
Total grains of which:	3,029.0	3,040.0	2,846.7	1,917.6	46.1
for consumption	2,171.0	2,249.0	n.a.	n.a.	n.a.
for feeds	759.0	0.0	n.a.	n.a.	n.a.
Oil cake and meal	1,342.0	1,334.0	1,279.0	512.9	147.2
Edible vegetable fats	107.7	123.3	119.1	46.4	13.7
Sugar	1,61.0	59.0	129.2	n.a.	n.a.
Rice	75.1	64.0	58.5	0.0	6.5
Butter	33.0	34.6	11.4	n.a.	0.0
Milk powder and milk mixes	0.2	0.0	0.0	n.a.	n.a.
Cheeses	4.4	0.0	0.0	n.a.	n.a.
Fish and fish products	189.0	201.0	635.0	72.8	29.0
Fish meal	35.0	41.6	261.8	45.3	2.9
Tea	32.2	33.7	38.7	15.6	7.9
Coffee	28.4	33.4	42.8	9.7	6.8
Cocoa	28.0	31.8	28.0	12.3	4.5
Tropical fruits	121.5	177.0	135.2	73.8	26.6
Meat	12.8	49.6	107.1	36.6	0.6

Source: GUS and Foreign Trade Research Institute.

Table A.3.2 Volume of imports of major agrifood products in 1987 - 1990 (index)

('000 tons)

	1988	1989	1990 (Jan - May)
Total grains of which:	100.4	93.6	2.4
for consumption	103.6	x	x
for feeds	0.0	x	x
Oil cake and meal	99.4	95.9	28.7
Edible vegetable fats	114.5	96.6	29.5
Sugar	36.6	219.0	x
Rice	85.2	91.4	x
Butter	104.8	32.9	x
Milk powder and milk mixes	x	x	x
Cheeses	0.0	x	x
Fish and fish products	106.3	315.9	39.8
Fish meal	118.9	629.3	6.4
Tea	104.7	114.8	50.7
Coffee	117.6	128.1	70.1
Cocoa	113.6	88.1	36.6
Tropical fruits	145.7	76.4	36.0
Meat	387.5	215.9	1.7

Source: GUS and Foreign Trade Research Institute.

Table A.4 Commodity pattern of Polish agrifood exports

(total agrifood exports = 100%)

	1984	1987	1990 (Jan - Mar)
Slaughter cattle	30.9	28.1	35.7
Slaughter lambs	4.6	5.4	11.7
Slaughter horses	5.0	3.5	2.9
Rapeseed	-	3.9	9.7
Rye	4.8	-	-
Food-processing industry goods	69.1	71.9	64.3
Pork (carcass)	0.9	0.5	1.0
Beef (carcass)	0.9	4.0	4.0
Horse meat	1.6	1.1	0.6
Poultry	2.7	3.0	1.3
Bacon	0.3	0.2	0.1
Hams and shoulders, canned	7.6	8.0	7.6
Meat, canned	1.7	1.5	2.4
Feather and down	1.2	1.2	-
Skim milk powder	2.9	2.3	2.1
Casein	1.7	3.0	2.2
Sugar	4.8	3.1	-
Frozen fruits	4.6	4.2	4.0
Frozen vegetables	1.2	1.4	0.9
Rapeseed oil	2.3	1.0	1.2
Fish, fresh and frozen	8.7	12.1	11.0
Juices and pulps of fruits and vegetables	0.9	0.5	1.0

Source: GUS and Institute of Agriculture and Food Economics.

Table A.5 Country destination of agrifood exports

(total = 100)

	1975	1984	1988
Western countries	67.4	77.2	81.9
Spain	0.4	0.4	2.4
Switzerland	4.5	3.0	4.0
Sweden	1.9	2.4	2.0
Italy	4.3	12.1	11.2
Japan	0.4	1.6	3.6
Lebanon	1.2	2.4	0.7
Austria	1.9	1.9	2.4
USA	12.1	12.8	10.5
EC countries together	31.1	34.6	50.1
Belgium - Luxemburg	0.6	0.3	1.4
UK	7.5	7.2	4.3
Germany, Federal Republic of	11.5	13.7	18.2
Netherlands	1.7	2.1	4.8
France	5.1	6.0	5.8
CMEA countries	32.6	22.8	18.1

Source: GUS and Institute of Agriculture and Food Economics.

Table A.6   Exports of major agrifood products to area I and area II in 1989 and 1990

	1989			1990		
	Total (,1000t)	Area I (%)	Area II (%)	Total (1,000t)	Area I (%)	Area II (%)
Sugar	47.8	0.0	100.0	5.5	0.0	100.0
Molasses	106.5	0.0	100.0	204.9	0.0	100.0
Rapeseed	120.5	0.0	100.0	326.9	0.0	100.0
Rapeseed oil	11.6	0.0	100.0	35.6	0.0	100.0
Rye	7.7	0.0	100.0	0.1	0.0	100.0
Potatoes	262.8	99.4	0.6	52.4	87.2	12.8
Fruit and vegetable products	117.1	31.3	68.7	85	35.6	64.4
Frozen fruits and vegetables	79.3	41.9	58.1	86.1	44.8	55.2
Fresh fruits and vegetables	n.a.	n.a.	n.a.	n.a.	n.a.	n.a.
Spirits[a]	228.3	1.4	98.6	239	11.3	88.7
Casein	4.7	0.0	100.0	6.2	0.0	100.0
Cheeses	n.a.	n.a.	n.a.	n.a.	n.a.	n.a.
Milk powder	17.0	0.0	100.0	13.8	0.0	100.0
Fish and fish products	52.3	1.7	98.3	50.6	0.8	99.2
Meat	26.2	0.4	99.6	30.4	0.1	99.9
Horse meat	3.2	0.0	100.0	2.0	0.0	100.0
Rabbit meat	1.0	0.0	100.0	0.5	0.0	100.0
Bacon	0.4	0.0	100.0	0.4	0.0	100.0
Ham and shoulders, canned	17.2	0.0	100.0	8.6	0.0	100.0
Meats and sausages, canned	7.3	0.3	99.7	7.0	0.0	100.0
Cattle for breeding	0.0	0.0	100.0	0.0	0.4	99.6
Sheep for breeding	6.7	0.0	100.0	6.5	0.0	100.0
Horses for breeding	0.0	0.0	100.0	0.0	0.0	100.0

a. in '000 hectolitres.

Table A.7   Imports of major agrifood products from area I and area II in 1989 and 1990

	1989			Jan - May 1990		
	Total (,1000t)	Area I (%)	Area II (%)	Total (1,000t)	Area I (%)	Area II (%)
Total grains of which:	1917.6	0.0	100.0	46.1	0.2	99.8
for consumption	n.a.	n.a.	n.a.	n.a.	n.a.	n.a.
for feeds	n.a.	n.a.	n.a.	n.a.	n.a.	n.a.
Oil cake and meal	512.9	0.0	100.0	147.2	0.0	100.0
Edible vegetable fats	46.4	0.0	100.0	13.7	0.0	100.0
Sugar	n.a.	n.a.	n.a.	n.a.	n.a.	n.a.
Rice n.a.	n.a.	n.a.	6.5	0.0	100.0	
Butter	n.a.	n.a.	n.a.	0	x	x
Milk powder and milk mixes	n.a.	n.a.	n.a.	n.a.	n.a.	n.a.
Cheeses	n.a.	n.a.	n.a.	n.a.	n.a.	n.a.
Fish and fish products	72.8	55.2	44.8	29	37.6	62.4
Fish meal	45.3	0.0	100.0	2.9	0.0	100.0
Tea 15.6	0.0	100.0	7.9	0.0	100.0	
Coffee	9.7	2.7	97.3	6.8	4.4	95.6
Cocoa	12.3	0.0	100.0	4.5	0.0	100.0
Tropical fruits	73.8	23.1	76.9	26.6	60.5	39.5
Meat	36.6	8.8	91.2	0.6	4.6	95.4

Source: GUS and Foreign Trade Research Institute.

Table A.8 Revenues and expenses of budget related to import/export activities in the domain of agricultural and food products

(Billion Zl)

	1988	1989	Index %
Area I			
a. revenue (to budget)	0.02	0.1	446%
tax on exports	11.6	32.1	177.3
tax on imports	-	22.8	-
duty	42.3	88.9	110%
turnover tax on imports			
TOTAL REVENUE	53.9	143.9	166.9
b. expenses	61.6	154.1	149.9
subsidies to exports	6.09	0.1	144.1
subsidies to imports			
TOTAL EXPENSES	61.7	154.2	149.8
* saldo in area I	-7.8	-10.3	-
Area II			
a. revenue (to budget)	2.0	0.3	-84.5%
tax on exports	141.7	258.0	182.8
tax on imports	21.6	75.0	247.5
duty	91.5	174.8	91.1%
turnover tax on imports			
TOTAL REVENUE	256.8	509.1	98.3
b. expenses	186.9	593.7	217.7
subsidies to exports	19.1	91.6	379.9
subsidies to imports			
TOTAL EXPENSES	205.0	685.3	232.7
* saldo in area II	+50.8	-176.2	-
Total saldo of budget revenue in import/export of agri-food industry	+42.95	-186.6	

Source: Ministry of Foreign Economic Relations.

Table A.9 Financial coefficient in agrifood trade (domestic to border price)

	1988		1989	
	I zone	II zone	I zone	II zone
Milk powder		1.01		1.14
Cheese	1.00	1.20	1.01	1.17
Butter	0.91	0.89	1.00	1.07
Casein		1.11		1.16
Meat		1.80		1.30
Pork	2.34		1.57	
Beef	1.75		1.26	
Lamb		1.12		-
Bacon		1.92		1.96
Ham and shoulder		1.58		1.46
Meat, canned		1.76		1.63
Live beef (cattle)		1.50		1.20
Horse meat		1.48		1.31
Sugar		1.16		0.91
Molasses		1.44		1.25
Rapeseed		1.51		1.04
Strawberry pulp		1.78		1.66

Source: Foreign Trade Research Institute.

Table A.10 Prices received by farmers, food processing enterprises and middlemen as percent of trade price paid and received on western countries markets

	1987	1989	1990 (Jan - Mar)
1. Wheat			
State procurement price	157.4	170.2	-
Free market price			59.0
Selling price of imported wheats on domestic market	151.0	69.2	107.6
import price (c.i.f. Polish imports)	100.0	100.0	100.0
2. Barley			
State procurement price	188.0	172.0	
Free market price			
Selling price of imported barley on domestic market	179.0	75.0	
Import price (c.i.f. Polish imports)	100.0	100.0	100.0
3. Oilseed cakes and meals			
Selling price of imported cakes and meals on domestic market	114.0	129.0	80.0
Import price (c.i.f. Polish imports)	100.0	100.0	100.0
4. Rapeseed			
State procurement price for oilseed	136.0	52.0	
Middleman sales price for export	195.0	94.5	87.0
Export price (f.o.b.)	100.0	100.0	100.0
5. Strawberries - frozen			
Free market price	56.0	44.0	
Selling price of processing industry for export (cooling houses)	102.0	115.0	90.0
Export price (f.o.b.)	100.0	100.0	100.0
6. Pork - carcass weight			
State procurement price	65.5	81.0	-
Free market price			71.0
Selling price of meat-processing industry for export	108.0	119.4	91.0
Export price (pl)	100.0	100.0	100.0
7. Young live cattle for slaughter			
State procurement price	115.0	120.0	-
Free market price			59.0
Middleman sales price for export	121.0	124.0	78.0
Export price (f.o.b.)	100.0	100.0	100.0
8. Live sheep			
State procurement price	96.0	70.0	-
Free market price			76.0
Middleman sales price for export	119.0	107.8	87.0
Export price (f.o.b.)	100.0	100.0	100.0

Source: Institute of Agricultural and Food Economics.

Table A.11 Export subsidies for selected commodities

Table A.11.1 Pork carcass (per 100 kg in zlotys)

Specification	1987 Value	1987 Structure %	1989 Value	1989 Structure %	I-III 1990 Value	I-III 1990 Structure %
Domestic price	53,980	100.0%	307,790	100.0%	1,198,161	100.0%
of which						
Farm-gate price	32,844	60.8%	208,334	67.7%	931,278	77.7%
Marketing margin[a]	21,136	39.2%	99,456	32.3%	266,883	22.3%
Border price[b]	50,068	92.8%	257,669	83.7%	1,325,404	109.8%
Net export subsidy		+7.2%		+16.3%		-9.8%

a. The difference between domestic price paid by the foreign trade agency to the final producer of exported goods and farm-gate price.
b. Trade price revised by the exchange rate.
Source: Calculation provided by Institute of Agricultural and Food Economics.

Table A.11.2 Live cattle[a] (per 100 kg live weight in zlotys)

Specification	1987 Value	1987 Structure %	1989 Value	1989 Structure %	I-III 1990 Value	I-III 1990 Structure %
Domestic price	24,366	100.0%	137,342	100.0%	618,840	100.0%
of which						
Farm-gate price	22,566	92.6%	127,166	92.6%	57,300	92.6%
Marketing margin	1,800	7.4%	10,176	7.4%	45,840	7.4%
Border price	18,670	76.6%	101,900	74.2%	738,000	119.6%
Net export subsidy		+23.4%		+23.8%		-19.6%

a. Exported in the live weight of 280 kg.

Table A.11.3 Live lambs[a] (per 100 kg live weight in zlotys)

Specification	1987 Value	1987 Structure %	1989 Value	1989 Structure %	I-III 1990 Value	I-III 1990 Structure %
Domestic price	30,740	100.0%	136,730	100.0%	951,660	100.0%
of which						
Farm-gate price	27,200	88.5%	121,000	88.5%	873,060	91.7%
Marketing margin	3,540	11.5%	15,730	11.5%	78,600	8.3%
Border price	29,433	95.7%	134,538	98.4%	1,004,498	105.6%
Net export subsidy		+4.3%		+1.6%		-5.6%

a. Lambs of export quality - 40 kg of live weight.

Privatization of agro-industrial enterprises

The Law on the Privatization of State-owned Enterprises, which was recently adopted by Parliament, provides a unique opportunity to carry out with urgency a large-scale program of structural reforms, including the privatization and demonopolization of socialized enterprises and a redefinition of the role of the state in economic activity.

The agro-industrial sector should be a priority for the privatization program of the government because the current situation in agriculture threatens to destabilize the macroeconomy.

While most of the agricultural land is in private hands, socialized enterprises still control the processing and commercialization of agricultural inputs and outputs. The price of industrial goods — determined by a monopolistic industrial sector — has increased relative to the price of agricultural goods, determined under more competitive conditions. Since the stabilization program was initiated, agricultural prices have remained constant or fallen, while industrial prices have increased substantially. The real income of farmers has fallen, as the industrial products they purchase have become more expensive in terms of their products. On the output side, the monopolies purchasing agricultural outputs have increased their margins of operation (the difference between the prices they pay to farmers and those they charge to consumers), further reducing the real income of producers.[1]

Unreasonably low prices for agricultural goods could prompt a decline of production in the next agricultural season, causing an unneeded aggravation of the food supply problems.

Furthermore, agro-industrial enterprises are hard pressed for cash. Rather than reducing their costs, they are asking for financial help from the government, threatening not to buy the incoming crop if they do not receive it. Such a threat presents the government with the uncomfortable choice of either accepting a collapse of supply of essential foodstuff in the immediate future, or surrendering to the pressures to finance the pervasive inefficiencies in this sector. The outcome, in both cases, would be the perpetuation of low growth and macroeconomic instability.

The recent Law on the Privatization of State-owned Enterprises provides the opportunity to avoid this uncomfortable choice by carrying out in a speedy fashion a large-scale program of privatization and demonopolization of socialized enterprises involved in agricultural marketing and processing. This paper provides suggestions concerning the implementation of this program, taking into account the provisions of the recent privatization law.

The long-term strategy

THE MAIN OBSTACLES TO AGRO-INDUSTRIAL DEVELOPMENT

The country's development strategy should be geared to removing the main obstacles now blocking the mobility of labor and capital. These obstacles are pervasive in the Polish economy. They should be removed quickly in order to liberate the growth potential of the country and ensure the success of the stabilization program. This is a particularly urgent task in the agricultural sector, where the rigidities remaining from the old regime threaten the success of the incoming harvest as well as the continued availability of dairy products and meat. The main structural obstacles in the agro-industrial sector are monopolistic power, labor management, housing, and a safety net for unemployed and rural workers.

Monopolistic power. The monopolistic and monopsonistic power of the agro-industrial enterprises has resulted in the increase in the margins between the prices paid by consumers and the prices paid to the rural producers. This effect will remain in place, regardless of the structure of ownership, as long as the agro-industrial firms wield monopolistic and monopsonistic powers. Thus, it is necessary to eliminate these powers as a first step in the structural reforms. This should be done by breaking up each of the enterprises into several new firms, each specialized in one aspect of the formerly integrated firm. That is, transportation, storage, milling, processing and distribution of inputs and outputs should be separated from each other.

Labor management. Even if the monopolies are dismantled, the set of incentives prevailing in the labor-managed enterprises would work against the mobility of factors of production and against efficiency in general. The experience in Poland and elsewhere has shown that labor-managed enterprises have the overriding objective of protecting and increasing the income of their workers, even if this means operating at a considerable loss.

In addition to introducing serious inefficiencies, the permanence of the labor management system has created an undesirable ambiguity regarding the ownership of the means of production.[2] Furthermore, the ambiguity and lack of control by the state of the way the enterprises are managed have led to the phenomenon known as spontaneous privatization, through which small groups of individuals appropriate the assets that lawfully belong to all Polish citizens. The Law on the Privatization of State-owned

Enterprises, which reasserts the ownership by the Treasury of the assets of those enterprises before proceeding to privatize them, has now cleared this ambiguity.

Under the pressure of the current stabilization program, labor-managed enterprises have gone to extremes (like falling in arrears with the banking system and with each other, selling needed assets, and giving license without payment to their employees) in order to avoid laying off workers. With these measures, the enterprises are avoiding making the permanent adjustments they need to improve their production methods. As a result, the adjustment program is failing to force the necessary gains in efficiency. In the longer run, the continuous strife of labor-managed enterprises to maximize wages at the expense of capital would continue to result in inefficient investment and in building up inflationary pressures. The Task Force is convinced that no progress can be made in improving the allocation of resources if this problem is not solved by initiating the privatization process as soon as possible and by eliminating labor management in the enterprises remaining in the public sector.

Housing. A third obstacle to factor mobility is the lack of a housing market. Two aspects of this problem are the linkage between employment and housing and the lack of an adequate supply of rental housing units. These problems deter labor mobility in at least two ways. First, they impose too high a burden on fired employees, who lose not only their jobs but also their dwellings. This makes it harder for the government to force labor cost reductions. Second, the housing problems make it almost impossible for people to migrate to other parts of the country, where they could have better chances of getting a new job. This applies both to the unemployed and to employed people who could move voluntarily out of their current jobs.

Safety net for unemployed and rural producers. The provision of social services was done through the enterprises in the old regime. This left social services out of the reach of the unemployed. In parallel with the reforms, the government is putting in place a safety net including a system of unemployment insurance. It is essential to provide the necessary budget and the administrative means to extend the provision of social services to all workers left unemployed and to all rural producers who lose their source of income as a result of the enterprise reforms. This will make the costs of adjustment less painful for them and their families.

CREATING A MORE EFFICIENT STRUCTURE TO MANAGE PUBLIC SECTOR ENTERPRISES

The ultimate objective of the government's strategy should be to remove these obstacles to factor mobility and encourage the development of a healthy private sector, where owners would maximize their profits by taking care of serving the needs of the economy in an efficient way. Current legislation allows the creation of private companies and the privatization of the socialized sector. In addition, since not all enterprises will be privatized, it is necessary to improve the management of the enterprises that would remain in the socialized sector.[3]

The differentiation between advocates for labor and advocates for capital within the enterprise is essential for any efficiency improvement. Neither privatization nor the needed improvement in the management of the public sector enterprises are possible as long as the labor management system remains in place. It is necessary to substitute labor management with managers appointed by the state. This should be done within a new and more efficient structure to manage public enterprises.

The new structure created to manage public sector enterprises should facilitate privatization and introduce mobility of factors of production in the enterprises remaining in the public sector. This requires changing the role of public sector enterprises and creating a mechanism to manage them more efficiently.

Changing the role of public sector enterprises. The role of socialist enterprises should be changed from that of providing specific goods and services to the economy to that of maximizing the return on the capital they use. The government should look at the socialized enterprises as a way of obtaining income. Consistent with this objective, the government should not expect from socialized enterprises any help in implementing macroeconomic or other general policies nor in supplying particular goods. Conversely, it should not grant any privileges to its enterprises. However, the mechanisms to give mo-

bility to capital in the socialized sector can exist only if the government assumes the role of the owner and makes the decisions required to shift resources across enterprises.

Two levels of management. Two levels of management should be established, both of them concerned with obtaining the highest yield from the capital they manage. One kind of manager is needed at the enterprise level, responsible for making their enterprise profitable and convincing investors (both public and private) to put resources into it.[4] The other level, which could be organized as a set of holding companies, would be needed to provide mobility of resources across the socialized sector and between it and the private sector. At the enterprise level, managers would work within a capital budget constraint, which they would be able to lift only by being profitable and by convincing their holding company that future operations will be more profitable than other alternatives open to the holding company. The two levels of management should be integrated so that they operate under the command of only one set of rules.

The holding companies should care only about maximizing the present value of the government's stock of capital. Their performance should be compared with the returns on capital in the private sector. They should not be created to coincide with economic sector or geographic areas. On the contrary, they should be diversified, equally so to the extent possible (that is, they should all have shares of enterprises in all sectors and regions, and the quality of their assets should be approximately equivalent).

The holding companies' initial portfolio would contain all socialized enterprises, most likely comprising 100% ownership of each of those companies. However, the holding companies should be free to sell the shares of those enterprises and get into joint ventures with other firms, private or socialized, domestic or foreign, in their efforts to maximize the value of the capital entrusted to them. Also, very importantly, the holding companies would appoint and fire enterprise managers as needed to attain their objectives.

Given the large number of enterprises in Poland, the number of holding companies that should be created would also be large. This could create problems in controlling them.

Without supervision, there is a risk that these holding companies would engage in unhealthy practices, such as spontaneous privatization, collusion, and so forth. For this reason, it would be convenient to put all the holding companies under the control of a single parent holding company that would answer to the government for the profitability of the totality of public assets. The parent holding company would demand from the subsidiary holding companies the return on capital the government demands from it, would transfer resources across holding companies, and would appoint the managers of those.[5]

Initiating massive privatization. The substitution of labor management by government control through holding companies would most likely improve the performance of socialized enterprises (if those holding companies focus their efforts on maximizing profits). However, it should be clear that a considerable number of rigidities would remain. As it was pointed out before, market forces cannot be expected to work if one owner, the government, controls most of the enterprises in the country. As recent experiences clearly demonstrate, decentralization of management of socialized enterprises does not solve this problem. Local monopolies have proven harder to break than national ones. Furthermore, it has become increasingly clear that managers of state enterprises tend to side with workers in wage and employment conflicts, to the detriment of profitability and efficiency.

Also, the enormous relative size of the socialized sector is hardly conducive to factor mobility. The diversity of responses to shifts in market signals, the entrepreneurial spirit so essential for a fast supply response, would still be missing if the government were to keep control of the enterprises. Given its gigantic size, the government would not tend to be a price taker in the market, even if it granted no privileges to its enterprises. Also, the management of public sector enterprises becomes extremely difficult if the private sector is not predominant because there is no valid reference point to judge the performance of the public sector corporations and their managers.

Therefore, it is necessary to reverse the relative sizes of the socialized and private sectors, making of private enterprises the majority. The establishment of holding companies should be considered only as an intermediate step in the achievement of the ultimate goal — the massive privatization of socialized enterprises.

Given the urgency of the structural change to ensure the success of the stabilization program, it is clear that privatization cannot be carried out using the conventional technique of selling the enterprises. It would take too long. Furthermore, selling the enterprises would pose problems, such as the valuation of the enterprises, for which no clear solution exists. Also, the acquisitive power of the population is not enough to buy the assets at any positive price. Selling the enterprises on credit would most likely result in an undesirable concentration of economic power in those individuals now able to obtain credit in the banking system.

These problems can be avoided by transferring the ownership of the enterprises to the population as a whole, as stated in the provisions of the privatization law. The implementation of the law can be done through a variety of the holding companies, turned into mutual funds.

Implementation of the privatization program

OBJECTIVES

Privatization has two related purposes. One is to improve the management of the enterprises. The other is to disperse economic power among a large number of agents. The relationship between the two objectives is complex. The dispersion of economic power is desirable in itself because it has direct benefits in terms of income distribution and political diversity. Also, up to a certain point, the objective of dispersion reinforces the objective of improving management, because the excessive concentration of economic power leads to inefficiency in the management of enterprises.

However, excessive dispersion of the ownership of individual enterprises would also lead to inefficiency. Without a controlling shareholder, management would be free to do with the enterprise according to its wishes, and the result could be chaos. Therefore, a delicate balance between these two objectives is needed.

As the experience in Poland painfully demonstrates, efficiency requires that the enterprise be managed by someone defending the interests of capital. That is, someone who would strive to maintain and increase the capital of the enterprise through economic management of its resources and judicious investment. In the absence of the owner, there is nobody that can play this role, because anyone else could benefit more by taking away from the owner's income than by defending the owner's interests.

To achieve the objective of efficiency in an economy with dispersed ownership of capital, it is necessary to allow private entrepreneurs to emerge and bid for the control of enterprises when they see a possibility of improving their management. Thus, the process in Poland should make it relatively easy for potential entrepreneurs to put together the resources necessary to take control of enterprises to improve their management, both when the privatization takes place and later on.

SPEED OF THE PROCESS

In the circumstances of Poland, the process should be fast. In economies where the private sector is already predominant, like the United Kingdom, speed is important but not crucial. The process can be slow because the benefits of privatization, although important, are marginal relative to the functioning of the economy as a whole.

In Poland, speed is crucial. The inefficient enterprise management system is causing rigidities that hamper stabilization and economic growth. Also, the socialized enterprises are perceived as a government responsibility, and their failure to spur economic growth is blamed on the government. Even if formally denied, there is also an informal perception that the government is financially responsible for the enterprises.

Enterprises understand this very well and play on this perception to ask for subsidies and privileges from the government. This behavior is quite clear these days. Enterprises have refused to carry out the reforms needed to improve their efficiency, even if the liquidity squeeze imposed by the government under the stabilization program would have forced them to do so in a private economy. Instead of adjusting, the enterprises — especially in the food industry — are using tactics that permit them to resist unchanged the liquidity pressures, hoping that the government will eventually bail them out if all enterprises are unable to operate for lack of liquidity.

The government should get out of this weak position as soon as possible. So, there is a premium to speed in the privatization process. The faster the privatization takes place, the better.

FAIRNESS OF THE PROCESS

Another requirement of the privatization process is that it be fair. That is, if shares are transferred without payment, they should be given equally to all citizens. If the shares are sold, the buyers should pay the market price for them.

RECOMMENDATIONS

This section offers some suggestions for the implementation of the privatization program. It should be clear, however, that there are many ways in which the transition to a market economy can be accomplished. All of these ways are risky because none has ever been tried.[6] Each of these ways emphasizes the attainment of some benefits. Each of them also presents risks of its own, and, although they can be modified to minimize them, each of the basic designs would still reflect a particular choice of which benefits should be given priority and which risks are worth taking. The ideas presented in this section give priority to creating conditions for the rapid emergence of private entrepreneurs and to the fast transfer of enterprise control to private agents. The risks of the approach suggested here are discussed later in this annex.

Of course, these suggestions for the implementation of the Law on Privatization of State-owned Enterprises are provided on the understanding that they are preliminary. They are an attempt to define the direction of the changes rather than specify them in detail. These and other ideas should be discussed exhaustively and compared with alternative schemes during the design of the program.

This section develops seven recommendations. The first two refer to general rules regarding the future development of capital markets, while the rest apply to the process of privatization itself. The recommendations are that:

• All shares should be given equal voting power.
• Banks should not be allowed to buy shares.
• The program should discriminate between different kinds of enterprises. A scheme transferring shares without payment to the

population as a whole can be an adequate solution for the large- and medium-size industrial enterprises, but not for the small ones nor for those engaged in services such as transportation, storing and retailing. State farms could also be treated differently.

- The role and number of the holding companies should be revised to ensure that they behave in a way consistent with the desired flexibility in the capital markets.

- The amount of shares to be sold to the population should be relatively small, so that the amount of savings transferred from the private to the public sector is minimized.

- A mechanism ensuring that entrepreneurs would be able to rapidly acquire control of the enterprises during the transition should be designed.

- A proper sequencing of the measures should be devised, especially with regard to the sequence of privatization and enterprise and bank restructuring.

In the remainder of this annex, these recommendations are developed in more detail.

Voting rights. Giving unequal voting rights to shares goes against transparency, opens the door for pressure groups to have their powers enhanced, may cause problems for foreign investment, and serves no purpose that cannot be obtained through other, less problematic means. If privileged voting rights are granted not to special shares but to groups holding positions in the enterprise (such as workers or managers), this would again give power to individuals who would not suffer the consequences of ignoring the interests of capital in enterprise decisions.

This recommendation should not preclude firms from issuing what is commonly called preferred shares, which are subordinated debt.[7] The sale of preferred shares, however, should be something that enterprises should decide in the future, and savers should decide if they want to buy them.

Banks should not buy shares. There would be a natural incentive for the managers of the holding companies to collude with each other to exercise a monopoly in the different markets of their enterprises. It is very easy to conspire against competition when five people control all markets.

There would also be strong incentives for managers of holding companies to collude with managers of banks, and for banks to use their financial power to maintain and expand their empires. This is an extremely grave problem because, on top of all the negative effects of having a small group of people controlling the economy, the collusion would create a serious conflict of interest for banks.

In the proposed scheme, banks would control 25% of the voting power, or about that figure, and they would have a substantial amount of money at stake in the enterprises. In such a situation, the banks would tend to give preference to their own companies in their credit and pricing decisions, and would tend to be lenient regarding the creditworthiness of such enterprises. This is a clear recipe for creating a financial crisis.

The example of Germany is frequently cited as proof that the linkages between enterprises and banks do not necessarily lead to bad credit decisions. This ignores the fact that banking supervision in Germany is very strong and puts substantial emphasis on ensuring that the relations between banks and enterprises are kept at arms' length. Furthermore, the banking regulators in Germany discourage banks from increasing their current stakes in enterprises and from acquiring participation in new enterprises (the banks acquired their current positions in enterprises as a result of the debt-to-equity swaps of the 1930s).[8]

On the other hand, the number of countries where ownership linkages between banks and enterprises have created financial crises is very large, and includes Spain, Chile, Yugoslavia, Mexico, and Poland (where public sector banks have a tradition of financing public sector enterprises to comply with implicit or explicit government wishes).[9]

Investment in shares is inconvenient for banks, even if they do not lend money to the enterprises they own, because shares are more risky than the assets normally carried by banks, their value is volatile, and both the cash flow and income they produce are unpredictable.

Selling shares to the banks presents serious problems. Such sales would most probably lead to inequity in the process, misallocation of resources and financial instability. Therefore, the government should not only refrain from selling shares to the banks, but should also prohibit them from buying them in the open market. At the very least, it should limit their ability to buy shares to a very small portion of their equity capital.

Furthermore, following the international conventions recently adopted on banks' capitalization (Cooke's committee), the capital requirements should be estimated in a piecemeal fashion, according to the risks of the portfolio of banks. That is, banks with a higher level of risk should have a higher ratio of capital to assets. This means that, the higher the authorized level of banks' investment in shares, the higher should be the capital requirement.

One exception to this rule should be the permission for banks to accept shares as collateral and their right to foreclose on them if needed to collect. However, regulators should ensure that the value of the shares is heavily discounted when accepted as collateral (to cover the risk of the volatility of equity stock) and that the foreclosed shares are sold by the banks to the public in general within a prescribed period (that should not exceed one year).

Discriminating between different kinds of enterprises. Currently, big conglomerates control the provision of many services that could be provided much more efficiently by specialized, smaller enterprises. Examples of these are transportation, retailing, storing, distribution and all kind of services that give mobility to products.

Typically, the big conglomerates provide these services only for their own purposes. That is, they transport, store and distribute only their own goods. This, of course, adds to their monopolistic power in their main line of business. Additionally, since nobody else provides these services for other purposes, this structure also constrains the development of other businesses that also need those services but cannot get them, either because they do not have the capital needed or because their demand for these services would not justify investing in them.

Although for some big enterprises it makes sense to have their own distribution network, it seems that at this time the rapid decentralization of these services is essential to lubricate the functioning of the economy. These services should be available to anyone and should be provided in a competitive way.

Since most of these services can be operated profitably on a small scale, it is probable that new businesses will be created to provide them. However, for the sake of speed, the process should be accelerated by separating these services from the big conglomerates and privatizing them quickly. Furthermore, the privatization of these services can be carried out efficiently by dismantling the units providing them and then transferring the individual assets. This may be true for trucking, for example, where trucks can be transferred individually. It may also be appropriate for retailing and storing facilities.

These assets should be transferred through sales. They are small enough to make sales easy. The problem of valuation does not exist, or is minimized, because the assets can be used for multiple purposes, thus facilitating the estimation of the profits they can generate.

In the case of trucks, for example, international prices can be used. Unlike complicated production facilities, it is clear that trucks will always be needed, and their opportunity cost is clearly their price in the international markets. Also, their price is low enough to attract many people to bid for them. Thus, the best course in this case would be to auction off the stock of trucks of socialized enterprises. A similar procedure can be followed with other assets involved in the distribution and commercialization of goods.[10]

The sale of these assets should be carried out as fast as possible. It is needed to facilitate trade. It can be financed by the banking system without any inflationary effect as long as the government does not spend the proceeds of the sales. These proceeds should be used to repay the government's debt with the National Bank of Poland (NBP). NBP should sterilize this money. That is, it should not grant credit, or create money in any other way, with these resources.

The suggestions of the Task Force regarding the privatization of state farms and cooperatives are included in two separate annexes.[11] State farms can be treated either as large business complexes and then be privatized with the scheme used for large industrial enterprises, or alternatively, the government may establish a system for leasing the land. Under such a scheme, the enterprise renting the land would not manage it for the government. Rather, they would operate for their own profits and losses, paying the government rent for the use of the land.

Small-scale industrial companies could also be sold in public auctions, following the same procedure as for the service enterprises. The following paragraphs discuss suggestions to privatize the medium- and large-scale companies in agro-industry and in other branches of industry.

The role and number of holding companies

Regarding medium- and large-scale industrial enterprises, the government should find solutions to two problems: how to privatize efficiently, and how to improve the management of those that would remain in the socialized sector. Holding companies can play a useful role in solving both problems. The identity and organization of holding companies solving one problem, however, should be different from those of the ones solving the other.

The role of holding companies managing enterprises that remain in the public sector. The management of the assets that would remain in the socialized sector may be improved if those assets are organized under one or several holding companies responsible for maximizing the returns on their capital.[12] The holding companies may be useful because mobility of factors of production requires that decisions on investment and disinvestment be made by representatives of the owner different from those that manage the enterprises.

Mobility of capital comes precisely from the owners' decisions on whether to invest the profits of their enterprises in the same enterprise or take them away to invest in other activities; on whether to liquidate or restructure loss-making firms; and on whether to sell firms or not. These decisions can only be made by an agent external to the enterprise whose fate is being decided. That is, by the owner, who should decide how much to invest and in what activity and enterprise.

Thus, managing socialized enterprises would entail two levels of management, both of them concerned with obtaining the highest yield from the capital they manage. One kind of manager is needed at the enterprise level, responsible for making their enterprise profitable and for convincing investors (both public and private) to put resources into it. The other level, which could be organized as a holding company, would be needed to provide mobility of resources across the socialized sector and between it and the private sector.

Thus, at the enterprise level, managers would work within a capital budget constraint, which they would be able to lift only by being profitable and by convincing the holding company that future operations will be more profitable than the alternatives open to the holding company. The two levels of management should be integrated so that they operate under the command of only one set of rules and, possibly, of only one institution.

However, it should be clear that just organizing the public sector enterprises into holding companies would not solve the overall economic problem of managing the Polish enterprises. Privatization is necessary to create a critical mass of economic agents reacting to market signals in an efficient way. Without large-scale privatization, factor markets would not emerge. The holding companies managing the public sector enterprises would not be forced to take the prices of factors of production as given quantities, established by the market. There would not be a point of reference to judge their behavior. As a result, they would easily become yet another layer of bureaucracy, following the experience of many other countries, such as Algeria and Egypt.[13]

The long-term role of privatized holding companies. For the privatization process, the holding companies present many opportunities but also many dangers. On the positive side, they can bring about all the benefits that institutional investors provide in market economies. However, they can also become an obstacle for the development of capital markets and the emergence of entrepreneurs.

The dangers: There is the problem of sheer numbers. Since, initially at least, the power of the other shareholders (the workers or the people buying shares from them) would be too dispersed to matter in the management of the enterprises, the management of the enterprises would most likely be carried out by the holding companies.[14] This means that each holding company would manage hundreds, if not thousands, of enterprises.

The logistical problem of doing this would turn each of them into a gigantic institution that most surely would become bureaucratized. Soon after the process was started, it would become difficult to distinguish these holding companies from the former branch ministries, the only difference being that (presumably) the enterprises owned by the holding companies would be diversified by activity while those of the branch ministries were not.[15]

The power of the managers of the holding companies would go unchecked because their ownership would be quite dispersed. It would take an astronomically large amount of money to control an important share of any of the holding companies.[16] As a result, it would be extremely difficult for potential entrepreneurs in the private sector to acquire sufficient voting power in these companies to have a say in their management. Realizing this, the likely reaction of the population would be apathy, which, of course, would ensure that nobody would challenge the power of the holding companies' managers.

The concentration of economic power would most likely become an objective in itself for those managers, even if formally their objective is to maximize their profits. As was discussed before, the objectives of managers are different from those of the owners. Commanding one-fifth of the industrial power of the country is more attractive than any compensation that the dispersed owners could give the managers as a reward for their efficiency. Clearly, the power of the managers would be so large that they could appropriate such compensation and more, and on top of that they would enjoy enormous political power.

Therefore, the tendency of these managers would be to hoard shares, as a way to keep and enhance their power, rather than trade them. The same would apply to bank managers if they share with the holding companies the management of firms. This would negate the objective of creating a flexible capital market.

There would be a natural incentive for the managers of the holding companies to collude with each other to exercise monopolistic power in the different markets of their enterprises. It is very easy to conspire against competition when five people control all markets. Acquiring control of individual enterprises would be even more difficult for potential entrepreneurs than taking over the holding companies. They would not be able to control the enterprises without the acquiescence of the managers of the holding companies, who, quite rationally, could refuse to sell.

Thus, the potential benefits of having institutional investors should be balanced with the dangers of creating institutions that would conspire against the market. This can be done by specialization.

The specialization of mutual funds: There are at least two aspects to capital markets. On the one side, they should be able to mobilize resources from the population to make them available for investment. To do this, they should offer a varied menu of instruments through which savers could invest in accordance with their attitudes to risk, liquidity and other preferences.

On the other side, the capital markets should promote the judicious investment of those savings. That is, they should encourage the efficient management of enterprises. In order to do this, they should promote the continuous emergence of entrepreneurship through a transparent competition for the use of the savings, including competition for the control of enterprises. The system should be very flexible, allowing for voluntary and involuntary takeovers.

Institutional investors could play a very useful role in both sides of the market. However, to be effective in this role, they should specialize more in mobilizing and allocating financial resources than in becoming enterprise managers.

Rather than being instruments to control enterprises, the holding companies should be mechanisms to offer diversified risks to savers. That is, they should become mutual funds, mainly concerned with providing a solid return on the savings of their participants. Their comparative advantage is that they can pool the resources of many people to invest in a bundle of instruments offering different degrees of risk and expected profitability, averaging a mix that offers lower profitability but also lower risks than investments in the shares of individual enterprises. That places their products somewhat between bank deposits and equity investments in individual enterprises. Many people would be attracted to them.

To achieve their objective of maximizing the return on the savings of their participants, given a level of risk, the mutual funds should remain independent of the enterprises they invest in. That is, they should be able to invest and disinvest quickly, basing their decisions only on risk and profitability. They would not be able to do that if they were concerned with controlling issues. Their interest in management should be limited to making sure that the companies they invest in are properly managed. They should vote on management issues through their investment strategies. If they do not like the management of a company, they just do not invest in it.[17]

The behavior of institutional investors is a powerful instrument to encourage good management, even if they do not intervene directly in choosing the managers. The power is transmitted through the price of the shares, which falls if savers do not buy them. If mutual funds disinvest in one company, or refrain from investing in it, the groups controlling the enterprises get a strong signal that they have to improve their management.

Thus, specialization on the savings side would not preclude the institutional investors from playing a useful role in improving the management of enterprises. A regulation prohibiting them the use of the voting power of their shares, on the other hand, would prevent their perversion into holders of monopolistic power.

Having strong institutional investors focusing on the profitability of their portfolios would be helpful for other reasons as well. By putting most of their resources in long-term investments, they would tend to be a stabilizing force in the market. Yet another role is that they would help in giving transparency to the market. Their relatively large size would allow them to invest time and money to gather information and analyze it in order to better invest their resources.

In summary, the role of the holding companies should be changed from that of controlling units to that of institutional investors, and the rules under which they would operate should be drafted accordingly. The use of their voting powers should be prohibited. If this role is adopted for them, they should be called institutional investors or mutual funds instead of holding companies. In the remainder of this paper, they are called institutional investors.

Linking the creation of mutual funds with pension reform: One possibility that the government may wish to consider is to link the creation of the mutual funds with a reform in the pension system. The wide diversification of investments that these institutions could have from the very beginning would make them safe enough to meet long-term responsibilities. If the government is thinking of giving away the ownership of these institutions, it might as well benefit from this action by transferring to them the pension obligations that currently are covered directly from the budget.

Presently, Polish pensions are based on a pay-as-you-go system. That is, current contributions are used to pay for the current obligations. No capital has been accumulated to cover the obligations. The problem with this system is that reductions in the growth rate of the population have a detrimental effect on the viability of the system, as pension liabilities increase while contributions decline. The government has to cover the difference. The United States Social Security system, for example, is facing a serious problem as a result of the decline in birth rates that occurred after the baby boom.[18]

In Poland, the government could capitalize the pension system with part of the shares to be given away. To make the transfer without payment equitable, such a pension system should cover the entire population. To make it more efficient, the management of the system should be privatized and made competitive, even if the system is public in nature. To do this, the government would pass laws forcing all workers and their employees to contribute monthly to a pension fund, but allowing them freedom in choosing which pension fund they will contribute to.

A portion of the institutional investors created during the privatization could be established as competing pension funds, while the rest would be straightforward mutual funds. Although a detailed discussion of how to do this is beyond the scope of this paper, some suggestions are given in the section on the role of holding companies in the process of privatization.

The number and size of institutional investors: Regardless of their shape as mutual funds or pension funds, the number of institutional investors should be increased considerably. A balance should be struck between making them numerous enough to encourage competitive behavior, and making them big enough to have a diversified portfolio. Some of them could be pension funds and the rest straightforward mutual funds. The size of these institutions, however, could differ, with the pension funds being bigger than the rest in order to accommodate the pension liabilities.[19]

Reaching for the individual entrepreneur

Even if there are one hundred of them, the size of the individual institutions would be too big if they keep most of their initial holdings. Most of the shares should be owned individually, at least at the start of the process. This would give more flexibility to the process. It would make it easier for entrepreneurs to emerge and take control of individual enterprises.

Also, this would give flexibility to individuals who prefer to have their shares pooled to organize their holdings the way they want. Some of them may want to establish true holding companies; others may prefer to have mutual funds specialized in certain types of businesses; others may prefer to have only friends as fellow shareholders. If the institutional investors keep most of the shares, the individuals would have to accept the government's design, at least in the short and medium terms.

Then, the institutional investors should start their career holding a minority of the shares of the privatized enterprises. Most of the shares should be with individual investors. However, they also can be used to transfer shares of enterprises to individuals, in addition to transferring their own shares to them.

To do this, the government could give the institutional investors two packages of shares. One would be for them to keep. The other would be for transfer. In addition, the institutional investors would transfer their own shares to the population.[20]

How much should be sold and how much should be transferred without payment?

Reasons to prefer transfer without payment. The Law on the Privatization of State-owned Enterprises offers the possibility of making shares accessible to the public through sales or otherwise. We have argued above that selling the shares is not a requirement to be met by the privatization process. This section argues that selling is not only unnecessary, but could be inconvenient and even contradict the objectives of the process.

There are at least three serious problems that would hinder the sale of the enterprises. First, as was mentioned before, since capital markets do not exist, the value of the enterprises, and therefore the price of their shares, is not known.

Second, privatization could not be carried out in a fast way. A third problem is the perception that the population does not have enough purchasing power to buy the enterprises, or that, if the purchasing power exists, it is unevenly distributed.

If the titles to the ownership of the enterprises are transferred without payment to the population, the problem of lack of purchasing power disappears. Also, if privatization takes place through distributing shares to all the citizens, there is no need to value the stock of capital. The shares distributed to the population would represent the right to a fraction of the net worth of the enterprise and to the profit it generates. The price of that share would change with time, as the value of the firm changes as a result of the success or failure of its operation. The problem of creating deep financial capital markets also could be solved if enterprises are transferred to the population. If a large transfer is effected, trade in shares can be expected to be heavy from the very beginning.

But there is another problem. Most importantly, selling the shares would run against one of the primary objectives of the reforms program, that of transferring the power of deciding on the volume and allocation of investment from the state to the private sector. Transferring the assets from the public to the private sector does not require the use of savings. However, if the assets are sold, savings would have to flow from the private to the public sector.

That is, in order to pay for the shares that the state would eventually sell, the private sector would have to use savings for investment. Those savings would then be at the disposal of the government. For example, buying 60% of the capital of most enterprises would take the better part of private savings for a long time to come.[21] This means that, again, investment would be commanded by the government.

Reasons to prefer transfer through sale. However, there are some reasons why the government should keep a portion of the shares for subsequent sale. One is that management should be controlled during the transition period. It will take some time between the moment the shares are given away and the emergence of groups able to control the enterprises through acquisition of shares in the free market. During that period, the government should keep a portion of the shares sufficient to ensure the control of enterprises. The government may exercise such control by either managing the shares itself, or, as is recommended later, by subcontracting their management to local or foreign entrepreneurs.

Another valid reason to sell part of the assets is that the government needs a certain amount of resources to clear the inheritance of the previous regime. Foremost among these problems is the need to restructure and recapitalize the banking system. This should be done by the government because nobody else will want to do it. The recapitalization of banks is essentially an absorption of past losses. No private investor would use his savings to cover the losses of others.[22] The government may use the proceeds of the sale of shares in enterprises to recapitalize the banking system.[23]

To achieve these objectives while minimizing the savings syphoned off the private sector, the government should aim at retaining the minimum that would be required to ensure control in a dispersed market. This should be no more than 10-20% of the shares. To further minimize the negative effect on private savings, the government should use the proceeds of the sale of those shares for recapitalization of the banks.[24] The determination of the precise amount that would be sold should be done estimating the amounts needed to recapitalize the banks, taking into account that the government would get revenues from the sale of small industrial and service enterprises, which would be transferred 100% through sales.

Introducing flexibility in the capital markets

It is very doubtful that the government's management would be very efficient during the transition. However, government control should at least help to avoid the chaotic situation that would develop if nobody exerted control over the enterprises. Nevertheless, the length of government control during this transitional period should be minimized. The process should be designed in such a way that private entrepreneurs would take control of the enterprises as soon as possible. This can be achieved in two complementary ways. One is using management contracts during the transition. The other is designing the distribution of shares in a way that facilitates takeovers.

Management contracts. To expedite the process, the government may sign management contracts with qualified foreign or local entrepreneurs, paying for the management services with options to buy, at a prespecified date (say, after three years), part or all of the retained portion, at a price specified in advance. This would give the managers a powerful incentive to manage the enterprise efficiently, thus increasing the market value of the shares. In the process, they will benefit all the holders of that enterprise's shares.

Doing this should not preclude takeovers from potential entrepreneurs buying shares in the free market. For this reason, the amount of shares kept by the government, and the amounts promised to the contracted managers, should be only what is necessary to ensure control when the initial trading in shares is taking place. If the contracted managers want to keep control in the face of potential takeovers, they should buy more shares in the market.

Distributing bundles of shares. As was suggested before, the government may distribute two kinds of shares without payment to the population. One kind would be the shares of the mutual funds. The other would be shares of individual companies. To simplify the process, the composition of the transferred shares of individual companies could be the same as that the mutual funds would keep at the start of the process.

If, as is proposed later, this composition is determined in a way that covers a wide range of activities and geographical locations of enterprises, the expected return to these shares would be close to the average that all the privatized enterprises would generate. This would be good for people who do not have a clear idea of what they would like to do with their shares. Just by keeping the bundle of shares, they would obtain the average rate of return. They would obtain the same return in their shares of the mutual funds.

Other people, however, would like to change the composition of their share holdings. This is good, because this desire is what will lead to trading in shares, ultimately establishing prices for the assets in Poland and transferring the control of the enterprises to emerging entrepreneurs. Since they would receive shares of individual enterprises, they would be able to trade in them without depending on the will to sell of the managers of the mutual funds.

Giving the public the right to unbundle the shares of mutual funds. An alternative way of achieving the same result in what seems to be a more practical way is to distribute shares of the mutual funds only, giving to the recipients the right to withdraw a portion of their mutual funds' shares. When taking their participation out of the mutual fund, people would be able to unbundle it into shares of individual firms.[25] People doing this could pool their shares together to either create new mutual funds or holding companies seeking control of particular firms. In order to avoid one of the problems of the alternative of giving shares of individual firms to the population from the very beginning (that of issuing shares with claims on each of the individual firms), a rule could be established that unbundling can take place only when a minimum number of people (5 or 10) ask for it.

The risks of the approach

Trusting that the market would quickly yield to a healthy concentration of ownership in individual firms, but not to an excessive concentration of economic power across enterprises, poses two symmetrical risks. One is that it would take too long for individuals to take control of the enterprises, either because the recipients of the shares do not want to trade them, or because trading is so disorganized that the accumulation of voting power gets going very slowly. The danger would be that managers would go unchecked during the transition period. The other risk is that knowledgeable people could take advantage of the ignorance of most of their fellow citizens to grab control not only of individual firms but of groups of them, generating a problem similar to that faced by Chile in the late 1970s and early 1980s.

Ensuring that the private sector rapidly takes control of firms. This risk would be addressed by the already proposed management contracts, involving options to buy shares. This solution is much better than giving control to managers of holding companies appointed by the government, because it would address the problem at the level of the individual firm, giving control to entrepreneurs who would have a stake in the future of the enterprise rather than in the accumulation of economic power across enterprises.

Protecting people who do not understand the process. There is a risk that a few individuals, probably with insider information, would very quickly acquire shares from ignorant people, creating conglomerates so large and powerful that they would prevent subsequent takeovers. This risk is not particular to schemes giving away the shares. It also exists in schemes involving sales.

A vivid example of the problems that such a scheme could bring about is provided by Chile in the late 1970s and early 1980s. In those years, the government sold many industrial enterprises and banks. Since only a few people were willing and able to buy these enterprises, they ended up being owned by not more than five groups, which also owned the banks. These groups used the banks to finance their own enterprises. The result was the largest financial crisis ever suffered by Chile, and one of the worst, relative to the size of the country, in any place in the world in the recent past. Not an example to follow.[26]

Protection of people who may not understand the value of what they are getting at the start of the process is also important for equity reasons. However, it should be done in a way that does not endanger the success of the process. This can be achieved by phasing the transfers without payment, so that the benefits and losses that people can have in managing their shares become clear before the second round of transfers takes place. This would be better than transferring bits of shares of all enterprises, because the value of shares of firms still controlled by the government would be zero or close to zero.

Also, the government may rule that, in the first three years, people cannot alienate their shares of the mutual funds (only shares of individual companies). This would ensure that, people will hold at least part of their patrimony for a reasonable period. Furthermore, these people could exchange all their holdings for shares of the mutual funds, which would carry low-risk, balanced portfolios.

An unavoidable risk

There would be, however, another associated risk. The entrepreneurs taking control from the government could find that it would be more profitable for them to transfer the assets of the enterprises to themselves than to go for the capital gains offered to them through the stock options. The risk is substantial in the case of Poland because the transition period would also be a period of fast restructuring of the enterprises. In order to improve the performance of enterprises, the new managers-entrepreneurs would have to dispose of unprofitable activities, selling unnecessary assets and streamlining the capital stock of the firms. This would create ample opportunities for abuse.

It should be clear, however, that this risk is not unique to the particular scheme proposed here. In fact, this is a risk that the economy is running right now. Taking advantage of managerial power to transfer assets for the benefit of managers can be done (and has been done) by managers of labor-managed firms in what is called spontaneous privatization. The same could be done by the managers of mutual funds, by the managers appointed by them in individual firms and by independent boards of directors. The problem will not be solved until managerial power becomes proportional to the equity stakes of the individuals controlling the managers.

Even so, this risk exists in fully owned firms in market economies. Owners always need someone to go over the accounts in detail when reviewing the performance of managers. This revision is carried out by auditors. Although certainly auditors would face a tougher challenge in Poland than in other countries, they can alleviate the problem substantially. Since it would be impossible to find qualified independent auditors in Poland, the country would have to rely on prestigious Western firms to do it. The government should hire auditors also for the enterprises that would remain in the public sector. The problem of logistics seems staggering but this is something that the government has to do anyway, regardless of whether it privatizes the firms or not.[27]

There are other measures that the government could try, such as imposing the presence of a minority of independent directors in the first three years of the process. Of course, these directors could be co-opted. As stressed before, a permanent solution would be achieved only when identifiable individuals control the management of the firm through ownership. To the extent that the scheme proposed here accelerates this process and provides ownership incentives to the people that would take control from the government, it tends to reduce the problem.

Sequencing and transitional problems

The problems of the transition should not be underestimated. The deep structural reforms needed to introduce market forces would surely cause considerable turmoil during the adjustment period. Many people may ask whether it would not be better to carry out the process in a gradual way, so that the economy has time to absorb some traumatic shocks before taking more of them. This paper takes the opposite opinion. The market is an all-encompassing system, and its benefits can be experienced only when all, or most, of the economy is functioning under its rules. Partial application of market forces is likely to misdirect entrepreneurship away from productive activities into speculative ones. This works against the completion of the reform.

Thus, it is better to suffer the turmoil all at once than to go through a protracted process where the benefits of the market are not obtained. Although a full discussion of the problems of transition goes much beyond the scope of this annex, the following paragraphs discuss a few of them.[28]

Accounting. Any privatization scheme requires a change in the accounting system. There is no need to invent new ways. Accounting is quite developed in Western economies. Establishing a new, basic set of books for the enterprises should be a relatively quick task if the government establishes a basic set of accounts that should be kept for tax purposes, and sets a deadline for the change. To make it fast, the government should allow companies to look independently for foreign consultants to help them in making the transition.

It should be clear that no reconstruction of records of past operations is needed, only that new operations start being recorded in a way consistent with the operation of the market and the taxing system. For bookkeeping purposes, the initial valuation of assets could be arbitrary, to be adjusted after, say, two years, when capital markets would be more developed.

Enterprise restructuring. The government should avoid investing in the restructuring and modernization of enterprises. This task should be left to the private sector. Managing the restructuring through the socialized sector would most likely result in inefficient investment and outright waste.

As long as the banks remain in the public sector, the socialized sector will enjoy considerable political power over the banking system through pressures exerted on both the central and the local governments. Consequently, the tendency of the banking system will be to lend to the socialized sector to the detriment of the private sector.

Since experience shows that the socialized enterprises tend to invest in very inefficient ways, most likely the flow of resources toward the socialized enterprises would not only starve the private sector of resources but would also result in substantial waste. To encourage the growth of the private sector and avoid wasteful investment, the government should prohibit the investment of public and banking system funds in enterprises where the government has a majority stake. Any investment in the socialized enterprises should be financed out of the enterprises' own resources.

Moreover, the government should stay away from the coordination of the restructuring process, limiting itself to facilitating the process through the fast privatization of the socialized sector, the cleaning up and privatization of the financial system and the creation of the infrastructure needed to attain mobility of resources. Creating interministerial committees to control or coordinate the restructuring and modernization of enterprises would most likely slow down the process and discourage the private sector efforts.

The fiscal effects of privatization. From a macroeconomic point of view, the transfer of ownership is a zero sum game. The public's increase in both wealth and in the income derived from it would be counterbalanced by matching declines in the wealth and income accruing to the government. If the government does not reduce its expenditures in line with its reduced wealth and income, or reduces it in amounts smaller than the increased expenditure in the private sector, there will be an inflationary effect in the economy. However, this effect is likely to take place independently of the method used to privatize. The government will lose the income from the enterprises even if it sells them.

Endnotes

This annex was prepared by Manuel Hinds.

1. A description of how the structural problems of the Polish economy have interacted with the stabilization program to produce the currently depressed state of the agricultural sector can be found in Annex 2.

2. For a discussion of the problems of labor-managed firms and their effects on stabilization and resource allocation, see Manuel Hinds, "Issues in the Introduction of Market Forces in East European Socialist Economies," The World Bank, EMENA Discussion Paper, Report No. IDP—0057.

3. The number and type of firms remaining in the public sector should be reduced to a minimum. Even public utilities can function effectively if properly regulated, as shown in the case of the United States and now the United Kingdom.

4. Investment, however, should be financed exclusively with resources generated within the enterprises. As is recommended later in this paper, the government should not invest further in these enterprises and should prohibit the banking system's lending to them.

5. The parent holding company, and all its subsidiaries, should also be audited by a specialized agency, which should ensure that the books of the holding companies reflect reality and that their transactions are carried out at arms' length.

6. As has been argued before, the experience gained from privatizations carried out in predominantly market economies, such as the United Kingdom, can provide useful insights for Poland, but is not applicable to an economy where most activities are socialized.

7. Subordinated means that the claims of the holders of these liabilities defer to any other liabilities, except those represented by common shares, in case of a liquidation. That is, if the enterprise is liquidated, all other liabilities are paid first, then those of the preferred shares, then those of the common shares.

8. Another example frequently cited is Japan. Of course, the economic and social organization of Japan is quite unique, and can hardly be taken as an example of what would occur in a western culture such as that of Poland.

9. When planning reforms, it is better to rely on the average experience of many countries rather than on that of exceptional ones. One clear example of this is the concentration of economic power in Sweden, where a small number of conglomerates controls a sizable portion of the country's GDP. This has not resulted in lack of competition or efficiency. On the contrary, many Swedish enterprises are among the most competitive in the world. However, not many people would use the Swedish example to argue in favor of concentrating wealth in a limited number of families to achieve competitiveness.

10. It could make sense for some big enterprises to keep parts of their distribution infrastructure in place, including storage facilities. However, the process should be biased toward complete decentralization to create a clean slate for all enterprises to have access to those services and to stimulate competition. If it is profitable for some enterprises to acquire distribution networks, they should do that in the future, as part of their natural expansion. The government, however, should avoid rebuilding the current monopolistic structure.

11. See Annexes 6 and 7.

12. This is a critical point. Efficiency would not improve if maximizing profits is not the sole purpose of the managers of the public sector assets.

13. For a more detailed discussion of ways to improve the management of public sector enterprises, and the need to create a critical mass of private enterprises to help improve the management of the public ones, see Manuel Hinds, op. cit.

14. Of course, even if management were shared with banks, each bank and holding company would still manage a very large number of companies.

15. Certainly, in large market economies there are mutual funds with investments in thousands of enterprises. But these funds do not intervene in the management of these firms. They are passive investors that hold shares just to get capital rents. On the other hand, holding companies effectively controlling the management of enterprises manage much smaller numbers of companies. In the scheme proposed for Poland, the holding companies would be of the controlling type.

16. Buying 20% of the voting stock of one holding company, for example, would be equivalent to buying 2% of the total enterprise voting stock in the country.

17. Specialization is desirable not only to avoid conflicts of interest. Also, the expertise needed to manage an efficient institutional investor is different from that of running a holding company. The former requires financial expertise, while the latter demands mainly skill in the management of real resources.

18. This problem affects only the pension liabilities of the social security system. Private pension funds are based on the accumulation of resources.

19. It is desirable to keep the number of pension funds small because they should be subject to close supervision as a result of their provision of a public good. A superintendency of pension funds should be created, responsible for supervising the prudent management of the pension resources.

20. The ways in which the mutual funds could transfer the shares of individual firms is discussed in the section on giving flexibility to capital markets.

21. The price of the shares kept by the government would be lower than that for shares in the hands of other owners, because the former would not have voting power. Still, buying them would transfer substantial savings from the private to the public sector.

22. For a discussion of ways to restructure and recapitalize banks, see Manuel Hinds "The Economic Effects Of Financial Crises," PPR

Working Paper WPS-104, The World Bank, October 1988.

23. Also, as was mentioned before, the privatization of small firms and services can be carried out more practically through sales.

24. The timing of the recapitalization of banks most probably would not coincide with the collection of revenues from the sales. This, however, is a financial problem that can be solved. See section on the recapitalization of banks.

25. This idea, which can be applied to this or other schemes involving mutual funds, was proposed by Professor Jacek Rostowski, adviser to the Minister of Finance.

26. To solve the crisis, Chile dismantled the large conglomerates that controlled banks and enterprises, sent to bankruptcy a large number of companies, took over control of the largest commercial banks, recapitalized them and sold them to new owners. After that experience, they changed completely their strategy of privatization, aiming at spreading ownership. Since then, enterprises have been quite successful.

27. The auditing problem can be used as an argument to delay privatization. It is not. On the contrary, it is an argument to accelerate privatization. Leaving the control of the firms under the current structure of ownership, or under managers without a personal stake in the firm's equity, is a sure way to maximize the losses in this account. Many important transitional issues, such as the sequencing of bank reforms and enterprise restructuring and needed fiscal and monetary policies are not touched in this section. See Manuel Hinds, op. cit.

Agricultural cooperatives

Background and recent developments

The first cooperatives in Poland were established in the middle of the nineteenth century. Until the First World War, the cooperatives followed different development patterns in each of the areas under Russian, Prussian and Austrian rules. After 1918, with Poland regaining its sovereignty and unity, these regional differences gradually became less significant. Between the two world wars, many new and different types of cooperatives developed and flourished. After 1945, the cooperatives were increasingly considered a transitional form of organization, advanced in comparison with individual ownership but still short of the final socialist development stage, that of state ownership. During this period the cooperative movement became part of the country's planned economy, and cooperatives were subjected to varying degrees of state control, despite the fact that Poland had the least rigid cooperative law of all Central and Eastern European countries. Furthermore, the state also initiated the establishment of both new cooperatives and different types of cooperatives with a view to accelerating the development of the socialized economy.

Structurally all primary cooperatives were grouped by subsectors into regional unions which in turn formed central (national) unions. Membership in the secondary and tertiary cooperative organization was obligatory. Generally, cooperative unions provided the links between the planning authorities and primary cooperatives by operating wholesale and processing enterprises. In addition, unions provided auditing and training services to primary cooperatives. The various cooperative subsectors are represented by the Supreme Cooperative Council vis-à-vis the state and international organizations such as the International Cooperative Alliance.

With the limited economic reform program of 1982, a new cooperative law was passed. This law with subsequent amendments in 1983 and 1987, granted primary cooperatives the right either to create unions of their own choice or to operate independently of any union. However, these legal changes had little impact on the top-heavy organization of the cooperative structure or on the low level of member participation in primary cooperatives.

At the end of 1989, more than 15,000 primary cooperatives with some 15 million members were operating in Poland, about 8,000 cooperatives in rural and 7,000 in urban areas. Primary cooperatives were affiliated to some 400 regional unions, which in turn were members of 17 different central unions each heading a cooperative subsector. Cooperatives in all subsectors contributed about 11% to the GNP and employed almost 1.8 million people.

The subsectors of agricultural cooperatives include about

• 2,000 peasant self-aid cooperatives supplying an estimated 90% of agricultural inputs and consumer goods in rural areas and buying some 60% of agricultural products

• 320 dairy cooperatives with about 700 milk-processing plants controlling the entire dairy industry

• 1,600 cooperative banks, the only institution offering small-scale savings and credit services in rural areas

• 140 horticultural cooperatives which buy and process the bulk of fruits and vegetables produced by private farmers

• 2,000 cooperatives of agricultural circles providing machinery services mainly for private farmers

• 2,000 agricultural production cooperatives cultivating some 750,000 hectares of land (4.6% of total arable area).

The performance of cooperatives in Poland has been rather mixed. Primary cooperatives have not been sufficiently service oriented and do not respond adequately to member needs and priorities. Most regional and national cooperative unions have operated at excessive costs, often undertaking activities at the request of state authorities which were not linked with the activities of village-level cooperatives. In addition, support services, such as management advice to primary cooperative organizations, were often neglected. While judging the past performance of cooperatives, however, it should be recognized that cooperatives can rarely rise above the political and institutional environment in which they operate.

With the change of government in 1989, and the introduction of a comprehensive economic reform program at the beginning of 1990, a cooperative law amendment was passed on January 20, 1990, which are intended to fundamentally restructure and democratize the cooperative sector. The two most salient features of the legal amendments are:

• the election of new member representatives at the level of primary cooperatives

• the liquidation of all cooperative unions at the regional and national levels, including the transfer or sale of the assets of the unions to new owners.

Potential, constraints and issues

POTENTIAL

The first indicator of the potential of agricultural cooperatives is their extensive institutional network in terms of buying and selling points and transport, storage and processing facilities. For example, the peasant self-aid cooperatives operate 70,000 retail shops, 40,000 purchase centers, 30,000 warehouses, and 5,000 processing and production plants. Until the end of 1989, agricultural service cooperatives were the only institutions providing inputs and marketing services to private farmers and supplying the rural population with consumer goods. The existing institutional network offers an excellent base to those agricultural cooperatives which have the commitment and the capacity to adjust to the new economic realities.

Several cooperatives have already seriously begun to adjust to market economy and competition, and to transform themselves into private and member service organizations. This high degree of flexibility demonstrated by several rural organizations constitutes the second indicator of the potential of agricultural cooperatives. Thus, cooperatives, in comparison with state enterprises, seem to be considerably advanced in reacting to the new rules of the economic game. This is evidenced, for example, by the increasing competition which is developing among the various types of agricultural cooperatives. Horticulture and farming cooperatives have begun to compete for products previously bought exclusively by peasant self-aid cooperatives, and vice versa. Since rural areas presently experience a general decline in business volume, cooperatives fight for market shares to maximize the use of existing capacities in terms of staff, storage and processing facilities. To a smaller degree, competition is also developing between cooperatives and state enterprises, for example, fertilizer companies bypassing cooperatives directly to supply bigger farms. Competition with the traditional private sector is presently occurring only on a rudimentary scale, usually limited to selected trade activities promising quick turnover and requiring little investment.

A third indicator for the potential of cooperatives are the several new rural organizations presently being established by farmers. In many regions, farm service enterprises are being organized which are similar to the independent cooperatives which existed before the Second World War.

CONSTRAINTS

The principal constraint which existing cooperatives face is their reputation of having been government-controlled organizations with little participation and control by members. Cooperatives will have to prove quickly that they did not fully lose their identity as member-oriented organizations during the period of command economy, and will need to demonstrate effectively that democratically elected member representatives have full authority over the organization. Due to the previous state interventions, many cooperatives developed into public service organizations as compared with member business enterprises. Cooperatives will have to refocus their activities on member needs and phase out any activity that is not sufficiently member-specific. Furthermore, cooperatives will have to develop a business approach and the corresponding managerial skills in conducting their activities to overcome the previous civil service approach and supply attitude. However, the lack of a business orientation and the inadequacy of managerial skills are not limited to cooperatives but are general problems in Poland which have developed during a period of 45 years of command economy.

The cooperative restructuring initiated by the cooperative law amendment of January, 1990, is inadequate in its concept and is rather poor in its implementation. The available and anticipated results of the restructuring do not adequately alleviate existing constraints, and in some instances they constitute new constraints for the development of agricultural cooperatives.

As referred to previously, the first objective of the law amendment was to democratize cooperatives by conducting new elections of member representatives in primary cooperatives. However, these elections were inadequately prepared and organized, with the result that only a minority of members participated. The subsequent changes in cooperative supervisory councils and management boards are not very significant. Therefore, several cooperative representatives will continue to lack credibility *vis-à-vis* members and outsiders. In addition, the Supreme Cooperative Council, which has been reconstituted on the basis of the elections in primary

cooperatives is similarly handicapped in its credibility.

The second objective of the law amendment, that is, the liquidation of cooperative unions including the transfer of union assets, has a clear overall negative effect. There is no doubt that these unions were inefficient in providing support services (that is, management support, audit services, etc.) to primary cooperatives, and clearly the decision to liquidate them was based on the assumption that it was not feasible to restructure these unions and improve their services. However, the law amendment does not allow the establishment of new unions until mid-1991; this provision results in primary cooperatives not receiving any support services during the current period of adjustment, which is precisely when they need such services more than ever. Furthermore, the liquidation of the unions made the numerous enterprises (wholesale, processing, transport) previously operated by the unions into ownership orphans. With the unions presently being liquidated and the new owners not yet determined, these enterprises operate in a vacuum, that is, without effective ownership representation. This situation has severely affected the operations and viability of the union enterprises, including the disruption of financial arrangements with lending institutions and export contacts with foreign business organizations. Finally, the restructuring of ownership of union assets, including enterprises, as presently planned raises considerable doubts as to its legal validity and will most likely result in a fragmentation of vital industrial and service chains.

SELECTED ISSUES

Cooperative ownership

When examining the financial situation of primary cooperatives, it is striking to see not only the many and substantial assets they have accumulated but also that these cooperatives are almost debt-free. However, the considerable net assets are not at all matched by an equivalent amount of member equity. In most cooperatives the total amount of equity held by members constitutes less than 1% of the net assets. The question then arises as to who owns the remaining 99% of cooperative assets. This question is highly relevant in the context of the above-mentioned constraints of inadequate member involvement, and weak economic bonds between members and their cooperatives caused by the state's previous interference. Furthermore, this ownership question needs to be answered whenever cooperatives are confronted with issues such as dividing into smaller units, merging with other cooperatives, or liquidating their organization.

Before attempting to answer the question of ownership, the financial policy of cooperatives needs to be briefly reviewed. To a large extent, the financial policy of cooperatives was indirectly or directly predetermined by cooperative legislation or state decisions. Central and regional planning authorities basically decided the kind and volume of commercial activities of cooperatives through the allocation of quotas. In return, cooperatives were granted fixed and guaranteed margins for their transactions. As a result, with reasonable management it was not difficult to generate surpluses in cooperatives. The system of surplus distribution was also to a large extent prescribed by the cooperative legislation and other regulations. Generally, 25-30% of the surplus had to be paid in taxes, 10-20% went into a development fund (administered by the central unions and used for several purposes such as investment lending to cooperatives, financing training activities, etc.), about 20% was used for financing social activities (for example, cultural centers, sport teams, young farmers and women's groups, kindergartens), and the balance of 30-55% went into reserves. Until recently, cooperatives did not pay any significant amount to members or users in terms of dividends or patronage payments. Of course, the nonpayment of dividends and patronage payments was part of the socialist policy of discouraging individual ownership. In line with this policy and according to the cooperative legislation, the assets financed out of reserves are considered as indivisible property which is owned by the entire group of members.

However, the ownership regulation of the cooperative law is presently being challenged by several groups. The first group consists of government representatives claiming that cooperative assets were financed in part by state subsidies or out of surpluses derived from monopoly profits; but these claims, if analyzed, do not seem to be justified. Subsidies were usually not entity-specific but rather intended to be passed on to farmers or consumers; and monopoly profits could not be generated where the kind and volume of cooperative transactions and their margins were determined by others than cooperatives. In conclusion, the state does not seem to have a justified claim on cooperative assets.

The second group of claimants is the cooperative employees who suggest that the surpluses financing assets were in part generated by underpaying staff. This claim does not seem to have any justification since cooperative staff were paid like other employees and similarly to civil servants in accordance with state regulations. If such claims by employees would be entertained, the state would be confronted with the following issue: Do civil servants have a claim on state property over and above the claim of other citizens for the very reason that civil servants are state employees?

The third group claiming part of the cooperative assets is the group of farmers who did business transactions with the cooperative but never paid the symbolic share to become members. Nonmember users of cooperatives would have to be treated as members as far as their claims relate to patronage payments. However, these claims should not be recognized in terms of shares but rather as redeemable loan stock.

The fourth and most important group of claimants is the cooperative members who have justified claims in their double capacity as shareholders and providers of business. Since, in the past, members were not rewarded either in terms of dividends or patronage payments, this should be undertaken retroactively by transferring a corresponding amount of the cooperative reserves into individual member share accounts. The remaining part of the reserves should remain undivided and continue to constitute group property, as is the usual case with cooperatives in Western countries.

Further research is required to determine the percentage of divisible versus indivisible cooperative property, and to provide guidance on the issue of whether to link the revaluation of member shares with a capital increase. The latter might be needed in the cases where cooperatives are not expected to be able to finance investments exclusively by loans.

For secondary and tertiary cooperative organizations, that is, regional and central unions, similar ownership principles should be applied as suggested for primary cooperatives. Primary cooperatives established regional unions which in turn established central unions. Whether primary or secondary cooperatives established unions on a voluntary basis or not is irrelevant in the ownership context. Consequently, central and regional unions are owned by primary cooperatives, that is, by the members of these cooperatives. However, the ownership claims of primary cooperatives on union assets should be considered as part of the indivisible group property.

Restructuring ownership of union assets

The assets of the cooperative unions under liquidation consist mainly of some 4,000 wholesale and processing enterprises. According to the cooperative law amendment of January 1990, the union assets are to be transferred to previous member cooperatives which apply for the property as individual units or as a group of several cooperatives, or which form a cooperative of cooperatives or to worker cooperatives consisting of at least 50% of the employees of a union's enterprise with each member having deposited three months' salary as capital contribution. Alternatively, the assets should be sold to any other individual, group of individuals, or company. Union assets which are neither transferred nor sold are supposed to be taken over by the Supreme Cooperative Council.

The task of restructuring the ownership of union assets is handled by individual liquidators who were appointed for each union under liquidation (in total some 400) by the Ministry of Finance and its regional tax offices. However, many liquidators seem ill-equipped for the onerous tasks they are expected to perform and are handicapped by lack of guidance, support, coordination and supervision.

To start with, most of the liquidators have a legal and/or civil service background and lack adequate knowledge and experience in management, organization, financial and technical knowledge of the fields for which they have been made responsible. The liquidators would need to be supported by teams of qualified specialists in areas such as valuation of the assets to be transferred, identifying and evaluating potential buyers of these assets, preparing and assisting in the negotiations for sales/transfer of assets and, above all, in managing the business of the unions until the transfers or sales are completed. In addition, liquidators should be given clear and comprehensive terms of reference, providing them with guidance and instructions on how to proceed, and holding them

accountable for their activities. However, such terms of reference and definition of responsibilities seem to exist only in a rudimentary form and are considered by the liquidators as inadequate in their coverage, depth and operational relevance. Liquidators also need to be supervised by an authority adequately equipped for this mammoth task, estimated to involve almost 4% of the total assets of the national economy. However, only a small unit within the Ministry of Finance is assigned to perform the function of supervision, as well as to provide guidance and support to the liquidators. Finally, the activities of the liquidators of the national unions need to be coordinated with the work of the liquidators of the regional unions within each cooperative subsector and among the various subsectors of the entire cooperative sector. However, adequate coordination mechanisms are not yet in place. The working group recently established in the office of the Vice Prime Minister/Minister of Finance to support the liquidation unit of the Ministry of Finance issued several papers providing some guidance to liquidators and assembled liquidators for discussions. These very commendable but limited efforts, however, only marginally improve the liquidation and restructuring process. To a considerable extent individual liquidators continue to struggle to interpret and apply the law as they think the special conditions in their sector or geographical area require.

The most important issue to be resolved before beginning any liquidation, including the transfer or sale of assets, is to establish clearly who owns the units to be liquidated. When the cooperative law was amended in January, 1990, the ownership issue was perceived to be extremely complex by assuming that the state and cooperative employees had claims on substantial parts of the union assets. However, as demonstrated above, the state and employees do not seem to have any justified claims, and the sole owners of union assets appear to be the primary cooperatives.

Once it is accepted that primary cooperatives are the owners of the unions under liquidation and their respective assets, the mandate of the state to liquidate these organizations and dispose of their assets would be open to question. Obviously, in enacting the recent amendment to the Cooperative Law, the Parliament treated cooperative unions like other state enterprises, which in theory are deemed to be owned by the population at large, represented by the government. The behavior or performance of cooperative unions in a manner similar to parastatals seems to have led to an incorrect perception of the ownership. The liquidation of unions could be legally challenged by primary cooperatives and be very costly if a court concludes that the state must compensate the owners for the damage caused by the liquidation. Therefore, before the restructuring process proceeds any further, the group responsible for the restructuring should seek the advice and involvement of the owners, that is, the primary cooperatives.

In addition to the doubts which can be raised concerning the representation of owners in the process of restructuring the ownership of union property, there are several issues related to the anticipated results and effects of this process, assuming the liquidation would be completed as presently programmed. Among others, these include the transfer as opposed to the sale of union assets, the sustainability of new ownership structures, and the fragmentation of industry and service chains.

In many cases, liquidators intend to propose transferring union assets to new owners at a purely symbolic value. For example, employees can become the new owners of a union enterprise by 50% of the employees establishing a worker cooperative and each employee/member depositing an amount equivalent to three months' salary. Thus the capital required to take over union assets might be less than 1% of the market value of the assets transferred. This demonstrates that the ongoing liquidation process is not geared toward generating revenues from the transfer of union assets, but rather to redistributing union assets and that the liquidation process does not provide for a compensation of legitimate owners whose assets are being distributed.

Furthermore, in addition to the extremely doubtful justification of employees' claims on union assets as demonstrated above, questions can be raised concerning the sustainability of enterprises owned by employees. In general, enterprises owned by employees have an inherent conflict of interest. The short-term objective of employees to maximize their gains from the enterprise in terms of direct remuneration conflicts with the long-term objective of an enterprise to build equity through maximizing profit and retaining part of this profit as reserves. Usually, worker-controlled enterprises give priority to the short-term objectives of employees over the long-term objectives of owners (thus neglecting the fact that employees and owners are identical), with the result that these enterprises become increasingly undercapitalized and uncompetitive. In summary, worker cooperatives are not a viable option of ownership structure.

An essential objective of the restructuring of the Polish economy is to allow the development of chains in industry and trade which efficiently link producers and consumers. The ongoing liquidation of cooperative unions and the redistribution of union assets does not seem to be consistent with that objective. Union enterprises involved in processing and wholesaling constitute vital elements in the trade and industry chains of most agricultural products. To a great extent, the restructuring of ownership of union assets is geared to break these links by establishing new owners, irrespective of the competence of these owners to sustain the operations of the transferred links and without assessing the potential of the links under new owners to become part of a rearranged chain. It could be expected that the final results of the liquidation and restructuring process will create a confusing puzzle of many largely independent operating chain elements, which after a long and costly process might eventually become again part of functioning trade and industry chains.

Strategic Recommendations

SHORT TERM

Redesign of liquidation and restructuring

The single most important issue affecting both the short- and long-term operations of agricultural cooperatives is the process by which cooperative unions are being liquidated and the associated restructuring of the unions' assets. So far, limited damage has been done, but if the process continues to be implemented as presently designed, the most likely result will be structural deficiencies in terms of long-term disruptions of essential services and industries for farmers and consumers, as well as substantial losses for the national economy. Therefore, the liquidation and restructuring process needs to be immediately and substantially redesigned and its implementation improved. The redesigning of the process should fully involve representatives of the legitimate owners of union assets and should aim within a realistic timeframe for an efficient and legitimate ownership structure of union assets and enterprises. As soon as possible, the implementation of the liquidation and restructuring process should be assigned to teams of competent professionals rather than continuing to rely on individual liquidators. During implementation, adequate efforts need to be undertaken to closely coordinate and supervise the work of the various liquidation and restructuring teams. Finally, while the liquidation and restructuring process is being redesigned and implemented, adequate management of union assets and enterprises needs to be ensured.

A national cooperative restructuring office should be established and charged with the responsibility of redesigning the liquidation and restructuring process and with coordinating and supervising its implementation. Additionally, this office should be responsible for supervising the management of union assets and enterprises until they are taken over by the owners. The working group for cooperative development operating in the office of the Vice Prime Minister/Minister of Finance could provide the nucleus of personnel for the proposed office. However, the proposed office should have adequate representation of primary cooperatives (for example, through the Supreme Cooperative Council), and it should be complemented in several areas by Polish and expatriate specialists.

Similarly, the implementation teams should consist of cooperative representatives, regional tax office officials, liquidators, and local and expatriate specialists. In principle, one implementation team should operate in each voivodship. However, small voivodships could be grouped and handled by one team. Once the principle of establishing a national cooperative restructuring unit and regional implementation teams is agreed upon, additional operational details would need to be developed.

Cooperative policy declaration

The existing cooperative legislation including the Cooperative Law of 1982, its subsequent amendments, bylaws, statutes and other regulations are to a great extent outdated and have hardly any relevance to the new political and economic conditions and trends. At the same time, however, cooperatives are in the process of adjusting to the new realities and becoming increasingly ready for their changed role in a market economy. To achieve this, cooperatives aim to restructure their organizations, reestablish their membership base and create new apex organizations. All these issues presently faced by cooperatives involve legal questions. However, the existing legal framework is outdated and a new or modified framework is not yet available. A new cooperative legislation will necessarily take time in order to be consistent with new potential and actual economic realities and to offer operational solutions for the transition period.

The present legal vacuum should be filled by a policy declaration on cooperative development possibly issued as a government decree or parliamentary resolution. This declaration should commence with a definition of a genuine cooperative organization and provide guidance on how existing cooperatives, which are still shaped to a certain extent by previous regulations, can transform themselves into genuine member-based organizations. Thereafter, the declaration should address the basic issues cooperatives presently are confronted with such as ownership, reestablishment of the membership base, division, merger and liquidation of cooperatives, transformation of cooperatives into share companies, the role of the state in cooperative development and the functions of the Supreme Cooperative Council, the procedure to be followed in establishing new cooperative apex organizations, and similar issues. Furthermore, the policy declaration should contain the key elements of the redesigned liquidation and restructuring process and establish the national cooperative restructuring office and the implementation teams. Finally, the declaration should provide the basis for establishing regional cooperative service centers which are proposed in the following chapter.

Cooperative support services

As mentioned above, the multitude of primary cooperatives operating all over Poland are presently facing without any guidance and support the tremendous task of adjusting to the new legal and economic environment and market conditions. Such a void is clearly not desirable since it is in the interest of the national economy to make the best use of the existing institutional infrastructure in order to minimize the disruption of essential services to rural areas.

The support services required by primary cooperatives will depend on their adjustment requirements and potential and will have to be determined by cooperatives themselves. On average, the following services are required by the majority of the cooperatives:

• management advice, including advice on legal, economic and organizational issues
• training for staff and management, and information services for members
• regular audit services and assistance in establishing internal control procedures.

These services should be provided as soon as possible by a network of regional service organizations. To distinguish clearly the proposed organization from the previous unions, the proposed organizations could be called cooperative service centers (CSCs). Any CSC should be a light and efficient service structure with a temporary mandate, that is, CSCs would be phased out as the new cooperative apex organizations become operational. CSCs could be established and made operational within a few weeks by recruiting core staff needed and renting offices from the union under liquidation.

In principle, primary cooperatives are expected to pay for the services rendered by CSCs. In the initial phase, however, some exceptions to this principle should be permitted. First, any external technical assistance made available to CSC should not be charged to primaries. This proposal is based on the assumption that technical assistance will be available on a grant basis. Secondly, initial training in basic skills introducing cooperatives to principles of market economy and member promotion should be provided at a nominal cost. Long-term training in specialized fields should gradually be charged at real costs. The costs of auditing services should be charged in full from the beginning. Any financial gaps in the cash flows of CSCs are expected to be bridged by donor assistance, revenues from enterprises previously owned by cooperative unions, and from sales revenues generated during the ownership restructuring.

The question arises as to who should establish and run the entities providing these services. In the medium term, primary cooperatives are expected to establish apex organizations performing these and similar functions. While waiting for these apex organizations to become operational, the Supreme Cooperative Council (SCC) should take the initiative to establish, in close consultation with primaries, a network of regionally based CSCs. The number of CSCs, their activities and locations should be decided according to the type of services requested by primary cooperatives. By recruiting the best qualified and motivated employees from the previous unions, CSCs concentrating on essential services would perhaps require not more than 15 to 20% of the staff previously employed by the unions.

While working with primary cooperatives, CSCs would also assist members and management in assessing the performance of these cooperatives and the potential improvements to be gained by refocusing cooperative services. These assessments would provide the basis for an eventual fundamental reorganization or rehabilitation of primary cooperatives. CSCs could also assist primary cooperatives in evaluating the possibilities of permanently taking over union assets, examining related financial issues, and delineating the problems associated with the management of these assets. Finally, primary cooperatives assisted and audited by CSC would gain credibility with the local banks, thus increasing their chances of obtaining funds for immediate requirements (for example, crop purchase funds for the ongoing agricultural season) and investments. By the same token, CSCs can assist foreign donor and finance organizations in identifying needs for technical and financial assistance and investment requirements of cooperatives at the primary, and reemerging secondary and tertiary levels.

The government and the Supreme Cooperative Council should consider establishing jointly a foundation for cooperative development in Poland. Such a foundation could be financed by the assets accumulated through the substantial contributions of cooperatives to the various development funds which are presently controlled by liquidators. The foundation could operate mainly as a credit guarantee scheme in assisting existing and new cooperatives to provide part of the collateral for loan financing of investments. Furthermore, and as an alternative to separately operating cooperative restructuring organizations and restructuring teams on one side and cooperative service centers on the other side, the foundation could assume both the responsibility for the liquidation/restructuring process as well as cooperative support services, and thus institutionalize the coordination of efforts aimed at the rehabilitation of the cooperative movement.

MEDIUM TERM

Cooperative legislation

The cooperative legislation consists of the Cooperative Law of 1982 and its subsequent amendments, the standard bylaws (statutes) of primary, secondary, and tertiary cooperatives, and other legal regulations concerning cooperatives. In comparison to other Central and Eastern European countries, the existing cooperative legislation in Poland is the least rigid. However, in the context of the new political and economic conditions the legislation is not at all appropriate since it is still based in many areas on socialist ideology. The existing cooperative legislation considers cooperative organizations as part of the socialized economy and consequently provides for state control over cooperatives. Furthermore, it does not recognize the business character and the full ownership of cooperatives by members and gives staff an excessive role in management.

A new legislation law is required which considers cooperatives as part of the private sector, owned by and doing business with and on behalf of their members, and managed entirely by their democratically elected representatives and appointed professionals. In addition to these generally accepted principles of genuine cooperatives, a new cooperative law needs to design a few additional structural elements by choosing, from the various cooperative models operating successfully in Western countries, the options that best suit the Polish conditions and requirements. Such structural elements include registration of cooperatives, and supervisory and management bodies, as well as audit requirements. Other aspects which are not essential for the definition of a genuine cooperative and go beyond some basic structural elements should be left to cooperatives in the various branches and at various levels to regulate in their statutes. Thus, the new cooperative law would provide an overall framework defining the general nature and basic structure of cooperatives and their movement, while the areas of organization, objectives, operations and movement-internal structure would be decided by members and their cooperatives.

In drafting a new cooperative law, the relevant legislation of other countries should be studied and the various cooperative branches in Poland should be involved. The aim should be to arrive at a legal framework conducive to cooperative development as one of several options available to individuals for establishing organizations. The proposed process of studies and consultation to arrive at an adequate cooperative law takes time. If such a process is well prepared, coordinated and given priority consideration, it can be achieved in about one year.

Structure of cooperative movement

A typical structure for a cooperative movement in a given country usually consists of primary cooperatives forming regional unions or federations (secondary cooperative organizations) to provide support services (management advice, training, and audit); and secondary structures establishing national branch federations to provide selected support services (for example, legal advice on key issues) and to represent the interest of the branch *vis-à-vis*. National branch federations often establish a joint confederation representing the entire cooperative movement within a country and in international organizations. Furthermore, groups of primary cooperatives, secondary and tertiary structures, and cooperative apex organizations often operate processing, trade, and service enterprises linked to their branch of activity or to the entire cooperative movement.

Presently, the cooperative movement in Poland consists of a multitude of primary cooperatives operating in various sectors and subsectors, a national apex organization (Supreme Cooperative Council), and thousands of cooperative enterprises previously controlled by secondary and tertiary cooperatives. The previous regional and central cooperative unions are presently under liquidation and the establishment of new unions is prohibited until July, 1991. Several primary cooperatives are discussing preliminary projects of establishing secondary units to provide on a permanent basis the support services they would like to receive. In this strategy paper no specific recommendations are made regarding the future structure of the cooperative movement, since these structures need to evolve according to the requirements of primary cooperatives, and their establishment should be left to the initiative of the cooperatives operating in the various regions and branches. The same applies to the eventual establishment of new central unions or federations.

The proposed cooperative service centers will fill the present void in terms of providing essential cooperative support services and, at the same time, will be at the disposal of primary cooperatives to advise on the establishment of a new secondary and tertiary structure. The proposed cooperative restructuring organization and the regional restructuring teams will manage, on behalf of the primary cooperatives, the existing enterprises previously operated by the unions under liquidation until such time as the ownership status of these enterprises is resolved. To arrive at efficient ownership structures it is recommended that primary cooperatives organize themselves as share companies and not as secondary cooperative organizations for taking over and operating union assets. A company structure reflects the different volume of equity contributions in the ownership representation and will facilitate joint-venture arrangements. Thus, regional and national cooperative enterprises would operate separately from secondary and tertiary cooperatives, thereby avoiding the conflicts of interest between the functions of providing support services and operating enterprises prevailing in the previous cooperative unions.

LONG TERM

In the long term, the cooperative movement is expected to be consolidated by primary cooperatives either having adjusted to market conditions or having exited, as well as new and genuine cooperatives having entered; new and efficient secondary and tertiary cooperatives being established, and the Supreme Cooperative Council being revitalized, together with the entire support structure; and a network of restructured and cooperative-controlled regional and national enterprises continuing to operate as essential elements of food, industry, trade and service chains. However, once the cooperative movement has consolidated, it does not mean that no further adjustments and evolutions are required. Cooperatives at all levels will have to continue to remain flexible to adjust to evolving market conditions and to further increase efficiency. Thus the cooperative movement as an integral part of the private sector is expected to substantially contribute to free competition and efficient resource allocation.

Implications of proposed strategy

The implementation of the proposed strategy, consisting of reprivatizing and consolidating existing cooperatives and facilitating the easy entry and exit of new cooperatives at all levels, obviously necessitates a complex and delicate process involving many political, economic, social and legal aspects. However, such a process is not limited to cooperatives but (in the context of the overall economic reform and privatization efforts) involves equally any other economic organization. Nevertheless, two implications of the proposed strategy for cooperative development warrant special attention, that is, the future role of the state and the need for technical assistance.

In the period from the mid-1940s until mid-1989, the state virtually hijacked the cooperative movement and used it as a tool in the implementation of its command economy. However, this has radically changed with the establishment of a new government and the economic reform program. The cooperative law amendment of January, 1990, aims at liberalizing cooperatives by liquidating the unions, which to a large extent controlled the cooperative movement on behalf of the state. The basic thrust of the law amendment and the good intentions of the lawmakers are beyond any doubt. However, it was mainly state representatives, that is, outsiders to the cooperative movement, who acted on behalf of the movement. Such an action without explicit mandate might have been justified at that time since the movement did not have a credible spokesman, but this has changed, though only to a limited extent.

By holding elections as provided by the law, primary cooperatives and the Supreme Cooperative Council do represent cooperative members and the movement. Therefore cooperatives and their representatives increasingly have to replace state representation in designing the restructuring and consolidation of the movement, as well as in drafting a new cooperative law. In the medium and long run the role of the state should be limited to providing a conducive environment to cooperative development as part of its private sector policy.

The tremendous and urgent need for technical assistance has been stressed while proposing (in the appendices) a national cooperative restructuring organization (including regional implementation teams), the network of cooperative service centers and the drafting of a new cooperative law. Additional technical assistance will be required for the establishment of a new secondary, tertiary and apex structure, as well as in consolidating the many enterprises previously controlled by unions. Since it appears to be government policy not to use loan funds to finance technical assistance, the interest of international and bilateral donor agencies and NGOs needs to be explored as soon as possible to provide on a grant basis experienced technical assistance. Several agencies have already indicated their interest in providing substantial technical assistance or, in fact, are already operating teams of management and cooperative specialists in the country. For example, an American cooperative organization presently provides some 100 specialists to agricultural primary cooperatives in one voivodship.

The first recipient of senior technical assistance should be the Supreme Cooperative Council to improve its knowledge base in technical fields related to the liquidation and restructuring process and cooperative legislation, and thus to strengthen its position in representing the interests of primary cooperatives. However, while waiting for external support, the Supreme Cooperative Council, together with the government, should develop a comprehensive program for the entire cooperative movement, identifying the needs for short-term consultancies and long-term technical assistance. The council should communicate this program to interested donor agencies.

Appendix 6.1 History of the cooperative movement

The first cooperatives in Poland were established in the second half of the nineteenth century, that is, at the time when Poland was partitioned among Russia, Prussia and Austria. Soon one could speak of prevailing cooperative models in various regions of the country. In the western region under Prussian occupation cooperative banks and agricultural marketing and supply cooperatives developed, while in the Russian part of Poland mainly consumer cooperatives developed both in the urban and rural areas. The south of Poland under Austrian rule had the most numerous saving and credit cooperatives.

After the Polish state regained independence in 1918, regionally developed cooperative models extended into other regions, and gradually a coherent movement evolved. As a result, most of the 20 basic types of cooperatives were associated at the central level in nine auditing unions and 25 different trading and financing organizations. By 1938, Poland had about 14,000 viable cooperatives united in various auditing unions. Outside these unions functioned several thousand weaker and generally short-lived societies.

During World War II, practically the whole cooperative movement of the country, with the exception of consumer cooperatives, was abolished by the occupants. A period of somewhat more independent rebuilding of the cooperatives from war damages ended as early as 1948 with the introduction of the socialized economy. In addition, the government forced the creation of a system of farming cooperatives as a form of collective economy. The communist system favored to a certain extent the development of cooperatives, but only as a tool of control over the economy — particularly in agriculture — and a means of transition from private to state ownership. Cooperatives of various kinds were assigned special tasks within the national economy. Among other things this resulted in a near split of the consumer movement into an urban movement (spolem) and rural peasant self-aid cooperatives. Evidently, the introduction of the command system into the cooperatives was destructive to self-governing functions and led to lack of involvement of the members.

The first abortive attempt to break away from the command system took place in 1956. For the cooperative movement, it resulted in dissolution of the majority of farming cooperatives and reestablishment of branches of the credit, dairy and horticultural cooperatives. However, the newly reestablished cooperative branches had their fixed place in the planned economy.

Structurally, all cooperatives were united in their respective regional branch unions, which in turn formed the central unions of different branches. Membership in the secondary and tertiary level organization was obligatory. Generally, the cooperative unions were used as an instrument for central management, thus regulating almost all aspects of activity of the primary cooperatives and at the same time providing them with some essential economic services.

At the end of the 1970s, under the pressure of the centrally planned economy, the cooperatives grew to be a gigantic network. The nine existing central unions comprised 11,000 primary cooperatives with 15.2 million members. The number of members in a primary cooperative ranged from 1,500 to 250,000. Generally, except for some local initiatives the leaders of primary cooperatives were increasingly controlled by central-level state and cooperative organizations.

The summer of 1980 witnessed the birth of Solidarity. However, in December 1981, the democratic processes were interrupted by imposition of martial law. Neither the new democratic mass movement of 1980 nor the government ever considered the cooperatives as a possible instrument for economic change. The economic reform declared by the government in 1982 had three basic principles: self-management, independence and self-financing, which incidentally corresponded to the basic principles of the cooperative movement. However, the cooperative movement did not take this opportunity to undertake any significant effort to transform or restructure. The reasons for this may be found in the fact that the cooperative leadership, elected in a way that might more accurately be described as appointment according to party recommendations, was not interested in changing the status quo.

Based on the new economic principles, a new cooperative law was passed in 1982; with subsequent amendments in 1983 and 1987, it guaranteed primary cooperatives freedom to associate voluntarily in unions different than the existing ones or remain outside any union structure. As a result of the new law, there were soon 17 central unions (instead of the nine previous ones) and some 200 independent cooperatives. However, the process of decentralization did not change significantly the dominant role of unions. The relationship between the cooperatives and their members had also hardly changed. As a result of enormous inflation at the end of the decade, the members' equity in cooperatives almost lost their value, thus decreasing further members' economic bonds to and interests in cooperatives.

With the change of government in 1989 and the first noncommunist prime minister in the postwar history of Poland, a new program for overcoming the deep economic crisis was established. Among its most urgent objectives was putting an end to inflation. At the same time, a parallel process was introduced to break up the monopolistic structures. With the objective of facilitating competition the cooperative was singled out since cooperative branches were considered monopolistic structures. The main reason for singling out cooperatives obviously was that it seemed to be an easier task to privatize the generally small- and medium-size cooperative organizations, than the usually large-scale government enterprises.

However, realizing the inevitability of fundamental changes, the Supreme Cooperative Council organized the Cooperative Congress in December 1989. The basic resolutions adopted by the delegates of this Congress, supported the idea of liquidating cooperative unions in their present form, however, they suggested alternative ways of implementing the liquidation. A strong protest was voiced against the planned ban on the possibility of forming new cooperative associations. However, the views expressed by the Congress were not taken into consideration by the government and the Parliament in drafting and passing the Act on Cooperatives in January 1990.

Appendix 6.2 Ownership of primary cooperatives and cooperative unions

Cooperatives are among the largest owners of assets in rural areas. Peasant self-aid cooperatives, which number 1,853, operate 71,452 shops and 5,444 restaurants. Dairy cooperatives, which number 323, operate 9,910 buying stations and 721 milk plants. Horticulture cooperatives (numbering 140) operate 210 processing plants and 6,455 retail shops. Agricultural production cooperatives (numbering 2,089) operate 774,601 hectares of agricultural land. The number of cooperative banks total 1,663, with total assets amounting to Zl 1,775 billion. The total value of fixed assets of rural cooperatives was reported to be Zl 2,609 billion in 1988. This amount represents 75% of the total fixed assets of the entire cooperative system if housing cooperatives were excluded.

This large value of assets is not matched by a high level of equity or liability. In most instances, the level of members' equity is but a fraction of a percent of assets. Many cooperatives are also debt-free. The question of ownership of cooperatives arises particularly in situations where the cooperative is to be liquidated, divided or transformed into other forms of economic organization. It is also essential to know who the real owners of these cooperatives are when increased capitalization becomes necessary or when the cooperatives enter into joint-venture enterprises with foreign capital. The issue of cooperative ownership becomes crucial in the overall effort of privatization as the economy moves toward a free market system.

To be able to determine the exact nature of ownership, it would be necessary to clearly determine specific characteristics of cooperatives in Poland, such as: the purpose for which cooperatives were organized; the type of membership; the internal structure, including the management system; the external structure, including the system of self-regulation; the extent of government control; the manner by which cooperatives were capitalized; and the system of profit sharing. The question which has to be answered is how the assets of the cooperative should be divided. And more importantly, the question is how the ownership structure of cooperatives should be revised if these institutions are to be able to meet the challenges of a free market system.

CHARACTERISTICS OF THE COOPERATIVE SYSTEM

According to the Cooperative Law of 1982, the cooperative "shall be a voluntary and self-governing association ...being guided by the needs of the associated members and by assumptions laid down in central and territorial socioeconomic plans...." In addition to serving the needs of members, it is inferred that the cooperatives would be used as an instrument of the state in the pursuit of the objectives of its socioeconomic plans. In addition, a provision in the law states that "the proper organ of state administration shall have a right to impose on the cooperative the obligation to introduce tasks into the plan or assign unplanned tasks if this is indispensable because of the demands of defence of the country or in case of natural calamity." In Eastern European countries, the sphere of activity of cooperatives is assigned to them by government

decision although it has been observed that in the case of Poland, the Cooperative Law provides cooperatives the greatest degree of independence.

The Cooperative Law does not make a clear distinction between types of members. The law allows either natural persons or legal entities to form cooperatives. The law even allows political organizations not having a legal status to become members of cooperatives. It would have avoided confusion if a separate set of provisions had been made to cover primary cooperatives formed by individuals and secondary-level organizations formed by cooperatives. There were 8,133 primary cooperatives and 225 secondary cooperatives in 1988.

The law provides for democratic voting at the primary level and allows other forms of voting at the secondary level but is not explicit that it should be capital voting. The secondary-level organizations (unions) combine the political and economic structures of the cooperative system. The unions were part of the political structure of the cooperative system but these unions created subsidiaries such as enterprises engaged in wholesaling, food processing, transportation, construction, etc. With the January 1990 law abolishing these unions for political reasons, these enterprises have become orphaned and it has affected their economic activities. A strong contender for ownership of these enterprises are the workers themselves, since they are the best organized. The original cooperative owners were prevented by law from forming new unions to make a bid for the assets of the liquidated unions.

There does not appear to be a very clear distinction in Polish cooperative law between membership/ownership, management and employees/workers of the cooperative. For instance, employees are allowed to become members of a cooperative even if they have nothing more to do with the business of the cooperative than being employees. There is a notion that employees have proprietary rights. As a matter of fact, a whole chapter is devoted to employee self-management where employees have powers over the manager.

The supreme body of the cooperative is the general meeting. The general meeting elects a supervisory council which in turn elects the board. Some powers of the general meeting and the supervisory council overlap. Day-to-day management of the cooperative could be vested in a member or members of the board. It is not uncommon for management to face election from time to time.

The Cooperative Law requires that a cooperative join a central union. The central union assesses the cooperative for a percentage of its income as its contribution to the development fund, which is at the disposal of the central union. The structure appears to be a self-regulating structure because member cooperatives elect the officials of the central union. However, the powers of the union are not entrusted by the cooperatives to the central union, but rather prescribed by law. While the objective of the Cooperative Law is to ensure the independence of cooperatives, the detailed provisions and structure of the cooperative system show that cooperatives are overregulated and are not in fact independent institutions fully controlled by their members.

The traditional definition of a cooperative in market-driven economies is that it is a business organization owned and controlled by its members operating for the benefit of its members. It will be noted that the Cooperative Law of 1982 does not describe the cooperative as a business organization. The use of the word capital is avoided in the Cooperative Law. The importance of capital as a prerequisite to the formation of a cooperative is downgraded. The requirement for registration is merely the intention of members to contribute a share or shares. There is also no differentiation as to the type of shares, whether subscribed or paid-up. Since all shares are paid-up shares, members do not have the responsibility for increasing the capitalization of the cooperative if and when this becomes necessary.

Traditional cooperative principles in market-driven economies specify a limited return to capital, provisions for reserves, and the balance of income distributed to members according to patronage that is usually called a patronage refund. The reason for the limit on the return to capital is to encourage members to join the cooperative for the benefits derived from patronizing the cooperative rather than for returns to investment. Most laws in other countries would specify limitations on the provisions for reserves. The patronage refund is the members' share of the profits of the cooperative based on the extent of patronage. It represents the difference between the initial price and the final

price paid or received by members. These refunds are distributed in cash or in the form of additional shares of stock.

The Polish Cooperative Law adopts the principle of limited return to capital by specifying that returns on shares shall not exceed 50% of the highest rate of fixed-term deposits. The profit-sharing arrangements specified in the Cooperative Law are key to the issue of ownership of the assets of the cooperative. After-tax profits are called the balance surplus. The law specifies that at least 20% of this balance surplus should be allocated to a resource fund, which is essentially the provision for reserves. It should be noted that it is a minimum rather than a maximum which is required. In addition, the Cooperative Law requires that cooperatives contribute to a development fund of the central union they are required to join. Furthermore, the law provides that what is left over may be used to create special purpose funds or may be distributed to members in the form of bonuses and rewards and to employees for social and housing purposes. The principle of patronage refund is not embodied in the Polish Cooperative Law.

The distribution of the income of the cooperative sector for 1988 shows the following: income tax, 25%; special tax, 2%; resource fund, 14%; investment fund, 9%; development fund, 9%; social purposes, 21%; and other, 20%. Two observations may be made. First, a significant proportion of income goes to nonbusiness or social purposes. Second, income is not shared by individual members and the remaining income is accumulated by the cooperative in the form of assets. It therefore becomes understandable how the members' initial shares, contributed when the cooperative was organized, became an insignificant proportion of total assets over several decades of existence of the cooperative.

CLAIMANTS TO THE ASSETS OF THE COOPERATIVE

As shown in the preceding section, the cooperatives in Poland were basically regarded as service institutions. Although cooperatives performed economic activities, these were for social purposes. Cooperatives were not regarded as profit-making businesses. It could be argued that cooperatives were instruments of the government which assigned them tasks to perform. It could therefore be argued that, being instruments of the government, cooperatives' assets (or a portion of them) belong to the government, particularly in lieu of the monopoly position and subsidies given to them.

The argument that the assets of the cooperatives were created by monopoly profits cannot be used in the case of Poland as it has been pointed out that cooperatives were not regarded as profit-making business enterprises. The argument that the accumulation of assets by the cooperatives was the result of government subsidies cannot be used either, because subsidies were not sector-specific, but spread over the entire economy. Furthermore, the subsidies to cooperatives were meant, ultimately, to be passed on to the consumers. Finally, subsidies cannot realistically be expected to be recovered.

Because of their service orientation, cooperatives conducted activities which were contrary to sound business principles. The peasant self-aid cooperatives established and operated more than 70,000 retail shops to make consumer goods widely available in rural areas in spite of the fact that a significant proportion of these stores incurred losses. There was no compulsion to produce a profit, although it was necessary for the cooperatives not to produce a loss in order to survive. Whatever balance surpluses they made could therefore be considered as a savings or reward for efficiency. Assets accumulated due to these balance surpluses therefore rightfully belong to the cooperative and not the state. The most the state may expect is to collect a tax on unearned increment on the value of assets.

As shown in the previous section, cooperatives had paid their dues to the state in terms of taxes. They were required to make transfer payments within the cooperative sector as contributions to the development fund. Cooperatives used a significant proportion for social purposes. Surpluses were accumulated by the cooperatives in the form of resource funds and investment funds. Members were never given a share of balance surpluses or profits of the cooperative. These were retained by the cooperative and a situation arose where the cooperative became its own owner. If balance surpluses or profits were refunded to members and reinvested in the cooperative, the level of equity would be extremely high. Perhaps this was not done during the previous economic order to discourage individual ownership of capital. This situation

should now be rectified and it should be asserted that the accumulated assets of primary cooperatives are owned by individual members.

A similar case can be made that the primary cooperatives own the cooperative enterprises previously owned by the cooperative unions now under liquidation. Primary cooperatives organized and registered cooperative unions as provided by the Cooperative Law of 1982. It follows that primary cooperatives own the cooperative unions. The decision of the unions to establish enterprises were made on the basis of economic necessity and these enterprises had to be operated in a businesslike manner. The success of these enterprises fully depended on the patronage of member cooperatives. Assets accumulated by unions over the years should therefore belong to the member cooperatives.

It cannot be claimed that the assets of these enterprises were the result of state subsidies. First, these subsidies were meant to be passed on to consumers. Second, cooperatives were heavily taxed. In 1988, 27% of the income of cooperatives went to payment of taxes. There were also indirect taxes as 21% of cooperative income was spent for social purposes. On the contrary, the cooperative system was largely self-financed. A total of 32% of the income of cooperatives was allocated to different funds (resource fund 14%, investment fund 9% and development fund 9%). The development fund averaged 9%, but sometimes as much as 25% of income for individual cooperatives went to the central unions, which in turn used the funds to finance the establishment and operation of enterprises. The total balance of this fund, reported to be Zl 800 billion, is now held by the state. This compares with the reported total value of fixed assets of rural cooperatives of Zl 2,600 billion. During the 45 years under the previous economic system, the development fund made the greatest contribution to asset accumulation. Furthermore, some of the assets of cooperative enterprises were confiscated by the state from other cooperatives and transferred to the present enterprises. It follows that these assets should be retained by the cooperative system.

There are also strong economic reasons for keeping the ownership of these enterprises in the hands of primary cooperatives. These enterprises (agroprocessing, wholesaling, transport, etc.) are part of a marketing chain. To break these linkages would create further disruption in the system and would aggravate the already difficult situation in the food industry. Furthermore, if an enterprise is removed from a primary cooperative, the cooperative can always organize another enterprise, thereby wasting existing assets.

State appropriation of the assets of these enterprises would be a step backward for the privatization process. Primary cooperatives are private enterprises and retaining the assets of cooperative enterprises by primary cooperatives would have the effect of reprivatization. Privatization in this sense means releasing these enterprise from state control. However, in reprivatizing union assets, the previous rules of the game should be changed. Redundant enterprises should be liquidated; those retained should be restructured under a set of time-bound performance criteria. Management should be dismissed if it cannot deliver. The enterprise should be dissolved if members cannot provide the necessary support.

Taking the historic, social and economic aspects into considerations, a small proportion of shares could be allotted to other interest groups such as employees and nonmembers who regularly patronized the cooperative. Employees could be rewarded with shares, not in recognition of any proprietary interest but as remuneration for their tenure with the cooperative. Nonmembers' support could also be recognized by awarding them shares according to the extent of their patronage. Since the cooperative provided social services to its members and the community, assets representing social amenities should be transferred to appropriate local government entities to separate the business and nonbusiness activities of the cooperative.

Another claimant to the assets of the cooperative would be previous owners of assets which were taken over by the state and handed over to the cooperative. There would appear to be legitimate claims by previous owners but this question should be settled under civil law rather than cooperative law.

PROPOSED OWNERSHIP CONCEPT AND STRUCTURE

The proposed ownership concept is based on a clear definition of the objectives of the cooperative. First and foremost is the principle that the cooperative is a business organization which must be able to generate a profit to survive in a competitive environment. Its objective is to serve its members by providing them with services vital to their welfare. The members are the owners as well as the ones who provide business to the cooperative. The success of the cooperative depends on the homogeneity of its members based on their need for the cooperative. This objective contrasts with the objective of a share company whose objective is to generate profit for its investors.

The second principle is a clear identification of the contributors of the factors which make up the cooperative. The factors which constitute the cooperative are: members, who provide capital as well as business to the cooperative; management, which is appointed by duly-elected representatives of the cooperative; and employees. It should be pointed out that employees have absolutely no proprietary rights or interest in a cooperative because they are neither owners nor do they provide business to the cooperative. The only exception would be agricultural cooperatives whose members have contributed land, capital and labor and receive remuneration as employees of the cooperative but also receive rental for the land they have contributed. Worker cooperatives are also possible in the industrial sector provided workers actually contribute the capital of the cooperative.

In a cooperative, the value of the share does not increase. To equitably distribute shares, it would be necessary to appraise the value of net assets of primary cooperatives in Poland and issue the corresponding number of shares to members in recognition of the fact that assets from income were accumulated by the cooperatives and not distributed to members. Employees may be given some shares as remuneration for their years of service but not in recognition of any proprietary rights. The procedures for evaluation of assets and distribution of shares should be developed by a competent authority.

Assuming shares of the primary cooperatives would allow cooperatives to restructure, divide or merge. A new cooperative may be formed. Members of the old cooperative would use their shares to purchase shares in the new cooperative. Those who would no longer continue their membership in the new cooperative would convert their shares into loan shares which would be redeemable within a certain period of time. A primary cooperative may also be able to transform into a share company: the shares of the cooperative would be used to purchase shares of the new share company, which in turn would be used to purchase assets of the cooperative. The new share company could issue additional shares in response to local and foreign investment. Two types of shares should be issued, subscribed and paid-up. Subscribed shares would establish the responsibility of members to meet additional capital requirements and to answer for liabilities of the company by requiring the shareholders to pay up subscribed shares when a call is made.

It is proposed that the primary cooperatives be governed by traditionally accepted cooperative principles such as democratic control, limited returns to capital, provision for reserves and patronage refund. For secondary cooperatives, it is proposed that the nature of the ownership structure be similar to share companies where there would be capital voting, mixed ownership and profits divided according to number of shares held. It should not be difficult to transform secondary cooperatives into share companies if these cooperatives have characteristics similar to those of share companies. Preferably, secondary cooperatives should be registered under company law or banking law, whichever applies.

Appendix 6.3   Restructuring the cooperative system

On January 20, 1990, the Polish Parliament passed an amendment to the Cooperative Law with a view to fundamentally restructuring and democratizing the cooperative sector. The features of the legal amendments are:

• the election of new member and cooperative representatives
• the liquidation of all cooperative unions at the regional and national levels, including the transfer or sale of the assets of the unions.

ELECTIONS AT PRIMARY COOPERATIVES AND TO THE SUPREME COOPERATIVE COUNCIL

The amendment made it mandatory for each primary cooperative to hold an election for representatives to its supervisory council, before March 31, 1990, irrespective of the expiration date of the mandate of the council already in office. Any cooperative not holding elections by that date would automatically be considered to be under liquidation.

The degree of participation of members in the elections and the results were reported to be disappointing. Only a minority of members, many of whom were either staff members or supporters of the council in office, participated in the elections. As a result, it appears that in most cooperatives the previous representatives were reelected.

The results of the elections of the primary cooperatives might be disappointing, but they are not surprising. The elections conducted under the amended cooperative law do not appear to have been adequately prepared and organized, or supervised by an independent external (to cooperatives) organization. Over the last 45 years, member participation and control were largely suppressed in most cooperatives in Poland. Informing and educating members about their rights, as owners of the cooperatives, and how they can exercise these rights are essential if members are to really exercise control. However, no systematic efforts seem to have been made to convey these messages to members. Most members were probably left with a helpless feeling that their participation in the elections would not make any difference. Furthermore, the elections obviously were not supervised by experienced independent observers. As with any elections, cooperative elections can be influenced in many ways without violating any laid down rules. Whether this was indeed the case, or whether manipulation of the elections may have taken place, as is felt by some observers, would be difficult to determine.

Considering the conditions under which the elections of member representatives at primary cooperatives were conducted, their results have limited credibility. The elections obviously did not contribute to a fundamental democratization of the basic units of the Polish cooperative movement, as intended by the cooperative law amendment. The limited democratization of primaries also limits the credibility of subsequent elections, for example, to the Supreme Cooperative Council (SCC).

The law amendment also made it mandatory for primary cooperatives to elect representatives to SCC. Previously, primaries were represented at the SCC by officials of the cooperative unions. According to the amendment the SCC could continue to represent the Polish cooperative movement, but had to be constituted by representatives directly elected by the primaries. During May 1990, the cooperatives in each voivodship elected two representatives, 98 in total, constituting the General Assembly of the

SCC. By mid-June 1990, the General Assembly had adopted new statutes and elected a new presidium of the SCC.

Previously, the SCC was financed by contributions from cooperative unions. With these unions under liquidation and the formal membership of primaries in the SCC only slowly evolving and not yet defined (for example, it is not known how many primary cooperatives will subscribe for membership in the SCC and what their financial contributions will be), the SCC is not yet fully established and its financing is still open. Furthermore, SCC presently works with a skeleton staff of about 15 professionals, several of whom lack adequate qualifications and experience. The result is that the SCC presently is only marginally operational.

To increase the credibility of member and cooperative representatives and to further advance cooperative democracy the elections should be repeated as soon as feasible. At that time, care should be taken to adequately prepare, organize and supervise the elections. Such elections are essential before primary cooperatives begin to establish a new secondary and tertiary structure to ensure that this new structure will truly represent the interest of primary cooperatives and their members.

Furthermore, the SCC will have to immediately undertake substantial efforts to prove that its leadership is committed to constructively participating in the efforts aimed at restructuring and rehabilitating (that is, reprivatizing) the cooperative movement by increasing the competence of the SCC staff and rendering relevant services to the movement. Since the SCC presently is cut off from any funding sources it will require some initial financial assistance until its services generate revenues. With the assistance of government, the SCC should also immediately explore possibilities of obtaining technical assistance in key areas to improve its capability of playing a leadership role in the ongoing efforts of restructuring the cooperative movement and defining a new concept of cooperative development.

LIQUIDATION OF COOPERATIVE UNIONS AND RESTRUCTURING OF UNION ASSETS

Background

After the cooperative law amendment became effective in February 1990, the Ministry of Finance and its regional tax offices appointed liquidators, one for each cooperative union (about 400 total). Each liquidator replaces and acts in the place of the supervisory council and the management board of the union under liquidation, that is, the liquidator has sole responsibility for the dissolution of the union he is appointed for, and for supervising the management of the union's enterprises until the latter is handed over or sold. In these functions, the liquidators are not answerable to anybody since the owners of the unions (that is, in the case of regional unions the primary cooperatives, and in the case of central unions the regional unions) are either not represented anymore or are themselves under liquidation.

In addition to dissolving the union and supervising the management of the union's enterprises, the liquidators have the task of establishing plans for the transfer or sale of union assets, including the enterprises owned by the union. These liquidation plans are supposed to include:

• establishing a complete inventory of the union's assets and liabilities
• listing the groups of employees or cooperatives interested in taking over, or the individuals or companies offering to buy assets of the union
• assessing the offers for takeover or purchase, and proposing a list of groups, cooperatives, individuals or companies who the liquidator thinks should obtain the assets.

According to the amendment, union property can be transferred to:

• previous union member cooperatives which apply for the property as individual units or groups of several cooperatives or who formed a cooperative of cooperatives, or
• worker cooperatives, formed by at least 50% of the employees of a union enterprise, with each employee member having deposited as capital contribution an amount equal to three months' salary.

Several liquidators indicated that most of the claims filed with them for taking over union assets are presented by newly formed worker cooperatives. Furthermore, as they interpret the amendment, liquidators intend to propose to hand over union assets, including enterprises, mainly to these worker cooperatives.

Once prepared, the liquidation plan will be presented to a meeting of representatives of primary cooperatives and of representatives of the groups and individuals who applied for union assets. If the liquidation plan is not approved by simple majority vote at this meeting, the plan will be forwarded to the appointing office of the liquidators (that is, Ministry of Finance or regional tax offices), which in turn can approve it or forward it to the courts for final decision.

Issues

In several key areas the liquidation and restructuring process of cooperative unions and their assets is inadequately designed and poorly implemented.

Competence of and support to liquidators. Satisfactory results from restructuring the extremely complex cooperative subsectors, including enormous amounts of assets, could be only expected if the liquidators charged with the tasks of liquidating and restructuring were competent. However, many liquidators seem ill-equipped for the onerous tasks they are expected to perform and are handicapped by lack of guidance, support, coordination and supervision.

Most of the liquidators have a legal and/or civil service background and lack adequate knowledge and experience in management, organization, financial and technical knowledge of the fields for which they have been made responsible. The liquidators need the support of qualified specialists for valuation of the assets to be transferred, in identifying and evaluating potential buyers of these assets, in preparing and assisting in the negotiations for sale/transfer of assets and, above all, in managing the business of the unions until the transfers or sales are completed. In addition, liquidators require clear and comprehensive terms of reference, providing them with guidance and instructions on how to proceed, and holding them accountable for their activities. However, such terms of reference and definition of responsibilities seem to exist only in a rudimentary form and are considered by the liquidators as inadequate in their coverage, depth and operational relevance. Liquidators also need to be supervised by an authority adequately equipped for such a mammoth task, one that involves about 40% of

the total assets of the national economy. However, only a small unit within the Ministry of Finance is assigned to perform the function of supervision, as well as to provide guidance and support to the liquidators.

Finally, the activities of the liquidators of the national unions need to be coordinated with the work of the liquidators of the regional unions within each cooperative subsector, and among the various subsectors of the entire cooperative sector (involving in total about 400 unions). Furthermore, the entire process should be linked to the overall program of economic reform and also be part of a sector program, involving state enterprises operating in these sectors. However, no mechanisms are in place to coordinate among the liquidators of the various cooperative unions operating in the same sector, or to link the restructuring of unions and state enterprises operating in the same sector.

The working group established in the office of the Vice Prime Minister/Minister of Finance, which supports the cooperative liquidation unit in the Ministry of Finance, issued several papers providing some guidance to liquidators, and assembled liquidators for discussions. These very commendable efforts, however, could not and cannot alleviate the structural inadequacy and inconsistency of the amendment to the Cooperative Law. To a considerable extent, individual liquidators continue to struggle to interpret and apply the law as they understand it, and as they think the special conditions in their sector or geographical area require. The result might be 400 different liquidation plans, which to a large extent will reflect these individual interpretations and will not fit into a consistent concept.

Representation of owners. The most important issue to be resolved before commencing any liquidation is to have a clear notion of who owns the assets of the units under liquidation. In drafting the cooperative law amendment of January 1990, the ownership issue was perceived to be extremely complex both because of the financial participation of the state in unions or union-controlled enterprises (for example, in terms of direct and indirect subsidies) and because of the different contributions in cash or kind of the union's member organizations.

In the efforts to establish the ownership of cooperative unions, however, one simple fact seems to have been overlooked. Central unions were established and are owned by regional unions and regional unions by primary cooperatives. The state does not buy into the equity of a cooperative by subsidizing cooperative activities. Therefore, regional and central unions are owned by primary cooperatives. However, primary cooperatives might have shares of different values when considering their equity contributions in cash or kind.

Once it is accepted that primary cooperatives are in fact the owners of the cooperative unions, the mandate of the state to liquidate these organizations and dispose of their assets would be open to question. Obviously, in enacting the recent amendment to the Cooperative Law, the Parliament treated cooperative unions like state enterprises, which in theory are deemed to be owned by the population at large, represented by the government. The behavior or performance of cooperative unions in a manner similar to parastatals seems to have led to an incorrect perception of the ownership. The liquidation of unions could be challenged in court and become very costly if the court concludes that the state has to compensate the owners for the damage caused by the liquidation. Therefore, before the restructuring process proceeds any further, the group responsible for the restructuring should seek the advice and involvement of the owners, that is, the primary cooperatives. These cooperatives could be represented by the recently reconstituted Supreme Cooperative Council.

It could be argued that the interests of the legitimate owners of the unions at the various levels are sufficiently represented if these owners make efficient use of two provisions of the cooperative law amendment:

• The amendment, and legal commentaries thereon, state that member cooperatives will have first priority in obtaining their unions' assets. By effectively applying for the union assets, member cooperatives would have all the possibilities of taking over, free of charge, the net assets of their regional and central unions.
• The liquidation plans must be approved by a meeting involving representatives of the cooperatives previously associated in the union concerned. Assuming that the representatives' cooperatives have the majority in these meetings, this provision could be interpreted to constitute a veto right of member cooperatives, giving them the power of blocking any handing over or

sale of union assets to anybody else than the member cooperatives.

However, in reality these provisions of the cooperative law amendment are not or will not be fully applied for the following reasons:

• The law amendment caught primary cooperatives by complete surprise (as it did many political and economic observers, who have far better access to information than small and remote cooperatives). Furthermore, the law amendment is very difficult to comprehend. This is evidenced by the conflicting interpretation of various provisions of the law by legal experts and liquidators. Therefore, it is not surprising that primary cooperatives have a delayed reaction and do not have a clear notion of their rights and options under the law amendment. On the basis of the information they received, many primaries are still not fully aware that they have first claim on union assets.
• In addition to being caught by surprise by the law amendment's provisions concerning liquidation of the unions, primary cooperatives were directly affected by the law. They had to organize and hold elections to their supervisory councils within almost one month (counting the time between publication of the law and the final date set for elections). Furthermore, the law amendment cancelling all monopolies subjected cooperatives suddenly to competition, and this in addition to the highly erratic development of other important economic parameters (interest rates, input and output prices, shifting of offer and demand). The compounded effect of all these multiple and highly significant legal and economic changes put many primaries in a state of trauma. Even several primary cooperatives who managed to remain calm understandably gave first priority to keeping their organizations afloat instead of formulating and forwarding claims to union assets.
• In comparison with primary cooperatives, the employees of union enterprises were in a completely different situation. Staff received firsthand information from liquidators and had ample time to discuss among themselves the options for takeover of the enterprises they work for, and to organize themselves into worker cooperatives. In addition, staff has insider knowledge on the value of assets, and recent trends on turnover and profitability. Finally, it

is relatively easy for staff to put aside an amount equivalent to three months' salary after having just received a severance pay equal to five to eight months' salary.

• The composition of the meetings which will be convened to decide on the liquidation plans, and the manner in which these meetings will be organized and conducted, is not clearly defined. In addition to cooperative representatives, other participants, including employees, will be invited to participate. The law does not specify the voting rights of the various categories of delegates and participants. Furthermore, even if these meetings were well organized and conducted according to legitimate rules, the decision of these meetings will not be final if the liquidation plan is not adopted by the meeting as proposed by liquidators. If the plan is rejected by the meeting (the meeting cannot alter or amend the plan) it will be forwarded to the agency which appointed the liquidator, which in turn can approve it or forward it to the court for final decision. This decision cannot be challenged.

The points listed above demonstrate that the cooperative law amendment is not effective in protecting the rights and bringing to bear the legitimate claims of the ultimate owners of union assets. In addition, there are several issues related to the results and effects of this process, assuming the liquidation continues to be implemented as presently programmed.

Value of assets. The valuation of union assets is important if the option being considered is to transfer/sell these assets, or part of them, to others than the legitimate owners, or only part of the owners (for example, 30 out of 40 primaries which were members of a regional union). In such a case, the entire group of owners should receive the proceeds of the transfer/sale, and a precondition for that would be that during sales negotiations the net market value of the assets is used as main reference. Presently, liquidators list union assets at their book value. This includes fixed assets, for example, an office building located in the center of a regional capital which might have been purchased 20 years ago at a price equivalent to three billion zlotys (adjusted to present prices). The present market value, however, might be in the vicinity of 30 billion zlotys. It also includes enterprises

which again are valued according to the book value of buildings, equipment and inventories. The valuation, however, does not take into account the immaterial assets of these enterprises such as market position, that is, value of orders, number and quality of clients, reliability of suppliers, established product names, etc. The value of an enterprise is often considerably higher than the combined value of its physical assets (minus liabilities) if the immaterial assets are taken into account. In summary, the valuation of union assets by liquidators presently is done according to the book value of material assets only; therefore, in most cases transfers would be made at a value far below the real value. That means the ongoing liquidation process is not geared toward generating and maximizing revenues from the transfer of union assets. Its only concern seems to be to dismantle unions and to redistribute union assets. Furthermore, the liquidation process does not provide for compensation of legitimate owners, whose assets are being distributed.

Worker cooperatives. The law amendment obviously is based on the assumption that in the past the employees of cooperative union-controlled enterprises were underpaid, and for this reason have a claim to the union assets. The basic question arises whether any employment contract, irrespective of its terms, constitutes a basis for any property claim. Generally, this question needs to be denied. Furthermore, the assumption of underpayment cannot be and presently is not consistently applied. For example, a previous employee in the office of a cooperative union who audited the union enterprises may not become a member of a workers' cooperative (which in turn can apply for the transfer of ownership of a union enterprise) because this auditor was not part of the work staff of this enterprise. However, the union auditor might also have been underpaid and might also have contributed to the accumulation of assets in that enterprise. It is difficult to see the logic which excludes union employees from the distribution of union assets.

In summary, it is highly doubtful whether employees have any ownership claims on union property; therefore, employees should not be considered candidates for taking over (at a symbolic value) union assets. If employees were to take over cooperative union assets, Poland would be faced inter alia with the serious issue of establishing a precedent which could not be generally applied. For example, would civil servants have an additional claim over and above the claims of all citizens on state property? Would farm labor have a claim on the property of private farms? However, if workers' claims were accommodated only in selected cases this would mean favoring one group of employees and discriminating others. This would be seen as an arbitrary decision and create social inequalities.

An additional issue relates to the anticipated results of worker cooperatives eventually taking over union enterprises. In general, enterprises owned by employees have an inherent conflict of interest: the short-term objective of employees to maximize their gains from the enterprise in terms of direct remuneration and the long-term objective of an enterprise to build equity through maximizing profit and retaining part of this profit as reserves. Usually, worker-controlled enterprises give priority to the short-term objectives of employees over the long-term objectives of the owners, neglecting the fact that in such a case employees and owners are identical. As a result, employee-owned enterprises become over time undercapitalized and uncompetitive and have to exit. In summary, worker cooperatives are not a viable form of ownership and, therefore, are not a relevant option in the present cooperative restructuring.

Industry and service chains. An essential objective of the restructuring of the Polish economy is to facilitate the development of chains in industry and trade to efficiently link producers and consumers. In agriculture the food chains link many agricultural producers with the multitude of food consumers.

The dairy and horticulture cooperatives as well as the peasant self-aid cooperatives operate such chains through their network of primary cooperatives and union-owned processing and trade enterprises. In addition, the peasant self-aid cooperatives operate a parallel chain (but working in the opposite direction) linking nonfood producers with the rural consumers through union-owned wholesale and repacking enterprises and primary-owned retail shops.

Nothing is wrong with the basic structure of the chains operated by agriculture cooperatives. On the contrary, Poland's agricultural economy performed relatively well because it had coop-

eratives operating these chains in parallel to the chains operated by state farms and enterprises. However, because of the limited autonomy of cooperatives, their dependency on planning authorities, as well as their relative inefficiency and the often monopolistic privileges they had, two trends developed:

• Cooperatives established several enterprises, purchasing centers and sales outlets to build cooperative empires, not for the purpose of better serving farmers or consumers, or to respond to the requirements of industries. This trend developed especially at the level of central unions and to a lesser extent regional unions, and included enterprises and units which were totally unrelated to the business of the chains they were part of (for example, restaurants, cultural centers, vacation resorts, etc.).

• In building and expanding their chains as vertical structures, cooperatives neglected the potential to establish horizontal linkages with other cooperatives or enterprises. Each cooperative subsector aimed for economic autonomy if not autarchy, by having its independent procurement, processing and sales network, allowing little room for division of labor and economies of scales. For these reasons, cooperative subsectors tend to be overequipped in terms of units and facilities.

To correct the picture with the aim of achieving business-focused chains and efficient service structures, the nonessential elements of the chain need to be cut off to improve the performance of the remaining structure. Unfortunately, the liquidation process initiated by the cooperative law amendment of January 1990 did not aim at such a slimming process focusing on reducing chains to their essential elements, but rather aimed at cutting chains into individually operating elements, including the essential elements. However, it is doubtful that the disparate links resulting from the liquidation will ever fit together again and form functioning chains.

The destructive, rather than constructive, focus of the liquidation is evidenced by the inadequate distinction between enterprises not essential for the chains and enterprises forming essential parts of the chain. All the enterprises, irrespective of their degree of relevance for functioning chains, are listed by liquidators for transfer of ownership. Before finalizing the restructuring it is absolutely vital to assess first the chain requirements per sector and subsector with the aim to retain the essential links of each chain. Such an assessment needs to include, in addition to union enterprises, state enterprises operating in the same sector. Furthermore, it needs to take into account the quantitative overequipment in many subsectors and their qualitative underequipment. Finally, the assessment should identify where and how new players could and should enter the chains.

It has been demonstrated above that the process of liquidation of cooperative unions, and the restructuring of the ownership of the assets previously held and the enterprises previously controlled by these unions is extremely complex and inadequately designed and presently poorly implemented. It will have serious negative consequences in legal, social and economic terms, handicapping to a significant extent the institutional infrastructure servicing agricultural production and food industries, as well as the development of rural areas. Furthermore, the cooperative restructuring is in the process of creating dangerous precedents for the restructuring of other parts of the Polish industry instead of providing a positive frame of reference.

Possible solutions

The crucial issue arises of how to respond sensibly to the challenge of restructuring the cooperative movement in Poland. There are three basic options:

• To continue and finalize the ongoing restructuring as presently programmed in spite of all its inconsistencies and contradictions as well as the serious consequences it might have. The advantage of this option would be that the present confusion prevailing at the various cooperative levels would be somehow over, accepting that the consequences of the restructuring process are an unavoidable byproduct of such a process.
• To judge all the problems and issues associated with the liquidation and restructuring as sufficiently serious to justify an immediate suspension of the Cooperative Law of January 1990, and subsequently freeze the ongoing liquidation.
• To accept that the problems are substantial and significant but instead of suspending the law, interpret it in a more flexible manner, for example, by extending some of the crucial time limits provided by the law, and considerably alter and improve the process of restructuring the ownership of cooperative union assets and enterprises.

The first option does not seem to be a feasible one, because it would mean neglecting the crucial issues and risking potentially disastrous effects of the present liquidation and restructuring.

The second option, that is, suspending the Cooperative Law of January 1990 would be, at least in legal terms, the cleanest solution. It would acknowledge the fact that the group drafting the law did not have sufficient time to present a well-thought-through and consistent document, and that the Parliament had to decide on the proposed law without having had the time and information to consider its adequacy and possible effects. However, if the law were suspended, a new law would have to be quickly drafted and passed, taking into account the new situation created by the partial implementation of the January 1990 law, and would have to be precise and comprehensive in its new regulations. Such a new law could, for example, provide that all assets of central and regional unions be managed during an interim period by a newly created holding company, which would oversee these assets as trustee on behalf of primary cooperatives. The assets and enterprises would be transferred to primaries whenever they were ready to take them over. The assets cooperatives are not interested in would be sold and the net proceeds of the sales distributed among primaries.

However, the suspension of the January 1990 law and the drafting and passing (again under great time pressure) of a new and adequate law seem to be extremely difficult for political and practical reasons. For example, the Parliament is completely backlogged with law proposals for the next six months or so. The only operational solution seems to be offered by the third option, that is, interpreting the law by government decree and thus modifying the law in the areas which are contradictory, against the original intention of the law or causing damage to the national economy.

Such a decree could be based on the assumption that the Cooperative Law of January 1990 has the constructive objective of providing a framework for cooperatives to develop into genuine member and efficient business organizations. Furthermore, the decree would set realistic time limits and provide adequate manpower for preparing and implementing the restructuring, and would provide for improved supervision and coordination of the entire process. Finally, the decree would also give guidance on how to apply parts of the 1982 cooperative law that are still valid.

On the basis of this decree, a cooperative restructuring organization (CRO) should be established and regional teams should be made responsible for the restructuring of each cooperative subsector rather than continuing to rely on individual liquidators. The main objective in establishing a CRO and regional teams would be to assist the Ministry of Finance and the liquidators with liquidation and the transfer/sale of assets, as well as with the continuation of essential economic activities of the union enterprises. Whereas the CRO would have an overall supervisory and coordinating role, the functions of regional teams would include:

• inventorying and evaluating, the assets and liabilities as well as management performance and staffing of each unit under liquidation or proposed for transfer/sale and preparing financial statements for each unit;
• clearly establishing the ownership of the assets of cooperative unions. This would include identifying the share owned by each member cooperative and the preparation of a plan for the distribution of net surpluses or recovering net deficits on liquidation;
• identifying and evaluating potential candidates (organizations, including cooperatives and individuals) for taking over or purchasing union assets that are not taken over by cooperatives; developing various options for transfer/sale and assisting with implementing the options chosen; and
• supervising and supporting the management of the organizations under liquidation or proposed for transfer/sale until the restructuring process is fully completed.

The advantages of establishing and efficiently operating regional teams supported by the CRO would include:

• providing liquidators with the professional support they urgently require in several fields and, by doing so, improving considerably the

chances of optimizing the cost/benefit ratio of the restructuring; and
• strengthening the ability to continue important economic activities until such time as adequate alternative arrangements are made, thereby considerably reducing the risk of disrupting essential services and important contracts, and halting any further declines in productivity during the period of transition.

Once the principle of establishing a CRO and regional teams is agreed upon, additional elements related to their establishment, functions, operations and staffing would need to be developed. Other issues to be addressed include possible linkages between the CRO/regional teams and the cooperative service centers proposed in Appendix 4.

Appendix 6.4 Cooperative support services

ORGANIZATION

Under the amended Cooperative Law of January 1990, the cooperative unions which provided some cooperative support services at the regional and central levels are being liquidated inter alia because of the inefficiency in providing these services. At the same time, the amendment does not allow the establishment of new cooperative unions before July 1991 to avoid the risk that the old structure of unions will resurface. Presently, the multitude of primary cooperatives operating all over Poland are facing without any guidance or support the tremendous task of adjusting to the new legal and economic environment and market conditions. Such a void is clearly not desirable since it is in the interest of the national economy to make the best use of the existing institutional infrastructure in order to minimize the disruption of essential services to rural areas. Support should be provided with the aim of facilitating the adjustment of the cooperatives that have the minimum requirements (that is, members' support, financial means and management capacity) and the exit of the cooperatives that do not have these minimum requirements. However, the provision of support to cooperatives should not hinder in any way the entry of new organizations intending to compete with cooperatives.

The kind and amount of support services required by primary cooperatives will depend on their adjustment requirements and potential and will have to be determined by cooperatives themselves. However, it is estimated that the following services are required by the majority of the agricultural cooperatives:

• management advice, including advice on legal and organizational issues
• training for staff and management, and information services for members
• regular audit services and assistance in establishing internal control procedures.

While awaiting the emergence of a new cooperative structure at the secondary and tertiary level, the support services should be provided by a network of regional service organizations. To distinguish clearly the proposed organization from the previous unions, the proposed organizations could be called cooperative service centers (CSCs). Any CSC should be a light and efficient service structure with a temporary mandate, that is, CSCs would be dissolved (or possibly evolve into rural business advice centers) as the new cooperative structure becomes operational. CSCs could be established and made operational within a few weeks by recruiting core staff needed and renting offices from the unions under liquidation.

The Supreme Cooperative Council (SCC) should take the initiative of establishing, in close consultation with primaries, a network of regionally based CSCs. The number of CSCs, their activities and locations should be decided according to the type of services requested by primary cooperatives. By recruiting the best qualified and motivated employees from the previous unions, CSCs concentrating on essential services would perhaps require not more than 15 to 20% of the staff previously employed by the unions.

In principle, primary cooperatives are expected to pay for the services rendered by CSCs. In the initial phase, however, there should be a few exceptions to this principle. First, any external technical assistance made available to CSCs should not be charged to primaries. This proposal is based on the assumption that technical assistance will be available through grants. Second, initial training in basic skills introducing cooperatives to principles of market economy and member development should be provided at a nominal cost. Long-term training in specialized fields should gradually be charged at real cost. The cost of auditing services should be charged in full from the beginning. Any financial gaps of CSCs are expected to be bridged by donor assistance, revenues from enterprises previously owned by cooperative unions, and from the sale of some of the union assets.

While working with primary cooperatives, CSCs would also assist members and management in evaluating the performance of these cooperatives and assessing potential improvements to be gained by refocusing cooperative services. This evaluation and assessment would provide the basis for an eventual fundamental reorganization and rehabilitation of primary cooperatives. CSCs could also assist primary cooperatives in assessing the possibilities of permanently taking over union assets, examining related financial issues, and delineating the problems associated with the management of these assets. Finally, primary cooperatives assisted and audited by CSC would gain credibility with the local banks, thus increasing their chances of obtaining funds for immediate requirements (for example, crop purchase funds for the ongoing agricultural season) and investments. By the same token, CSCs can assist foreign donor and finance organizations in identifying needs for technical and financial assistance and investment requirements of cooperatives at the primary, and reemerging secondary and tertiary levels.

MANAGEMENT ADVICE AND SUPPORT

The single most important factor determining the success of efforts to privatizing cooperatives in Poland will be the capacity and flexibility of cooperative management to adjust to business and market requirement. The previous statutory integration of the cooperative sector into the centralized economy led to a significant diffusion of managerial skills and unfamiliarity with business practices. This lack of management knowledge and experience is part of the general behavioral and cultural effects of many years of command economy.

Commercial management of a cooperative organization is no different from the management of any other business organization. The technical and managerial skills necessary to run any successful business are equally required in cooperatives. However, cooperative management differs in its objectives and structures from management in other organizations and imposes additional responsibilities on management in serving user members and reflecting the cooperative ownership structures without compromising commercial competitiveness.

A cooperative is a business organization which operates with the purpose of providing benefits to its members. The members are the owners and at the same time the main group of clients of the cooperative. Therefore, the benefits of cooperative activities can be provided in terms of preferential conditions for business transactions between the cooperative and its members (as compared with transactions with nonmembers or users) and in terms of return on capital contributions of members. The main objective of a cooperative is to protect members interests by providing efficient services. However, cooperatives must also offer an adequate reward for capital, labor and management — sufficient to attract and retain members who then profit from business services. In an investor-driven business the main objective is maximizing the return on capital. Therefore, cooperative management working for a people-centered business has an additional set of objectives as compared with the management of capital-centered firms, which can concentrate exclusively on the profitability of the business.

The structure of cooperative representation and management consisting of a general assembly, supervisory council, elected board and appointed management, reflects the purpose and objectives of cooperative organizations. For example, cooperative board or committee members represent members not primarily as shareholders but rather as service entities. The task of cooperative management consists of achieving through business efficiencies a sustainable balance between member services and capital formation.

The challenge presently facing cooperative management in Poland is threefold:

• to transform cooperatives from public-service organizations to member service organizations;
• to realign membership with the new realities; and
• to apply business criteria in order to provide efficient services and to be able to compete with other players in the market.

To respond to the first challenge, many cooperatives have to redefine their purpose. In the case of peasant self-aid cooperatives, for example, the logical purpose seems to be to assist farmers in procuring inputs and marketing agricultural products, including primary processing. The needs expressed by the group of members of the cooperatives will finally determine the business purpose.

The realignment of membership includes the establishment of adequate economic bonds between members and their organization. To achieve this, it is essential that the capital contribution of registered members be substantial. Previous members who decide not to continue their membership will obtain repayment of the current value of their shareholding in terms of redeemable loan stock. Once the membership of a cooperative is clearly established, the management can concentrate on servicing these members by performing member-relevant business activities.

The third challenge consists of reorientating management from providing minimum services in many fields to efficient services in selected fields, as well as to change from an order-receiving (through the national planning system) to a decision-making, market-oriented behavior. In defining the business purpose and reestablishing its membership, cooperatives obtain a framework in which to operate. Cooperative activities can now be clearly defined, including the requirements for their implementation, in terms of staff, facilities and finance. On this basis, the projected profitability of the various activities can be calculated. According to these definitions and projections the existing cooperatives will need to be reorganized and restructured. These adjustments need to include considerably reducing overall staff and recruiting new staff for key posts, selling or renting out facilities unrelated to the commercial role now being set, and purchasing new equipment. However, the most substantial adjustment requirements will be establishing organizational and managerial systems that will permit cooperatives to respond efficiently to the evolution of member needs and market changes.

It will be the prime function of CSCs to assist and advise member representatives and managers in identifying the options best suited for the specific conditions cooperatives work in. In addition, CCSs should be at the disposal of cooperatives to assist and guide in the implementation of the options chosen.

TRAINING OF COOPERATIVE MANAGEMENT AND STAFF

In addition to providing advice and support to cooperatives, a second essential function of CSCs is to provide training for member representatives and fulltime managers and staff in fields where an immediate upgrading of knowledge and skills is required.

Elected representatives constituting the supervisory committee and management boards should develop through some basic training a good understanding in fields such as:

• overall legislative, commercial and sectoral conditions in which the cooperative operates and to which it must increasingly adjust;
• reconstitution of membership, including the issues of transformation of part of the cooperative reserves into member equity, and increasing member equity by additional contributions of members;
• selection of cooperative activities, including the elimination of marginal or nonbusiness activities and the inclusion of additional member-oriented activities;
• reduction of overall staff and recruitment of new managers and senior staff in key areas; and
• potential forms and degrees of vertical and horizontal cooperation with other primary cooperatives and integration into the new secondary and tertiary structure, including the possible takeover of assets previously controlled by cooperative unions.

The professional skills of fulltime managers and senior staff should be advanced in fields such as:

• design and implementation of an adequate management information system including accountancy and periodic financial statements;
• establishment of cost and profit centers;
• evaluation of employees;
• development of remuneration schemes compensating staff according to performance.

Employees require immediate training in fields such as:

• accountancy and record keeping;
• stock control;
• maintenance of facilities.

Most of the training should be conducted in the form of seminars and short-term courses. Ample training facilities previously operated by cooperative unions are available in rural areas. CSC should rent these facilities and recruit professional trainers. However, the first priority would be to provide training for trainers in fields related to the new knowledge and skills required in cooperatives, such as management, information systems and profit centers. Training of trainers requires the involvement of technical assistance.

Part of the training should be provided on the job by combining the advisory functions of CSC with the assistance provided in the implementation of options, systems, etc., adopted by cooperatives. A combined, advisory and training system operated by CSCs can provide services in the following fields:

• collect and communicate to cooperative managers relevant information and data on changes in legislation, macroeconomic trends, prize developments and marketing opportunities;
• advise managers on legal and organizational issues, assist in the development of appropriate management systems, and guide the implementation of these systems; and
• provide on-the-job training for senior staff on key issues, and organize external training opportunities.

AUDIT OF COOPERATIVES AND ACCOUNTING

Since the global economic crisis of the 1920s, it has become an international requirement and practice to audit in regular intervals the financial statements of organizations by independent and professional outsiders. The justifications for external audits include:

• determination of solvency, capital adequacy and liquidity;
• state authorities' interest in ascertaining whether economic organizations are operating in compliance with legislation, and especially whether they are calculating correctly and transfering fully the taxes due to the state or

local authorities, contributions to social security schemes, etc.

• providing (potential) creditors and investors in these organizations with an independent verification of managements' financial statements;

• application of objective and universal standards to the financial data of different organizations to facilitate interbusiness comparisons.

In many countries the audit of cooperatives is perceived to have an additional feature: the multitude of individual owners of cooperatives and their lack of experience in business activities require that the audit include not only the formal evaluation of whether financial statements reflect a true picture of the organization's transactions but also a judgement on the performance of management, including an assessment of the performance of the service mandate of cooperatives.

Until the end of 1989, the audit of cooperatives in Poland was undertaken by the cooperative unions. The cooperative law amendment of January 1990, suspended the audit requirements with the liquidation of the unions. Presently none of the agricultural cooperatives is being audited. However, the auditing requirements are greater than ever before during a time when previous systems are being dismantled, legal and economic changes occur rapidly, and new cooperatives try to adjust to these new conditions. Members, management and staff feel lost in such an unstable situation and mistrust and conflicts are developing. The audit requirements are especially evident in cooperative organizations under liquidation. Liquidators desperately need help in establishing the value of the assets and liabilities of the units under liquidation. Furthermore, regular audits at more frequent intervals than before could provide some stabilizing elements by providing objective and reliable information on the financial situation of cooperatives to all concerned: members, supervisory council, management boards, state, creditors, business partners and aid organizations. Auditors can compare the situation and performance of one cooperative with other similarly structured cooperatives, and develop average and other performance criteria with performance standards cooperatives can aim for.

Aggregates of the audited results of cooperatives would provide valuable information on trends of cooperative development in Poland and their rate of success in their restructuring efforts. Qualitative judgments provided by auditors could assist in defining training requirements of management and staff, and identifying gaps in areas where existing legislation might require modification.

A sound cooperative development requires, as soon as possible, establishment of an efficient audit service and the implementation of regular audits in every cooperative organization. While the need for efficient audit arrangements is obvious, opinions vary on the extent of cooperative audits (including the frequency) needed and the kind of organizations which should perform the audits. In the short run, however, the extent and the frequency of audits will be determined by the limited availability of competent auditors. Many of the auditors previously employed by cooperative unions work for other organizations or changed professions. Commercially operated auditing companies are extremely costly and in short supply, and some are of doubtful quality. For the coming years, even minimum audit standards in terms of coverage and frequency will be difficult to achieve for all the cooperatives operating in Poland. Minimum requirements will have to be further lowered and external audits in many cases will have to rely heavily on internal auditors.

The immediate audit requirements should be met by the proposed CSCs. In the medium term, however, the quality of cooperative audits should become increasingly closer to international standards and should be performed by the new cooperative structure. Considerable efforts should be made as soon as possible to attain these standards, for audits are not only a formal requirement but were established in response to business requirements, and therefore are of vital interest for cooperative members and management, and would contribute to the gradual integration of the Polish economy into the international economy.

Appendix 6.5 The need for new cooperative legislation

The Cooperative Law of September 16, 1982 and its subsequent amendments is not substantially different from the previous law. This is the legal framework within which cooperatives were formed and developed in Poland. It was conceived, passed and implemented in a fundamentally different political and economic system. With the introduction of the system of market economy, cooperatives will have to operate in a competitive environment. Existing legislation has become inadequate or inconsistent with the requirements of the new economic order. There are numerous questions such as the ownership of cooperative assets which have to be answered before cooperatives can be restructured to effectively compete in a market economy. The fundamental character and the basic principles under which they operate have to be completely changed. Unless new cooperative legislation is prepared in an appropriate manner, cooperatives cannot adjust to the new economic environment.

The purpose of this appendix is to identify the weaknesses of the present legislation and point out what has to be changed or avoided. It further proposes the essential elements which have to be incorporated in new legislation. It then proposes the procedure which should be used in preparing proposed legislation for it to receive the benefit of local consultation and international experience.

COOPERATIVE AS A USER-OWNED BUSINESS ORGANIZATION

Existing legislation does not regard the cooperatives as business enterprises. Rather, cooperatives are regarded as public service institutions that have a social purpose. Cooperatives have carried out social activities without regard to economic considerations and have been unable to respond to market signals. The word business does not even exist in the present law.

The new law should require that cooperatives be established and operated as business enterprises with the aim of efficiently serving members' economic needs. Their continued existence would be based solely on their success as user-owned businesses.

OWNERSHIP OF COOPERATIVES

The question of cooperative ownership manifests the most glaring defect of existing legislation. The cooperative law amendment of 1990 which liquidated cooperative unions created a situation where thousands of cooperative enterprises are without owners. In Western countries, this law would be regarded as a violation or infringement of the constitutional right to private ownership and the law itself would be declared illegal. The fact that such a law could be passed magnifies the defect of the existing legislative framework.

Existing legislation entertains the concept that employees have proprietary rights to cooperatives; that worker councils could take control of management. The law also allows political parties to become members of cooperatives.

The new law should observe the principle that only the members own the cooperative; that the cooperative operates for the benefit of the members. It should also recognize that the success of a cooperative would depend on a certain level of homogeneity of membership who have a common purpose in forming and operating a cooperative. Members and employees in most types of cooperatives cannot mix as owners as there would be a clear conflict of interest. The only case where employees can become members is in the case of producer cooperatives where all members are employees. Political parties should be banned from any involvement in cooperative enterprises.

CONTROL OF COOPERATIVES

While the existing law states that cooperatives are voluntary and self-governing associations, the law also opened the possibility for state intervention. The law states that cooperatives shall conduct economic activities in accordance with central and territorial socioeconomic plans. Furthermore, the law provides authority for the state to assign tasks to cooperatives. In reality, cooperatives were controlled by the state. Cooperatives until lately were required to join a cooperative union and contribute a significant portion of their earnings to a development fund.

The new law should categorically state that cooperatives are private enterprises and should be completely independent of the state. There should be no state intervention except for regulations concerning their legal status. The principle of democratic control at the primary level should be preserved. The manner of member representation in governing bodies should be made more in line with Western concepts.

Qualifications for membership on the board of directors should be specified. At the secondary level, capital voting should be allowed.

ROLE OF CAPITAL

The present law avoids the use of the word capital. The law does not recognized that capital is the basis for any business enterprise. In the registration of a cooperative by the courts, the requirement is only the intention of members to contribute at least a share to the cooperative rather than actually paid-up shares. While the law provides a limited return to members' shares (dividends may not exceed by more than 50% the highest rate of interest on personal fixed-term deposits), in practice this was not done. As a result, members' equity contributions became insignificant and in most cases were a fraction of a percent of total assets. Assets of cooperatives were accumulated as reserves, resulting in a situation where cooperatives owned themselves. This may have been a ploy of the previous regime to discourage private ownership.

It must be made explicit in the new law that members are to provide sufficient capital as a requirement of registration. Cooperatives should issue not only paid-up shares but also subscribed shares. Subscribed shares would allow the cooperative to call on the members for additional capital if and when the need arises. Unpaid portions of subscribed shares would also answer for the liabilities of the cooperative.

Members should be given a remunerative return to their capital investment. However, it is proposed that the principle of limited returns to capital be retained as a traditional feature of cooperatives. The principle that the value of shares should not change should also be retained. If the purpose of organizing a business venture is solely for the purpose of generating a return to capital, it is proposed that the organization be registered as a share company.

PROFIT SHARING BASED ON PATRONAGE

According to the existing law, cooperative profits or balance surpluses are divided as follows: state taxes, resource fund, investment fund, development fund and various social purposes. It is not explicit in the law that a portion of profits should be distributed to members in accordance with the extent of their patronage.

Whatever unallocated profits were accumulated as reserves resulted in a situation where the initial share contributions of members became a fraction of a percent of total assets. This situation has now raised the issue of ownership of cooperative assets.

The traditional cooperative concept of distribution of profits in accordance with the extent of member patronage does not exist in the present law. The essence of a cooperative is to provide goods and services to members at the best price. However, cooperatives cannot and should not engage in cutthroat competition. Cooperatives will therefore have to operate at prevailing prices. The concept calls for a division of profits at the end of the year in accordance with the extent of patronage of each member. This sharing of profits by members is usually called patronage refund in Western countries and in many instances cooperative laws in those countries specify a minimum percentage of profits to be distributed to members in this form. It is also common practice that the patronage refund is reinvested in the cooperative to increase capitalization. This cooperative concept should be made an essential element of the new law.

COOPERATIVE STRUCTURE

The existing legislation does not distinguish between primary and secondary cooperatives. It also does not distinguish between business and nonbusiness cooperatives. Cooperative unions were therefore engaged in both nonbusiness activities such as support services, and business activities such as economic enterprises operated in support of primary cooperatives. When the unions were abolished for political reasons, the economic enterprises were likewise affected. This would not have happened if there were separate nonbusiness and business structures.

Cooperatives should also be free to form central unions as they see fit. It is proposed in the new law that cooperative unions be registered as nonbusiness cooperative institutions which would represent member cooperatives and provide for support services. Secondary enterprises should be registered as business cooperative institutions which can take a form similar to share companies. Capital voting at this level should be allowed.

TRANSFORMATION OF COOPERATIVES

There are no provisions for cooperatives concerning the transformation into share companies. Provisions in the new law should provide for primary cooperatives to transform into share companies, for primary cooperatives to form share companies, and for secondary enterprises to transform into share companies and divide, merge and/or enter into joint-venture arrangements.

COOPERATIVE REGULATIONS

The present provision of law provides for self-regulation of the cooperative system. The highest body is the Supreme Cooperative Council. However, the cooperative law amendment of 1990 has abolished everything between the primary cooperatives and the Supreme Cooperative Council (SCC). Furthermore, SCC has been weakened as it lost its source of funds with the dissolution of the unions. At the present time, primary cooperatives are unregulated. For instance, there is an absence of auditing of accounts. It is therefore necessary that the regulatory structure be rebuilt. Consideration should be given to having a governmental office perform specific regulatory functions concerning the legal aspects of cooperatives. The powers of the Supreme Cooperative Council should be clearly spelled out.

FORMULATION OF THE NEW COOPERATIVE LEGISLATION

It is proposed that a formal body be constituted to formulate the proposed legislation. Members of this body should come from various sectors of the cooperative system, government and other concerned parties. It is also proposed that the international community be called upon to assist in the preparation of the legislative proposal to learn from successful experiences in other countries. An international conference for this purpose could be organized.

In terms of form, it is proposed that the new law which will replace the Cooperative Law of 1982 be limited to the fundamental concepts and essential elements needed for the restructuring and development of the entire cooperative system. Less important provisions should be relegated to a body of the state to avoid lengthy legislation that may take too much time in preparation and consideration by Parliament. This body would be required to consult SCC. Such provisions could be issued in the form of government decrees which should have the force and effect of law but should have the flexibility of being modified from time to time. SCC should develop its own internal regulations to supplement such provisions.

In the meantime, studies and discussions necessary for the preparation of a comprehensive legislative proposal should be started. It should be recognized that the process of formulating and passing a new law will take time. Corrective amendments to the present law should be resorted to in the meantime.

Endnotes

This annex was prepared by Lorenz Pohlmeier, assisted by Tadeusz Kowalak, Orlando Sacay and Anna Tuz, with support from Tadeusz Borek.

1. In Western countries, cooperatives usually pay an initial price for agricultural products after the harvest. At the end of the financial year, when the amount of profit is known and the final price can be calculated, the difference between the initial and final price is paid in terms of patronage payment.

Annex 7

Structural reform of state farms

Current structure of state farms

State farms are an important element of Polish agriculture. They were formed by the nationalization of lands belonging to large estates, or by absorption of land taken over by the National Land Fund, and as such are very much associated with the previous economic order. They utilize about 18% of the arable land, although the percentage varies greatly between regions — higher in the west and north (40%) and lower in the central and southern regions (10-15%).

State farms are generally very large (5,000 ha to 6,000 ha is not uncommon) and tend to be horizontally integrated in groups of several large farm parcels, as well as vertically (*kombinats* with feed mills, seed farms, poultry processing, livestock fattening, and so forth). They produce a significant proportion of marketed product and exports. They have benefited from privileges and subsidies, and are in general less efficient than private farms. They possess substantial, and in many cases excess, assets in buildings and equipment.

LAND AND REGIONAL PATTERNS

Currently, 1,271 state farm groups cultivate 3.3 million ha, 18% of the arable land, and graze an additional 1 million ha. The farms produce some 19% of farm output and market, in crops such as wheat, over 50% of off-farm sales.

The number of state farms in 1970 was just over 5,300. Most of these state farms have many production enterprises as well as services like repair shops, grain storage, livestock, food processing, etc. In addition, many state farms are divided into small production parcels, from 100 ha to 400 ha, often located from 5-30 km from central administrative headquarters.

The administrative structure on state farms has been consolidated (Table 7.1), with groupings of parcels and enterprises under a single administrative umbrella. During the past 15 years, some 25% of these state farm holdings have been grouped into *agrokombinat* administrative units. A more realistic estimate of state farm parcels and enterprises, if they were divided into cost and profit centers, is probably on the order of some 10,000 units — 5,000 farm parcels and some 5,000 processing, repair, storage and fattening enterprises. The dispersed and divided structure prevalent in 1970 is be-

Table 7.1 Number of state farms, area and size

Year	Number (ha)	Average size ('000)	Area cultivated
1960	5,734	423	2,425
1970	5,374	535	2,895
1980	3,698	837	3,095
1985	1,258	2,886	3,531
1988	1,226	2,872	3,521
1989	1,271	2,768	3,507

Source: Ministry of Agriculture and Food Economy.

Table 7.2 Production on state farms as percentage of total Polish farm output
(Zl billion in fixed prices)

Year	Total	State farms	%
1985	2,732	519	19%
1987	2,812	548	19%
1988	2,848	542	19%

Source: Ministry of Agriculture and Food Economy.

Table 7.4 State farm profits and losses and Treasury subsidies
(Zl milliard)

Year	Profit and losses	Subsidies	Net transfer
1980/81	(21.9)	26.8	(48.7)
1981/82	28.1	27.1	1.0
1985/86	53.8	80.6	(26.8)
1987/88	220.6	140.7	79.9
1988/89	2381.3	410.1	1,971.2

Source: Ministry of Agriculture and Food Economy and Ministry of Finance.

ginning to reemerge spontaneously as the *kombinat* grouping of state farms is split into smaller administrative units.

While the land in state farms accounts for 18% of arable farmland in Poland, these farms account for more than 40% of arable area in 14 voidvodships, mainly in northern and western Poland, producing primarily grains and some livestock products.   The distribution of state farm holdings is shown in Table 7.3.

The 1,000 ha Kalisz state farm near Poznan is an example of an agribusiness type of the state farm structure in western Poland.   Its operations comprise the following parcels and enterprises:

* onion production and packing for export (1,000 m tons annually to France, Germany, and England);
  * dairy unit (200 ha) milking 200 cows;
  * pig fattening unit of 2,000 animals;
  * cereal production on 300 ha;
  * vodka plant;
  * tractor and equipment repair unit; and
  * worker housing and day care center.

Table 7.3 State farm holdings by size in 1988

less than	
100 ha	7.2%
100-199	5.2%
200-399	10.9%
400-599	7.8%
600-799	5.5%
800-999	3.4%
over 1,000	60.0%

Source: GUS.

CONTRIBUTION TO THE AGRICULTURAL ECONOMY

State farms are active in export development, accounting for an estimated 28% of Poland's US$1.2 billion in farm exports.   State farms are especially important with shipments to other countries in Eastern Europe, accounting for nearly half of the US$240 million shipped to CMEA countries in 1988.

Only limited data on the current and potential financial viability of the state farms was available.   The Polish Bank for Food Economy estimates that perhaps 40% of state farms are experiencing financial difficulty, though this was disputed by Ministry of Agriculture analysts.   Until the new economic reforms of 1989 and

Table 7.5 State farm contribution to agricultural output by crop and livestock

Wheat	25%
Rye	10%
Barley	25%
Buckwheat and millet	18%
Maize Corn	39%
Sugar Beet	14%
Rapeseed	60%
Vegetables	7%
Potatoes	7%
Orchards	10%
Berries	4%
Greenhouses	4%
Livestock	(No)
Cattle	21%
Pigs	33%
Sheep	42%
Horses	2%
Poultry	9%
Milk	14%

Source: GUS, 1988.

1990, state farms did not have to be profitable and could cross-subsidize loss-making farm operations and enterprises.

Direct transfers from the state budget to the state farms are running at about US$50 million. A fair portion of these financial transfers are being given to loss-making farms. These transfers do not account for the imputed rental value of farmland, interest on loans, and so forth. Even at US$10 per ha annually, land rental receipts by Treasury would amount to US$33 million.

Thus, direct and indirect state subsidies are likely to be approaching US$100 million annually, a figure which some in Poland consider conservative. For example, state farms have normally had preferential access to new farm tractors and equipment, usually at lower capital costs than the private sector. In addition, the state farm sector does not properly account for depreciation. State farm administrators are thus selling these tractors after 2 to 3 years use to the private sector at a handsome capital gain.

The high profits in 1989 may have been caused by inventory gain in grain and cattle sales with the extensive inflation pressures occurring in that year.

LABOR AND MANAGEMENT ISSUES

Wages and other payments. State farms account for 27% of rural employment and 36% of farm employment in the country. Wage rates on state farms are similar to wages paid in industry, with small differentials between labor, mechanical, and machine operators. State farm workers also receive free garden plots (100 sq meters), and often get a free milk allowance, potatoes, and occasionally meat. Managers receive about 10% more than the average paid to workers, a differential that provides little incentive to management.

Housing. Key to recruiting workers on state farms is the provision of adequate housing. In an economy with severe housing shortages, availability of on-farm housing was crucial. Nearly 200,000 housing units, mostly apartments averaging two to three rooms, are currently provided essentially free for state farm workers and managers.

Restructuring state farm operations will require carefully accounting for the value to on-farm workers of this housing. Workers and

Table 7.6 The structure of the state farm workforce in 1988

Category	No.
Total	473,000
Workers	375,000
Management	9,000
Technical	39,000
Finance	26,000
Administration	24,000

Note: The estimate above for administrative workers on state farms may be much lower than actual cases. Some economists estimate that up to 33% of the state farm labor force is administrative.
Source: Ministry of Agriculture and GUS.

administrators will need to eventually pay market rents for the value of this housing. In the meantime, it may be most difficult to separate such workers from this housing tied to state farms.

Reduction in labor force. In visits to state farms and in discussions with specialists in labor management, it appears that a reduction of 20-30% in the state farm labor force over the next five to seven years will be necessary. Most farms have at least 50 excess workers. In what sectors and where this work force will be deployed and the question of their current housing are critical issues facing the Polish government.

Worker attitudes toward state farm employment. Several studies of worker attitudes toward state farm employment have been undertaken in recent years. Dr. Elzbieta Piotzowaska, sociologist at the Institute of Sociology in Lodz, writes that worker attitudes vary, from indifference to the land, to passivity toward work with a preference for segmented tasks. Workers on these farms have major concerns about losing their jobs and particularly their housing and public employee status, with the associated public benefits. Their principal attitude toward employment on the state farm is "determined by salary and especially the social benefits of housing, collective holidays, day care for children and bonuses."

CURRENT EFFICIENCY OF STATE FARMING SECTOR

While accounting for nearly 20% of agricultural GDP, state farms received an estimated 40% of capital investment and annual operating allocations over the past two decades. This resulted in substantial capitalization of these farms, particularly in worker housing, workshops, livestock housing and especially farm machinery. "Per hectare inputs of capital goods on state farms are twice as high as the average for Polish agriculture..." (RGZ, 1987)

State farms also are involved with some value-added activities, particularly feed milling, tractor and machinery repair, some vegetable processing, vodka making, starch production, and so forth. State farms sell and purchase from local private farmers and often are important economic nodes in their areas.

Cash flow analysis, profit and loss accounting, and balance sheet auditing on state farms basically do not exist. Financial controls are reporting and inventory management systems. State farm managers are judged on production and yield performance, not on profitability.

In 1988, yields on state farms in basic grains and potatoes were estimated at some 15-20% greater than the private farming sector. Private farmer yields in Poland are low, primarily due to lack of inputs. Input use is substantially higher in the state farm sector (with 18% of the cultivated area, they use 45% of the fertilizer). Yet even on state farms yields are not high, reflecting inefficient use of these scarce input resources.

Tractor usage on state farms per 100 ha is about the same as on private farms (6.4 tractors per 100 ha compared with 6.5 tractors per 100 ha on private farms). State farms have some 170,000 tractors (16% of the national tractor stock of 1.1 million), with the private sector owning 932,000 units.

Legal clarification of land leasing and ownership

Clarification of the land-leasing and ownership issue is particularly critical in the forthcoming state farm restructuring and privatization effort. With some 3 million ha cultivated, the arable land involved is worth roughly US$600 million, at US$200 per ha. If the state farms paid rent to the state for the use of this land, at a low annual rate of 5% of estimated value, the state Treasury would gain some US$30 million per year.

Currently, all land is owned as social property by the state. Before any discussion of ownership of assets and new forms of management and shareholding can take place, decisions on the recasting of the legal status of state land-holding needs to occur.

This top down legal restructuring of state farms (legal, institutional, and fiscal) is necessary as the rural private sector is fiscally unable to spontaneously alter the ownership pattern of the state farm sector. The legal structure must be clarified, following the options of land use, leasing, and ownership; and management of existing assets and, perhaps in some cases, assets divested to local, national, and possibly external firms and owners. Natural evolution would be too slow to permit state farms to restructure themselves without some top down change in the land leasing and land ownership question.

Since it will take considerable time to develop a program for the orderly freehold sale of the state farm land base, an interim option would be for the government, in reasserting its ownership over state farm assets, to specify that all state-managed farmland be placed on a leasehold basis and managed by a new state landholding agency and that economic rents (payable to the Ministry of Finance) be instituted.

This option has the benefit of delinking the land base from the enterprise operation, making it easier for the divestiture of state-managed farmland via medium-term leasing to private farmers, joint ventures, and remaining privatized state farm agribusiness units.

Farmers in Poland have expressed interest in leasing and buying land in some regions from local state farms. Until the legal issues are sorted out, the option of leasing this land (under an auction or bidding for a medium term lease) should be made available. Parcels in economic blocks with road or vehicle access could be made available and the lease payments set by an open auction or by written sealed bids.

This lease/purchase option is also available for the equipment and perhaps some of the building assets of the state farm. Tractor and equipment pools, together with the repair facilities, could be leased at market rents to a person or group of persons keen to run a farm equipment repair and contract hire business.

State farm restructuring

Should the state farm system be privatized and then dismantled? An unplanned, sudden break-up of state farms would be difficult, but for the medium and longer term, privatization and restructuring is essential.

The reasons for a carefully managed approach to state farm privatization and restructuring are the following:

• Private farmer and purchase/leasing. Private farmers are interested in enlarging their farms (purchase or leasehold), but only if the land they acquire is connected or not too far from their present land. Neighbors of state farms (most notably those who lost land to them during the nationalization process) are those most interested in getting land from the state farms.

• Employment. State farms provide a significant portion of rural employment (nearly 500,000 jobs), and there is clear recognition that suddenly breaking them up would create additional short term unemployment.

• Agri-service centers. State farms sell and purchase from private farmers, and are very important economic actors in their areas. In some areas, such as cattle assembly for export, this linkage to the private sector is growing rapidly.

In addition, the buildings and equipment of the state farms were conceived for the needs of these large operations and could not easily (if at all) be used by private farmers. Any break-up of state farms would make this equipment partially or totally redundant (unless leased at great cost for the economy) and would also entail investment costs to equip or reequip the farmers who would take over the land.

Because state farms are so large compared with the size of the individual farms (current Polish law limits the size of any private farming to 100 ha), it would not be possible in most cases to sell or lease all the state farm land immediately to those farmers who already farm in the neighborhood.

Nor does it seem reasonable to expect that a substantial number of state farm employees have the will or are capable of becoming efficient self-managing farmers in the short term. (See: *Worker attitudes toward state farm employment*, above.)

Reconstituting the former large estates does not seem a very desirable option either. Breaking up the state farms would cause a migration of population to other areas, at the same time causing additional unemployment in the receiving areas. It would at any rate result in a major

disruption in the subsector, and thus substantial needs for transfer of resources. This is not possible now, since agriculture must be an important engine of economic development and cannot count on any significant transfer of resources from the other sectors. It seems thus that prudence dictates caution regarding any decision about the sudden physical breaking up of the state farms.

Leasing state farmland may be a preferable short-term option, ensuring the land would remain public property until a broader land market develops and this land can be sold or leased on a long-term basis.

The question of what to do with the state farms therefore becomes the following: how can the state farm sector become more efficient in the short term, and how can a land market (including the rental market) be developed in the medium term, allowing the more efficient private farmers to purchase or lease land from the state farms, subject to such limits of size of ownership as will be decided for social reasons?

BASIC ISSUES

The general privatization law for Poland was passed in late July, 1990. However, it excluded the state farm system from its provisions. Additional legislation will be required for the privatization and restructuring of the state farm system. New laws, regulations, and policies will need to take into account the following principles:

Financial controls. No privilege should be given to the state farms that is not enjoyed by the private farming sector. This means that preferential access to inputs, equipment, credits, markets, and the like should be rescinded. Controls are also needed to ensure that interfinancial transfers between state farms are put on a sound accounting basis and that such loans and cross-transfers are not used to circumvent normal operating losses and to avoid worker layoffs. Controls also are needed to ensure against losses from asset stripping during the privatization and restructuring process.

To ensure that the state farms become economic entities competing more equally with the private sector, the financial and administrative links with the state should be severed, so that the financial consequences of mismanagement do not become government responsibilities.

State farms must be allowed to go bankrupt if mismanaged, while safeguarding the integrity of public ownership. These farms should then be divested by sale or lease or allotted by government to a management team for reorganization.

Regional differentiation of state farm privatization. There are seven major agro-ecological zones in Poland that have been identified and mapped. State farm divestiture criteria needs to be adjusted to recognize the regional differences in agro-ecological potential. In addition, the land market for divesting portions or all of state farmland differs greatly, with demand higher in the south and central regions and lower in the west and north.

Profit centers. The notion of a financially autonomous profit and cost center should be introduced, and cross-subsidizations among different units should be actively discouraged since it generally reduces the overall financial efficiency. An accounting system should be introduced to accurately reflect the profitability of the units.

Worker housing. A policy decision is needed to establish a clear separation — a delinking — of the state farm housing and the land on which it stands from the commercial operations of the farm enterprise. Housing for state farm workers, in an economy short of housing, has been an incentive for recruiting and retaining workers in rural and in some remote areas. With the shortage of housing in urban areas, demand will continue to be high in the short and medium term for this housing. In a restructuring program, state farm housing will need to be legally separated, delinked, from the new commercial entity and set up as a separately owned housing cooperative financially independent of the farm enterprise.

Land ownership and leasing. As disposal of the state farmland is likely to be a difficult legal and political issue, state farmland should be separated from the farm enterprise by the government into a new state landholding agency and then leased on terms determined on a case-by-case basis. Rentals would then be paid to Treasury.

Establishment of a state farm agribusiness restructuring group. This task force, similar in concept to the industrial restructuring task force, needs to do an immediate analysis of current book values of state farms, undertaking an immediate inventory of all assets including land, buildings, livestock, equipment, and crops.

This inventory analysis is critical to (1) prevent unauthorized disposal of state property; and (2) determine what assets, especially excess equipment and uneconomic crop and livestock inventory, can be auctioned off and at what values reserve prices should be established. Currently, accounting on state farms is designed only for reporting and inventory control purposes, not for determining profitability. Establishing systems for developing appropriate profit and loss statements and balance sheets for state farms and their individual related on-farm enterprises is crucial.

Finally, there needs to be guidance documentation prepared by the state farm agribusiness restructuring group for individual state farm managers to set the rules during the longer-term period of major organizational and ownership change within the state farm system.

RESTRUCTURING OPTIONS

Three scenarios are apparent for restructuring and privatization of the state farm system:

Laissez-faire (continuation of spontaneous division). In late 1990, a number of state farms per month are spontaneously dividing into smaller managed parcels and independent enterprises. Farms made up of separate land parcels are splitting off under independent management. Enterprises on state farms such as feed mills, poultry processing, and livestock fattening units are also organizing into separately managed units. This is occurring without guidance or approval from the Ministry of Agriculture and Food Economy if the local voivodship and the farm workers' council agree to a split. Only if there is no agreement does a state farm division question get referred the Ministry of Agriculture and Economy in Warsaw for a decision.

Laissez-faire division of state farms and enterprises into separate management units has the benefit of obtaining separate accounting entities that contract with other units (farm machinery and repair, for example) for services. This makes it easier to identify those units that are profitable or potentially profitable.

On the negative side, it is unclear whether the division is taking place with any sort of rational business planning as to efficiency of scale in parcel size or and the viability of basic services or processing units. This division is taking place without financial restructuring. Also, no land rent is being paid to the state.

Contract management. Until the longer-term structure and ownership is settled, there is an option of contract management of state farms. This has the benefits of tighter management controls, of establishing viability of accounts and inventory, and of tighter worker supervision.

However, the contract management option lacks the benefit of incentive management. The contractors, receiving a small percent of the overall gross, may lack serious incentives to ensure improved profits in the short and medium term. It would also be questionable whether internal management teams would be available, and, if the government were to reach outside Poland, whether enough quality management teams would be available and whether this option could in fact be achieved for all the state farms. In a few specific cases, such as those state farms that need to be managed in an interim manner pending policy decisions on longer-term management, there might be a limited role for contract management services, particularly by EC younger farm managers experienced in similar size operations. Such operations could serve as useful models to demonstrate modern agribusiness management techniques.

State farm restructuring and privatization. Phased privatization and restructuring is a third option. As mentioned, this requires state reassertion of legal ownership into state farm(s) state holding group or groups and creation of joint-stock ownership for state farms. This redefinition would then enable the state to legally privatize the state farm system.

A sudden privatization and full divestiture of all 1,300 state farms' assets to the primarily local private sector farm owners may be difficult to arrange in the short term. Funds are unlikely to be available for complete privatization at reasonable market values, especially with credit unavailable or at very high real rates. Full sale might also result in a decline of food output in grains as new owners would need

several years of transition.

Nonetheless, a number of state farms meeting the following criteria should be immediately restructured into contract management, leased, or placed into conservation and forest reserve status. This includes state farms that:

• are not meeting their 25% tax payments to the Treasury; or
• are in areas of extensive private landholding whose owners are keen to expand their landholdings and would be able to lease or purchase state farm landholdings. This is especially the case for those smaller and disbursed state farms in central and southern Poland.

In addition, in the next several years, leasing of land to local private farmers and sale or leasing of excess machinery by some form of auction with reserve pricing should be encouraged, especially for state farms in areas of:

• high numbers of private farms wishing to expand their landholdings with leasing or purchase of portions of or entire smaller state farms;
• state farms with dispersed and parcelized holdings that are logistically uneconomic to farm;
• state farms whose cropping pattern and comparative efficiency cannot compete with private farms, such as in horticulture; and
• excess equipment on state farms. Many state farms have accumulated excess stocks of farm equipment. Managers are hoarding this equipment as a source of spare parts and backup as major repairs are difficult to get done in a timely manner. Even with a modest excess inventory, spare capacity exists. A detailed inventory farm by farm, with auction sales to other farms (with reserve prices specified), would ensure a more rational and efficient pattern of utilization of farm equipment.

Phasing: what needs to be done

Changing the land use and ownership system will take time. Because of this, and also because one needs to insulate government from the risks of production, a phased approach along the following lines might be considered:

• Separate worker housing, its land, and other social benefits from the commercial farming enterprise.

• Reassert Treasury joint-stock ownership over the fixed assets (buildings, processing equipment, offices, repair facilities, storage, and so forth) as well as moveable assets (such as farm equipment). These enterprises and assets would then be restructured and offered for lease or sale to the private sector. Land underpinning these assets would be leased at market rents.

Appropriate legislation should be enacted (if need be) to authorize the creation of private corporations with the objective of managing state assets (Ref: Société fermière in France). Those companies should have full legal personality and be properly capitalized. They should also be authorized to purchase land.

The above mentioned corporations would compete through bidding for the management of all or part of the state farms. They would take responsibility for all the assets not belonging to the agency, would ensure maintenance of the land, and would be entitled to all the profit of the exploitation after payment of the fee to the agency and all taxes.

• Separate farmland from the farming enterprise and place it into a new state landholding agency that would be empowered to lease this land to the restructured farm enterprise, to the private sector, or to joint ventures. Public ownership of state farmland should be formally disconnected from its management. The state landholding agency should make sure that land is maintained in good agricultural condition; when appropriate legislation is passed, the agency will be empowered to sell it.

One major problem to resolve as soon as possible is the confusion created in the mind of the public regarding who owns what. There is clear indication that workers and managers of state farms tend to believe (or want to believe) that under the previous laws, they acquired legal rights of ownership to the assets they managed. This confusion applies to the state farms, but also to the cooperatives and to their industries. It is of utmost importance to clarify this point as early as possible, for it not only affects the present problem of transfer of ownership, but might very well deter future investors if it appears that an employment contract generates rights to the assets of the enterprise.

Clear declaration of intent and appropriate legislation is necessary to clarify that an employment contract does not create any property right to the assets of the entity in which the employee works. This does not preclude the granting bonuses in the form of shares to employees if the company so decides. Neither would it preclude granting a minority shareholding to the workers of those companies or entities being privatized, if such an action were deemed essential for political reasons. But this must be defined as a gratuity, not as a right.

Not all state farms will attract experienced managers, and thus it will be necessary to implement interim measures to ensure efficient management until appropriate divestiture of the assets occurs. Since it is essential to reaffirm the property rights of the state over those units, it would be essential to rescind the 1983 self-management rules, and reestablish the responsibility of the authorities for overseeing management, with a clear mandate to find private managers, and a deadline after which mandatory sale of the land will take place. It is essential that the transitory nature of those measures be clearly affirmed and strictly enforced.

Future of state farms

In the short term (1990 and early 1991), the rural policy questions are those of employment stability in rural areas, maintenance of production for domestic and export markets, and the development, in the short term, of the legal and financial framework for transferring land ownership and management from the state farm sector to different forms of private management and ownership. Immediate policy steps are required as follows:

• Tightened financial controls. The government should not provide any preferential financial or input provisions to state farms that are not also provided to private farms on similar terms.

• Accounting systems to replace current reporting and inventory control mechanisms. It is critical to undertake an inventory of assets on each state farm. These accounting systems are needed to develop financial criteria to assess: profitable state farms; potentially profitable state farms; and bankrupt state farms, especially those unlikely to become profitable in the medium term.

• Identification of nonprofitable state farms. Listing the state farms that are effectively in bankruptcy through nonpayment of legally owed taxes to the Treasury is essential. These farms need to have priority identification and asset valuation, and then be given priority for apartment delinking and sales, building and land leasing where possible, and, most importantly, equipment auctions with reserve pricing. They cannot, in fiscally austere times, continue to be a drain on the state Treasury.

• Establishment of a state farm agribusiness restructuring group. This is critical to prevent unauthorized disposal of state property (asset stripping) and determine what assets, especially excess equipment and uneconomic crop and livestock inventory, can be auctioned off, and at what values reserve prices should be established. There needs to be guidance documentation prepared by this restructuring group for individual state farm managers to set the rules during this upcoming period of major organizational and ownership change within the state farm system.

• Worker housing separated — delinked — from the question of state farm ownership. An important consideration on state farms is the eventual ownership and management of worker housing. Housing standards in rural Poland, both in private and public sectors, are relatively high. Apartments on state farms for the most part are well constructed. Rents and utility costs are minimal.

With a severe housing shortage in Poland limiting worker mobility, state farm workers are likely to be most reluctant to give up their on-farm housing. However, privatization of state farm housing is an option, with sale by the state with lease/purchase options available.

• The land issue. Clarification of the legal status of the leasing statutes is imperative (for example, the right to lease land in perpetuity — the usufruct rights inherent in leasing). Some joint ventures are proceeding with a form of usufruct in constructing joint ventures with external and internal firms, but further legal clarification is needed as to the rights of the lessor.

• Treasury joint-stock ownership. Once basic and realistic book values of state farms are determined, the state ownership in those farm assets would need to be reregistered in Treasury-held joint stock shares. Only in this legal structure can future restructuring occur.

In this process, state farms (enterprises) would have to apply to the office of privatization in the Treasury for permission to register as a joint stock company. This board would then appoint new management, introduce normal commercial codes in transacting business, and prepare regular operating statements and balance sheets under generally accepted international accounting standards.

MEDIUM-TERM STATE FARM RESTRUCTURING

In the medium term (1991-1995), restructuring of the management and ownership of state farms will be done in the context of the wider policy of public sector asset management reform and privatization strategies. The need for developing both a market economy and a functioning capital market, as well as the resolution of the transferability of property rights, will be crucial in the medium term and will shape the rate and structure of privatization of the state farm sector.

Joint ventures. If the short term legalization measures outlined above take place, then joint ventures between state farms, private Polish farmers, and external investors will be markedly easier. Efforts to establish joint ventures during the medium term should be fostered to introduce modern management, accounting and agronomic standards.

Management restructuring. Regardless of the longer-term structural form of the state farms, a strong and consistent introduction of management and accounting reforms on state farms is necessary. Once the joint-stock ownership is settled, it is imperative that an individual state farm board of directors be appointed, with state farm workers not to exceed 20%. The new board should develop criteria for restructuring management, appoint new management where necessary, and develop separate and accountable profit and cost centers (financially independent units) for all identifiable enterprises and farm parcels on the state farm.

Linkages and contracts with external agribusiness management training institutes is critical. Adequate funding for these linkages appears to be offered from currently available external aid packages.

Asset and inventory valuation. Valuation of each state farm operation should be completed no later than the end of 1991, guided by the recommended state farm agribusiness restructuring group.

Liquidation. Bankrupt state farms should be placed at auction, with moveable assets sold and fixed assets leased or sold, especially worker and management housing. Land for which there is no private market and which cannot be worked should be placed in protected crops or, if continued production is not feasible, should be placed in pasture or forestry reserves. The national land fund would be restructured to enable such land to be managed to avoid soil erosion.

LONGER-TERM STATE FARM RESTRUCTURING

In the longer term (1995 and forward) and from the perspective of economic efficiency, the preferable option would be to permit individual, exclusive, and freely transferable property rights, with capital markets and markets for corporate control assuring market valuation of the state farms assets and liquidations as necessary. Until this environment is achieved, the shaping of the state farms may evolve in a variety of management and ownership patterns.

Full privatization of land, buildings, and equipment. Some state farms on productive soils in zones of extensive private farming are likely to be liquidated and the land auctioned to local farmers in the area. Currently, the larger private farmers appear to have ample equipment and would be able to farm additional acreage. If full payment is not feasible due to liquidity issues, a lease/purchase option for farmers wishing to buy land is likely.

Agri-service centers. Some state farms are beginning to act as service centers to their local private farming communities both in the state, cooperative and private sectors. Machinery repair firms, storage, livestock assembly and buying stations, and feed milling and distribution could be privatized from existing state farm units and serve a larger local market than just the state farm. Enterprises with horizontal integration with a restructured state farm provide agro-processing for neighboring larger-scale and smaller-scale farms.

These agri-service centers should be encouraged, but not in a manner that substitutes a state-run repair shop with a private firm that enjoys a local or regional monopoly.

Privatized state farms with land owned or leased from the state. In some cases, complete dismantling and selling of state farms to local farmers or to the local or foreign private sector may not be feasible. Sale of such farms over time to local farmers, farm managers and possibly to external technical partners working as joint shareholders, and then appointing independent management may be feasible. Several pilot operations along these lines are being developed currently, although it is far too early to assess the outcome.

State ownership of land and enterprises with independent management. A fourth option might be government hiring of skilled, independent, internal and external farm management firms to manage state farm enterprises for an agreed fee plus a percentage of the net revenue. This is done frequently by trusts, insurance firms, and banks in other countries. In most cases, these are interim arrangements until a sale of enterprises can be effected. It may have some applicability in Poland as an interim measure to restructure loss-making state farms prior to privatization, until a longer-term sale can be arranged.

The government is receiving a number of such proposals from Polish entities and from other countries.

Conclusions

Generally, the state farm sector is inefficient in its use of factor inputs. Privatization, if managed well, should result in efficiency gains and lower cost production, especially for basic grains. As the government develops its policies for restructuring the extensive state farm system through the proposed state farm agribusiness restructuring task force, a series of privatization, sale/leasing, and management contractual arrangements will be developed, all under an agreed set of basic clear laws with enforceable regulations. Regionally, the approaches will differ: what might work for a state farm divestiture in an area of many private farmers keen to expand may not be applicable in the northeast where the local farming population has little interest or is aging rapidly.

As market mechanisms develop, the recommendations of the state farm agribusiness restructuring task force will have increasing importance as the state farm system evolves though a variety of means; some undertaking full privatization, including the sale of land to local farmers; others selling enterprises to local and external investors in joint-venture formats; and still others developing into agri-service firms, undertaking assembly, storage, processing, and repair with separate, privately owned enterprises on former state farms.

A regional pattern may evolve, with small state farms in central and southern Poland being sold off to local farmers, with uneconomic state farms in eastern Poland being converted to conservation areas, and those with more economic and better managed farms in northern and western Poland being privatized, restructured, and put on a sound management and financial basis.

Endnote

This annex was prepared by August Schumacher (World Bank), assisted by Andrzej Kolodziej (Agricultural Academy of Wroclaw) and Ryszard Rozwadowski (Agricultural Academy of Warsaw).

Annex 8

The agricultural and food marketing system and the agrifood industry

The functioning of the agriculture and food-marketing system is of fundamental strategic importance to the Polish agricultural and food sector. It affects the overall distribution of resources, economic welfare, and the efficiency and competitiveness of the agriculture and food industries.

The agrifood industry is also of considerable strategic importance. It employs an estimated 800,000 employees, produces roughly 20% of total value added in the Polish economy, and accounts for 13% of all convertible exports. In addition, consumers spend roughly 50% of their income on food of which an estimated 75% of the volume is processed in some form. Thus, the performance of the agrifood industry, and the policies which affect it, have major economic, political, and social implications.

As will be seen below, there are some serious deficiencies in the operation of the food-marketing system and the agrifood sector within it, and this short paper addresses these and proposes measures which should be key components of an agricultural strategy for the Polish agriculture and food sectors.

This annex is restricted to a consideration of the broader strategic issues affecting marketing and the agrifood industry. It focuses attention on the institutional framework rather than the detailed exploration of the operation of individual sectors. With one exception, exploration of the detail seems unjustified in the process of defining an agricultural strategy. The exception is the dairy sector where the crisis in confidence

as a result of liberalization has warranted a more detailed consideration of the options for rationalization (see Annex 21). Other sectors might need similar detailed examination, but only after the main framework of strategy has been developed.

It should also be emphasised that under the current situation of the stabilization program and the transition from command to market economy there are rapid and fundamental changes taking place within a very unstable set of external circumstances. The sector is in transition and in these circumstances it is often difficult to clarify the underlying economic position. Consequently, in a number of areas we will recommend further examination of aspects of the marketing system and agrifood sector.

The recent historical context

The agricultural and food marketing system has been subject to a fundamental change in function and modus operandi. Previously, under the command economy, it was simply a means of delivery of products on the basis of directive, and subject to manipulation by distortion of input and output prices.

Most of the production going onto the market was channeled through the state-controlled co-operatives and the processing sector was dominated by state enterprises. Subsidies were given throughout the system to reflect the central perception of what was needed. Within this system, the decision of what was produced and the price of sale was determined by balancing the subsidies on production, distribution, processing, and consumption. No market mechanism operated to provide an allocation function.[1] The command economy had little need for many of the institutions required in a market economy to facilitate the exchange of goods at prices determined by the state of demand and supply. Much of the transfer of goods along the food chain was at predetermined prices and was based on a complex set of administerial, regulated, and contract prices. Wholesale exchanges existed but only to facilitate the physical transfer of goods along the food chain. Small private markets existed for the sale of produce, which was residual to that required through the state system, and there was a limited development of farmer markets for vegetables, fruits, flowers, and eggs. Wherever processing was involved, the socialized sector and channels to the market represented the only possible alternative sales route. Farmers were under considerable pressure to use the state channels because of the access this granted to inputs and other services.

The extent of the distortion caused by this system varies by commodity. In some commodities (particularly basic foods) there was a much heavier subsidy and degree of control. In others, such as fruit and vegetables and some processed foods, the subsidies were less, although they still made a significant impact.[2] No part of the agricultural and food marketing system was left untouched by the command economy because of the size and nature of the distortions in operation.

But the impact of such a system extends far deeper than distortions of commodity markets. The people involved in the system were also strongly influenced by it. The criteria of adjustment of production was not connected in any way to market conditions by the concepts of price and profits but by what was perceived to be required. Thus, managers of enterprises were not accustomed to examining and analyzing their organizations on the basis of profitability, and the extent of subsidizing enterprises often meant that those who had the largest deficits at the end of the year ended up with a higher surplus than many others after the end-of-year negotiation of subsidy. Not only did this result in a serious misallocation process, but it also generated a management attitude and approach which was both administrative and, inevitably, political in emphasis. The rationale for an enterprise was its function (a conduit to the market) and its social contribution (local employment and other social services). The managers of these organizations were subject to pressure for increased efficiency, but they were also subject to conflicting claims on them which led to substantial compromise on any efficiency criteria.

The level of distortion to economic incentives is made clear by Schaffer, (European Economy, March 1990). He studied the 1988 data on the largest 500 state enterprises. This showed clearly that food enterprises were most likely to be loss makers and that those which made losses were paid supplementary payments which resulted in the loss makers having better results than many profit makers. Under these conditions, it is hardly surprising that individual enterprises were not run effectively or efficiently.

The adjustment to liberalization

The speed and magnitude of change have been considerable. The system has been subject to rapid liberalization of farm input and output prices and the removal of price subsidies at the retail level, beginning in August 1989. On their own, these measures caused considerable disturbances throughout the system, with some stockpiling of storable products, and later a sharp drop in consumption of some products. However, of much more fundamental importance were the implications of liberalizing the system before any changes in the structure and ownership of the marketing chain had been initiated. As might be expected given the background, the system was hardly capable of responding to the new circumstances of liberalized prices and the market economy.

The management situation throughout the system is critical. For any of these managers to adjust to the disciplines of a market economy demands a considerable metamorphosis in motivation. However, in addition to this, managers are faced with the uncertainties arising from restructuring.

The liberalization was also accompanied by the first moves in the privatization and restructuring program of the government. State enterprises were broken up and individual units were under autonomous management. Similarly in the cooperative sector, cooperative unions were liquidated and individual cooperatives were left to operate independently. As a result, throughout the marketing system, managers who have been highly dependent on state control and assistance from the center have had to survive on their own in a completely new management environment.

On top of this, the position of management within various parts of the food chain has been undermined. Those in charge of autonomous units have little freedom to manage with true executive authority. In the autonomous state enterprises the managers ultimately report to the voivodship and the social role of the enterprise is reinforced by the powers of the workers committees. Management responsibility is divorced from ownership and the result is lack of motivation and commitment to organize the enterprises efficiently. The hiatus over ownership because of the recent reforms and the attempts to break up the state monopolies result in considerable uncertainty and inhibit any management initiatives. Throughout the food chain, managers await clarification of their position before taking positive action.

Despite the liberalization of the market, the lack of market exchange infrastructure is still evident at many parts of the food chain and farmers have few opportunities to sell on wholesale markets, which are subject to competitive bidding. While wholesaling facilities exist for unprocessed and processed products there are imperfections in the way they operate and, in some, the number of participants is limited and there is little open determination of prices. It has not proved possible for the task force, within the time period, to obtain a reliable full and comprehensive description of the current status of market exchange facilities and this remains a high priority.

Another characteristic of the current system is the extended links in the food chain. This is a legacy of the previous system where, for example, the milling sector traditionally purchased from cooperatives rather than directly from farmers because of the historical pricing and margin system for grain. Some of these redundant links in the chain still exist, although the liberalization of the pricing system and the greater autonomy of the individual grain-processing state organizations have brought some pressure to introduce more direct links between farmers and processors. Contradictorily, there is also a strong tendency for vertical integration in some parts of the marketing system. Such a feature exists partly because of the attempts to bypass the existing monopsonistic channels (see below) and partly because of past designation as the chosen channel to the market.

A serious flaw in the existing situation is the absence of reliable and comprehensive sources of market information or the necessary vehicles of dissemination of this information. The old system required a certain degree of market transparency, but the emphasis was on volumes flowing through the system and costs and there was no need to disseminate any information throughout the marketing system as the decisions were made centrally. Currently, the emerging market system desperately needs the development of a comprehensive market information structure which will help provide market transparency and provide a rational base upon which individuals in the system can make their production and selling decisions. There is evidence that farmers have little idea of what alternative prices are available and some spend a considerable amount of time finding out the best place to sell their products. The costs of inadequate market transparency are enormous in terms of both time wasted and the overall misallocation of resources.

Competition in the food chain

One of the objectives of the restructuring of enterprises is to increase competition in the sector. However, this has met with only limited success. In some areas the national monopolies have simply been replaced by the autonomous regional or local monopolies and competition has hardly been affected. Indeed, as might be expected, where large national organizations have been broken up, the local management, which depended on the support of the central services, has continued to seek help from within the old 'family'. Thus, there is strong evidence of collusion and anticompetitive behavior that reduce the level of competition.

The extent of competition varies by area and industry branch and also there are substantial differences at the various stages of the food chain. The spatial distribution of competition appears to result from historical and geographical accident. In some areas, single cooperatives will supply a town with much of their basic foodstuffs, while in other areas cooperatives compete with other cooperatives, state farms, and private traders.

The extent of competition in the food-processing industries will depend on the form of previous organization and the capital intensity of the branch. In most cases, the processing capacity was evenly spread throughout the country in order to provide adequate processing facilities to absorb production. Where branches of the food industry were capital intensive, restructuring has left the relatively few autonomous management units with well-defined local or regional monopolies.

The flour milling and edible vegetable oil branches, both of which retain strong regional oligopolies despite restructuring, are oligopolistic sectors. In the edible vegetable oils sector, the old national monopoly has been broken into a small number of autonomous enterprises, each of which holds a strong regional position with very little competition in the production of margarine, except from imports. Each of these have combined to form a service company which plans new investment in manufacturing capacity. This investment will consolidate the oligopolistic nature of the branch. The national grain-milling enterprise (PZZ) was divided into separate milling companies. However, each of these mills has a local monopoly of storage, drying, and milling facilities. Farmers selling their grain have little option except to use the same channels that they have used for years and the prices paid are not competitively determined.

In other branches competition may be greater. For example, small-scale meat processing (for example, sausage making) has always included some private participants and here conditions can be more competitive. Estimates of the structure of the meat-processing sector suggest that the private sector is relatively well-represented (about 10% of throughput), largely through very small-scale sausage making plants. Although this feature is probably more highly represented in the meat sector, small-scale manufacturers can be found in other branches such as baking and the fruit and vegetable processing sectors. Much interest in setting up enterprises in those sectors is motivated by the desperate attempt by producers to identify alternative outlets for their products in the face of the local monopsonist buyers. Field visits at the beginning of June 1990 revealed substantial interest in investing in small-scale slaughtering, meat cutting, and processing facilities among private farmers and state farms. However,

these and other new entrants are constrained by a wide range of barriers to entry such as lack of capital, skills, and access to market outlets.

The frustration experienced in finding marketing outlets has been one factor leading to the widespread development of the street markets that abound throughout Poland. These markets offer an alternative way of selling and have resulted in the development of competition to the established channels at the retail stage in some areas. These informal retail markets represent an encouraging development in the food economy and a concrete indication of the extent to which the rules of the market economy can be adopted. However, many of the street markets need to be supervised and formalized so that public hygiene and other consumer protection issues can be introduced and the standards of markets raised. All food markets should have access to water and facilities for ensuring hygienic handling and presentation of food.

The export and import of agricultural and food products have been handled by a number of foreign trade organizations. These had monopolies for designated commodities and were primarily established as state enterprises. Competition in this area was severely limited as these state export agencies had considerable monopolistic power with regard to trade. Because of the monopoly powers all exporters became dependent upon them and did not need to invest in any aspect of export development. The monopoly agencies charged margins but their role was buttressed by state export policy, which included heavy subsidization of exports. These monopolies have now been broken down and in most product areas anyone can export, but the old foreign trade organizations still hold an important and influential position simply because of their dominant position in this activity and their widely developed existing trading relations. There is also evidence that they retain their old powers, including control over the granting of export licenses in some products. In some areas liberalization of controls on exports has encouraged many to export directly, independently, and in competition with the established state-owned agencies (with its well-developed network).

Deficiencies in the current marketing system

The legacy of history and recent reforms can be summarized as follows. The main problems arise from the failure of the markets to function as a result of:

• the absence of certain preconditions for the functioning of a market such as adequate market transparency and market exchange infrastructure;

• the absence of competition; and

• the problems of the individual management organizations adjusting from a command to a market economy.

Such problems are to be expected given the rapid transition of the Polish economy from command to market economy and the extent of the changes required from individuals and institutions. It is difficult to separate the marketing system from the more general problems of the economy. The economy still lacks a fully functional competitive credit system and many of the institutional features of a normally operating market economy (for example, insurance, capital market, and corporate legal framework). All of these are taken for granted in a developed market economy and each dovetails with the others to provide cohesion to the marketing system.

The explicit malfunctions of the market as it now exists in Poland are the following:

• There is poor price transmission throughout the system, with large trading and processing margins and obvious price distortions at various points in the chain.

• There is a lack of feedback through the food chain from consumers to producers, with many of the participants in the chain being production rather than market orientated. The range of products is very narrow, the quality is often poor, there is little attention to added value, and the presentation of products is poor.

• There is little market transparency; in other words, there is little reliable information available that will allow the individual actors participating in the market to determine what the true market position is. This results in very high costs of marketing and misdirection of effort.

• There is little market exchange infrastructure to stimulate the development of competitive markets.

• There are excessive links in the chain between consumer and producer.

• There has been misdirected investment to provide for the needs of the command economy rather than those of the market economy; thus, processing plants are inappropriately located and some essential investments are not evident.

The situation in the agrifood industry

It is difficult to separate the problems of the agrifood sector from the specific market deficiencies itemized above. The predicament of the sector arises from the inheritance from the past and the consequent lack of preparedness to face new circumstances in the future. In general, the condition of many of the enterprises is poor, with buildings in need of refurbishment, and outdated and obsolete equipment and facilities often falling below acceptable standards of hygiene, safety, environmental protection, and employee health and safety. Many of the enterprises in the food-processing sector have a serious lack of financial resources for investment. The combined subsidy and taxation and distribution policies have greatly contributed to this situation. In years of deficit, subsidies made good any losses while in years of surplus taxes penalized success. In effect, these policies have combined to prevent enterprises from undertaking long-term strategic planning and investment.

It is clear that the food-processing industry represents a major constraint on the development of the entire agricultural and food sector. The food industry is not geared to the market economy and the ownership hiatus referred to earlier (management responsibility divorced from ownership) continues. These are serious problems and require urgent attention if agriculture is to achieve its full potential within the market economy.

It is very difficult to get a clear picture of the financial position prevailing in the sector. Despite the observed problems of the industry, official data suggest that investment levels in recent years compare with historical averages. 1989 was characterized by investments almost 15% higher in real terms than in the previous year, although much of this was generated because of the hyperinflation of that year. Investment in milk, vegetable oils, grain elevators, cold storage, and freezer facilities predominated (as in previous years). Much of this investment took place in the first half of the year and interest in investment halted with the introduction of the economic changes at the end of the year.

There is substantial interest in capacity as might be expected in a centrally-driven economy. Institute of Agriculture and Food Economy data suggest that these investments, coupled with the reduction in demand in 1990 ensure that there is adequate capacity for the current supply (except possibly grain in a very wet year or with a large stock overhang). We are concerned about the capacity for processing rapeseed oil, future capacity constraints on the margarine, brewing, pasta, and cheese sectors, the poor quality of and losses in much potato storing, and the low level of vegetable and potato processing. Whether higher levels of investment in these areas would be economically justified is difficult to assess.

All parts of the food chain have been put under financial pressure by the adjustments required as a result of the implementation of the stabilization program. The distribution channels are mainly cooperatively owned (their position is discussed in Annex 6). In the agrifood industry there has been very little investment since the autumn of last year, largely because of the uncertainty, the economic reforms, and the very high interest rates. Demand has dropped considerably as real incomes have fallen by 35% (see Annex 3). As a result, many processing plants are operating at low capacity and some are carrying large stocks and are in a difficult financial situation. Statistics collected by GUS for the socialized sector suggest that the current financial situation is generally worse than last year, but varies between branches for a number of reasons:

• The economic position of industries where the competition is low or demand has not been seriously hit is not strong but neither is it critical (for example, in the meat industry and the beer and milling industries, profits continued at the same level as last year). The absence of real impact on the financial results of these branches of the food industry companies is quite astonishing considering the extent to which the rest of the economy has been hit. It is uncertain whether these results are real or illusory; it is true that companies in a monopoly position can simply mark up their sales prices without pressure to increase their efficiency; however, accounting practices may give a false picture of their current position. Where fixed costs are either written off or inadequately accounted for by depreciation, the impact of lower capacity utilization (usually a key criteria in determining food industry profitability) may be less critical in determining profitability. Irrespective of this, the absence of competition has undoubtedly shielded parts of the processing sector from the full financial effects of the stabilization plan.

• In certain higher value grocery products (nonessential basic foods which were previously unsubsidized), margins are compressed (for example, confectionery, dehydrated products, frozen products, etc.).

• In industries that are exposed to competition from substitutes, financial problems are greater (for example, where margarine competes with butter and starch, in the form of glucose, competes with sugar).

• In industries with campaign processing and heavy seasonal stockholding (for example, sugar and starch) financing costs have caused serious problems and there is similar concern over financing this year's cereal crop.

• In the dairy industry there are very serious structural problems (see Annex 21).

It is clear that there is a need for some form of short-term action to assist those industries whose liquidity has been most seriously hit to ensure that the 1990 crop can be purchased. Such assistance should be temporary and clearly targeted to avoid the perpetuation of serious distortions.

Currently, the agrifood industry is already benefiting from a number of specific taxation and credit provisions not available to other industries:

• an allowance against profit tax equivalent to 50% of the annual investment in equipment;

• exemption of industries manufacturing products previously subsidized from turnover tax (normally charged at 20%);

• a temporary tax holiday (until January 1, 1991) for new private enterprises in selected activities (including meat and distributive trades);

• credits for small-scale private companies from the EC Counterpart Fund (75% of commercial interest rates).

In addition, the food industry is influenced directly by the general arrangements for foreign investment and joint ventures, although no special arrangements exist.

The potential of Polish food products

The underlying longer-term comparative advantage of Polish food products is uncertain and needs systematic study. In particular there is a marked absence of up-to-date strategic marketing studies upon which to assess the market potential, a deficiency which should be corrected.

However, a number of general observations can be made that help to clarify the current situation and the nature of the future challenge. First, unprocessed or slightly processed products are a significant part of agricultural exports.

Second, Polish exports are usually commodity-type products of low value and positioned at the bottom of the market; in this market, their position is fragile as price is the key determinant of success. If they are not the cheapest they are displaced from the market. This allows little prospect for extracting value-added and higher profits.

Third, Poland has very few natural marketing advantages. While there is a feeling that Poland has some potential in serving the market for low input (organic) products, major hopes based on this premise are unlikely to be fulfilled. The market opportunities are there, but competition will be very tough. Moreover, the general image of Poland in this market is unfortunately compromised by its general reputation for serious atmospheric pollution.

Fourth, there are big uncertainties associated with the development of export markets (particularly trading relationships with western economic blocs and the Soviet Union); these two markets are likely to demand different strategies (see Annex 4).

Fifth, there are a number of niche and added value market opportunities in the domestic market despite the contraction in demand. These opportunities are illustrated by the importation of a number of higher quality products selling at substantial premiums to domestic products (for example, high-quality long-life milk selling at 10 times the domestic price. Finally, there can be little doubt that the domestic market will develop all the characteristics of western markets in the medium/longer term (for example, demand choice, convenience, added value).

In addition, there are several other important aspects to take into account. Exports figure very prominently as a macroeconomic objective for Poland and this particularly applies to agricultural and food exports. However, it is clear that the industry is unprepared for developing new markets and products. The industry has not had to innovate in new product development previously, and it lacks many of the capital and know-how resources to prepare for this. If the industry is to exploit any opportunities and to defend its own market it needs to invest in the necessary plants and equipment and also, of critical importance, to develop human resources. Thus, no matter what the comparative advantage for Polish products, progress in domestic and foreign markets will not come easily. There will need to be a considerable effort to adjust the industry so that it performs well in both price and marketing terms.

The desired future situation

There are many deficiencies in the Polish marketing system and its agrifood sector when judged against market economy criteria. It is true that the performance of agricultural markets in other developed countries is often not good, largely because of the impact of massive subsidization and control of competition. However, the macroeconomic environment for Poland precludes such an interventionist policy framework, at least in the short term. Because of the tendency toward liberalization of world agriculture, this applies in the longer term also (see Annex 1). In any case, the fundamental challenge for the Polish economy is to make the transition to a true market economy so that the entire marketing system is able to respond to market developments.

In the medium term — subject to social, political, and macroeconomic considerations — the marketing system should develop so that it is competitive and effectively serviced. The dynamic effects of enhanced efficiency, innovation, and entrepreneurial activity will result from such a development. Those who operate successfully will be rewarded with profitability rates providing the basis for further necessary investment to improve their overall position. The benefits for consumers will be a greater range of products at lower prices. The processing sector will provide greater market opportunities for the farm sector and can provide more general benefits for the country as a whole as a result of the positive impact on export revenues. The precise distribution of these benefits will depend on the terms of trade between Poland and the rest of the world and between agriculture and other sectors of the Polish economy.

The nature of demand will change as the benefits of the current economic policy program are revealed. Consumers will demand a wider range of products with considerably higher added value. Niche markets will be more prevalent and better presentation will yield regular price premiums. The marketing system and the main components of it will need to be able to respond to these changes.

The policy options

It is important to distinguish between two different levels of issues in identifying policy options and strategies for the marketing system:

- those that concern marketing system malfunction; and
- those that concern individual enterprise management.

Many of the latter arise because of the former and recognition of this is an important consideration in the identification of the desirable phasing of policy reforms. Resolving the system malfunctions will also specifically contribute to improving the position of the agrifood industry. Clearly the priority is to ameliorate the system malfunctions and this implies making the market work.

However, in addition to this it may be necessary to consider various policy options that involve proactive interventions in the workings of the market. The degree of flexibility to intervene in the operation of the market represents an important strategic issue. Since all actions in the short term must be undertaken within the very tight constraints of the stabilization program and the macroeconomic targets of the economy as a whole, any special assistance or concessions which are requested demand very careful examination and justification. Each action granting special assistance for any sector must pass the test: might the objectives be achieved by market forces?

If the answer to this is no, or only after a long period, then the issues come down to the precedence of government objectives within the overall constraints of the macroeconomic parameters. It is well recognised that the temptation to alleviate such politically sensitive effects as unemployment by reintroducing new subsidies is there, and this represents a threat to the shorter-term economic strategy.

Having said this, the support of objectives that have an important effect, for example, on food consumption, rural employment, farm diversification, and related income distribution issues may justify a high priority for the Polish government. With some important qualifications, strategies that provide special assistance to further such objectives might be justified, especially as one moves from the short to the medium term.

THE MAIN ELEMENTS OF STRATEGY

The underlying assumption of the strategy is that the marketing system would perform better if competition were increased and certain market infrastructure encouraged. This applies equally to the agrifood sector as an integral part of the marketing system. Consequently, the key priority is to encourage competition and to help markets function.

This will be achieved by:

- increasing competition throughout the food chain;
- improving marketing system infrastructure and institutions (in the form of both physical and forward markets); and
- improving general marketing services.

In addition, it will be necessary to bolster the ability of the agrifood industry to adjust to the challenge that lies ahead.

TYPE OF MEASURES RECOMMENDED

Much of the strategy reinforces what is currently in progress. In keeping with the development of the overall strategy for agriculture a key consideration has been to identify measures that accord with the stabilization program in the short term and that, in the medium term, do not substantially distort resource allocation in the economy as a whole. The emphasis is on developing the necessary institutions to help the markets function. The key characteristics of the components of the strategy are:

- that they involve modest financial assistance (primarily start-up financing as many of the institutions can be self-funding or run as private businesses themselves);
- that they may involve some enabling legislation (to facilitate raising funds from a sector for self-help);
- that they involve some regulation (for externalities such as food quality and public health).

To meet the special needs of the agrifood industry we propose additional measures that serve to modify the outcome of current market structure, namely special temporary concessions for new entrants and, eventually, reestablishment of equipment investment incentives in the agrifood industry.

MEASURES FOR INCREASING COMPETITION

Under the heading of increasing competition, we emphasize the need for pursuing several reforms which are already in progress. There are five broad areas of priority:

- First, and most essential, the privatization of all state enterprises in the food chain (including the foreign trade organization) should be undertaken. This stage warrants the highest priority in view of the wide range of benefits that will result. The mechanisms of privatization are discussed in Annex 5. Here, it is sufficient to note that the stages required are:
  - affirmation of state ownership;
  - establishment of state holding companies; and
  - state disposal of assets.

The implementation of this timetable should be as rapid as possible to avoid further uncertainty over ownership and to ensure that market-driven incentives are adequately installed in the management of these enterprises. Should any delay be foreseen in this process, adequate provision should be made within the holding companies for encouraging more efficient, motivated management.

- The second measure to increase competition is to implement antitrust regulations and monitor competitive conditions. As far as the food sector is concerned, it is very important that this extends to, and is effective at, regional and local levels through the food chain. An antitrust law has been introduced with this objective, although the agency charged with administering

the law has a major challenge in developing its capability within a relatively short time and with only limited experience in such activities. Clearly, if the agency is to be effective technical assistance will be required. It has been indicated that the agricultural sector is a high priority for the agency. In fact, in terms of criteria of industry concentration, the agricultural sector comes fairly low compared with other more capital-intensive industries. However, concern has focused on agriculture simply because of the political importance of food and food prices and the potential of antimonopoly rules to improve the competitive situation.

- The third set of measures to increase competition is the lowering of barriers to entry, particularly by offering:
  - encouragement to joint ventures (this is not specific to agriculture);
  - a sound legislative structure for cooperatives; and
  - special provisions for new entrants.

As far as joint ventures are concerned, it is clear that the balance of interest must be adequate to attract technical assistance and new capital, and to have access to markets. This is a critical issue as foreign partners can provide considerable technical assistance as well as much needed capital. Currently, this issue is receiving the priority attention of the government. As far as cooperatives are concerned, a separate annex (Annex 6) addresses what is needed to convert them into more enterprise-oriented organizations.

The provision of temporary encouragement to new entrants is one of the areas where special assistance is justified. It is justified by the following premises:

- the importance of the food sector both economically and socially (as food is such an important part of the budget of the less well off);
- the nature and magnitude of the barriers to entry into the food industry and the perpetuation of oligopoly and oligopsony; and
- the fact that privatization alone will not be enough to increase competition; there is the likelihood that in certain sectors private monopolies will replace public ones, at least in the short to medium term.

In addition, we concur with others about the need to give small- or medium-scale enterprises special assistance, at least for a temporary period. These types of enterprises are not appropriate to all processing activities or markets; however, with some assistance, they may be well suited to:

- meeting emerging niche market requirements;
- identifying gaps in the markets of the large state enterprise;
- they may offer additional diversification activities to farm businesses; and
- providing rural employment.

However, care must be taken in the way these concessions are offered because of the problems of targeting and the implications of distorting the credit system. Despite the problems of distortion, we consider this issue of sufficient importance to justify some assistance at the point where it will mean most, namely in facilitating better access to finance for new entrants.

For new entrants the major constraint is in the area of access to finance. While we are aware of the problem of introducing distortions into the credit system we consider that some action is required here. In preference to subsidized interest rates, we support establishing a temporary fund that can act as a bank guarantee for small- and medium-size agrifood investments. This fund can be administered by an agency that helps in the selection of projects. The service can be made available to any bank that applies for the fund, thus preventing any distortion by designating privileged channels. The agency can also provide technical assistance to the banks in assisting the appraisal of investment proposals and in this way help provide the much needed assistance required by the newly emerging commercial banking sector. In addition, the conversion of future EC counterpart funds or of counterpart funds from bilateral sources to such a purpose should be considered.

• The fourth measure to increase competition involves ensuring there are no special concessions for the current players in the sector (for example, cooperatives). Such provisions are essential for a truly competitive environment to evolve.

• As a final measure to increase competition it might be appropriate in some product areas to allow competition from imports (with appropriate antidumping protection). The qualification on antidumping is particularly important in view of the protectionist nature of agriculture and trade policy in many parts of the world.

MEASURES FOR IMPROVING MARKETING SYSTEM INFRASTRUCTURE AND INSTITUTIONS

The promotion of appropriate marketing system infrastructure and institutions represents a major objective. The main aim here is to facilitate the development of a comprehensive market information service and a rational spot, forward, and (eventually) futures trading and market exchange system throughout the food chain. There are several specific areas that need priority attention:

• First, there is an urgent need to develop market transparency throughout the food chain. This means to collect and disseminate the information that will be necessary for all the players in agricultural markets to make their production and marketing decisions. Such information is the essential oil on the cogs of the marketing system. The precise details of this initiative deserve special study that will take into account the needs of the system, the current procedures, and the areas of development, including market information dissemination mechanisms.

• Second, there is a need to encourage and regularize local retail market facilities. The growing retail street markets are a positive aspect of the economy. They are to be fostered and encouraged by providing better sites and basic facilities and making them subject to adequate public hygiene regulations.

• Third, the marketing system is desperately in need of market exchange facilities, especially at the producer/primary wholesaler, producer/processor stage, and these should be encouraged. The feasibility of establishing such formal and supervised means of exchange should be examined to extend and encourage markets. Strengthening the markets should be accompanied by the development of forward markets, but a precondition of this is a better, more reliable market information system. Eventually, more sophisticated markets may be developed to help the sector cope with risk and to tie in with credit facilities. The precise form of these should be explored in some detail. The market information service will demand public investment. This is justified as it is a public good. The development of market facilities may require initial assistance with government funds, but the markets should eventually be self-financing institutions.

A large number of market services are required to ensure that a market system works well. At the outset it is important to clarify the responsibilities for these. There are strong arguments for restricting government responsibilities to a limited range of activities that involve the public good. For example, we support the case for government supervision in maintaining minimum public health standards, because if the government does not do this, no one else will. In the same way, the government has a responsibility to ensure that an adequate unbiased and independent statistical and market information service is maintained.

There is strong argument for a commodity sector to assume responsibility for certain activities for the common good of all the professions in the sector (for example, farming, trade, processing, and retail). In order to carry out these sectoral responsibilities it will be necessary to provide opportunities for the establishment of interprofessional organizations (IOs). These agencies of sectoral self-help, which can adopt responsibility for activities for the common good, exist in most of the agricultural sectors within developed countries. Establishing these agencies will require appropriate enabling legislation. This legislation should enable sectors to establish such organizations and to collect the required funds. The best model would be a form of the *produktschaps* that exist in the Netherlands, although other models exist in France, West Germany, Belgium and the United Kingdom. Thus, there would be an IO covering each of the major commodity sectors should the sector decide to establish one.

The sort of activities that could be usefully covered are considered below. Such an organization can establish sectoral quality standards. These may be essential to protect the sector from adverse effects on demand arising from poor-quality products coming onto the market. This is not a priority area in the short term on the home market but it is extremely important in developing and maintaining export markets. In addition the IO can provide some additional market analysis and information services. These services, supplementing those provided by a state-funded organization as part of the development of market transparency, do not have a public good character since they cover commercial issues such as country market shares, export market assessment, and information.

IOs also have a role in the organization of exporting and promotion of exports, either acting separately or in concert with other IOs for other agricultural commodity sectors. In view of the importance placed on exports in the macroeconomic framework, the organization of export market development is a key issue and one for which Poland is not well established with the existing foreign trade organizations. These trading organizations can still restrict competition and discriminate against others as well, holding conflicting interests through their role in importing. They should be fully privatized and any anticompetitive activities should be restricted. They should act only as export agents in competition with others.

However, there remain certain key activities that need to be undertaken on behalf of the sector in the area of export market promotion. It is important to separate industry promotion activities (with interprofessional responsibility) from trading (with private responsibility). If this is not done it is inevitable that conflicts will arise since an organization driven by its own incentive to maximize profits or commission will inevitably be tempted to discriminate against others. Generic industry promotion should be undertaken with interprofessional responsibility by the IOs. This generic promotion can cover both promotion of Poland as a source of supply or promotion of the commodity itself. Again the Dutch model seems most appropriate, although other export promotion organization models may be as suitable. The emphasis should fall on control of export quality, development of export market information systems, market analysis, and market promotion. Very careful consideration should be given to defining the role of the IO and of private organizations to ensure that there is no overlap of responsibility. As in most other models, there may be a need for some government assistance to ensure that Poland adequately competes. In addition the IOs have a role in developing the internal market where generic promotion may be necessary.

Some note should be made of the possible participation of IOs in market regulation activities. Where such activities are envisaged they may be ideal agents because they represent the different participants in the sector and they should have the means of raising funds from the sector to contribute to the financing costs. The issue of price stabilization and the role of the new Agency of Agricultural Marketing is discussed in a separate annex (see Annex 1 on macroeconomic adjustment and agriculture).

Finally, there are a number of activities that have traditionally had state involvement but for which private sector responsibility will be critical in the future. In particular, storage and transport; although there may need to be some public provision for strategic stocks and cover for short-term concern over storage capacity.

MEASURES FOR DEVELOPING HUMAN RESOURCES

The development of human resources is critical. It is possible to identify needs throughout the different levels of human resources, but of key current significance is the absence of management resources geared to operating in the market economy. Investment in management development can improve efficiency (for example, more marketing-oriented management, more rational raw material purchasing procedures, and promotion and market development).

In the area of human resources we consider it important that a coordinated program for the development of food industry management be prepared. Technical assistance from individual countries needs to be very closely coordinated in this area. Much of the technical assistance currently provided is aimed at developing human resources although there is little evidence that it is being directed in a coordinated way to ensure that it meets Polish priorities. The tendency for promotion of local or regional activity may lead to a patchwork of programs that are not integrated into national objectives.

The management development programs should be targeted at young middle management and emerging management resources. Business school education would seem to need high priority. A range of food industry management and marketing activities needs to be covered, with priority given to applied corporate management development rather than academic approaches.

SPECIAL MEASURES TO ENCOURAGE RATIONAL INVESTMENT IN THE AGRIFOOD SECTOR

Wherever one turns in the food-processing industry it is easy to identify possible areas for investment to improve efficiencies and to enhance value. Much of the equipment is out of date, and there is a serious deficiency in basic packaging investment to facilitate better presentation and marketing of products. In addition to this, there is a serious lack of capital and this constrains investment. In these circumstances we would argue for concessions. Specifically to assist investment in the food-processing sector we consider it necessary to argue for the retention of the principle of tax concessions for investment in the food-processing sector. However, we consider it important that this concession be rescinded or reduced for state enterprises until adequate management is installed. There is little point in making these concessions if we cannot be certain that they will be adequately utilized. This is a controversial issue and is very closely linked to the issue of privatization and the methods which will be adopted to achieve that. One argument would hold that adequate management cannot be achieved until the organization is in private hands (or at least a majority private shareholding). It must be noted, however, that some members of our group felt that such a criteria was unnecessarily dogmatic and that some state enterprises could provide adequate management.

Sequencing

In terms of sequencing there are some urgent short-term problems to be faced. There is an argument for providing special temporary arrangements to ameliorate the stock and new crop financing problems of the sugar and potato industries (and also grain). Of more important significance are:

- the reinforcement of privatization as so many improvements will follow from this;
- the initiation of a major review and reform to the market information system;
- strengthening the new entrant incentives for small- and medium-sized agrifood industries; and
- coordinating an agrifood management development plan.

In the medium term and after privatization, the reintroduction of investment incentives should be reconsidered. Any consideration of the sequencing of policy in the area of marketing and the agrifood industry depends on the nature and speed of the privatization program adopted. A summary of priorities, phasing, and legislative and public funding implications follows.

Summary of strategic areas, priority and phasing

Strategic area	Priority (1=high)	Planning	Legislation required	Public finance	Comments
Increasing competition in food chain:					
• Ensure enterprise structures are outside control of state	1	S	Yes	None	Implies privatization program (see Annex 5) Privatization laws under discussion
• Ensure competition in food chain locally by implementing antitrust regulations	1	S	No	None	Antimonopoly agency established; implementation of rules for food chain awaited. Agency competitiveness to be developed
• Ensure lowering of barriers to entry for new entrants: a) special provisions for new entrants to food processing sector (bank guarantees for small and medium-sized enterprises)	1	S	Yes	Major	Agency to be developed Possibly to incorporate EC Counterpart Fund
b) encouraging joint ventures that introduce foreign capital	1	S	Yes	None	Joint venture arrangements under review
c) ensure the cooperative legislation provides realistic incentivised corporate status and encourages private enterprise development	1	S	Yes	None	(See Annex 6)
• Ensure no special concessions offered to those in a dominant position in the food chain (e.g., cooperatives or exporting foreign trade organizations)	1	S	None	None	(See Annex 6)
• Allow competition from imports	1	S	No	None	
Improving marketing system infrastructure and institutions:					
• Develop framework for providing market information base and dissemination mechanism	1	S	Possibly	Minor/ startup	Review requirements and information base to develop basis of new market transparency framework
• Encourage development of supervised retail market premises	1	S	Possibly	Minor/ startup	Depends on status of legislation affecting establishment of retail markets and their supervision
• Examine potential for development of a) supervised auction markets for farm products b) supervised forward physical markets for certain products c) supervised auctions for certain processed products d) market facilitating activities	1	S/M	None	Minor/ startup	Potential and opportunities to be examined in detail with recommendations brought forward
Improving marketing institutions and services					
•Develop commodity-based interprofessional industry development associations to carry out key activities for common good (no trading, no market management)	2	M	Yes	None	Legal framework probably requires allowing such organizations to assume responsibility on behalf of industry promotion (possibly in collaboration with other interprofessional bodies
Developing human resources					
• Coordinating management development program for agrifood sector	1	S/M	No	Major	To be coordinated with other initiatives on development of enterprise management expertise in Poland
Special agro-processing support					
• Bolster agrifood sector's ability to invest by allowing continuation of tax concessions on investment in in equipment on enterprises that are either private or adequately managed	1	S	No	Major	

Further research required

The following areas are priorities for further examination:

- detailed description of the structure of the channels of distribution and ownership;
- detailed examination of comparative advantage and particularly up-to-date assessments of strategic marketing opportunities;
- review of the market information requirements of the sector and the establishment of a formal market reporting service and agency; and
- exploration of the feasibility of establishing more commodity exchanges in the Polish food chain.

Endnotes

This annex was prepared by Nick Young, assisted by Malgorzata Ellert, Karol Borzuta and Karol Adamik.

1. A detailed account of the channels and procedures operating in the agricultural and food marketing system is given in World Bank, *Poland: Agricultural Sector Study*, August 1989.

2. Historically, 10 major sectors of the food industry have been under the control of the state: cereals, sugar, potato, oilseeds, tobacco, meat, fish, beer and alcoholic spirits. In addition, dairies, fruit and vegetable processors and bakeries were traditionally controlled by cooperatives.

Annex 9

The transformation of grain marketing

Poland has declared its intention to rapidly adapt its economic institutions to function according to the logic of the market. The full, detailed implications of this are difficult to foresee for the economy as a whole and for the grain sector in particular. Uncertainty is increased by the move within Eastern Europe from ruble trade to hard currency trade. In the long term, the status of Poland as a net exporter or importer of grain will only be determined by the actions of the market. However, the dominant role of domestic production in satisfying demand suggests that the development of the grain sector can make a significant contribution to the national drive for increased efficiency.

The problems of the real economic adjustment in Poland have been compounded by major macroeconomic instability. The emerging hyperinflation of 1989 has been met by sharp counterinflationary measures. These measures, including an increase of real interest rates, have resulted in a dropoff of aggregate demand, and this in turn has led to some reduction in consumption of grain-based products. Furthermore, high real interest rates, instability of rates, and uncertain prospects for grain prices have all tended to discourage the willingness to hold grain stocks. Finally, shipment of grain aid to Poland from the EC and the United States appears in retrospect to have been unneeded.

As a result of these conditions, the grain market in Poland has been depressed in the first half of 1990. Furthermore, the significant holdover stocks from the 1989 harvest combined with the continuing uncertain prospects for aggregate demand have made producers very concerned that the situation could continue to erode after the 1990 harvest. This difficult situation has been exacerbated by the long-standing resentments of the private sector farmers against the state farms and grain merchandisers and processors, Panstwowe Zaklady Zbozowe (PZZ).

The result has been a significant political crisis that threatens to undermine the adjustment toward a market-based economy. In Poland's current situation, the first issue posed is whether the fragile consensus in favor of the transformation toward the market will break down. This, in turn, raises the prospect that the authorities would respond with short-term measures that, on their own, may undercut the market system and that, if perpetuated in new institutional forms, could become sources of economic inefficiency for years to come.

The heart of agricultural marketing, and of grain trade in particular, is the problem of allocating a seasonally produced good to consumption that takes place continuously through time. Thus, the medium-term adjustment issue in this area is whether and how the former state procurement and storage mechanism can be reorganized to be carried out by institutions that are responsive to prices. Beyond this, the issue is the creation of pricing structures that efficiently aggregate the information needed to make the link between the original grain production and consumption.

The grain sector in Poland

In recent years, Polish grain production has been about 25 million metric tons. This consists predominantly of soft wheat comparable to French wheat or American soft red wheat. In addition, there is a substantial production of rye, barley, and oats. Additionally, rapeseed is grown as an animal feed. Of the total harvest, somewhat more than 5 million tons enters commercial channels. The remainder is produced and stored locally for use largely as animal feed. Poland routinely imports grains, in particular high gluten hard wheat, which are used for mixing with local soft wheats in flour production and for production of pastas.

The organizations that are predominant in the production and processing of grain are state farms, the regional state grain merchandizing companies (PZZs), and independent private farmers. The state farms tend to be large, vertically integrated organizations. They produce a substantial proportion of wheat destined for human consumption. There are 41 PZZs organized largely by voivodship. These organizations clean, dry, store and ship grains. In addition, their mills yield much of Poland's flour output. Independent farmers generally operate on a smaller scale and produce grains, including wheat, for use mostly as animal feed. However, smaller-scale storage units can serve for the storage of human consumption grains if they have been first dried to reduce moisture to 14% to 18%. It should be noticed that, since much of Poland's capacity for the intermediate stages of grain processing, including drying, are concentrated in the hands of state companies, any radical steps toward privatization of these organizations would pose a risk of significant disruption in the supply chain. On the other hand, the same initial state also implies there may be significant efficiency gains if local monopoly power is undermined.

The profile of the PZZs has important implications for both short- and medium-term analysis of the Polish grain sector. The PZZs have a total grain storage capacity of 4.5 million tons. Of this total 2.9 million tons are in high capacity storage silos, and the remaining 1.6 million are in flat storage. The PZZs have 849 drying units of which 479 are Russian-built units that are moveable. These latter work on the basis of diesel exhaust, which has been found to pose a health risk. In principle, these are to be phased out of operation. The total PZZ drying capacity is 145 thousand tons per day of which 50 tons per day is located at flat storage facilities. Thus, using full drying capacity, grain sufficient to fill total storage capacity could be dried in about 31 days. It is estimated that, at the start of July 1990, there was a total of 1.7 million tons of grain in PZZ warehouses. However, these estimates should be treated with some caution.

Wholesale prices within the grain sector were liberalized starting in 1989. Table 9.1 presents the price pattern for 1989 and 1990.

Table 9.1 Polish average wholesale wheat prices, 31/7/89-25/6/90

('000 Zlotys)

Date	31/07	28/08	25/09	30/10	27/11	25/12
Price	121	168	172	213	321	372
Date	29/01	26/02	26/03	30/04	28/05	25/06
Price	809	807	731	701	705	660

Source: Ministry of Agriculture.

The sharp rise during the latter half of 1989 coincided with the rapid general inflation. Since that time general inflation rates have slowed, reaching approximately 3% for June. This implies the fall of 20% in the nominal price of wheat represents a real drop of at least 41% from the end of January to the end of June.

In 1989 the 41 separate PZZs were given the freedom to independently set prices. Furthermore, the newly developed antitrust laws and administration are an official impediment to horizontal price restraints. It is often alleged that informal cooperation exists in setting prices among PZZs. However, the absence of an obvious coordinating framework and the necessity of frequently revising prices during the period of rapid general price rises all represent obstacles to tacit collusion. Average prices by voivodship reported by the governmental statistical office (GUS) for May 1990 indicate significant geographic price dispersion. While this is not necessarily inconsistent with monopolistic price (for example, if regional markets are segmented and have different elasticities of demand), it suggests that there may be independence in price setting implying responsiveness to local market conditions.

The Agency for Agricultural Marketing (ARR)

BACKGROUND

The Agency for Agricultural Marketing (Agencja Rynku Rolnego, ARR) was created by an act of Parliament in May 1990. The agency has the potential for being a major new player affecting the production and merchandizing of agricultural products. On the one hand, it has the potential for developing new institutions that can supplant the traditional, monopsonistic state procurement system and that move in the direction of free markets. On the other hand, there is a risk that the agency may develop into a vehicle for massive state intervention, which would protect production and merchandizing decisions from market prices as effectively as under central planning. Consequently, while the agency is in its formative stage, it is extremely important to ensure that it be organized along lines that are consistent with the desired adjustment to a market economy.

The scope of the agency would be to intervene in the storage and trading of primary agricultural commodities, initially limited to grains. The purposes of the agency in the grain market are to: (i) increase storing and drying capacity; (ii) increase competition in grain merchandizing by facilitating the creation of new enterprises or producer groupings; and (iii) stabilize grain prices. These three objectives are not necessarily mutually consistent, and the priority among objectives, should conflicts arise, remains to be resolved.

As it is currently conceived, the agency will engage in the following operations: (i) buying grain on either a spot or deferred basis from qualified organizations; (ii) certifying quality; (iii) facilitating the provision of credit for participating producers and merchandisers; and (iv) selling grain to processors, private domestic merchandisers or for export. In order to qualify as a seller, an organization would be required to possess acceptable storage facilities that are available for storage of the grains sold. In conjunction with these operations the agency would perform the following separate functions:

- establishment of purchase prices;
- establishment of offset prices for established contracts;
- qualification of storage facilities;
- establishment of a system of warehouse receipts; and
- monitoring of market conditions for grains to facilitate selling and trading.

The agency is being organized under the auspices of the Ministry of Agriculture; however, formally it is an autonomous state agency. There is a supervisory board of 20 members drawn from diverse producer and consumer interests. In practice, these seats are likely to reflect the major political groupings. The governing council officially is to be provided a role in determining the pricing structure, particularly at the beginning of the crop year. The administration is to be organized into a central office and five regional offices. The regional offices are to have the responsibility for administering the storage facilities and effecting payments.

The agency budget from the state sources is ZL876 billion (approximately US$87 million) for its first year of operations.[1] In addition, under the agency enabling act, 1 million tons of grain out of the PZZ system's 4.5 million ton long-term storage facilities would be transferred to the agency. This would be an asset transfer with no compensation paid by the agency. For the current year, the government has authorized credits for the acquisition and processing of food of 20% annually. Grains stored in agency-certified warehouses would automatically qualify for these credits.

PRELIMINARY ASSESSMENT

Independent of how well the proposed organization of the agency will fulfill the intent of the Polish Parliament is the question of the consistency with the goals of the economic transformation program, namely: (i) stabilization; (ii) structural reform to promote a market economy; and (iii) restoration of Polish creditworthiness. We will discuss this issue with respect to five separate dimensions.

The original conception of the agency gave a central place to direct ownership of grain that would be stored in private warehouses. Since the agency is to be a public organization with no profit-making purpose, there would appear to be a very serious and fundamental difficulty in making it reach its decisions in response to market principles for grains that it would own itself. It would appear to suffer from the same failing of traditional state procurement: there is no clear incentive to carry out its activities in a cost-effective manner. Furthermore, as a new organization with relatively established expertise, there is little indication that it will be effective in maximizing the value of a given stock of grain by discovering the highest-price uses for the product.

The key to this original conception is that ownership of the grain would be transferred from private hands to public ownership. In this way private merchandisers who participate in the agency's program no longer have an incentive to find the highest value use of the grains. Consequently, their network of information on supply and demand conditions is effectively lost in determining the final disposition of the grain. Beyond this, once they have transferred ownership, the private storers will have the incentive to minimize the actual cost of storing grain subject to the constraint that they continue to qualify for the storage fee paid by the agency. The agency will have the burden of inspecting the storehouses and the grains in store; however, its incentives to perform this contract enforcement function are again compromised by its lack of a clear profit motive.

The second mode of operation of the agency involves contracting for delivery on a deferred basis. This has fundamentally different implications for incentives. Since there is provision for making offsetting trades to cancel the original contract, this gives an opportunity for the merchandiser to protect the collateral value of the grain and therefore have access to credit. Furthermore, while the grains are in store, the merchandiser can evaluate local market conditions and find the best marketing opportunity for the grain. Again, this is made possible through the facility for secondary trading.

If the agency is active, this will likely imply that a significant amount of storage capacity will be owned by private organizations of one form or another. Storage facilities are an integral part of private grain merchandizing. In this way, the effect of the agency would be to aid the private economy in meeting one of the preconditions for the creation of larger-scale private grain markets (which until now have not existed). More broadly, after a period of operation the agency may have contributed to the growth of larger, better capitalized private merchandisers who then would be in a position to compete on a national or even international scale.

The forward contracts can become the basis for pricing transactions not directly involving the agency. Agency prices can help to better aggregate information and facilitate potentially superior decisions based on agency-based profit calculations.

A FORWARD TRADING MECHANISM

The basic institutional features that are at the heart of the forward pricing mechanism are as follows:

• The agency maintains a price list at which it is willing to buy grain at certified warehouses at specified dates in the future as well as for spot delivery. At the same time, the agency maintains a price list at which it is willing to offset (sell back) contracts established previously;

• Parties who have contracted to sell to the agency for deferred delivery will be required to post as collateral grain that is stored in certified warehouses. The agency would have a lien on this grain so long as the party has a sale contract outstanding with the agency. However, the private party retains ownership of this grain and has the right to arrange for use of this grain in any way it sees fit. In particular, it can sell to another private party on a spot or forward basis in any way it wishes. In order to effect such transactions, the party would have to arrange for the withdrawal of the agency's lien on the grain;

• The combined physical grain and sale contract with the agency would be sufficient basis for the private party to borrow up to a specified fraction of the contracted selling price from participating banks. The practice of preferential credits, which is a familiar practice and which is in effect for the food sector at this time, would facilitate this practice.

Central to the agency's forward pricing mechanism is the possibility of an offset transaction. In essence, the participating party would have the possibility of secondary trading, which would allow him to undo his initial transaction should a better alternative use of his grain become available. This form of liquidity would be an important means of stimulating the development of the private markets for grain transactions.

The offset transaction in combination with the initial sale would imply a profit or loss depending upon how the posted price for the stated delivery date had changed. If the price list for the stated month rose, the offset price would be above the sale price and the private party would have incurred a loss. They would have to pay this to the agency before the lien on their physical grains would be released. If the price list had been lowered, the contracting party would have made a profit. The agency would have to pay this to the party and also release the lien. If by chance the price list had not been revised in the time between initial sale and offset, the private party would make a small loss reflecting the difference between the price listed for agency purchases and the higher offset price. This could be a small transaction cost that would help cover the actual costs of administration.

Perhaps the best way to understand the operations of the proposed agency pricing system is with examples that would illustrate the basic principles involved. Suppose initially it is September and a merchandiser owning a certified warehouse can acquire wheat in the local area at Zl600,000 per ton. Suppose also that the agency price list at this time is Zl600,000 for spot delivery and Zl670,000 for November delivery. Suppose that the merchandiser also can obtain a loan through a bank participating in the agency credit network for up to 90.9% of the contracted sale price at a rate of 10% for two months. Once the merchandiser has located a willing supplier of the grain, he can have it delivered to his warehouse, have it inspected, and create a certified warehouse receipt, which at this point is the property of the original seller of the wheat. Given this, the buyer and seller go to the participating bank and arrange for a deferred delivery sale of the wheat to the agency for Zl670,000 per ton. On this basis, the bank will grant a credit of Zl600,000 per ton. The merchandiser uses this credit to pay the grain supplier; the warehouse receipt is then assigned to the merchandiser, who posts it at the bank as collateral for his credit.

This initial transaction can come to fruition either by allowing the sales contract and loan to mature or by offset. If the transactions are allowed to mature in November, the agency pays to the party Zl670,000 per ton at his bank and in return acquires the warehouse receipt. The proceeds of the sale to the agency are used to pay back the loan principal and interest of Zl660,000 leaving the merchandiser a small profit of Zl10,000 as a return on his capital

invested in the storage facility.

Alternatively, transaction can be closed out by offset. For example, suppose that in October the prices have generally risen. The agency is now quoting Zl700,000 for spot delivery and Zl735,000 for November delivery (which for simplicity we assume applies for offset as well as initial sales). However, suppose that the merchandiser has located a willing buyer of the wheat at a price of Zl720,000 for spot delivery. In order to effect the transaction, the merchandiser goes to the participating bank and carries out the offset transaction, which incurs him a loss of Zl15,000 per ton which must be paid to the agency. The bank will allow him to prepay his loan for Zl630,000 of principal plus one month's interest at 5%. However, now that the lien has been withdrawn on his warehouse receipt, he can assign that to the buyer in return for Zl720,000. The net proceeds on the transaction are Zl720,000 - Zl630,000 - Zl75,000 = Zl15,000 per ton.

Note that the details of the transactions described above can be routinized and standardized so that in actual practice they work smoothly. Properly packaged, the participating parties can simply view this as buying grain on credit. Furthermore, note that the procedure can be facilitated if the agency can operate through the offices of banks participating in its credit network.

The offset example given above made the assumption of a rise in the price level. The same principle will also work in the case of a falling price level. Suppose the initial September transaction took place under the conditions assumed above. However, now assume that prices had fallen so that the agency price list in October is Zl500,000 spot and Zl125,000 for November. However, the merchandiser has a willing spot purchaser at Zl520,000. If the merchandiser offsets his agency sale, prepays his loan, and sells his warehouse receipt spot, the mechanics are precisely as above. In this case, however, the merchandiser has made a profit on his offset of Zl145,000 (= Zl670,000 - Zl525,000). His net proceeds from the transaction are Zl520,000 - Zl630,000 + Zl145,000 = Zl35,000.

In the examples just given, the principal reason that the merchandiser is able to realize a profit in the face of either a price level rise or fall is that during the time he has held the grain in storage, he has been able to locate a buyer who is willing to buy the grain at a Zl20,000 premium over the price quoted by the agency for spot transactions. This price differential (merchandiser's spot price less agency's spot price) sometimes is known as the merchandiser's basis. In the operations of forward trading, the smart merchandiser will soon realize that he can make money from the system by engaging in sales to the agency when he expects his basis to rise. When he expects his basis to fall, he should avoid agency sales and rent his storage facilities for a fee. This is the logic of trading. Note that unless the merchandiser is very well capitalized, he is unlikely to be able to simply buy and store the grain uncovered as a speculation on grain price levels; the reason for this is that banks are unlikely to lend to him if his collateral is subject to substantial price risk.

An important part of the functioning of the agency is the determination of the price list. This can be done to accomplish a variety of objectives. First, it should be noticed that the differentials between prices for various delivery dates will determine the incentives to store or to deliver to the agency. In particular, if the agency spot price is below the spot price prevailing in the private market, no private agent would ever have an incentive to deliver to the agency. Nevertheless, if the premium of the agency-deferred price over the private spot price is sufficient to cover carry costs, including interest from participating banks, there will be an incentive for merchandisers to engage in agency deferred sales. Thus the agency has the means of guiding resources into holding stocks of grains in private hands. The agency itself need never take possession of any grain.

These general points are best illustrated by means of an example of the calculation of a price schedule. Table 9.2 gives the steps in the creation of a price list based on information available at the end of July. All contracts are due at the beginning of the month. The components are a price base, an interest rate, and a storage cost schedule.

In this table the price for immediate delivery generally should be set below the highest price competitor, usually PZZ, in order to discourage deliveries and to encourage participation in the deferred delivery pricing system. The prices rise along with the time until the maturity. This reflects a concession needed to encourage the storing of grain. Notice that the carry (the steepness of the price increment as maturity

Table 9.2 Determining agency contract prices at 20% simple interest
(1,000 Zl per ton)

Delivery date	Storage	Credit	Contract price
August 1	15	11.67	700.00
September 1	14	11.67	726.67
October 1	13	11.67	752.33
November 1	12	11.67	777.00
December 1	11	11.67	800.67
January 1	10	11.67	823.33
February 1	9	11.67	845.00
March 1	8	11.67	865.67
April 1	7	11.67	885.33
May 1	6	11.67	904.00
June 1	5	11.67	921.67
July 1	4	11.67	938.33

increases) is the sum of two parts. The concession for credit cost is calculated on the basis of simple interest. In actual practice, it should reflect the way interest is calculated by Polish banks. The marginal monthly concession for storage costs is decreasing as of the time since the last harvest. The reason for this is to give a reduced incentive to store as the crop year progresses, therefore assuring a flow of the good out of storage and into processing channels.

To the extent that the market environment in the grain sector remains fragmented and inefficient, the agency can exercise considerable power in setting prices. Basically, the agency can vary the level of the schedule and the steepness of the schedule. The steeper the schedule, the greater the incentive to store. The higher the level of the schedule, the greater the number of dealers who will find it desirable to do spot sales to the agency. In the current environment, it is likely that the agency would like to determine the level of the schedule by setting a spot price just under the prevailing cash market spot price, thereby avoiding physical trading at this early time in its existence. On the other hand, setting a steep schedule implies a strong incentive to store grain. This may be deemed desirable at early stages of development as an inducement to enter into the agency trading system.

A crucial issue is the extent to which agency prices will fully reflect market forces. By setting its deferred prices sufficiently high, it can induce agents to produce grains and keep them in storage. However, to the extent that it is more attractive to carry grain within the agency system than through storage in private channels, the agency will tend to make a systematic loss. This operating loss must be met by the agency's budget. This implies that if budgetary discipline is maintained, the degree of price distortion is limited by the extent of the agency budget. This simple fact implies that, should the agency evolve to become a long-standing, very expensive government body, it would have considerable power to introduce significant price distortions.

A more positive outlook would be for the agency to become progressively self-financing, which would be possible only if the agency respected the market environment it found itself in. In principle, nothing stands in the way of the agency being an independent private company. Furthermore, once established, there could be a very natural way for the agency's operations to evolve into a modern futures market. As was the case in the development of a number of markets, the two crucial steps in this direction would be to introduce a margin system and to open the way for trading by agents without posting physical goods as collateral. This would invite forward purchases so that demand forces would be more immediately transmitted to the pricing apparatus. A more obvious, but no less important, point is that, to the extent that external grain trade is liberalized, the agency should and would be forced by arbitrage to conform to world prices.

The foreseeable cost to the agency per contract written is simply the carry of that contract over the period held. Consequently, we have a clear basis for estimating what that budgetary cost might be. Assuming that the agency established in August 1990 a price schedule running from Zl680,000 spot to Zl900,000 per ton for June 1991 delivery and that the agency carries long contracts that represent 33% of those stored by PZZs in 1989-90, we conclude that the approximate budget cost excluding administration would be some Zl108 billion. The details of the calculation are given in Table 9.3.

The other potential drain on the agency budget would be trading losses. If the agency maintains forward purchases equal to, say, 1 million tons, it faces the risk that the price may fall. For example, on the basis of the stock holding assumptions given in Table 9.3, if the agency trading operation lost 10% of its forward

Table 9.3 Estimated agency losses through storage report
(billion Zl)

	PZZ stocks	Agency stocks	Carry (1000 Zl)	Agency costs
August	1.95	0.65	26.35	17.13
September	1.9	0.63	25.35	16.05
October	1.62	0.54	24.35	13.15
November	1.43	0.48	23.35	11.13
December	1.37	0.46	22.35	10.21
January	1.27	0.42	21.35	9.04
February	1.34	0.45	20.35	9.09
March	1.22	0.41	19.35	7.87
April	0.95	0.32	18.35	5.81
May	0.65	0.22	17.35	3.76
June	0.35	0.12	16.35	1.91
July	0.05	0.02	15.35	0.26

Note: Total estimated storage funding cost is Zl 105.4 billion.

purchases (Zl70,000 per ton per month), this would equal approximately Zl329 billion. Consequently, we see that imperfect hedging could easily swamp other costs. For this reason, as the agency grows, it is important to get successful trading procedures in place.

The principles of hedging the agency forward purchases are those that apply to any physicals-oriented trading operation. The best hedge for a given long position is a short position that matches the long as closely as possible with respect to maturity date, grade, and location. The main alternative is to hedge in a liquid market that may not match the characteristics of the existing position. In the case of the agency, it is likely that its hedging operation should be directed toward developing forward trading with the major users of grain. Alternatively, it should be seen whether Chicago Board of Trade grain futures contracts can hedge the agency's price risk. The major potential impediments to this may be the imperfect connection between Polish and world prices because of quality differences, trade restrictions, and substantial transportation costs. Furthermore, there is considerable foreign exchange risk. These are significant issues that require expertise that is not currently within the agency.

Competitive issues

Under the former state procurement mechanism, the PZZ for grains was effectively a state monopoly with 41 branches under its control.

Producers of grain for commercial purposes had little choice but to sell to the PZZs, at the single state price. The competitive outlook for the grain sector to this point has been affected by two important acts:

• the old grain trust has been divided into 41 independent PZZs in most cases organized at the level of the voivodship [2] or in a few cases for a region consisting of several voivodships; and
• there is no longer any legal impediment for any new or existing organization to engage in grain trading, storage, or transportation in any region of the country.

On the face of it these acts move toward reducing concentration in the grain sector and removing barriers to entry. Thus there would appear to be the basis for considerable competition in this area.

Nevertheless, it is frequently doubted that effective competition will quickly establish itself. There would appear to be three main possible justifications for such fears. First, the long working association of managers at the newly separated PZZs may be conducive to the emergence of collusive practices. This is exacerbated by the fact that managers may exercise considerable managerial discretion since their organizations have not established clear profit-seeking ethos. Second, the existing PZZs are generally highly vertically integrated and have significant storage and milling capacity. To the extent that there are important economies of scale in these activities, these existing assets would represent significant effective entry barriers that would discourage potential competitors. Finally, even if technical scale economies might permit additional plant investments or might even require the consolidation of productive capacities, private entities may be unable to have access to the required credits under the current conditions of high real interest rates. Consequently, the existing entrenched position of the PZZs would tend to be perpetuated.

These are hypotheses that are difficult to assess without more information and, probably, more actual experience. Here, the specific question to be asked is more limited: will the emergence of the agency have significant pro-competitive benefits? The answer depends critically on the proportion of grain that would be owned by the agency relative to that held privately. If the non-PZZ storage capacity were

routinely filled with agency-owned grain, the net effect would be to add an additional, larger trading partner to the existing 41 PZZs. Since none of these 42 bodies would have a clear profit motive, it is not clear that this would have a significant effect in reducing possible price distortions due to collusive activities of these producers.

On the other hand, if, as a result of the program, there were a significant increase in privately owned storage capacity that was largely utilized in storing privately owned grain, the net effect would be to add a new competitive force in the sector that would be responsive to market forces. This could serve as a significant discipline on the incumbent PZZs. This is particularly the case with respect to local elements of monopoly power for cleaning and drying grains. The key to this is the level of the support price established by the agency. If the agency sets a relatively low support price most storage would be for privately owned grain in normal circumstances. Nevertheless, there may be significant interest on the part of private merchandisers either to have the option to sell to the agency when market conditions are unusually bad or to have access to credits for investment under favorable terms.

Policy approaches to the current situation

In the current depressed situation in the grain market, the natural question to ask is the extent to which the agency's activities will aid in lending support to grain prices. The agency's program tends to raise grain prices for three reasons: by setting the premium of deferred prices sufficiently high the agency encourages storage; the expectation of higher prices as more agents add to storage tends to reduce hasty selling in depressed conditions; and by providing price insurance the agency helps to channel credits to producers and thereby reduce sales caused by farmer illiquidity.

In the very near term the main supporting effect of the agency is on expectations. Full operations of the agency are still months away. Consequently, it is prudent to prepare a contingency plan. The main additional steps that could be taken are to arrange for exports of grain or to force the PZZs, explicitly or through indirect means, to directly increase their prices. This latter method is very undesirable since it is an extreme form of administered prices. The exports appear to be an option. The main problem with rapid exports at this time is that current market conditions could lead to a rush for exports. Potentially, this could put Poland in the position of importing at high cost later in the crop year. Consequently, it would be desirable to be ready to allow export licenses in September if the grain markets erode further.

Conclusions

The Agency for Agricultural Marketing has the potential to exert a powerful influence on the grain sector either in the development of market institutions or to undercut those institutions. Its current emphasis on trading on a forward basis with offset, using certified grain, offers a reasonable prospect for stimulating market institutions. However, should political pressure lead to excessively high prices, especially for immediate delivery, the agency could fairly quickly degenerate into a traditional state grain acquisition company. Consequently, additional efforts by the World Bank and others to support its development toward market forms could be very beneficial.

Given its newness, there are very significant concerns about its administrative capacity to operate successfully in the near term. There is the need for improved administration at all levels. In particular, there is a very pressing need to develop expertise in hedging and trading. Strong consideration should be given to contracting for outside hedging expertise for a period of six months to one year.

Given the apparent willingness of important farm groups to cooperate with the agency, there is some chance that a support will be established for the market. Consequently, the decision to export on a large scale should be deferred to late August at which time more will be known about the harvest.

The grain sector faces numerous potential sources of inefficiency at the micro level. In particular, the concentration of drying capacity could promote monopolistic practices at the local level. Analysis of this is required before it is possible to assess the truth of the claim that PZZs exercise monopolistic power.

Endnotes

This annex was prepared by Ronald Anderson (Université Catholique de Louvain and City University of New York). Claude Blanchi (World Bank), Odin Knudsen (World Bank), Wales Mack, Knud Munk (EC), and Wojciech Pawlak (Agency for Agricultural Marketing) have helped in providing information and in discussing the issues.

1. At the time of this report the official zloty exchange rate was Zl9,310 = US$1.

2. Poland is divided into 49 voivodships, for administrative purposes.

Agricultural research

The current situation

Agricultural research in Poland is primarily the responsibility of the Ministry of Agriculture and Food Economy (MAFE), although some work is undertaken at the nine agricultural universities, and by the Polish Academy of Science (which supports an animal research institute). Other ministries may also be involved, particularly the Ministry of Industry with respect to machinery and pesticide development. Some adaptive trials are undertaken by the Voivodships Agricultural Progress Centers (VOPRs).

By far the most important component of the national agricultural research system is the complex of 16 institutes, six central laboratories, and eight other central research-related units under the aegis of MAFE (Annex 1). In addition, there are about 90 substations of research institutions, and 80 variety testing stations. These institutions employ a total staff of 8,325, of whom 1,693 are scientists, supported by around 4,000 technicians, and 1,170 administrators. In 1989 the ratio of technicians to scientists was 2.16:1, adequate but not lavish, whereas the administrator:scientist ratio of 0.63:1 was high.

Data on the breakdown of the scientific staff by level of training are not available, but most have an M.Sc. or Ph.D. The 1989 report of the Foundation for the Development of Polish Agriculture (Borlaug Report) gives them a generally high rating and credits them with a considerable number of significant achievements. The Bank report endorses this view of their technical quality, but qualifies this by listing a number of organizational and financial problems.

Total funds allocated to agricultural research under the 1990 plans are Zl516.399 million: equivalent to approximately US$54 million at an exchange rate of 9500. For comparison, the French agricultural research system, which is approximately the same size, has a 1990 budget of US$324 million.

Research is funded principally from the Central Fund for Science and Technology Development, and decisions about allocation of funds to research programs are made at present by the Praesidium of the Science and Technology Development Committee, with some advice from MAFE with respect to agriculture. In 1990, the MAFE institutes are to receive Zl442,788 million from this fund, of which Zl312,000 Million are channeled to them directly by the S&T committee for central programs, while Zl130.755 million is allocated to MAFE for redirecting to branch programs at institutes and to support some central services. There is also a popularization fund of Zl70,000 million paid to institutes by MAFE out of the state budget for outreach activities—including links to WOPRs and state farms, publications, information bulletins, meetings, statistical analysis, etc.

There is some resentment in MAFE concerning the allocation of funds to agricultural research by the Science and Technology Development Committee. Agriculture generates around 13% of the GDP and 28% of employment; while 30% of S&T funding is currently from a 1.2%

cess on sales of agricultural products. Yet all of the direct research needs of agriculture receive only about 9.5% of the fund's money, although apparently some research by the Polish Academy of Science, and also industrial research related to fertilizers, pesticides, tractors, and vehicles used in agriculture may also be charged to agricultural research by the S&T committee. Data on this expenditure could not be ascertained, but it may be about Zl76,000 million (the difference between the total allocation of Zl516,399 million and the allocation of Zl442,788 million to the MAFE system from the S&T committee).

It is probable that the cess system will be abolished at the end of 1990, after which all research funds will be derived from the state budget, although mostly channeled through a proposed new scientific research council of the Council of Ministers which will replace the present Science and Technology Development Committee.

Constraints to the effective use of research resources

There is a lack of a comprehensive national agricultural research policy, with medium- and long-term horizons as a framework for developing programs geared to national priorities for submission to a scientific research council for funding.

There is considerable instability in the agricultural research system because there is no central management unit such as an agricultural research council, and no core fund to pay salaries. Research tasks are contracted to specific programs, and program coordinators assign staff once those programs are accepted for funding. Overheads such as institute directors' salaries, administrative costs, vehicles, equipment, etc., are prorated among programs. Directors' salaries are determined on a points basis according to the number and size of programs, so there may be considerable inequalities from institute to institute. The directors of institutes have some latitude to suggest programs, and are responsible for their administration overall, but there is little cohesion among the institutes; nor is there any central authority in the ministry to coordinate effort, provide guidance, training and other services to the institutes, maintain records of expenditure, staff and equipment, evaluate results, and perform other functions of

sound management. Until the present Director of Research and Extension took office no financial records were maintained. Uncertainty about future funding arrangements and rumors about reorganization of the MAFE institutes are causing further instability.

The MAFE system is too dispersed and lacks integration and focus. Some institutes deal with commodities, some with disciplines, and some with mixtures of the two. In addition, there are various laboratories — mostly commodity-oriented, but not forming part of related production programs. There is little evidence of interdisciplinary interaction at the institutes or of collaboration among institutes; nor is there any network of regional stations working across commodities with a farming systems approach. Several institutes may have substations located in close proximity to others without any contact. Senior MAFE staff feel that a more rationally structured system is urgently needed, leading to better use of resources with economies of scale, and a committee of scientists has prepared a proposal for reorganization (Annex 2).

Research has been largely production oriented, and geared to large state farms and cooperatives, which received preferential treatment for inputs. Hence widening gaps have opened up in recent years between actual and potential yield, as inputs have been in short supply and these large agricultural entities have ceased to receive preferred status. The research system is not attuned to economic analysis; there is only one institute directly charged with economic work, which receives only 4% of the total MAFE allocation, and other institutes have little or no economic capability. Hence, much of the information needed to assist farmers in managing their resources efficiently, and to assess the real costs of government support to the agricultural sector to optimize future use of resources by government and farmers, is not available.

There are gaps in research coverage which have become more apparent as economic conditions and the structure of farming change, and more attention is being directed to private farms. These gaps include economics and social sciences, farm management, integrated pest management, small-scale mechanization, grassland and fodder crops, and animal management. Research on livestock production seems to receive an unduly low share of research resources: about 16% of funds, and 17% of staff, compared with 45% of staff for crops. Yet in 1988 animal products comprised 62% of commercial sales from the agricultural sector. However, the issue is not simple, since crop production provides the majority of livestock feed in Poland, and crop research has contributed substantially to this. Agricultural processing, with only 12% of total staff, receives the largest share of scientific resources after crops and livestock. It is not clear that marketing is allocated a significant proportion of this, nor that marketing receives sufficient attention from the three institutes dealing with production of vegetables, fruit and herbs, where quality and consistency of supply are crucial.

Links between research and extension need reappraisal and reinforcement. The nine agricultural universities have no extension responsibility. The WOPR research-extension demonstration farms bear little resemblance to private farms, and there is not much cooperation between research institutes and extension workers in on-farm trials on private farms. WOPR farms are used by individual research institutes for experimental work by mutual agreement, but interinstitute coordination is limited and there is no systematic feedback process from extension to research or vice versa. The WOPRs themselves do some adaptive research, but it is not clear that this is linked to work by any institute.

There is virtually no research by the private sector, although it seems desirable to encourage it in order to reduce the burden on the public budget, and to stimulate innovation through competition.

Scientific salaries and operating costs are very low by international standards (about US$27,500 per scientist), and much of the equipment is obsolete. Per scientist costs at INRA (the French national agricultural research organization) averaged US$215,000 in 1988 and costs at the 13 international agricultural research centers exceed US$200,000. Hence there is a drain of good scientists from the MAFE to the universities and elsewhere. The program-oriented system of financing tends to favor short-term expediency over needed capital investment across programs at the institute level.

Strategic recommendations

A first issue which needs to be addressed is whether Poland needs a large agricultural research system funded from the public budget, or whether it could progress by borrowing technology from other countries with analogous ecological situations and by offering incentives to the private sector to engage in research.

Reports suggest that there is a considerable underexploited potential to raise yields of existing crop varieties and breeds of livestock, owing to constraints outside research, especially high prices and some shortages of production inputs and animal feed, farm structure, deficiencies in market infrastructure, inefficient processing industries, and uncertainties concerning prices of fresh and processed products. Consequently yields of several major crops and livestock are well below those in other Eastern European countries, and significantly below Western European countries even though Polish genetic material is rated as good and sometimes better.

No computation of the internal rates of return to agricultural research in Poland has been undertaken, either for individual commodities or for the research system as a whole. Nevertheless, it is possible to infer from the World Bank sector survey and from the Borlaug report that the agricultural research establishment has served Poland well, at least with respect to the genetic base for production. It might further be inferred that a good deal of progress might now be possible with respect to increasing output per hectare of the major staple commodities without much investment in research beyond testing for local adaptation.

This is a plausible but untenable hypothesis in the light of the social and economic implications of the transition from a centrally planned to a market economy and from a predominantly state-controlled agricultural sector to one led by private enterprise. Not merely an adaptation of existing agricultural production techniques but a fundamental realignment of agricultural policy with emphasis on owner-occupied farms, on economic efficiency rather than maximization of yields, and on radical improvement of marketing and processing methods, will be needed to meet future needs. In restructuring its agriculture Poland faces many problems which are not encountered in the Western industrialized countries with which comparisons are sometimes made; some may be transitional, but many, for example the necessary upward adjustment of farm size, are long term.

Research will be essential to find solutions to these problems, both at the conceptual level of agricultural policy and at the practical level to apply science to develop more efficient and cost-effective production and processing techniques. At this juncture there is no clear need to invest more heavily in basic science, for example, in biotechnology for DNA transfer; there is an adequate base of knowledge to achieve the goals outlined above without this. Nor is a larger agricultural research establishment necessary: we believe that considerable economies are possible in the size of the system while increasing its effectiveness. To achieve this, however, will require a significant re-ordering of Poland's considerable agricultural research resources to create a more manageable, better-equipped, and better-integrated national system able to respond flexibly to new challenges. The remainder of this chapter will concentrate on how this might be achieved.

SHORT-TERM RECOMMENDATIONS

Shift the emphasis of research policy to efficiency. New research programs need to be developed as a matter of urgency, to be submitted for funding to the proposed new scientific research council of the council of ministers. While those programs should be designed to fill certain important gaps in research on commodities, the central objective should be to improve the efficiency and economic viability of Polish agriculture, and to clarify some of the crucial issues which impede determination of economic parameters needed to reach domestic agricultural policy decisions and to indicate comparative advantage in external trade. Highest national priority must be given to applied research, and to the adoption of up-to-date technology in Polish agriculture. Programs include:

• seeking approaches that will lead to a more efficient use of inputs and minimize pollution hazards. These may include improved application methods, more responsive crop varieties, more efficient feed conversion by livestock, and integrated pest management. Identification of economic response levels to inputs must form part of all production research, and the results must be applied rapidly in the formulation of recommendations for advice to farmers.

• testing imported or locally manufactured agricultural machinery of modern design for adaptation to small farms, including equipment for harvesting and preparing products for feed, silage, hay, and forage production; herbicide and fungicide application including seed treatments; and lime and fertilizer application;

• testing new materials and modular designs for on-farm storage of grain, oilseeds and potatoes.

• promoting specialist horticultural and livestock products for local markets, for processing, and for export. Market demand analysis, market organization, and quality control, are particularly important areas for research but are often neglected.

• expanding interdisciplinary research, with particular emphasis on social and economic aspects of technological change, and the development of improved farming systems for private farms, integrating crops, livestock and possibly trees.

• Incorporation of some aspects of biotechnology into research programs at existing institutes, for example, to reduce costs in certain processing industries or to accelerate multiplication of genetic material (tissue culture). However, the government should not create new biotechnology facilities requiring major investments. Large sums have been spent by both private and public institutions in Western countries with relatively limited commercial success. Patent issues and environmental controls have sometimes impeded the application of successful results. This is a field of research which seems particularly amenable to joint ventures between agricultural research institutions and other public (university, etc.) or private organizations having proven capability in biotechnology research, as well as the equipment, legal, environmental and other knowledge required for successful application of the results. Contractual arrangements between appropriate government agencies and private firms should be considered, probably in cooperation with the new science and technology council. In the short term, such arrangements would have to involve external expertise, as private firms with experience in biotechnology do not yet exist in Poland.

Reinforce existing procedures at MAFE for policy formulation and resource allocation to research. This could be done by creating a policy-making and management unit to coordinate the national system, through the establishment of an agricultural research council under a deputy minister. This council would have both an advisory and an executive role, including policy analysis and policy formulation, coordination, financial oversight and evaluation, the provision of central services to the institutes; training and human resource development; and international linkages. It is most unusual for an agricultural system as large as that in Poland to have no apex management organization.

Establish an improved procedure for evaluating research proposals from institutes. This would take place before their submission to the National Scientific Research Council for funding. At present programs are submitted ad hoc by scientists after scrutiny by a scientific advisory council at their institutes. Proposals are subsequently reviewed by a technical consultative committee in MAFE, but do not have to conform to an established national policy and related priorities, since no overall framework exists. In the future, all proposals from research institutes should be channeled annually by a set deadline to the Technical Advisory Committee (TAC) of the agricultural research council for scientific evaluation according to defined criteria, and for conformity to established national agricultural research priorities. Recommendations of the TAC concerning programs would be reviewed by the council for approval before submission of a consolidated request to the Scientific Research Council on behalf of MAFE. This is of particular importance at the moment as all programs are currently funded for a five-year period by the existing Science and Technology Development Committee and will be terminated at the end of 1990 when that committee is replaced by a new scientific research council. If, as has been reported, information of how research funds are actually spent is lacking, an important task for the agricultural research council should be to improve accountability and to establish financial monitoring procedures.

Develop a blueprint for a more rational structure of agricultural research. A comprehensive review of the current structure and facilities of institutes, laboratories, research stations, and substations should be initiated immediately by MAFE to make detailed recommendations for creating a new national agricultural research system. A first step should be to review the mandates, functions, and locations of the com-

ponents of the national system in the light of national agricultural research policy, so as to identify gaps or overlaps in subject matter coverage and also in the coverage of agro-ecological regions and areas with special needs. This would provide the basis for a plan to redeploy existing resources to cover priority commodity and environmental management research more effectively, and to establish an integrated network of main institutes and regional centers to achieve economies of scale and enhance research capability. A major objective must be to create better conditions for interdisciplinary research and for interinstitute coordination and cooperation.

A possible structure of a future national agricultural research system in set out in Annex 3. It should be feasible to commence implementation of a plan developed along the lines indicated above within 12-18 months from the initiation of the proposed review of the current structure of the system.

MEDIUM- TO LONG-TERM RECOMMENDATIONS

Establish a new regional research organization. This would be based on well-equipped centers in each of the main agro-ecological regions of Poland. These would replace the existing uncoordinated mass of nearly 200 substations of research institutes and variety testing stations scattered all over the country. Characterization of ecological zones permits the results of research done at central institutes to be tested for local suitability with much greater precision; moreover, those zones can be further subdivided to cater to varying socioeconomic situations. Good work has already been undertaken in Poland to define the seven major ecological zones. A network of regional research centers based on those zones would not have to be very large to cover national needs economically and effectively.

Each regional center would be located strategically to represent a specific subset of conditions within a major agro-ecological region, if possible at a site where land and facilities could be transferred to it from a state farm or a VOPR. Regional centers' staff would consist of a manager and administrative unit, and a small interdisciplinary scientific team with supporting technicians. Program staff of the national institutes could be outposted to the regional centers to conduct research relevant to their mandates with facilities provided by the centers; the regional staff would also undertake on-farm work to test suitability of new varieties and techniques to local conditions, and to develop improved farming systems integrating crops and livestock. Promising new technology would be transferred directly to farmers through an extension service unit based at each regional center. Regional research centers would not be subject to the jurisdiction of regional governments.

The whole regional center network would be managed and administered by a regional directorate of research under a director, based at the agricultural research council, and the staff of the regional units would be members of that directorate. Funds for the directorate and regional center staff would be provided from the MAFE budget, not from the national scientific research council; funds for research conducted at the regional centers by program staff of the national institutes would, however, be charged to their programs out of the National Research Council support to those programs.

Strengthen technology transfer procedures. It is essential to improve linkages between research and the various agencies involved in extension. The latter should not undertake research of their own, but should work with staff of the institutes and regional centers in adaptive testing and monitoring of new technology, and transferring successful new techniques to farmers, and should provide feedback of information on research needs and problems to research staff to help set national and regional research priorities. Measures to achieve these goals will have to be phased with the proposed changes in the structure and responsibilities of the extension agencies (see Annex 12 on agricultural extension), and with the creation of the new agricultural research system of national institutes and regional ecological zone centers described above. However, the overall aim must be to strengthen both the research and the extension services to cooperate more effectively, and to work out jointly new conceptual approaches to achieve this. The proposed regional research centers should play a key role in linking the work of the national institutes to the extension staff. Funding for improved technology transfer procedures might be provided from the existing MAFE popularization budget, currently Zl70 billion, which seems to be used by insti-

tutes for numerous purposes, many of them not closely identifiable with outreach.

Update scientific and management competence.

• **Exchange arrangement.** There is a consensus among visiting agricultural scientists that Polish scientists are well trained and capable of good scientific work. Nevertheless, scientific and managerial capability needs to be updated to meet new knowledge and changing technological and socioeconomic dynamics, and more frequent exchanges between Polish scientists and those from research institutions in Western industrialized countries would be a valuable aid to this end.

• **Training arrangements.** In addition to exchange arrangements, which can often be made on relatively short notice on the basis of personal contacts, there is a need for a more structured training effort to introduce new knowledge and methodology to the institutes' staff, and especially to bridge major disciplinary and subject matter gaps. The latter include research management; policy analysis; animal management; farming systems techniques; agricultural processing and marketing; agricultural machinery design — especially for small farms; and biotechnology. Since the training program is likely to involve PhD-level studies, it should be planned with a ten-year horizon and closely aligned to national research priorities and the new thrusts outlined under *Short-term recommendations* above. Twinning arrangements between appropriate international research institutions or national institutions in countries with advanced scientific capabilities should be encouraged as part of this program.

• **Instituting an award system for demonstrated research achievements.** The present approach to review of agricultural research performance is mechanistic and program oriented. There is some annual internal peer review of progress and new proposals for adjustments to the 5-year program budgets; but there are no external reviews of institutes, and little systematic evaluation of research impact at the farm or user level. The system seems to leave little room for movement of staff among institutes or for recognition of individual or team excellence; royalties to plant breeders go to institutes, not to individuals. The S&T council has an award scheme: it would be useful for

MAFE to retain some of its S&T research budget to reward outstanding performance, particularly for evidence of adoption and impact of applied research, rather than for academic publications. Royalties earned on sales of their seed varieties or improved breeds of livestock should be shared equally by the breeders and their institutes.

• Encouraging private enterprise in research. Although some research in plant breeding and horticulture and some industrial research on design of agricultural machinery and new plant protection products is done outside the formal institutional research system in Poland, little of this is truly private. Yet in most industrialized countries, and some other countries with an important agricultural sector, particularly in Latin America and Asia, a substantial share of research related to agricultural production and processing is privatized. An extreme example is the recent sale of the Cambridge Plant Breeding Institute in England to Unilever. Fields of research particularly well suited to private enterprise are plant breeding, especially where hybrid techniques are involved; biotechnology; horticulture; machinery design and development — including processing machinery; and certain agricultural chemicals — pesticides and veterinary medicines. It must be emphasized, nevertheless, that because private involvement in agricultural research in Poland is practically nonexistent, and because research is not generally the first activity pursued by the private sector when entering new markets, significant progress in this respect is likely to be slow, and will probably require incentives to its development.

Action to stimulate private involvement in research in Poland could be via joint ventures with Polish agricultural or industrial companies, contracts on competitive bidding to undertake specific research tasks, commissioned research to private companies, and incentive measures to encourage investment as long as these do not involve economic distortions. Alternatively, taking indirect action by phasing out redundant or ineffective elements of the public sector research system and withdrawing research funds from quasi-state enterprises such as tractor manufacturers, could stimulate private entrepreneurs to fill the gap.

Implications of the strategic recommendations

The proposed major reorganization of Poland's agricultural research system, implies:

• creating an agricultural research council as the management, policy-making and coordinating unit of the MAFE to develop and implement an agreed national agricultural research policy, and to provide central services to research institutes and programs. An important objective would be the improvement of financial management, accountability, and evaluation procedures for the research system;

• initiating new research programs for submission for financial approval by the new National Science Council, with the aim of closing existing gaps in crop research, strengthening economic inputs, reinforcing livestock research, and improving environmental management. These programs should be the key components of the national agricultural research policy, and not an *ad hoc* collection of ideas submitted by individual scientists or institutes;

• developing a more rational structure of national agricultural research institutes, backed by regional centers representative of the principal agro-ecological zones. A main objective would be to increase efficiency and cost effectiveness by reducing the number of national institutes to minimize duplication of effort, and promote interdisciplinary and systems-oriented research programs. A second objective would be to achieve a sweeping reorganization of substations by eliminating a large number, and collapsing the bulk of the remainder into fewer but better-equipped regional centers which could accommodate research programs from several national institutes instead of being affiliated to only one, as is frequently the case at present;

• rethinking approaches to technology transfer and links to extension with a new and important role for the regional research centers;

• expanding MAFE' s linkages with the universities and the private sector to commission work on aspects of basic research, including biotechnology, as well as on applied research related to agriculture-related industries, through contractual or joint ventures to be financed by the National Science Council.

Consequences of the above proposals would include:

• a greater role of the Ministry of Agriculture in the articulation, coordination, and implementation of agricultural research policy;

• a cohesive set of research programs submitted to the National Science Council for financing, more closely aligned to identified national priorities;

• a tighter management structure, with the national institutes as the key instruments rather than the research programs, so as to improve accountability and provide better services and management stability. Each major research program would be headquartered at an institute, with elements of that program being undertaken as necessary at other national institutes and/or at regional agro-ecological zone centers (Appendix 10.1);

• a reduction of at least 50% in the number of research institutes and laboratories, and a much larger reduction in numbers of substations. Some institutes would be amalgamated, for example, animal production and veterinary science; horticulture and medicinal plants; but in particular it is foreseen that a majority of the laboratories dealing with processing would be phased out by integrating them with related institutes responsible for research on production (for example, cereal, potato and sugar technology with the field crop institute that deals with breeding and production of those crops); and meat technology with animal production research;

• a substantial redeployment of existing staff, and some staff redundancy. There would also be buildings and equipment at stations or laboratories which would be closed down and which could not be used *in situ* for other purposes or transferred to the remaining institutes.

• an anticipated saving in total annual costs of operating and maintaining the national agricultural research system, resulting both from a reduction in the number of institutes and laboratories and in their total staff, and from improved management and efficiency in the remaining national institutes and regional centers. Most important, the economic and financial returns to research are expected to increase as a result of the impact of the new research organization on agricultural productivity, income growth and the balance of payments. Thus the share of agricultural research expenditure in agricultural GDP would decrease.

This does not mean, however, that no new expenditure will be necessary. It is expected that economies resulting from the reorganization will enable the reorganized national institutes and newly created regional centers to be better equipped to modern standards; that the proportion of operating costs can be raised to 40% that of salaries; and that expenditure per scientist (remuneration, operational and administrative support) can also be increased.

The share of research funds obtained from the Ministry of Agriculture budget may also increase. This is because the proposed agricultural research council, the management and other fixed costs of running the national institutes, and the regional research centers are not program costs *strictu sensu*, and may therefore not be provided from the resources of the new scientific research council of the council of ministers. This, however, remains to be decided, since that council has not yet commenced operations and its rules are not clear. In any case, the total national cost of funding agricultural research is expected to decrease even if the share of MAFE in that cost rises. The costs of running the agricultural research council and servicing both its committees and those of the institutes is expected to represent about 3% of the total national agricultural research expenditure. This is a reasonable overhead charge for providing policy guidance, efficient management coordination, and essential services to a large national agricultural research system.

Concluding comment

A proposal with many similar features to those suggested in Appendix 10.3 has been developed by a committee of scientists for consideration by MAFE's research advisory committee This would reduce the total number of research institutes from 16 to 12, and would retain only four other units of the remaining 15 laboratories and other research-related entities (Appendix 10.2). In effect it would halve the number of institutional components. However, the scientific staff would remain about the same, with savings being effected by some 2,400 cuts in administrative and support staff. While some further consolidation might be envisaged, for example, combining animal production and veterinary science in one institute and reducing numbers of substations, implementation of this proposal would achieve many of the objectives recommended in this annex. It does not, however, provide for a management organization (agricultural research council) for the system as a whole, nor for a drastic reorganization of regional research. Both of these provisions must be considered essential to the establishment of a more cost-effective and efficient national system.

Endnote

This annex was prepared by Peter Oram, John Hayward, Oskar Honisch and Marian Krol.

Appendix 10.1
Situation of MAFE agricultural research system, 1989

Institutions	Head quarters location	Number of Sub-stations	% of Total 1989 ag/res budget	Total staff	% of total 1989	Scien-tific staff 1989	% of total 1989 ag/res staff
Institute of Agronomy and Soil Science	Pulawy	17	4.8	745	8.9	170	10.1
Institute of Plant Breeding	Radzikow	16	8.4	770	9.2	145	8.6
Institute for Potato Research	Bonin	7	4.1	441	5.3	63	3.7
Institute of Vegetable Research	Skietniewice	5	2.3	395	4.7	90	5.3
Institute of Pomology and Horticulture	Skietniewice	15	6.7	518	6.3	123	7.3
Sugar Beet Research Institute	Warsaw	0	0.6	79	0.9	21	1.2
Institute of Medicinal Plants/Herbs	Poznan	0	0.9	162	1.9	42	2.4
Institute of Plant Protection	Poznan	1	2.3	412	5.0	99	5.9
Center for Cultivar Testing and Certification	Slupia Wielka	81	n.a.	134	1.6	15	0.9
Center for Forestry Research	Konstantin-Jeziorna	0	n.a.	38	0.5	13	0.8
Institute of Land Reclamation	Falenty	8	3.9	506	6.1	106	6.3
Institute of Animal Production	Krakow	12	10.1	310	3.7	92	5.4
Veterinary Research Institute	Pulawy	3	2.3	438	5.3	126	7.5
Inland Fisheries Institute	Kortowo	2	1.2	189	2.3	50	2.9
Center for Poultry R&D	Poznan	10	n.a.	513	6.2	24	1.4
Meat and Fat Research Institute	Warsaw	1	4.9	267	3.2	55	3.2
Institute of Food Industry Biotechnology	Warsaw	0	2.2	241	2.9	51	2.9
Institute of Agriculture and Food Economics	Warsaw	0	6.5	265	3.2	67	4.0
Institute for Building and Mechanization	Warsaw	4	5.2	672	8.1	129	7.6
Center for Animal Mechanization	Gdansk	0	n.a.	165	2.0	16	0.9
Center for Technical Services R&D	Zolzary	0	n.a.	205	2.5	0	0.0
Central Lab for Cereal Technology	Warsaw	0	n.a.	38	0.5	12	0.7
Central Lab for Food Concentrates	Poznan	0	n.a.	86	1.0	17	1.0
Central Lab for Potato	Poznan	0	n.a.	54	0.6	10	0.6
Central Lab for Tobacco	Krakow	0	n.a.	78	0.9	18	1.1
Central Lab for Refrigeration	Lodz	0	n.a.	96	1.2	18	1.1
Central Lab for Feed Industry	Snopkow	4	n.a.	70	0.8	27	1.6
Extension Methodology Training Center	Brwinow	2	n.a.	277	3.3	86	5.1
Central Library	Warsaw	2	n.a.	78	0.9	8	0.5
Museum	Szreniawa	-	n.a.	83	1.0	0	0.0
Total Ratio of Nonscientific Staff to Scientists		190	100.0	8,325	100.0	1,693	100.0

Appendix 10.2
Reorganization after 1990 proposed select committee of MAFE scientists

	Number of sub-station	Total staff	As % of all components of system	Scien-tific staff	As % of all components of system
Institute of Agronomy and Soil Science	4	750	15.4	250	15.2
Institute of Plant Breeding	4	650	13.4	200	12.2
Institute of Horticulture	0	600	12.3	200	12.2
Institute of Medicinal Plants	0	150	3.1	50	3.0
Institute of Plant Protection	2	300	6.2	110	6.7
Institute of Animal Production	2	550	11.4	160	9.8
Veterinary Research Institute	0	400	8.2	160	9.8
Inland Fisheries Institute	2	160	3.3	60	3.7
Institute of Food Industry	1	450	9.3	150	9.1
Institute Agriculture and Food economics	0	250	5.1	100	6.1
Institute of Mechanization and Amelioration	3	600	12.3	200	12.2
Extension Methodology Center	1	n.a.		n.a.	
Central Library	3	n.a.		n.a.	
Museum	0	n.a.		n.a.	
Center for Cultivar Testing and Certification	n.a.	n.a.		n.a.	
TOTAL		4,860	100.0	1,640	100.0

Appendix 10.3
Possible future structure of national agricultural research system

Agricultural Research Council

(i) **Council:** Executive & Finance Committees; Technical Advisory Committee; **Secretariat** (Policy, Administrative, Finance, Central Services)

(ii) **Central Services**[1]: Data base/Management Information System; Library; Training & Staff Development Unit; Computer and Equipment Services; External Relations and Meeting service; Directorate of Regional Research

(iii) **Central Funds**[2]: **Core Staff Budget** for Council staff, Regional Research staff, and Management staff at Institutes; **Contract research** fund to encourage joint research with universities, private sector, etc. **Technology transfer fund**[3]

Agricultural research institutes[4]

(i) Plant breeding, genetic resources, seed technology and varietal certification
(ii) Field crop production and protection (cereals, potatoes, sugar beet, oilseeds, legumes)
(iii) Horticultural production and protection (vegetables, flowers, herbs)
(iv) Ruminant livestock production and health, (Including pasture and fodder crop management)
(v) Land and water resource management and agricultural mechanization
(vi) Food and agriculture policy and socio-economic strategy
(vii) Food technology and agricultural processing

Regional agro-ecological zone stations[5]

---

1. Services provided by the Council to the research institutes and centers.
2. Funded from the MAFE regular budget provided by the State.
3. Currently known as the "popularization" Fund, derived from the MAFE budget.
4. Research programs funded mainly by the Science Council Central Fund: Core management/administration costs of institutes by MAFE Central Fund.
5. Decision as to number to be based on national review, but probably not exceeding 21. A small number of special purpose substations might be retained in addition, e.g., for atypical ecological or socioeconomic conditions; tree crop research, and so forth.

Seed production and distribution

Strategic importance

Good quality seed of well-adapted varieties is fundamental to achieving economic returns to crop production. If the seed is diseased, or has poor germination because it has been badly harvested or stored, plant population will be poor and returns to the use of other inputs will be low. If the seed is affected with seed-borne diseases or impure due to mixtures with other crops or weeds, yields at harvest time will be low. If the varieties used are not well adapted to local ecological conditions, the crop may have poor resistance to weather, pests, diseases, or weeds, and may even fail completely.

Conversely, the choice of a well-adapted variety may offer the cheapest insurance against catastrophic losses, and provide a reasonable assurance of an adequate yield to risk-averse small farmers reluctant to apply substantial inputs of fertilizers or pesticides. Seed is not only a relatively cheap input, but one which is understood by all farmers and which is environmentally benign.

Satisfactory arrangements to develop, test, and maintain ecologically well-adapted varieties of the major crops, with good yield potential, genetic resistance to the main pests and diseases, and good consumer acceptability, and an efficient organization to multiply and distribute high-quality seed to farmers, are therefore basic components of a sound agricultural development strategy.

It is noteworthy in this context that the World Bank sector study report states that seed breeding and seed multiplication in Poland is at an internationally recognized high level of quality, and may have been the single most important contributor to expansion of cereal production over the past eight years.

Current situation

VARIETAL DEVELOPMENT

Other reports, notably the 1989 Borlaug report, conclude that the genetic base for crop production in Poland is good, and that scientific competence is satisfactory. Some objectives for crop improvements by breeding are suggested in Annex 10 on research, and in addition to those goals there is a continuing need for breeders to maintain existing standards of varietal quality, pest and disease resistance, and to adjust to changes in demand.

Before varieties are released for multiplication they are normally tested at substations of the parent institutes, then submitted to the National Institute for Cultivar Testing and Certification which has 81 testing stations all over Poland. After three years of testing by this institute, varieties which have performed satisfactorily are added to the national list of approved varieties; conversely some which have become obsolete, or broken down due to biological stress, are removed from the list.

Once approved for general release, seed developed by the plant breeders may be bulked up at research institutes where land is sufficient to do so, at least up to elite standards, before being channeled to state farms, or sometimes to other contracted growers, for further multiplication.

SEED MULTIPLICATION

Seed production in Poland is organized along conventional lines and within legal standards which conform to those of Western Europe or the United States. However, with the exception of some horticultural crops, private firms have no role in either plant breeding and varietal development or in seed production and distribution.

State farms are particularly concerned with producing elite and original seed of cereals (the stage beyond elite), which they are especially well equipped to produce economically. They are also concerned with seed potato and rapeseed production. Smaller contractors deal either with the two subsequent stages of cereal seed production, which require less stringent standards, or with other crops (horticulture, grasses, sugar beet, legumes).

Until recently, seed was mainly purchased from state farms and contractors by Seed Production Central, an organization belonging to the voivodships with 17 main depots throughout Poland, supported by funds from the Ministry of Agriculture budget. This organization sold seed to farmers. It also maintains around 70 breeding stations with 200,000 ha of land for creation of new varieties and maintenance breeding of registered varieties. There are also a number of smaller companies in the seeds business, which originally belonged to the State Union of Agricultural and Horticultural Seed Production. This has been dismantled since 1988, but it seems to maintain its existence as the Polish Agricultural Plant Breeding and Seed Production Company (Ltd), CENAS, which has its own offices in Warsaw, as well as in the Ministry of Agriculture. It maintains a catalogue of associated companies, listing the species and varieties of seed which are available from them. Some are plant breeders, some do both breeding and seed production, and some are only involved in multiplication. They all appear to be quasi-governmental in nature, although it is reported that at least one successful breeder would like to become independent. CENAS maintains 2,000 ha for breeding and variety testing, plus their own laboratories, and 100,000

ha of land for seed multiplication in rotation with commercial crops for sale. The breeding work is partly state subsidized, but seed prices have not been subsidized since 1986. Sale prices of certified cereal seeds are reported to be 15-20% above those of commercial crops. This is an adequate return on seed production except for potatoes, which may require a higher mark-up because of heavy transport and storage costs.

Seed inspection and certification is the responsibility of a separate organization of the Ministry of Agriculture — the Seed Service. It has 17 regional divisions based on the old distribution of voivodships, but effectively covering all voivodships by overlap. This organization, which is funded from a surtax on sales of certified seeds, sets and enforces standards for seed quality and seed inspection as laid down in the national seeds law. It trains seed inspectors who field inspect seed being grown throughout the multiplication chain, and carry out spot-checks of seed at harvest before it is sealed for sale to farmers.

As far as could be ascertained, the current arrangements for varietal certification, testing, and seed inspection are adequate and in line with generally recognized international standards. On the whole seed development in Poland has a good record. Some very mixed cereal crops were seen on farms during field trips, but the main cause seems not to be inadequate seed inspection of contractors' seed, but poor standards of combining, leading to mixtures of cereal varieties and species in harvested seed where farmers save their own seed, and poor tillage practices allowing seed shed at the previous harvests to germinate in the following year's crop. Inadequate and poorly constructed storage facilities (silos difficult to clean, and the like) also contribute to this problem.

However, concern must be expressed at the trend toward mixing research on plant breeding and the production of breeders' seed with large-scale seed multiplication at research institutes, experimental stations, and state farms, which also use their land for commercial crop production. To quote the recent report of a team under the aegis of the Economic Council, led by Professor Anton Leopold, "The structure and management system of the enterprises encompassing genetic stations and commercial entities has deprived them of autonomy as well as abolished the breeders' control over and responsibility for the reproduction of their products. The whole system, including the evaluation, was subordinated to a centrally planned command and quota economy." Paradoxically, there is a further cause for concern if the dissolution of the centralized seed multiplication organization and the break-up of state farms leads to a vacuum in supply of certified seed. The current situation therefore calls for very careful monitoring by the government.

THE ADEQUACY OF SEED SUPPLY (TABLE 11.1)

Production of certified cereal seed is adequate to allow farmers to renew their seed from stocks every 2-3 years in the case of barley, oats, and triticale, and every 3-4 years in the case of wheat. These replacement rates are within those recommended for normal husbandry, but below need for the high technology package. The situation with rye is unsatisfactory: it is a cross-pollinated crop and therefore needs seed renewal more frequently to prevent genetic dilution, yet certified seed supply is only enough to replace farmers' seed from stock every 6.3 years. Currently about 30% of wheat, 40% of barley and oats, and 66% of triticale area is sown to improved seeds, but only 15% of the area of rye, and 12% of the potato area. Seed imports are small, mainly consisting of hybrid maize varieties from Hungary, Western Europe and the United States and horticultural seeds from Holland. Exports of seed are negligible, although once domestic supplies are adequate, seed exports of specialist crops might be an area with growth potential.

Reports that sales of certified seed have dropped significantly in recent years are confirmed by the statistics with respect to potatoes, but not in the case of cereals. Potato seed sales have fallen from 618,000 MT in 1986/87 to 455,000 MT in 1988/89. However, over the same period the total area planted to potatoes also declined by about 80,000 ha, although the percentage reduction in their area is a good deal smaller than that of seed. Since seed represents about 25% of potato production costs it is clearly a target for economies by growers, although those economies could prove false if the use of home grown seed leads to increased virus and other disease problems resulting in a serious decline in yield.

In the case of cereals, changes in the use of certified seed by farmers seem to be related mainly to technological change. Sales of triticale seed have increased from 6,000 MT in 1985 to around 50,000 MT in 1989; this has mainly replaced rye, sales of which fell from 78,000 MT to 60,000 MT over the same period. Sales of winter wheat declined from 104,000 to 88,000 MT; but spring wheat sales rose from 27,000 to 58,000 MT. Sales of spring barley declined by 1.5% but oats showed little change. The total sales of cereal seed in 1988/89 were 403,000 MT compared with a 5-year average of 398,000 MT. A note of caution is necessary with respect to 1990. There are reports of a serious decline in purchase of certified seed by farmers but this cannot yet be confirmed because the system of data reporting has been disrupted.

Table 11.1 Seed Requirements and Production (1988/89 data)

Crop	Area Sown ('000 ha)	Average Seedrate (kg/ha)	Seed Required[a] (total MT)	Seed Produced (total MT)	Adequate for replacement (years)	Minimum Desirable replacement (years)	Minimum Desirable Need (MT/year)	Ha Change
Wheat	2,196	275	604,000	163,500	3.7	3-4	155,000	-1,700 (5)
Barley	1,175	175	205,625	109,300	1.9	3-4	60,000	-12,325 (4)
Oats	803	160	128,480	55,700	2.3	3-4	37,000	-6,233 (3)
Rye	2,275	180	407,500	64,800	6.3	2-3	163,000	+32,733 (3)
Triticale	649	230	149,270	56,900	2.6	1-2	99,000	+10,525 (4)
Potatoes	1,859	2,500	4,647,500	542,500	8.6	3	1,555,000	+40,500 (25) +63,50

a Assuming that entire crop area is planted with new original seed each year. Seed of sugar beet and rapeseed is adequate to meet annual replacement requirements.

Main constraints

• Inadequate production of seed potatoes and rye seed. There is a need to triple annual output of seed potatoes and to almost triple that of rye seed. Triticale is marginally adequate, but special care needs to be exercised to maintain genetic stability and avoid dilution of seed stocks with other cereals, especially rye.

• Insufficient and/or unsuitable storage, especially for smaller seed producers and horticultural crops.

• Shortage of handling facilities and cool stores for seed potatoes.

• Inadequate supply of seed dressing materials, lack of proper equipment for treating seed for small farmers, and short time bottlenecks for treatment of winter-sown cereals between harvest and seeding. It is reported that seed in bulk storage is not treated during processing, with treatment being left to the farmers. Sometimes farmers simply mix seed treatment chemicals with seed in the farmyard, or even in the seeddrill. This leads to poor coverage of seed and can even reduce germination. Only about 4.2 million hectares of cereals were treated in 1988/89, about 50% of total area. The government target for the year 2000 is approximately 80% of cereal area. It is estimated by MAFE that a 10-fold increase in supply of seed treatment equipment to farmers is needed to overcome these problems. A new mobile pedal-driven machine capable of treating 2 tons of seed per hour, costing 1 million Zl is to be manufactured by joint venture; and now, broadly effective seed treatment materials are available costing only 16,000 Zl per 100 kg seed treated.

• Seed impurity, which is increased on farms by unsatisfactory equipment for combine harvesting and by inefficient seed cleaning during processing by larger contractors during bulk handling and storage, as well as during transport.

• Transportation bottleneck for seed potatoes being shipped from the low disease areas of northeast Poland to other production areas, according to the Bank Sector Study, which also states that a considerable expansion of transport capacity is required to remedy this.

• Seed industry in a state of transition from state control and centralized organization to a more dispersed system composed of associations of smaller operators. State Farms are reported to be interested in producing and selling seed directly to farmers rather than acting as contractors to the bulk purchasing depots. None of these seed producers is a private company, although in some respects they seem to be moving in that direction. It is not possible at this moment to determine how these changes in the structure of the industry will affect output and quality of certified seed, but the situation should be monitored carefully by the agencies responsible for seed certification.

Strategic recommendations

SHORT TERM

Fill gaps in seed supply. Seed availability of rye and potatoes should be increased as rapidly as possible consonant with sound quality control. Wheat seed production, which is only marginally adequate for renewal every 3-4 years, should also be expanded. There is a surplus of barley and oat seed production so that about 20,000 ha could be shifted from those crops to producing seed of the other cereals (see Table 11.1). Triticale seed breeding and multiplication should be monitored carefully to guard against genetic degeneration and against physical mixtures with other cereals. Pasture seed quality is also reported to be affected by dilution, and there may also be limitations in terms of quantity. Economy in cereal seed use might be achieved by reducing the current rather high seedrates, especially for wheat. However, this probably depends also on the improvement of seeding and seed dressing equipment, and more widespread treatment of seed. This is an important area for research. Research on production of true seed of potatoes should also be considered. There are reports that the quality of pasture seed is poor. Small quantities (0.3-2.5 tons) of most temperate pasture grasses are listed as available in the seeds catalogue, and these appear to exceed demand. However, it was not possible to check their quality. No seeds of clovers are listed. Annual forage and grain legumes are produced in quantities from 15,000-40,000 MT depending on the species; supplies of these seeds seem adequate to meet demand.

Improve seed storage and handling facilities. Bulk storage capacity, location, and equipment should be evaluated to determine the adequacy and quality of the facilities, as a basis for an investment program to modernize the resource and to expand capacity where necessary. Cool storage facilities for seed potatoes should be included in this review. On-farm storage is generally inadequate, particularly on smaller private farms. New storage technology based on plastics should be tested in collaboration with importers, with the help of appropriate consultants. Small-scale portable equipment is available for quantities from 5-50 MT; at costs from 65-40 US$/MT plus transport; and silo storage from 25-1,000 MT at a cost of 80-200US$/T (costs per ton decrease as the storage capacity rises). The material is reported to be insect and vermin proof, moisture proof (when properly installed), simple to install and easily cleaned. MAFE is considering seeking help from FAO for testing such equipment, and this project merits support.

Reduce seed-borne diseases. High priority should be given to expanding the availability of small-scale seed treatment equipment to farmers, and to a campaign to upgrade standards of application and to expand total coverage of cereal seed to 80% by 1995. Seed under bulk storage should be treated routinely by seed merchants before bagging and sale to farmers, and labeled accordingly. Routine spraying of potatoes grown for certified seed against potato blight should be enforced; and farmers growing seed for their own use should be encouraged to spray whenever conditions favor blight.

MEDIUM AND LONG TERM

Initiate a national review of the current state of the seed industry in all its aspects.

• Plant breeding: What is the role of the MAFE research system and how do other organizations involved in breeding complement the national institutes? Are there any major breeding problems or bottlenecks requiring special priority?

• Seed multiplication: Research institutes, other breeders, state farms, cooperatives and private farmers are all involved in some phases. Who does what? How adequate are their facilities? What is their competence and what standards do they maintain? To whom do they sell their seed? Do they have storage facilities?

• Seed purchasing, storage and distribution: What is the chain of supply prior to storage? How is seed stored? How adequate are facilities

for transport, cleaning, storage, seed treatment, and transport to buyers? What is the distribution network?

• Seed quality control: What is the role of government? Are the current arrangements for field inspection of seed being produced by contractors and at various state enterprises adequate to ensure seed quality? Is seed properly inspected and certified before bags are sealed for sale to farmers? Is labeling clear and are there minimum standards of labeling which must be met? Are there satisfactory arrangements for spot-checks and growing-on samples of seed taken from seed suppliers at point of shipment to farmers. Can farmers have seeds tested independently if they wish? Do they have any recourse to law if they are sold bad seed? Can seed companies be fined for lack of quality? Are there sufficient and well-trained field inspectors? Should their training be expanded or upgraded? Would external assistance to government be helpful in establishing standards, preparing legislation, and training seed inspection staff?

The object of this review should be to provide the basic data for the preparation of a national seed development program, and a related investment package to ensure the future supply of quality seed of the principal crops.

Improve standards of farm equipment for sowing, weed control, and harvesting. Seed is wasted when improperly sown and poor plant populations may result, leading to higher weed infestation and low yields. Lack of weed control through cultivation or herbicide use causes further problems and weed seeds or seeds of other crops contaminate seed at harvest time, especially as combining and seed cleaning standards are low. The important issue of improving farm equipment and raising standards of operation to reduce those losses is dealt with in Annex 18 on mechanization

Privatize the seed industry. An important objective should be to identify activities suited to private involvement in seed breeding, multiplication, and distribution, and to activate measures to stimulate private investment in the seed industry.

In most developed countries the private sector now plays an important part in breeding new varieties of seed, and has the major role in seed production and sale; but this is not yet the case in Poland. In many ways the industry there now seems ripe for privatization: large state-controlled centrally managed seed organizations have been dismantled and numbers of loosely associated companies of a quasi-public nature seem to be taking their place. It is expected that the review of the industry proposed above will clarify their current role and activities, and the extent to which they are suited to private ownership in the future. It will be necessary to introduce a system of licensing companies to ensure the maintenance of quality throughout the industry, from breeding to sale of seed. Even in countries where the seed industry is predominantly private, governments play a key supporting and regulatory role.

To encourage the transformation of seed enterprises from state or para-statal control to private ownership various incentives could be offered. These might include royalties to breeders (which should also be available to breeders at the national research institutes), patent rights on new varieties and on machinery or other innovations in seed technology, tax holidays for entrepreneurs, joint ventures with foreign companies, and credit availability on suitable (nondistorting) terms.

Endnote

This annex was prepared by Peter Oram.

Agricultural extension

This annex sets out the rationale for developing a new approach to extension in Poland. The approach is proposed in the form of a strategic program reflecting immediate and longer-term actions to support the approach.

The annex addresses some basic questions which the Polish government must face:

- Does Poland need an extension service?
- If so, what functions should extension perform?
- Who should provide the extension — the public or private sector of both?
- Who are the future clients of extension?
- What should be the ownership and structure of extension?
- What strategic steps should the government take in the short, medium and long term to enable extension to meet it objectives?
- What are the implications of the strategy?

The annex begins with a brief review of the present extension system and examines constraints on the system which are relevant to answering the above questions.

Present situation

Agricultural extension in Poland is provided through 49 Voivodship Agricultural Progress Centers (WOPRs) and their field agents at *gmina* level, by livestock services, by quarantine and plant protection services and by agrochemical centers. The public sector system is loosely supervised by the Ministry of Agriculture and Food Economy (MAFE). Many public and private sector agents operate at farmer level: specialized extension is provided by commodity and field crop services of the agricultural and food industries such as the sugar beet industry, and advisory services are also provided to farmers by village cooperatives and private sector agricultural unions. In January 1990, estimates of the total extension workforce were:

Voivodship advisers at WOPR headquarters	1,792
Field advisers at *gmina* level	8,017
WOPR administrative and service employees	3,068
Total WOPR	12,877
Agricultural union advisers	1,500
Quarantine and plant protection staff	1,900
Commodity and field crop service advisers	4,500
Village cooperative advisers	3,500
Agrochemical service advisers	330
Total	24,607

Precise numbers of individuals charged with the responsibility of advising farmers is not known, as the service is fragmented and uncoordinated even at voivodship level. For example, in addition to WOPRs, commodity and cooperative advisers, research institutes also employ specialist extension advisers to coordinate with WOPRs and to promote research messages, for example, the Institute of Plant Protection has 1,800-2,000 field staff located in about 50 field stations. What can be said is that the ratio of trained specialists capable of providing technical information to farmers in Poland is extremely high. With a private farm population around 2.2 million, it is estimated that the WOPR advisers, union advisers, commodity advisers and private cooperative advisers alone total almost 20,000; a ratio of one to every 110 farms. It is accepted that rigid ratios are meaningless in work program development, but they can be used as a rough planning indicator. Considering the average size of farm and level of sophistication of farming, a planning level of one adviser to about 200-250 farms suggests that a reduction in extension staff numbers is possible. Such a step has already been taken in some voivodships (for example, Jelenia Gora, where half the extension staff has been laid off). A rationalization program which would determine precise advisor members and match numbers to needs is urgently required.

The WOPRs are the official lead agency for extension. About 80% of WOPRs have training centers attached to them and all are combined with production farms which may include dairy and pig units in addition to full-scale arable areas ranging from about 500 ha to over 6,000 ha, and land for adaptive research trials and demonstration areas. The total arable land farmed by WOPRs exceeds 40,000 ha. These farms, however, do little for extension as they are quite unrepresentative of the great majority of private farms.

About half of all WOPR staff have received a university-level education. Training has, however, been mostly limited to academic disciplines and not directed to the problems of practical farming. Particularly lacking is farm cost analysis and farm business planning skills. Subject matter specialists at WOPR headquarters are usually well-qualified technical staff who mostly maintain a good theoretical knowledge of their subject through personal liaison with appropriate research institutes. Few, however, have practical farming experience and, hence, take a narrow view of farm enterprises. A range of opinions suggest that very few exten-

sion staff at *gmina* level know as much about farming as do the better farmers themselves.

Funding of WOPR. Each WOPR is funded through the voivodship from taxes which are supplemented by the state. The activities and funding of WOPRs are theoretically divided into two parts: production and extension, each having different accounts.

The production units of WOPRs are supposed to be self-financing, and profits after taxes should be used partly to finance extension. Salaries and bonuses of production farm staff, including the WOPR director and production advisers, depend on gross production of the farm. As a consequence the farms have attempted to maximize production through the high use of inputs and bear little relevance to typical farms of the voivodship. Indeed, pressure to produce profits has encouraged some production units to invest in operations only distantly related to agriculture, for example, to develop commercial distilleries and brick-making operations.

The deputy director for extension of the WOPRs is responsible for all training and extension and is paid from the state (voivodship) extension budget which is supplemented by sales of publications and accommodation receipts from training centers, which at times also serve as hotels. All extension and training expenditure is funded from the budget but is expected to be supplemented from farm production. There is tension between the production and extension sides of WOPRs because production teams feel that investment in farm operations, and therefore in their bonus potential, should take precedence over investment in extension.

In 1989, the state budget allocation for WOPR operations was Zl 51.6 billion, which is expected to rise to about Zl 250 billion in 1990. This increase does not keep pace with inflation and there is therefore significant pressure on WOPRs to cut costs. All cuts will fall on extension, not on production. Of this budgeted amount an increasing proportion, between 75% and 90%, is used for salaries. No financial records are maintained at the state level for individual WOPRs, although each WOPR must legally maintain its own financial records. The sources and application of funds are poorly defined, and the allocations from state and profit centers and the ownership of assets between production and extension seem inextricably intertwined. Extension advice is provided free to all farmers irrespective of their ability to pay.

Organization of extension programs

A large part of the extension effort involves extracting information from research literature and preparing technical packages for dissemination. Headquarter subject matter specialists hold regular monthly seminars at which *gmina* extension agents are presented with these packages. *Gmina* extension staff then disseminate this information by means of a network of innovation and extension farms. Throughout Poland there are about 3,000 innovation farms, at least one per *gmina*, where new packages are first tested, and about 40,000 extension farms, one per village, selected in agreement with local authorities, where technology packages, which must be approved by the voivodship and by farmers' union representatives, are introduced.

Several problems affect the performance of what, on the surface, appears to be a satisfactory dissemination pathway:

• All packages are designed for output maximization and not farm operation efficiency. This problem stems from the production target mentality of previous administrations and the maximization philosophy of research. It is also continued by WOPR agricultural economists whose computer programs test only the financial returns to the total package rather than search for component combinations which maximize financial returns. The packages are therefore only applicable to those farms that can afford high input levels and are not necessarily the most efficient. The existing recommendation packages are of limited value to farmers in today's economically constrained environment.

• Innovation and extension farms are chosen largely on the basis of farmers' willingness to accept packages; this implies that the farmers are able to take risks and are therefore atypical. Furthermore, extension staff have mobility problems and understandably choose farms that are easily accessible. Such farms are therefore rarely representative of the majority of local farm conditions. Small, traditional farms are not adequately covered by extension.

• Extension agents are not trained to interpret farmers' needs and to feed information back to research. Information transfer is therefore overwhelmingly one way.

• Evaluation of staff performance is subjective and weak. Evaluation of extension campaigns relates only to voivodship production targets and numbers of training programs held. Evaluation analysis to assess the impact of specific WOPR campaigns on rural clientele is not conducted.

• WOPRs have their own field information centers dealing with the production of extension materials for the local press and radio stations. Much of the information produced, however, appears ad hoc and frequently duplicates information produced from other sources such as research stations. A high proportion of farmers own or have access to television but too little use is made of television in the dissemination of farm innovations or for illustrating the problems faced by farmers in their day-to-day activities.

• There is a general lack of trust among farmers for everything associated with the government. Farmers clearly identify WOPRs with government control and treat WOPR agents more as regulators than as advisers. This particularly affects smaller farmers who do not believe the WOPRs and its associated farms, training and service functions are designed for them. These shortcomings have caused the WOPRs to be heavily criticized at all levels: senior government officials consider them wasteful of resources; farmers' unions see them as self-serving institutions; and the majority of farmers consider WOPR advice and WOPR farms as irrelevant to their needs.

Constraints on the extension service

The most severe constraint on the effectiveness of extension in Poland is caused not by structure or procedure but by attitude. In response to centrally determined production targets, the drive for maximum production is pervasive throughout the extension and research services. All targets, programs and incentive systems are geared to crop and livestock production rather than to farm efficiency and this has promoted a misguided respect for maximum yields, for high input systems and for so-called commercial farmers. The extension system has therefore evolved to be in tune with the objectives of state farms and the small traditional farmer is largely held in disdain.

This attitude problem cannot be overcome quickly; time, training and exposure to other approaches will be needed to turn technicians into farm advisors. Many will be unable to make the necessary adjustment, and evaluation programs will need to be designed to distinguish fairly between staff. New incentive systems must recognize and reward contributions to local farm efficiency, with particular emphasis being placed on identifying representative farm clients and catering to their needs. Farm business planning, in physical and financial terms, should be recognized as a professional skill which is as valuable to the Polish economy as that of a doctor or engineer. In Western Europe and America, and increasingly in the more advanced agricultural areas of Asia and Latin America, farm planning advisors are in demand and are supplied by the private sector. Problems of career pathways for such specialists in government service are therefore minimal. In Western Europe and America, university curricula have responded to these changing needs and certificates and degrees in farm management economics are commonplace. In Poland, curricula will similarly need to be revised to reflect this change in attitude.

The extension and production service system in Poland is duplicative and wasteful of financial and skilled manpower resources. Furthermore, its procedures are inflexible and not responsive to changing economic conditions or changing local farm needs. There needs to be a clear distinction between production work, advisory roles, research and regulatory functions. There are no position descriptions, lines of command are blurred, and there is little professional or financial accountability.

Poor communication and transport facilities waste personnel time, discourage staff, and distort the advisory program. Few *gmina* extension officers have adequate transport, and telephone connections to villages and households are extremely scarce. Inadequate operating expenses also constrain extension's ability to interact effectively with more remote farms.

Linkages between WOPRs and research institutes appear ad hoc, mostly depending upon personal contacts between subject matter specialists and institute scientists. WOPR farms are in charge of the execution of adaptive research trials and of demonstrations of innovations in crop and livestock production techniques. However, on-farm trial programs are designed by individual programs of research institutes and there is no real coordination into a coherent on-farm strategy. Recent financial constraints have resulted in institutes being asked to pay for the running of WOPR trials and in innova-

tion farmers having to pay for inputs on demonstration areas. This has tended to sour relations over the on-farm development programs.

Addressing the problems of Poland's extension

DOES POLAND NEED AN EXTENSION SERVICE?

In view of the problems and constraints listed above the answer must be certainly not in its present form. However, there has perhaps never been a more pressing need for an effective advisory service. The current dramatic shifts in farm input-output price relationships has generated great uncertainty throughout farming communities. This makes it even more important for farmers to make the right decisions regarding optimizing scarce resources; they need advice urgently on minimizing risk. The shift to a market-driven economy will bring differential pressure on different farm groups; poorer farmers will leave the land and better farmers will look for ways of meeting market demands. Undoubtedly farmers will obtain information from unofficial and union sources but the extension service should be the basis for rural advice. There is clear evidence of large regional differences between crop and livestock production technology and particularly large differences between production levels in large and small farms. The extension service has an important role to play in raising small-farm production by interpreting research results and commercial farm practices to the small scale, and in moving information rapidly between regions.

In addition to these well-understood roles, extension has a critically important responsibility in the current circumstances of feeding back information on farm problems from the field to research and to government policymakers. Research programs will have to change to respond to farmers' needs and extension must articulate those needs. Similarly, the government should be able to assess objectively the impact of policies on rural conditions, and a countrywide network of extension staff should provide this feedback as part of a normal work routine.

Polish farmers urgently require access to analytical and diagnostic services. Some WOPRs have developed farm model computer programs which are popular with advanced farmers. These programs are based on packages of prescribed inputs and allow little flexibility. Nevertheless they illustrate the type of assistance which extension should offer. This need for farmers to interact with computer-based farm model programs will become increasingly important as the pressure for farm efficiency builds. Diagnosis of soil nutrient deficiencies, plant disease problems, etc., and advice on fertilizer and lime application rates designed for specific field conditions are just indicators of the main advisory functions which extension should offer.

The present shift from a centrally regulated to a market-driven economy will undoubtedly bring about major changes in farm households and in rural communities. The needs of these communities and individuals for qualified advice will increase enormously. Initially such advice will relate to technical farming but its emphasis will shift rapidly to broader needs, such as how to establish cottage industries, how to set up small businesses and, indeed, how to make the move out of farming. The rate of this shift in emphasis cannot be predicted as it depends on government policy toward maintaining rural employment. However, the Polish extension service must position itself, through retraining programs and through evaluation and incentive schemes geared to emerging social needs, to become the front-line advisors to rural communities. The challenges to the administrators and the trainers of extension are great. One thing is certain, however, an effective extension service is needed and will be needed in the foreseeable future.

WHAT FUNCTIONS SHOULD EXTENSION PERFORM?

At present, WOPR functions are spread across a wide range of activities, with the split between production and advisory services being particularly divisive and disruptive. It is essential that all farm production functions be removed physically and financially from the advisory and diagnostic service.

Furthermore, it is important that extension advisors be welcome on farms. Therefore, advisors should not have government regulatory functions, for example, checking produce quality standards, reporting transgressions of environment protection laws, etc. The confidence of farmers in their advisors must be built up as a central theme of government strategy.

Extension functions should therefore be confined to:

- farm and household advice;
- formal and informal training of farm families;
  - analytic and diagnostic services including:
    - farm planning
    - farm budgeting and investment appraisal
    - simple soil testing and advice on lime and fertilizer advice
    - accessibility to livestock feed testing
    - pest and disease identification and advice on plant protection
- ensuring a two-way flow of information between farmers and research;
- articulation of farm problems for the government;
- assisting research agencies with on-farm testing and demonstration;
- cooperating with scientists in research program planning.

WHO SHOULD PROVIDE EXTENSION?

Ideally, at a high level of farm and farmer development most, if not all, extension advisory functions should be paid for by the users of such advice, reflecting the value farmers place on the advice and at least covering full costs. Such a situation is increasingly being employed in Western Europe where ministry of agriculture advisors are expected to take on the partial role of paid private consultants. The degree to which this ideal situation, of extension being provided as a private service, applies, however, depends on the technical sophistication of farming, farm profitability, and farmers' education levels. Above all, however, it depends on the professional competence of extension and the level of confidence which farmers have in their new advisors.

In Poland, many commercial farms are capable of paying for advice and services. However, these are normally the more prominent farms with greater access to government services and benefit from free advice. Small, poorer farmers cannot pay and would rely on government extension if it were made available to them, which it mostly is not. It should be a recognized and carefully monitored policy that government extension advice to private farms, operating at profit levels which generate income tax liabilities, and to all state farms, should be fully costed and that these costs should be paid by the recipients of advice and services. Costs of advice and services should, as in Western Europe and North America, be a legitimate farm expense deductible from pretax farm profits. In these circumstances private competition for provision of services by the private sector would be encouraged.

Government advice and services would continue to be provided free to those farms whose enterprises were not profitable, the intention being to make them profitable or to assist the poorer farmers in making the transition out of farming. The practical aspects of distinguishing between those farmers who can and should pay for advice and those who cannot, are difficult and often subjective. When development reaches a stage where farmers pay income tax, the problem becomes easier; in the meantime, however, the system must rely on the judgment of extension managers. Pressure on the budget to encourage partial self-financing is a common practice (for example, in Britain) but must be carefully monitored to ensure that such pressure is transferred to commercial farmers. Determining priority clients for government-supplied free extension and monitoring the frequency of contacts with those poorer farmers is essential. Increasingly the successful commercial farmers will employ their own advisors as government services become harder and more expensive to obtain.

In the foreseeable future, therefore, extension will be available to farmers through a combination of government agents and private sector consultants, with the latter gradually increasing in importance. Government extension will continue to be required by less well endowed farms. It is unfortunately true that the best advisors will move first to the private sector, where their value will be recognized and rewarded. If the government wishes to offer a good professional service to poorer farmers it must reward good staff appropriately. Some form of differential bonus based on performance criteria is essential.

WHO ARE THE FUTURE CLIENTS OF EXTENSION?

The most obvious clients of extension are farmers. However, an extension service should cater to the needs of government, research, farmer servicing agencies and particularly farm families — rural youth, farm spouses, etc. As explained above, some clients can more appropriately be dealt with by private extension and some by government extension. Extension

strategy should identify major client groups, their characteristics and needs. Work programs, budgets and training programs should be geared to identified needs.

Government extension has to date focused exclusively on the needs of more progressive and commercially minded farmers. These groups have quite different needs from the majority of farmers, needs which can increasingly be filled by private sector initiative. Shifting the emphasis of government extension staff to cater specifically to the needs of disadvantaged groups will require strong direction, revised training programs, appropriate support from research and revision of staff performance criteria.

WHAT SHOULD BE THE OWNERSHIP AND STRUCTURE OF EXTENSION?

Farmers rightly feel that they have no ownership influence over the WOPR services and that in many ways the WOPRs reflect the worst aspects of former central planning. This situation is fully recognized by the government, whose intention it is to change WOPRs radically.

A widespread network of WOPRs does, however, exist throughout Poland, and each WOPR has a substantial infrastructure, training, accommodation and printing facilities, and access to areas of undisputed state land. The essential feature of any strategy should be to work with this network; attempts to break down the network, to replace it with something new or operating in parallel, would be disruptive and unnecessarily expensive. The strategic plan for the WOPRs should therefore be to change their structure, management, staff, procedures and ownership as rapidly as possible but without destroying the basic service network facilities. At present each voivodship has a WOPR. As part of the restructuring of the extension service some rationalization of the geographical spread of responsibility is needed; this could lead to budgetary savings. Clearly differences in the geographical spread of WOPRs' responsibility should reflect regional differences in farm structure. A review of the physical network is therefore needed but should not take precedence over a review of institutional and procedural matters.

As a first step, all farm production functions — including arable farm, dairy units, pig production, seed production, machinery and ancillary production units such as distilleries, etc., should be completely removed from advisory and diagnostic support services. The production facilities, including staff and physical assets, should be treated in the same way as state farms Management and physical assets should be divided: WOPR headquarters buildings, training facilities, accommodation and catering facilities, and audio-visual units should be allocated to the new advisory service. Farm building and equipment would be allocated to production units. Land allocated to the advisory service for operating research trials should be adjacent to headquarters. In order to illustrate this clear separation and new approach, the farmer support service should be renamed: the Agricultural Service Agency (Agencja Uslug Rolniczych or AUR) would seem appropriate.

The AUR should be financed from the budget; staff salaries should reflect qualifications and responsibilities. A budget commitment of 65:35, salaries to operating costs, should be maintained to ensure adequate provision for mobility. The ratio of frontline AUR advisory staff to farmers, taking into account private extension, gradually improving communications, and the opportunities offered by mass media programs, should not exceed 1:400. This would imply a *gmina*-level advisory force of about 5,500 backed up by about 1,400 voivodship advisors in addition to the analytical and diagnostic technicians who are essential to supply extension with farm support services. It is anticipated that the existing work force could be significantly reduced by accelerated retirement, by movement of some technical staff to the private sector and by retrenchment of frontline extension staff at *gmina* level — especially those incapable of being trained in the new methodology of giving farm management advice to typical small farmers. Early training program results should be used as a basis for retrenchment, which would accelerate the shift in emphasis to the small-farm program.

Extension work programs should be strictly stratified according to farmer types and the number of farmer contacts related to the proportion of specific farmers in the rural community. For example, if half of the farms are below 5 ha and are mixed livestock and cereal farms, then about half of the extension time, visits and resources should be spent advising this type of farmer.

Much more attention should be given in ex-

tension programs to the interaction of livestock and crops. Technical specialists should be trained to see their specialization from a holistic, farm efficiency standpoint, taking into account farmer goals, not technical production standards.

An inventory of extension staff at all levels should be prepared, showing qualifications and a record on in-service training and performance evaluations. Position descriptions and performance criteria should be prepared for all staff categories.

Greater use should be made of local newspapers, radio, television and, increasingly, of telephones to communicate with farmers. Television and local video programs are powerful, cost-effective tools for information dissemination and feedback. The effective use of communication tools requires analysis of farmer perceptions; therefore, careful training of operatives, even for telephone communication, should be budgeted to make the best use of new technology. Extension strategy should recognize, however, that farmer skill development requires personal contact, and a combination of extension advisors and mass communication media will be essential throughout the long term.

Farmer ownership of extension is at present being proposed by the government through the reinstatements of the system of Chambers of Agriculture (COAs). Various proposals are being put forward for these COAs and a draft bill is being prepared. The essential features of the COAs as proposed are that they would be self-governing bodies with voluntary membership drawn from government agencies, the private sector and farmers' unions or associations. Membership would be flexible so that the composition of the COAs could reflect the needs of rural communities. Different voivodships would require different COA composition to reflect local circumstances.

A draft bill anticipates that the COAs would come into legal operation in January 1991. They would operate mostly in a single voivodship but could stretch their influence beyond the boundaries of the voivodship if necessary. Within one voivodship the COA would be supervised by the voivod, but if working in an area exceeding the voivodship, the Ministry of Agriculture would supervise. This arrangement is administratively unworkable; it has obvious problems of administration and accountability in time and space. When a COA is established it must have a defined area of influence and must also have specifically defined accountability.

The draft bill proposes funding the COAs from:

- members' contributions;
- subsidy allocations from state and local budgets; and
- income from commercial and service operations.

Such funding raises issues on two counts. First, only wealthier farmers are likely to contribute and therefore have voting rights over all voivodship agricultural matters (the Poznan model COA has only 500 farm members). Secondly, under this model state budget allocations would become subject to private sector disbursing procedures. Thus private farmers would make decisions about the allocation of state funds, a situation which would be unacceptable to the government and to potential donors.

It is further anticipated by the draft bill that the COA itself may carry out its own production activities and in addition will "take over all matters relating to agricultural extension and production organizations — including financing." This would be satisfactory if the COAs were self-financing or operated entirely with farmers' contributions; it could not apply to government budgets which have a responsibility to all taxpayers.

Important questions arise over the COA: its relationship to the voivodship; its funding and accountability, and whether it could have executive and financial authority over government agencies such as the AURs and their associated agrochemical centers, plant quarantine stations, etc. The last proposal could clearly bring about conflict of interest situations: conflicts might arise where government policy, for example, over environment protection, did not coincide with the short-term interests of farmers over pest control and fertilizer application — an issue in which agrochemical centers could become entangled. Such problems are occurring in Western Europe and North America and should be anticipated in Poland. The system of combining government extension with farmers' unions was tested for several years in North America but the experiment was abandoned as unworkable largely because of conflict of interest problems.

The concept of developing a mechanism for ensuring coordination between public and private sector activities, and for increasing the direct influence of farmers over their service and advisory agencies, is sound. However, there is a real danger that the COA as presently conceived could become another central authority with little representation from smaller farmers. Criticisms to this effect are being charged in the Poznan case. The COA could easily become a self-serving, profit-making organization, an end in itself rather than a means to an end and with little relevance to the problems of the majority of farmers.

Chambers of agriculture are operating in Western Europe and the details of their financing and operating procedures should be reviewed to determine whether they are immediately applicable to Poland. The concept of chambers of agriculture should be seen as part of a long-term experiment — one of several possible means of achieving the goal of deemphasizing the influence of the state on local agricultural affairs. It should be tested at a voivodship level to see if the COAs can become self-financing but its introduction by legislative means throughout Poland appears premature. The administration of the voivodship, however, is already fully equipped to deal with the many bureaucratic requirements of administering and accounting for staff and finances. It is recommended therefore that, in the short term, the AUR work directly with the voivodship administration. The voivodship should be advised in its operations and in setting priorities in its budget allocation by an agricultural advisory board comprised of a true cross-section of farmers.

WHAT STRATEGIC STEPS SHOULD BE TAKEN?

The above outline suggests that government strategy should be aimed toward gaining easy access for all rural families to an efficient professional advisory and diagnostic service which is responsive to their needs. Steps to be taken are:

Short term

- Issue government instructions to all extension staff to redirect the extension effort toward farm efficiency and away from the simple attainment of high production target goals. Voivodships should refrain from issuing production target objectives.

• Employ technical assistance to develop re-training programs for extension staff in business-oriented farm management, including farm planning and budgeting; there should be support for this effort from equipping extension economists with appropriate computer software.

• Employ technical assistance to develop new performance criteria for extension based on identifying and servicing the needs of representative farms and farm households, and on improving farm efficiency. Publicly introduce these criteria and a system of extension evaluation by representative client farmers.

• Remove all WOPR advisory and diagnostic functions, administratively, physically and financially, from production functions. Rename the advisory and diagnostic service to reflect its new focused role: the Agricultural Service Agency, Agencja Uslug Rolniczych (AUR), would be appropriate.

• Review staff levels at AUR to rationalize the number of advisors to farm families based on revised work programs. A ratio of around 1 advisor to 250-400 farmers, depending on region and farm complexity, would seem appropriate.

• Demonstrate support for the AUR by a full budget commitment; ensure that the operating budget is about 50% of salary costs (that is, a ratio of about 65:35 for salaries:operating costs).

• Review extension client characteristics and needs; together with research, develop appropriate technology options and promote these through mass media and personal communication campaigns.

• Review the entire diagnostic and analytical network of services offered to farmers to avoid duplication and waste of resources.

Medium term

• Review the emerging needs of farming communities and categories of individuals such as pensioners, rural youth, farm women, and failing farmers in the light of changes in government policies, and develop training programs to prepare extension staff to meet these advisory needs.

• Equip AURs with training materials, video equipment and technical assistance to demonstrate to farm community members how to manage the transition from a controlled to a market-driven economy. Cross-referencing experiences from different parts of Poland and from interna-

tional experience would be essential to stimulate rural development.

• Revise agricultural curricula at agricultural secondary schools and universities to emphasize farm economics and efficient farm management.

• Encourage twinning arrangements between appropriate international institutions and agricultural teaching, research and extension establishments in Poland.

• Review AUR operations and develop full cost assessment of advisory and diagnostic services. Phase in full-cost payment for agricultural advice and diagnostic services, payment for such services to be tax deductible.

• Establish agricultural advisory boards at voivodships. Boards should act as a coordination mechanism for all voivodship agricultural operations in the public and private sector, to review functions of farm support services and to make recommendations to the government. Board members would be drawn from representatives of major farming groups, government agencies, research and private agribusinesses, etc.

• Reequip diagnostic facilities and AUR laboratories as appropriate to enable efficient and rapid analytical and diagnostic services to be offered to farmers at *gmina* and AUR levels. This local level voivodship service to be coordinated with the more complex services offered by the research network.

• Review details of the operations of chambers of agriculture in appropriate Western European countries (for example, Spain and Austria). Assess to what extent chambers of agriculture could be self-financing and to what extent all farmers could achieve full representation. Introduce a chamber on a test basis within the jurisdiction of a voivodship and monitor its operation. If the model were found acceptable, the chamber of agriculture could take over from the agricultural advisory board. However, to the extent that public funds are being used for extension, the voivodship administrative mechanism would be required to administer and account for such funds.

Long term

• Change full-cost advisory and diagnostic services to commercial farms. Facilitate the gradual takeover of extension advice and diagnosis by the private sector. Government services should continue to be made available for poorer farmers at subsidized rates.

• Government advisory service should be equipped to advise rural households on all aspects of farming, including environment and resource protection, low energy agriculture and rural society management.

Implications of the strategy

The proposed strategy would have implications for the government, for the existing WOPRs and for commercial and poorer farmers.

• Government and voivodship administration would be faced with the responsibility of WOPR staff retrenchment and retraining. It is anticipated that the numbers of extension staff might be halved. However, the remaining advisory and diagnostic staff of the AUR, plus an additional 50% of salary costs for operating expenses would have to be taken fully onto the government budget.

• Technical assistance would be required to assist the government in developing position descriptions and performance criteria, training programs and new curricula for secondary schools and agricultural universities.

• WOPR production farms remaining after the split from AUR facilities would be treated in the same way as state farms. Some land in specific agro-ecological zones would be retained by the AUR for research and demonstration purposes but the WOPR farm, staff and management would be treated as independent units with no budget support and no linkage to the AUR.

• Commercial and poorer farmers would be better off but in different ways. Commercial farmers could expect more farm management advice and more efficient diagnostic facilities; but at full cost, which they could offset against taxes. Smaller, poorer farmers would have greater interaction with AUR staff, whose performance rewards were geared to increasing farm efficiency. All farmers and private agencies should gradually increase their influence over extension through the agricultural advisory board and eventually their own self-supporting chamber of agriculture.

Endnote

This annex was prepared by Wladyslaw Korcz and John Hayward.

Rural finance

Background

The financial sector has been dominated by the banking system, although the banks operated as financial agents of the government under the previous regime, rather than as the independent financial intermediaries found in market economies. In the past, the National Bank of Poland (NBP) supervised the preparation of credit plans in support of the government's annual production and investment plans, and these were reviewed by the Council of Banks (chaired by NBP's president) before being submitted for approval of the Council of Ministers and Parliament. The credit plans were then implemented by the banking system under the general guidance of NBP. NBP provided financial services to the commercial and industrial sectors; the Bank for Food Economy (BFE) and the cooperative banks (CBs) served agriculture and agro-industry; Bank Handlowy was the primary bank involved in foreign trade; PKO Savings Bank provided services to households; and Bank Polska Kasa Opieki (PKO-SA) primarily served as a channel for foreign exchange provided by Poles living abroad. The portfolios of BFE and the CBs together represent about 23% of total bank loans outstanding at the present time, and their deposits amount to approximately 18% of the total (about two-thirds of which are deposits in CBs).

Finance in the rural sector has been dominated by the Bank for Food Economy (BFE), with its 95 branches located in provincial capi-

tals, and the CB system of cooperative banks (CBs), with 1,660 banks, 495 branches, and 2,700 cash counters. (A CB or CB branch is present in every community in the country.) BFE was formed in 1975 through the merger of the Agricultural Bank and the Central Union of Savings and Loan Cooperatives; the Ministry of Finance holds 51% of its shares and the CBs the remaining 49%. Under this arrangement, BFE served as the central union for the CBs, which was a violation of the cooperative principle of voluntary organization and prevented the CBs from operating as independent institutions. BFE provided services to social sector agriculture and agro-industry (state and cooperative farms; state enterprises; and dairy, horticultural, and agricultural circle (machinery service) cooperatives).[1] CBs provided services for private sector farmers, craftsmen, and rural households; employees of social sector enterprises; and local governments.

BFE mobilized savings directly from the social sector (15-20% of total resources) and indirectly from the private sector through the CBs (15-20% of resources), but the major part of its resources (over 60%) was provided by NBP. BFE granted loans in accordance with the annual credit plans, and the government sometimes intervened in individual loan decisions. BFE bore little risk in its loans since the founding organizations of state farms/enterprises and central unions of cooperatives normally provided funds to allow entities to repay their loans, if they had insufficient funds of their own.[2] Of BFE's total loan portfolio, about 45% was in agriculture (including machinery services) and 50% in agro-industry. In agriculture, about half of the portfolio was in production credit (at year end) and half in investment credit. In agro-industry, approximately 75% was for working capital and 25% for investment.

The important role of CBs in the rural economy is the result of a long history of cooperative tradition in Poland. (Some of the CBs are over 100 years old.) The forerunners of the present CBs went through several setbacks but emerged as relatively sound rural financial institutions. They have survived government control exerted through BFE and local administrations. Their strength is based on the fact that they thrive on their own resources. This exemplifies the merits of the cooperative spirit of pooling resources of members to serve a common goal. CBs have succeeded in assembling small amounts of savings which would not have been possible otherwise. They are community-based organizations, and they were the only financial institutions providing services to private entities in the rural sector. The CBs have a widespread membership with about 2.5 million individuals, of which about 75% are farmers and the rest artisans, employees of the social sector, and other residents of rural communities.

The CBs mobilized savings from the private sector, some social sector entities, and local governments, but they were required to deposit their funds with BFE, and their lending was constrained by the national credit plans implemented through BFE. They obtained refinancing from BFE in individual cases but were net depositors with BFE in the aggregate and thus provided funds for the social sector. (At the end of 1986, over 60% of deposits — including net deposits of local governments — amounting to the equivalent of about US$1.0 billion, had been diverted to the social sector.) The CBs provided financing for agricultural production and investment, consumption, housing, land, and budget support purposes, and they also recorded the value of farm output sold to the state (for purposes of calculating pensions) and served as agents for land sales. CBs operated on a negative margin between deposit and loan rates, and received a subsidy from the government in compensation. The environment for CBs was riskier than that for BFE, but they required farmers to assign receipts from output sold to the state for repayment of loans. About 60% of

the consolidated portfolio of CBs was for agriculture (roughly 15% in production credit and 45% in investment credit), 25% for housing, and less than 10% for craftsmen and other small businesses.

Current data are not available, but in the past, virtually all state and cooperative farms received production credit from BFE amounting to nearly 50% of their material production cost, on average. About 50% of their average investment expenditures also were financed with credit. While the number of private farmers who received production credit through the CBs is not available, only about 5% of their material production cost was financed with credit. In accordance with past priorities, credit for private farmers was allocated largely to investment. A larger amount of credit was made available to private farmers for investment. Thus roughly 40% of farmers received credit for investment purposes, amounting to somewhat less than 25% of expenditures.

Recent developments

Substantial changes are being introduced in the financial system, with major implications for rural finance. In early 1989, NBP was converted into a central bank, and its commercial banking operations were taken over by nine independent banks established with former NBP staff and facilities. Sectoral credit ceilings have been eliminated, and all banks are allowed to operate in all sectors. Some expansion into other sectors has occurred, although banks have tended to concentrate initially on their traditional sectors. NBP has approved licenses for 26 new banks, of which two are wholly private domestic banks and two are joint ventures between domestic and foreign interests. While license applications indicate that the new banks intend to operate as universal banks, the Agricultural Development Bank of Poznan and Agrobank of Warsaw appear to be aiming at the agricultural sector. It seems that the number of banks being formed may be excessive and that closer scrutiny may be warranted to ensure that new banks are financially sound and that they are not being formed to serve narrow interests of the owners. A program for the establishment of a system of credit unions is being prepared and is likely to result in a broad network of such institutions focusing on personal finance.

Under the new banking law of January 1989, interest rate policy was gradually liberalized beginning in August 1989. Preferential interest rates (including those for agricultural credit) were raised and unified with other rates at the beginning of 1990. During the first half of this year, NBP's refinancing rate has been set on a monthly basis, at the level of inflation expected for the month. (In practice, the rate has been below the rate of inflation, although the real refinancing rate has increased from around -24% per month in January to perhaps 0% per month in May.) Banks are allowed to set their own loan rates, but because of the high nominal rates charged by some banks in January of 45-50% per month (about -19% to -16% in real terms), NBP has been recommending a level for the prime lending rate. BFE's rates generally have been below the recommended level and were set at 4.4-5.0% in June, compared with the refinancing rate of 4.0%. The loan rate of CBs has varied among individual banks but has tended to be somewhat higher than BFE's rate.

Subsidized credit for agriculture continues under at least two programs. NBP allocated Zl 900 billion for a program initiated in April to provide credit to farmers at fixed rates of 24% for six months (3.7% per month) and 36% for nine months (3.5% per month). In July the rate on six-month credit was reduced to 16% (2.5% per month), and the nine-month credit was eliminated. Farmers have the option of paying interest at the market rates in effect during the loan term if that proves to be lower. Banks receive the difference between the fixed rates and the market rate from budget funds. BFE was given an allocation of Zl 250 billion which it utilized in April and May; the commercial banks were allocated the remaining Zl 650 billion but reportedly have utilized very little of it. BFE has applied for an increase in its allocation, although the seasonal demand for the summer crop is largely over. The other program is based on the funds generated by the EC food assistance program amounting to about 800 Zl billion. Credit is available to the private sector for small-scale production, trading, and processing through both BFE and the CBs at 75% of the prevailing interest rate.

A number of initiatives are being undertaken to improve the infrastructure of the banking system. A clearing system involving electronic processing of transactions is to be established by beginning 1991. Accounting and auditing stan-dards for banks are being developed within the program to bring general accounting and auditing standards in line with international standards, and they are expected to be introduced as of January 1, 1991. Computerization programs are being designed to enable the banks to generate the information required by the new accounting standards, the reporting requirements of NBP, and modern management information systems. Prudential regulations are being developed to address major aspects of sound banking such as loan classification, provisioning, and capital adequacy, and are to be introduced by the beginning of 1991. A review is being undertaken of the present system of government deposit guarantees (primarily on savings deposits in state banks such as BFE and household deposits in CBs), with a view to developing an appropriate deposit insurance system. Financial markets are being introduced, as NBP has begun to issue bills and rediscount commercial bills, and bond and stock markets are to be established.

A bank restructuring program is to be implemented following diagnostic studies (including audits according to international standards) to determine the status of banks (particularly with regard to loan portfolios), in conjunction with the restructuring of social sector enterprises. A major part of the program will be the assessment of loan portfolios to determine potential loan losses, the allocation of these losses, and the recapitalization necessary to establish a sound financial basis for future operations. Special financial audits already are being arranged for banks participating in the Agroindustries Export Development Project (AEDP) and Industrial Export Development Project (IEDP) being supported by the World Bank. (BFE and Bank Handlowy are the participating banks at present.) Ownership structures also will be modified during implementation of the program, as state banks acquire capital from the private sector and from foreign sources, and as the government divests itself of its shareholdings.

As a result of the amendment of the cooperative law at the beginning of this year, BFE no longer serves as the central union for the CBs. It has attempted to continue its arrangements with the CBs by signing agreements of association with some 1,400 of them, although these agreements do not constitute a permanent link and can be terminated on a year's notice. The other 260 CBs have signed agreements with commercial banks or are planning to form regional banks.

A process of disintermediation has occurred at an accelerating rate as political and economic uncertainties have grown, budget constraints have taken hold, nominal interest rates have increased as part of the general adjustment of relative prices and in response to rising inflation, and real interest rates have become highly volatile. Total assets of BFE and the CBs declined by more than 10% in constant terms between 1982 and 1988, and 44% between 1988 and 1989. At the end of 1989, the CBs had deposits of Zl 2.9 trillion and loans of only Zl 1.2 trillion (about 40% of deposits). The dramatic increase in nominal interest rates at the beginning of 1990 caused many borrowers to repay outstanding loans, resulting in a contraction of both deposits and loan portfolios. (BFE's nominal loan rate jumped from 85% per year — 5.3% per month — at the end of 1989 to 39% per month in January.) High nominal and volatile real rates also led to a decrease in credit demand for the spring planting season, as farmers reduced the use of purchased inputs and used own funds to the maximum extent. (BFE's real loan rate decreased from -11% per month in December to -22% per month in January, then climbed to about 5% per month in March before declining again to around 0% per month in May.) Investment decisions probably were postponed. BFE has utilized only about 70% of its refinancing allocation with NBP, although the general credit ceilings imposed by NBP may have restricted the full use of the allocation.

The current excess stocks of agricultural commodities resulting from factors such as the decline in domestic demand and the inventory management policies of farmers, processors, and distributors (supplies apparently were held from the market following the 1989 fall harvest in anticipation of continued price increases) has caused problems for borrowers and banks. Borrowers were unable to dispose of surplus inventories when nominal interest rates rose, were therefore unable to repay their loans, and were forced to incur unaccustomed high finance charges. Banks (including BFE) were left with substantial amounts of nonperforming loans. This situation will be aggravated by the 1990 fall harvest and needs to be managed carefully to ensure that additional burdens are not placed on the banking system.

Potential

The goal in rural finance would be to provide efficient financial intermediation services, integrated into the overall financial system and encompassing the processing of transactions; mobilization of savings through the provision of financial instruments with appropriate characteristics of safety, liquidity, and return; and allocation of resources through the provision of credit on appropriate terms and conditions for production, investment, and consumption purposes. These services should be provided by a network of competing commercial and cooperative banks, all operating in the private sector. While substantial improvements can be expected in the relatively short term through broad measures such as the introduction of the clearing system (see below), institutional development of BFE/CBs and the CBs and the expansion of commercial bank operations in the rural sector will require a longer period. Therefore a banking system which is reasonably satisfactory for operating in a market environment will develop only over the medium term.

A clearing system involving the electronic processing of transactions is being designed and is to be introduced at the beginning of 1991. BFE and the CBs will need to install the necessary equipment to participate in this system, and the CBs will need varying amounts of time to acquire direct access, but an efficient means of effecting payments will become available to an expanding clientele in the rural sector over the short to medium term.

Effective credit demand will rise as a result of factors such as the elimination of constraints imposed by credit plans under the previous regime; increases in relative prices of some agricultural inputs and outputs; expansion of private sector involvement in input supply, output marketing, and processing; and enterprise restructuring. The potential for mobilization of resources to meet this demand appears substantial, provided adequate returns are paid on deposits and other financial instruments.

BFE and the CBs can play an important role in the rural sector if they undergo substantial modification. BFE will need to become much more energetic in adapting to a competitive market environment and acquiring the capability of dealing with the private sector, but it has extensive experience with state and cooperative farms and agro-industrial enterprises, and it has a broad network of branches. It could be a major factor in the restructuring of state and cooperative entities, since it knows their operations and holds their outstanding debt. If BFE is able to overcome its present deficiencies, it could develop into a full-fledged commercial bank, with a solid base in agriculture and agribusiness but also providing a range of services to the public and to commerce and industry.

Because of their roots in the cooperative tradition and their integration into the life of rural communities, as indicated above, CBs have been able to survive the attempts to incorporate them into the state control system over the past 45 years. While loan decisions under the previous regime were made by managers selected with the concurrence of local party structures and sometimes influenced directly by these structures, and although high repayment rates were achieved because of CB involvement in the payment process for state procurement of agricultural commodities, the CBs have extensive experience in lending for agricultural production and investment, craft enterprise requirements, and consumption needs. Of particular importance during the restructuring of the economy is the role CBs can play in supporting employment generation through the financing of rural businesses. In general, provided adequate strengthening is undertaken at the level of individual banks and a suitable superstructure is put in place, the CBs should be able to provide effective services to rural households and businesses. As the superstructure is established, the CB system can extend its coverage at the regional and national levels and thus compete on an equal basis with the commercial banks.

The nine commercial banks spawned by NBP reportedly have started to serve a few of BFE's former farm and enterprise clients, and are likely to expand their involvement gradually. Other banks, such as Bank Handlowy, Export Development Bank, and PKO-SA also are beginning to finance agro-industries to a limited extent, and new banks may become involved with agriculture and agro-industry. Over time, local banks will be established to serve towns and villages. Thus, the commercial banking system is likely to extend its coverage throughout the rural areas. The system of credit unions which is likely to be established will probably provide substantial competition for CBs and other banks in the field of personal finance.

Constraints

Financial intermediation. A basic constraint is that financial intermediation as known in market economies essentially did not exist under the previous regime. CBs mobilized resources from the private sector but were not allowed to determine the allocation of those resources. Instead, the utilization of resources was determined in a national credit plan which allocated funds between social and private sectors and between production and investment goals. As a result, substantial sums were transferred from the private sector to the social sector. BFE received demand and savings deposits from social sector entities but provided a much larger amount of credit to these entities. Thus, the financial system served as part of the planning mechanism, and BFE channeled government and private sector resources to the social sector. Financial intermediation in the sense of mobilizing and allocating financial resources in an increasingly efficient manner in a competitive market environment must now be established in the rural sector in order to provide households and businesses an opportunity to obtain a satisfactory return on financial assets and access to funds for viable production/investment activities and consumption needs. Other sectors should also benefit, since the rural sector is likely to provide a net outflow of funds. The process of introducing financial intermediation has only just begun and needs to be accelerated through measures such as the elimination of agricultural credit subsidies and the strengthening of BFE and the CBs. Competition for BFE and the CBs needs to be increased through judicious licensing of additional banks, including foreign banks.

Subsidized credit. A policy of providing a subsidy to agriculture through the credit mechanism would be a major constraint on development of the financial system in the rural sector and would have a wide range of negative consequences. It would interfere with the transformation of existing banks into efficient financial intermediaries, since they would be dependent on a flow of government funds and would be subject to government intervention, and the subsidy would preclude satisfactory assessment of bank performance through profit and other measures. The subsidy would discriminate against poor farmers, since it would favor borrowers over nonborrowers and large borrowers over small borrowers. Furthermore, since subsidized credit must be rationed administratively, large influential farmers tend to benefit the most, and the system generally is subject to abuse. Subsidized credit encourages farmers to engage in production and investment activities which are not viable and cannot be sustained. When the subsidy ceases, farmers are confronted with the necessity of shifting production patterns and may be stuck with unutilized facilities. The incentive of banks to pursue recovery of subsidized credit is weakened, as is the credit discipline of borrowers. The public must bear the cost of a subsidy, either through inflation or through taxes. And finally, subsidies create vested interests which make it extremely difficult to remove the subsidies, as current experience demonstrates. Substantial progress has been achieved to date in the reduction of agricultural credit subsidies, and the opportunity should not be missed to phase out the remaining subsidies, to the long-term benefit of farmers, banks, the government, and the public.

Excess commodity stocks. The situation on excess stocks was described above. While credit to viable borrowers may help to carry these stocks, care needs to be taken not to burden the banking system with additional bad debts.

Adequacy of credit. The demand for credit has declined precipitously because of the high nominal and widely varying real interest rates which have been in effect since the beginning of the year, as noted above, and it appears that the supply of funds presently is adequate to meet the reduced demand. It is unclear whether the volume of credit was adequate to meet production and investment needs previously, because of factors such as the restrictions imposed by the credit plan and the scarcity of inputs. However, the demand for credit should rise substantially with the return of stability; the gradual accommodation to relative price changes; acclimatization to market uncertainties; expansion of private sector involvement in input supply, marketing, and processing; enterprise restructuring, etc. A segment of credit demand which was virtually nonexistent previously is the need

for financing of private land sales; this can be expected to develop with the expansion of the private land market and to form a significant portion of aggregate credit demand in the future. Resources to meet this demand may be supplied in part by refinancing from NBP, but these funds will be limited by the constraints of monetary policy. If agricultural production and investment are not to be unduly constrained by a shortage of credit, a major effort will be needed to generate resources through deposit mobilization, as discussed below. Furthermore, the banking system currently is not prepared to meet the private sector credit requirements for land and enterprises because of factors such as the term structure of CB resources, the CBs' lack of experience with enterprise analysis, and BFE's lack of experience with the private sector. The institutions will need to develop the capability to meet these requirements.

Resource mobilization. At present, rural sector entities tend to invest surplus funds in tangible assets or foreign exchange, affected in their behavior by factors such as experience under the previous regime, inflation, and uncertainty. In addition to the resulting serious misallocation of real resources, the banking system is deprived of financial resources which could be channeled to viable production and investment activities. In general, banks have not provided a positive real return on deposits and have offered a limited range of financial products. Their incentive and capacity to pay a suitable return in the future will depend in part on the government's credit subsidy policy. At least they now have control over the allocation of funds and can expand the range of financial products.

In the past, BFE obtained most of its resources from NBP and the CBs (15-20% of its resources from CB deposits and over 60% from NBP). In the future, it will need to expand greatly its mobilization of deposits from households and enterprises to compensate for dwindling supplies from the CBs and NBP and to meet the growing needs of clients in the private sector. CBs no longer are constrained in the use of their resources by a national credit plan and therefore can utilize the deposits formerly retained by BFE to increase lending to the private sector. However, they will need to expand the mobilization of deposits to accommodate the growing requirements of farmers and rural enterprises, as well as the demands arising from the privatization and restructuring of state and cooperative farms and enterprises. Since individual CBs are unable to meet the needs of medium-size and large clients, some form of superstructure is required to consolidate resources for lending to these clients.

Inadequate institutional capability of existing banks. BFE has virtually no experience in risk management or in assessing enterprise creditworthiness in a competitive market environment. Furthermore, it has only a limited capability of assessing the viability of production and investment activities since analysis of such activities was previously undertaken in a planned environment, with government involvement extending to individual lending decisions. Its network of some 95 branches affords national coverage, but all branches are located in provincial capitals. Thus, BFE presently is not well suited to providing full services to the rural sector and will need to undertake major changes to perform satisfactorily in that role. Yet BFE does have an institutional basis and branch network on which to build and could grow into the role. The process of institutional development has been initiated, but it needs to be accelerated substantially.

The CB system is built on the foundation of previously existing cooperative banks (some of the CBs are over 100 years old), but it was decapitated when BFE was formed to serve as apex institution. In addition to the central control which was exerted through BFE, CBs were subjected to the influence of local administrations in the selection of managers and in individual loan decisions. Thus there appears to be a dearth of professional management expertise in some CBs, and they have retained little expertise for operating within a risky, competitive environment. Information systems are rudimentary. The CBs' ability to assess risk is virtually nil, and their experience in assessing the creditworthiness of enterprises is limited. Portfolios contain loans granted on nonbanking criteria. Furthermore, defaults were minimal under the previous system, and CBs will need to establish provisions to absorb losses on loans granted in a risky environment. The capital of CBs has been eroded and needs to be replenished. (At the end of 1989, the consolidated net worth of CBs was less than 3% of total resources.) Since BFE no longer serves as the central union for the CBs, there is uncertainty about the

future evolution of the CB system, but there is also an opportunity for the CBs to determine their own development. In spite of the deficiencies, the CBs appear to have operated reasonably well within all the constraints and seem relatively well suited to serve as financial intermediaries in the rural sector. Nevertheless, substantial institution-building is required, and a superstructure is needed. Initiatives are under way and should be supported.

The existing commercial banks have institutional limitations similar to those of BFE, and they have major problems with their industrial and commercial loan portfolios. They have little experience in the rural sector, except for their financing of trade cooperatives such as the peasant self-aid cooperatives. Thus, they will need to undertake substantial institutional development programs and resolve their portfolio problems in order to become a significant factor in the rural sector. NBP will need to be judicious in granting licenses to new banks in towns and smaller cities to ensure that they are viable and are intended to serve a broad range of clients, not just the owners. No credit unions exist at present, although they might be established fairly rapidly on the basis of the program now under preparation.

Strategic recommendations

A series of measures needs to be implemented to strengthen rural finance and integrate it into the national financial system. They are described briefly below in terms of short-, medium-, and long-term time horizons.

SHORT TERM

Phasing out subsidized credit. As noted above, there is an opportunity to build on the substantial progress which has already been achieved and to phase out subsidized credit, thereby contributing to efficient agricultural development and benefiting all concerned (with the possible exception of larger influential farmers who receive most of the subsidy and who can afford the cost of adjustment when the subsidy is removed). The special credit program which was introduced for the spring planting season with NBP funds now has served its purpose and should be terminated. Any further financing from NBP should be in the context of the general program available to all banks and all sectors on uniform terms and conditions. In addition, the terms and conditions for the counterpart funds generated from the foreign food assistance programs should be adjusted to market levels (especially the interest rate). If the government considers it necessary to provide support to poor farmers beyond the benefit they would receive from an increase in demand which would result from, say, a food stamp program, a targeted income subsidy might be considered. In any case, the subsidy should not be provided through the credit system because of the discriminatory and distortionary effects.

Financing excess commodity stocks. The present situation of excess stocks of agricultural commodities may be aggravated at the time of the fall harvest. The fixed interest rates now in effect for the second half of this year, together with forward prices announced by the agricultural marketing agency, may provide sufficient incentive for farmers and merchants to hold stocks, and there may be a case for accommodating the resulting credit bulge within the macro credit ceilings for the economy. However, any losses resulting from the marketing system should be borne by the budget and should not be a burden on the banking system. If this marketing system cannot be introduced in time for the fall harvest, the government may need to utilize budget funds to procure commodities.

Commitment of government to reform of rural banks. While the government has indicated its intention to reform the financial system and has initiated a variety of measures at the sectoral level, it needs to reaffirm its commitment at the level of individual institutions and proceed accordingly. In the case of BFE, the government should exercise its rights as majority shareholder to ensure that prompt action is taken to begin the rehabilitation of the bank. With respect to the CBs, the government should act to promote their development through such measures as ensuring that: obstacles are not placed in the way of establishing regional banks; suitable technical assistance is provided for the strengthening of CBs and the formation of the regional banks; BFE provides appropriate support to CBs which remain associated with it; and associated CBs are not prevented from terminating their arrangements with BFE and joining regional banks.

Introducing professional bank management expertise. Perhaps the most important measure to be taken at the level of the institutions is to introduce management expertise for operating in a competitive market environment. For BFE, such expertise might be provided through a small group of advisors with suitable experience in market economies. At the same time, training at foreign banks and banking institutes should be provided to existing managers with appropriate qualifications and for the next generation of managers. In the case of the CBs, members need to exercise their rights through the supervisory councils to replace unqualified managers who were imposed on them under the previous regime. Technical assistance for CB managers should be provided under the foreign assistance programs, and training should be provided at foreign institutions and the proposed domestic banking institute.[3]

Repatriating profits. At present, returns on foreign equity participation in banks are not allowed to be repatriated by the foreign investors. While this is not the only obstacle to foreign participation in banks, it is a major one, and it is likely that the direct involvement of foreign banks will be important to the development of a suitable banking system in Poland over the medium term. Therefore an appropriate modification in the legislation should be made to allow the repatriation of bank profits.

Establishing information systems. Basic information on loan approvals, commitments, disbursements, repayments, etc., currently is not available in a timely manner for BFE or the CBs, and systems to provide such information should be introduced as quickly as possible. A major constraint on the collection of appropriate information is reported to be the control which the Central Statistics Office (GUS) exercises. Apparently, BFE cannot even collect data from its own branches without having the format approved by GUS. The relevant regulation should be changed immediately to remove GUS from the process, and systems should be designed and implemented for BFE and the CBs which utilize the existing manual and partially computerized capabilities of the institutions. Subsequently, more complete management information systems should be introduced in conjunction with the computerization programs. If

NBP is coordinating the computerization programs for banks, NBP should ensure that there is adequate flexibility for meeting the information needs of individual institutions. Technical assistance should be provided to BFE and the CBs for the design and implementation of the information and computer systems.

Creating separate BFE and CB structures. In view of their separate histories, different ownership structures (BFE's majority ownership by the government), and different sets of clientele, it seems likely that BFE and the CBs will evolve into separate institutional structures, and such development should be encouraged. Some groups of CBs apparently are in the process of establishing their own regional banks, and although some 1,400 of the 1,660 CBs reportedly have signed agreements of association with BFE, most of them probably do not have any alternatives at present. Additional groups of CBs are likely to form regional banks over time. In the meantime, both BFE and the CBs which remain associated with it will benefit from the relationship. Eventually, the separate BFE and CB structures will be in a position to provide a full range of financial services to the rural sector, in competition with each other and with other banks.

BFE has a base of clients and branches on which to build a separate existence. It should focus initially on its traditional clients and should seek to meet the full range of their financial needs, including restructuring or liquidation, as appropriate. It should also give attention to expanding its client base by providing financial services to larger farmers, processing enterprises, and trading enterprises in the private sector. Subsequently, BFE should extend its reach to smaller clients and develop its operations in other sectors, becoming a full-service commercial bank. BFE's branch network of some 95 offices affords it national coverage, which gives it an advantage over existing commercial banks. In addition, it will have a presence in towns and villages during the transition period through the associated CBs. BFE's branch network should expand gradually, in accordance with its capabilities, to allow it to reach clients in towns and villages directly.

The CB system should be completely independent of government, should determine its own evolution, and should operate within the framework of the banking law, without any special privileges. There are various options for developing the system (see Appendix 13.2), but it appears that regional banks would best meet the needs of CBs, and initiatives to form such banks reportedly are under way in Poznan, Bydgoszcz/Torun, and Rzeszow. The regional banks should be formed as joint-stock companies, since they then would be able to attract other investors, including foreign banks. As regional apex institutions for the CBs, these banks would provide access to NBP refinancing facilities, assist in the upgrading and computerization of accounting systems, provide training for management and staff, coordinate the retention of external auditors, etc. (Those CBs which remain associated with BFE during the transition period should receive similar assistance from BFE.) The regional banks also should develop their own branch networks for deposit mobilization and for lending to larger rural and urban borrowers. Some degree of uniformity in the regional banks should be achieved for purposes of developing a well-coordinated cooperative banking system and to facilitate the formation of a national apex institution at a later stage. Management information, accounting, auditing, and computerization systems should be considered in this respect. In order to address CB development systematically at the individual bank and regional levels, it might be desirable for a national development program (or perhaps regional programs) to be prepared. Foreign cooperative organizations and banks might provide assistance to CB task forces in formulating such programs.

MEDIUM TERM

Expanding the supply of credit. In the medium term, as the price shock fades, stability is achieved, the private sector expands, and enterprise restructuring proceeds, the demand for credit will rise and the banks will need to increase their efforts to meet this demand. They will need to give special attention to satisfying the requirements for purposes such as land transactions and for clients such as private sector enterprises which were not significant in the past. BFE probably is in the best position to finance land transactions because of the size and diversification of its portfolio, and because of its potential ability to mobilize long-term resources. Such transactions could be financed directly and through refinancing of CB loans. BFE will need to make a substantial effort to gear itself up for lending to the private sector because of its previous lack of experience with the sector and with the assessment of the creditworthiness of enterprises operating under competitive market conditions. The CBs will also need to expand substantially their capacity for assessment of enterprise creditworthiness.

Mobilizing additional resources. BFE and the CBs will need to undertake major efforts to mobilize additional resources in order to expand the credit supply. In part, these resources will come from foreign sources, in the form of both equity investments and debt financing, and in part from NBP refinancing. But the major portion will need to come from households and enterprises. Savers will need to be provided adequate incentives to hold financial assets, and thus the banks will need to offer a range of products which provide a satisfactory return in real terms and are suited to the needs of their clients. Furthermore, banks will need to mount deposit mobilization campaigns to inform savers about the products they have to offer and to convince savers of the desirability of holding financial assets. Banks can no longer sit and wait for savers (or borrowers) to walk in the door.

Restructuring BFE. BFE is likely to undergo a major restructuring as a result of the assessment of its loan portfolio (already initiated under the special financial audit now in progress) and the disposition of loan losses. Its total assets have declined about 50% since 1985 in constant terms and are likely to shrink much further as loan losses are addressed. Current thinking is that BFE should be transformed into a joint-stock company. Additional capital will need to be mobilized from the private sector, foreign banks, and/or the government so that the bank can initially help meet the needs of larger farms and enterprises and, in the medium term, serve larger clients and participate in the restructuring of social sector farms and enterprises. The capacity to perform this role will need to be developed through extensive institutional development measures (described below). Provided such measures are undertaken, BFE would be in a position to expand its operations in the private sector and gradually begin to extend its branch network, as appropriate. As BFE demonstrates its ability to operate on a profitable basis in the new environment, the government should sell its shares to the private sector.

Strengthening BFE and the CBs. In order to operate successfully as profit-oriented, risk-assuming financial intermediaries in a competitive market environment, BFE and the CBs will need to undertake major institutional development programs. The magnitude of BFE's task is considerably greater because of its lack of experience with the private sector and the problems of its social sector clients. But the large number and disparate capabilities of individual CBs also complicates their situation.

BFE and the CBs will need to adjust to the changes occurring in the financial sector, including the introduction of new accounting standards and systems, new auditing standards and procedures, computerization programs, and prudential regulations.

They also will need to acquire professional management expertise, as discussed above. In addition to the training of managers, banks will need to provide training to all staff who have the potential to contribute in the new environment. A particular need is training in the assessment of enterprise creditworthiness.

BFE's loan portfolio problems will be addressed as described above, and the CBs will also need to review their portfolios, perhaps in the context of preparing the development programs mentioned above and the auditing arrangements.

CBs will need to replace the BFE audits with more permanent arrangements, perhaps by retaining private sector auditing firms to undertake annual audits for groups of CBs.[4] Where regional banks have been formed, these auditing arrangements could be introduced in conjunction with those for the regional banks.

BFE's capital requirements will be considered in the restructuring process. The CBs' need to expand their efforts to mobilize additional capital from members to meet their individual requirements and to establish the regional banks. CBs can obtain additional capital through direct contributions, which many CBs are doing at present, and they could also consider converting a portion of deposits to equity, as well as requiring borrowers to contribute a small percentage of loans to equity.

Multilateral and bilateral assistance programs

should be utilized to the maximum extent possible to provide support to BFE and the CBs in their institution-building efforts.

Growth of competition. Although virtual banking monopolies currently exist at the level of large-scale (BFE) and small-scale (CBs) agriculture and agribusiness, it appears that competition is growing under the present framework and that intervention to promote competition is not needed. The role of the government and NBP should be to provide an environment conducive to the growth of competition, that is, to ensure that there are no obstacles to the growth of competition (including competition from joint-venture and foreign banks), that new banks are sound, that there is effective prudential regulation and supervision, etc. As noted above, the commercial banks derived from NBP are beginning to finance some state/cooperative farms and enterprises; other existing banks (for example, Bank Handlowy, Export Development Bank, and PKO-SA) are beginning to finance agro-industry; and new banks may become involved in both agriculture and agribusiness (two of the new banks seem to be aimed at these sectors). In time, regional banks formed by CBs also may provide competition for larger clients. Some competition has developed among CBs, BFE, and commercial banks for medium-scale clients in localized areas, and this competition is likely to increase gradually and extend to smaller clients as well. PKO (savings bank) also might begin to serve smaller clients in agriculture and agribusiness. Furthermore, banks will be facing competition in the realm of personal finance from the burgeoning credit union movement.

Establishing a commodities market. As money, bond, and stock markets become established, attention should be directed to the design and introduction of a commodities market to provide an alternative to negotiated sales of agricultural commodities and to facilitate the establishment of prices.

LONG TERM

Integrating rural finance into the financial sector. In the long term, the rural sector should be served by a range of universal, private sector banks, among them BFE and the CB system. Some of them will have national coverage, while others will have regional local coverage. They should all operate under the same prudential regulation and supervision of NBP, and they should receive no special support from NBP or the government. Thus, rural finance should be an integral part of the financial sector.

Creating a national apex for the CB system. A national apex bank for the CB system should be established, as a joint-stock company with its own branch network, to enable the system to compete more effectively for large national clients, to mobilize debt resources on a broader scale, to facilitate international operations, to represent CB interests with NBP and the government, etc. With the establishment of a national apex, the CB system would have full coverage at the national, regional, and local levels.

Introducing a comprehensive deposit insurance scheme. If a national deposit insurance system is introduced, due attention should be given to the needs of the CBs and adequate provisions for them should be adopted.

Endnotes

This annex was prepared by Orlando Sacay and Gary Luhman, assisted by Andrzej Scislowski, Bozena Chelminska, and Elizeusz Karp (National Bank of Poland — NBP); Tadeusz Wyszomirski, Janusz Dedo, and Stefan Kobylinski (Bank for Food Economy — BFE); and Roman Rak (Rural Solidarity). It draws on information provided by a number of organizations, especially NBP, BFE, the cooperative banks (CBs), and the World Bank.

1. NBP provided financial services to trade cooperatives, notably the peasant self-aid cooperatives (Samopomoc Chlopska), through its commercial banking department.

2. The founding organizations generally were provincial governments in the case of state farms and MAFE in the case of state enterprises.

3. A banking institute is being established at Katowice with assistance from the French government and is scheduled to initiate operations in October of this year.

4. A number of private accounting and auditing firms are being formed, some as joint ventures with foreign firms.

Appendix 13.1
A Vision of BFE's Future Development

Environment

BFE's future will lie in the environment of an open, competitive market economy, a liberalized financial sector, and an increasingly sophisticated international financial system. BFE must now reorient its operations toward a profit objective. It must assume the risk on the loans it makes to individuals and enterprises also operating in a competitive market environment (in which they may go bankrupt). It must compete with other domestic banks (since banks are no longer limited in the services they can offer or the sectors they can serve), foreign banks, and increasingly with other types of financial institutions. And it must manage its assets and liabilities in the context of the uncertainties of developing domestic financial markets and the cauldron of international finance. It will need to strive hard to survive in this environment, and it is not well-equipped to meet this challenge at present. BFE's future also will be affected greatly by the government's policy regarding subsidized agricultural credit. This vision assumes that a targeted income subsidy or other relatively nondistortionary subsidy will be introduced if the government decides that a temporary or permanent subsidy for farmers is necessary. It also assumes that the government, as the majority shareholder, is committed to allowing BFE to develop as an effective, efficient, self-reliant financial intermediary. Within this framework, BFE will need to achieve and maintain financial viability to survive.

Financial sector adjustment

The major restructuring of the financial sector, which is currently under way and will accelerate in the future, will require substantial changes in BFE. In the context of the Agroindustries Export Development Project, supported by the World Bank, a special financial audit of BFE is being undertaken by an international accounting/auditing firm in accordance with international accounting and auditing standards and will form part of the basis for an action plan to strengthen BFE's management, operations, and financial situation. As part of its program for further development of the financial sector, the government is likely to pursue major initiatives in accounting, auditing, bank restructuring, and bank regulation and supervision. Accounting standards for enterprises and banks are to be revised to bring them into conformity with international standards, as of the beginning of 1991. BFE will need to revise its accounting system to conform to these new standards and will need to ensure that the computer system which it is establishing will meet the requirements of these standards. Similarly, standards for financial audits are being adapted to international standards, and BFE's annual financial audit will need to conform to these standards. The program of bank restructuring is in the early stage of design but is likely to have a major impact on BFE because of the bank's former role as channel for government financing of social sector farms and agricultural enterprises and the resulting potential losses to its portfolio. The BFE action plan mentioned above will assist BFE in meeting the requirements of the restructuring program.

Strategy and business plan

At the same time as it is undertaking actions to address problems of immediate concern, BFE needs to develop a strategy for achieving its vision and a business plan for implementing that strategy. This process was initiated when BFE held a conference of managers to discuss its future development; and now, a concerted, sustained effort will be necessary to ensure that the process continues until it results in a well-conceived and fully formulated strategy and plan. The special financial audit will contribute to the process by providing information on BFE's financial situation which is not currently available, recommendations of measures to improve it, and broader recommendations for organization and management. The review of BFE undertaken by Rabobank under the Netherlands' assistance program for Poland will also contribute to this process (the report is expected shortly).

Relationship with cooperative banks

On the basis of historical development, different ownership, different sets of clientele, and the present initiatives of cooperative banks (CBs), it seems likely that BFE and the CBs will evolve into separate institutional structures. The CBs were independent of BFE prior to 1975 and appear to be in the process of reestablishing that independence, as evidenced by the actions being taken by groups of CBs in Poznan, Bydgoszcz/Torun, and Rzeszow to form regional banks. While some 1,400 of the 1,660 CBs reportedly have signed agreements of association with BFE, most of these CBs probably do not have any alternatives at the present time and will benefit from association with BFE during the transition period. However, the agreements do not constitute a permanent link between BFE and the CBs, and can be terminated with a year's notice. Conceivably, a few of the CBs might become sub-branches of BFE, but most are likely to form their own regional groups over time. BFE should not be concerned about this process, since it has a basis for a separate existence, and both BFE and the associated CBs will benefit during the transition. The CBs will provide BFE a correspondent presence at the community level for purposes of resource mobilization and lending (through refinancing for such purposes as land sales which CBs would have difficulty financing with their own resources) to customers which BFE could not reach directly at present. BFE should continue to support CB development by providing services such as clearing, financing, management and staff training, computerization, and auditing. As more and more CBs form their own regional banks, and BFE strengthens its institutional capacity and gradually extends its branch network, the BFE and CB structures will be in a position to provide a full range of financial services to the rural sector.

Clientele

BFE should focus initially on its traditional clients in the social sector of agriculture, to secure its client base. On the one hand, it will need to assess the present and likely future viability of its state and cooperative farm and enterprise clients. Some are already experiencing difficulties in operating in the new environment and others will encounter problems in the future as relative prices continue to adjust

and competition continues to grow. BFE will need to address the potential losses on existing loans to these clients in the context of the government's bank restructuring program and the clients' restructuring programs, and establish provisions as appropriate. Furthermore, it will need to ensure that any future loans to these clients are made in the context of restructuring programs and have a high probability of repayment through achievement of financial viability by the clients or through liquidation of assets, in order to ensure the soundness of its future portfolio. On the other hand, BFE will need to ensure that it meets the needs of its viable clients for a full range of financial services, or they will switch to another bank.

Next, BFE should expand its client base by providing financial services to larger farmers, processing enterprises, and trading enterprises in the private sector of agriculture. Larger farmers may be the easiest group for BFE to serve, since it has some knowledge of farming operations, although farmers too, are now confronted with a risk environment. Private processing enterprises will be more difficult because BFE has little experience in analyzing the performance of enterprises in a competitive market environment. Trading enterprises will be the most difficult, in the sense that BFE has no previous experience in dealing with such enterprises.

After BFE has developed its activities in the agricultural and agroprocessing sectors that it knows, it can look toward expanding its operations in the commercial and industrial sectors. It will need to select its clients in these sectors carefully, perhaps initially on the basis of existing clients who operate in more than one sector, and will need to expand its capacity for analyzing enterprises in these sectors. Finally, BFE might expand its involvement in personal financial services. This effort is likely to be aimed at the provision of various savings instruments in the first instance but might also extend to consumer finance. As BFE's branch network gradually expands, it will have a growing capability to reach smaller clients for both resource mobilization and allocation.

Branch network

BFE's present branch network of some 95 offices affords it national coverage, which none of the existing commercial banks can claim, and allows it to reach large clients in every part of the country, as well as medium-size clients in local areas. In addition, BFE will have a large, albeit declining, number of CBs associated with it during the transition period, through which it can reach smaller clients. Thus, BFE is in a solid position to develop its banking business from the perspective of its geographical coverage. Provided BFE is able to address the institutional development and financial issues and consolidate its traditional client base, it is likely to need a restructured branch network to serve its clients adequately in the future. Some existing branches may be in areas with too few clients to be profitable and should be closed. (CBs may wish to take over the facilities in some cases.) In other areas, the expanding client base may warrant extending the branch network to additional towns. In general, the decision to open or close a branch must be based on the profit it can generate from the range of financial services provided to clients, and will require detailed analysis of each case.

Loan portfolio

BFE needs to undertake a full assessment of the quality of its existing portfolio, adopt appropriate measures in collaboration with the government and NBP to deal with loan losses, and ensure the quality of its future portfolio. A preliminary classification into suitable risk categories will result from the review undertaken by BFE and the external auditor in the course of the special audit now in process; this assessment will allow an initial estimate of losses. The estimate will be refined as more detailed analysis is undertaken of borrowers in difficulty. The decision on allocation of these losses will have a major impact on BFE's financial structure and ownership. Whatever the outcome, BFE will need to participate in the design and implementation of restructuring programs for farm and enterprise borrowers who have problems repaying their loans. In addition, BFE will need to strengthen its appraisal and supervision of loans (particularly with respect to the creditworthiness of farms and enterprises operating in a competitive market environment) in order to improve the quality of its future portfolio. Adequate provisions for future loan losses will need to be established.

Resource mobilization

BFE's capital is less than 3% of total assets, and its action plan is to include measures for increasing capital to at least 8% of risk assets, as agreed under AEDP and IEDP. This matter will be addressed in part during the restructuring of the loan portfolio, and might involve the assumption by the government of BFE's debt to NBP and the conversion of the debt to equity, for example. However, since substantial loan losses are likely to be involved, additional capital may be needed to allow BFE to provide the level of financing required by agriculture and agro-industry. This additional capital could be provided by a foreign bank (or banks) interested in becoming involved in Poland's banking business through association with an established institution, by the domestic private sector, or even by the government. (Although CBs contributed about 49% of the capital for the establishment of BFE, that contribution has been eroded by inflation and is now insignificant. CBs will be fully occupied with rebuilding their own capital and establishing their own superstructure; they are unlikely to be interested in expanding their stake in BFE.) To facilitate the mobilization of additional capital (as well as to provide an appropriate basis for future development), BFE should be converted to a stock company. As BFE demonstrates its ability to operate on a profitable basis in the new environment, the government should sell its shares to the private sector and thus allow BFE to become a private bank.

BFE's borrowings from NBP amount to over 60% of total assets. To the extent that these liabilities are not converted to equity, specific terms should be agreed to for the repayment of this debt, whether by BFE or by the government. In the future, BFE should participate in NBP's refinancing program on the same terms and conditions as any other bank. BFE will also have access to the interbank market, loans from foreign institutions (including the World Bank), and perhaps international financial markets. Eventually, it may be able to issue its own bonds.

Deposits of CBs account for some 15-20% of BFE's assets, and deposits of social sector clients account for another 15-20%. Formation of regional banks by CBs is not likely to have a significant impact on CB deposits in the short term, although these deposits will decline over the medium term as growing numbers of CBs form such banks. More significant in the near term will be the control that CBs now exercise over their own resources, since this is likely to result in an expansion of lending and a decline in deposits with BFE as economic stability increases. (CB lending previously was governed by the national credit plan, as administered through the BFE branches.) Moreover, competition for enterprise deposits is growing. Therefore BFE will need to be aggressive in mobilizing deposits by offering present and prospective clients a range of products at competitive prices and mounting campaigns to promote these products.

Operational efficiency

It is assumed that BFE will not be provided with a subsidy from any source and therefore that it will not have access to preferred refinancing from NBP. Thus it will need to compete with other banks on an equal basis and must raise the efficiency of its operations to survive on a shrinking margin between deposit and loan rates. Such operation is made more difficult by factors such as variable interest rates, a growing range of financial instruments, rapid development of domestic financial markets, and the continuously increasing sophistication of international financial markets. In order to perform satisfactorily, BFE will need to acquire rapidly expertise in competitive market banking (particularly with regard to risk management, financial management, and credit administration), introduce appropriate policies and procedures, and establish systems (management information, accounting, auditing, etc.) required for prompt, informed decision-making and sound operation.

Institutional development

BFE previously operated as a channel for government financing in a planned economy and must now transform itself into a profit-driven financial intermediary operating in a competitive market environment — a staggering task. Perhaps the first requirement is management expertise in operating in such an environment. Such expertise is a highly scarce commodity in BFE at present; it must be brought in from outside the institution and developed from within. One means of taking advantage of outside expertise could be the appointment of a small group of advisors with extensive experience in banking in market economies (including recent experience in international financial markets). Then the next generation of decisionmakers (existing staff with appropriate qualifications and new staff recruited on the basis of potential for management in the new environment) must be trained at foreign banks and banking institutes, and in sound domestic training programs. The entire range of staff who have the capability of performing adequately in the new environment also must be trained, both abroad and at home. In all cases, care must be taken to select trainees on the basis of their potential contribution to the future success of BFE, rather than as a reward for past service.

BFE needs to introduce a set of policies suitable for its new role. These policies must be geared to achieving and maintaining a sound financial position and performance and need to encompass such matters as mobilization of resources in the form of deposits, borrowings, and equity; placement of resources in various forms of investments and loans; interest rates and management of assets and liabilities, portfolios, and liquidity. Particular attention needs to be devoted to lending policies and procedures, especially to loan appraisal, supervision, and collection (including assessment and liquidation of collateral). Appropriate personnel policies need to be introduced to address issues such as compensation, training, recruitment and termination, performance evaluation, and promotion.

Management systems need to be enhanced. Accounting and auditing need to be adapted to the requirements of the banking system, as mentioned above. The internal auditing system needs to be strengthened to complement the external audit in keeping with international standards. A new management information system adapted to the needs of management in the new environment should be introduced. In particular, the computerization program must meet the requirements of the new accounting and management information systems.

The cost of the institutional development program will far exceed anything BFE has attempted in the past, because BFE has not had to face such a challenge before and because of the changes in relative prices. Management seems reluctant to incur this cost but must recognize that the program is absolutely essential for BFE's continued existence. Fortunately, assistance is available from a variety of sources.

Multilateral and bilateral assistance

Many multilateral institutions, including the IMF, World Bank, European Community, and various United Nations agencies, are providing a range of technical assistance in the banking system and to individual banks, including BFE, under grant and loan financing. Many bilateral assistance programs are also supporting development of the banking system and specific banks. For example, support for BFE's institutional development program is being provided in the form of the review undertaken by the Rabobank team, and training and equipment under the Netherlands' assistance program. The German Cooperatives Bank (DGB) has explored various types of cooperation with BFE. A twinning arrangement between BFE and an appropriate foreign bank could bring substantial benefits.

Appendix 13.2
A Vision of the Future Development of Cooperative Banks
Environment

The CBs also will be operating in a new environment, as described for BFE. They have an advantage, since they have been dealing with the private sector, but they still have been operating within the framework of central control exerted through BFE, particularly with regard to the credit plan, and the web of state-controlled prices, input supply, and output procurement. Furthermore, local administrations have influenced loand decisions and the selection of bank management and loan decisions. Now the CBs and their clients must operate in an uncertain, risky environment. And since BFE no longer serves as their central union, the CBs must decide on their future affiliations for purposes such as linkage to the national and international banking systems, resource mobilization, and representation of CB interests at regional and national levels.

Clientele

The CBs have a long history and a solid base of private farmer and craftsmen clients in the rural sector. They should focus initially on expanding the range of services provided to these traditional clients and extending the client base to encompass trade and processing enterprises. As the CB system evolves, it will serve larger clients and operate in other sectors.

Superstructure

A superstructure for the CB system is needed for such purposes as liquidity management; refinancing arrangements with NBP; joint services (for example, clearing, data processing, training); and representation at national and international levels. There are various options which the CBs might consider for their superstructure. One would be to remain linked to BFE, either in the form of the loose association represented by the present agreements or through the transformation of main BFE branches into regional banks with CB and BFE ownership. This would represent an evolution of the relationship which has been built up over the past 15 years and would be the easiest path to follow, but it is unlikely to bring maximum benefit to either BFE or the CBs. The CBs were independent of state control prior to the advent of the previous regime, and are likely to thrive best as an independent system in the private sector. Another option would be for CBs to become associated with existing commercial banks, perhaps on a regional basis, but the CBs would not have any influence on the operations of the commercial banks (which would likely channel CB resources to the urban sector). One possibility for an independent CB system would be to have regional associations to provide management advice and technical services to individual CBs, and a national apex bank for purposes such as mobilization of debt resources, international operations, and representation of CB interests *vis-à-vis* NBP and the government. However, it would be difficult and time consuming to establish such a structure all at once, and the system would not be well suited to mobilizing resources or serving borrowers in regional urban centers.

Thus, CBs are likely to develop best by forming secondary banks at provincial or regional levels and, subsequently, an apex bank at the national level. Secondary banks at the provincial level might have too small a coverage, since they would have an average of only 34 CB shareholders and could have difficulty meeting the NBP's minimum capital requirement of Zl

10 billion for a new bank. On the other hand, regional banks would have an average coverage of perhaps 100 CBs and would have a much better chance of raising the necessary capital. A national apex bank is unlikely to be feasible in the initial stage, since it would have no intermediate structure and would need to deal with 1,660 CBs on an individual basis. Thus, it seems that regional banks would best meet the needs of CBs, and initiatives to form such banks reportedly are already under way in Poznan, Bydgoszsc/Torun, and Rzeszow. A stock company format for regional banks would be most appropriate, since they then would be in a position to attract other domestic and foreign investors. Furthermore, the regional banks should be full-service banks, with their own branch networks, to mobilize deposits in urban centers and meet the needs of borrowers operating on a regional basis. After the regional banks have been established, a national apex bank should be formed to give the CBs a presence at the national level. This apex bank could also operate as a universal bank.

Capitalization

The capitalization of CBs presently is very low at less than 3% of total resources, and additional capital is needed to allow individual banks to operate satisfactorily in the new environment and to establish the regional banks. In the short term, CBs need to obtain additional capital from members, and many have initiated this process by raising the value of shares from the low levels resulting from past inflation. The payment of dividends providing a positive real return on shares would aid this effort. In the medium term, CBs might consider requiring borrowers to contribute, say, 5% of loans to equity. Such a procedure would provide a foundation for expanding operations at the base and regional levels, as well as provide capital resources for establishment of a national apex bank. Capital for regional banks might be mobilized in part from foreign banks, especially cooperative banks, which also could provide a range of services and technical assistance for regional banks and their CB shareholders.

Deposit mobilization

In order to meet the expanding credit requirements of existing clients and those of new cli-ents such as traders and processors in the medium term, CBs will need to undertake major efforts to mobilize deposits and other debt resources from households and businesses. In order to do this, they will need to provide deposit rates which are positive in real terms and will need to mount promotional campaigns. Over time, they also will need to expand the range of financial instruments offered. Furthermore, they will need to retain or establish borrowing relationships with banks such as BFE and the commercial banks. As regional banks are formed, they may be able to participate in NBP's general refinancing program. CBs also may have access to debt resources from foreign multilateral and bilateral sources, initially through other domestic banks and subsequently through the regional banks.

Loan portfolios

In general, CBs probably are not confronted with the problems with existing loan portfolios that BFE faces. Nevertheless, there are likely to be short-term difficulties as borrowers grapple with the present situation of excess commodity stocks and the medium-term difficulties borrowers experience in adjusting to a competitive market environment. Furthermore, CBs have started to lend to agricultural circle cooperatives (which previously borrowed from BFE) and the peasant self-aid cooperatives (which previously borrowed from the commercial banks), and have even assumed previously outstanding loans to these cooperatives. Since they have not lent to these entities in the past, they may not be in a position to assess properly their creditworthiness. In addition, some of the past medium- and long-term loans were made at low nominal interest rates which cannot be converted to variable rates (as was done in the case of the social sector), and some loans were made on the basis of nonbanking criteria. Therefore, CBs need to undertake portfolio reviews and address issues of cooperative and enterprise restructuring (especially regarding the cooperatives) and loan losses. In order to ensure the quality of their future portfolios, they need to strengthen loan appraisal, supervision, and collection (especially with regard to new types of borrowers), and they need to establish appropriate provisions for potential loan losses.

Institutional development

In order to perform successfully in the new environment, CBs will need to undertake substantial institutional development programs. A major requirement will be professional management expertise. In some cases, unqualified managers have been imposed on CBs for nonbanking reasons, and these managers will need to be replaced by persons with suitable qualifications. Managers and staff with appropriate qualifications will need to be trained for operation in a competitive market environment in a revamped BFE training program for CBs, in other domestic training programs, and in foreign banks and banking institutes. A particular need is for training in the assessment of enterprise creditworthiness. Policies suited to the new environment will need to be introduced, particularly with regard to financial, credit, and personnel management. Management information, accounting, and auditing systems need to be upgraded and adapted to the requirements of the banking system, regional banks or BFE, and the CBs' individual situations.

Auditing

The system of financial auditing for the CBs needs special attention. BFE's responsibility for auditing the CBs was terminated by the recent amendment to the cooperative law, and the responsibility has passed to NBP. However, NBP does not have the capacity to perform this function and has requested that BFE undertake the audits on its behalf, for both associated and nonassociated CBs. This arrangement is satisfactory for the present but should be replaced by more permanent arrangements. Private sector auditing firms should be retained to undertake the annual audit for groups of CBs. In the case of CBs that have formed regional banks, the audit of the CB shareholders can be included in the arrangements for the audit of the regional banks. For those CBs which remain associated with BFE, BFE can assist regional groups of CBs in preparation of terms of reference for the

audit and retention of auditors. The CBs will need to pay the full cost of these audits as part of their normal operations. Initially, because of the adoption of international accounting and auditing standards (at the beginning of 1991) and the lack of experience of domestic firms in performing audits in accordance with these standards, foreign expertise is likely to be needed in the audit teams.

Development programs

Because of the large number of individual units involved, it might be desirable for a development program to be prepared for the CB system or perhaps for regional groups of CBs (as with the program being prepared by the World Council of Credit Unions). Such a program or programs would need to address issues at the level of the CB and of the regional bank, and could provide suggestions for the national level as well. The programs could provide recommendations on such matters as strategies, preparation of business plans, management, advice, training, information systems, capitalization, deposit mobilization, and portfolio assessments. Foreign cooperative banks might provide assistance to CB task forces in formulating these programs.

Multilateral and bilateral assistance

Assistance for the CBs will come from a variety of sources. BFE will provide substantial assistance in areas such as computerization and training for those CBs which remain associated with it, at least during the interim (although BFE will need to revise its training program to meet the needs of operating in the new environment). Various multilateral and bilateral assistance programs will have an impact on the CBs — the banking institute to be established in Katowice with French assistance is a notable example. A major source of assistance to CBs that form regional banks could be the foreign banks which might become involved with these regional banks.

Agrarian structure, land consolidation, and farmland management

Current situation

FARM STRUCTURE

Polish farm structure (18.9 million ha) is divided in three sectors:

- state farms (1,300 central units), with 4.1 million ha;
- cooperatives (800 central units), with 0.4 million ha; and
- private farms (2.7 million units), with 14.4 million ha.

The rural population has been surprisingly stable since 1950, still representing 40% of the total population. Area per person employed in farming has been steady at 3.8 ha since 1950. Over 75% of the land area is privately operated, with an average farm size of 6.4 ha and with farm size distributed indicated in Table 14.1.

Wide regional differences exist, tied to the different history of Poland's regions, to unequal industrial development and to the extensive multi-plot character of the private sector. Land consolidation has been a slow process.

While the majority of land is in private hands and production in a number of sectors is primarily private (such as in horticulture and pigs), the extent of the private sector in the overall agribusiness system (inputs to consumer) is very limited. Agribusiness in Poland is overwhelmingly dominated by the state sector. Inputs, as well as marketing, processing and, until recently, all retail, were in the state sector.

Overall, average farm size in the private sector is 6.4 ha with the larger of the private sector farms (those over 12 ha — that is, the top 30% in size) producing 70% of the output of the private farming sector.

Table 14.1 Farm structure

	Size (ha)	No. ('000)	%	Area (ha, million)	%	Avgerage size (ha)
Very small	1-5	1,108	48.7	2.7	19.9	2.4
Small to medium	5-10	692	30.4	4.4	32.4	6.4
Medium to large	15+	183	8.0	3.3	24.3	18.0

Source: Institute of Agricultural and Food Economics, Warsaw.

Fragmentation of private sector holdings is extensive, with the average size farm of 6.4 ha divided into some three parcels, varying substantially by region. Regionally, the smaller farms (3-4 ha average) are in the southern part of the country with larger farms (15 ha average) in the northern sectors. According to cadastral data, some 4 million persons own Poland's 2.7 million farms. The 110,000 land registration books contain a reported 30 million individual parcel numbers (Zrobek 1990).

The extent of very small farming is substantial, at over 1 million farms below 5 ha. These small farms have remained relatively constant despite 20 years of land consolidation efforts. Such farms are likely to persist and, in a rapidly restructuring economy, probably should continue to exist in the short and medium term to

- foster social stability;
- provide alternative employment, even at low efficiency levels; and
- assure household and local food supplies.

Such farms, often with reasonable housing, also provided residency for extended families when housing is scarce in urban areas and likely to remain so.

These very small farms are divided by Polish sociologists into peasant farms (older farmers nearing or at retirement, producing primarily for home and local consumption) and part-time farms, or pluri-active farms. These latter farms include 4.7 family members living on the farm, with some working off farm, compared with 3.5 family members in the average small farm under 4 ha. These pluri-active farms, Dr. Anna Szemberg writes, are "not in conflict in running the farm and absorb work of those persons which do not find full employment on the family farm." She argues that with limited off-farm employment opportunities and lack of labor mobility due to housing shortages, the sociological importance of the pluri-active farm sector of Poland will be important in the 1990s.

Surveys of these part-time farm families indicate considerable interest in farm expansion, especially by sons and daughters (Szemberg, 1990).

The definition of the family farm was changed in June 1989 to exclude farms below 1 ha from the national farm statistics. This statistical redefinition reduced the number of officially reported farms by some 250,000.

Polish economists forecast that numbers of private farms are likely to drop by 500,000 by the year 2000 (Szemberg, IERIGZ, et al.). Larger farms are likely to expand (farms over 15 ha, reaching an average size of 30 ha). Szemberg predicts over 66% of the farmland by the year 2000 will be farmed by operators of farms in excess of 10 ha and will constitute 33% of the private farm numbers. Another group (RGZ) makes a similar projection with small farmers (below 2 ha) showing a small increase, the 2-10 ha farm size declining, and those farms above 10 ha doubling in number over the next two decades.

Very small part-time and retirement farms are likely to persist, with the major reduction coming in the full-time farming sector in the range of 4-15 ha. The rate of diminuation is projected at 2% annually, with a drop in cultivated farmland from this sector of 500,000 ha, 3% of the private sector farmland by the turn of the century.

The result of this restructuring will be an increase in the average size of farms from 6 to 8 ha overall in the private sector, the latter being the farm size now prevailing in Italy. With unemployment increasing, it is unlikely that labor shortages in most rural areas will be a problem. Structural change will be more likely in northern and central Poland compared with the south.

OPERATIONS OF THE NATIONAL LAND FUND

Most farmland in Poland continues to be in private hands. The government, however, over the past 40 years, has attempted to regulate and, at times, to socialize private land holdings. The National Land Fund was organized for this purpose, offering private farmers an opportunity to sell their farm, while keeping their house, to the National Land Fund in return for a pension at retirement.

These policies were recently delinked and farmers can obtain a pension of 70% of the normal pension offered without having to sell their lands; they can transfer the land to a successor, sell or lease on the private market.

Currently the National Land Fund manages some 800,000 ha, about 50% rented to private farms. The fund manages little land in the more populated south and central regions.

The fund's acquisitions have been mostly poorer Class 4-6 lands, in small tracts, with no buildings, in some cases in fragmented pieces. In 1988, some 58,000 ha were sold to the fund, often for cash rather than retirement pensions. Private market land sales with bank financing were reported as 12,800 ha in the same year.

Sales from the fund are structured to bidders on favorable terms to local farmers, particularly if the parcel, when added to existing parcels, improves the viability of the parcel currently owned by the buying farmer. About 75% of the sales from the National Land Fund are for farm enlargement.

The price of the land for sale is set on the basis of the value of 100 kg of rye per ha at the official procurement price. The local government administration determines to whom the sale will be made. The Bank for the Economy(BFE) acts as agent of the state Treasury, receiving a 5% margin on each sale.

Constraints and potential

PRIVATE SECTOR RESTRUCTURING PATTERNS

In order to create a more orderly and market-driven land market for private farms, the government will need to take a number of policy steps. Currently, farm size is limited by law to 50 ha in central Poland and 100 ha in western Poland. These size limits will need to be increased and eventually eliminated. To foster improved sales, the government should consider selling or leasing land in smaller blocks to facilitate transfer, for example, in blocks of 25 to 50 ha in central Poland and in larger blocks, perhaps at 100 ha, in western and eastern Poland.

RESTRUCTURING THE NATIONAL LAND FUND

As the government moves the economy to a more market-driven structure, the private land market is likely to develop. This should make it easier to transfer farmland via sale and lease/purchase to the private sector.

Also, as the farmer pension scheme for land exchange is delinked from farmer pensions, the rationale for the current role of the National Land Fund will cease to exist. Alternative roles for the National Land Fund could be as follows:

• Eliminating the fund, with transfer of cur-rently leased land to farmers holding the lease title. Remaining land would be placed on the market for auctioning to the private farming sector. The problem is that much of the land is in areas of low farmland demand. Complete elimination of the fund is not favored.

• Continuing the fund's operations and focusing its operations more deeply on the consolidation issue, but delinking its role in land for pensions. There was some support for continuation of the fund in its current role, but the majority of the Task Force felt that the fund's current role is too passive.

• Restructuring the fund into a regional land management and conservation agency. A considerable amount of the land held is lower quality land which could be beneficially placed in a long-term conservation program, under permanent grass, and in appropriate cases, in a reforestation program. Existing land holdings under lease to farmers would be converted in lease/purchase or direct purchase arrangements.

In addition, this restructured and more regionally activist regional land management and conservation agency could be constituted to examine regional development alternatives, for farming, in villages and in the rural sector, particularly in regions where it has had previous operational experience, such as northeastern Poland.

LAND CONSOLIDATION: DIRECTION AND RESTRUCTURING

Poland has had a long-term policy of land consolidation — the so-called policy goal of improving the agrarian structure. Some 40,000 to 60,000 ha have been consolidated annually over the past decade at a cost of some US$15 to US$75 per ha.

While the smallest farms have also been targeted, the principal effect has been on middle-size commercial farms that depend mainly on farming for a living. These farms, ranging in size from 5-15 ha, are declining in number as they are consolidated with official support, bought by larger farms (over 15 ha), or purchased in exchange for a pension through acquisition of the retiring farm by the National Land Fund.

Until recently, land consolidation was also fostered by restricting access to inputs, operating and development credit, and extension services; by encouraging older farmers to retire and sell their land to the National Land Fund in exchange for a pension; and by consciously not producing the appropriate-size machinery for smaller farms. The overpowered equipment used on medium-size Polish private farms is particularly noticeable.

These middle-size farms (4-15 ha) are still critically important in Polish agriculture, making up 43% of private farms, cultivating 56% of private sector land, and producing over half of private sector output.

The larger farms (over 15 ha) comprise only 8% of private farms, but cultivate 25% of the arable land, that is, some 3.3 million ha—about the same as all the state farms in the country.

On many private farms, land is not farmed contiguously, but rather is divided into a number of separate plots. Prior to the recent economic reforms, Polish economists expected certain trends to continue: stability in the peasant and part-time farming sector (farm size up to 5 ha), with such farms serving as residences and retirement homes and providing local and family food security; retrenchment in commercial farms up to 15 ha; and some expansion in farm size of farms in excess of 15 ha. With the reforms and with the likely sale and leasing availability of state in areas of private farms, it is likely that farmland holdings by farmers holding in excess of 5 ha will expand, particularly those in excess of 15 ha.

Current structure and equipment in the Land Consolidation Group of the Ministry of Agriculture enables only 60,000 ha to be consolidated annually. To expand this capability to 100,000 ha annually, modernization of land consolidation is necessary.

Using the Global Positioning Systems (GPS) methodology will yield the following: substantial time savings (up to 10 times); increased geodictic accuracy; 60% cost savings and multipurpose output in survey, design, cadastral specification, and support data for land registration, mapping output and basic information for decision makers. The estimated cost is about US$1 million initially for GPS receivers, field computers, software and digital mapping technology. The Task Force recommends that GPS technology be introduced to assist in the land consolidation program in Poland.

An institutional linkage with the French SAFER (Society for the Management of Rural Lands) also be might be considered. This society has been most successful over the past two decades in effective rural farm consolidation through buying, holding, and then reselling lands to improve farm structure in France.

Land taxation to encourage land consolidation. Another option to foster land consolidation is a land tax. Such a tax has a number of advantages over other forms of rural taxes:

• it is easily understood as it relates to physically measurable parameters;
• it is easily administered as land ownership is normally identifiable and fairly static;
• it promotes the efficient long-term use of a major resource — land; and
• rates of land tax can be adjusted rapidly to influence land usage such as implementation of land protection programs.

Poland has a number of major advantages vis-à-vis a land tax:

• it already has a land tax legislative mechanism in place (albeit not at meaningful tax levels);
• it has a land registration system which records land ownership; and
• it has a land capability classification system which is known to farmers and on which land valuation could be based.

Administering a land tax. Later in this decade, as industrial development stabilizes and the owners of small farms reach retirement, land on these small farms may not be optimally used. Even if the land market were to be stimulated, it is unlikely that there will be real pressure on self-sufficient, retiring small farmers to consolidate plot holdings or to lease underutilized plots. Realizing the value of land through sales is only attractive if the opportunity value significantly exceeds the emotional risks involved in selling and leasing. If, however, unused or unprofitable land is a cash liability, then farmers will take steps to reduce that liability. A land tax would apply just such a pressure.

Furthermore, if the land tax were administered not just on area and classification (as is done in most countries), but on classification and the ratio of perimeter length to area, then pressure would be applied to (1) reduce long thin fields to square fields and (2) reduce many small plots into fewer larger plots.

ATTITUDES ON CHANGES IN AGRARIAN STRUCTURE

In recent years, surveys of youth, clerk, and peasant attitudes to current and potential changes in rural agrarian structure were done at Lodz University. This data is currently being updated. In the opinion surveys of these three classes of rural groups, "all three categories indicated that poorly managed, financially stressed state farming operations should be restricted and administratively released of their land" (Pilichowski, Lodz University, unpublished paper, June 1990).

However, Lodz researchers did not find a similar consensus on the management of inefficient private sector farming operations. The consensus of interviewed persons indicated that economic pressures (a more active rural land market, support for consolidation and leasing law changes) rather than compulsion would be a preferred solution. The youth and clerk category of interviewees favored the economic fostering of smaller farm consolidation, with older farmers favoring intensified intervention and support to assist such farmers in managing traditional, diversified farms.

Interviews also indicated that there were not strong views about setting land holding ceilings (that is, maximum peasant farm holdings), with clerks rather than farmers and youth leaning toward farm size ceilings within areas. For those favoring farm acreage ceilings, the recommendation was for ceilings in the farming area parish not to exceed 3 times the average size farm in the area. Thus, if average farm size were 10 ha, farm ceiling size would be suggested at 30 ha. However, these views were held by a minority of those interviewed, with over 66% of interviewed persons in rural areas suggesting that larger farms (in excess of 20 ha) enabled more economic use of factors of production, improved efficiency, and improved chances of organization. Concerns with availability of farm labor were seen as limitations on larger farms, especially those of a mixed livestock and cropping nature.

Younger farmers and younger members of the rural population also favored continued prospects of land consolidation. The data from the surveys indicated continued support for consolidation, with older farmers being the principal category expressing caution on an expanded consolidation process.

Surveys indicated little support for farm re- settlement between regions in Poland. Interview respondents, especially younger persons, expressed interest in exploring resettlement in other parts of Poland, but included reservations on how this might be carried out effectively in the current situation in Poland.

Finally, surveys indicated a strong desire amoung younger farmers and full-time farmers to cooperate more intensively with state farms, with less such inclination by older smaller-farm farmers. Interest in cooperating was expressed for both horizontal and vertical, for example, input provision, tractor rental, marketing and, in some cases, processing.

As expected, the updated surveys indicated a discrepancy of viewpoints: younger farmers and younger persons in rural areas expressed interest in adapting farming operations; and older farmers expressed their desire to maintain the traditional production techniques.

Strategic recommendations and policies

Overall, farm structure is likely to change markedly in the latter years of this decade (after 1995), as the state farm management and ownership is changed, as cooperatives return their farm production functions to members, and especially as the private farm sector continues to consolidate, both with modest government assistance and particularly in light of an aging group of farm owners and as longer-term opportunities become available in industrial and service sector development and employment growth.

But from 1990 to 1995, the overall restructuring of the nonfarm industrial and service sector will likely create extensive unemployment and related social dislocations in rural areas.

If a similar and simultaneous restructuring in the major private sector of the Polish economy, its private sector farm economy, were to take place, the likely employment and social dislocations would be great. Thus, an adjustment and land ownership restructuring strategy, particularly for the partial divestiture of the bankrupt and financially stressed state farm sector, is proposed—one that is especially phased to take this labor absorption strategy into account.

A green model composed of small-scale peasant and part-time farms would be fostered to take advantage of their potential for rural labor stabilization and their low use of farm chemicals. These very small and part-time farms come under the category of the government's developing the so-called green farm model, a strategy to ensure stability of a minimum input, sustainable small farming sector and to stabilize the rural labor force during the upcoming national economic stabilization adjustment period.

A limited market of chemical-free farm products exists in Western Europe and North America, especially for higher value products such as the small fruit sector. This sector should be encouraged with modest government interventions, especially in the provision of support to export-oriented small fruit-processing facilities and locally for an extensive network of market places and market shops.

For the smallest of these farms, the Task Force recommends continued focus on land consolidation at current levels (in real terms) of fiscal support from the government, with emphasis on improved technical support, especially through introduction of GIS (computerized geographic information systems).

For the part-time farming sector, in the short and medium term, such farms are likely to play an important labor adjustment role, as labor is divested from inefficient state enterprises. Interim encouragement is needed for these farms to act as a labor sponge.

A diversification model would be encouraged, with private farmers farming efficiently, and with support for diversification into alternative crops and on-farm processing and cottage industries.

The diversification model of assisting full-time private farmers in consolidating their farms, improving their existing crops, diversifying their cropping patterns where possible, and adding on-farm small-scale processing and cottage industries has short- and medium-term benefits. This has also been called a pluri-active rural model by Polish sociologists. In a time of limited financial resources, it focuses national farm and rural policy on fostering productive, efficient farming enterprises, enabling them to sell to a wider range of more competitive market enterprises and to diversify cropping patterns as market and price signals indicate.

Accompanied by policy measures to create a more competitive input industry, and especially more modern and competitive market infrastructure and assembly enterprises in rural areas, this pluri-active diversification model makes the most sense for sustaining short- and medium-term rural employment, for developing a market for divesting state farm and national land fund lands, and for supporting a private sector short- and medium-term strategy of employment and income stabilization.

For commercial private farms (15 ha and above), farm size is likely to increase during this period as peasant farmers retire and state and cooperative farms sell and lease land for these farmers to add to existing holdings. By the end of the current decade, these farmers are expected to number 500,000, accounting for 70% of farm output from an estimated 8 million ha, up from the 6 million now currently harvested.

A rural development model is a related strategy to encourage more urban based industries to expand or relocate into rural areas to take advantage of the substantial part-time farm labor force as well as nonfarm workforce. The rural development model of providing incentives for industry to locate in rural areas of substantial off-farm and part-time workers is being extensively fostered in Western Europe by the EC.

It is an expensive strategy and one that may need to be considered later in the decade at the conclusion of the current stabilization strategy.

The fostering of large-scale production units (1,000 ha and upward) of primarily former state-farming operations, operated with centrally appointed administrators, using intensive inputs and farming on a relatively large scale, has been government policy until recent political changes.

Wide-scale adoption of this model, however, has been rejected by the majority of Polish farmers over the past 50 years.

The Task Force rejected wholesale support of this production model for the future agrarian structure of rural Poland, with the exception of continuing to privatize and restructure the larger, well-managed farms in western Poland whose ownership structure and farm-financing system would need to be altered (see Annex 7).

For state farms, a major adjustment in both structure and ownership will occur. It is likely that at least 20% of the state-owned farmland area will be leased or sold over the next 5 years to private commercial farmers, most living near these farms. Furthermore, the ownership pattern will change, with a variety of approaches being used to effect the changes. Principally, the government needs to immediately specify rules for changes from social property to share ownership, in keeping with the legal definition in recently passed privatization legislation.

Phasing

SHORT TERM AND MEDIUM TERM

Several legal changes are required in the short and medium terms terms to legalize and improve the functioning of the private land market and to foster legal transfers from the public to the private sector:

• Eliminate the ceilings on private sector holding (currently at 100 ha). In the medium term, consider a higher limit perhaps up to 200 ha in central and southern Poland and 400 ha in eastern/northern and western Poland.
• Permit farmland to be purchased by natural and legal persons, reducing the requirement of farmer qualifications. The point is to enable workers on existing state farms to acquire freehold or long-term leases on farmland and to enable persons, especially younger farmers, to enter farming.
• Establish up-to-date regulations for long-term leasing of farmland to protect the interests of the smaller farm sector of renters and to encourage the renters to invest in the farms.

PRIVATE FARM SECTOR

Green sector of smaller farms. Stabilization of this subsector is valuable as it acts as an employment sponge. This sector is mainly producing for on-farm consumption and limited off-farm local market sales.

Development of an extensive private town and rural farmer market system will enable this sector to sell directly. While somewhat inefficient in longer-term labor utilization, fostering direct market sales is also employment intensive in a period of increasing rural labor unemployment.

Commercial private farming. The 100 ha restriction on size of land-holding should be removed. The government may wish to set some limits on the size of farms to avoid speculation and reselling, say, no purchases in excess of 200 ha during the period of privatization.

Steps should be taken to improve cadastral and land title registration systems as well as the financial system to improve sales, transfer and consolidation of land holdings. Income should be stabilized through programs in dairy and pig modernization.

Land sale and lease markets. Critical to the restructuring of the uneconomic state farms and cooperatives is the development of financial mechanisms to ensure smoother institutional support for land purchases and longer-term leaseholds for expanding private farmers, land acquisitions to include purchases from nearby state farms and from retiring (green sector) smaller and less economic farms.

STATE FARM SECTOR

Legal and accounting changes should be completed and major management reorganization begun. Leasing should be started and programs initiated to begin the sale of lands to local private farmers in areas of private land holdings. In cases of bankruptcy, operations should be closed down, with land and equipment leased and sold to private farmers and possibly joint-venture partners, or poorer lands allocated to conservation and forestry.

National Land Fund. Farmland being sold or leased by the National Land Fund should be first sold to farmers in the vicinity of the land being sold and should be sold via an auction or bidding system. Legislation should be passed to wind down this fund in 1991 and sell and lease its assets by December 30, 1995.

The organization of the National Land Fund should be restructured into a national regional land and conservation management agency that would control the lands in its portfolio of lower-farm quality and place and manage them for conservation purposes — in both grass and, in appropriate cases, for forestation. Grazing and forage cutting would be limited to best management practices.

As part of this restructuring, consideration of a pattern of organization and structure along the lines of the successful French SAFER (Society for the Management of Rural Lands) might be considered, maintaining direct linkages to SAFER in the interim medium-term period. For conservation and reforestation programs, linkages to the Bureau of Land Management and to the Forest Service of the United States Department of Agriculture might be considered.

Land consolidation. These efforts would include:

• maintenance and modest expansion (from 60,000 ha to 100,000 ha) of current land consolidation efforts, expansion of current modest budgetary levels (in real terms), improvements in administrative efficiency, and the addition of Global Positioning System (GPS) computer mapping capability. This capital cost will run about US$1 million — modest considering efficiency gains achieved.

• complete restructuring in a national regional land management and conservation agency;

• final sale and lease/purchase of existing lands; and

• developing possible linkages with external groups such as SAFER in France or the USDA's Bureau of Land Management and Forest Service.

LONG-TERM STRUCTURE AND IMPACT OF PROPOSALS

The impact of the proposals outlined above are likely to be as follows:

• Development of an improved market for farmland transactions in Poland, especially for smaller parcels. Some limitations on size of blocks may be necessary on land sales to private farmers and new start-up farmers. This would not be a ceiling on size of land holding, but rather a restriction on the size of parcel which the government would be divesting from bankrupt state farms and from national land fund holdings.

• Fostering a rural structure of primarily family-owned farms of sufficient size (depending on the region) to assure a living comparable with skilled industrial workers in urban areas.

• The sale/lease of lands to private farmers of currently leased National Land Fund lands and of state farms located in areas of substantial private land holdings.

• Development of financial intermediaries to foster land sales between farmers and from holdings (land fund and state farms) to farmers.

Endnote

This annex was prepared by August Schumacher, Jr. (World Bank), Maria Nowak (Caisse centrale de cooperation économique/EC), Rysard Zrobek (Agricultural University of Olsztyn) and Andrzej Pilichowski (Lodz University, Institute of Sociology).

Farm production and profitability

Current Situation

Poland lies in a transitional climate zone, influenced in the west and north by the Western European maritime climate and in the east and north by the Eastern European continental influence. As a result, weather is highly variable. Annual precipitation averages between 500 and 650 mm over most of the plains, and usually more than 60% of rain falls during April-September. Over some 80% of the country, total precipitation exceeds potential evapotranspiration. Relative humidity can be high in the critical hay, cereal and root crop harvesting periods, complicating operations and often necessitating postharvest drying. Topography is generally flat and favorable to farming, but flatness can lead to poor drainage, a problem affecting about 50% of Polish agricultural land. Only about 30% of Polish arable area is on soils rated as good, another 30% has major inherent problems. Soils are mostly light textured, of low natural fertility, often with a high water table and requiring drainage. Soil acidity is serious in more than 60% of the soils and requires corrective measures for optimising crop production. Polish scientists estimate that the overall agroecological conditions in Poland are about 30% less favorable to crop production than in most Western European countries.

A further limiting factor to agricultural production is farm structure. More than one half of the 2.2 million private farms are smaller than 5 ha. These farms occupy almost 20% of agricultural land but contribute little to marketable output because they produce largely for their own consumption. Many of the small farms are part-time operations with the household depending primarily on industrial employment for its income. The hitherto inadequate availability of agricultural inputs and services to private farms has been an additional serious limiting factor to agricultural production.

Despite these limiting factors, Polish agricultural scientists have had success in developing improved varieties of the major food and industrial crops, as well as in pig breeding and the maintenance of animal health. Polish farmers have proved willing and able to adopt promising new genetic material and agricultural technology, as exemplified by the widespread use of improved large white pigs and the remarkable expansion of the area under triticale. This is an entirely new synthetic cereal crop, with which farmers everywhere are unfamiliar, yet in the space of only 5 years its use in Poland has risen from zero to 700,000 ha, making Poland the world's largest producer. Overall, yields have risen significantly in the last decade: cereals by 37%, potatoes 10%, sugar beet 17%, and rapeseed by 69%, the latter with a major transformation in quality. Changes in yields, areas, and production are shown in Table 15.1 (more detailed figures, encompassing all the crops and giving percentage changes, are included in the appendix).

These figures, and those in the appendix, show some important trends. One of the most

Table 15.1 Changes in area, yield, and production in a decade

	1979-81			1989		
Crop	Area '000 ha	Yield t/ha	Production '000 t	Area '000 ha	Yield t/ha	Production '000 t
All cereals	7,875	2.35	18,466	8,377	3.22	26,958
Wheat	1,525	2.76	4,189	2,196	3.85	8,462
Rye	2,970	2.07	6,166	2,275	2.73	6,217
Barley	1,362	2.62	3,563	1,175	3.33	3,909
Oats	1,082	2.20	2,387	803	2.72	2,186
Triticale	-	-	-	649	3.71	2,404
Rapeseed	259	1.62	434	583	2.74	1,597
Potatoes	2,347	16.81	39,508	1,859	18.50	34,391
Sugar beet	461	28.99	13,387	423	34.00	14,374

obvious is that yields have increased in all crops. In the group of major crops, yield gains have been quite satisfactory in most of the cereals (in grain legumes, oil seeds, and sugar beet), while the progress in potatoes has been slow and disappointing. However, in relative terms these figures do not provide any reason for complacency as can be seen from a comparison with:

• the average yield potential according to soil suitability classes as estimated by IUNG (1988) (Table 15.2)
• yields achieved in research and on best farms in Poland using complex technology (Table 15.3); and
• national yield averages achieved in some European countries (Table 15.4).

Because of its natural resource constraints it may be unrealistic, however, to expect Poland's

Table 15.2 Average yield potential by soil suitability classes
(t/ha)

Soil class	Arable land	Grass land	Percentage of area	Wheat	Rye	Barley	Oats	Potatoes
I	0.06	-	0.4	5.2	4.9	5.2	4.7	N/A
II	0.47	0.07	3.2	5.0	4.7	5.0	4.6	30.4
IIIa	1.49	0.56	10.5	4.7	4.4	4.7	4.3	28.5
IIIb	2.05		14.1	4.2	4.1	4.4	3.9	27.6
IVa	3.26	1.74	22.5	3.5	3.9	3.7	3.6	25.5
IVb	2.42		16.7	-	N/A	N/A	N/A	N/A
V	2.97	1.29	20.5	-	2.8	2.3	2.6	22.6
VI	1.78	0.47	12.4	-	1.8	-	-	18.4
TL	14.50	4.13	100.0					

Table 15.3 Research and best farm yields in Poland, 1986-88

Crop	Yield	Soil Suitability Class
Winter wheat	6-8 t/ha	I - IIIb
Rye	5-6 t/ha	IIIb - IVb
Spring barley	5-6 t/ha	I - IVa
Oats	5-6 t/ha	IIIa - IVb
Triticale	5-6 t/ha	IIIa - IVb
Rapeseed	3-3.5 t/ha	I - IVa
Potatoes	35-40 t/ha	IIIb - V
Sugar beet	40-50 t/ha	I - IIIb

yields to match those of Western Europe, although selective support to lime application and to drainage should open the way to higher yields, both directly and through improving responses to the use of other inputs — especially fertilizer and organic manure.

In Poland there are considerable yield differences between the socialist and the private sectors. The socialist sector yields are superior in cereals, legumes, and potatoes, while the private sector yields are higher in all the other crops. The socialist sector tends to have superiority in high input crops with potential for complex mechanization, as shown in Table 15.5.

These comparisons indicate that there is still a considerable potential for yield improvement in cereals; in fact, under conditions of good crop husbandry the yield of all the four traditional major cereals could be increased within a few years by at least 15 to 20%. The major constraints appear to be low levels of fertilizer use, and lack of adherence to the optimal agricultural calendar, particularly to recommended sowing dates. The root crop data also indicate a good potential for improvement: a yield increase over the next 3 to 5 years of at least 20% in potatoes and 10% in sugar beet does not seem unrealistic, provided the essential inputs can be used in ad-

Table 15.4 Average yields in selected European countries, 1988
(t/ha)

	Wheat	Rye	Barley	Oats	Rapeseed	Potatoes	Sugar beet
Czechoslovakia	5.3	3.7	4.3	3.3	2.9	20.6	33.6
East Germany	5.1	2.8	4.2	3.8	2.6	25.8	23.3
Poland	3.5	2.4	3.0	2.6	2.5	18.6	34.1
West Germany	6.8	4.2	5.2	4.3	3.1	31.7	54.8

Table 15.5 Yields by sector in 1988
(t/ha)

	Total	Socialist	Private	Percent difference (Ss/Ps)
Cereals	2.90	3.41	2.81	+ 21
Grain legumes	1.55	1.75	1.51	+ 16
Potatoes	18.60	21.20	18.40	+ 15
Sugar beet	34.10	30.70	34.80	- 12
Oilseeds	2.52	2.53	2.52	0
Fodder (roots)	46.90	41.60	47.50	- 12
Hay (grasslands)	5.57	4.09	6.00	- 32

equate quality, quantity, and timeliness. An augmentation of the rapeseed yield of at least 10% in the next few years should not be a problem, provided improvements can be achieved in crop nutrition, timeliness of field operations and crop protection. There is good potential for further improvement in vegetable yields, but that is more likely to come from expansion of glasshouse and plastic cover technology, and improved crop protection, than from agronomy. Development of vegetable yields has been satisfactory over the past decade; increases were between 17 and 50% for the six main vegetables, with the exception of tomatoes where yields doubled.

The data in the appendix indicate satisfactory growth of production in wheat, triticale, and cereal mixtures, but only a small increase in barley, and a sizeable decrease in oats and rye. Rapeseed production has gone up by over 80%, sugar beet has remained largely unchanged, while potatoes have decreased by almost 20%. Among the minor crops, production of grain legumes has increased about 2.5 times, tobacco is up by 13%, hops remained unchanged, while flax has plummeted by about 60%. Most of the forage crops increased in production only slightly, although the natural pastures and meadows are believed to harbor good potential for increased production. Total vegetable production went up by almost 24%, while production in greenhouses and under plastic cover (representing only 5% of total production) doubled. Fruit production shows a mixed picture, with large variations between years: apples increased modestly; there was a strong increase in sour cherries; but there was a clear decrease in pears, plums, and cherries.

The appendix also shows that during the decade the area of grain legumes increased by 80%, and rapeseed by over 40%, whereas cereal area changed by only 8%. Potatoes decreased by 20%, sugar beet by 10%, flax by more than 60%, tobacco by almost 20%, and forage crops on arable land by 17%. Area under vegetables remained virtually unchanged.

Apart from triticale, attempts to introduce new crops (sunflower, soya bean, hybrid maize) have had little success. While this does not mean that attempts to diversify the agricultural economy should be abandoned, it suggests that for the immediate future Poland should continue to capitalize on its comparative advantage by reinforcing research and extension on wheat, triticale, rapeseed, potatoes, grain legumes, fodder crops (including maize), and horticultural crops; and that it should strive to improve its considerable area of poorly managed permanent pastures.

Constraints and Potential

FARM INPUT SUPPLIES AND PRICES

Inadequate quantity, quality and timeliness of inputs are the greatest constraints to higher crop production. To the major deficiencies belong insufficient quantities of lime for correcting soil acidity, inadequate amounts of macronutrient fertilizers for proper crop nutrition, and lack of pesticides for pest control, certain areas are still isufficiently drained, and some field operations are still inadequately or inappropriately mechanized. The genetic potential of some excellent varieties cannot be satisfactorily exploited because of all the above reasons, and because of infrequent use of certified seed. Long intervals of exchange for quality seed exist notably in potatoes and rye, and mainly in the private sector. The private sector also suffers from lack of advice, or infrequent advice, from extension services. Good production technology is available, as is evident from the very satisfactory yields achieved in research stations and on good farms. The technical potential for production increases in virtually all crops does exist and conditions have to be created so that it can be properly utilized.

Under the centrally planned economy inputs were often in short supply, and preference was given in their allocation to state farms and cooperatives rather than to the private farmers who manage about 75% of Polish agricultural land. Inputs were heavily subsidized, leading to a situation where yield maximization to meet production quotas, rather than economically optimum use of inputs, was the main goal. Thus in 1988, fertilizer use in the socialized sector was approximate to the technical optimum recommended by research, whereas that in the private sector lagged far behind.

Experimental evidence indicates technically optimum fertilizer (NPK) levels of 250kg/ha, and a similar level of lime (CaO) application, compared favorably with actual 1987-80 averages of 183 kg/ha and 178 kg/ha, respectively. In the case of NPK the 1986 European average was 230 kg/ha. It is very important to note that where soils are acid, lime and fertilizer must both be applied or the benefits of the latter will be small.

Fertilizer application in Poland is not well balanced in terms of the elements applied, mainly due to weaknesses in formulation by manufacturers. There are also very large regional differences in levels of application, with those in the eastern regions being much lower than in the central and western regions. Evidence as to the optimum economic levels of use is lacking, reflecting serious weaknesses in economic research throughout Polish agriculture, as well as the production-oriented mentality of the socialist sector. Much therefore remains to be known before the real potential contribution of fertilizer and lime to agricultural growth can be determined, although theoretically it appears considerable. This knowledge has to be developed in relation to specific agroecological zones of Poland and farming conditions, and not to broad national averages or administrative units.

Pesticides vary in importance with crops, but herbicides are likely to have a high payoff in view of the high levels of weed infestation in most crops, especially in cereals. And fungicidal seed treatments are one of the most effective as well as the cheapest means of controlling several important cereal diseases. Neither herbicides nor seed dressings are used widely enough— only about half of the cereal area receives seed treatment. This seems to be largely a question of lack of suitable low volume sprayers for herbicide application and of cheap, simple on-farm equipment for seed treatment. Efficient and safe spraying, particularly of herbicides, is difficult on small, fragmented holdings, and the scattered nature of fields make custom operations unprofitable.

Due to inflation and the removal of subsidies, input prices have risen sharply, to levels which have led to cutbacks in their use by farmers. These have extended to seeds, most significantly to seed potatoes, which represent about 25% of potato production costs. Because spraying against potato blight has also been cut back, the repercussions on potato yields could be serious. It is also reported that sales of certified cereal seeds have fallen. Since use of healthy seed of well-adapted varieties is the foundation of good yields, and seed is the most environmentally friendly of all inputs, such an economy by farmers seems most unfortunate.

Generally speaking there is a cost-plus rather than a cost-saving attitude to assessing farm profitability in Poland; consequently, little data is available to show how costs could be reduced without reducing productivity. Some privately sponsored research suggests that considerable economies are feasible in tillage and seeding practices (seed rates seem high, seed treatments inadequate, and plant populations are often unsatisfactory), that wider use of herbicides could have a high payoff (weed populations are generally too high and treatment costs relatively low), and that possibilities of combining herbicide and fertilizer application and introducing integrated pest management (IPM) practices should be explored. Since the current dilemma facing the government with respect to farmers is to a great extent one of how to improve or at least stabilize farm incomes in the face of rising input costs, without restoring subsidies or increasing prices to consumers, cost-reducing approaches should be accorded high priority.

LIMITATIONS IMPOSED ON PRODUCTIVITY BY FARM SIZE AND STRUCTURE

There is also considerable scope for reducing costs, without reducing yields, through more effective mechanization. On unmechanized holdings labor costs are higher, and timeliness of practically all farm operations is more difficult to achieve — thus, losses are higher both during the growing season and at harvest. Inefficiently designed and serviced machinery, as is the case in Poland, also leads to higher costs and reduced yields.

The advantages of scale for crops which benefit most from mechanization (cereals, legumes, sugar beets, potatoes) are apparent when yields on large farms in the socialist sector are compared with those in the private sector, where over 50% of farms (1.2 m) are under 5 ha in size. No other large European country has such a high proportion of small holdings. This is another reason for the lower average yields in Poland, and one which is less within the power of individual farmers to address than other problems of input use.

The future of both the large state and cooperative farms (24% of total cultivated area) and of farms under 5 ha (20% of area), is in doubt; however, nearly 60% of the area is under larger private farms, on which the future of Polish agriculture depends heavily. At the lower end of their size range there are opportunities for multi-farm-use machinery, but its economics are problematic where farms are fragmented, with small, scattered, and awkwardly shaped fields. Priority must be given in machinery design (or import policy) to meeting the requirements of such farms, and particularly of custom operations on smaller units of land. In addition, agricultural land and tax policy must be directed to action which leads to amalgamation of holdings, consolidation of plots, effective custom operation and other measures which provide economies of scale in farming.

MARKETING AND PROCESSING BOTTLENECKS

Under the command economy Polish farmers depended very heavily on state-controlled marketing and processing outlets for the sale of their products. In the crop sector wheat, rye and barley among the cereals, and sugar beet, rapeseed, flax and tobacco among industrial crops are all processed; only potatoes, food legumes, and horticultural crops can be marketed directly. Even more important, 70% of crop output is fed to livestock; and sales of milk products and meat are almost entirely dependent on an organized marketing and processing chain.

Under the socialist system all agricultural input manufacturing and agroprocessing industries were state-controlled, and some of the latter were owned by state farms or cooperatives. Although they tended to give preferential treatment to farmers in the state sector rather than to private farmers, they seem to have provided reasonably secure markets at state-controlled prices. Neither quality of product nor cost-effectiveness and profitability of processing operations were at a premium.

At present these industries have largely been uncoupled from state support, and some are having crises of liquidity, as well as worker-management problems. Their equipment is often obsolete and unsuited to quality operations and their ability to provide effective market linkages to private farmers is questionable. Lack of modern processing capacity for oilseeds is a bottleneck to the expansion of rapeseed production and thus to increasing home-produced supplies of concentrated feed for livestock; while the extremely low extraction rates of sugar from beet make the upgrading of processing standards a prerequisite for the success of any attempts to increase sugar yields by breeding.

The weaknesses of the processing industries are particularly obvious in the livestock sector, especially with respect to milk, and are well described in annexes 20 and 21. The inability of the individual dairy cooperatives to finance their own stocks at relatively high interest rates following the abolition of the cooperative dairy union and the fall in demand following reduction of the consumer subsidy on milk, have had repercussions throughout this critically important agro-industry, with farm-gate prices falling dramatically and lower purchases by the processors. Consequent slaughtering of dairy cows has caused a corresponding fall in beef prices. Export opportunities for milk are limited by poor quality and lack of an effective export organization. The potential for exports of pork is restricted by inefficiencies in the meat-processing industry; and both pig and poultry production is hampered by poor feed-processing and mixing industries. The issues are discussed in more detail in Annex 20, but it is clear that the built-in inefficiencies of obsolete equipment under capacity operation, and lack of quality in feed composition, are now being reinforced by problems of transition from a command to a free market economy, which are similar to those affecting the dairy industry. Processing margins have become excessively high as inefficient plants try to maintain liquidity in the face of decreased demand for element feed in an unsubsidized economy, leading to further massive cutbacks in demand by producers. The situation is likely to get worse in the short term, before rationalization and upgraded technology restores competitiveness and efficiency to a streamlined industry.

For the livestock industry it is clear that the rationalization of the feed industry, and the improvement of supply management and markets, are sine qua non to the intensification of smallholder animal production and the improvement of economic standards of production on medium-size farms. For crop production, the upgrading of processing standards is no less essential, even though the social effects of inefficiency in the main agro-industries are not as immediately obvious. For the agricultural sector as a whole, the magnitude of the inefficiencies of input and machinery manufacturing and the product marketing and processing industries is the major obstacle to exploiting the potential for improving productivity and promoting efficiency at the farm level.

PROBLEMS WITH OTHER SERVICES TO AGRICULTURE

Most services to agriculture are state controlled and either fully state financed or heavily subsidized. They are also overstaffed. These general comments apply to the research, extension, veterinary and artificial insemination (AI) services; although in 1990 farmers have been expected to contribute 40% to the costs of AI, and consideration is being given to privatization of health services like clinical interventions and vaccinations.

The strategy recommended for institutional development is described in detail in the annexes on research, extension, livestock development and mechanization and will not be repeated at length here. However, in each case substantial restructuring and streamlining of the service is proposed, involving consolidation of resources and a reduction in staff numbers. The objective is to make the most efficient use of scarce resources, rather than simply to achieve financial economies, by creating modern management structures, eliminating redundant or ineffective components of the system, strengthening coordination within as well as between services, and improving linkages between national, regional and farm levels. Suggestions are also made concerning the scope for and possible approaches to privatization of support services to farmers.

STRATEGIC CONSIDERATIONS

Because of Poland's lack of comparative advantage in export crop production the present strategic orientation toward supply of basic food for the population and provision of feedstuffs for animal production should continue. Presently, about 70% of crop production (including cereals and potatoes) directly or indirectly supports livestock production, and the rest is essentially used in human consumption. Whether these proportions should remain as they are or whether there should be some changes should be determined entirely by market forces.

In technical terms, there is a case to be made for a number of crop interventions (summarized in the table below) which should be tested economically, including:

• concentrating cereal development mainly on intensification of wheat and triticale because of their good adaptability to Polish conditions and high yield potential;

• expanding the production of double-zero rapeseed, while developing varieties with even better winter hardiness, disease resistance and yield potential (accompanied by a corresponding expansion of crushing capacity);

• concentrating potato production in the most suitable agroecological areas, usually outside the wheat and sugar beet zone, and increasing yields through better supply of high quality seed, crop nutrition and plant protection. The potato development program must include breeding high yield varieties with much better blight resistance; better adapted mechanization, notably for the private sector farmers who are the major producers (over 90% of area and production); and improved marketing services and processing facilities;

• concentrating sugar beet production in the most favorable agroecological areas, breeding for high sucrose content as well as yield, improving marketing through introduction of differential payments based on sucrose content; and improving processing facilities, which are reported to have extremely low sucrose extraction rates of around 12%, while the cultivated beet hybrids are yielding around 18% of sucrose;

• increasing the grain legume area, notably in private sector farms, from the present 1.1% (the socialist sector has 6.4%) of arable land, to at least the national average of 2.4% in order to provide more high value vegetable proteins for human and animal consumption and to improve soil structure and fertility; a simultaneous improvement in mechanization technologies will be required, notably for the private sector farms;

- paying more attention to grassland management (natural meadows and pastures) through better research, crop nutrition, and introduction of appropriate harvesting and conservation techniques;

- exploring the justification for increased production of some of the more important minor crops having either an export or export substitution potential, such as malt barley, hops, tobacco, flax and hemp; and

- increasing production of vegetables, flowers, fruits and berries, with a view to supplying potential increased domestic demand, and capturing some of the nearby export markets.

- The following table summarises the major priorities in crop production up to the year 2000.

Crop	Area Change	Yield Change	Processing and storage
Wheat	+	++	+
Triticale	+	++	+
Other cereals	-	+	+
Rapeseed	+	+	+++
Potatoes	-	+++	++
Sugar beet	-	++	+++
Grain legumes	++	++	++
Fodder crops (incl. grassland)	+.	+	++
Vegetables, fruits berries, flowers	+	+	++

These priorities will have implications for research and extension, investments in agroprocessing, and input supply and services. Greater efficiency in production and processing will enable Poland to meet its food and feedstuff demand at lower unit costs.

Farm Profitability in Mid-1990: A Preliminary Analysis

Agricultural profitability has been affected since 1989 by devaluation of the zloty, rising prices of farm inputs and machinery, removal of subsidies, high interest rates, and falling consumer demand for farm products by urban consumers. The situation has become so volatile that it is difficult in July 1990 to make valid comparisons with 1989 or even the first quarter of 1990; the actual status of farmers' incomes, compared, for example, with the earnings of an industrial worker, is a matter of controversy.

Thus, although it is hazardous to draw conclu-sions as to which enterprises or farming systems are profitable, as a basis for suggesting guidelines for future agricultural strategy, it is nevertheless all the more necessary to attempt to do so. Therefore, as a concluding section of this annex, a brief review of the probable returns to certain key enterprises and farming systems in Poland is presented, based on a model developed by the Agricultural University of Wroclaw, using mid-1990 Polish product prices and July 1990 input prices derived from international sources and applicable to Poland.

NATURE OF THE ANALYSIS

The calculations were based initially on small private farms of 10 ha or below, which represent 40% of the agricultural land in Poland, and 78% of all private farms. Farm sizes of 6 ha (about the national average farm size), and 10 ha (a likely minimum target size for the future), were selected as the basic units of analysis. If enterprises or farming systems did not appear profitable at either of these two farm sizes, the analysis was extended to define the minimum size required for a farmer to break even, using the same parameters for inputs, yields and prices. Scenarios are presented in relation to selected 6 and 10 ha farms, both for good and for poor (predominantly acid) soils.

As discussed earlier, Polish farmers do not have as wide a range of enterprises to choose from as farmers in countries with more benign climates and better soils. The cropping pattern is dominated by cereals, with nearly all of the remaining arable land taken up by fodder crops, potatoes and industrial crops. Thus the 18 farm types discussed here are based on a fairly narrow range of typically grown crops; the majority also have a major share of their crop output used for feeding home-reared animals, principally dairy cattle and pigs — the two main livestock enterprises.

No attempt was made to introduce exotic crops or livestock into the farm models since, at least in the short term, they would be unlikely to improve returns to farming on a significant scale. However, it was considered worthwhile to examine farms where there were no animals, as well as various combinations of crops and livestock, and situations where animals were supported entirely from home-grown produce versus those where the bulk of their feed was purchased.

RESULTS

Profitability is defined as total costs, including interest and amortization, minus total revenue during one year. All labor is assumed to be provided by the farm family. It is important to note at the outset that the results are valid only to the extent that the relative price structure does not change significantly. Price instability resulting from changes in import duties, taxes, removal of subsidies, devaluation, etc., or from overproduction within agriculture will obviously have immediate impact on the profitability of enterprises.

The results are summarized in Tables 15.6 and 15.7 for 18 model farm situations. The salient points are the following:

- Even at present prices and input costs it appears possible to make a living equivalent to that of an industrial worker from a small private farm in Poland. Five of the 18 model farms achieve a net profit of Zl 712,000 (US$75) a month or more, up to Zl 1.9 million (US$200) a month on the most successful unit. Another four farms yield only a marginal profit of Zl 380,000 (US$40) a month or less, and all of the remaining nine farms lose money — up to Zl15 million (US$1,578) a year in one case.

- Choice of enterprises and quality of management may be a more important determinant of profitability than farm size. Three of the six most profitable farms are only 6-hectare units; two are 10 hectares and one is 12 hectares. However, for farms with the same basic enterprise mix there are indications from sensitivity analysis that increasing unit size leads to increasing net returns. This seems to be due to economies of scale, particularly with buildings, labor, and machinery use, although these gains may be lost or reduced when increasing unit size forces management to add new buildings or buy more equipment to cope with the additional load.

- Quality of soil is probably more influential on profitability than farm size since it not only holds down yields, but may also force management to restrict the choice of enterprises. There is only one poor soil farm in the top six farms that yields a reasonable living wage at current

Table 15.6 Specifications of model farm units: farming systems and financial returns

Farm Number	Soil type	Farm size	Animal units		Crop units (ha)									Financial data (M Zl)			
			Cows	Pigs	Wheat	Barley	Rye/triti-cale	Potato	Sugar beet	Rape-seed	Peas/faba bean	Fodder	Grass land	Gross income	Total costs(3)	Profit	Loss
1	good	10	-	-	3.3					3.3	3.3			na	na	3,987	
2	good	10	5	-	2.0	2.0			2.0			2.0	2.0	32,723	39,167		6,444
3	good	10	5*	1*	2.0	2.0			2.0			2.0	2.0	46,761	53,610		6,849
4	good	10	5	1	2.0	2.0			2.0			2.0	2.0	41,898	40,341	1,557	
5	good	10	5*	3*	2.0	2.0			2.0			2.0	2.0	64,300	51,971	12,329	
6	good	12	4	-	5.0	2.0				3.0			2.0	54,031	45,663	8,368	
7	poor	10	3	-			4.0	2.0				2.0	2.0	22,473	36,611		14,138
8	poor	10	3*	1*			4.0	2.0				2.0	2.0	34,899	46,744		11,845
9	poor	10	3	1			2.5R 1.5T	2.0				2.0	2.0	32,009	37,832		5,823
10	poor	10	3	2			1.0R 3.0T	2.0				2.0	2.0	41,559	38,589	2,969	
11	poor	10	3	3			4.0T	2.0				2.0	2.0	52,265	42,244	10,021	
12	good	6	1	-	2.50	1.25		1.25					1.0	19.505	28,277		8,772
13	good	6	2	1	1.86	1.14		1.00					2.0	29,085	30,422		1,336
14	good	6	2	2	0.7	2.3		1.0					2.0	37,727	31,214	6,513	
15	good	6	-	2	1.6	2.3		1.1		1.1				36,807	27,725	9,082	
16	good	6	-	4		2.0		2.0				2.0		56,152	33,663	22,489	
17	poor	6	1	-			3.0	1.5			0.5		1.0	12,741	27,775		15,034
18	poor	6	1	1			2.0R 1.6T	1.0T			0.5		1.0	22,092	27,963		5,871

Table 15.7 Order of profitability: 18 farm models

Farm Number	Soil Type	Size	Cows	Pigs	Percent area cash crops	Ranking		Total costs as percent of gross income	Gross returns	Comments
						Gross income	Total costs			
16	good	6	-	4	0	2	10	60	+25.5	All crops fed to pigs; legumes improve feed use; no grassland
5	good	10	5	3	20	1	2	81	+13.3	Wheat sold
11	poor	10	3	3	20	4	5	81	+10.0	Rye sold; no grassland
15	good	6	-	2	43	9	18	75	+9.1	Wheat and rapeseed sold
6	good	6	2	2	12	8	12	83	+8.4	Wheat sold
14	good	12	4	-	66	3	4	85	+6.5	Wheat and sugar beet sold
1	good	10	-	-	100	0	0	-	+4.0	Wheat, sugar beet, rapeseed sold
10	poor	10	3	2	10	7	7	93	+2.9	Rye sold
4	good	10	5	1	20	6	6	96	+1.6	Wheat sold
13	good	6	1	-	42	13	13	105	-1.3	Wheat sold
9	poor	10	3	1	25	12	9	118	-5.8	Rye sold
18	poor	6	1	1	33	15	15	126	-5.9	Rye sold
2	good	10	5	-	20	11	11	120	-6.4	Wheat sold
3	good	10	5*	1*	20	5	1	115	-6.8	Wheat sold; feed bought
12	good	6	1	-	42	16	14	145	-8.7	Wheat sold
8	poor	10	3*	1*	40	10	3	134	-11.8	Rye sold; feed bought
7	poor	10	3	-	40	14	10	163	-14.1	Rye sold
17	poor	6	1	-	50	17	16	217	-15.0	Rye sold

* Feed for livestock purchased.

prices, and five out of the seven poor soil farms are among the eight least profitable units compared with only three of the 11 good soil units. Where farms of similar basic type are delineated on both good and poor soils (models 12 & 17: 13 & 18: 2 & 7: 4 & 9), the returns from the farms on poorer soils are consistently and significantly inferior. Both of the profitable poor soil farms are 10-hectare holdings, and neither is as profitable as the nearest good soil comparator unit. In general it seems to require at least 10 ha of land on poor soils to produce a return equal to most 6-hectare units on good soils. The number of animals which can be kept on a better soil farm seems to be the principal factor determining profitability, especially with respect to pigs.

• At prices around 820 Zl per kg of meat, pigs are, at the moment, the most profitable enterprise for smaller farms, and dairy cattle are probably the least rewarding. The top five units in terms of net profits all have at least two pigs; and all of the bottom 50% have either no pigs or only one pig. The most successful farm by far, with profits nearly twice as high as the next best, has four pigs fed entirely off 6 hectares, with no cattle, and no crops sold. It has the second highest gross income, but only the tenth highest cost — partly the result of increased efficiency of feed conversion by including a legume in the rotation to provide high protein. The number of pigs in a farm unit is thus directly related to profit or loss. It should be noted, however, that small family farms are likely to be very vulnerable to the pig cycle: a 15% price reduction per kg of meat reduces the return per pig by 20%, and makes a considerably greater difference (nearly 40%) to the net profits from a 6-hectare, 2-pig holding with no cattle (see Figures 15.4 and 15.5).

• Increasing the number of cattle on a holding does not have a beneficial effect comparable to that of increasing the number of pigs. Among the six least profitable farms, two have 5-cow units, and two are 3-cow units. The profitability of farms with the same number of cows is determined largely by the number of pigs on those holdings, declining progressively as the number of pigs decreases — whether on good or poor soils (see farms 5, 4 and 2 with 5 cows each on good soils, and farms 10, 9 and 7 with 3 cows each on poor soils). It should be noted, however, that the value of animal manure has not been included in the analysis.

• Farms that purchase the bulk of their feed for livestock are less profitable than similar farms that grow all their own feed.

• Only one model 10-hectare farm on good soil

was assumed to have no livestock with all crops being sold. The net profit on this farm was modest (about 4 million Zl), placing the farm seventh of 18. Figure 15.6 presents the profitability of an arable farm with no livestock and shows that below 8 ha all such farms would lose money. To achieve a profit of about 1 milllion Zl per month a farm area of 14 ha is needed. The 6-ha farm would lose about 4 million Zl annually compared with a 6-ha arable farm with two pigs (see Figure 15.5) where, at a pig price of 800 Zl per quintal, a profit of almost 9 million Zl per annum can be achieved. Analysis of individual crop enterprises suggests that at current input-output price relationships and on good soils, wheat and rapeseed are profitable with break-even points well below existing product prices of 73,000 and 125,000 Zl/q respectively (see Figures 15.2 and 15.3). The current potato prices are already below the break-even point at 12,600 Zl/q (see Figure 15.1). Rye appears to have a rather low profit margin at 57,000 Zl/q, since its yields are lower than those of wheat; triticale at a slightly higher price and with higher yields is in a more competitive position. Returns from a grain legume such as peas, with a current price about double that of wheat, would be below those from wheat, because grain yields of legumes are only about a third of those of modern wheat varieties. However, the value of the nitrogen supplied by the legume, and its role as an improver of feed conversion ratios in the animal feed-mix should be taken into account in the calculations.

• One other interesting point emerges from the analysis. Table 15.7 shows the rank order of the various farm models in terms of gross income and total costs, as well as net profits. It seems that some of the most successful units have achieved their net profits more through maintaining relatively low costs than through high gross income. This strongly supports the strategy recommendations for research and exten-sion work on efficiency and cost saving rather than the yield maximization and cost-plus approaches that have prevailed under the command economy.

A CAUTIONARY NOTE

While these findings indicate that farm modelling can be valuable in determining the actual or potential productivity of crop, livestock, or whole-farm enterprises as an aid to formulating price structures and other policies, it is important to bear in mind its limitations. The results of modelling are heavily dependent on the assumptions made concerning crop and livestock yields, input-output relationships, and the levels of investment needed in buildings, equipment, and machinery, which determine fixed costs. Unstable price relationships in a volatile socioeconomic situation imply that the model parameters must be updated frequently to avoid misleading conclusions. It is difficult to cover adequately all current permutations of crops, livestock, and farming systems in a large and fairly diverse country such as Poland and even harder to foresee potential new situations several years ahead. Thus the results, although interesting, should be treated with caution as indicative rather than definitive. The analysis described here illustrates the principles of decision-making based on models. Research and extension in all voivodships should be equipped with similar models and desktop computer facilities to allow farmers and advisers to make their own decisions based on quantitative data rather than intuition.

Endnote

This annex was prepared by Marian Krol, Andrzej Kolodziej, Oskar Honisch, Peter Oram, John Hayward and Wales Mack.

Figure 15.1 Profitability of potatoes on good soils

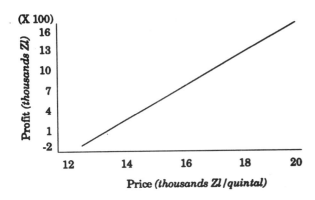

Figure 15.2 Profitability of wheat on good soils

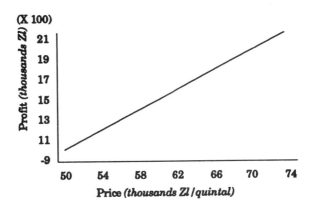

Figure 15.3 Profitability of rapeseed

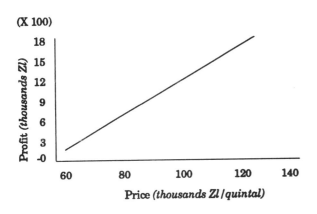

Figure 15.4 Profitability of pigs

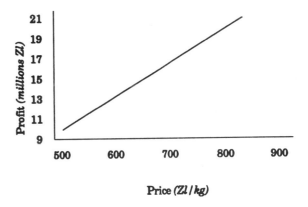

Figure 15.5 Sensitivity of a 6 ha farm to the changes in pig prices

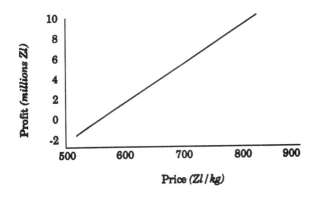

Figure 15.6 Profitability of arable land with no livestock

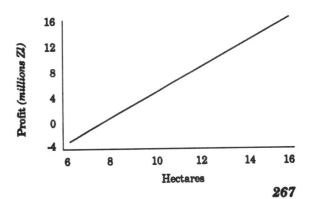

Appendix

Crop area, production, and yields (1980 & 1988)

Crop Area Development ('000 ha)	1980	1988	%
Total cereals,	7,847	8,439	+ 8
of which:			
Wheat	1,609	2,179	+ 35
Rye	3,039	2,325	- 25
Barley	1,322	1,250	- 5
Oats	997	850	- 13
Triticale	0	549	(new crop)
Mixtures (grain)	737	1,185	+ 61
Maize	16	40	+250
Grain legumes	188	339	+ 80
Potatoes	2,344	1,866	- 20
Sugar beet	460	412	- 10
Oilseeds (99% rapeseed)	336	478	+ 42
Flax	82	31	- 62
Tobacco	52	42	- 19
Hops	2	2	0
Forage crops	2,628	2,188	- 17

Production ('000 t)	1980	1988	%
Total cereals,	19,495	26,504	+ 36
of which:			
Wheat	5,089	7,582	+ 49
Rye	6,474	5,501	- 15
Barley	3,560	3,804	+ 7
Oats	2,434	2,222	- 9
Triticale	0	1,731	(new crop)
Mixtures (grain)	1,710	3,387	+ 98
Maize	165	204	+ 24
Grain legumes (edible)	81	108	+ 33
Grain legumes (fodder)	143	457	+220
Potatoes	42,742	34,707	- 19
Sugar beet	14,149	14,069	- 1
Oilseeds (99% rapeseed)	655	1,206	+ 84
Flax	273	108	- 60
Tobacco	80	90	+ 13
Hops	2	2	0
Forage crops	9.055	9.867	+ 9

Yield (q/ha)	1980	1988	%
Total cereals,	24.8	29.0	+ 17
of which:			
Wheat	29.3	34.8	+ 19
Rye	21.6	23.7	+ 10
Barley	27.6	30.4	+ 10
Oats	22.8	26.1	+ 14
Triticale	n.a.	31.5	(new crop)
Mixtures (grain)	25.5	28.6	+ 12
Maize (grain)	38.4	53.1	+ 38
Grain legumes (edible)	15.5	20.0	+ 29
Grain legumes (fodder)	10.8	16.0	+ 48
Potatoes	177.0	186.0	+ 5
Sugar beet	280.0	341.0	+ 22
Oilseeds (99% rapeseed)	19.5	25.5	+ 31
Flax	32.8	34.6	+ 5
Tobacco	15.9	21.6	+ 36
Hops	10.0	10.6	+ 6
Forage crops	352.0	469.0	+ 33

Soil fertility, acidity, and requirements for fertilization

Current situation

Soils in Poland generally have poor fertility. Basic nutrients such as phosphorus and potassium exist at low levels and have to be regularly supplied. Soil organic matter content is low and a regular supply of manure is required to keep organic matter at an acceptable level. Microelement deficiencies are not common at present yields but potential shortages of boron, zinc, manganese, copper, molybden and iron may occur to certain crops in some soils.

An extremely serious problem is soil acidity. Over 26% of all arable soils are classified as very acid (pH 4.5 or less) and another 35% are acid (pH 4.6 to 5.5). Such soils are largely predominant in northwestern, south-central and eastern parts of the country and reach levels of more than 80% of arable land in some voivodships. Soil acidity has a negative effect on two accounts: first, it limits yields because of a lack of CaO as plant nutrient; second, and more important, it limits efficiency in uptake by plant roots of other nutrients. Many soils are deficient not only in calcium but also in magnesium, and additions of substantial amounts of dolomitic limestone are essential for full utilization of applied fertilizer and production of satisfactory yields.

Fertilizer is supplied to the agricultural sector from domestic production as well as from imports. Nitrogen and phosphorous fertilizers are produced in at least 12 industrial plants in Poland, using imported raw materials — primarily natural gas from the Soviet Union and phosphate rock from North Africa, the Soviet Union, and the United States. Potassium fertilizers are imported in finished form from Germany and the Soviet Union. Calcium products are readily and easily available in Poland but their wider use has been hampered by constraints in processing and distribution facilities.

Organic fertilizers, mainly farmyard manure (FYM), deserve particular mention. FYM's periodic but regular application in required quantities is of the utmost importance to farm production, particularly on the lighter textured soils. FYM increases organic matter content of soils and provides conditions for better temporary storage of nutrients and a more gradual release of macro- and microelements; it delivers around 5-6 kg of N and 3-4 kg each of P_2O_5, K_2O and CaO, and about 1.5 kg MgO per ton applied. FYM further improves soil structure, waterholding capacity, and microbial activity. Although FYM is widely used, particularly in the private sector, it appears that through better education of farmers and more efficient distribution equipment the efficiency and effectiveness of its use could be improved and nitrogen losses reduced. Extension devotes too little time to advising on proper production, storage, application and general husbandry of FYM and this should be improved. Other methods of organic fertilization, such as composts and green manures, should also be more widely promoted.

Constraints and potential

The average supply of NPK over the 3-year period 1987-89 was 3,435 million (M) t, providing about 183 kg NPK per hectare of agricultural land. For comparison, the European average in 1986 was around 230 kg/ha, while France used about 310 and West Germany 430 kg/ha. In 1988, Bulgaria, Czechoslovakia and Hungary used 233, 292, and 218 kg/ha, respectively.

The overall, mean, technical optimum level on a national basis, as recommended by research following several thousand critical field trials, is about 250 kg/ha in Poland. This would indicate a current annual national shortage of NPK on technical grounds of about 1.2 M t. The Research Institute of Soil Science and Crop Cultivation (IUNG) at Pulawy, estimates (1990) that national yield losses due to inadequate fertilization represent on the average about 3 cereal units per hectare (equivalent to 3 q/ha of cereals), which would signal a good potential for yield and production increases under conditions of better fertilizer supply. However, a clear precondition to this level of fertilizer response is improvement of soil acidity, followed by maintenance of favorable soil pH, on more than 60% of Poland's soils.

Optimum economic fertilizer use depends on yield response to fertilizer application and the relative prices of fertilizer and crops. Optimal economic application levels, thus, vary by crop and ecological condition. No analysis of economic application optima was carried out in the past or is available at present. Initial impressions are that application levels tended to be too high in the socialist sector and too low on private farms, with consequent reduced overall profitability in the sector. In the future, fertilizer recommendations to farmers need to be formulated strictly on economic grounds, based on relevant technical information, which means frequent review of recommended levels in times of volatile prices.

Another important issue is the origin of the country's fertilizer supplies and the future of its fertilizer industry. A comprehensive approach is needed for analyzing the cost and benefit of the potentially locally produced fertilizers (including imports of raw materials and energy), as compared with the alternative of increased or even full imports of ready fertilizers. Such an analysis is quite complex as it involves foreign trade, the fertilizer industry, agriculture and the environment. We recommend, therefore, that a national fertilizer subsector study be carried out with the assistance of appropriately qualified experts. The team should include a foreign trade specialist, an agricultural economist, two fertilizer industry specialists, and an agricultural production specialist. The latter two team members should be experienced in environmental protection. The team would require about 4 weeks of field work in Poland and about 6 weeks for analysis and report writing.

Research has established that in order to compensate for the mean annual CaO used for crop uptake and lost through leaching (which is about 200 kg/ha), and to provide a surplus for soil improvement, it would be necessary to apply as a national average about 250 kg/ha of CaO per year, preferably in the form of dolomitic limestone. The mean application rate for 1987-89 amounted to only 178 kg/ha. The year 1989 was, however, a considerable improvement over 1988, with 30% more of overall CaO production (4.1 M t compared with 3.1 M t) and a 20% higher application rate (202 kg/ha compared with 169 kg/ha). The average national yield loss due to soil acidity and unsatisfactory lime application has been estimated by IUNG (again in 1990) at 1.6 cereal units (equivalent to 160 kg of cereals) per hectare. It is evident that with improved liming alone the technical potential for yield improvements is substantial. A further, cumulative yield increase can be expected with improved NPK fertilization as stated in the previous paragraph.

Average fertilizer application figures mask a substantial inequality in fertilizer utilization between sectors as well as between regions and voivodships. For example, the private sector used in 1987 only 60% of NPK and 57% of CaO when compared with the socialist sector. Average use in the socialist sector of N, P2O5 and K2O has, over the last 3-5 years, been almost identical with the technical (that is, not economic) optimum as recommended by research. In 1987, however, only 83%, 63% and 56% of recommended levels of N, P2O5, and K2O were used in the private sector. The limited use of fertilizer in the private sector is without doubt one of the major reasons for low yields. The very limited use of phosphorous, potassium and lime fertilizer is of particular concern because proper response to nitrogen can only be expected if these nutrients are available in adequate quantity. The eastern part of the country uses much less fertilizer than the western part, as documented by two extreme cases: in 1988/89 the voivodship of Nowy Sacz used only 107 kg/ha of NPK, while Poznan applied 291 kg/ha. Mean cereal yields in Nowy Sacz and Poznan were correspondingly 2.55 t/ha and 3.74 t/ha, of which wheat yields were 2.59 t/ha and 4.64 t/ha, respectively.

The following are the major deficiencies in chemical composition, type, and physical form of some fertilizers currently in use:

• In 1989, about 12%, or 180,000 t of sulphate of ammonia was used. This product is known to increase soil acidity and its use should, therefore, be minimized in Poland. Ammonium nitrate, enriched with calcium, and another type containing additional magnesium, represented only 14% of the N supply, while the share of pure ammonium nitrate was 53%. This has implications for soil degradation and for environmental contamination.

• Most fertilizers are produced in Poland with low concentrations of nutrients. For example, urea (46% N) represented only 21% of total supply; in the phosphorous group, the share of the high concentration triple superphosphate (45%) was only 9%; the rest was made up of single superphosphate with less than 20% P2O5. These figures do not adequately demonstrate the economic losses due to higher transportation costs. For example, if in 1989 all the P2O5 delivered as single superphosphate had been transported as triple superphosphate, more than 2.7 M t of transport capacity could have been saved. It is of equal importance that farmers could have transported to and spread on the field only 40% of the total material they had to use with the single superphosphate formulation.

• Physically, much of the fertilizer is still delivered in powder form (for example, more than half of the phosphatic fertilizer). Fertilizer in powder form is difficult to store, difficult to apply, and is detested by farmers. Similarly, all potassium chloride comes in the form of crystal salt, again difficult to store for any length of time in usable condition.

• Only one compound fertilizer is on the market, although the factory can reportedly produce any nutrient combination. It is sold under the name Polyfoska and has an NPK composition of 8:24:24. It is apparently in high demand but the supply covers only about two-thirds of farmers' requirements. More compounds should

be produced, particularly for large, homogenous areas that grow major crops.

• Liquid nitrogen fertilizer, consisting of water-based urea and a mixture of urea and ammonium nitrate, is being tried in the vicinity of chemical factories in southern Poland. An estimated 5,000 to 10,000 t is being used annually, and various pesticides are being added in the process. Technical results are reported to be good, but economic evaluation and comparison with high concentration granular solids is not available.

A further constraint seems to be in packaging and storing fertilizers. Potassium chloride, all lime fertilizer and about 90% of phosphorous fertilizers are reportedly delivered in bulk. Fertilizer storage is said to be insufficient, and as a result potassium fertilizer has to be stored in the open or in pits covered with foils, while lime fertilizers are stored outside without any covering. Only nitrogen fertilizers and compounds are reported to be delivered in bags, facilitating storage and handling. The degradation of fertilizer in these circumstances represents a serious economic loss and can contribute to environmental contamination.

Another problem frequently mentioned by farmers is the unsatisfactory machinery for fertilizer application and particularly for lime distribution. The machinery circles, which were charged with the responsibility of lime application and were equipped with corresponding spreaders, have been performing poorly. Evidence of uneven fertilizer application is apparent; this leads to uneven growth and poor harvesting conditions. A clear need exists for high-performance, high-quality fertilizer spreaders.

The notion of crop rotations is very familiar to research and extension. However, the closely related concept of fertilizer rotations, so critical to proper husbandry on fragile, light textured and infertile soils, does not seem to be commonly applied. The majority of the country's soils require a well-planned and balanced fertilizer regime, based on natural soil nutrient content, crop rotations, and replacement of nutrients that have been removed by the crops. For each farm there should be established by the extension service (with the help of soil diagnostic and economic data) quantities, periods, and times of application of FYM, lime and industrial fertilizers. This would promote proper soil husbandry, increased yields, and greater economic utilization of fertilizers.

Strategic Considerations

Task Force recommendations to the Polish government for effective soil fertility management are as follows:

Short-term strategy recommendations

• Recognize that nutrient application on highly acid soils is wasteful; promote and support lime application as an immediate priority;
• Promote measures to ensure more equitable access to fertilizers between the state and private sectors, among voivodships, and among regions;
• Minimize the use of highly acidifying forms of fertilizer, such as ammonium sulphate;
• Promote the use of higher concentrate single element fertilizers and appropriate compound fertilizers;
• Develop national packaging and handling standards for all fertilizers;
• Undertake a comprehensive national fertilizer subsector study, encompassing trade, industry, agriculture and environment;
• Reorient research, extension and farm practices toward the economic use of fertilizers.

Medium-term strategy recommendations

• Subject to confirmation by the above study, change domestic production of fertilizers to higher concentration products and to compound formulations;
• Packaging and handling standards;
• Discontinue the use of powdered fertilizer; promote the use of granular formulations;
• Instruct the extension service to prepare fertilizer rotation schedules based on the need for sustainable and environmentally sound soil fertility management;
• Improve national macronutrient supply to economically, technically and environmentally optimum levels.

Long-term strategy recommendation

Verify and implement recommendations of the national fertilizer subsector study.

Expected Implications

The impact of the above measures is expected to be clearly demonstrated in increased yields, production and profitability, and in substantial savings to the sector and to the economy as a whole. Under the technical assumption of a yield increase of about 4.6 cereal units (460 kg) per ha, which IUNG estimates will be achieved as a national average using currently calculated liming and fertilization levels necessary to reach those projected yields, on the 8.4 M ha of cereal area alone the incremental production would be on the order of more than 3.5 M t of cereals annually. Another 230,000 cereal units (corresponding roughly to 2.3 M t of cereals) could be expected to be harvested from the remaining 6 M ha of arable land cultivated under various other crops. An extension of an appropriate fertilizer regime to the 4 M ha of grassland could bring in further production increases of about 120,000 cereal units (equivalent to about 1.2 M t of grain). Thus, the gross incremental production that could be expected from these application rates of lime, organic fertilizer, and industrial fertilizer is on the order of about 7 M t of grain equivalent. Actual application rates and resulting production responses consistent with maximizing profitability would need to be calculated based on current costs and prices, however.

Endnote

This annex was prepared by Oskar Honisch, assisted by Marian Krol.

Land amelioration

Current situation

Poland has 18.7 million ha of agricultural land, 76% of which is cultivated by some 2.2 million (in 1989) private farmers, and the remaining 24% by various state and cooperative farms. The topography, characterized by an average elevation of 173 meters above sea level, is favorable for agriculture. The annual precipitation exceeds potential evapotranspiration over most of the country by an average of about 14%; an exception is the central-western belt, extending approximately between the towns of Ostroleka and Gorzow, where evapotranspiration is higher than precipitation by some 9%. Generally, over most of the country there is adequate water storage in reservoirs and underground aquifers.

Land amelioration in the national context includes major water management works but also agricultural water management, consisting of irrigation and drainage. Land amelioration works are, therefore, divided into (i) basic infrastructure, consisting of about 73,000 km of major canals and river protection works, and of flood embankments, pumping stations and storage reservoirs; and (ii) specific rural infrastructure, comprising drainage networks of about 290,000 km of secondary ditches and canals, and subsurface drains and collectors. This annex is concerned mainly with the specific rural infrastructure.

In the purely agricultural context, land amelioration in Poland is generally understood to be equivalent to drainage. Because of the prevailing climatological, pedological and topographical conditions, many areas are poorly drained. Periodic excess of water in agricultural lands has been historically one of the factors limiting crop production by adversely affecting soil structure and crop nutrition, and shortening the growing period. To alleviate the problem, drainage efforts have traditionally been widespread. Subsurface drainage is the preferred method, based on a herringbone design with a central buried collector and subsurface lateral drains. Compared with drainage, from which almost half of the agricultural land could benefit, irrigation plays a minor role. Irrigation works (sprinkler schemes and extensive subsurface irrigation) serve only about 0.56 million ha.

In the 1986-90 Five Year Plan, US$581 million (1984 constant prices) have been earmarked for land amelioration, representing 16% of total agricultural investments. Economically justified investment levels currently are not known, but are likely to be in the range of US$100-150 million per year.

Basic infrastructure (as described above) is paid for entirely by the state. Cost recovery from beneficiaries (farmers) for investment cost on specific infrastructure is officially required to be at 15%, but is believed to be in reality less than that. Payment by farmers is currently spread in equal amounts over a 10-year period, without adjustment for inflation. Reform of cost recovery policy is needed, with a view to increasing recovery from beneficiaries, especially as there exists inflated demand for drainage works from private and nonprivate farms alike.

The Department of Land Use and Amelioration (DLUA) of the Ministry of Agriculture and Food Economy (MAFE) estimates that, technically, about 9.5 million ha of the country's 18.7 million ha of agricultural land would benefit from amelioration. Of these 9.5 million ha, 6.6 million ha (of which, 4.3 million ha on arable land) have already been ameliorated. In 1989 the amelioration program actually implemented included 129,000 ha of drainage, of which 38,300 ha was for grassland amelioration.

The DLUA estimates that over the next 20 years some 2.4 million ha (after an exclusion of about 0.5 million ha was judged clearly uneconomic) of new agricultural land will require drainage, and old structures will have to be rehabilitated on 1.2 million ha. To the latter group belong areas in the southwestern and western part of the country, where existing drainage facilities are reputedly 60-80 years and, in some cases, up to 100 years old. A program has been worked out to ameliorate in each of the four 5-year periods up to the year 2010 between 0.8-1.2 million ha of land. The plan for 1991-95 calls for 800,000 ha, of which 70% is arable land and 30% grassland. The annual average target of 160,000 ha over the next five years is 26% higher than the mean achieved over 1986-89 (127,000 ha), clearly indicating that good planning, organization and financing would be required if this target were to be achieved.

However, it is unlikely that amelioration is justified on the above large area. Some technical professionals and economists recommend that more attention be paid to the preservation of the natural environment and that particularly some ecologically important swamplands be excluded from potential drainage. It is obvious that not only technical, financial and economic, but also environmental criteria will have to be applied in future selection of areas to be ameliorated. Furthermore, in some areas farmers are concerned that drainage might accentuate drought during dry summers. In some countries, farmers are converting their drainage systems to provide the dual benefit of drainage in the spring and fall and subsurface irrigation in dry years during the summer. This is mainly done by installing water level control structures in risers and exercising water level control when summers get

dry. This method should be tested further in Poland.

The DLUA is responsible for coordinating all land amelioration infrastructure. At provincial (voivodship) level, the Provincial Boards for Investment in Agriculture have jurisdiction over selection and design of specific projects, construction of infrastructure, and organization of operation and maintenance activities. The Research Institute for Land Reclamation and Grassland Farming (IMUZ) performs an important function in research and extension, and in standardization and promotion of technical aspects related to land amelioration. Most of the amelioration works are undertaken under contract from farmers by 94 state-owned contractors in cooperation with 13 equipment rental enterprises and five workshop enterprises. However, private sector design bureaus and private contractors are reported to have lately started operating in increasing numbers. Maintenance of drainage and irrigation infrastructure is entrusted to some 2,400 district (gmina) associations for water use and infrastructure maintenance.

The cost of new drainage is currently (mid-1990) estimated to be about US$1,000 (Zl 10 M) per ha of arable land. The cost of draining grassland tends to be about 16% higher than that for arable land due to additional infrastructure required (for example, levelling, roads). Labor is estimated to account for only about 15% of total drainage cost; the foreign exchange component is approximately 35%.

Constraints and potential

Among the issues and constraints identified is drainage design, which until recently was based on methodology developed in 1978. Standard norms and assumptions have featured strongly in design, giving insufficient weight to local conditions and resulting in inappropriate design parameters, for example, the interrelationship between depth and spacing of lateral drains. Technical criteria used in drainage are being reviewed again, taking into account most recent research findings in this field, with a view to introducing improvements.

The feedback process between existing drainage networks and the design of future schemes is largely lacking. To collect data on recently completed drainage and improve future feedback, a drainage monitoring and evaluation program would be useful, possibly under the leadership of IMUZ and involving all Provincial Agricultural Investment Boards.

The method of trenchless drainage with plastic pipe is not used much, mainly because of equipment problems and the high draft power requirements. Since this cost-saving type of drainage seems to be particularly adapted to the lighter soils with a certain clay content, there appears to be good potential for its selective introduction, using latest design machinery.

Methods of land improvement other than drainage, for example, bedding, levelling, subsoiling, etc., have been given little attention in the past. Such methods tend to be less costly than drainage, although their effects are shorter lived. These alternatives to drainage should be studied and their range and conditions of applicability identified. Some pilot work with bedding has already started, for instance, in the Elblag voivodship, and such efforts should continue. It would be desirable for IMUZ to strengthen its field experimentation activities, both to gain better insights into land amelioration alternatives and to improve the design of amelioration works.

The criteria used for selecting areas to be drained are weak. The evaluation methodology should be improved by establishing an appropriate framework for financial and economic analysis of drainage investments. The structure of the cost of works needs to be desegregated to permit analysis of basic cost components, determine the impact of taxes and duties, and assess the foreign exchange content. Yield responses to drainage should be more accurately measured, based on more research evidence. Land areas currently identified as requiring drainage on technical grounds should be subjected to an economic review, first to establish whether drainage is economically justified and, second, to distinguish priority areas for implementation to achieve the highest possible returns on drainage investments.

There are also constraints related to drainage materials which adversely affect the cost and effectiveness of drainage works. It might be advantageous to give more emphasis in the future to plastic materials for drains — and less to tiles — and to vibrated concrete for collectors. Opportunities for improvement in this area should be identified through a review of the availability and costs of raw materials for drains and collectors. Included in such a review should be the national plastic pipe industry as a step toward restructuring and streamlining of the industry to assure adequate least-cost future supplies (including from foreign sources) of plastic pipes.

Laying drains and collectors is done with a fleet of about 630 drain-laying machines, which are technically obsolete and in poor repair for lack of spare parts. Consequently, drain-laying performance is relatively poor at some 450 - 600 ha per year per machine, representing one-third to one-fourth of a modern high-performance standard. Questions of supply of new machinery (that is, type, source and cost) and of spare parts need to be resolved for future drainage operations. As a preliminary step, it is recommended that a detailed inventory of heavy drainage machinery in the country be completed. The situation with regard to heavy maintenance equipment for drainage networks is similar to that for drain layers and thus should be dealt with similarly.

There are signs of inefficiency in the organization of drainage contractors, particularly in operating and maintaining their heavy equipment. Private, specialized rental enterprises which could operate sophisticated workshops and procure spare parts more efficiently, should be encouraged. Another source of inefficiency and high cost is the absence of a competitive bidding process. Bidding procedures should thus be established and competition promoted; private companies should gradually take over all functions.

Although drainage is by far the most important amelioration work, irrigation has a certain role to play as well. Irrigation benefits about 60,000 ha of arable land under some 700 schemes, mostly sprinkler systems, in the north and central-western parts of the country, primarily for intensive vegetable production. Additionally there are some 500,000 ha of extensive subsurface irrigation of grassland consisting of open ditch networks, equipped with regulating gates to allow control of the water table for the dual purpose of irrigation and drainage. Irrigation is not expected to make a major contribution to agricultural development in the near future, as adequate economic benefits can be derived only on a minor scale under specific soil and climatic conditions and for certain high-value crops. However, technically, there appears to be a potential for further development of irrigation, notably in the driest part of the country, where the average summer precipitation is less than 300 mm. This area is situated in the country's central belt and is approximately delimited by the major towns of Gorzow, Poznan, Bydgoszcz, Ostroleka, Warszawa, Sieradz and Leszno. According to DLUA's estimates, the area comprises about 20% of the country's agriculture land. Development of irrigation is, however, not a high priority and should only be considered with respect to strict economic criteria and undertaken by private investors.

Strategic considerations

A number of measures have been identified that should be considered in developing a strategy for land amelioration. Some of them are of an organizational and planning nature with relatively little cost involved, others will require investments. They are all designed to assist in proper selection of drainage areas and in achieving high quality amelioration works. It is anticipated that particularly the introduction of one measure — the higher participation of beneficiaries in covering the investment cost for drainage works — will act as a regulatory factor and will ensure that only areas with highest economic potential will be drained. It is conceivable that under this scenario the annual drainage requirement of 160,000 to 180,000 ha, estimated by DLUA for the next 20 years, will be considerably reduced.

SHORT TERM

Short-term strategic considerations include:

• Establishment of strict economic, technical and environmental criteria for selection and prioritization of areas to be drained; efficiency of drainage must be the prime strategic consideration;
• In support of the above, training at appropriate institutions of 20-30 Polish agricultural economists in advanced economic analysis, with special emphasis on project appraisal methodology;
• Introduction of a drainage monitoring and evaluation program to gather reliable technical and economic data for further work;
• More intensive work on land improvement methods which are less costly than drainage, such as bedding, levelling, and subsoiling;
• Preparation of a detailed inventory of heavy drainage machinery (trench diggers, drain layers, bulldozers) and maintenance equipment (drain flushers, booster pumps) as a basis for making decisions on gradual replacement by more modern and efficient machines, preferably to be done by the private sector; and
• Support for privatization of land improvement design bureaus and amelioration contractors.

MEDIUM AND LONG TERM

Medium- and long-term considerations include:

• Handing over the total drainage design and implementation function to the private sector, including selling the state-owned drain laying and canal and drain maintenance machinery fleet to private entrepreneurs;
• Introduction of higher-quality plastic materials for drains and vibrated concrete for collectors;
• Gradually increased beneficiary participation in the recovery of cost for amelioration investments (from the present 15% to about 50% as a first step, and to full cost as a second step at a later stage), and allocation of full responsibility to beneficiaries for covering operation and maintenance cost; and
• Modest development of private sector irrigation in selected areas for selected crops.

Expected implications

Technical and economic benefits which can be expected from drained fields are several. On the technical side, experience has shown that soil in drained fields dries and warms up about two to three weeks faster in the spring, thus extending the growing period and allowing for increased yields. Mechanical operations can be done under more optimal soil moisture conditions and heavier machines and multipurpose equipment can be used with less risk of soil compaction. Fertilizer is generally less leached and better utilized by the plants. Harvesting operations can be carried out more smoothly because soils are accessible to mechanization more quickly after rainfall. After three to five years, soils can be generally upgraded by one or two classes (on the Polish land suitability scale of eight classes for arable land and six classes for grassland). According to data from the Research Institute for Land Reclamation and Grassland Farming

(IMUZ), the increase in production from draining one ha of land is on the average equal to about 1.2 t of cereals.

Endnote

This annex was prepared by Oskar Honisch, assisted by Marian Krol.

Agricultural mechanization

The current situation

FARM STRUCTURE AND AGRICULTURAL MECHANIZATION

Because of the problems of owning and operating tractors and other mechanical equipment on the 2 million farms of less than 10 ha, where only one farmer in three owns a tractor, much field work in Poland is carried out by hand or with animal traction. Thus, there are 1.1 million working horses on Polish farms, principally on holdings of less than 5 ha. Special equipment is still manufactured for animal traction. The agricultural labor force is also high: 40% of the Polish labor force is in agriculture. In small farming alone there are 2.3 million families, of which 35% is fully engaged in farming, and a farm labor force of 4 million.

Even though the agrarian structure presents difficulties to mechanization, tractor density in Poland is fairly high. In all there are about 1.1 million farm tractors. Tractor ownership is highest on smaller private farms of 5-10 ha where there is an average ratio of 7.4 tractors per 100 ha. On bigger private farms the ratio is 6.2 per 100 ha; here every farmer has a tractor. On state farms the average ratio is 2.3 tractors per 100 ha.

It is revealing to compare the current situation in Poland with that in the northern continental region of the EC, where climatic conditions are rather similar, but crop yields are about 40% higher.

	Poland	N.C.EC*
Number of workers per 100 ha	21	7
Number of work horses per 100 ha	6	0

* Northern Continental region of the EC.

It is clear from these figures that if Polish agriculture is to move toward the northern European mechanized system, considerable changes are likely to be required in the nature of the energy component. In particular, priority would have to be given to the development of tractors and equipment better suited to farms of less than 10 ha, where fields are often scattered, small, and irregular in shape. As the cost of labor increases, the energy component will have to shift from manual to mechanized methods if Polish agriculture is to be economically competitive.

Analysis of the methods adopted by Polish farmers, particularly the smaller ones, with respect to the major farm operations during the production cycle — land amelioration, tillage, seeding or planting, fertilizer distribution, application of herbicides or pesticides, and harvesting — shows that the practices adopted are often wasteful or inefficient due to farm size and layout (with regard to drainage); outdated methods dictated by obsolete equipment (tillage); lack of precision due to old or inefficient machinery (fertilizer distribution, planting, seed treatment, spraying); high losses during harvesting (poorly calibrated equipment, lack of spares) or during storage (inadequate, poor quality, on-farm storage, lack of drying facilities). Thus there is great scope for farming improvement through better mechanization—reducing losses, saving money and raising output.

FARMSTEAD OPERATIONS AND AGRICULTURAL BUILDINGS

On small farms under 5 ha, farmstead operations, storage facilities, and housing of livestock are mainly traditional and at a low technical level. Technical standards and the degree of specialization of facilities and equipment increase progressively as private farms become larger; and the large state farms have good facilities and well-equipped specialized production systems.

AGRICULTURAL MACHINERY MANUFACTURING AND SERVICING ORGANIZATION IN POLAND

More than 75% of the tractors and nearly all other equipment used in Poland is manufactured in Poland. There are 30 medium- to large-size state-owned companies with between 1,000 and 20,000 workers each, and about 300 small, private workshops. The largest company, URSUS, has a manufacturing capacity of 70,000 tractors per year; in 1989, 7% of its output was exported. In 1989, 75,000 tractors were sold including some 15,000 imports, mainly from Eastern European countries. Due to inflation and highly subsidized equipment prices, the demand was greater than in the previous year (60,000), but because of lower farm profitability, general uncertainty in the economy, and high interest rates, sales for 1990 are expected to be only 25,000. Under the central planning system all domestically produced equipment and imports were targeted and scheduled according to an annual assessment of farmers' demand, depending on the available supply of raw materials. State-owned and operated factories were grouped under a central apex organization known as AGROMET.

In this system of manufacturing to order the large farm sector had preference; private farmers were not allowed to buy tractors prior to 1975. The specific needs of the small farmer were neglected.

Each voivodship has two state-controlled distribution centers for tractors and other equipment; one for the private sector (Zaklad Zaopatrezenia); and one for the state farm sector (AGROMA). Parastatal farmers' circles exist at the village level. The function of these monopolistic entities includes sales and after sales services such as training of the users, repairs under guarantee, normal repairs and spare part supply. Like the manufacturing companies, they have good facilities as far as buildings and other storage space is concerned. However, their technical equipment and shop management is not up to date. Spare part supply was unsatisfactory in the past; small farmers in particular received poor service. More recently the spare parts service has become extremely poor, as wholesale distributors are not maintaining their inventory for financial reasons. Sales are only about 50% of estimated needs. With the main harvest season about to start, this could be a serious constraint.

Because of the dominance of relatively small private farms with limited scope for self-contained mechanization, the promotion of multifarm use of equipment should have high priority in Poland. State-hire services for this purpose have proved bureaucratic and inefficient and are not popular with farmers; private sector farm machine and equipment combinations—a type of mutual neighbor assistance — have proved more successful. However, there appears to be much scope for larger and more professionally managed operations by private contractors or private farm machinery cooperatives.

The present prices of Polish agricultural tractors and equipment — of comparable power size to those working in the EC — are only about 20% of West European and North American prices. Based on present relative prices of wheat and tractors, it is evident that Polish farmers can pay for a Polish tractor with the equivalent of 37.5 tons of wheat; the Western farmer needs the equivalent of double that weight to pay for a Western tractor. There is, however, a great difference in design and construction quality between Polish and foreign equipment; the latter is far superior.

	Price of tractor	Equivalent tons wheat
Poland	US$3,000	37.5
EC	US$15,000	75.0

For medium- and low-income countries (those in the early stages of the development of tractorization) that need tractors primarily for tillage and transport, Polish tractors and equipment have some export potential. However, Poland's tractors could not find buyers in sophisticated markets. Until recently imports were mainly confined to specialized equipment from Eastern Europe (horticultural tractors, drainage machines, etc.), but with the present open market economy it is becoming evident that Polish farmers are increasingly more interested in buying better quality Western tractors and equipment. Because of the high prices of new machinery, the secondhand market is expanding, especially for imports from Western Europe.

It is in the interest of the farmers, and of the Polish economy, to liberalize the introduction of foreign tractors and other agricultural equipment that better serve local needs, especially those of the small farmers. Particular attention needs to be paid to imports of machines that lead to cost savings in farm operations, and to those most suited to multifarm use.

Because domestic sales of tractors have fallen by about 40% in 1990 compared with the two previous years, surplus stocks have accumulated at factory level; these cannot easily be sold locally even at discounted prices, or readily exported. [1] With raw material price increases, subsidy reductions and expensive credit, Polish manufacturers face difficult times. Nevertheless, this inefficient industry should not be protected; trade liberalization and privatization should be pursued without special tariffs, barriers or duties on imports or export subsidies. Such protection will only delay the time when Polish manufacturers become competitive and innovative. The quality of their products must be raised, possibly by seeking joint ventures with overseas companies. In the long run the Polish economy will bear the burden of attempts to safeguard the local industry.

PUBLIC SERVICES TO FARM MECHANIZATION

In addition to services provided by the manufacturing and commercial sector, the national research and extension services are involved in supporting the improvement of agricultural mechanization.

Agricultural mechanization research is the primary responsibility of the National Institute for Buildings, Mechanization and Electrification in Agriculture (IBMER) at Warsawa. It reports to the Ministry of Agriculture, along with the 16 other research institutes and numerous laboratories forming the Polish national agricultural research system. In addition to IBMER, other institutes work on aspects of mechanization, especially the Institute of Crop Production and Soil Tillage at Pulawy, and the Institute of Animal Production at Krakow, which specializes in forage harvesting, feedmixing and mechanization of animal feeding. Some research is also undertaken at the universities, and by the Ministry of Industry through an institute (IPMR) at Poznan, which specializes in design and construction of agricultural machinery. It is reported, however, that collaboration among the various institutes under the Ministry of Agriculture, and between these and the universities and industrial research institutions, is extremely limited.

Regional experiment stations and substations are attached to the national institutes. Some of these have a special national task, for example, the soil tillage station at Wroclaw.

IBMER has six divisions (faculties), 21 departments, various other units, and three experiment and testing stations. In December 1989 its staff totalled 672: 129 scientists including 20 professors and 47 other staff with PhD degrees. Due to financial stringency, the total staff has been considerably reduced from its 1987 level of 952.

Under the command economy system, IBMER was the only official agricultural equipment testing institute. Without its certificate of approval no equipment could be imported or manufactured in Poland. Another official duty was the planning of the future demand for tractors and agricultural equipment. In addition to research and testing the Institute is in charge of training and technology transfer. In 1987, 21 inventions of IBMER were submitted for a patent; 20 requests were granted. Like other Polish institutes of research, IBMER has the right to promote candidates for a doctorate in agricultural science.

Agricultural mechanization extension. Extension subject matter specialists in agricultural mechanization are stationed at national and district levels. However, discussions with private farmers and WOPR-level extension officers show that the extension service provides insufficient support to the private sector with respect to mechanization.

Constraints to effective agricultural mechanization

GENERAL CONSTRAINTS

• Farm size and structure in the private sector: too many farms under 10 ha (2.0 million); dispersed, small, and awkwardly shaped parcels which make mechanization technically difficult and raise its costs. Poor drainage and poor agricultural road systems are further cost-increasing factors.

• An inefficient parastatal manufacturing industry producing tractors and equipment of poor quality and obsolete design.

• A serious and increasing shortage of spare parts for agricultural machines.

CONSTRAINTS TO MECHANIZED FIELD OPERATIONS

• Lack of a dynamic land consolidation program, including computer programs to help in calculating the economic feasibility of mechanization.

• Shortage of ditchless drainage machines (for laying perforated plastic pipes) and lack of laser levellers.

• Too many tillage operations with traditional implements, leading to: high labor, tractor, and machine hours; high energy costs; soil compaction; and unnecessarily prolonged exposure of equipment to weather hazards. Modern tractor-mounted multitiller sets, which largely avoid these problems, have been used successfully in Poland and demand is high, but access to small fields is often difficult. Operation on irregular small parcels raises costs; smaller capacity sets are required for such conditions.

• Seeding and precision planting equipment is often of low precision due to old age or poor design. The match between seed and equipment is frequently poor due to lack of cooperation between the seed and machinery industries. Planters for leafy crops are not available in Poland. Chemical seed treatment against seedborne diseases is inefficiently performed, due mainly to lack of the inexpensive equipment needed to apply it on small farms. In general, the needs of the smaller farms have been seriously neglected.

• Fertilizer is often badly and unevenly spread, sometimes by hand or by poorly designed centrifugal spreaders. In addition, Polish fertilizers, including lime for land improvement, are

poorly suited to precision distribution because they are formulated as soft granules of unstable sizes, or as sticky powders.

• There is a need to increase availability to small farmers of safe, small-scale, motorized knapsack or tractor-mounted sprayers.

• Haymaking practices often lead to late cut, over-cured hay. It has been shown that early cut, wilted silage gives a much better quality product, but this depends upon limiting curing time after cutting and rapidly filling and sealing silos. Special equipment (rotary cutters, tedders, self-loading tractor trailers with choppers) is needed, and mutual assistance among neighboring farmers or other forms of multifarm use of equipment is required for various corn silage and high moisture corn treatments, depending on the nature of the product and whether it is for cattle or pigs.

• Family farmers unable to afford a combine still harvest grain by hand, mowers, or binders with stationary threshers. Such methods are labor intensive and lead to grain losses of 10% or more. Even Polish combines, which theoretically should cut losses to below 4%, often have much higher losses due to their age or poor maintenance. Family farmers urgently need efficient small combines or contracted multifarm access to larger combine harvesters.

• Roots and tubers present similar harvesting problems. Significant losses result due to spinner damage on smaller farms and to old or poorly operated harvesters on larger holdings. Poor preharvest practices (suboptimal row spacing, poorly aligned rows, insufficient ridging, etc.) can compound losses from inefficient harvesting. Further losses can be caused during inefficient mechanized loading of roots and tubers into trailers and transportation by old equipment. This is particularly important if seed material is being transported.

CONSTRAINTS DUE TO FARMSTEAD OPERATIONS AND AGRICULTURAL BUILDINGS

• Increases in crop yields in the last decade have overstrained on-farm storage facilities in traditional barns. Lack of drying and inadequate storage capacity or poor quality storage are a serious cause of losses with stored grain, especially on smaller farms. Modern metal or hard plastic storage containers with forced ventilation are an important requirement.

• Although farm size is likely to increase

progressively over time, there is not expected to be a rapid transformation of agrarian structure with a concomitant consolidation of holdings and replacement of obsolete buildings and equipment. Impetus toward specialization and improvement of facilities is nevertheless likely to be generated by changes in the nature of market demand, especially for better-quality produce, and the enforcement of quality standards through price, legislation, or other means. This in turn will lead to a need for better livestock sheds with improved feed mixers, milking machines, and milk coolers; controlled grain storage and drying facilities; cool stores for potato, vegetable, and fruit storage; greenhouses; mushroom barns; grading equipment; and specialized transportation equipment.

Small, mixed farms have limited opportunities to produce a wide range of high-quality products, nor can they afford many specialized facilities for handling and storage. Specialization is essential and must be achieved by cooperative or other group systems of production and processing where specialization at the individual farm level is not technically or economically feasible.

Constraints affecting the manufacture and distribution of farm equipment

• Lack of competition in a monopolistic, state-controlled industry has resulted in production of equipment of low quality both in construction and in performance, as well as to lack of innovation and obsolescence in design.

• The same causes have led to extremely low labor productivity in manufacturing and trade compared with industry in high-income countries with a market economy. Prices of Polish equipment are about 25% of those in the international market due to low wage rates.

• The system of production and distribution in Poland favored state farms over the private sector in both sales of equipment and after-sales service, including the supply of spare parts.

Research

• The large gap that exists in Poland, between theory and practice in the design of tractors and equipment, has so far not been bridged by research efforts.

• On-farm research by IBMER has mostly been limited to the state farm sector and has failed to address the practical problems facing private family farms.

• Cooperation among research institutes of the Ministry of Agriculture, and between those institutes and researchers in the universities and other ministries, is unsatisfactory.

• The quality criteria applied by IBMER in its machinery testing operations are far below international standards.

• IBMER's present structure is inefficient: it has high administrative overheads because its nonscientific service units are overstaffed, and it has to undertake regulatory duties (for example, in obligatory machinery testing) which are not related to research.

Extension

Links between the national and district level extension service staff and IBMER are weak. Extension staff at voivodships, who have specialized training in mechanization, are insufficient in number to work effectively with research staff in transferring new technology to farmers.

Strategic recommendations

Short-term imperatives

Agricultural mechanization in Poland faces a difficult short-term situation in which manufacturing is in transition from state control to private ownership; and distribution and servicing of tractors and farm equipment is shared between two other state-controlled organizations, one dealing mainly with state farms and the other with private farms. Neither of these entities is directly linked to a manufacturer in a manner comparable with dealerships in market economies.

The farm equipment industry is currently in crisis: a large stockpile of unsold tractors and equipment has developed as demand has fallen by 40% since 1989; the scope for exports is limited by poor quality; and manufacturers face serious liquidity problems at a time of high interest rates. In order to cut their losses, they have been retrenching on production of spare parts, and, as much farm equipment is old, there are concerns that there will be serious losses during the forthcoming harvest if the supply of spares is not improved.

High priority in the immediate future therefore needs to be given to easing the transition from state to private management in manufacturing and distribution — including the supply of spares — while laying the foundation for full privatization.

Priority must also be given to redressing the past neglect of private farmers by the state-controlled manufacturing and distribution organizations. This implies both meeting the most urgent current needs of private farmers for tractors and equipment and looking ahead in research and testing to a situation where quality of produce will be paramount and farms will be more specialized (even if not much larger); and where the problems of finding capital for mechanizing individual farms may be mitigated by group sharing of equipment (informally or formally through private machinery cooperatives), or through multifarm operation by professional contractors.

Specific actions that can be taken to achieve these objectives include:

• Maximize use of available tractors. The level of tractorization of Polish agriculture is higher than can be justified socioeconomically. For the short and medium term the primary objective should be to make better use of all available resources. Therefore, replacements should be limited to 2-3% per annum and more efficient tractors should be introduced.

• improve spare parts and servicing facilities. Priority should be given to overcoming the present serious constraints in the supply of spare parts, especially the spare part supply for the small-farm sector.

In order to achieve this goal a number of actions will be needed by the government, that is:

- Domestic, state-owned manufacturers should be immediately required to improve the supply of spares produced in their plants.

- The government should establish a licensing system for importers and for domestic manufacturers of tractors and farm equipment. A condition of granting a license would be a satisfactory assurance from the firm concerned that its products will be backed up by training of maintenance staff, free servicing and repairs under extended warranty, and an adequate inventory of spare parts available at short notice to customers without surcharge.

- Manufacturers and importers should be encouraged to establish dealerships at local level either through privatization of existing farm equipment trade centers (AGROMA), or through private entrepreneurs. Buildings, workshops, and storage space previously occupied by state-controlled enterprises might be leased to private operators by the government; such leases would offer an option to purchase after a set period and extended credit for modernization of workshop equipment and establishment of a spare parts inventory. Manufacturers and importers should provide training to managers and operatives and might also assist their dealers with loans or by supplying equipment and spares on credit.

- In order to ascertain the reasons for current problems, IBMER, in cooperation with staff of the agricultural extension service, should be instructed to conduct a survey of the adequacy of spare part and after-sales and maintenance services during the coming harvest season and report its findings and recommendations to the Minister of Agriculture for appropriate action.

• Liberalize imports of foreign tractors and agricultural equipment.

Because much of the agricultural machinery produced by Polish manufacturers is obsolete or poorly designed, even though relatively inexpensive compared with foreign equipment, it is in the interests of the Polish farmers to introduce foreign tractors and other implements that serve their needs better, especially those of the smaller farmers. Therefore, it is recommended that imports of new and secondhand agricultural tractors and equipment (including materials such as plastics for agricultural use), as well as spare parts, should be liberalized completely. As a spur to improving product design and quality, Polish manufacturers should not be protected by tariffs or import duties.

• Establish a national agricultural mechanization council to advise government on medium- and long-term strategy for the future development of agricultural mechanization in Poland, including both the farm sector and the manufacturing and service sectors.

Such a body should have representation from the government, farmers' organizations, the farm machinery industry, the agricultural research and extension services, and universities. Practically oriented foreign experts might be invited to assist the council.

The council should advise on the implementation of medium- and long-term recommendations, for example, the future development of the multifarm use of equipment to give family farmers better access to the benefits of modern technology.

• Priority should be given to the types of equipment required for the family farm sector. These include small to medium-size tractor-mounted fertilizer distributors; drum-type seed treaters; precision planters; modern portable sprayers; rotary cutters, tedders, and rakes; self-loading and unloading tractor trailers; general-purpose tipping trailers, maize choppers, and pickers; windrow potato diggers; and hay and grain ventilators and modern plastic grain storage containers. Small-capacity processing equipment is also needed: mobile milking and cooling sets to improve quality and marketability at the farm and local levels for milk; mobile grinders and mixers for animal feed; and grading and packing equipment for fruits and vegetables.

• Priority should also be given in the short and longer term to the multifarm use of agricultural equipment. In addition to the promotion of the combined use of equipment among neighboring farmers, encouragement should be given by the government to establishing private farm contractors and private farm machinery cooperatives. Analysis is needed of the effectiveness of existing operators: their equipment standards, operating procedures, and rates charged. Measures to assist and extend successful ventures would include extension service advice on appropriate equipment, business management training and training of operators, establishing rules of service and safety standards, recommendations concerning fair rates for contract work, and access to credit or bank guarantees.

• The government should organize training programs in multifarm use of equipment, with the help of experts from European and other advanced countries with practical experience in the actual running of contract machinery operations.

• Reinforce research on farm mechanization and postharvest technology.

- IBMER should be supported at approximately its current scientific strength so that its capacity to undertake an expanded research program is not reduced.

- IBMER should be required by the Ministry of Agriculture to formulate a practically oriented work program for 1991-92 geared to the most urgent needs of Polish agricultural mechanization and directed primarily at serving the private farming sector. This program should include: (i) reduction of product losses with harvesting and postharvesting equipment; (ii) improved systems of forage harvesting and storage; (iii) improved and new systems for harvesting and storing maize; (iv) analysis in cooperation with extension specialists of the actual spare parts supply and other after-sales services; and (v) evaluation of the performance of imported technologies.

- IBMER should cooperate more closely with other national institutes of the Ministry of Agriculture working on aspects of mechanization, as well as with the universities and with industry. It should actively seek to promote interinstitute cooperation, and should, in formulating its work program, specify to the Ministry of Agriculture how this will be achieved at the program and project levels.

- In order to strengthen its base of knowledge, IBMER should develop linkages with institutes for research on agricultural mechanization in the EC and other European countries, and overseas (United States, Australia, Japan, etc.).

- Safety testing for Polish equipment should be continued by IBMER only where no other Polish institution is better qualified to undertake it (for example, safety testing of electric appliances should not be done by IBMER but by the official testing institute for these goods). This will relieve IBMER of unnecessary regulatory duties, allowing it to concentrate on research.

• Develop closer linkages between research and extension in agricultural mechanization.

- Locate, at IBMER, a small but efficient national extension unit specialized in farm mechanization to transfer the results of IBMER's research to farmers and processors and promote their adoption. This unit should have linkages to the regional agro-ecological zone stations (recommended in Annex 10 on agricultural research) as a means of attuning research at the national institutes more closely to local farming needs.

- In order to develop these linkages, voivodship extension offices should each have mechanization specialists in the various areas of activity indicated in the future work program of IBMER. These should work closely with IBMER and the regional agroecological research staff in transfering technology to farmers.

MEDIUM- TO LONGER-TERM RECOMMENDATIONS

• Action should be initiated by the government to encourage privatization of the tractor and agricultural equipment industry. This should include manufacturing, wholesale and retail trade, maintenance and repair services, and the parastatal machinery cooperatives and circles. An important step in this direction would be to abolish AGROMET as the dominant public body and grant full freedom to manufacturers to select the equipment they wish to produce. Incentives should be provided through tax holidays, access to credit, or other appropriate fiscal measures.

• Polish agricultural equipment manufacturers — united in a private association — should apply for membership in the European Federation of Agricultural Machinery Manufacturers.

• Promotion of joint ventures between Polish and foreign entrepreneurs should be encouraged by the government as a means of accelerating privatization. This might include legislation concerning freedom of import/export; definition of rights of ownership of the managers, employees, and foreign partners; and maintaining and strengthening safety rules in manufacturing, operation, and maintenance of equipment, including road safety standards for agricultural vehicles.

• The government should adopt the EC regulations as well as the ISO and EC safety standards on agricultural tractors and equipment, including universal components. Poland should apply for membership with the European Patent Office.

• The Polish agricultural machinery industry should become fully integrated with the international market. Exports of Polish agricultural equipment should be promoted, particularly to lower- and middle-income countries. In the short run, markets should be sought for the present large stock of tractors and machinery with due regard to safety, after-sales service, and the supply of spares. As the quality of Polish equipment is improved, good longer term export opportunities appear possible.

• Obligatory performance and quality testing of agricultural equipment should be abolished in Poland. The new free market will rapidly impose its own acceptable quality standards.

• IBMER should be reoriented as an institute for applied, practice-oriented research with emphasis on the private family farmers. It structure should be simplified: all scientific staff should be concentrated at its headquarters, and the nonscientific services united in one department of management and administrative services. IBMER's research should be regrouped into five departments in place of the current 21. These would be: agricultural machinery; agricultural buildings; mechanization systems; ergonomics, including safety; and mechanical and civil engineering, including the management of the engineering workshop.

Technical assistance should be sought to help IBMER design and implement a revised research program, practically and institutionally well geared to the mechanization needs of small farms. Experience of industrial research planning would be essential for such assistance.

• Reorientation and refocusing of extension's mechanization effort is also recommended in order to devote special attention to:

- growing and harvesting maize for grain (at various moisture and maturity levels), and for silage;

- making silage in preference to hay;

- on-farm inspection of equipment (especially crop sprayers), fertilizer distributors, grain and potato harvesters, and milking installations — including equipment for cooling and transportation of milk at the farm level;

- measuring and identifying the main causes of product losses during harvest and postharvest operations and finding ways of reducing them;

- improving arrangements for effective seed treatment at farm level;

- developing economical on-farm storage for the major crops.

These activities should be undertaken in close cooperation with the appropriate research institutes, industry, and farmers' organizations.

Endnotes

This annex was compiled by Peter Oram, using information provided by Adrian Moens, Jan Pawlak, and staff of the Ministry of Agriculture, IBMER, Institute of Agricultural Scientific Research, Krakow, the University of Warsaw, Agromet, and Agroma.

1. Polish agricultural machinery exports have always been a low proportion of total production: about 5% in the case of tractors.

Annex 19

Agriculture, pesticides, and the environment

Overview and current situation

ENVIRONMENTAL POLLUTION AND FARMING

Much has been written in the national and international press about environmental pollution in Poland and there is great awareness and sensitivity to the problem at both government and grass roots levels. Attention has mainly centered on the destruction of farmlands and forests near major industrial plants. However, the chronic debilitation of the productive farmland resource base by heavy metals and acid rain is a more insidious problem, which has widespread implications for farming.

The present socioeconomic and political situation in Poland is promoting decentralization of authority and minimizing centralized legislation and regulation. However, experience worldwide has demonstrated that governments must develop and enforce regulations to protect the environment, for example, against the indiscriminate importation, production, and use of chemicals.

At the present time, Polish agriculture is not a major contributor to rural environmental degradation. Farm chemical use in Poland is only about 20% of levels applied per ha in EC countries and chemical use is mostly widely dispersed. Industry is by far the greatest source of rural pollutants that have important consequences for agriculture. The government is taking steps to regulate against industrial pollution but should also ensure that agriculture itself does not become a source of pollution.

Projections of the extent of sulfur damage to forests range as high as 50% of Poland's forested area by the 1990s. Some 80% of Polish forests are coniferous and are particularly subject to industrial pollutants, much more than deciduous species. Nevertheless, the obvious damage to coniferous forests can be taken as a clear indicator of pollution levels of deciduous forests, farm land, and water supplies. The long-term implications for agriculture and for the image of Poland's farm produce, particularly for potential exports, are serious.

Of immediate concern in the farmlands close to the industrial areas in southern Poland is soil contamination from industrial pollution. A Polish report (Godzik 1987) cites soil tests on vegetable plots with concentrations of lead, zinc, cadmium, and mercury between "30% and 70% higher than World Health Organization norms for soil used in growing food." Polish scientists estimate that some 700,000 persons in the Upper Silesia industrial region may be at risk from eating produce grown in home garden soils with unacceptable levels of industrial pollution.

To be competitive in its agricultural exports, especially when exporting to markets which are becoming increasingly food safety conscious, Poland must demonstrate a commitment to the health safety of its agricultural products.

Pesticide use

The use of pesticides in Polish farming has steadily increased, from 0.63 kg of active ingredient per hectare in 1980 to an estimated 1.64 kg of active ingredient per arable ha in 1989. This compares with about 6.5 kg of active ingredient per hectare in EC countries. Some 22,000 tons of pesticides were used in 1989, mostly on cereals, potatoes, sugar beets and rapeseed. Domestic production and formulation of pesticides in 1989 reached 15,400 tons and an additional 6,000 tons were imported. Imports are now basically free of tariffs. Imported products, in many cases identical to locally produced materials, are being sold at 42-50% of world prices.

The government is encouraging the decentralization of pesticide purchases. Any organization or individual with foreign exchange can import pesticides, and business with these organizations can be on the basis of direct sale or over-the-counter trade. Similarly, state farms and commercial farmers are increasingly buying pesticides directly from both foreign and local agrochemical firms.

There is, therefore, a free market in pesticides which must be carefully regulated to protect individuals, the environment and the economy.

Table 19.1 The use of pesticides in Poland in 1989

Crops	Product type	Millions of hectares treated
Cereals	Herbicides	5.2
"	Fungicides	1.9
"	Seed dressing	4.4
"	Growth regulators	0.7
Potatoes	Insecticides	1.0
"	Fungicides	1.1
Sugar beet	Herbicides	0.7
Rapeseed	Disease and insect control	0.6
Total		15.6

According to official estimates, domestic production and imports together amounted to about 21,400 tons (see Table 19.2), which closely matched use. There are, therefore, theoretically very few leftover stocks, although there is no official inventory of old unused material

Table 19.2 Production and importation of pesticides (1989)

	Domestic Production	Imports
	tons a.i.	
Insecticides	500	500
Fungicides	4,500	1,800
Seed dressing	1,100	
Herbicides	9,100	3,400
Miscellaneous compounds	200	300
Total	15,400	6,000

According to these figures, 58% of production and imports were herbicides. Sales figures of pesticides are not available at present but a comparison of production and use suggests that there is a mismatch in terms of product needs. A review of actual sales and stocks by product is needed to determine the status of supplies for the 1991 season. According to international commercial sector estimates, trends in pesticide use in Poland are as follows:

Table 19.3 Trends in pesticide use in Poland

Type	Tons	Trend
Herbicides	11,500	increasing
Fungicides	6,000	increasing
Insecticides	4,000	decreasing slightly
Others	500	increasing

A similar comparison of these figures with those in Table 19.2 also suggests that, while the production and use of fungicides may be reasonably balanced, insecticides may be in short supply and there may be an oversupply of herbicides.

To assist in crop protection efforts, the EC donated some US$55 million of crop protection materials in late 1989. These were distributed through a foundation and three cooperative groups and sold at subsidized prices. Despite this, demand for these products is low, with only some 20% of the materials purchased as of early summer 1990. The main reason is ascribed to farmers' unwillingness to purchase expensive inputs under agricultural marketing uncertainty.

Chemical input use, for both fertilizers and pesticides, varies markedly by category of user. State farms use more inputs generally, while the majority of private smaller farmers make minimum use of crop protection chemicals. They also use substantially less chemical fertilizer, relying largely on their own sources of farmyard manure. However, although the use of manure has many benefits — it contributes much needed organic material to sandy soils and helps bind chemicals in surface layers and minimize leaching into aquifers and rivers — it should be recognized that careful management of manure is an important part of environmental protection. Grazing animals, by the nature of their feeding habits, tend to concentrate in their bodies any chemical pollutants which may be present on grass and fodder, and these chemical residues in their manure can be a potent source of contamination.

Pesticide registration

Pesticide registration is not as tightly controlled as it should be. The registration process is far less stringent than that required in most western countries. For example, temporary registration of products can be issued for three years without evidence of long-term toxicological data, and based on certificates of registration in countries of origin. Some countries of origin have lax registration procedures; it would be safer if Poland's requirements were the same as or similar to those in OECD countries.

Toxicology studies for pesticides in various stages of development are carried out by the Research Institute of Industrial and Organic Chemistry (IPO) both in Warsaw and Pszcyna. The facilities at the Warsaw branch are minimal and not at all satisfactory; those at Pszczyna are better, but neither unit is capable of operating at the internationally accepted standards of Good Laboratory Practice (GLSP) which would render their studies acceptable in other countries.

Work on ecotoxicology (that is, effects on birds, bees, aquatic organisms, soil organisms, etc.) for the IPO is done at the Pszczyna branch. However, it appears that there are substantial gaps in their ability to carry out this technically difficult work.

Environmental chemistry (the study of the fate of chemicals in the environment) is done at both the Warsaw and Pszcyzyna branches. This,

like most areas of pesticide safety study, is technically very demanding. The work being done consists mostly of residue analysis; little is done on pesticide metabolism, hydrolysis, photolysis and leaching. Analytical laboratories are poorly equipped by modern standards.

Pesticide registration is conducted by the Bureau of Pesticide Registration, a special unit of one researcher and four technicians in the Institute of Plant Protection in Poznan. Considering the lack of sufficient equipment and immediate online linkages to the pesticide registration data bases of the EC, the FAO, and the United States (EPA), there is excessive reliance on chemical firms' assurances as to safety and efficacy under Polish conditions.

Pesticide residue testing is also undertaken by the Institute of Plant Protection, conducted by the Department of Research and Control of Pesticide Residues, with a staff of 14 professionals and technicians supported by regional staff.

There is no effective legislation on the use of restricted products; nor are there enforcement laws related to safety practices in the use of such products. Protective clothing is not readily available in Poland. Contract sprayers and applicators apparently do not need to be certified and trained prior to purchasing restricted-use products (which are readily available to anyone wishing to purchase them off the shelf).

Also, there appears to be no enforcement of the safe disposal of older or unused or deregistered pesticides and pesticide containers. This is a serious concern. It is important that such materials and containers be disposed of properly and, especially, that they not be dumped in unlined soil pits near aquifers or other water resources.

As Polish agriculture recovers from recent stabilization efforts, increasing use of chemical inputs is likely. As farm chemical use expands in the coming decade, it is critical that Poland establish a code of conduct to ensure that:

• pesticide regulations are brought to international standards; and
• imported and locally produced farm chemicals meet international standards for registration, both on crops grown for domestic consumption and for export.

Training in careful pesticide use by farmers should be undertaken, especially in applicator protection; groundwater, household wells, and river protection from runoff; and sprayer calibration. Training in the proper disposal of obsolete, unused pesticides is critical, as is the correct disposal of empty pesticide containers.

Initial efforts in integrated pest management and biological control need to be expanded, particularly in those major Polish crops such as apples, small fruit, greenhouse crops, and potatoes, where experience in IPM techniques has expanded in recent years. Informal initial discussions with local fruit research stations indicated interest in pursuing initiatives, a step that would likely attract foundation and international funding support.

Pesticide rotation programs are also needed to avoid pest resistance.

CONTAMINANTS AND ADDITIVES IN ANIMAL FEEDSTUFFS

A critical issue facing many countries that trade in livestock and livestock products is loss of markets because of unacceptable chemicals in meat, milk, eggs, etc. In some cases problems arise through the accidental contamination of feedstuffs, particularly with farm pesticides, but in other instances illegal feed additives are used. In Poland, there appear to be no regulations covering inspection and control of local and imported animal feeds with high levels of antibiotic and other chemical contaminants. This is particularly important for the dairy industry, but also affects pork, beef, and poultry. Such legislation is urgently required to safeguard the livestock industry and to enhance its reputation as a provider of health products. Legislation could be prepared as part of the total farm chemical regulation package or as a specific need of livestock legislation; the important point is that such legislation be prepared quickly.

RURAL WATER SUPPLY PROTECTION

Most farms use farm wells for water supply for households and livestock. A number of wells are not adequately protected from manure runoff from farm barnyards.

Improved manure management on farm is important. The recent initiatives of the FDPA to introduce small-scale manure disposal tanks are a step in the right direction.

ECOLOGICAL AGRICULTURE

The current relatively low use of farm chemicals in Poland and the designation of the smallholder farming sector as the green sector, may result in a targeted niche in Poland and externally for the development and promotion of green food products. This market is small and specialized but likely to grow.

Poland should take steps to place itself appropriately in this market. Given the interest in EC and Eastern European markets for lines of ecologically produced foodstuffs, exploration of a classification system for organic production and processing would be appropriate. This certification effort is likely to require limited financial resources, which local and external foundations are likely to support once a more formal plan is prepared.

Strategic recommendations

SHORT TERM

Continuous monitoring of pollution levels in representative farmland and forests is essential. Small permanent soil and foliage testing sites should be established throughout Poland, particularly in areas of higher risk from industrial emission, but also in relatively uncontaminated farms and water sources. Such sites should be regularly tested to evaluate changes in contamination levels over time. Only with such continuous records from permanent sites can objective statistical analysis of the pollution problem be presented for national and international arbitration.

Soil and foliage testing for heavy metals should be carried out in high-risk areas so that farm produce from such areas can be isolated as appropriate. This is particularly important for farms selling milk products and fresh export commodities.

A code of conduct for pesticide manufacture, sale, storage, and use and disposal at industrial and farm levels should be prepared and implemented as a matter of urgency. The FAO's Guidelines for Pesticide Registration and Usage should be employed to develop the code of conduct for Poland. This code should ensure that pesticide regulations are brought to international standards and that imported and locally produced farm chemicals meet international standards for registration and use on domestic and export crops.

Pesticide registration and integrated pest management should be upgraded in legislation, studies, and research. The existing small Bureau of Pesticides at the Institute for Plant Protection in Poznan should be upgraded to a full department of pesticide registration and control. The department should be reequipped and linked with FAO, EC and U.S. (EPA) pesticide registration data files. A twinning of this new Department with an EC or U.S. registration group would greatly assist in this process.

MEDIUM TERM

The code of conduct should be employed nationwide and legally enforced. Copies of Poland's code of conduct should be made available to all potential importers of pesticides and all major international pesticide manufacturers.

Training programs in safe pesticide use and integrated pest management should be prepared by research in collaboration with extension. These programs should be designed for farmers and for staff of those agencies handling, storing, and selling pesticides. Instructions should take the form of classroom teaching combined with practical demonstrations. A systematic program of training should be undertaken in all voivodships. Certification of successful completion of the course should be a prerequisite for authorization for sale and use of more toxic chemicals.

- Pesticides should be sold at unsubsidized rates irrespective of origin. Concessionary imports should have no retail price advantage.
- All pesticide importers and manufacturers should be registered; the six Polish pesticide manufacturers need to be restructured and privatized.

LONG TERM

- The Polish government must strengthen its regulation of pesticide availability and use.
- All pesticides produced and used in Poland must be recognized worldwide as conforming to international standards.

Endnote

This annex was prepared by John Hayward and August Schumacher, Jr.

Livestock production sector

Summary

IMPORTANCE

Livestock is fulfilling a key role in Polish agriculture: (i) economically, it provides 46% of the value of agricultural production and 50% of agricultural exports, and it uses 70% of domestically produced grains; (ii) socially, it is the main source of cash income for small farms; and (iii) ecologically, it maintains soil fertility on the majority of the Polish soils.

KEY CONSTRAINTS

Key constraints to livestock development at the farm level are: (i) inefficiencies in input delivery (especially in the feed industry), which depresses overall feed use efficiency and limits stock numbers to the amount of feed that can be grown on the farm, thus hampering intensification and curbing farmers' income; (ii) inadequate management of farm feed resources; (iii) poor product quality (mainly as a result of inadequate quality control and the small farm size), which precludes adequate investments in quality improvement; (iv) inadequate supply management, which results in wide variation in dairy prices and will probably do the same for prices for pigs and poultry in the near future. The drop in milk prices is hurting above all the medium-size specialized dairy farmer, who has fewer oppor-tunities to diversify into other activities than the small mixed farmer; (v) breeding services, which have not fully adapted their program to changing economic conditions; (vi) inadequate marketing systems, in particular in the live animal sector; and (vii) an inefficient and almost bankrupt milk-processing industry, with low product quality and a very narrow product range, and without the necessary flexibility to look for other markets, or the capacity, under present credit systems, to finance its stocks.

STRATEGIC CONSIDERATIONS

The short- and medium-term strategies proposed in this paper are based on the following considerations: (i) with a rather poor physical resource base compensated by a good genetic potential and excellent health status of its livestock population, and with the poor quality and image of its products in the world market partly balanced by below-the-world-market production costs, the Polish livestock sector has modest comparative advantages in the world market for dairy and beef, maybe somewhat better for pork. In any case, export should be seen as a secondary objective and a means of achieving better supply management and price stabilization; (ii) increases in farm size are unlikely over the next five years, as increased unemployment in the industry will augment the pressure on the small farm, as many part-time farmers will have to rely on their farm as their sole income source; and (iii) livestock will need to remain an essential part of the agricultural system for the sandy soils in the east and south.

OVERALL STRATEGY ELEMENTS

At the production level, this would lead to the following strategic elements: (i) enable, through a greater reliance on purchased feed and less land-dependent livestock activities (pigs and poultry), the intensification of livestock production beyond the number of animals the farmer can keep on the basis of farm-grown fodder and cereals. This is especially relevant to small farmers; (ii) consolidate, and subsequently increase, production efficiency on the medium-size (especially dairy) farms; (iii) improve on-farm product quality, marketing, and supply management, especially for pigs; and (iv) improve the efficiency of breeding, health, and research services needed by the sector.

SPECIFIC STRATEGIES

Feeds and feed industry. The development of more efficient feeding systems will be the key factor in developing sustainable livestock production in Poland. Some of the main specific elements are to: (i) improve, through research and extension, the quality of on-farm roughage (especially grass) and conservation methods; (ii) address the structural deficiency of protein supplements at the national level, by an in-depth assessment of the comparative advantage of rapeseed processing versus soya meal imports; (iii) rationalize the feed-mixing industry, so that compound feeds become competitive with home-grown feeds, and introduce improved technology to allow inter alia the use of high-energy compounds, cereals, and oil seed meals substitutes; and (iv) increase quality standards and labeling of compound feeds and supplements.

Quality, markets and supply management. Improvement of product quality at the farm level and improved marketing will be the key to maintaining domestic market share and gaining increased access to international markets. Key aspects would be: (i) increasing the price differentials and standards for first class products in pigs and beef cattle to include a carcass evaluation; (ii) the privatization and breaking up of the present de facto state monopolies in the domestic and export livestock trade and the strengthening of market infrastructure and market information flows; and (iii) the establishment of an industry-financed and managed price stabilization fund, initially for pigs, created and maintained by a levy assessed on all pigs at slaughter when the price is above a certain reference price; this would be used to partially compensate between periods of high and low prices and between domestic and export markets, to avoid the worst excesses of the hog cycle.

Support services. The key strategic elements for breeding and veterinary services, to improve their cost effectiveness and make them more responsive to present sector needs, would include, for the breeding services: (i) the introduction of a new set of selection criteria and indices, which includes protein content (cattle) and feed conversion (pigs), and which integrates the different indices into one overall economic index; (ii) a separation and privatization of semen production, insemination and milk recording, and herd book functions (now combined into one organization) into three different organizations; and (iii) introduction of full cost recovery for these services over the next two years. The veterinary strategy focuses on the privatization of the private good services and the strengthening of the public good services to maintain Poland's excellent animal health status. The livestock research and extension strategy focuses on (i) the necessary rationalization of the institutional framework, greatly reducing the number of research institutes; (ii) increased emphasis on feeds and grassland management and economic evaluation of technology as key priorities; and (iii) greatly increased industry involvement in extension.

The above proposals would attempt to increase the efficiency of private sector livestock production in Poland through an active intensification and diversification policy for small- and medium-size farms. It would bring about these improvements through a number of interventions, but above all through the rationalization of inputs and services for the livestock industry. The proposals would capitalize on Polish traditions and skills in livestock production, would not require increased state subsidies, and would attempt to mitigate some effects of the transition toward a market economy.

The livestock sector

OVERVIEW

This annex outlines a proposed strategy for the Polish livestock sector. First, it emphasizes the economic, social and ecological importance of livestock in Polish agriculture and describes the key structural and technical constraints to its development. Second, it postulates the basic assumptions under which the sector needs to develop. Third, it identifies the principal strategies, that is, the development of more intensive production on small farms and the consolidation and strengthening of ruminant production on medium-size farms, as the building blocks for future livestock production in Poland. Fourth, it provides specific recommendations for the necessary adjustments in the crucial input services of feed, marketing, breeding, veterinary health and livestock research, and extension.

IMPORTANCE OF THE SECTOR

The Polish livestock population of about 10.5 million cattle, 19 million pigs, 67 million poultry, 5 million sheep and 1.4 million horses fulfills a key role in Polish agriculture, as it:

- provides 46% of the value of agricultural production;
- provides 50% of agricultural exports;
- uses 70% of all domestically produced grains:
- is the main source of cash income for 1.2 million small farmers; and
- is the principal source of organic fertilizer, an essential input under the Polish conditions of sandy soils and low soil fertility.

STRUCTURE OF PRODUCTION

Small farms. Most livestock is raised on about 2 million private farms, of which 1.2 million farms are small (less than 5 ha) family farms and 800,000 are medium-size, more specialized operations. The typical small farm grows its own feed (cereals and roughage) to milk up to two cows, keep one to two sows, and to finish the progeny of those sows. Housing is generally inadequate. Livestock is the principal source of cash for the small farmer. The small farm size, together with the almost exclusive reliance on home-grown feed, is a severe constraint to future livestock development, as it:

- limits investments in efficiency improvements, especially in the areas of feed conservation (silage) and quality improvement (milk cooling equipment), absolutely necessary if the sector is intended to compete with international markets, as it should. This disadvantage would become even more acute if the proposed bigger price differential for quality milk as part of dairy sector policy (Annex 21) were implemented;
- hinders the efficiency of technology transfer and provision of services for a farming system already characterized by a risk averse attitude;
- limits the number of stock per farm and causes competition for feed between different species. These feed limitations are exacerbated by an inefficient compound feed industry. As a result, the present cattle and pig stock on the small farm is too low to provide adequate income. For example, a farm of the average size of 5 ha would provide enough feed for only about three to four cows or 15 fatteners (twice a year), stock levels that are not producing — and cannot be expected to produce in the future — adequate levels of income; and
- leads to poor feed conversion (kg of feed per kg growth) because of the prevailing structural imbalance in home grown feeds (protein quantity and quality deficit and mineral deficiencies) and thus to an inefficient use of the home-grown cereals.

However, while the long-term strategy needs to aim for farm size expansion, in the short term the pressure on the small farm can be expected to increase. A large part of the small farmers are also employed in industry, and with growing unemployment, an increasing number of hitherto part-time farmers will have to rely in the near future on the small farm as their sole source of income.

Medium-size farms. The typical medium-size farm has 5 to 20 cows or 5 to10 sows with followers. Beef is produced as a by-product of dairying, and sheep are sometimes kept, although especially in this category we find more specialized enterprises. Those farms are generally highly mechanized, as an inheritance from the prestabilization economy when machinery was subsidized. The medium-size farms have the best genetic quality stock and the best husbandry skills, and are critical to future livestock and, especially, dairy development in Poland. Key features of these farms include poor grassland management and the precarious state of the specialized dairy producers, who have been hardest hit by the recent drop in price. About 18% of milk and 30% of the pork and poultry production come from state farms and production cooperatives, which achieve high levels of production (for example, in milk production, 3,996 liters per cow per year versus 3,156 liters per cow per year on the private farms), although frequently without due regard for economic efficiency.

PRESENT SITUATION

The national economic stabilization program has put especially dairy and beef production under acute stress, as it caused a dramatic deterioration of producer prices and input/output ratios as shown in Table 20.1:

Table 20.1 Approximate prices and feed/output price ratios for the main livestock products, 1988-1990

	Price (US$/kg) June 1988	Percent change June 1990		Price ratio kg feed/kg product	
				June 1988	June 1990
Milk (lt)	0.14	0.03 – 0.08	-60	2	1
Beef (kg lw)	1.00	0.16 – 0.50	-50	14	4
Pork (kg lw)	0.80	0.90	+10	9	7.5
Broiler (kg lw)	0.75	1.00	+30	6	6.5
Eggs (piece)	0.05	0.04	-10	4	3

a. Farm gate price of barley plus appropriate protein supplement.

In dairy production and processing, the situation is critical. The fall in real household income and the reduction of the consumer subsidy on milk has caused a 10% drop in the consumption of dairy products, from the very high level of 270 liters per capita per year. The abolition of the Cooperative Dairy Union has suddenly left the individual dairy cooperatives with the task of financing their own stocks, and that at very high nominal interest rates. These high financing charges have especially hurt those cooperatives that specialize in butter production. The consequences of the market decline and the high financing charges have mostly been passed on to the producers, and, as a result, farm-gate prices for milk have plummeted (60% in US dollar equivalent over the last two years). This in turn has led to a fall in production, and a 9% drop in sales is reported by the industry over the first five months of 1990, compared with the same period in 1989. The sharp drop in producers' price hurts above all the medium-size specialized dairy farmers, who have fewer opportunities to diversify into other activities than the small mixed farmer. This is shown by the March 30, 1990, livestock census figures, which, while not yet showing a decline in the total cattle population, show a 5% decline in the number of cows kept on state and medium-size farms, and an overall decline of the number of calves and heifers. A much steeper decline has probably been prevented by the extremely low producer prices for cattle.

In meat production the situation is more varied. Beef production (at least 80% of which comes from dairy cattle) already suffered in Poland from consumer preference that is lower than for pork. It has now been further hit by excess dairy cows being slaughtered because of the unfavorable milk price. Beef prices are currently about one-fourth to half of world market prices, and at present levels beef production is unattractive to farmers. On the other hand, pork production benefits currently from favorable price relationships with a better live weight/feed price ratio (1:7.5) than the 1:5 generally found elsewhere. The key issue is whether in an open market economy, the supply and demand can be adequately balanced, or whether significant variations, following the classical pattern of the hog cycle, will emerge. The first indications of a high piglet price and 10% more sows and piglets compared with the same month last year raise fears that substantial overproduction will emerge in this sector in the near future. Also, a similar situation might arise in poultry production. Present feed/broiler price ratios are extremely favorable, and poultry is currently highly profitable in Poland. This high profitability is likely to encourage increased production in the near future. At present prices, export opportunities are limited; on the contrary, there is a possibility that, in the near future, Polish markets will attract substantial imports.

PROSPECTS

The genetic potential of Polish livestock is good, the disease status excellent, and Polish farmers have first-class husbandry skills. Furthermore, the livestock sector benefits from low labor costs. These advantages are balanced with the drawbacks of a short growing season, dominance of poor soils, and severe feed quality constraints. As a result, Polish livestock consistently performs below its genetic potential, with milk production of about 3,250 liters per year (versus potentially 4,500 liters/year); a feed conversion of about 4.5-5 kg feed per kg growth in pigs (versus potentially about 3.5 kg/kg growth); and 3.5-4 kg per kg growth in poultry (versus potentially about 2.25 kg/kg growth).

On the basis of Poland's physical resource base, structure of production, and a rough assessment of production costs in relation to world market prices (Annex 1), the following tentative picture emerges regarding the comparative advantages of the different livestock operations:

• Dairy. With a short growing season and small farm size, Poland is disadvantaged to produce, at low costs, high quality products for the world market. On the other hand, it is expected to maintain for the next decade a comparative advantage in lower labor and land costs. It is, therefore, expected to be able to produce competitively for the domestic market (except in the case of dumping) and, provided quality standards and marketing are improved, export its modest surpluses. Present exports are severely limited by poor quality products and inadequate export organization. Because of the resource base and structural farm limitations, export should not be seen as the major objective in the dairy sector, but rather as a secondary objective and a means of achieving better supply management and price stabilization.

• Beef. Beef, as a by-product of the dairy sector, is also dependent on home-grown roughage and is, therefore, similarly affected as dairy by the short growing season. The small farm size precludes beef cattle as a principal farm enterprise, although beef cattle can be easily kept as a secondary activity. More attractive opportunities might exist for the export of live animals and specific types of intensive beef production (veal on the basis of milk replacers) and in the export of live breeding animals for dairy production to countries, building up their dairy industry.

• Pork. Low labor cost, good skills, and a surplus production in cereals and potatoes, combined with an excellent internal market, augur well for pig production. Furthermore, pig production is well adapted to small farms and would provide the necessary organic matter to maintain soil fertility. Present exports, already benefitting from a good image and the relative low levels of protection in the world (for example, EC import levies for pork in carcass are currently only one-fourth of those of beef carcasses), could be maintained and possibly increased, provided the key inefficiencies in the feed- and meat-processing industry are addressed.

• Poultry. The poor status of the Polish feed-mixing industry and the low winter temperatures mitigate against the development of a competitive broiler industry, as the main world market producers command more sophisticated feed and breeding technologies and are increasingly shifting their poultry production to regions with more favorable warmer temperatures. It is, therefore, not expected that Polish poultry (broilers) can successfully compete in the world market, and the recently introduced import liberalization measures might even open the local market for substantial imports. Egg production seems at par with the world market.

• Sheep and horses. Although sheep and horses comprise a minor part of the livestock industry, sheep have some potential for export to the Mediterranean countries (Poland has an 8,000 ton export quota to the EC) at remunerative prices. Horses, while declining as a power source for farms, might continue to be exported to the EC for meat (although in decreasing numbers because of the shrinking herd and in view of Poland's low labor costs), and for recreational purposes.

A key issue in this context is to what extent Poland will be able in the near future to improve its volume of livestock exports. Present below-world-market domestic prices for milk, beef, and pork have generated an increase of export volume of over 20% over the first quarter, but other factors like inferior quality, truncated marketing channels, market unfamiliarity of potential Polish exporters, and cumbersome export procedures seem to be important constraints for the sector to fully realize this potential.

In designing a strategy, it is assumed that:

- for the short term, (i) increases in farm size are unlikely and should not be accelerated in the face of increased unemployment in industry, which will increase the pressure on the small farm, as many part-time farmers will have to rely on their farm as their sole income source; (ii) increases in government subsidies are not available; and (iii) the relative profitability of the different subsectors will not change substantially;
- for the medium and long term, (i) livestock must remain an essential part of the agricultural system, in particular for the sandy soils in the east and south; (ii) Poland will maintain its comparative advantages regarding labor costs. Provided quality is improved and inefficiencies are adequately addressed, there are modest prospects for exports of dairy, beef, and pork.

The preceding analysis and considerations lead to an overall strategy at the livestock production level, which would:

- enable a diversification and intensification of production, especially on the small farms;
- consolidate and, in the medium term, improve the efficiency of production on the medium-size farms;
- improve product quality and marketing, to make Polish products more competitive in the world market; and
- improve the efficiency of the inputs (especially feed), markets and services (breeding, health and research) needed by the sector.

For the small farms, the diversification would focus on other agricultural and cottage industry activity (for example, horticultural production and small-scale food processing) because of Poland's comparative advantage in low labor costs.[1] But for soil fertility considerations, especially on the sandy soils of eastern and southern Poland, small farms also need to include livestock. Pigs and poultry have proven, in Poland as elsewhere, to be interesting options for small farmers, as they are less land-dependent. With an estimated return to labor of US$15 per pig fattened (Annex 2), a 30-pig fattening unit (twice a year) would provide an income of US$900, or close to the present indus-

trial wage. Additional opportunities might exist in the production of veal on the basis of milk replacer and in intensive beef production on the basis of cereals and silage. Required actions include a rationalization of the feed industry, an improvement of marketing and supply management, and an improvement of the support services.

For the medium-size farms, measures urgently need to be introduced, to avoid a total collapse of dairying. In brief, they include the introduction and application of (i) stricter quality standards, and (ii) a set of measures (for example, stronger quality price differentials, concentration on high milk density regions) that would favor the medium-size milk producers. They are complemented by a set of measures to bring the producer price back to a higher price than present, rationalize the processing and marketing chain, and improve exports. For the medium term, the success of this type of enterprise will depend to a large extent on the availability of (i) high quality farm grown forage, which will reduce dependence on concentrates; (ii) milking and cooling equipment, which will allow the production of high quality milk; and (iii) the provision of efficient breeding and health services.

The specific measures needed to improve feed (concentrate and roughage), marketing, breeding, animal health and livestock research, and extension are described in the following sections. The specific strategies for other inputs like credit and agricultural mechanization, the dairy sector, and agroprocessing and marketing are detailed in a separate working papers, and will be touched upon only if relevant in the overall strategy for the sector.

Feeds and the feed industry

PRESENT SITUATION AND PROBLEMS

Overall feed situation. Most feed in Poland is home grown. In 1989, all roughage and about 80% of all concentrate feed[2] was fed on the same farm that produced it and only about 10% was bought from the feed industry. Early 1990 figures show a further decline of the feed industry. While this very high reliance on homegrown feed is fully justified for the bulky roughage for ruminants and is even quite rational in view of present margins on concentrate feeds for nonruminants because of the structural deficiency in protein on the farm, it reduces the efficiency of overall feed utilization and puts severe limits on the possibility of intensification, especially on small farms raising pigs and poultry.

Protein

Farm-grown fodders. A general deficiency in protein (both in roughage and concentrate feeds) severely depresses the overall efficiency of feed utilization. Poor grassland management leads to low protein contents of grass and hay. More specifically:

• long grazing or cutting intervals lead to a sharply reduced protein content of the pasture. Research data show a decline in the digestible protein content of natural meadows from 10% (or good for about 15 liters of milk per day) under a three-cuts-per-year regime to 7% digestible protein (or good for about 7 liters per day) under a two cuts-per-year regime. The higher total grass (dry matter) yield under a longer interval does not compensate for this loss in quality;
• the heavy reliance on hay making, instead of silage, causes further losses of the conserved product. Silage making, especially in its prewilted form, is constrained by the heavier equipment needs;
• the extreme fragmentation of the parcels (up to eight lots per farm) precludes grazing, and makes the production of farmyard manure necessary; and
• the rather high input in N fertilizer (60-80 kg N per ha per year) on private farms could at least in part be replaced by the development of grass/clover mixtures, provided the appropriate clover cultivars would be identified.

Concentrate feeds. In concentrates, the absolute deficiency in the quantity (estimated in 1989 at about 600,000 tons or the equivalent of 1.4 million tons of soya meal) and quality of the protein are the prime causes of the 30-50% higher feed conversion rate (that is, Polish pigs and poultry require at least 1 kg feed more per kg growth than elsewhere). Thus, for the same amount of pork and broiler production, 3-4 million tons more cereal are required than necessary if protein quality and quantity were optimal. A (partial) solution to this problem could lie in increasing the oil crushing capacity for rapeseed, of which now only 500,000 tons of the total 1,500,000 tons produced in Poland is pro-

cessed, provided the industry can bring its crushing margins to a level at which it can effectively compete with imported vegetable oil and soya meal. Additional protein feed imports would free some feed cereals for export, thus realizing a classical efficiency gain from trade.

The feed industry

Some of the main characteristics of the Polish feed industry are described below:

• The Polish feed industry is about equally divided between members of a state association, Bacutil, which produce a full range of products, and the cooperatives, which produce mainly protein supplements. Together they operate over 1,100 plants, with a total capacity of about 9 million tons, but normally operating at about 50% of their capacity. They employ about 10,000 persons. Furthermore, some state and cooperative farms have small mixing plants.
• Most of the feed mills are using obsolete technology (the newest feed mills are about 16 years old) and are in a bad state of repair. As a result, feed quality is poor and inconsistent, and there is a severe lack of farmer confidence in feed quality.
• Concentrate feeds contain a high %age of cereals. Cereal substitutes (tapioca), coarse grains, and oil meal substitutes (corn gluten) are not used, and although under present export constraints (including an export ban on wheat) it might be more attractive to include cereals, an increased use of cereal substitutes and coarse grains in the feed could be considered when the constraints are alleviated and domestic cereal prices move closer to the world market prices. Technically, such a shift would benefit feed utilization, especially of poultry feed, which is now deficient in energy.
• Up to 1989 concentrate feed was so heavily subsidized that protein-enriched compound feeds could be sold at the price of cereals, thus providing an incentive for farmers to purchase these better feeds. This subsidy is now eliminated and, as a result, demand has plummeted below the already weak feed industry capacity utilization in normal years. Overall demand for the first five months of 1990 has fallen to only 44% of the demand for the comparable period last year, and some mills are working at only 10% capacity. The fall in demand was about the same for all feed categories, including the feeds for the

currently profitable pig and poultry industry. The industry was further hit by the very high nominal interest rates during the first months of 1990.

• In an effort to maintain liquidity, feed mills have greatly increased their prices, which now are more than double the cost of the ingredients, and even triple for protein supplements (versus a processing and distribution margin of 20% in Western Europe). At these margins, it is not attractive for the farmer to purchase compound feed, and it is clearly more attractive for him to use his own feed (even if that means 25% higher feed use); only if feed costs come down 25% over the farm gate price of the cereals will it become economically justifiable for him to purchase feeds from the feed mills.

• The envisaged privatization of state farms (which in 1989 purchased over 60% of the production of the feed mills) and the proposed importation under the EC ffood aid program of 40,000 tons compound feed will most likely lead to further drops in demand for concentrate feeds.

Thus, it seems likely that a substantial rationalization and reduction of capacity, followed by a technology upgrade, will be necessary to enable the remaining feed mills to produce at acceptable capacity rates and become again competitive with home-grown feed.

RECOMMENDATIONS

In the short term it is recommended that:

• the process of rationalization be allowed to take its own course, accelerating decentralization and privatization of the state enterprises (Bacutil) and cooperatives involved in the sector;

• stricter quality standards be introduced regarding key nutritional parameters (energy, digestible protein, essential amino-acid composition, minerals, and growth promoters), that labeling of these parameters be made obligatory, and that an industry-based control system be established to enforce these standards;

• the contents of the feed component under the EC food aid program be modified from compound feed to essential ingredients not produced in Poland (amino acids, growth promoters, and vitamins).

In the medium to long term it is recommended that:

• enabling mechanisms (joint ventures) and commercial credit be provided for investment in technologies like pelleting, the use of animal fat, the production of minerals, and the production of milk replacers for steer fattening in conjunction with the dairy industry;

• cereal substitutes be increasingly incorporated in compound feeds, with due regard for economic considerations;

• local capacity for rapeseed extraction (and, hence, production of local rapeseed meal as a protein supplement) be increased, provided the earlier studies of the comparative advantage of rapeseed extraction over the import of soya meal and vegetable oil are also confirmed under current input/output price ratios;

• the research and extension effort on grassland management and conservation be considerably strengthened; and

• the development of vertically integrated production (the feed enterprise providing the piglets or day-old-chicks and extension providing a minimum price guarantee for the finished product under a subcontract with the farmer, although the risk remains for the farmer) be encouraged in pig and poultry production, to give the feed mill industry a direct interest in producing high quality feed, and to provide farmers with guaranteed outlets for their produce.

IMPACT

The short-term impact of these measures will be industry contraction. A number of feed mills will close, increasing unemployment and limiting the availability of balanced feed in some regions. The latter in turn will increase the use of cereal-only rations, and therefore further depress temporarily the already poor feed conversion rates. It is, therefore, essential to accelerate the adjustment. The medium- to long-term impact would be positive. Improved quality control, lower processing margins, and increasing specialization should increase the demand for high quality feed, and the impact on the production efficiency is expected to be positive. The proposed vertical integration would result in a decrease in public funding for extension, as the industry would take over this task. Finally, the proposed introduction of cereal substitutes would push cereals into cash crops and broaden the basis of Polish agriculture.

Livestock markets and supply management

PRESENT SITUATION AND CONSTRAINTS

The development of more efficient market channels will be, together with improved feeds, the key to a balanced growth of the livestock sector. Livestock trading and slaughtering, was until the recent introduction of the economic reforms, the monopoly of the state, and still remains heavily dominated by the state. For example, over the first month of 1990, the state bought for the domestic market 78% of all animals (and in some voivodships 90%) and for export 90% through one company, ANIMEX. Purchasing is done on about 3,000 markets or directly from the farm on the basis of a fixed-price scale according to live weight and sometimes exterior confirmation. Livestock processing for export (mainly canned ham) is carried out in 29 large USDA-approved state slaughterhouses; for domestic consumption, processing is done in 45 large slaughterhouses and a large number of small meat works. The meat-processing industry employs about 90,000 persons. Key constraints to the system are:

- the de facto monopoly of the state in livestock exports — and in certain regions also in domestic livestock trade — stifles a transparent price transmission, leads to inefficiencies, and is, for example, one of the major reasons for the excessive (60%) difference between border prices and farm-gate prices for live animals;
- the absence of any supply management system threatens to cause major fluctuations in producer prices, especially for pigs, where the first indications of a substantial oversupply, according to the hog cycle, are appearing. Such wide price gyrations would be a major impediment to an expansion of pig production by smallholders and a major threat to long-term consumer loyalty and market share;
- the lack of flexibility of existing meat-processing plants, which are all geared to the production of one product (canned ham) and, as they are all about 15 years old, use outdated technology;
- lack of adequate market information;

- inappropriate quality standards, especially for the pork export market, which demands a leaner animal of lower live weight than is acceptable as first class under the present grading system; and obviously inadequate enforcement of prevailing standards, as 99% of the pigs were classified as first class (although in 1989, under government monopoly); and
- poor sanitary standards, especially in the smaller, privately owned meat works.

RECOMMENDATIONS

For the pig, poultry, and beef industries, the short-term strategy would imply:

- introduction of an industry-financed and -managed price stabilization program for pigs, which would impose a levy (3-4%) on all animals slaughtered, to be used to alleviate the worst excesses of the hog cycle. It would therefore serve as a partial (about 50% of price differential) transfer payment (i) between periods of high and low prices, and (ii) between market sectors (domestic versus export market) to balance supplies. The reference price below which no levy is assessed would be set by the industry (producers and meat works) and tied to the cost of production of the most efficient producer and to world market prices. It would be financed exclusively from a levy on the pigs and would require no state subsidy. It would be audited by an independent audit firm. The 3-4% level of the levy would be low enough not to cause evasions of slaughterhouses. The partial character of the transfer payment would provide a buffer mechanism, but would not prevent some cyclical movements. As such a fund is working satisfactorily in the Republic of Ireland, an early visit by a Polish delegation there to become familiar with the details of such an operation would be recommended;
- the breaking up of the livestock export company, to allow other livestock exporters to enter, and the review on a regional basis of the domestic livestock markets, abolishing de facto state monopolies, wherever they prevail;
- the introduction of an industry-enforced improved grading system, which for first-class export pigs sets 105 kg live weight as the upper live weight limit and a maximum of 5 cm total back fat at the two normal measurement places as the minimum requirements. The grading system for slaughter cattle seems correct — the

key issue here seems the correct application of the existing scale; and

• the stronger enforcement of sanitary regulations, especially for small private meat works.

For the medium term this would imply:

• improvement of market infrastructure, mainly to develop current livestock purchasing points into efficient markets and livestock auctions;

• development by the Ministry of Agriculture of an active information dissemination service on market prices and volumes;

• increased involvement, through active promotion, of private traders in livestock exports;

• increased investments, through the private sector and commercial credits, to keep the export slaughterhouses and meat works up to international standards and increase their product range and flexibility.

IMPACT

The price stabilization program would require no government subsidy and would lead to increased smallholder production and thus reduce social suffering incurred by the increasing unemployment. The provision of market infrastructure and market information is a public good and would require additional state funding, although only in limited amounts. The proposed tighter quality standards and market liberalization, combined with increased slaughterhouse investments from commercial sources, would lead to increased exports of high quality products. Without the latter, Poland might lose its export markets.

Support Services

BREEDING SERVICES

Present situation and problems. The Polish artificial insemination (AI) service is technically of high quality, but breeding policies are suboptimal and have not been adapted to recent changes in demand conditions and efficiency requirements. The technical efficiency is demonstrated by the good (72% for cattle and 80% for pigs) nonreturn rates and high (80%) share of the cattle population covered (only 10% of are covered). Major efficiency concerns are:

• Sire selection. Production of the dams of the bulls selected for insemination seems not to reflect the production level of the superior farms in Poland. Foreign semen with superior genotypes is little used (20% of inseminations).

• Selection criteria. In cattle, the goal of increasing the fat content of the milk is no longer necessary, in view of the current butter surpluses in Poland and in the world. In pigs, although data are recorded for the most important efficiency parameter — feed conversion — this information is not properly disseminated. There is no economic evaluation of the different characteristics.

• Organization. Milk recording, selection and artificial insemination are covered by the same organization. Furthermore, the producers have limited influence on breeding policies and overall sire selection. The 52 autonomous state insemination centers are too numerous to permit effective bull selection and achieve economies of scale. Considerable savings could be obtained by reducing the number of centers;

• Staffing. The 8,504 inseminators carry out an average of 718 inseminations per year. This number should be about 2,000, even taking into account prevailing poor telecommunications and transport.

• Farmer participation. Farmer participation in sire selection for individual inseminations is minimal. This is the result of (i) continuing subsidies (about 60% of the costs, that is, 50% of insemination and 75% of milk recording costs) that induce farmers to see insemination and milk recording as free and therefore not valuable; and (ii) lack of advice by the extension service regarding appropriate attention to sire selection.

Recommendations. In view of the above, short-term recommendations are to:

• Increase the fee charged to producers to 60% of the total costs for insemination and 50% for milk recording;

• Prepare an action plan to separate and privatize the semen production, insemination, and milk recording and herd book functions, now covered by one organization, among three different organizations. Private operators (including, but not restricted to, the herd books) would produce or import the semen. This would include a reduction in the number of breeding stations. The proposed chambers of agriculture or the dairy centrals in the regions with high dairy production density would take responsibility for the actual insemination and milk recording. And private breed-specific herd books would continue with the herd book activities and eventually take over semen production; and

• Introduce a new set of selection criteria and indices that include protein content (cattle); more completely disseminate the feed conversion data; and integrate the different indices into one overall economic index on the breeding value of the sires.

The proposed strategy for the medium term:

• Increase the fee to be charged to the producer for AI services to 80% in 1992 and to 100% in 1993. Milk recording fees should be increased gradually to full cost over a 5-year period;
• Implement the action plan proposed above concerning the rationalization and privatization of the service;
• Open possibilities for other private operators (veterinarians, the regional dairy centrals) to become involved in the service; and,
• Strengthen the extension effort to increase farmers' awareness of the value of sire selection.

This medium-term strategy would need to be refined in the long term.

Impact. The introduction of these measures can be expected to decrease farmers' participation in the service, but accelerate overall genetic progress. The January 1990 introduction of 40% producer contribution (although to some extent confounded by the general dairy crisis) has been followed over the first three months of 1990 by a 15% drop in the service compared with the same period last year. A further drop can be expected. However, this will not affect overall genetic progress if the selection intensity is improved along the lines proposed above, and if at least one-quarter of the cattle and 5% of the swine population remain in the service (to provide adequate trickle down of improved genetic material toward the rest of the population). The cost recovery and privatization would signify a saving of Zl 70 billion in 1991 and Zl 150 billion (June 1990 rates) afterwards.

ANIMAL HEALTH SERVICES

Present situation and issues. The Polish livestock sector benefits from excellent animal health. The country is free of the main contagious diseases and can, therefore, export live animals and meat to most parts of the world, including the EC. The main disease constraints include management diseases like mastitis, internal parasites, and mineral imbalances as a result of environmental pollution. An eradication program for leucosis is under way and 10 of the 52 voivodships are now free of the disease. Until now, veterinary care has been the responsibility of the state, and provided mainly free of charge at a cost of US$15 million (1989). The key proposed policy includes privatization of private good services (presently requiring 70% of budget) like clinical interventions and vaccinations, combined with the introduction of full cost recovery for these services. Public good services (requiring the remaining 30%), like sanitary control, food inspection, and further eradication of leucosis, would remain in the public domain.

The main issues include the:

• pace of privatization, including the need for an intermediate decentralization of responsibility to the local governments, before launching full privatization at the level of the individual veterinarian;
• conditions under which private veterinarians could start;
• employment opportunities for veterinarians (including 300-400 new graduates each year) and, in particular, for veterinary technicians, who cannot be absorbed in the private sector. The present coverage of one veterinarian per 1,400-1,800 cattle is too dense to provide an adequate income for a private veterinarian.

It appears that little gain can be made by an intermediary step, and that immediate and full privatization of the privatizable services would be preferable. It is therefore recommended that in the short term:

• an action plan be prepared to define the conditions of transfer. As it is essential that private veterinarians be fully represented in the preparation of such a plan, a national order of veterinarians should be created immediately to represent the private sector. The minimum size of veterinary practices in different parts of the country should be established, and then actual practices established. Allocation of these practices (including existing housing, equipment, and vehicles) could be on the basis of an auction for interested, certified veterinarians. Additional incentives (tax relief and subcontracting of certain public sector tasks like meat inspection) could be envisaged, and;

• a manpower requirement study be prepared before year-end, with the possibility of an immediate limitation on the number of students admitted to the veterinary schools or the closure of some faculties.

Impact. Experience elsewhere has amply shown that producers are quite willing to pay the full price for veterinary services of good quality. No negative impact on the animal health situation would therefore be expected. An adequate public sector capability in preventing and controlling infectious diseases would need to be maintained, however. The program of privatization would result in savings for the public sector of about Zl 100 billion (1990 prices) per year.

LIVESTOCK RESEARCH AND EXTENSION

Present situation. Livestock research is currently spread over a large number of institutes:

• the Institute of Animal Husbandry Research, headquartered in Balice near Krakow with 12 experimental stations throughout Poland, which, with 350 scientists and 300 technicians, is the main livestock research institute, concentrating on breeding and nutrition;
• the Veterinary Laboratory in Pulawy, with 150 scientists and 450 technicians, involved mainly in disease prophylaxis and food hygiene;
• the Feed Evaluation Laboratory in Lublin, concerned mainly with industrial feed mixing and the use of additives in animal feed;
• the Poultry Institute in Poznan, with 30 scientists and 500 technicians, involved exclusively in poultry breeding and feeding research;
• the Dairy and Meat and Fat Technology Institutes, both in Warsaw, involved mainly in the processing side of livestock products; and
• the Institute of Animal Nutrition in Warsaw, belonging to the Polish Academy of Science,

with 40 scientists and 100 technicians, which carries out basic research in animal nutrition.

A preliminary review indicates that:

• Livestock research, with an estimated 20% of the total agricultural research budget and the same share of scientists, seems to be underfunded in relation to its contribution to agricultural GDP, the technology gap and its capacity to generate results;
• Livestock research in Poland has focused on intensive modern production methods, at the expense of smallholder production technologies; has given priority to breeding over nutrition (for example, most animal husbandry research at Krakow is directed toward genetic improvement); has neglected grassland research; and has given only scant attention to the economics of new technologies.

Livestock extension, carried out by the Agricultural Progress Centers (WOPR), has similar problems of large farm and production maximization focus. Similarly, livestock extension seems to be a second class citizen, as reflected in the number of livestock specialists and the general crop orientation of the field extension staff. The influence of the industry (producers, feed, and processing) on the focus and operation of the service and the content of its message is weak.

Recommendations. In this context, it is recommended (in addition to the recommendations included in Annexes 10 and 12 on agricultural research and extension) that:

• the institutional framework for livestock be restructured, consolidating the different institutes into far fewer and merging all production oriented institutes with agroprocessing institutes, so that the total livestock food chain is covered. This would involve closing a number of substations and reducing staff, but at the same time the budgetary allocation per scientist would increase. With an increased importance of the production and management type diseases, one could argue that veterinary research should also be merged with livestock production research. However, the need for specialized equipment and laboratories, and the need to maintain units of a manageable size, might necessitate a continued separation of production and veterinary health research. In that case, a close cooperation mechanism needs to be established.

• a Livestock Research Strategy be developed, which will review present status and define the main priorities for future research. A key element of this strategy would be to determine how to make the research more relevant to the small farmer, with special attention in livestock production research to feeding and grassland management and conservation (for example, varietal research on clovers and other protein sources, such as beans, etc.), silage making for the small farm, appropriate animal housing, and the economic evaluation of these technologies.

• besides the reorganization proposed in Annex 12, on extension, the possibility of subcontracting specific key extension programs (that is, the installation of chilling equipment on medium-size dairy farms, better compound feed use with available farm feed resources, and issues related to the vertical integration in the pig and poultry industry) to dairy and feed mill industries, should be explored.

Conclusion

The above proposals attempt to set the framework for the next decade and seek to intensify smallholder production and consolidate and improve production on medium-size farms. They would bring about these improvements through a number of interventions, but above all through the rationalization of the feed industry, the improvement in supply management and markets, and the reorientation of the other support services to farmers' needs. The proposed package would aim to alleviate the impact of price volatility in the dairy sector and the general increase in unemployment by providing alternative forms of livestock production, while at

the same time maintaining soil fertility. They would not require increased state subsidies. The proposals would capitalize on Polish traditions and skills in livestock production and attempt to facilitate the transition toward a market economy.

Endnotes

This annex was prepared by Cornelis de Haan, assisted by Zdzislaw Piasek, Franciszek Brzozka, Jan Malkowski, Tadeusz Kowalski, and John McCarrick.

1. Specific measures might include the eventual introduction of special investment support for intensification (not restricted to livestock) as part of the unemployment benefits for former part time farmers now being redundant.

2. On the basis of the feeding value (Oats Units).

Appendix

Approximate production cost and market prices of main livestock products
(US$/kg live weight equivalent)

Product	Market price	Production cost	World market f.o.b. price	EC price
Milk	0.03 – 0.09	0.10	0.14[a]	0.35
Beef	0.12 – 0.50	n.a.	1.00[b]	2.00
Pork	0.90	0.75	1.00[c]	1.50
Broilers	1.00	0.70	0.8[d]	1.20

a. Based on New Zealand export prices.
b. Based on Australia prime beef prices.
c. Based on Chicago market prices.
d. Based on New York prices.

The dairy sector

Summary of dairy strategy

BACKGROUND

The Polish dairy sector is of major economic and social importance. With an annual production of 15 billion liters, dairy represents 19% of agricultural GDP and 32% of the contribution of livestock to GDP. It is a major source of income for 2 million farmers — two-thirds of the farming community. Besides direct on-farm employment, the dairy industry, with 712 plants spread throughout the countryside, provides over 110,000 jobs and is thus a major source of rural employment. Finally, milk and milk products are an important part of the diet of the Polish population. With 270 liters per year, per capita consumption is among the highest in Europe, and over 10% of the average household income is spent on dairy and dairy products, giving the dairy sector an important sociopolitical dimension.

Trends over the last two decades show a gradually declining cow population (25% since 1970) compensated for by a proportional increase in production per cow, which now stands at about 3,250 liters per cow per year. Over the last 20 years, the amount of milk processed has almost doubled, from 37% of total production in 1970 to 73% in 1988, with a much greater supply from private farms. This is partially caused by an increase in the number of suppliers, which rose from about 1.2 million in 1970 to a current level of 1.4 million. Collection stations have declined in number from 30,000 in 1970 to the present level of about 10,000 (although this number is still too high).

PRESENT SITUATION

This important sector now faces serious problems, partly as a result of deep-seated structural problems, and partly as a result of the national economic reform program. The structural problems are:

- the small average farm (5.2 ha) and herd size (2.4 cows per farm) with 1.1 million farmers having only one to three cows and producing 30% of the milk, 0.3 million farmers with four to 10 cows, and only 7,500 farmers with more than 11 cows. This small farm size puts severe limits on investments in improvement of production efficiency — for example, feed conservation, livestock housing, and milk quality improvements — as described in the following paragraphs;
- the severe imbalances in livestock feed supplies, caused by poor grassland management and conservation, and exacerbated by an inefficient feed mixing industry. Poor grassland management, especially the Polish practice of long grazing and cutting intervals, leads to low quality roughage deficient in protein and adequate for a production of only five to 10 liters per cow per day, whereas grass in this environment should provide for at least 15 liters of milk production per day. Further feeding value

losses (on average, 10% of protein) result from the predominance of hay making (80% of all fodder conserved), rather than silage making. Finally, the feed mixing industry, with low productivity and high overhead costs, cannot supplement these deficiencies with a competitive concentrate feed of reliable quality;

• the poor livestock housing conditions and lack of adequate machinery and equipment, resulting from the small farm size;

• the extreme fragmentation of milk collection, with 1.4 million farmers delivering on average 12 liters of milk per day to 10,000 milk assembly points, greatly increasing collection costs and impairing quality control and improvement;

• the precarious status of the dairy processing industry: 712 plants, over 500 of which are more than 30 years old, are operated by 323 dairy cooperatives, generally function with unclear ownership and management responsibilities, and operate commercially with a very narrow product range. Over the last years, investments have not kept up with need and, while low labor costs could enable some smaller units to maintain their production costs at reasonable levels, production costs are not nearly so critical in the dairy sector as product mix is in determining viability and the ability to pay farmers a competitive price. This will become increasingly important under the recently introduced, more liberal import regime. This imposes a much higher requirement of scale, and new investments, once the industry has been rationalized, are necessary;

• the inappropriate price structure, which gives only a very low weight to quality (equal to the payment of 1% fat), no weight to milk protein content, and only a minimum premium (Zl30-Zl50 per liter) for winter milk, despite a high peak to valley ratio of 1.6:1, which even seems to have increased over the last years. The absence of any weight given to milk protein content is repeated in genetic improvement and artificial insemination (AI) services, where up to now the main breeding goal has been to increase the fat content in addition to milk yield; and

• the inadequate quality enforcement, which means that on average about 80% is classified as Class I milk, whereas independent tests showed that only 30% would classify as Class I according to a strict application of the standards.

As a result, Polish dairy products are of low quality and can be sold in the world market only at a severely discounted price, normally at 40-60% of U.S., European, and Cairns Group prices, as shown in the Table 21.1 below.

Table 21.1 First quarter 1990 world market and Polish export prices of dairy products

(US$/ton)

	World market	Polish export
Skim milk powder	1,200	350-750
Whole milk powder	1,250	860-900
Butter	1,350	600-950
Low-fat cheese		1,900
Gouda cheese	1,700	1,100
Casein	2,700	1,500

Economic reform has exacerbated these problems and led to a situation of acute stress:

• the dramatic reduction of the subsidy on milk products from US$1 billion in 1988 to an estimated US$70 million in 1990, together with a fall in real household income, caused a drop in the consumption of dairy products of 9% over the first five months of 1990;

• the application of the remaining subsidies to low-fat milk (although recently changed) stimulated the production of butter;

• the liquidation of secondary cooperatives — hitherto responsible for stock management and financing — left the widely scattered primary cooperatives in disarray over stock management and export, leading to the present large number (260) of small exporters and to price cutting to gain access in the highly cartelized world market for dairy products. While Lacpol, a federal cooperative with 72 dairy members, claims to be responsible for 40% of dairy exports with sales of US$100 million, there are at least 10 other state or quasi-state agencies exporting some dairy products and 250 private exporters operating without any form of bonding or licensing, thus damaging the image of Polish dairy products in the world; and

• the extremely high nominal interest rates, coming at a time of peak production — under normal conditions also a time of stock building — put many primary dairies in great financial difficulty.

As a result, dairies producing butter were confronted with extremely high financing charges for a product that, because of poor quality, could not be exported and which they are now disposing on the domestic market at one-third of the milk-equivalent price of those producing cheese, skim milk powder, or other exportable products. Over 50 of the dairies producing for the collapsed butter market have gone bankrupt and several more are facing the same fate. As the cooperatives passed the financial crisis on to the producers, a wide range of producer prices emerged (Zl300-Zl900 per liter). This compares with a world market equivalent price of Zl1,350 per liter, a producer price under the relatively undistorted market of New Zealand of Zl 1,800 equivalent per liter, and a U.S./EC subsidized price of Zl3,500 equivalent per liter.

The lower producer price range in Poland of Zl 300-600 per liter, paid by dairies producing butter (frequently with two to three month delays) severely threatens the solvency of the supplying farmers, affecting above all the more specialized medium-size farmers. These farmers depend more heavily on milk and are more likely to be hurt in their farm investments by high interest rates than are the small one-to-three-cow operations. However, medium-size farmers have the best genetic stock and sufficient scale to justify the crucial investment in milk quality improvement. They are therefore the cornerstone of future dairy development, and the substantial reduction in this category of dairy farm, which threatens to occur, would have a long-term negative effect on the future development of the sector.

PROSPECTS

Short term. Management problems and financial issues relating to the normal summer peak stock (rather than a mismatch between supply and demand, as often argued) seem to be the key issues. Although the analysis is hindered by inadequate information on the present stock position of the different dairy products, present information shows that the 9% fall in demand has already been followed by an adjustment of 11.3% in the supply purchased by the dairy industry. If a more detailed inventory of current stock levels would confirm, as expected, that the levels are normal — or even below normal for the time of year[1] — then it would become crucial

first to address the current stampede selling, especially of butter stocks. If no support measures are taken, it is likely that this present distress selling of butter in the domestic and world markets will continue, resulting at the end of the peak season in much lower stock levels than required to bridge the winter season. The necessity of importing substantial quantities at much higher world market prices over the winter is then a real threat. This undesirable situation might be prevented by the introduction of a set of measures (described below) that would lead the industry to conserve their stocks.

Medium and long term. The Polish dairy industry's strength lies in the husbandry skills of its farmers and the excellent disease status and good genetic potential of its herd — factors which could put the industry on a par with many other producers in the world. The Polish dairy sector also benefits from low labor and energy costs, and the low income levels of its farmers, which give the Polish dairy sector a margin of advantage over some of the more efficient producers. Demand projections can be summarized as follows:

• For the domestic market, dairy product consumption is expected to equalize at Western European levels over the next decade, which, when combined with population growth, suggests that the market will not regain even by the end of the century the consumption levels of the 1980s.

• For the world market, much will depend on (a) how successful the major dairy exporting countries will be in maintaining restrictions on their own production and continuing their satisfactory performance of the last years in the management of exports and export pricing; (b) whether the current Uruguay round of negotiations of the GATT will be effective in liberalizing trade; and (c) to what extent Poland is able to improve product mix and quality and evolve a structure capable of carrying stocks and matching supplies to the market. With present comparative advantages, modest prospects exist for expanding current volumes slightly and using exports as an effective supply management tool to stabilize prices.

Overall strategy

Within this overall framework, the strategy would be to produce a full range of high-quality competitively priced products; this will allow the industry to hold the domestic market and export as opportunities arise, and at the same time provide a viable income from milk production to the maximum number of farmers. This strategy would need to satisfy its principal stakeholders, that is, (i) the consumers, who will want a reliable supply of a full range of competitively priced products; (ii) the farmers, who will want security and the opportunity to earn a comparable income; (iii) the dairy industry management and staff, who will want attractive working terms and conditions; (iv) bankers and investors, who will want the security of loan repayment and adequate returns on their investments; and (v) the government, which will want to withdraw as soon as possible from the sector (in operational and subsidy terms).

To achieve these objectives, a number of short-term tasks are necessary to (i) restore industry confidence; (ii) start restructuring the industry; (iii) improve quality; and (iv) rationalize exports. These short-term tasks would need to be complemented by medium- to long-term measures to address the structural production and industry constraints identified above. These tasks and measures are discussed in detail below.

Short-term objectives

The first task will be to restore industry confidence and, especially, to stop stampede selling if this would lead to deficits in the winter. It is therefore proposed that:

- the industry immediately make an inventory of available stocks;
- the industry set a credible and viable milk target price — one that would reflect the discounted export price available for dairy products other than butter;
- the state guarantee until spring 1991 exportable butter stocks at the set price level up to the world prices minus 20%. At current prices this would provide a guarantee of about US$1,000 per ton of unsold butter in March 1991. The guarantee would only apply to butter of exportable quality, as certified by the Na-

tional Dairy Institute in coordination with the recently established Agricultural Marketing Agency (ARR). It would be stored by the individual dairies at their cost and risk, in bonded warehouses. Stock movements would be under the supervision of ARR. The state guarantee would be dependent on the industry's assurances that (a) it will implement a new pricing structure, increasing the premium for quality and reducing the premium for fat; (b) it has made satisfactory arrangements to avoid a recurrence of present market conditions in 1991; and (c) it will implement a quality improvement scheme. This price guarantee should enhance the collateral value of stocks and facilitate their financing. On the other hand, the price levels chosen are such that it is not expected that any government subsidy will actually be required.

The second immediate task will be to start restructuring the industry to arrive at economies of scale, greater product flexibility, and better export organization. To that effect, a rapid move to a system of regional rationalization is recommended, to be induced by granting dairy licenses on a regional basis to up to a dozen equal milk pools created through the amalgamation of existing dairy cooperatives (giving these milk pools exclusivity of collection and processing in their regions for a fixed period — say two years). These regions would be selected on the basis of milk density and social and infrastructural integrity. Immediate actions in this respect would include:

- the recruitment of technical assistance to prepare the plans and prospectus for the regional milk pools with the goal of winning the support and participation of farmer investors, bankers and government staff and to assist the amalgamated cooperatives in the initial management of their business;
- the immediate clarification and rationalization of the ownership of the existing dairy cooperatives, attributing the total net worth of the existing cooperatives to the original subscribers in proportion to their share of initial capital. Those continuing in the dairy industry would be issued shares in the new rationalized cooperatives up to their share value and might be required to subscribe for further shares, depending on the investment requirements. Those not continuing in milk production or as

members of the new cooperatives would be issued redeemable loan stock for the value of their holding in the new cooperative;

• the passing by the government of dairy licensing legislation, which would underpin the amalgamation of the dairy cooperatives and enforce the collection and processing exclusiveness of these milk pools for two years;

• the passing of cooperative legislation, reiterating the ownership rights of shareholders and enabling the amalgamated cooperatives to enter into joint ventures, supply management, licensing franchises and technology transfers with international partners.

The third task would be to start improving quality standards. This would include changes in the price structure and a well-directed investment program, supported by concentrated extension efforts. More specifically it is recommended that:

• the price differential for Class I milk be increased to 30% over the value of basic milk;

• stricter enforcement of the prevailing international standards be introduced. In the short term, it may be necessary to support the dairies in ensuring that payments are based on quality, by applying a system of random checks by an independent institute (the Dairy Institute, for example); and to exclude from the government support program those dairies whose milk classifications (and therefore payments) are not supported by these random tests. It could be expected that in 1991 about 40% of the milk would fall into Class I;

• an industry-supported quality logo be introduced;

• payment for the protein fraction be at about 50% of the value of the milk, thus halving the fat premium;

• testing procedures be adjusted so that milk contaminated with antibiotics can be detected before it is bulked up and that strict suspension rules be applied to suppliers of milk containing antibiotics;

• commercial lending be encouraged for the improvement of chilling facilities on farms (estimated at US$200 million), in the dairies (estimated at US$100 million) and in the distribution and stock management (estimated also at US$100 million). For the on-farm investment in chilling equipment, the minimum economi-

cally justifiable herd size is a 4-cow unit. With the price differential for first class milk proposed above, the equipment is paid back in three years; and

• this quality improvement campaign be supported with an active extension campaign, focusing on (a) farmers with problems meeting the quality standards—to help them to improve milk hygiene; (b) small farmers, who want to continue with milk production—to increase the scale of the milking operation with technologies such as group milking and a milk bank, and to assist this class of farmers in introducing the use of chilling equipment at an affordable price; and (c) farmers who want to abandon dairy production — to advise them on alternative enterprises, for example, horticulture and more intensive pig and poultry farming (see Annex 20).

The final immediate task would be to rationalize imports and exports. This would include:

• passing antidumping legislation, in accordance with GATT regulations, imposing a variable levy to adjust for the subsidy of the exporting country;

• suspending all food aid in the form of dairy products;

• creating a dairy or food export promotion board for information and coordination of dairy or food exports to improve the image of Polish dairy or food products in the world market;

• launching a study to review possible export coordination mechanisms. This would mean assessing the efficiency and profitability of existing state export enterprises and their role, if any, in future exports, versus the desirability of an industrywide food export joint venture, subject to antitrust legislation. The move from a dairy export enterprise to a food export consortium would bring about significant intersectoral synergies as meat, dairy and horticulture products are drawn from the same stores using similar transport and financing arrangements, complying with the same customs and import requirements, and, in many cases, being offered to the same customers. Such a food export agency could also provide a ready-made forum in which voluntary industry stabilization levies could operate and within which stock financing and management or public warehousing functions could be discharged more cost-effectively, thus freeing up the capital of individual firms, which would otherwise be committed to working capital, for quality improvement, product development and growth.

IMPACT

These measures should lead to more competitive and sustainable industry. On the positive side, it should lead over the next year to a more stable market, that is, to a narrower producer price range, with the average producer price reaching, or coming close to, the present top price of Zl 900 per liter. It should also improve quality and reduce the present 40% price discount for Polish dairy products in the world market. On the negative side, these measures could squeeze out the small producer and those dairy cooperatives which cannot increase quality and broaden their product range. The small farms would be put under pressure through the greatly increased price differential for quality milk, as the size of their operations would not justify the necessary investments in quality improvements. The rationalization of the dairy industry in milk pools will exclude producers in lower milk density areas and will render a substantial number of existing plants and processing facilities redundant. The rationalization will lead, however, to more efficient on-farm production and processing. But, as supply and demand are in a precarious balance, care should be taken to monitor supply and demand so that policies can be adjusted as the market develops.

MEDIUM-TERM STRATEGIES

Recommendations for the medium term are that:

- the industry further rationalize assembly and processing plants in the milk pools under the new structure;
- the state encourage, after the 2-year exclusivity for the regional dairies in the milk pools has elapsed, the entry of new enterprises to develop niche products and markets and thus maintain a competitive industry;
- the industry agree on an industrywide stock management and export structure, in accordance with results of the study on export coordination mechanisms (recommended above);
- the state abolish the milk subsidy. An

interim step could be the establishment of a subsidized school milk program;
- the industry implement over a 3-year period the investment program;
- the AI services reorient their selection program toward a stronger emphasis on protein production and integrate the different selection criteria into one overall selection index, taking into account the relative economic value of the different production traits; and
- the state develop a strong extension program for grassland improvement as the basis for cost-effective milk production.

LONG-TERM STRATEGIES

In the long term, the emerging dairy cooperatives could get involved in other food-related activities; have a stronger farmer focus, integrating other farmers' input services into their package of services; or, through joint ventures, acquire access to other dairy markets outside Poland. These activities need to be supported by an active product and market research program.

Introduction

Economic restructuring has had a traumatic impact on the dairy industry. In 1988, Zl 760 billion were paid to farmers for raw milk. The state paid Zl 653 billion in subsidies to dairies that offered dairy products for sale to consumers, realizing in total Zl 447 billion. In that same year, butter and cheese imports accounted for 12.5% and 7%, respectively, of domestic market requirements while approximately 1% of domestic production was exported.

During economic restructuring in 1989, subsidies were removed, with the exception of a subsidy applied to low-fat milk. This exception was later extended to standardized milk because of declining butter prices. The withdrawal of dairy subsidies from all but liquid milk led to a reduction in government spending on dairy products from almost US$1 billion to about US$70 million. Milk accounted for almost half the food subsidy allocation.

The situation was further exacerbated by the liquidation of the secondary cooperatives responsible for stock management and wholesaling, by very high interest rates, and by inadequate storage capacity. The market was left to balance supply and demand even as the stock management and marketing of the dairy cooperatives was dismantled. The resulting level of uncertainty and indecision was not conducive for the dairy industry to address the issue of how best to cope with market changes and sudden adjustment needs.

The result is that dairies producing butter for the domestic market — hitherto topped up by imports — saw no other remedy than to dispose of products at prices that could only justify one-third of the raw milk price paid by those producing cheese, skim milk powder or other exportable products. This lower price linked to the collapsed butter market and inadequate stock-financing threatens the solvency of those dairies and the supplying farmers and is the central cause of the present crisis in the dairy industry.

The problem of the dairies can only be resolved through rationalization and adaptation of production, restoring order in stock management and marketing capacity and focusing on quality. The impact on milk producers is heaviest on the more specialized high-input dairy farmers whose liquidity was already seriously strained by premature repayment of loans in the face of interest rate increases in December 1989. The subsistence smallholder milking one to three cows on low inputs is less likely to be hurt over the long term by the economic squeeze. Indeed, he may not be exposed to it at all because the problem applies mainly to butter production.

The viability of the dairy industry depends on an improvement of product quality at the export level. This can only be done by building an industry based on farms of sufficient scale to invest in quality milk production. Such an investment can only be justified by having a price structure that sufficiently differentiates among qualities so as to remunerate that investment. Only on this basis can the domestic market be maintained and the full world market price for exports be obtained.

Through a combination of market management and rationalization of processing capacity, it is possible for the dairy industry to pay Zl 900 per liter for all first-quality milk without further subsidies or other forms of government support. With effective export marketing and improvement in quality, it is possible to further increase this basic price by Zl 500 at today's discounted world market prices. This would allow the government to withdraw the 400 Zl subsidy that currently applies to about 15% of milk which, presently, accounts for only approximately 6-10% of industry revenues.

The determinants of world market prices, however, will change over the next decade and whether they will be favorable or not for Poland is a matter of some conjecture. In any event, to cope with the world market situation, Poland must protect its domestic market from the vagaries of highly protected and discounted foreign markets, while positioning itself to compete profitably in foreign markets where possible.

To summarize, the present problems of the dairy sector arise from a combination of factors: withdrawal of subsidies, high interest costs, milk harvest effect arising from seasonality, and abolition of the traditional storage and stock management system carried out by cooperatives. As a result of these changes, the underlying weaknesses of the sector — poor product quality and poor industry structure — have been exposed, and sales are possible only at a deep discount for key commodities on both domestic and export markets.

If four essential actions are taken, the price of Class I milk can be brought back to Zl 900 per liter (or even higher at present world market conditions), thus offering good prospects for farmers with an average-size farm milking four cows or more. The four essential actions are:

• immediately supporting a stock buildup with a target price of Zl 900, and restructuring the pricing system;

• investing in the production of Class I milk on farms right through the assembly processing, distribution and retail system (with a full chill chain), so that this investment can be converted into better products and, hence, higher milk prices for farmers;

• restructuring the dairy industry by creating strong farmer-controlled regional dairies and facilitating their involvement in external joint ventures since these organizations must quickly make the shift from a command to a market economy;

• creating an industry-based stock management and commodity export mechanism to enable recovery from the present deeply discounted position of Poland's major dairy commodities.

Production strategy

It is difficult to assess the competitiveness of any dairy industry today given the distortions in world markets. The world market price for dairy products — resulting from U.S./EC disposal policies—has fallen dramatically over the past year. The outlook is that production restrictions and some fine-tuning in the support mechanisms will enable the major dairy-exporting countries to stabilize world market prices and perhaps bring about a recovery. In the longer term, a liberalization of trade in agricultural commodities, including dairy products, is envisaged, whether or not the current Uruguay Round of GATT negotiations, due to be concluded by the end of 1990, achieves its ambitious goal. Even if the goal is not achieved, trade restrictions will be less effective in curtailing the movement of consumer food products in international trade. But if protectionist policies in agriculture continue unabated, it is unlikely that production of agricultural commodities for subsidized export will be expanded. In either case, the likely result is that world market prices will tend to equalize within and between the major dairy markets and, thus, increase to something nearer the full cost of production in the most efficient industry.

Presently, remunerations of Polish milk producers are in the range of Zl 300-900 per liter. The lower price reflects today's value of butter on the highly distorted domestic market, and the higher price the value of Polish skim milk powder, casein, and cheese on the export market. The returns at this higher price are comparable to returns for pig, poultry, and grain production at prevailing prices and would be sufficient to sustain supplies. Thus, at Zl 900 milk is competitive with other farm enterprises. The Zl 900 price, however, reflects a 40% discount applying to dairy commodities from Eastern Europe relative to prices in the United States, Europe, or Cairns Group countries (Australia, New Zealand, etc). This is based on a perceived quality differential and on disorderly exporting.

The first challenge facing the Polish dairy industry is to reorganize its supply and processing capacity to close the Zl 600 domestic price gap within the industry. This requires improving milk and product quality and excluding contaminants that result in rejection of large product batches.

The second challenge facing the Polish dairy industry is to close the Zl 600 quality perception gap between the world market price (which is the result of US$10 billion in export subsidies spent worldwide) and prices received by Polish dairy exports. This is not merely an internal dairy industry issue. It extends across all food products and includes wider quality stock management and marketing considerations.

With good market and product management, the quality of products sold on the domestic market can be brought into line with that of other European countries at or under world market prices. This is the best form of market protection, although it will require the support of effective antidumping legislation. This combination of forces would leave the Polish dairy industry uniquely positioned to trade profitably in an unprotected and unsupported dairy market, provided it can resolve its twin problems of product mix and product quality, while creating a structure capable of carrying stocks and matching supplies to the market. The fundamental economic reason for Poland's position is not any inherent advantage in milk production or high productivity. Rather, lower income levels give the 4-cow Polish dairy farmer a margin of advantage over the 120-cow New Zealander. Achieving this position requires comparable quality, however. As the economic situation improves, this advantage will be eroded

Table 21.2 Polish dairy competitiveness

	Zlotys
US/EC price	3,500
New Zealand price	1,800
Distorted World price 1990	1,400
Base price 1990 — provides returns comparable to other farm products	900
Discounted price 1990 — unsustainable	300

as better income alternatives arise, and greater productivity will be required of dairy farmers to achieve comparable incomes. This continuous process of adjustment is likely to gradually concentrate the national cow herd in fewer hands, rather than threaten the dairy self-sufficiency of Poland.

DAIRY INDUSTRY STRUCTURE

Agriculture accounts for 28% of employment, 12% of exports, and 13% of GDP. Milk is a major income-generating activity for two-thirds of the farming community and for the 113,000 employed in milk processing. Consumers spend 10% of their income on dairy products — hence, the social, economic, and political importance of dairy.

Dairy product consumption at 270 kg/head p.a. is among the highest in Europe. It declined in the first months of 1990 by about 9%. It may be expected to equalize at European levels over the next decade, which, when combined with population growth, suggests a market that will not regain — even by the end of the century — the consumption levels of the 1980s. In March 1990, food accounted for 50% of consumer spending. Meat and dairy products account for 45% of spending on food, half of which is for dairy products.

Over 15 billion liters of milk (accounting for 19% of agricultural output) are produced in Poland by some 4.8 million cows, and 2 million farmers. The marketed portion sold for processing has doubled over the past two decades. Over the same period, the cow herd and milk output have fallen by 1 million head and 1 billion liters, as has the average herd size — even though farm size has increased from 4.7 to 5.2 ha. Today, 1.4 million farmers offer milk for sale, accounting for 84% of the milk that is processed. The balance is sold by state and cooperative farms.

The average yield per cow has been rising very gradually and is now about 3,165 liters/cow, with average sales per cow estimated to be 900 liters less. Thirty percent of the milk is provided by the 1.1 million farmers who own one to three cows. Three hundred thousand farms have four cows or more and account for 55% of milk supplies. Only 7,500 farmers carry more than 11 cows. Seasonality varies by region from 2.5 to 1 in the northeast to 1.3 to 1 in the southwest and averages 1.6 to 1. There is evidence of an increase in seasonality over recent years.

Milk is assembled in average lots of 12 liters per day, through about 10,000 milk assembly points to 712 plants (500 of which are over 30 years old), operated by 323 dairy cooperatives. The milk is graded according to quality and fat content and is paid for on that basis, with a lower differential applying to quality than for 1% fat. Seventy-nine percent of milk is paid for as Class I but independent assessments suggest that not more than 30% complies with the 4-hour methylene blue test, which is the main yardstick used to determine milk quality.

The dairies produce, according to their capacity, a range of products for the local market with some marginal volumes going for export. In the past few years, exports have been outweighed by imports by three- or fourfold. Because of the combination of donor aid in the form of milk products and the impact on demand of the removal of subsidies combined with high interest rates, many dairies have been forced in 1990 to seek export outlets for unsuitable products and/or to dispose of them on the domestic market because they lack either the physical or financial capacity to carry stocks. This has resulted in unprecedented price cutting for Polish dairy products—both on domestic and export markets.

The product mix is the result of a combination of investment restrictions and output maximization to match the domestic market, and import minimization. The following profile emerged from these factors:

Most liquid milk is presented in one-liter bottles, at 2% fat, unchilled, although one plant is offering cartons, a few offer sachets at a higher price, and at least two importers are offering UHT milk in plastic bottles. The government subsidy of Zl 400 per liter, applied until recently to low-fat milk, only accentuates the fat problem. Apart from price and margin controls on milk and cheese, no other government restrictions or supports apply to the dairy sector.

Table 21.3 Product mix

Product	Percent of Milk and Supplies	Output
Skim milk powder*	53.4	204,000 tons
Liquid milk	15	2.5 billion liters
Cheese	10	360,000 tons
Quark	9	
Cream	8	
Other	10	

*equivalent to 264,000 tons of butter

Table 21.4 Polish milk production trends

	1970	1988
Cows (m)	6,082	4,806
Milk output per cow	2,384	3,165
Milk output (million)	14,499	15,177
Purchase of milk	5,309	10,949
of which		
state farms	1,209	1,915
private farms	4,100	9,034
Percentage of production offered for sale	36.6	72.6
Percentage of fat	3.35	3.63
Number of suppliers (000)	1,189	1,399
Milk assembly points	31,236	9,749
Milk carriers	16,239	31,611
of which, motors		13,131
Price per liter (Zl)	2,64	69,45
Percentage of first class total	33	79,5
of which		
private farms		77.0%
state farms		81.5%

Table 21.5 Polish milk supply network

Supplier size (thousands)	
0 – 4,000 liters p.a	1,070
20 – 50,000 liters p.a.	315
over 50,000 liters p.a.	7.5
Membership of cooperatives (thousands)	323
Dairy plants	712
Membership of cooperative councils	6,900
Membership of suppliers	
Committees	72,186
Number of advisors	2,149
Milk as percentage of sales	86.6%
Dairy retailing — shops	315
Cocktail bars	47
Assembly points	
By volume (liters per day)	
0 – 1,000	1,738
1 – 5,000	7,214
over 5,000	797
By equipment	
Own water	8,755
Refrigeration	7,039

SUPPLY AND DEMAND CONDITIONS

Despite the very substantial price rise for dairy products in 1990 arising from the combination of high inflation and withdrawal of subsidies, the data for the year to date suggest that the fall in supply has in fact been greater than the fall in demand (see Table 21.5). Imports in 1990 were insignificant.

The evidence of the past few years is that seasonality is on the increase. Given the unsustainable margins (average supply price of Zl 595 per liter), this trend is likely to be accelerated this year unless some corrective action is taken.

Stock levels should be higher this year if the market demand from the latter part of 1990 until the new milk season is to be met from domestic supplies. Were the market to be supplied from imports, this would represent at today's world market prices a dramatic increase in the average consumer price since world prices are running substantially ahead of prevailing Polish prices, particularly in butter and skim milk powder.

The outcome of the present situation could well be a stampede out of milk production. Therefore, the market situation requires a steadying influence to restore butter prices and to build up stocks. This, however, cannot be achieved immediately because of difficulties relating to product quality, stability, and shelf-life, and the additional problem arising from contaminants (including antibiotics) resulting in the disposal of batches of rejected products. These problems further weaken an already seriously weak market. The rigorous enforcement of quality standards is likely further to reduce supply to well below the level of domestic demand in the short term. The situation is therefore critical and in need of immediate and sensitive handling. It must be emphasized that this is not a problem that subsidies can solve, that we are not facing a problem of oversupply, but rather one of a lack of stock management to meet a seasonal situation exacerbated by poor quality and high interest rates.

PRODUCTION STRATEGY AND CONSTRAINTS

Despite the serious problems mentioned above, the Polish dairy industry has a number of strategic strengths on which to build a viable and competitive future:

• the excellent cattle husbandry tradition, the large number of dairy farmers, and the relatively low cost of milk production in the private sector;
• the excellent disease status of the Polish herd and its good genetic potential;
• the capability of on-farm concentrate feed production provided that the market comple-

Table 21.6 Dairy product market adjustment
(January – March 1989 and 1990)

Amount (kg)		Consumption				Quarter Adj., %	March Adj., %	Weighting
		January	February	March	Total			
Milk	1989	13.80	13.27	14.67	41.74	-6.6	-9.1	20
	1990	12.67	11.97	13.33	37.91			
Butter	1989	0.71	0.66	0.75	2.12	-5.6	-4	50
	1990	0.66	0.62	0.72	2.00			
Cheese	1989	1.18	1.15	1.29	3.62	-18.5	-18.6	20
	1990	0.97	0.93	1.05	2.95			

		January – May	5 month adj., %	3 month adj., %	Market Adj. March
Total Milk Supplies	1989	4.4 billion liters	-11.3%	-8.7	-8.4
	1990	3.9 billion liters			

ments it with appropriate supplements;
- the low labor, transport, and energy costs;
- the large domestic market for dairy products.

Though not an advantage as such, one can also add that the dairy industry will benefit for some time from the lack of higher income alternatives.

Taking these strengths into account, it is possible to envision that the Polish dairy industry would be capable of producing a full range of world class dairy products; satisfying the domestic market; and availing itself of export opportunities as they arise, while providing the opportunity to earn a decent income from milk production to the greatest number of dairy farmers.

However, the dairy industry must satisfy its main stakeholders. Consumers will want reliable supply of a full range of quality products competitively priced.

Farmers will want security—the opportunity to earn an income comparable to other agricultural and nonagricultural activities. Dairy industry management and staff will want attractive working terms and conditions and career opportunities.

Bankers and investors will want stable repayment of loans and the opportunity of return on investment. The government will want to withdraw from direct involvement in the sector at the earliest opportunity, both in operational

Table 21.7 Milk utilization
(tons)

	1970	1988	1989
Total supply	5,309	10,949	11,305
Liquid milk (M liters)	483	2,580	
Whole milk powder	14,600	49,500	49,400
Skim milk powder	20,100	158,900	175,000
Butter	127,000	266,000	298,000
Cream	91,700	266,800	
Regional cheese	43,000	124,700	412,000
Cottage cheese	69,000	312,000	
Processed cheese	14,000	23,800	
Condensed milk	5,000	20,400	
Milk drinks	63,800	107,000	
Casein	18,800	23,800	32,700
Calf milk replacer	3,500	38,800	

and fiscal terms, but also to ensure consistency and adequacy of supplies for consumers and to establish the dairy industry on a basis that will maximize its contribution to social and economic development.

Prerequisites. To satisfy the requirements of these stakeholders in a realistic manner and to pursue the vision described above, a number of prerequisites must be met:

- Enforceable milk quality and hygiene regulations that reflect the value of quality in the premium paid must be developed. This will

Table 21.8 Milk markets
(tons)

Exports	1970	1988	1989
Butter	12,400	-	-
Cheese	2,200	5,100	700
Skim milk powder	-	44,200	39,900
Casein	5,400	12,300	7,100

Table 21.9 Domestic consumption
(kg per capita per year)

	1970	1988
Liquid milk (liters)	45.0	66.7
Butter	3.8	7.6
Cheese	1.6	3.5
Cottage cheese	2.1	7.9
Cream	2.8	6.9

mean that milk farmers will need to invest in milk cooling storage.

• A new cooperative legislation framework within which to resolve the ownership issue and restructure the dairy industry must be passed.

• Provision for licensing or other control of dairy processing plants must be made, both to ensure standards and to establish a critical mass at the level of the industry.

• An industry-guided market management mechanism must be developed, in order to help match total volumes and product mix to available market conditions; this must be combined with strict legislation that prevents dumping.

• Reliable credit facilities for farmers, processors and retailers must exist, as well as a climate within which they can undertake repayment commitments. This requires a high level of predictability and confidence.

• Industry commitment to rationalization at the assembly and processing levels, with the aim of increasing milk density and consolidating the processing capacity (but with continuing strong farmer ownership involvement), must exist.

• Finally, a well-focused extension service must be put in place for both categories of farmers affected:

- those who have a future in quality milk production;

- those who must seek alternative enterprise.

If these conditions are met, this will inevitably lead to the following:

• Milk for processing will cease to be an option for many smaller producers of poor quality milk in lower milk density areas furthest from processing facilities and markets.

• A substantial number of existing assembly and processing facilities will become redundant.

• There will be international involvement in the Polish dairy industry, whether through joint ventures, licence franchise, or technology transfer agreements.

Critical success factors. Some elements in the chain of the dairy industry are of strategic importance in the restructuring process.

Inputs. Expanding dairy farmers need a good support service and an uninterrupted flow of least-cost, high-specification inputs. This will require:

• rationalizing the veterinary and AI services;
• rationalizing and developing the feed supplement concentrates, fertilizer, and other farm input sectors, including farm machinery;
• access to credit for dairy farmers investing in quality.

Grassland. Better grassland management and conservation is essential to low cost milk production. This will require special attention from the extension service.

Quality. A chill-chain from farm to retailer and cleaner, higher quality milk are essential to improved products. This will require investment in training and in plants, and enforcement of standards through stiff penalties imposed by the dairies (on delinquent farmers) and by the government (on delinquent dairies). It will also require an industry-regulated quality assurance campaign.

Scale. Since the objective is to maintain the maximum number of farmers in milk production consistent with the development of an internationally competitive industry, this will require scale and density at the production level, and scale and product spread at the processing level.

To achieve this, milk assembly must be rationalized by a combination of extension and price measures, assisting those with no future in quality milk production to identify alternative enterprises and offering a price premium based on quality and credit terms to those who must invest in quality and expansion. New technologies that help reduce costs of small farm assembly (such as milk banks, together with group milking) should be examined.

At the processing level, rationalization can only proceed after new cooperative legislation has been passed. This legislation should recognize the prior right of dairy farmers to organize dairy processing, provided they can combine milk supply, management, plant, and money in a proposal for a strong, stable dairy enterprise.

Transferring facilities to new cooperatives (or joint ventures) should take account of the existing equity, distinguishing between past and future shareholders by converting to loan stock. Thus, in providing for the rationalization of the dairy industry in a given region, the net worth of existing dairy cooperatives would be attributed to the original subscribers in proportion to their share of capital.

Those who will continue in milk production would then be issued shares in the new rationalized dairy cooperative to the extent of that value and may be required to subscribe for further shares depending on both investment and membership requirements. Those who will not continue in milk production or as members of the new cooperative would be issued redeemable loan stock in proportion to the value of their holding in the old cooperative.

Constraints. The major production constraints in pursuing the approach outlined above are the following:

• Volumes will inevitably suffer as quality standards are enforced, possibly threatening supply adequacy and raising new market problems.

• The investment levels for on-farm cooling and storing of milk is substantial. This comes at a particularly bad time for all dairy farmers. Such investments in milk refrigeration are unlikely to be a financially viable proposition for farmers with fewer than four cows. Other alternatives, including reliance on higher hygiene standards, direct delivery (rather than collection), group refrigeration, and milk banks, can also be considered, provided they are self-funding

and result in higher quality milk.

• The existing electricity system may exclude on-farm refrigeration in some key areas.

• The payback from this investment and for the parallel investment in processing will arise, through the market, only if quality improvements are transmitted to stocks and to the market place. It is therefore essential that farmers, in making their investments, be assured that the proper industry structure to ensure market recovery and a premium for quality are in place.

• Many smaller dairy farmers who cannot achieve quality milk will receive an uneconomic milk price. In the longer term, there will be no future in dairying for them except that provided by the local market.

Although these constraints are formidable, to neglect them would be to continue to undermine the viability of Poland's dairy industry with unacceptable quality standards. This would have disastrous consequences for dairy farmers, for the dairy industry, and for consumers in the long term.

SPECIFIC ACTIONS

Target price. The immediate task is to restore order and stability in product quality and pricing. This requires industry coordination to determine stock levels and demand-supply positions until next spring and to fix a winter price premium to suit the situation. The traditional premium of Zl30-50 will have no effect in enhancing winter supplies. Given the growing seasonality and the likelihood of shortages, a more realistic premium is warranted by market conditions. To that effect, a sustainable target price should be set.

At Zl900 per liter of Class I milk, dairying compares about equally with alternative farm activities. This seems to be, given todays' conditions, the minimum price at which commercial milk production can be undertaken even by Poland's most efficient dairy farm. This price is broadly reflected in the domestic market price of dairy products with the major exception of butter, the sales price of which should be doubled to justify Zl 990/liter to producers. This price also reflects the discounted export price available for dairy products, with the exception of butter, some of which is exported at prices 50% lower than the general 40% discount that applies to Polish dairy products. Setting a target price of

Zl900 per liter, therefore, would give transparency to the pricing system, distinguishing between those dairies capable of meeting the target price and those that, through inefficiency or poor product quality, cannot.

Such a price, however, cannot be achieved even by the most efficient dairies without first restoring market stability. Restoring market stability will require the combined efforts of the industry and the government in order to make it more attractive (or feasible) for dairies to carry seasonal stock surpluses.

To that effect, the following mechanism is proposed. The government should meet with the dairy industry and outline the broad strategy for industry rationalization and ask, as a matter of urgency, that the industry identify the appropriate target milk price for Class I milk and establish the present stock position. The government should offer to support the target price by guaranteeing key dairy products of exportable quality up to the equivalent of the target price.

This price guarantee should enhance the collateral value of stocks and boost industry confidence, therefore making it possible to carry stocks at the level necessary for seasonal stabilization. This would remove the surfeit of stocks on the domestic market and stop export sales under that price. The government should only provide this guarantee if the industry agrees to three conditions:

• to implement a new pricing structure, increasing the premium for quality and reducing the premium for fat;
• to make arrangements satisfactory to the government to avoid a recurrence of the present market conditions in 1991;
• to implement fully the quality testing system outlined below and to institute a quality assurance campaign.

The government's risk could be covered by sampling all dairy products going into storage under the guarantee scheme and inspecting dairy stocks in storage. It should exclude products that do not meet minimum export standards.

The role of seasonal stock management would revert to the industry by the summer 1991 stock buildup and may in time become the task of a wider food export corporation.

Enforce quality standards. Dairies must immediately adjust their testing procedures to be in a position to reject contaminated milk before it is bulked up and apply suspension penalties to suppliers of milk containing antibiotics.

International standard milk tests are used in Poland but they are not enforced. These standards should be enforced with a substantial premium over the base price for Class I milk. Class II milk should be priced so as to ensure balance. A quality extension service should then be focused on those farmers having difficulties meeting the standards.

It may be necessary in the short term to support dairies in enforcing payment based on quality, applying a system of random checks on milk samples by the Dairy Research Institute, and to exclude from any government-supported program those dairies that do not meet quality standards during the tests.

Milk pricing. As a matter of urgency, it is essential to revise pricing within the constraints of the market as follows:

• target price at about Zl 900 for Class I milk, which, as indicated above, should be agreed to by the industry and require government underwriting;
• a winter milk premium reflecting the 1990-91 winter circumstances;
• a protein fraction representing about 50% of the value of the milk, halving the fat premium;
• a premium for Class I milk of about 30% of the value over basic.

Each dairy should set its price, within these parameters, with reference to the target price, which is based on prevailing discounted export prices for stable commodities. Dairies with higher value added products and marketing/processing efficiency should be able, in time, to exceed this target price by a considerable margin.

Quality program. The higher milk price will probably be earned by up to 40% of milk suppliers in 1991. But dairies have an obligation to adjust the price structure along the lines mentioned above to assist farmers in meeting the new standards. This will involve organizing a major quality campaign supported by an investment and credit package devised to be repayable through the quality premium within a 3-year period. It would be appropriate for the government to seek grant support from donor agencies to reduce the cost to farmers of installing refrigeration and storage equipment.

Management. Apart from quality, the key management actions to be taken at the farm level are the following:

- assist in financial management those farmers who are considering borrowing to expand in dairying;
- assist farmers in grassland management and conservation. This is central to least-cost milk production and seems to be the weak link in the Polish system;
- assist farmers unable to meet the quality standards and having no long-term future in milk production in seeking alternative ventures. These farmers may in the interim find local outlets, but in time they will need alternative cash enterprises if they are to stay in farming;
- design and implement a new extension program, in which these farm management issues would be the central focus, to assist in the stabilization of the dairy industry and the rural sector.

Processing and marketing strategy

DAIRY SECTOR ISSUES

The dairy industry has been operated until recently by a network of primary and secondary cooperatives. The secondary cooperatives were dissolved and placed under government management in early 1990, liquidators were appointed, and new elections for cooperative committees were called as a first step in the transition of cooperatives toward a market-oriented operation. Further changes are necessary to complete this transformation, and new industry structures must be developed to replace those designed to serve the past planned economy. The present institutional vacuum has contributed in no small way to the many problems of the dairy industry (high variance in milk prices received by farmers, collapse of the butter market, etc.).

The following issues must be resolved under the new institutional structure:

- Product quality. Standards for the domestic market must, for practical reasons, be indis-

tinguishable from export market requirements. This will enable the industry to export without discounting and, in time, to face competition on the domestic market.
- Management. In the past, management focused on technical performance and on social and political requirements dictated by the planned economic system. The new situation involves a significant shift in management culture and skills. Provisions must be made to meet these requirements. The summary dairy accounts presented in Table 21.10 show the extent to which the concepts of management information systems, financial control systems and cost/profit centers must be developed.

Table 21.10 Dairy profits, 1988

Loss	Zl546.7 billion	+ 171%
Subsidy	Zl653.4 billion	
Profit	Zl108.6 billion	+ 139%
Subsidies as percentage of sales:		169.3%

- Investment. Table 21.11 summarizes the investment program for 1988. It is highly diverse and clearly not sufficient to meet the needs of the industry, which has many obsolete and inadequate plants and equipment. New investment will be required for quality enhancement, assembly and processing rationalization and realignment of the product mix with the market. Caution is in order so that investment can be increased without threatening the supply-demand balance and, therefore, the viability of the industry.
- New products and packaging. Though there has been some new product development in recent years (see Table 21.12), it will be neces-

Table 21.11 Dairy industry investment, 1988

Buildings	47.2 billion Zl
Machinery	12.1 billionZl
Transport[a]	4.5 billion Zl
Total[b]	63.8 billion Zl (*)

Note: Investment in 2,024 separate projects including: 25 new dairies; 27 large modernization projects; and 205 building projects of 100 million Zl +.
a. Total dairy transport fleet: 12,602 vehicles. This investment involves replacing 635 of the vehicles with 856 vehicles of which 784 were new. Transport involves 28% of the work force.
b. At the average 1988 exchange rate, this is equivalent to US$100 million.

Table 21.12 New Dairy Products, 1988

Salad cream
Longlife cottage cheese
Low-fat flavored cottage cheese
Semi-mature cheese
Instant SMP
Kortowski cheese
Low heat WMP
Cheese made from WMP
SMP milk additives
Ultra filtration SMP

sary to extend and develop considerably the range of product and packaging options if relatively free market conditions are to prevail in the domestic market. This will require flexibility of response on the part of the dairy sector and of the packaging, printing, and retail sectors.

• Scale and competitiveness. The main dairy products require large-scale production to achieve economies of scale, particularly as quality and hygiene standards increase. The scale required is greater than that of individual production plants: each milk pool must reflect the broad market mix and achieve scale in each product in order to offer a competitive milk price to it suppliers in all circumstances. The scale required for market competitiveness is even greater. This suggests an integrated regional approach to rationalization rather than a functional or plant approach.

• Competition. A lively market—with choices available for retailers and consumers as well as for farmers—is essential in the dynamics of any industry. This must be taken into account, side by side with scale, if the industry is to be responsive to change, and it is essential for competitiveness.

• Stock management. Seasonality of supply imposes special requirements in terms of stock management if both its suppliers and customers are to be well served and the industry is to find stability. Stock management requires occasional access to international markets and a steady, predictable access to warehousing transport and stock finance. This must be done at the industry level but does not require government involvement.

Of all the issues raised, management has the highest priority since it conditions rationalization of the industry, better product development and market management. Meeting this need

and the need for capital are the major challenges, assuming quality enforcement.

RATIONALIZATION OF THE DAIRY INDUSTRY

The present dairy structure broadly reflects the country's administrative structure: ultimately all the components were supposed to combine into a dairy monolith. It is not surprising therefore that the individual dairies fared rather badly after the liquidation of the cooperative union. The prewar structure of the dairy industry was based, as in other countries, on emerging regional dairies designed to match a milk pool to a marketplace as cost-effectively as possible.

To facilitate the emergence of the new milk pool structure requires guidelines or rationalization proposals to provide a framework within which amalgamation and acquisitions could take place. Once this initial restructuring is in place and the industry is stabilized, market conditions will determine future mergers and acquisitions and the establishment of new dairies to develop new products for niche markets.

Because labor costs are low in Poland and labor productivity is a key determinant of the economics of scale, smaller units could survive better in Poland than in Western economies for some time to come. However, production cost is not nearly as critical a factor in the dairy sector as product mix in determining viability and ability to pay farmers a competitive price. This imposes a much higher requirement of scale.

Options. The dairy industry could be left to its own devices over the next few years to achieve a more rational balance of scale, product mix and market position. A number of large, efficient units would emerge and many weaker dairies would fail, probably precipitating in the process the failure of large numbers of milk suppliers. But this approach is unlikely to ensure, in all regions, supplies for the market in the short run, and is not consistent with industry stability and investors' confidence.

Another option is to pursue a lower scale of rationalization. This is likely to lead to plant investment, which will be written off in a few years as the domestic market becomes more exposed to competition and a greater premium is placed on competitiveness.

A national structure for milk procurement and pricing — including contracts on quotas —

could be established, with farmers selling milk to each dairy plant in accordance with its production options. But this is unlikely to lead to the adaptation of the product mix to market circumstances.

Finally, regional rationalization based on prevailing scale requirements could be facilitated by granting dairy licenses on a regional basis and giving exclusivity for a fixed period. This option seems to represent the most balanced approach to improved competitiveness, competition and stability. It presents, however, a new challenge to cooperatives that will need to maintain effective farmer involvement in what will be large organizations.

Regional rationalization. Milk production in Poland is concentrated in a belt across the center of the country from the northeast to the southwest. Consumption per head is greater in the northwest and west. More information would be required before conclusions could be offered as to the broad regional lines likely to give the best dairy structure. But it is clear that the southeast and northwest are the main deficit areas and that the supply belt is across the center suggesting that a cartwheel-shaped regional structure might emerge. Such a shape would have the disadvantage, however, of fragmenting the areas of highest milk density and intensifying interregional dairy competition both for supplies and market in the center. The regions should be designed to coincide with milk pools and consumer markets rather than with geography. They should have social, infrastructural, and cultural homogeneity.

Whatever shape the regions would ultimately have, they should reflect commercial reality and combine coherence with scale. This might result in approximately eight to 12 regions, the final shape of which will be determined by the amalgamation decisions of existing cooperatives. These decisions would result in the emergence of up to a dozen new regional dairy cooperatives formed from the amalgamation of selected existing dairies. These new cooperatives should be structured so they could accommodate joint ventures, supply management, and license franchise and technology transfer agreements with appropriate international partners. This would accelerate necessary changes in management, product, and plants that the new market situation demands.

The emergence of these regional dairies will require considerable emulation and assistance, but will not require financial support beyond that available through technical assistance and commercial means. The best form of support that the government could provide would be to introduce new dairy processing legislation and issue licenses exclusively to newly emerging dairies.

The scale of the investment needed to modernize plants and improve product mix and quality can only be determined in the context of the commercial prospects of the emerging dairy cooperatives. But it is unlikely to be an investment of less than US$100 million within the dairies or less than US$200 million in providing refrigeration and storage on dairy farms. In addition, up to US$100 million in warehousing and chilled distribution — with some provision for additional seasonal stock-carrying capacity — is required. This suggests total investment requirements of up to US$150 million per year over the next three years to bring Polish dairy products up to the international quality base line. If this one-time investment is successful in bridging the gap between Polish dairy product prices and discounted world market prices (the alternative source of supplies), the annual benefit could be several times the level of the investment.

MARKETING ISSUES

Marketing will, of course, become a central management function of each of the emerging dairies. The first task facing managers is to make the best of the products they have. Then they will need to achieve a steady improvement in product quality, presentation, and range; and to encourage investment by wholesalers and retailers in chilling to ensure that quality is maintained throughout the chain. Over time, the market for chilled, cultured and dessert products will expand, and market leaders will develop strong brand positions. This process may result in further market-driven rationalization amalgamations. If the Polish dairy industry is not well structured, the dominant brands are likely to be based on imports.

Without adequate provision for seasonal stock financing and management, however, the task of domestic market development will be impossible. The market overhang of summer stock buildup threatens any investment in quality or product development. While this is part of the marketing function, it cannot be tackled by firms acting unilaterally and, therefore, involves some level of industry coordination.

International trade. Table 21.13 shows levels of recent dairy imports with the breakdown by commodity and source. Table 21.14 lists the main outlets for Polish dairy exports, and Table 21.15 sets out the prevailing world market prices and the prices now being realized for Polish exports (at present market and discounting conditions). These figures clearly point to the need for corrective action and for a more structured market management.

Export marketing. While dairy exports are likely to be marginal in the foreseeable future, a link between the Polish dairy industry and the world market is nevertheless of critical importance to the stability of both producer and consumer prices.

In the recent past, imports substantially exceeded exports, but in the last few months there has been an increase in export discounting. While Lacpol, a federal cooperative with 72 dairy members, claims to account for 40% of dairy exports with sales of US$100 million, there are at least 10 other state or quasi-state agencies exporting dairy products and a further 250 private exporters operating without any form of bonding or licensing. These exporters undercut each other, and this situation is responsible for the discounting observed today. Ironically, although there is increased competition among the whole range of export agents, the competitiveness of Polish dairying has been seriously eroded.

The previous pattern of export sales was based on stock management positions taken by the Central Union. Since its liquidation, 326 individual dairies are left to make their own decisions on stock disposal. Given the very high interest rates, the very low domestic butter prices, the large number of newly independent butter producers, and the seasonal pattern of milk supply, these dairies must decide for the first time whether to carry increased butter stocks for winter sales or whether to take the netted back value realized on the depressed domestic market. This represents a discount of up to 50% on prevailing world market prices. The problem has been exacerbated by nonenforcement of milk quality standards, re-

Table 21.13 Dairy imports
(tons)

Commodity	1988
Butter	36,460
Cheese	8,248
Processed cheese	1,920
SMP	5,879
WMP and formula	3,507

Source Butter and powdered milk	Cheese
Netherlands (butter only)	Netherlands
Norway	West Germany
Finland	Soviet Union
West Germany (butter only)	Finland
Ireland	Norway
Switzerland	
New Zealand	
Austria (powdered milk only)	

Table 21.14 Main export markets for Polish dairy products

Cheese	Casein	SMP	Total (tons)
USA	Japan	Austria	13,245
	Germany	Algeria	4,000
	France	Japan	13,260
	USA	Tunisia	4,724
	Netherlands	Netherlands	1,500
	Italy	Sri Lanka	
	Mexico	Syria	
		Switzerland	
		Yugoslavia	427
		Germany	

sulting in low grade or even unstable products and extends beyond butter into cheese, skim milk powder, and casein.

Options. Under the restructuring proposal mentioned above, a small number of strong dairy cooperatives are likely to emerge. They will have direct responsibility for their own marketing operations and will concentrate on the domestic market, as will most of the emerging niche product producers. It will be their responsibility to decide on what basis they can best discharge their market responsibilities with respect to commodity exports as the need arises. They may choose to act independently or through one of the existing agents (parastatal or private)

Table 21.15 World market prices and Polish prices for dairy products
(in US$, per ton)

	World	Polish
SMP	1,200	350-870
WMP	1,250	860-900
Butter	1,350	600-850
Low-fat Cheese	1,900	-
Gouda	1,700	1,100
Casein	2,700	1,500

Note: World SMP and WMP prices are equalized by the effect of EC export restitution in an effort to reduce fat surplus.

or through channels created by joint-venture partners.

However, bringing prices of Polish dairy products back to world market levels from their present deeply discounted position is unlikely to result from such a multiplicity of independent channels given the managed character of the world dairy products market. There is, therefore, an urgent need to rationalize the present export marketing system and to assess the various options. These are:

- the dissolution of existing export boards;
- the establishment of a state-sponsored dairy or food export promotion board;
- the facilitation of a (food-industry-wide or sectoral) commodity export joint venture subject to antimonopoly legislation;
- the rationalization of existing state or quasi-state export boards, offering all or part of the equity to prospective food supply firms and other investors.

Whatever the option finally adopted, it is essential to the interests of the industry to require exporting agents to be bonded in order to ensure that their capital adequacy matches the scale of transactions they undertake.

The overall objective of the export rationalization process should be to rapidly provide for coordination and information — with the least further disruption in dairy exports — so that exports can be undertaken in the context of the prevailing stock and domestic market situation, while at the same time reducing the role of public organizations as fully and quickly as possible. How this can best be achieved can only be determined after a full appraisal of the quality of the business of existing state and quasi-state agencies. It should be established whether — jointly or individually — they represent a means by which individual firms can delegate their stock management and commodity exports responsibilities.

In any event, branded consumer-ready products should be the subject of direct transactions between the dairy and the customer, whether domestic or foreign. If after assessment, it appears that the existing quasi-state export agencies offer little or no real export-marketing advantage, their dissolution should not be further delayed. Firms should make their own arrangements on a voluntary basis within their own sectors to coordinate export sales. As the exports in the dairy and other key sectors are likely to be variable over the next few years — as domestic supply and demand settle down under the new market regime — this is unlikely to be the most cost-effective or stable form of export arrangement for the dairy sector (or for any other food exporter in similar circumstances). However, it will represent a considerable improvement over the present situation.

If, after assessment, it appears that the quasi-state food export agencies, through rationalization and restructuring, provide a good basis on which the industry could build a strong food export agency, it would benefit from significant intersectoral synergies since meat, dairy, and horticulture products are drawn from the same stores using similar transport and financing arrangements, complying with the same customs and import requirements and, in many cases, being offered to the same customers.

The restructured export agency could also provide a forum in which voluntary industry stabilization levies could operate and within which stock financing and management or public warehousing functions could be delegated in a cost-effective manner, thus freeing up the capital of individual firms which would otherwise be committed to working capital. Such an agency could also create over time a commodity futures market as part of its stock funding system.

Despite the range of advantages that would apply to such an agency, it could become bureaucratic and monopolistic (even under antitrust legislation and without any special statutory powers) and this should be a cause of great concern. How best to achieve the objectives of minimum state involvement and maximum industry marketing effectiveness is a matter of practical assessment to be made by the individual exporting firms. As for the government, it should reappraise its role in food exporting and rationalize it in pursuit of these objectives, with a view to speeding up the privatization process and maximizing industry marketing efficiency.

SPECIFIC ACTIONS

Short term. Even if the recommendations proposed in this document were fully and speedily implemented, they could not resolve the immediate problem of the industry, which is to build the summer butter stock to meet the winter demand. Nor could they dissuade commercial dairy farmers from leaving milk production at prevailing prices.

• The most immediate requirement for restoring industry stability is to set an attainable and viable target milk price. A price of Zl 900 for Class I milk is suggested with additional provision for winter premium. This will be financed through enforcement of the tests reducing the fat premium.

• Such actions will involve government action in the form of guarantee of export-quality butter stocks at a price level sufficient to justify Zl 900 per liter (up to world prices minus 20%) until the spring of 1991. This would suggest a price guarantee of less than US$1,000 per ton for butter (the world price is US$1,350 and the Polish discounted price is US$600). The government would not be involved in financing the stocks, but the process would require samples and warehouse inspection. The guarantee should only be given by the government if the industry fulfills the following conditions:

- agreement on the target price and implementation of the revised milk pricing system, based on enforced quality tests;
- establishment of a dairy industry quality logo to apply to products that meet voluntarily implemented standards;
- industry agreement for 1991 on stock management without government support;
- introduction of a credit scheme for farmers investing in quality.

In order to discuss these conditions, an industry forum should be convened as soon as possible to agree on the terms of government support. In the absence of a cooperative union, the industry personnel who would have the authority to negotiate may be difficult to identify. However, it should be possible to find them among the dairies forming the supreme council or in the 72 dairies which are members of Lacpol.

• Technical assistance for dairy industry rationalization should be provided in two key areas:
- the preparation of plans and prospects for regional groups of dairies, the object being to win the support of farmers, investors, bankers, and government for the new, changing regional dairies;
- management consultancy and development programs in each of the newly emerging dairy cooperatives.

• It will be necessary to provide the legislative framework within which this restructuring can take place, including:
- cooperative legislation recognizing the ownership right of shareholders;
- food hygiene legislation;
- milk processing licensing to regulate dairy processing;
- legislation in the areas of taxation, ownership and provision for tax treaties in order to facilitate investment.

Medium term. The industry must in the medium term:

• rationalize its assembly and processing plant network under the new structure;

• agree on an industry-wide stock management and export structure. (Whether that involves investing in a new food export company emerging from the rationalization, and privatization of state and cooperative export agents, or merely an informal dairy industry network, is a decision to be made by the industry.)

As these developments take place and order is restored to the market, it should be possible for the government to eliminate milk subsidies (an interim step which could be considered is a subsidized school milk program).

The dairy industry is part of a chain of interdependent industries and services. While the immediate focus must be on eliminating the internal bottlenecks, it will be necessary in the medium term to give more attention to critical linkages, including:

• adequacy of electricity and water sources on farms to support a modern quality dairy industry;
• rationalization of essential input services;
• development of domestic sources of dairy equipment;
• development of the packaging and labeling sector;
• development of public warehousing and the wholesale and retail sector;
• development of private transport, maintenance, catering and other support services, including banking and insurance.

Long term. In the longer term, the regional dairy organizations emerging are likely to become involved in other food sectors through acquisitions in order to develop a food product range and enhance their market positions. The alternative is to build a strong regional farmer network resulting in the integration of farm inputs in the regional dairies. A third possibility in the long term is that — through joint ventures — many of these regional dairies become involved in the dairy sector outside Poland selling newly developed products in export markets.

It is important to allow new entrants into the industry to ensure the development of niche products and markets and maintain a diverse and competitive dairy industry. This will require an active policy of encouraging and facilitating product and market research and development.

Dairy farmers will seek to increase their incomes through increased productivity. This will involve a continuous process of on-farm investment and is likely to result in significant further concentration of dairy production in fewer farms. As this process eliminates the dairy option for smaller farmers, it is essential to develop other alternatives for these families, in agriculture or elsewhere in the rural economy.

Conclusions

In a market economy, the right of consumers to choose on the basis of perceived value outweighs the technical and social considerations of the production system. The strengths of Polish dairy farmers and of the Polish dairy industry, therefore, must be translated into transparent pricing and quality advantages for their products.

Because dairying is both land and labor intensive, this enterprise is often viewed in Europe as the backbone of a smallholder rural economy. For this reason and because of the importance for consumers of dairy products, dairying is extensively supported throughout the world at both the production and market levels.

The Polish dairy sector is not in need of government financial support. Rather, Poland's dairy sector requires better product quality and better marketing. Despite prospects of freer world trade, the world dairy market is highly distorted, volatile and generally unfavorable to producers. Making quality improvements dependent on the world market, therefore, is unlikely to serve the interests of either producers or consumers. The best tools to improve quality and marketing are, on the part of the industry, domestic market management and, on the part of the government, protection against dumping and other legislative safeguards.

The current situation in the Polish dairy sector requires industry coordination in order to maintain a reasonable balance of supply and demand at prices below those at which dairy imports can enter the country and to manage stocks in a way that balances seasonal supplies and thus ensures a stable year-round price. These functions can be performed without government involvement in any well ordered industry provided that it is supported by antidumping legislation. The role of public entities in the dairy market should be rationalized in the shortest possible time, taking this framework into account.

Endnotes

This annex was prepared by John McCarrick, assisted by Leonard Kalinowski, Karol Adamik, Cornelis de Haan, Jean-Jacques Dethier and August Schumacher. The summary of dairy strategy was written by C. de Haan.

1. Taking into account that Poland's imports this year are insignificant, compared with normal imports of 40,000 tons of butter per year.

Distributors of World Bank Publications

ARGENTINA
Carlos Hirsch, SRL
Galería Guemes
Florida 165, 4th Floor-Ofc. 453/465
1333 Buenos Aires

**AUSTRALIA, PAPUA NEW GUINEA,
FIJI, SOLOMON ISLANDS,
VANUATU, AND WESTERN SAMOA**
D.A. Books & Journals
648 Whitehorse Road
Mitcham 3132
Victoria

AUSTRIA
Gerald and Co.
Graben 31
A-1011 Wien

BAHRAIN
Bahrain Research and Consultancy
Associates Ltd.
P.O. Box 22103
Manama Town 317

BANGLADESH
Micro Industries Development
Assistance Society (MIDAS)
House 5, Road 16
Dhanmondi R/Area
Dhaka 1209

Branch offices:
156, Nur Ahmed Sarak
Chittagong 4000

76, K.D.A. Avenue
Kulna

BELGIUM
Jean De Lannoy
Av. du Roi 202
1060 Brussels

BRAZIL
Publicacoes Tecnicas Internacionais
Ltda.
Rua Peixoto Gomide, 209
01409 Sao Paulo, SP

CANADA
Le Diffuseur
C.P. 85, 1501B rue Ampère
Boucherville, Québec
J4B 5E6

CHINA
China Financial & Economic Publishing
House
8, Da Fo Si Dong Jie
Beijing

COLOMBIA
Infoenlace Ltda.
Apartado Aereo 34270
Bogota D.E.

COTE D'IVOIRE
Centre d'Edition et de Diffusion
Africaines (CEDA)
04 B.P. 541
Abidjan 04 Plateau

CYPRUS
MEMRB Information Services
P.O. Box 2098
Nicosia

DENMARK
SamfundsLitteratur
Rosenoerns Allé 11
DK-1970 Frederiksberg C

DOMINICAN REPUBLIC
Editora Taller, C. por A.
Restauración e Isabel la Católica 309
Apartado Postal 2190
Santo Domingo

EL SALVADOR
Fusades
Avenida Manuel Enrique Araujo #3530
Edificio SISA, 1er. Piso
San Salvador

EGYPT, ARAB REPUBLIC OF
Al Ahram
Al Galaa Street
Cairo

The Middle East Observer
8 Chawarbi Street
Cairo

FINLAND
Akateeminen Kirjakauppa
P.O. Box 128
SF-00101
Helsinki 10

FRANCE
World Bank Publications
66, avenue d'Iéna
75116 Paris

GERMANY, FEDERAL REPUBLIC OF
UNO-Verlag
Poppelsdorfer Allee 55
D-5300 Bonn 1

GREECE
KEME
24, Ippodamou Street Platia Plastiras
Athens-11635

GUATEMALA
Librerias Piedra Santa
5a. Calle 7-55
Zona 1
Guatemala City

HONG KONG, MACAO
Asia 2000 Ltd.
6 Fl., 146 Prince Edward
Road, W.
Kowloon
Hong Kong

HUNGARY
Kultura
P.O. Box 149
1389 Budapest 62

INDIA
Allied Publishers Private Ltd.
751 Mount Road
Madras - 600 002

Branch offices:
15 J.N. Heredia Marg
Ballard Estate
Bombay - 400 038

13/14 Asaf Ali Road
New Delhi - 110 002

17 Chittaranjan Avenue
Calcutta - 700 072

Jayadeva Hostel Building
5th Main Road Gandhinagar
Bangalore - 560 009

3-5-1129 Kachiguda Cross Road
Hyderabad - 500 027

Prarthana Flats, 2nd Floor
Near Thakore Baug, Navrangpura
Ahmedabad - 380 009

Patiala House
16-A Ashok Marg
Lucknow - 226 001

INDONESIA
Pt. Indira Limited
Jl. Sam Ratulangi 37
P.O. Box 181
Jakarta Pusat

ITALY
Licosa Commissionaria Sansoni SPA
Via Benedetto Fortini, 120/10
Casella Postale 552
50125 Florence

JAPAN
Eastern Book Service
37-3, Hongo 3-Chome, Bunkyo-ku 113
Tokyo

KENYA
Africa Book Service (E.A.) Ltd.
P.O. Box 45245
Nairobi

KOREA, REPUBLIC OF
Pan Korea Book Corporation
P.O. Box 101, Kwangwhamun
Seoul

KUWAIT
MEMRB Information Services
P.O. Box 5465

MALAYSIA
University of Malaya Cooperative
Bookshop, Limited
P.O. Box 1127, Jalan Pantai Baru
Kuala Lumpur

MEXICO
INFOTEC
Apartado Postal 22-860
14060 Tlalpan, Mexico D.F.

MOROCCO
Société d'Etudes Marketing Marocaine
12 rue Mozart, Bd. d'Anfa
Casablanca

NETHERLANDS
InOr-Publikaties b.v.
P.O. Box 14
7240 BA Lochem

NEW ZEALAND
Hills Library and Information Service
Private Bag
New Market
Auckland

NIGERIA
University Press Limited
Three Crowns Building Jericho
Private Mail Bag 5095
Ibadan

NORWAY
Narvesen Information Center
Book Department
P.O. Box 6125 Etterstad
N-0602 Oslo 6

OMAN
MEMRB Information Services
P.O. Box 1613, Seeb Airport
Muscat

PAKISTAN
Mirza Book Agency
65, Shahrah-e-Quaid-e-Azam
P.O. Box No. 729
Lahore 3

PERU
Editorial Desarrollo SA
Apartado 3824
Lima

PHILIPPINES
National Book Store
701 Rizal Avenue
P.O. Box 1934
Metro Manila

International Book Center
Fifth Floor, Filipinas Life Building
Ayala Avenue, Makati
Metro Manila

POLAND
ORPAN
Palac Kultury i Nauki
00-901 Warszawa

PORTUGAL
Livraria Portugal
Rua Do Carmo 70-74
1200 Lisbon

SAUDI ARABIA, QATAR
Jarir Book Store
P.O. Box 3196
Riyadh 11471

MEMRB Information Services
Branch offices:
Al Alsa Street
Al Dahna Center
First Floor
P.O. Box 7188
Riyadh

Haji Abdullah Alireza Building
King Khaled Street
P.O. Box 3969
Dammam

33, Mohammed Hassan Awad Street
P.O. Box 5978
Jeddah

**SINGAPORE, TAIWAN, MYANMAR,
BRUNEI**
Information Publications
Private, Ltd.
02-06 1st Fl., Pei-Fu Industrial
Bldg.
24 New Industrial Road
Singapore 1953

SOUTH AFRICA, BOTSWANA
For single titles:
Oxford University Press Southern
Africa
P.O. Box 1141
Cape Town 8000

For subscription orders:
International Subscription Service
P.O. Box 41095
Craighall
Johannesburg 2024

SPAIN
Mundi-Prensa Libros, S.A.
Castello 37
28001 Madrid

Librería Internacional AEDOS
Consell de Cent, 391
08009 Barcelona

SRI LANKA AND THE MALDIVES
Lake House Bookshop
P.O. Box 244
100, Sir Chittampalam A. Gardiner
Mawatha
Colombo 2

SWEDEN
For single titles:
Fritzes Fackboksforetaget
Regeringsgatan 12, Box 16356
S-103 27 Stockholm

For subscription orders:
Wennergren-Williams AB
Box 30004
S-104 25 Stockholm

SWITZERLAND
For single titles:
Librairie Payot
6, rue Grenus
Case postale 381
CH 1211 Geneva 11

For subscription orders:
Librairie Payot
Service des Abonnements
Case postale 3312
CH 1002 Lausanne

TANZANIA
Oxford University Press
P.O. Box 5299
Dar es Salaam

THAILAND
Central Department Store
306 Silom Road
Bangkok

**TRINIDAD & TOBAGO, ANTIGUA
BARBUDA, BARBADOS,
DOMINICA, GRENADA, GUYANA,
JAMAICA, MONTSERRAT, ST.
KITTS & NEVIS, ST. LUCIA,
ST. VINCENT & GRENADINES**
Systematics Studies Unit
#9 Watts Street
Curepe
Trinidad, West Indies

TURKEY
Haset Kitapevi, A.S.
Istiklal Caddesi No. 469
Beyoglu
Istanbul

UGANDA
Uganda Bookshop
P.O. Box 7145
Kampala

UNITED ARAB EMIRATES
MEMRB Gulf Co.
P.O. Box 6097
Sharjah

UNITED KINGDOM
Microinfo Ltd.
P.O. Box 3
Alton, Hampshire GU34 2PG
England

URUGUAY
Instituto Nacional del Libro
San Jose 1116
Montevideo

VENEZUELA
Libreria del Este
Aptdo. 60.337
Caracas 1060-A

YUGOSLAVIA
Jugoslovenska Knjiga
P.O. Box 36
Trg Republike
YU-11000 Belgrade